HOW MEN FEEL

HOW MEN FEEL

THEIR RESPONSE TO WOMEN'S DEMANDS FOR EQUALITY AND POWER

Anthony Astrachan

ANCHOR PRESS

Doubleday

NEW YORK

1988

Grateful acknowledgment is made to the following for permission to use copyrighted material:

Little, Brown & Co.: Poem 613 by Emily Dickinson, from *The Complete Poems of Emily Dickinson,* edited by Thomas H. Johnson, 1935 by Martha Dickinson Bianchi, renewed 1963 by Mary L. Hampson. Reprinted by permission of the publishers and the Trustees of Amherst College from *The Poems of Emily Dickinson,* edited by Thomas H. Johnson, published by The Belknap Press of Harvard University Press, © 1951, 1955, 1979 and 1983 by the President and Fellows of Harvard College.

Harvard Business Review: passages from "Two Women, Three Men on a Raft," by Robert Schrank, © 1977 by Robert Schrank.

Jane Lazarre: passage from "Fathers as Mothers: On Being a Father in the Year of the Woman," by Jane Lazarre, first published in *The Village Voice,* 1975.

Joseph Riener: passage from "Those Mixed-Up, Painful Feelings of Being a Parent," by Joseph Riener, first published in the Washington *Post,* 1982.

Times Change Press: passages from "The Socialized Penis," by Jack Litewka, © 1972 by Jack Litewka, first published in *Liberation,* March–April 1974, reprinted in *For Men Against Sexism,* edited by Jon Snodgrass.

Ellen Willis: passage from "Women Are Denied the Right to Express Lust," by Ellen Willis, published in *Ms.* magazine, 1982.

Macmillan Publishing Co., Inc., New York; Macmillan (London) Ltd.; A. P. Watt, Ltd., and Michael Yeats: seven lines from "No Second Troy," by William Butler Yeats, from *Collected Poems,* by W. B. Yeats, © 1912 by Macmillan Publishing Co., renewed 1940 by Bertha Georgie Yeats.

Farrar Straus & Giroux, Inc.: seven lines from "Jean Stafford, a Letter," by Robert Lowell, from *Day by Day,* © 1975, 1976, 1977 by Robert Lowell, and twelve lines from "Mermaid," by Robert Lowell, from *The Dolphin,* © 1973 by Robert Lowell.

Doubleday & Company, Inc.: six lines from "The Indigo Bunting," by Robert Bly, from *Loving a Woman in Two Worlds,* © 1985 by Robert Bly.

Black Sparrow Press: eight lines from "making it," by Charles Bukowski, from *War All the Time,* © 1984 by Charles Bukowski.

Michael Blumenthal: five lines from "Kol Nidre" and thirteen lines from "Stones" by Michael Blumenthal, from *Sympathetic Magic,* © 1980 by Michael Blumenthal, published by Water Mark Press.

Viking Penguin, Inc.: five lines from "Couvade" and six lines from "Weeding" by Michael Blumenthal, from *Days We Would Rather Know,* © 1980, 1981, 1982, 1983, 1984 by Michael Blumenthal.

New Directions Publishing Co.: three lines from "The Ivy Crown," by William Carlos Williams, from *Pictures from Brueghel,* © 1955 by William Carlos Williams.

Portions of this book appeared earlier in slightly different form in *Advertising Age, Brother, Geo, Ms., Newsday, The Nation,* The Washington *Post* and *Working Woman.*

The first edition of *How Men Feel*
was published in hardcover by Anchor Press/Doubleday.

Library of Congress Cataloging-in-Publication Data

Astrachan, Anthony.
How men feel.
Bibliography: p.
Includes index.
1. Men—United States—Attitudes.   2. Sex role—
United States.   3. Feminism—United States.   I. Title.
HQ1090.3.A88   1986   305.3′1   85-22944
ISBN 0-385-23334-5

To the memory of my parents
IRVING ASTRACHAN and MANLEY AARON ASTRACHAN

who first showed me the joys and pains
that men and women feel
when they try to love as equals

CONTENTS

ACKNOWLEDGMENTS

The Ford Foundation and the Rockefeller Foundation both gave me research fellowships which provided financial support for the completion of this book. I am deeply indebted to them, and I particularly wish to thank the men in charge of the fellowship programs during the periods of my grants, Richard Sharpe at Ford and Joel Colton at Rockefeller. Both were unusual in their recognition of the need to extend foundation resources to scholars and writers who are not associated with academic or government institutions.

I wish to thank the Writers Room, where I wrote several chapters free of the distractions that often plague writers working at home, and the Center for Policy Research, which gave me an institutional umbrella and office space for a year.

Susan Jacoby's career tribulations and subsequent triumphs led to my first look at men's feelings about women who are changing society simply by demonstrating their competence at work that they take as seriously as men do. I am profoundly grateful for the personal support and professional help she has offered my work on this book through every stage of marriage and friendship.

Robert Brannon, Robert Crease, Marguerite Feitlowitz, Sara Ann Friedman, Mary Lee Grisanti, Lesley Hazleton, Ron Hollander, Percy Knauth, Laurie Lisle, Charles C. Mann, and Page Wilson were members of a writers' group who over two years read several chapters and offered the best kind of criticism: it made me go back to work and improve what I had written.

Jim Covington, Sara Ann Friedman, Joan Rizzo, and Claudia Sisson were my fellows in what we called a "genders group," where our talk improved my understanding of many of the ideas and feelings that went into the book.

Carolyn Grillo offered helpful suggestions for several chapters.

Several other people helped me find resources or led me to valuable ideas. I want particularly to express my thanks to Herb Gutman, whose untimely death robbed scholars in and out of academe of insight and enthusiasm that illuminated our work. I am also indebted to Boris Astrachan, Sandy Close, Lisa Cohen, Martin Duberman, Ellen Frankfort, Betty Friedan, Laurence J. Gould, Alan Gross, Jean Herskovits, Lucy Komisar, David Lutwin, Sid Miller, Martha Nelson, Joseph Pleck, Letty Cottin Pogrebin, Grace Schulman, Barry Shapiro, Alix Kates Shulman, Alan Stamm, and Meredeth Turshen.

My editor, Paul Bresnick, gave me two things that a writer needs, perceptive criticism and continuing encouragement.

Thanks to my sons, Owen and Joshua Astrachan, whose daily lives give me hope that men and women will do a better job of treating each other as equals in the future.

And thanks especially to Rhea Gaisner, with whom I have learned that it is possible to love as equals and be happy.

PREFACE

This book tries to show how men feel about women's quests for independence, equality, and power. My methodology was simple: I kept looking for men who had had some experience of women demanding changes, at work or at home. I found them through friends, through scholars who had done work in related fields, through members of women's and men's organizations. I advertised for respondents in *The Wall Street Journal* and *The New York Review of Books* (with meager but usable results). In many cases, I also met the women in their lives, who usually offered a different perspective. I sought and found a population diverse in age, race, income, education, and occupation, in four different parts of the country, and I interviewed close to 400 people, about 350 of them men. My sample, however, was in no way representative or statistically random. My goal was not a scientific survey but illuminating examples.

The interviews usually took an hour and often longer. I followed no rigid pattern, although I made sure that I covered the whole range of subjects I thought might cast light on the issues of work and love, of equality and power. I used models as different as Robert Coles's *Children of Crisis* and Gail Sheehy's *Passages,* but I never spoke to either of those pioneers.

It took me seven years to search for a full spectrum of people, experience, and insights, and five years to organize what I found and write this book. The two tasks overlapped, so *How Men Feel* took nine years from start to finish. It was fascinating to see that while relations between men and women in the United States went through many swings back and forth on the surface in those years, the underlying emotions remained the same and the social dynamics changed only slowly but relatively steadily.

I promised anonymity to all the people I interviewed for this book, and except for the few who asked to be identified, I have given each person a pseudonym marked by an asterisk the first time it is used in each chapter.

ANTHONY ASTRACHAN
Hoboken, New Jersey
December 1985

Part One
WHAT, WHY, AND HOW

Chapter 1
WHY THIS BOOK

For almost twenty years, women in America have been claiming rights that society denied them for millennia: to traditionally masculine jobs, to a share of power, to the two fundamentals of equality and choice in both public and private life. These changes constitute one of the fundamental revolutions of this century in the United States, one as important as the revolution in race relations.

The women's revolution is challenging men's hold on power and reshaping men's roles in society. But few people have examined the way men respond to this revolution, in real life and in their own souls; we take it for granted that some men welcome it, while more feel threatened by it and resist it. The idea of threat and resistance is perversely like a security blanket—it comforts us and protects us from looking beneath it at the specific emotions we feel when we confront these changes and the specific behaviors they produce.

This book attempts to tear away the blanket and face those specifics. I learned my first lessons about them by looking inside myself, at my own anger at women making changes, my fear and anxiety, my envy and shame—and at my own pride and pleasure in many of the things that women are doing, my admiration for many women, and my identification with some. I went on to talk with and listen to other men—my father and my sons, the men I worked for and with, about 350 other men and the women in their lives. I saw that we feel more pain than pleasure about the changes women are making, that in most of us the negative feelings are stronger than the positive, and I wanted to understand why. Why do we have so much difficulty treating women as equals in work and in love, why do we waste so much of their energy and talent and feeling and so much of our own, why do we inflict so much pain on them and on ourselves? I wanted also to understand why we achieve such joy when we succeed in creating a dynamic of equality with women, and how some of us do it. The answers, I discovered, had to do with male power and male powerlessness and the way we see the power of mother in women's challenge to both. The process of discovery was long, but the questions of how men feel about the changes that women are making, and why we feel that way, would not let go of me.

FIRST LESSONS: MY WORK AND MY WIFE

Those questions got their first grip on me in 1969 and 1970, just as the new feminists were making themselves heard in the United States. I was overseas at the time as a correspondent for the Washington *Post,* so the media blare about the women's demands barely nudged my consciousness a little higher. But something happened to a woman at work that blew it up. She was my wife, Susan Jacoby.

Susan and I met at the *Post.* We had known each other for a year and a half when the paper sent me to Africa, and we decided to get married two years after that when the *Post* transferred me from Nairobi to Moscow. Meanwhile she had proved herself one of the paper's best young reporters. In four years she moved upward from cub assignments to the education beat to finding her own in-depth local stories. At the age of twenty-two (she was thirteen years younger than I) she was covering important education stories all over the country. When she applied for a leave of absence to go to Moscow with me, we thought it would be granted as a matter of course to ensure the return to the paper of one of its better talents.

But the *Post* tried to refuse. "Why should we give you a leave to go to Moscow?" asked Ben Bradlee, the executive editor. "You won't learn anything there you'll be able to use when you come back." Properly decoded, that meant "No woman is going to cover foreign affairs for us." Flora Lewis had already been a foreign correspondent for the *Post,* and since then it has had other women foreign correspondents and a woman foreign editor, but there was no mistaking Bradlee's real, if unconscious, meaning in 1969.

Eventually, with a nudge from another editor, Bradlee softened enough to give Susan her leave. The *Post* even agreed to pay her stringer rates for stories she wrote herself. (A stringer is a nonstaff correspondent who files regularly or frequently and is paid space rates.) But there was never any thought of accrediting her as well as me as a correspondent in Moscow. The first reason was that the *Post* had no budget for a two-person bureau. Even if it had had, and even if it had been willing to give Susan the assignment, the Soviet authorities might not have agreed; they based their accreditation of American correspondents on the number of Soviet journalists allowed into the United States.

Later, when the Soviets had shown they would not make a formal objection to Susan's writing as a stringer, we again asked the *Post* to accredit her—as other media had accredited other stringers already present in Moscow. By then their refusal was part of a larger struggle between the newsroom and the Moscow bureau, which began when Susan helped me report and write a story about people dancing in the street in front of the Moscow synagogue to celebrate the Jewish holiday of Simchas Torah. I telexed it with a byline that read "By Susan Jacoby and Anthony Astrachan." The foreign desk removed her name and refused to pay her for her work on that piece. Acrimonious telexes and letters flew both ways. Among other things, the editors claimed that joint staff-stringer bylines had caused a host of problems in other places and were being discouraged as a matter of policy. We found that hard to believe, if only because stories continued to appear with the combined bylines of a male correspondent and a male stringer. More important and more aggravating, we were told, in writing, that other correspondents' wives were professionally qualified and still helped their husbands—without pay and without a credit line. Whatever their professions, none was a journalist and none had been a reporter for the *Post*. It only rubbed salt in our wounds when we were told that the wife of a Saigon correspondent, who had once worked as a news desk assistant—the same level as a copy girl—had been given a color television set for her help in transcribing her husband's stories when he phoned Saigon from the field.

We had to live with the situation, of course. Susan wrote less for the *Post* than she had originally expected and spent most of her time writing magazine articles and collecting material for what became her first two books. But the insult and the injury continued to rankle, exacerbated when the authorities and our professional colleagues in Moscow insisted on treating her as a wife —that is to say, as an unperson. As a "wife," Susan was usually excluded from all-male business lunches given by diplomats and other correspondents. This was doubly ironic, because she spoke Russian better than I did and knew more about Soviet life than half the men at the table.

That was the start of Susan's fears that her personal and professional identities were being submerged in mine, as so often used to happen and sometimes still happens to the wives of assertive husbands. Susan was such a good journalist, and such a strong personality, that I found it hard to take those fears seriously. I began to understand them near the end of our stay in Moscow. A young Associated Press correspondent, in his first interview with the press department of the Foreign Ministry, was asked if he was married. He said he was not and the official replied, "Good. Then you won't write stories under your wife's name the way Astrachan does."

Susan's transformation in the eyes of others from reporter into "wife" was an outrage to me because it was an insult to the woman I loved and because it was an insult to a professional colleague of proven competence. It hurt all the more when she blamed me for the trauma. Years later she said to me, "None of the things that happened to me were your fault, and you did everything you could to show the paper how you felt, but I still blamed you. I too was professionally fascinated by Moscow and wanted to be there, but I felt that I was enduring these insults because we were in Moscow for your career. No intellectual knowledge made up for the emotional battering." While we were still in Moscow, the injuries to both of us remained fresh for me whenever she refused to collaborate on stories in which I could have used her help because she would be given neither money nor credit for joint efforts, and on the few occasions when I passed up a story that she wanted to do or could do better than I. I thought that made me sensitive to her sufferings, and I learned only later that I was not sensitive enough.

My outrage was one of the reasons I decided to give up being a foreign correspondent and return to the United States. I couldn't be happy in work that prevented my wife from doing her work. I expected the *Post* to give us both good assignments in Washington. Instead, Bradlee offered me a choice of a tolerable assignment in New York, covering the United Nations and Canada, with no job for Susan, or—after I had raised the question of her job—an intolerable assignment for me in Washington with the possibility of an acceptable job, even a promotion, for Susan. From the company's viewpoint, sending me to New York was the easiest thing to do: a job was open, while finding a decent assignment in Washington would have meant juggling people or creating new slots. We knew that, but we were stunned by the corollary: the paper had never taken seriously its commitment to give Susan her job back after the leave of absence. I was outraged anew, and my anger grew sharper at Bradlee's response to our attempt to set up a third choice. We suggested that we would try a commuter marriage if he would give me the New York job and her the good assignment in Washington. Ben said he'd be damned if he'd take the blame for breaking up our marriage, and that if Susan held him to the promise of a job in Washington while I stayed in New York, she'd be writing obituaries—the journalistic equivalent of Siberia.

My outrage was not strong enough to refuse the New York assignment, of course. I knew I'd hate myself and the job, and that Susan would hate the person I'd become, if I went back to Washington and a demotion. She agreed, and we went to New York. It was a long time before I understood that she went through agonies in our first two years there, as she had in Moscow, from fear that her identity was being submerged and her career seriously damaged. Later Susan became successful as a free-lance magazine writer and author of books (two of them about the Soviet Union), and I left the *Post.* By then I had begun to understand her earlier rage. It fed my own anger over the behavior of other men, without always making me change my own behavior to meet her needs better.

One thing made our adventures and misadventures with the *Post* important: we resembled all couples whose personal relations were affected by the assaults of institutions shaped by a society that took sex discrimination for granted. We happened to be the first couple that confronted the *Post* with the problem of husband-and-wife careers. The *Post* continued to do silly things with two-journalist couples for several years, but like many American corporations, its consciousness was eventually raised.

It now recognizes, for instance, that a man may have to follow the turnings of his wife's career as often as she follows his. In 1980 it transferred its Peking correspondent, Jay Mathews, to Los Angeles because the Los Angeles *Times* had brought home its Peking correspondent, his wife, Linda Mathews, to be the editor of its op-ed page. The paper now understands that it need not deprive itself of a woman's talent when her husband is transferred. In 1985 it made foreign editor Karen de Young its London correspondent when her husband's employer assigned him there. At least three male correspondents have married experienced reporters on their way overseas, and the *Post* has used their wives as stringers more enthusiastically than it ever used Susan. It now seems to understand that husbands and wives who work in the same newsroom may be a synergistic asset to their employer. (That happened after Ben Bradlee married one of the *Post*'s best-known reporters, Sally Quinn.)

In general, the *Post* has become more appreciative than it was in our day of talent that happens to be female. It was almost ten years before women achieved some equity in promotion. But between 1981 and 1985 the paper filled fifty-four positions in the category of "assignment editors, critics, and columnists," the key newsroom level, and nineteen of those appointments, or 35 percent, went to women. Five women have passed through the fourteen main supervisory positions in the 1980s, though feminists on the staff are quick to note that de Young is the only woman who has ever occupied a hard-news slot of the kind that is important to Bradlee. Women had 26.3 percent of the page-one bylines in the *Post* in a 1984 survey of eleven major newspapers; *USA Today* had the highest rate, 41.5 percent, and the New York *Times* the lowest, 10 percent. The *Post* also gives far more play to feminist issues in its news pages and opinion columns than does the *Times*, usually considered the yardstick of American journalism.

Yet Howard Simons, then the managing editor, was uncomfortable when I applied the phrase "consciousness raising" to the *Post* in a conversation, though he was glad I thought things had improved. He said it was more a question of having the right people in the right places. I thought, of course, that he had had two of the right people in the right places ten years earlier but hadn't been able to recognize them. To me, the *Post*'s unquestionable change for the better is a bitter irony. Susan and I suffered, and I became fascinated by the problem, because we were on the cutting edge of a change that has become commonplace in business life. Sometimes we both marvel at the innocence we showed fifteen years ago. Our naïveté made us ill-prepared to deal with what happened to us, which I hope is true of fewer couples today.

My innocence certainly increased the anger I felt when I realized the *Post* had penalized me for trying to hold it to the promise of a job for Susan. My difficulties with the management in my last three years at the paper had many causes. The editors said I had filed too many stories from Moscow on Jews and dissidents. I was bad at the game of office politics and didn't realize how important it was. Foreign news and the care of returning foreign correspondents was seldom high on Bradlee's list of priorities, and he believed in what he called "creative tension." That meant forcing some reporters out on the theory that he would get better performance by letting the staff know that years of good work might not protect someone whose stories no longer excited him. Several senior reporters left about the same time I did. But it was clear that whatever the faults of employees, bosses, and the system, the *Post* was also punishing me for having had the temerity to support a good reporter when the paper wanted to forget its promise to my wife. To the editors, that meant only the temerity to quarrel with their unquestionable power to make whatever assignments they wanted.

My anger at what the *Post* had done to me was inseparable from my anger at what men had done to Susan and my anger at the way men had wasted talent because it happened to be female. I could not understand those men's behavior, because it's insane to waste any talent. And I failed to understand them for an additional reason. It makes me feel good to deal with a woman who is competent at her job, and I assumed my bosses felt the same way. (Over the years, as I saw how hard it was for women to advance at the *Post* and the New York *Times,* I learned how wrong I was. I wonder if any of those men feel that way now.) Before I married Susan, I got an equal charge from the woman reporter who taught me something about covering Congress and the woman reporter who said I'd taught her something about covering the Organization for African Unity. Almost all the women in my personal life have had careers, and I have enjoyed their achievements almost as much as my own. When Susan wrote a good article, it gave me pleasure that was professional, because I enjoy good work in my own field; personal, because this good work was done by someone I lived with; perhaps even sexual, because it was done by a woman I thought beautiful and exciting. It also caused me anxiety and envy because she and I competed so hard with each other, but that never erased the pleasure. Our marriage has ended, but I still take pleasure in her writing.

Pleasure in someone else's work is always vicarious compared to pride in one's own, and there is always the danger of paternalism when a man takes pride in a woman's work. But I believe people really can identify, in a way that transcends unconscious or ulterior motives, with the achievements of others whom they love or admire or respect.

FIRST LESSONS: MY PARENTS

Long before I met Susan, my father's example led me to that belief. My father, Irving Astrachan, was a high school teacher—a great classroom teacher and a remarkable school administrator, literary magazine adviser, and college-entrance counselor. He was a teacher who cared deeply about his students, at least the students who responded to him. I felt my father's identification with me from my earliest years. Then I came to feel it more strongly because I heard about and saw so much of his identification with his students before and during my own years as a student at Stuyvesant High School, where he taught. His identification with me and mine with him overrode the classic father-son struggle. His ability to identify with his students is one of the reasons that I believe in the possibility and the reality of identification, not only between parent and child, but between men and women—even husband and wife, even men and women in the same occupation.

My father was a gentle man who tried, in contrast to the masculine stereotype, to make me less aggressive and less ruthless as a child. He was the first man who taught me that it was as important, and as pleasurable, to appreciate a woman's intellect as it was to appreciate her body. He did a larger share of the housework than most husbands did in the 1940s, after my parents could no longer afford a full-time maid—washing the dishes when my mother cooked, cooking breakfast and making lunch himself, running the vacuum cleaner. He was a nurturing parent. My mother told me, when we were talking about this book a few years after my father died, "Pop had *maternal* feelings about you. He would hurry home to spend an hour with you before he went off to his second job. Before you were four, you told people, 'I love my father. He laughs so much.' " And my father was a sensualist who rubbed my back and taught me to rub his when I was a boy, teaching me without words that touch between males was not only licit, but healthy and healthful.

Clearly my father laid the groundwork for much of my interest in the changes women are making, for much of whatever ability I have to support those changes. I knew that even before I decided to write this book. It took me much longer to realize that my mother had had as much to do as he had with my involvement with this subject. I didn't admire or identify with her as much as I did with my father, so I didn't look for similar association. She was not one of the premature superwomen who combined a glamorous career with child raising fifty years ago, so I didn't see her as an innovator. In other words, even after I started studying this subject, I found it hard to see that my mother had followed her own difficult quest for equality and choice. Most men have troubled vision when it comes to seeing that quest in the lives of the women they know best.

My mother, Manley Aaron Astrachan, was a woman of forceful personality and great energy—nervous energy rather than physical, but still energy, capable of transformation into love and work. Her energy often took the form of ego drive; it was she who gave me much of the aggressive spirit that my father tried to curb. Her life showed how keeping aggressive energy bottled up, as traditional Western culture demands of women, creates the danger of explosion.

My mother was a woman of sharp intelligence who did not go beyond high school, so that her intellect lacked the shape that either college or disciplined self-education might have given it. But she became assistant to Alfred Knopf, the paragon of American book publishing. In later years she loved to talk about the work she had done with writers like Willa Cather, Bernard De

Voto and H. L. Mencken. She developed my father's ability to appreciate a woman's mind, which he tried to pass on to me.

That makes it all the more astonishing, as I think about it today, that my father asked my mother to stop work when I was born. It would not be too much to say that he and Knopf conspired to make her quit her job and stay home with me. As a result, my father had to work at two and sometimes three teaching jobs at a time to make the money needed for our standard of living. That meant that he had to forgo a lot of the maternal or nurturing pleasure he found with me. It also meant that I never had much of the nurturing I needed. My mother did not have the natural gift for nurture that my father did. She resented me as the reason her career was cut off, so she gave me less mothering than she might have if she had continued with Knopf. Having to stop work contributed to her coming close to a nervous breakdown when I was two and to her developing colitis when I was five. But the energy that made it impossible for my mother to be "just a housewife" helped cure her illnesses and manifested itself first in arts and crafts and volunteer work, traditional outlets for women of her class and generation. Then, when I left college, she started a second career as a travel agent. Through it all she never stopped loving me and my father, and they had nearly fifty years of unusually close and happy marriage. But she felt the hurt of her aborted career through all those years.

My father was dying and I was already germinating this book when I learned what he had forced my mother to do after I was born. I asked him why he had done it, and he could only say that he was the victim of his culture, Jewish and Western. He didn't use the words "sex-role stereotypes," which the social scientists see as the parts of the culture that operate here, but he was talking about them. He hoped that if he had known in 1932 what he knew in the 1970s, he would have behaved differently, but he was too honest to say he was sure he would have. He had behaved differently in the years before he retired: when Stuyvesant went coed after more than sixty years as a boys' school, my father—unlike many of his contemporaries—was able not merely to adjust to the girl students, but to enjoy their presence, to identify with them, and to inspire the kind of response in them that male students had always given him. My discoveries about the events after my birth eroded some of my identification with my father, but they led me to see and love both my parents in new dimensions, and this gave me new angles of vision on today's changes.

MAN IN THE WOMAN'S POSITION

Some of the feminists I met in the early 1970s gave me yet another new angle of vision. They suggested that my interest in the changes women are making, and my efforts to support women, owed a great deal to my being in the kind of positions that women are usually in—and to my recognizing that I was. They thought, for instance, that my experiences at the Washington *Post* made me identify with women, who are often more exploited by employers than men.

I found it hard to accept this idea, perhaps because I knew that men often are exploited and feel exploited more than women, concerned with their own treatment, recognize or admit. I also knew that most men who are exploited do not consciously feel they're in a woman's position. If anything, they behave in a more aggressive or more macho manner away from their jobs. Later I came to feel the feminist analysis might have some validity. I felt the *Post* had abused Susan and me in the same action, so I identified with her; perhaps through her I identified with other women, with all exploited women. And I sometimes said to myself that the *Post* had "screwed me." That put me in a primary female position—or in the situation of a man who sees male weakness as a female position, the archetypes being men who rape men and men who are raped in prison. This in turn brought me back to the exploited men who become more macho. I saw that such behavior is compensation for our exploitation, an attempt to deny the powerlessness that in our eyes impeaches our manhood because we think it is a feminine condition.

The feminists also suggested that I was often in the same relationship to Susan as many wives were to their husbands, rather than the reverse. For the first four years of our marriage, I was much further up the career ladder than she was, but after 1974 she was often more in demand as a free-lancer than I was. The one year of our life together that she made more money than I did, I was delighted on one level but felt that she saw me as less powerful on another. And I was certainly in the economic position of most wives vis-à-vis most husbands. That may have reinforced the resentment I felt through all the years I free-lanced during our marriage, even when I made a reasonable living, even when I made more money than Susan did. I feared that I would not survive economically without her, and I resented that even as I applauded her success.

There was a period when I felt she lacked respect for my work, particularly my work on this book, perhaps because she had moved from feminist subjects to others. Later she repeatedly came back to them and to encouragement for me. At the same time, my admiration for her writing was increasing, but when I expressed envy of some of her work, she seemed to regard it as an invasion of her territory. There was a time when I felt Susan was shaping my thoughts and my behavior so much that she was limiting my independence, threatening to submerge my personality, even without intending to.

All these things fed the competition between us that helped destroy our marriage (see Chapter 8). In that competition, if I lost I felt damaged, and if I won I felt guilty—an experience that was new to me but commonplace for women. My feelings in the periods I've described were close to classic feminist complaints about husbands. My feminist friends said that the combination of love and resentment I was feeling was the kind of experience that produces a feminist, as Ingrid Bengis described becoming a man-hater in *Combat in the Erogenous Zone.*[1]

I think the feminists were right, in part. But just when I was going through "female" experiences, I was thinking like a male. I didn't like being weak, and I found it hard to reconcile the sensation of weakness, which I saw as one part of the feminine in me, with the assertiveness, the claims to mastery and dominance, the "masculine" elements that I continued to show. In other words, I was going through the same problems integrating the masculine and feminine in me that Daniel Levinson found characteristic of men in mid-life crisis.[2] Like traditional men whom I had both pitied and censured, I found it much easier to support my wife when she ranked below me professionally than when she became my equal. Consciously, I wanted her to be my equal. I tried to help her professionally, both by editing her writing (which she some-times asked me to do and sometimes resisted my offers to do) and by lobbying for her to get assignments. I felt I was giving her permission to surpass me. Only later did I realize that that was what my father had done for me, what parents often do for children rather than slay them or be slain in the struggle with authority figures—and that like many parents but not like my father, I was blaming her for being ungrateful.

Still later I realized that parental analogies seldom augur well for relations between man and woman. My feeling like a male was encouraged by Susan's difficulties in empathizing with the role reversal that the feminists had dis-cerned. She couldn't accept my feeling that she had surpassed me because she was still stuck emotionally in the first years of our marriage in Moscow and New York, when I was in the dominant position and she resented it. There were periods when we did manage to function as equals, but we often became so competitive that it corroded our love. My difficulties in accepting her as my equal were one of the reasons our marriage broke up. (There were others, some of them of equal importance, that don't belong in this or any book.)

PERSPECTIVE

My belief that men and women can treat each other as equals, in work and in love, has survived that pain. Such belief is one of the specific feelings and behaviors in men that this book looks at in a new perspective. I have learned from my own life and from other men that the effort to complete the women's revolution, and the men's revolution that must accompany it if it is to reach fruition in equality and independence for both sexes, is very difficult. It's difficult because power is involved, in public life and in private relationships. It's difficult because both profound and primitive emotions are involved. But it is not impossible. The structures, the dynamics, the processes of Western society can be changed. The evolution of economics and technology seems to demand such change. A few men and many women are trying to achieve such change, and both numbers are increasing. Such profound change is not free of social and emotional cost, however. This book is in part about the pleasures and rewards that men too can find in the changes women are making. It is even more about the costs that men feel we, and women, and society in general, will have to pay.

Chapter 2
A FRAMEWORK OF IDEAS

I couldn't understand what men had done to Susan and my mother, and how I felt about it, until I had a framework of ideas. I couldn't understand what women were doing to society, and how men felt about that, until I had a framework of theory and history. Not a web of abstractions, but ideas that would fit the real people I had interviewed, the people whose lives this book is about. I found I had to make a framework for myself; other thinkers had many illuminating perceptions, but none considered men across a wide enough range. I've made a few discoveries of my own, and I've metabolized them and many of the others' concepts into a new whole, a new view of an old universe.

Many ideas came from men, but most of the sharpest insights came from women. Few men are as willing as some women to immerse themselves in the difficult, often painful work of looking honestly at their own lives and the world's. Few men seem to recognize that ideas articulated by women may be true for all humans, may match male experience as well as female. We often act as though only the reverse were true.

One fundamental view that women have emphasized seems a bit obvious to be called new, but it's so often ignored or denied by men that it needs to be put in focus once more: changes in relations between the sexes are not only matters of role and emotion. They are also matters of power. The comparative success or failure of women and women's programs in the politics of the 1980s neither measures nor impeaches the truth of this idea. Power is not a matter just of offices and legislation, but of relations between people, control of the economy, social norms and social behavior, the power to name and define. Women are demanding an ever-increasing share of all these powers. Rulers have always been men, but women are challenging the assumption that that means the rulers will always be men.

Men have begun to sense and to talk about one kind of change—the personal, which we often see as a threat to our gender identity. We usually insist on remaining blind to political change, or pretending blindness. Some of us do quite a bit to fight this kind of change, and a few of us actually do things to encourage it. But most of us say almost nothing directly and explicitly about it, despite or because of the threat it poses to the power that we believe is also part of our identity. We can neither play an equal role in bringing the changes to fruition, nor block those we may think it imperative to resist, until we see clearly the shifts in feeling and in the struggle for power.

MORE PAIN THAN PLEASURE

The most important generalization about emotion needs more carefully qualified phrasing than I gave it in Chapter 1: most men tend to have more and stronger painful feelings than pleasurable ones about these changes. It is fashionable not to voice such emotions, but we feel them. Even men who are predominantly positive about these changes also have intense negative feelings that complicate their relations with women.

Strictly speaking, no feeling is negative. Anger and fear, for instance, serve a primary purpose: they warn us of the approach of something we see as a danger. But it's easy to call emotions that make us behave badly "negative," as a kind of shorthand. When we fight women and the changes they are making in work and love and power, we are feeling negative about them.

Our emotions fall into specific patterns that no one has identified in this context before. When we are negative about what women are doing, our feelings make patterns that emphasize different and changing combinations of anger, fear, anxiety, envy, shame, and guilt. When we are positive, our feelings fall into patterns that emphasize some combination of relief, pride, admiration, identification, and—though it surprises many men—pleasure.

The shifting patterns of emotion produce different patterns of behavior; every chapter of this book looks at the ways they occur in real life. I have encountered three behavior patterns that seem important on the negative side. Hostility is the most obvious, whether it be gross and physical or subtle and Machiavellian. The second is sometimes harder to deal with—abandonment or denial of the reality that we face, of women's competence at work, of women's capacity for power. The third is often the most fascinating. It's the compulsion to transform women into something we can deal with in order to avoid treating them as peers or powers—into nuns or whores, wives or lovers, daughters or sisters or mothers. The cause is obvious even when the emotions and the behavior are startling: most of us identify our masculinity so completely with our work and our traditional modes of dominance that we start to feel unmanned—which is to say, we start to lose our identities, our selves, our very humanity when women show that they can do the same work or exercise the same power.

The positive feelings and the patterns of behavior they produce tend to be less dramatic. Three kinds of behavior seem important: acceptance, support, and association. Sometimes they are undramatic because they seem natural, based on a man's identification with a wife or a daughter. Sometimes they are undramatic because they avoid confrontation. A man accepts his wife's taking a paid job because the family needs more money and represses the feeling that he should be the sole breadwinner. Support begins when a man realizes that there is something more at stake than money if a woman goes to work in a new field or asks him to share responsibility for housework—that she is demanding equality and choice, and that he wants her to have them. Association is a man's identification in action as well as feeling with a woman who is making changes. It may be pride in a lover's accomplishments, or admiration for a peer's achievements. It may become more complex when a man does what has traditionally been a woman's work. If he sees this as weakening him, it may lead to intense negative feelings and behavior. But it can also be the occasion for one of the strongest kinds of pleasure a man can feel in this context—the joy of raising children. Finally, association may bring men and women truly to join together, in an effort to achieve something better within the system than they can in opposition to each other, or to change a system that oppresses them both.*

The mixture of positive and negative feelings and behaviors varies from moment to moment and person to person, but it tends to sort men into fairly simple categories. In every class, every region, every race, and every age group, I found men who were opponents, men who were ambivalents, men who were pragmatists, and men who were supporters of the changes women are making. A man is likely to move from one category to another as he moves from one area of life to another, or to adopt the mask of one to hide feelings that place him in another.

Still, these stereotypes have their uses. Opponents are men who explicitly deny the equality of women, or who claim that it can be established only by destroying society as we know it. The purest examples cite the Bible and biology to "prove" that women shouldn't work at paid jobs, or that if they must work in order not to starve, it shouldn't be in "a man's job." Ambivalents probably form the largest of the four groups. They recognize intellectually that women have a legitimate claim to equality, but they can't live up to it. They know, for instance, that women are competent at many traditionally masculine jobs, but in their guts, they don't like working with women who take those jobs and they often don't want to live with them. Pragmatists are men who often say, "I'm not for women's lib"—and then add a "but" and a statement that feminists could accept or support. They would approve of a woman's earning money, and they would recognize the need for

---

* "Oppress" is a word loaded with overtones. In the language of women's movement ideologues, men oppress women. In this context there are few if any cases where women collectively oppress men. But in any system the powerful always tend to oppress the weak (if less harshly in the American system than in most others), and there are almost as many men among the weak as there are women. That is the sense in which I am applying the word to both sexes.

a woman to be able to change a flat tire by herself or acknowledge that a women's bank might help turn the right to equal credit into a reality. Supporters are men who like the idea of women's asserting their equality and their right to choices. They want women to have careers that mean something to them. They try to be sensitive to women's thoughts and feelings, and if they are married, they give their wives' careers equal weight when it comes to changing jobs or locations and take responsibility for a major portion of housework and child care.

There are also men who try to change the system on their own initiative or for their own reasons, like the rebels against gray flannel suits or the *Playboy* philosophers (see Chapter 9). It's important to recognize that they are not responding to women, and indeed often ignore women or contradict what women see as their interests. But as their ideas seep out into the general culture, they get caught up in the broader changes in male-female relations. The men who follow them fall into one or another of the categories from opponent to supporter as they face women challenging our psyches, our culture, and our political system.

IT IS A STRUGGLE FOR POWER

In our culture and our political system, rulers have indeed always been men. This does not mean that male rule is biologically based. It does not mean that male rule is morally imperative or historically inevitable.[1] It does not even mean that all men are rulers. Our response to women's demands for change is profoundly affected by something that Elizabeth Janeway has shown with new and compelling clarity: in truth, only a few men hold power.

The vast majority of men may identify with the powerful, may have explosive fantasies of power, but in reality we have little or no power. We never have had. We belong with women in the category of the weak, and as Janeway puts it, the weak are the second sex. We too, we men, are limited in our choices, dependent on the powerful, and dubious about our ability to change the rules. We find it hard to accept the idea that women are changing the rules themselves. In Janeway's words, women are invading the corridors of power "as if, merely being human, they had a right to be there. But most men have given up that right in return for a quiet life and some sense of security, for government by law as an acceptable bargain between the weak and the powerful. The idea that women are now refusing to accept this bargain acts as a terrifying, a paralyzing challenge to men. Either they too must revolt or they must acknowledge themselves lacking in the courage and ambition being shown by their traditionally inferior sisters."[2]

We have not been quick to rebel ourselves or join their revolt because we do indeed identify with our brothers who rule. Power, in the view most often shared by the powerful and the weak, is a matter of haves and have-nots, of what Lenin phrased as *kto kvo*—who does what to whom, who uses or abuses whom. We want to be haves, doers, users rather than used. Men who are powerless—blue-collar workers, the unemployed, racial minorities, certain homosexuals at certain moments are only the most obvious examples, as the middle class and the yuppies learn soon enough—are likely to feel more anger or fear than more powerful men at the changes that women are making. Men with less power often have a greater need to think of women as inferior; almost everybody needs to feel superior to somebody as part of his or her definition of self, and we spend a lot of aggressive energy treating women, consciously or unconsciously, as an underclass.

When these people whom we label inferiors rebel, we become angry not only because they challenge the power that we have, or that our myths compel us to pretend that we have. They also expose us to the reality of our own powerlessness. Denial and hostility are all too expectable results. Some of us yield to compulsive fantasies of power—unlimited, uncontrolled power. A few of us translate those fantasies into life. Wife beating is an obvious example. Rape and murder are possibilities.

Men have made four kinds of power our domain, whether by actually holding it or by identifying with the male holders. The most important is one that neither men nor women have put into clear focus. It is the power to name, which Janeway calls "the valuable power to define the elements of our world and to declare how weighty, how urgent and how pressing they are." That is the power, she emphasizes, that has made the aggressive, thrusting penis the symbol of active, assertive power, and the "hidden inwardness of women's sex organs the mark of the passive receiver and nurturer."

The power to name and define, though little discussed, underlies the three other, obvious kinds of power whose holders are predominantly men. Violence is inherent in the most palpable, the power to mobilize destructive aggression—the ability and intention to hurt or kill others, individually or collectively—in groups ranging in size from pairs to the modern state. The next most visible is the power to organize life—society, economy, and polity —for both destructive and constructive ends. The third is closely related to what I will call constructive aggression: the power to direct others' use of their skills, to command others' manipulation and control of the environment, to select what is to be changed, to choose the desired goals, to measure efficiency and effectiveness.

In some cases, men have begun to share these four kinds of power with women, and in others, women have seized or invaded areas that men did not offer to share voluntarily. There is a fifth, private kind of power, which men have not tried to preempt: the capacity to develop oneself, to deal with one's own emotions and weaknesses, to master one's own skills and strengths. Only the last aspect of power over the self traditionally appeals to large numbers of men in Western society. The expression of emotions is a power we have often left to women, as the male stereotypes of our culture encouraged us to repress our own feelings. The women's movement, the current spread of the psycho-therapeutic subculture, and the age of narcissism, which includes both healthy and unhealthy aspects of concern with self, may all increase male interest in the power to develop oneself and deal with one's emotions.

There is no single or unequivocal answer to the question why human society has encouraged men to dominate the exercise of these four kinds of power, or why men's attempts to monopolize rule have been so successful. Perhaps positions of rule or leadership are men's reward for the strength and skill needed for the hunt and for warfare, which tend to be male monopolies even in societies where women have a share of authority. Perhaps leadership is the incentive that makes men risk their lives in those dangerous occupations. Both ideas seem to me to be valid anthropological speculations. But I think that Dorothy Dinnerstein and Nancy Chodorow go deeper and are more probably right when they say that male rule grows out of the long infancy of individuals in the human species.[4] Until recently, biological and technological conditions forced women to care for the young while men worked, warred, and ruled; men and women have both made this division of labor a matter of political inequality rather than simple role differentiation. Going deeper yet, to a psychological level that sounds crude but still has the ring of truth, I think men may have claimed leadership long ago, and kept it through the ages, to compensate for our inability to bear children.

DIFFERENCES THAT MATTER

That inability is one of the sexual differences on which the biological existence of *Homo sapiens* depends. It's so obvious that it seems silly to state it, but it's important to make it explicit so we can see its limits: women can bear and breast-feed children; men cannot.

One other sexual difference is also real and important: males are more aggressive than females.

(Males' heavier musculature and greater strength is a biological difference that throughout history has been associated with the division of labor between men and women. It reinforces the perception of male aggressiveness, and we use it as an excuse to deny female demands for equality. But it is seldom a determinant in today's society unless men exploit it to commit violence against women. There are also differences in the way male and female brains function. For instance, girls tend to be better at languages and boys to be better at visual and spatial tasks. These affect education and job testing and can contribute to social tensions—or social harmonies. Both body strength and brain function are like other biological differences: they are usually small, and differences among members of the same sex are usually greater than average differences between the sexes.)

If we see these differences clearly, we may stop acting as though sharing work and power with women threatens the existence of the species. We have this fear for only one reason: over the millennia Western society has used the real differences between the sexes to create forces of immense strength in our psyches, our culture, and our politics.

First among these forces is the process of psychological development in which the infant starts to become adult by struggle with the mother, the female. Closely related are both the division of labor that makes women the child rearers as well as the child bearers while men go to work and war, and the male tendency to bond together and exclude women. The division and the bond crystallize into social structures in which men work and act in public, and rule, while women labor in private.

None of these forces is truly biological, in my opinion. They still run with great depth and strength in us and our society, but we can change them without endangering the species. We need only ask, do we want to pay the immense cost.

Some of the male feelings that go into that reckoning operate in the individual psyche. Some operate in the group—the couple, the family, the work organization, the religious community, the race, the nation-state, any and all of the different groups to which we belong by virtue of being human. The most important emotions function in both individual and group—the anger and the fear, for instance, that men often feel when women challenge our control of work and politics.

These strong but simple feelings become explosive because we see women as claiming not one power (or a share in our one power), but two. The second is the power to bear children. We fear that power because it is mysterious to us, and we fear it because we don't have it. Only they do. We cannot separate our anger over female political power from our fear of female reproductive power. But we seldom articulate either the distinction or the link.

Janeway sees female power as a myth, a male projection onto the "other" sex that is used to keep women in submission in the world of reality.[5] It certainly is a reason that men deny women power, that we resist the changes women are making. But the fear of female power is real in the individual psyche, and it reflects power that men—and women, too—see as real. This is clearest in the ancient myths and beliefs. Wolfgang Lederer has assembled what might be described as a catalogue raisonné called *The Fear of Women.* Even a fragmentary selection shows the strength of the fear, and sometimes of the actions men take to deal with it. The Norns and the Fates, female figures able to cut off the life of man, were prime examples. So was Pandora, the female gift whom Zeus sent to man as retribution for Prometheus' theft of fire from the gods. She came with a box or jar; in the age of Freud it is easy to say we know what that stands for, especially when the myth says that she took the lid off the jar and scattered all the evils through the world. Witches were irresistibly attractive and inhumanly destructive, as children still know today from Grimm's fairy tales, and as the inquisitors knew when they burned witches by the thousands across Europe between 1258 and 1782. Tribes around the world have myths of females whose vaginas have teeth—and of heroes who learn how to master them. Menstrual bleeding is part of the mystery of birth, but almost every culture has incredibly detailed rules for avoiding what men once saw as a deadly curse, a curse of amazing variety. A menstruating woman kills one of two men she walks between, according to one passage in the Talmud. Today we smile rather than shudder at that thought, or at the idea that menstrual blood can sour wine, curdle mayonnaise, dim mirrors, or kill garden pests.[6]

Men associate women with death as well as birth. This central strand in the fear of women derives in part from the intuition that to be sexual is to be mortal, embodied in the story of Adam and Eve and other male-shaped religious myths.[7] The French call the male sexual climax "the little death"—the death of "the little man," the penis, that humans discerned even before modern biology told us there is a half death in the act of reproduction, the gamete's throwing away of half of its paired chromosomes in the linking with the half from its mate. The intimation of mortality sees the psychic merger of selves in love and in the sex act as threatening the death of the self—a threat that men feel more than women do. And each time the human organism passes beyond the little death, it moves closer to the large death that awaits it.

THE POWER OF MOTHER

The male identification of sexuality and death with woman begins at the same source as the division of human activity into public and private and all the other practices and institutions from which our ancient myths and our contemporary anger and our fears about females grow: the fact, the function, the role, the image, the mystery of motherhood. Men ascribe power to a female figure not only because she is other, but because she is Mother.

Almost every man I interviewed for this book thought of his mother as an important figure in his life. Only a handful, however, had ever thought about development in the infant, the very process that makes the mother so important, or the way that process affects the daily life of everyone entangled in the revolution and resistance that this book is about. The mother gives the child the first food and the first "no," and draws the first love and the first rage. The infant experiences her as omnipotent, and particularly as having the power to destroy as well as create. This makes her both the Terrible Mother and the Good Mother of myth and folktale. But the child also learns to devalue the female in order to separate from her. Men's responses to the changes that women are making—and women's responses too—are shaped by the way adult relationships between them repeat, in attenuated form, the infant's struggle, the vital need to separate from the mother it cannot bear to leave.

Chapter 10, on the new fathering, includes a closer look at the development process. Here I want to make only one point: the dominance of mother in childhood is literally the first cause of men's anger and fear and our other negative feelings about women's demands for independence and equality. There is another major cause, centering on aggression, and several minor ones, but the power of mother is primary. That is where the window of possibility for revolution opens widest. Dorothy Dinnerstein, Nancy Chodorow, and Lillian Rubin are absolutely right when they say that the way to change men's responses to the new challenges posed by women, and the profound human dilemma beneath them, is to have men share primary parenting responsibilities and participate as deeply as women "in the initiation of infants into the human estate."[8]

If we did this, boys and girls would be able to identify with figures of both genders. They would rebel against and separate from parents of both genders. Men might then be less obsessive about their masculinity than they are now, and less compulsive about devaluing women. The subconscious fear of women that is really fear of maternal omnipotence would diminish. Men would then be less inclined to set up public spheres that define women as secondary and powerless.[9]

Such a profound change will be difficult, painful, and costly. Human society has shaped a myriad of institutions over thousands of years, and Western society has shaped its economy, around the assumption that women do the mothering. But this revolution is not impossible.

TRUTHS ABOUT AGGRESSION

The power of mothering is just one of two basic reasons that men resist women's claim to equality in work and rule. The second is connected with another misconception about a genuine biological difference. Work and power both spring from aggression. People think of aggression as masculine, and men fear the thought that women may become masculine. People think of aggression as destructive, and men fear the thought of women as destroyers.

Two truths, if we accept and make use of them, may reshape the carelessness of that kind of commonplace thought. The first is that aggression is, along with self-preservation and sex, one of the innate drives in humans. Both sexes have it, which we forget when we think of aggression as something peculiar to our masculine identity, something that women do not or should not have. Men are *more* aggressive than women, according to the preponderance of the evidence, but women too are—or at least can be—aggressive.

The second truth is that aggression is not only destructive; it is also creative. It is the force behind humanity's efforts to master nature, to move toward goals of any kind. Aggression is the drive to change or transform external objects, as psychiatrist Jay Rohrlich says in *Work and Love: the Crucial Balance.*[10] In changing things, it may seek to hurt and destroy. But it can also seek change in the present in order to enhance or create life in the future. (It's interesting that the most prominent advocates of the idea that aggressiveness is an ineradicable part of human nature, the sociobiologists, pay so little attention to the constructive kind of aggression. They usually talk of aggression only as a matter of dominance or hurtfulness.)

I want to emphasize how basic the drive to change the external world is to humans. We are biologically capable of planning, neurally organized for purposeful effort, and such effort, such enterprise, "gives us pleasure as straightforward as the pleasure of lovemaking."[11] Dinnerstein, who puts it so clearly, does not use the word "aggression," but the enterprise she speaks of is a product of the aggressive drive.

This kind of aggression, when it is sufficiently organized, is called work.[12] Rohrlich defines work as "the skillful organization, manipulation and control of the external and internal environments, to achieve a desired goal most efficiently and effectively."

The evidence that men are more aggressive than women comes from the destructive side of aggression. This is the side usually emphasized in everyday and diplomatic language—the side that leads to rage and hostility, which in turn may produce attack, invasion of others' space, injury, and death. Eleanor Maccoby and Carol Jacklin, defining aggression as a loose cluster of actions and motives whose central theme is the intent of one individual to hurt another, report that males are more aggressive than females in all human societies for which evidence is available. They don't say this difference is purely biological, but it has a biological aspect: a high level of the male hormone testosterone is associated with aggressive behavior as cause or effect or both.[13] Maccoby and Jacklin are quick to point out that women can injure other people, that in any group some women will be as aggressive as men, and that an individual's aggressive behavior is modified by his or her unique experiences. They make these points in order to conclude, "All we mean to argue is that there is a sex-linked differential readiness to respond in aggressive ways to the relevant experiences."[14]

I believe that this readiness applies not only to the destructive forms of aggression they consider, but also to the constructive forms, the side of aggression connected with work. Males and females both have the basic drive to plan and achieve, but it is stronger in males.

The greater male readiness to respond to the demands of the enterprising drive is reinforced by the way humans develop. As infants we turn from delight in our "omnipotent unity" with the mother to delight in our new constructive aggressiveness, which underlies both the child's first steps in a nursery and the adult's first steps on the moon. The delight we have abandoned was, of course, provided by a female. These facts of infant life make both boys and girls see this new delight, the aggressive enterprise, as nonfemale, which further devalues women.[15] Society reinforces the feeling by contrasting work, concerned with the world of things, which it tends to make masculine, with love, concerned with people and attachment, which it tends to make feminine (girls repress their need for attachment less than boys do). In this way every human in our society re-creates the old division of labor anew.

HUMAN ACTIVITY, PUBLIC AND PRIVATE

Another perspective on the division of labor and indeed on the entire human condition comes from looking at the different kinds of human activity. Hannah Arendt calls them labor, work, and action, in ascending order. I think we must add language to her list.

Arendt defines labor as the production of necessities for the growth, metabolism, and decay of the human body, assuring both individual survival and the life of the species. Work provides a world of artifacts that outlast and transcend the individual lives that they house collectively, bestowing a measure of permanence on the "futility of mortal life." Action is activity between people without the intermediary of things or matter, activity that "corresponds to the human condition of plurality, to the fact that men, not Man, live on the earth. . . ." This plurality is *the* condition of political life, and action, "in so far as it engages in founding and preserving political bodies, creates the condition for remembrance, that is for history."[16]

Rohrlich's definition of work applies to all three of Arendt's concepts, though her definition of labor bases it in the drive for self-preservation as well as in aggression. The definition of work does not apply to language, which I have put atop her list. But it is language that enables us to organize labor, work, and action, that grows more complex and sophisticated as we move up the scale of activity, that on occasion becomes a fourth kind of human activity in its own right. It is language that makes possible remembrance of action, and it is language that enables us to conceive, talk about, and plan—that is, to take action—for the future.

The future is one of many realms of language that contemporary philosophers call the "counter-factual"; George Steiner mentions among others the conditional, the lie, the fantastic, poetry, fables, stories, dramas, novels.[17] Creating them is a form of human activity that can be differentiated from work and its artifacts, from action and its plurality—though it overlaps with both. Language needs both the factual and the counterfactual for its gift to humans of the power to name and define—one of the powers that men have preempted and made a base of our dominance.

These different kinds of human activity are keys to defining the boundary between public and private. This boundary is fundamental in the division of labor, in the changes that women are making, and in the male response to those changes. It operates at profound philosophical depths and in everyday life. For most of the history of Western society, men have spoken and acted as though women belonged on the private side of the line.

Arendt notes that in classical times action took place in public and work often emerged into the public sphere. Labor, however, was kept hidden in privacy, as were "the laborers who 'with their bodies minister to the [bodily] needs of life,' and the women who with their bodies guarantee the physical survival of the species. Women and slaves belonged to the same category and were hidden away not only because they were somebody else's property but because their life was 'laborious,' devoted to bodily functions."[18]

This changed somewhat in the centuries when the household was a productive economic unit and women did so much "public" work in the privacy of the home. Then the industrial revolution shifted economic effort from the household to the factory 150 years ago. The women who stayed home not only to bear but also to raise children were again relegated to the private, the domestic. Whole ideologies developed in America in the 1830s and again in the 1870s to enforce the split. These ideologies reinforced the tendency to segregate those women who did go out to work in certain jobs or industries, which testified to the strength of the desire to keep them away from the "public" that was male.[19]

Men's determination to hide women in the depths of the laborious and the private has compelled us to rewrite history—to hide, for instance, the role of women in the invention of nets, baskets, textiles, pottery, mortar and pestle, the plow, and bread.[20] Those inventions were female achievements in the world of work; our refusal to acknowledge them is ironic, because that work merely provided women with tools for the lower activity of labor to which we confined them.

Men also tried to restrict women's use of language to the private. The best-known of a myriad of examples may be St. Paul's injunction, "Let your women keep silence in the churches: for it is not permitted unto them to speak; but *they are commanded* to be under obedience, as also saith the law. And if they will learn any thing, let them ask their husbands at home: for it is a shame for women to speak in the church."[21] Paul was repeating an idea that echoed from millennia before Christ, which has in turn reverberated down to the present. Only two centuries ago, in most Western countries, the entry of women into social and political debate verged on obscenity.

Women were long barred not only from such public forums as religion and politics, but also from literature. When women did begin to speak and write in public, men tried to return them to the hiding place of the private by caricaturing them. Sheridan's Mrs. Malaprop and Fielding's Mrs. Slipslop "implied that language itself was almost literally alien to the female tongue. In the mouths of women, vocabulary loses meaning, sentences dissolve, literary messages are distorted or destroyed."[22] Emily Dickinson offered touching testimony to the plight of women presuming to enter the male world of poetry in the first stanza of a poem, and to the futility of male-constructed barriers in the next two:

> They shut me up in Prose
> As when a little Girl
> They put me in the Closet—
> Because they liked me "still"—
>
> Still! Could themself have peeped—
> And seen my Brain—go round—
> They might as wise have lodged a Bird
> For Treason—in the Pound—
>
> Himself has but to will
> And easy as a Star
> Abolish his Captivity—
> And laugh—No more have I—[23]

Today the effort to restrict women's use of language to the private continues. It is changing as women enter "masculine" occupations and political life, and as the women's movement and the therapeutic subculture join forces to persuade men to listen better to the women in their lives. But it is still very much part of the main cultural tradition. Women and men speak in different languages, or at least in different styles, and the women's style is perceived, even by feminist linguists, as less precise and less forceful. This enables men to devalue women's speech. It helps justify, even subconsciously, restricting women's access to public forums. It is part of a system by which females learn their place as they learn language.[24]

There is a terrible irony here, since girls are superior in verbal skills to boys, at least in elementary school. The process by which women learn their place intensifies at puberty; many girls in high school and college often seem to hide or discard those verbal skills in coeducational classes, though that too is changing. Some men do recognize that women are "a hell of a lot more verbal than men are" even as adults—which "scares the hell out of men when it begins to be used in specific competitive ways. As long as it's corralled into private activities it isn't threatening," observed Carl Woodman,* a wise businessman (see Chapters 7 and 9). Men who feel that fear reward women who remain silent and penalize women who speak out. The penalty may be no more than calling them "shrill" or "strident," or as serious as dismissing them from jobs.

BOUNDARIES AND FEARS

When a woman speaks out in disagreement with her male supervisors, the men may see her as threatening male power in the organization. If she is fired, they are responding with anger. She threatens their male bond, too, and they respond by excluding her—which can also be taken as a hostile act. (For more on the male bond, see Chapter 5.) But she also threatens the boundaries that the men at the top draw around themselves, and if threats to power lead to anger, threats to dissolve boundaries lead to fear.

This happens because the disappearance of boundaries can lead individuals to insanity and societies to chaos, a prospect that indeed arouses primal fears. Work is the part of adult life where boundaries are most clearly drawn. In our society, men define ourselves and others know us primarily by our occupations, their labels, symbols, and products, by what we do and what we make. We define women and force them to define themselves that way too. But when women invade the traditionally masculine function of earning a significant portion of family income, and even more importantly, when they do it by engaging in traditionally masculine occupations and rising to traditionally masculine levels in the work hierarchy, many men feel that they are dissolving important boundary lines.

Men usually identify work boundaries with the demarcation of our gender identity, and we fear the dissolution of the boundary between those with penises and those without. Many of the interviews in this book show that unconsciously we fear the disappearance of the boundary that separates us from our mothers, whom we fear and long for, and that groups us with our fathers, whom we fear and long for in different ways. The link on this side of the boundary is important. We often overlook it because we must forget the wounds our fathers inflict on us and the deaths we inflict on the father-as-authority. But I like Lederer's idea that the competition to be as good as a strong father, or better—a competition that takes place on this side of the boundary—establishes a sense of adequacy in the son.[25] Father was big enough and strong enough for mother, and we need our identification with him to know that we can conquer our own fear of women. That identification, that assurance, depend on the work boundary and the boundary between the powerful and the powerless. They are threatened when those boundaries are dissolved. These boundaries will change as our identification with our fathers changes—if men take a full share in the process of initiating children into humanity.

ROLES AND ANXIETIES

If threats to male rule lead to anger and the erosion of boundaries to fear, changes in sex roles more often lead to anxiety. Indeed, the most sophisticated research on the subject suggests that *sex-role strain* is today's paradigm. Sex roles produce strain and strain produces anxiety, Joseph Pleck points out, because sex roles are inconsistent and because conformity can be psychologically harmful. The proportion of individuals who "violate" sex roles is high; violations lead to social condemnation that is more severe for males than for females. Sex roles are shifting from traditional to modern versions; everything that produces strain can be found in both, and historical change itself produces further strain.[26] Many, though not all, of these anxiety-ridden changes in roles have been stimulated by women demanding changes in their own roles.

Even as they change, sex roles are still defined by stereotypes—widely shared beliefs about what the sexes actually are like—and norms—widely shared beliefs about what the sexes should be like.* Male sex-role stereotypes continue to operate even as the role changes. Robert Brannon suggests that there are four important ones. First, a man should avoid the stigma of anything feminine, especially emotions that make him appear vulnerable. Second, a man should work and support his family (the breadwinner role), and should have the skills and knowledge to achieve success and status. Third, a man should have, and show, physical strength, toughness, confidence, and self-reliance. And fourth, a man should be venturesome, willing to take risks and engage in violence without hesitation.[27]

Men saw the breadwinner role, for instance, as one in which they provided status and economic security for women. A man may feel anxiety that a woman who works for her own status and security threatens his entitlement to the role and the status he found in it, if she is a peer. If she is his wife, as often happens, he may feel anxiety that his dominance in the family is psychologically, sociologically, or economically threatened—that his wife has less need for him.

Roles and boundaries alike are involved in the anxieties that arise from the seeming opposition of work and love, the segregation of the two that is both cause and effect of the division of labor, and the attempt to bridge it that sometimes seems to be part of the changes that women are making. Work is a product of the aggressive drive, love of the sexual drive. Work demands boundaries; love dissolves boundaries in seeking union. Work uses intelligence

---

* Sex roles are matters both of the individual's psychological development and of what is learned by socialization, of the individual's internalizing society's mandates.

and skills to change the external world in order to achieve a goal in the future, functions our society has associated with the male role more than the female. Love uses emotions and senses for internal experience in the present, things the culture has put into the female role more than the male. Civilization and personal well-being are rooted in both work and love, of course, and individuals are always seeking some balance of the two. But at some deep, almost always unconscious level many men feel that if women become our peers at work they will no longer be able to function in love, or we will no longer see them as desirable, no longer *want* them to function in love. Some women feel that if men become their peers in mothering or other aspects of love, then we will no longer be able to give women what they need. These feelings produce anxiety in many men and in women too.

Yet another kind of anxiety percolates from our feelings about power, about love, about roles and boundaries. If women become our peers, men may have to modify or give up our use of women in relations between males. We use women to symbolize our power, to validate our masculinity, to mediate between us and our fathers, brothers, sons, peers, rivals.[28] In all these ways, we use women to express the emotions we have long taught ourselves to conceal, to repress. In today's culture we are learning to experience and to express our emotions in ways that should make us healthier, but we still use women to *receive* the feelings we can now bring out.[29] What would we do if we couldn't use women in these ways? The very question provokes anxiety. But it is the wrong question. If men and women become true peers, emotions and power would flow both ways. But we would have to give the emotional functions we have until now assigned to women higher value, higher rank, and higher pay. The real question is, can we do that?

ENVY, SHAME, AND GUILT

Some men fear that placing a higher value on emotion will mean giving the functions of women a higher value than those of men. That creates the possibility of envy. Some men already envy women for the changes they are making—or perhaps for our perception of their achievements, for combining masculine work and feminine emotionality (the fear of their having both political and reproductive power is echoed in a fear of their having both economic and emotional power). Many women would consider this ironic, since they feel they have seldom gained much enviable power in reality. But there are men who feel envy as Willard Gaylin describes it: a bitter, resentful feeling toward the person who has something we do not.[30] Envy involves our feeling that we have been denied what we want; that others have what we have been denied; that we are impotent in the face of disparity; and that we do not have what we want just because others have it. I have heard men talk that way about women's advances under affirmative action programs, even though the advances are truly token. And I have heard men talk that way about some women's significant new ability to combine mastery and nurturance.

Some men take the idea of equal value between men and women, of the mere possibility of higher value for women, as part of a threat that we will become like women or indeed be transformed into women. Even without the often misinterpreted concepts of penis envy and castration fear, the fear of becoming like women can lead to a sense of shame in men. It is important to remember here that shame is a public emotion, involving the public exposure of some sin, some wrongdoing, some failing. It incorporates the community, the other, directly into the feelings. It fuses humiliation and anger.

We feel shame at becoming like the other. Men struggle against identification with the female, which implies the desire for such identification.[31] We repress this desire, which makes shame all the more likely if such identification occurs and is revealed. It may be shame at identifying with the mother from whom we want to separate. It may be shame at becoming like a feared and mysterious other, or at degrading a beautiful and admired other, making it like our (unconsciously seen as shameful) selves. It may be shame at becoming entrapped in emotionality, in sexuality, in weakness and vulnerability, in the function of serving and the function of caring—in qualities we make women carry for the whole society.

These qualities are intertwined in a Gordian knot with powerlessness, a powerlessness that men have done so much to create. If we become like women in any sense, we are in danger of being "not male," which may make us feel psychologically like being no person at all. If we become like women in the sense of being powerless (as in fact most of us are), we are in danger of being almost nothing. Feeling like nothing, feeling we may be exposed as nothing, makes us feel shame for ourselves. Feeling the powerlessness that we have mired women in makes us feel shame for them. We know that powerlessness, which we have made congruent with incompetence, is synonymous with low self-respect. We deny women self-respect even as we seek to love them and ask them to love us, both of which depend absolutely on their self-respect. When women claim power, they remind us of the wrongs we have done them as our intimates and as a class. Before and beyond shame, we feel anger at the threat to deprive us of some of our power, and we also feel guilt that we have denied women power.

People often think of guilt as a negative emotion, but it's not. It shapes much of our goodness and generosity because it informs us when we have failed our own ideals and prods us to try again. Guilt, like love, is an unselfish emotion. In Gaylin's words, it testifies that "for Homo Sapiens community is not an ideal, but a biological necessity. There is no such thing as individual survival. The human being is human because of the nurture of other human beings.

. . . Guilt parallels the sexual drive. Here one sees the most primitive, the most central and essential fusion between individual pleasure and group needs."[32]

It's a pity that so many people regard this emotion as negative—as a burden, as a confession of blameworthiness, useless at best and branding us at worst with wrongdoing and sin. It's a pity that so many men deny we have anything to feel guilty about so far as women are concerned, as though guilt were a declaration of weakness and wimphood. Guilt is one of the things that impels us to recognize women's claim to equality and power, independence and choice. Only a strong man can feel it and put it to uses that benefit himself and society.

POSITIVE EMOTIONS

The positive emotions that men sometimes feel about women's claim to equality and independence are, like guilt, part of the drive toward fusion between individual pleasure and group needs, part of the drive toward the community we must find if we are to be truly human.

There is, significantly, almost no literature on this: no anthology of myths and rituals that resonate to our positive feelings, few psychology texts on the joy that can flow, if we are both wise and lucky, from the most complex and delicate of relationships. Perhaps this happens because psychiatry is part of medicine, which traditionally studies disease and not health. Perhaps philosophers, especially in this era, find pain more interesting than pleasure. If we experience any positive feelings, we tend to have them about the women we live with—our wives and lovers, particularly our daughters, sometimes our sisters and mothers—before or more than we do about the women we work with (see Chapter 9). The arrival of women in the traditionally masculine work place is eroding the old polarization between work and love, which often makes us uncomfortable, and sometimes we still feel horror at the violation of taboo. But the erosion of that boundary is also one of the things that sometimes make it easier for men to feel good about the changes women are making at work.

The first positive feeling that I have identified is relief. People seldom think of relief as an emotion, but there is no doubt that it feels good to lay a burden down. Power is a burden. Responsibility is a burden. Many of the stereotyped male sex roles are burdens. They are also sources of pleasure and pride, of course; they give us the heady sense that power is its own reward, and they are parts of our sexual identity, so that shedding them or lightening them may be painful and threaten to rip apart our manhood.

But if we take the risk, we may find that sharing burdens can also make our lives easier. If a wife takes a paying job, it eases her husband's financial

burden. If she participates in family decision making, it eases his emotional
stress. If we share our power, we validate it and feel a special kind of relief:
reassurance. If we are forced to resolve the cognitive dissonance between our
claim to superiority and the behavior that shows we are really no better than
women, it may feel at first like excruciating torture. But we can transcend the
pain—if we are persistent and use both our brains and our hearts, and if the
women we love or the women we work with are generous—and experience
the relief of giving up an equally excruciating pretense. If we then discover
that our essential manhood is undamaged despite the pain, we again feel that
important emotion, reassurance.

The next positive feelings men are likely to develop about the changes women
are making are pride and admiration. In ancient times, pride was a sin. Webster's New Collegiate Dictionary has not completely escaped from the notion
and gives as its first definition of pride, "Inordinate self-esteem." It quickly
goes on, however, to "a reasonable or justifiable self-respect" and "delight or
elation arising from some act, possession, or relationship."

Ideally, pride is first an emotion about one's self. Self-respect is an essential
for mental health and the good life. Pride springs from achievement and
mastery—the mastery of doing and creating, not mastery over another person. As Gaylin says, pride is essential to maturation, to abandoning the pleasures of dependency, to discovering the pleasure in achievement that supports
independence. Ironically, the pride that men can feel in women—from the
third definition, delight arising from a relationship—is in constant danger of
paternalism, of creating a new dependency. Men as a class are not the parents
of women as a class, of course, and if our pride in a woman's achievements
has a paternalistic flavor she won't tolerate it for very long. But a parent's
pride in a child is pride in the child's progress toward independence. Some
men feel pride in a woman's *assertion* of independence, equality, and choice.

Admiration—esteem, delighted approbation—is a more impersonal emotion than pride, and unlike pride it is usually other-directed. It is important
because it is a positive feeling we can have about a woman who achieves
mastery in our own kind of work, an emotion that avoids some of the dangers
of mixing work and love just because it is impersonal. It recognizes the independence of the person we admire in a way that pride cannot, since pride is
more closely and more obviously involved with the relationship between self
and object. But admiration is still a pleasurable feeling because it associates us
with another and implies generosity and thus enhances our sense of our
selves.

Beyond pride and admiration, often growing out of them but even more
closely related to love, is identification. As I noted in writing about my father,
identification is the process by which we fuse our sense of self with those we
admire and envy and above all with those we love. The love of parent for

child may be the highest form of identification, but it is not the only one. Men can also identify with wives or lovers, with friends, with colleagues and peers. We are not used to identifying with female colleagues, but we can. We can share their achievements, and share our own with them. We can share their pains and pleasures, their joys and sadnesses.

Gaylin remarks that identification binds us to others in a common fate and enables us to feel compassion, sympathy, and empathy. These have not been common male responses to women who demand equality and choice. We might come closer to thinking and feeling that women are humans if we had more compassion and sympathy and empathy. But we have to be careful, because those feelings slide quickly into behaving charitably toward women and expecting them to be grateful. Janeway makes an important point: sympathy for the stigmatized devalues their emotions, and men stigmatize women as the Other almost every day. We, the powerful and the normal, say it's natural for the stigmatized to be angry. Who wouldn't be resentful in their position? Their resentment then becomes a background noise that the powerful take for granted. If we see women as objects of charity, we won't see them as enemies—or as agents of change.[33] Nor will we see them as lovers or comrades in the fullest sense. Charity is one of the opposites of identification.

My list of positive feelings concludes with pleasure, but it's hard to distinguish pleasure from the other emotions. It is part of most kinds of feeling good. Five kinds of pleasure affect men's feelings about women, starting with the sensual.[34] Women bring us the joys of touching and being touched, the joys of taste and smell and sight and sound. God forbid we should abandon these joys, but they have only one connection with the changes we are talking about. Women searching for independence and equality, women asserting themselves and taking initiatives may give us greater sensual and sexual variety, either in a relationship with one woman, or in increasing the possibilities of relationships with many women.

The pleasure of discovery, of using our distance perceptors and our intelligence to fuse the sensory and the intellectual, is something we probably have to experience in order to feel good about women as our peers. So is the pleasure of mastery, which produces the sense of growth.

The pleasure of immersion, the profound involvement of self with something or some activity we care about, increases our capacity for the highest forms of sharing. Immersion in the same activity is not a prerequisite for feeling good about equality with women. Indeed, it may make positive feelings harder to cultivate because we may feel threatened by their invasion of yet another of "our" territories. But if we do share immersion with a woman peer, it can make our positive feelings more intense.

Gaylin moves from immersion in things and processes to fusion with people. His examples are playing in an orchestra, singing in a choir, being part of a team activity. We do not disappear into a crowd but enlarge ourselves in identifying with the larger body. If men experience this pleasure with women, it may teach us yet more about women as peers. That would carry with it the possibility of a simpler and more dangerous kind of fusion. It is a profound pleasure for a man to love a woman who is talented, successful, achieving. If there is no exploitative conquest, if she gives herself to him, he receives a richer gift than he would find with a woman who had not developed that side of her self. I am assuming that such development need not be at the expense of her sensual, nurturing, or emotional sides, as it is so often and so sadly. A woman of course also receives a richer gift if she loves a man who has developed all these aspects of his self. Traditionally that has been even harder for a man than for a woman. One of the benefits we may find in these changes is that it may become easier for us.

POSITIVE BEHAVIOR

The behavior that grows out of these positive feelings often starts as paternalism. Acceptance, for instance, may begin with a man's pragmatic decision to "let" his wife work and to put the money she earns to family use. Often it is earmarked for luxuries, and only later does she gain the equal status of putting her income into necessities, just as he does. He may not immediately "give" her an equal voice in deciding how to spend the money, but most women soon demand that equality, and most of their husbands eventually agree.

Support for a woman's career, for her quest for equality and choices, is likely to be voiced at first in the tones of a member of an elite giving charity to the poor or handicapped, or of a parent enjoying a child's steps toward independence. This attitude changes fastest when a woman demands that her husband show his support by doing an equal share of the housework and child raising. Support also moves away from paternalism when a man trains a woman to master a profession. There is obviously something paternal in the mentor-protégée relationship, but it soon ceases to be paternal when the younger person moves onward. That may threaten the mentor and give him pain, or it may reward him and give him pleasure, depending on many things in his soul and in the external world.

Association, joining together, is the form of behavior that loses its paternalistic flavor the fastest. Otherwise it wouldn't be true association. Sharing the housework moves from support to association when the man takes equal responsibility instead of just "helping" his wife. (That is still relatively rare.) Doing traditionally feminine work when a man has no woman in his life, no woman to share it with, is association in the abstract more than in the concrete or the flesh-and-blood. Hearing single fathers complain about doing the shitwork of child raising, hearing them realize that it is the price of the joy of child nurture, makes me think it is very real association all the same. Women have known those things forever. Association with women as peers at work will become more common as more women enter traditionally masculine occupations, though men are resisting more than expected as the number of women passes the token level (see Chapter 7). Women are still so new and so few at the higher levels of business and the professions that it is hard to find concrete examples of happy association.

DEALING WITH REALITIES

The emotions and behaviors sketched here are not only matters of theory. Men and women experience them every day. But neither sex sees these feelings and the acts that flow from them clearly enough. Those who dwell on the negatives seldom recognize that the positives do happen. Those who are proud of their positives often deny that the negatives also operate and are significant in their souls and their lives. This book shows the workings of both positive and negative in daily life, in different kinds of workplace, in marriage and sex and parenting. I hope it will help both men and women decide if they want to pay the high but subtly calculated cost of the changes that I think add up to revolution---a revolution that I would like to see come to fruition.

Chapter 3
A MAN GOES CRAZY

Once I saw a man go crazy when women took power. Literally. A man went into a psychotic episode when women occupied the seats of power in a world we had made ourselves. His craziness and the consequences for the group are prime examples of how hard it is to change the traditional dynamics of power and how much it can cost.

We were thirty men and thirty women who had come together to study the dynamics of men and women at work, the way gender and sexuality affect the exercise of authority and leadership. The conference was conducted by the A. K. Rice Institute, which studies group relations and trains people to deal with them. We met for five days in a former convent in rural Maryland, where we saw no one who was not connected with our work.

I had been told that the meeting would become a world of its own, which would come to life and draw me in, a small Sargasso Sea. Despite the warning, I was surprised at how quickly it happened. Isolation from the real world helped make it a world of its own. The way it worked brought it to life: every person became a member of several different groups, and every group's processes stripped away our usual defenses and compelled us to recognize more than we normally do the attitudes, beliefs, fantasies, and feelings that operate in our worlds "back home." As a result, personal relationships in these groups flared quickly and were remarkably intense.

Every group had its own time and place to meet and its own seating arrangements. In this conference, each of us belonged to a small group of people of the same sex, who sat in a close circle, and to a spontaneously formed group with members of both sexes, who sat haphazardly. We also belonged to a group composed of all conference members of the same sex, where we sat in rows like those of a classroom, and to a large group that included every member of both genders, every member of the conference. There we sat in three concentric circles. By the third day I realized that each seating arrangement provided a different field on which power and leadership might emerge in different ways.

By the third day I also felt as though I were in a Buñuel movie. Our primary task was to study our own behavior; it led us to act like characters in one of his bizarre scenarios. It's relatively easy, say, for a management consulting firm to study the behavior of a bank or a newspaper. It is much harder to sit in a room in a group of people with nothing to do but study what all of you do or say as you do it. You express your ideas and your emotions about the subject of the meeting—in our case, the intersection of gender, work, and power. You talk about what you think your group and the other groups are doing, or should be doing. You dream up ways to examine your subject and yourselves, and sometimes you act them out. In any case, you feel and act weird.

Staff behavior created another bizarre flavor (which the staff itself said was like John Fowles's *The Magus* rather than Buñuel). The staff, usually psychologists and psychiatrists with special training, acted as consultants but not as leaders to the different groups. That meant they never gave orders or suggestions or answered pleas for guidance. They usually maintained silence except for carefully timed, often barbed, comments on the group's behavior. The idea was to see how leadership emerged among the members as the group regressed under the staff's refusal to lead. (The staff softened a little and explained a bit more toward the end, but by then many of us had developed elaborate fantasies of snubbing, punishing, or overthrowing them; at one famous early A. K. Rice conference, the members kidnapped the director, tied her to her chair, and locked her in a closet.)

The distinction between staff and members was the main internal boundary of this conference. The numbers of male and female members were equal; so were the numbers of male and female staff. In a conference on gender and power, numerical equality was essential to making men and women true peers. But it was the boundary that made us know we were equal. On one side, all members clearly had the same status regardless of gender. On the other side, all the staff had a contrasting status that was also the same regardless of gender.

CRAZINESS

This only intensified the Buñuel-like characteristics of the conference that many members felt were "making us crazy." Yet we were almost all surprised when Jack Paynter* appeared to go crazy in a more clinical sense.

It happened in a session of the large group. The innermost of the three circles, perhaps twelve chairs, were the seats of power. I knew that's what they were because almost nobody wanted to sit in them. The members had perceived that those who sat there were leaders and that leaders were often crucified—figuratively, of course, but still painfully. In the end the seats of power had to be filled because there were exactly as many chairs as people, but they were usually filled last.

At the first three sessions of this large group, the few members who took seats in the inner circle early, by preference, included three or four men and occasionally one or two women. (I was one of the men the first two times around, but then I withdrew to the middle circle.) In all three rings, men seemed to take the lead; at least, several men talked more often and longer and louder than most women. (The director of that conference was a man; his deputy was a woman. Both acted as staff consultants to the large group. At another A. K. Rice conference on gender and authority two years later, they switched roles, and the women members, I was fascinated to see, asserted much more claim to leadership.)

At the fourth session, things changed. Ten women, all members of the same one-sex small group in the conference, occupied ten of the chairs in the inner circle of the large group. Jack, sitting in the outer ring, had been mumbling. When the women sat down, his voice moved up a notch to back-of-the-classroom level and then turned into a shout. He moved back and forth between mutter and shout for a couple of minutes, but none of it made any sense. (He had been mumbling for three days, but I had not paid him any attention. Nor had anyone else; 90 percent of the participants were psychiatrists, psychologists, or counselors back home, but none of them recognized the problem. It was one more irony that Jack himself was a psychotherapist.) Then he rose and pleaded that one of the women change seats with him. One did, feeling that it might help him return to sanity, and he entered the circle of power that was also a circle of women.

The group started to discuss Jack's and its own behavior. Someone said, "Look, the group can't function with Jack here, and it would be better for him too if he weren't in the center." That would have meant changing seats once more. Jack moaned, "Don't make me change again." I felt a chill when I heard that. His anguish evoked first pity and then fear in me, even though I like to think that I favor change in the matrix of power. Others said later that they had also felt a chill then.

A. K. RICE AND REAL WORLD

That chill, like Jack's first change of seats, strengthened the bizarre flavor of the conference. But I never doubted that it was a model of the real world. Women were claiming a share in power, doing the same kind of work as men, demanding equality and choice, and this threatened many of the men. Rice confrontations between men and women as peers were more vivid and dramatic than they normally are, but the emotions we felt and the things we did were of the same kind we feel and do back home. Jack's feelings were of a rare intensity, depth, and sharpness, but they were still very much like those I had found in quieter form in the people I had interviewed for this book. The resemblance held as the interviews increased from dozens to hundreds. Jack's psychosis had many causes, but it came to symbolize for me the welter of conflicting and often painful emotions that we feel, that *I* feel—but that we seldom face and seldom recognize—when we face the revolution women are making.

Jack's episode also illustrated in a perverse way the postulates of the A. K. Rice model of the real world, which apply not only to Rice conferences, but to this woman's country club, that man's bowling team, the company you work for.[1] These postulates begin with the idea that every group has boundaries—spatial, temporal, and psychological. Every group has a structure, a hierarchical organization with leaders of different kinds—for example, executive and spiritual, figurehead and power behind the throne. Every group has tasks, among them a primary task that it must perform if it is to survive. A group has a culture arising from the values and attitudes brought into it by each member, and it forms images of itself, public, private, and unconscious, which change continually. Among the important functions of a group are selecting members and making rules for membership, shaping and being shaped by members' individual and collective relations to authority, and conducting transactions within the group. Transactions between any members affect the whole group.[2] The last is particularly important when the transaction is between male and female, and therefore likely to bring into play social and psychological forces of great power.[3]

Transactions in a group are irrational as well as rational. Members' irrational, defensive acts fall into patterns. The most important are fight-flight, in which members destroy the group or escape from it; dependency, in which members try to follow a leader without assuming responsibility but display helplessness and ignore the powers of the weak; and pairing, in which members form subgroups irrationally, with unconscious fantasies of producing a new group leader. All groups under stress regress to infantile behavior that is usually characterized by anxiety, rage, and depression.

Jack's outburst violated the group's boundaries, overturned its structures, derailed it from its primary task, and reshaped its culture and its images of itself. The women were certainly pairing. The episode produced examples of fight and flight and a host of irrational transactions.

On another level, what happened illuminated the most important aspect of the changes that women are making in the real world: their being a matter not just of sex roles, but of power, of women's challenging the power that a few men have at the same time that they force us to face the uncomfortable reality in which most of us are powerless. Elizabeth Janeway said our alternatives were to rebel ourselves or to acknowledge that we lack the courage and ambition that women show.[4]

We also have a third choice: we can go into a psychotic episode, as Jack did in a moment when women refused to accept the bargain between the weak and the powerful that most people see as government by law. Many participants understood that this was happening. One man related the events to the real world even as he expressed the model's departure from reality. He said,

"We created a society in which men and women were truly equal, and it drove a man crazy." When the women took the seats of power, many of the men saw it as an attempt to assert their claim to leadership and end the apparent male domination. I remember seeing it as a deliberate maneuver to confront men; I think now that the perception of confrontation came before the perception that they were taking power, or some of the power. I must have sensed that the confrontation was not only with male leaders, but also with the majority of male conference members, who avoided the seats of power and exercised no leadership. When I read Janeway much later, my memory of that at the Rice meeting was one of the things that gave me a shock of recognition.

Some of the women who took the seats of power said later in the conference that they had simply decided to experience what would happen if women banded together in the large, two-gender group.

FEAR AND DENIAL

What happened was that Jack went into his episode. One of his main problems was homosexual panic, in the view of some of the psychiatrists there. He was afraid of men, fearing both their subconscious homosexual designs and his own buried homosexual urges. He might also have seen the women in the seats of power, the very women he had asked to take him in, as women with penises. Then he might have feared *their* penetrating him, again evoking his terror of homosexuality.

That touched on the question of gender and power that fascinated me and everyone at the conference. But it seemed a bit fanciful and at the same time a bit too clinical for me as a nonpsychiatrist. I was more interested in the simple fact of Jack's slipping over the edge of psychosis, abandoning reality, when the women occupied the powerful seats. I thought that in one sense he recognized their power, appealing to them first not to shut him out and later not to make him change again. In another sense, he denied their power because his appeals were a form of asking for care—asking them to return to the power of the Good Mother, perhaps, but denying their new power in the group with its subliminal image of the Terrible Mother. He also denied the gender boundary, asking women not to shut him out and changing seats with a woman rather than with a man, which would have asserted his power as a man. The diagnosis of homosexual panic was made partly because he acted worse when men were present, a further denial of the gender boundary.

Other men produced another, perhaps more significant kind of denial after Jack went over the line. First, Eleanor Allen,* a psychiatrist; Kathy Barnes,* a psychiatric nurse; and three other women took over the care of Jack, using their clinical skill from back home. They had come together in the Institutional Event, in which all members met together and were then told to break up into new, spontaneous, two-gender groups. Jack had been a member of the same Institutional Event group as these five women; the dominance some of them showed may have helped lead him to the edge of his slide. It was they who first diagnosed an element of homosexual panic and asked men to stay away from him. For twelve hours they watched over him.

Meanwhile, some members and staff put in hours of effort, in and out of the scheduled conference events, to decide what to do about Jack. Some people wanted to remove him from the conference and turn him over to a doctor who could medicate him or hospitalize him there in Maryland. Others wanted to keep him in the conference until his wife could come and take him home.

Finally, close to midnight, two men—Mark Mason,* a psychoanalyst back home, and Walt Smith,* a consultant who was a psychologist and educator— came to a basement lounge where members were drinking and talking. Mark proposed that members take turns keeping watch, in male-female pairs, outside Jack's room that night. They were to make sure he did not injure himself or anyone else. Mark had clearly won staff approval for the idea. Walt made consultantlike statements about task and role and boundary, central elements of the A. K. Rice view of groups and of the events of real, conference, and psychotic life that were taking place. Eleanor's group had departed from its membership roles to take care of Jack, and the all-night vigil would mean other changes in role and task that might distort the shape of the conference. One male member argued that we should put Mark's plan into operation immediately. Another argued strongly for the opposite course, Jack's removal. It was already plain, however, that the staff had decided to keep him in the conference building, though he could hardly participate in conference events. Hospitalizing him would have been much harder on him, and risked much more damage to the A. K. Rice Institute.

As the men spoke, I grew angrier and angrier. They were totally ignoring the work that had been done, rightly or wrongly, by Eleanor and her "brood," as she called the women in the care group. I saw the men as obliterating that work. My anger reminded me of the rage I had felt years earlier, as a correspondent in Moscow, when my journalist colleagues and the Soviet authorities treated Susan only as a "wife" and obliterated her competence and her activities as a journalist.

At the conference the same kind of waste of female talent produced the same kind of rage. My voicing my rage over Susan had been one of several things that alienated my editors from me and me from them and led to my leaving the paper. Perhaps because I had hurt my career by expressing that anger in real life, I suppressed my anger at the conference, with classic results —my face grew red, my body grew hot, and my pulse quickened. After the vigil over Jack had been organized, I opened a figurative valve and eased the pressure by talking to Walt, the consultant. I indicted him and Mark for making no acknowledgment of the women's work in caring for Jack. I charged that only men had participated in the debate and the decision to adopt the analyst's plan, further obliterating the women's work. I argued that these men had abandoned both the real purpose of the conference, the study of gender and authority, and the theoretical equality of the sexes that demanded in order to talk about task and role and boundary. They had done this, I said, in the hope of protecting the conference—by keeping its wheels turning even if they turned away from the task, and by forestalling contamination from the real world that would have occurred if an outside psychiatrist had taken over Jack's care. Walt looked at me, his eyes widening, and after a few seconds said, "You're right." It made me doubly conscious of the male tendency to obliterate women who seek power or even demand autonomy. Back home I've seen some men learn to curb that tendency. Perhaps the people of the Institute have too; Eleanor, the psychiatrist who first took charge of Jack, has since directed A. K. Rice conferences herself.

Jack's psychotic episode was a dramatic example of a man's retreat from reality when women reached for power, of the denial that is one of the consequences of our feelings about the changes that women are making. When the men wiped out the women's work in caring for him, I saw it as another kind of denial of female power. I saw a third kind in one of the spontaneously formed groups of that same conference.

Ken Garner* became the group's gatekeeper simply by standing by the door. That made him a de facto leader controlling entrance to or exit from the room. (In this event, any group could send envoys to observe or negotiate with other groups for some specific purpose, some secondary task that supposedly would help pursue the primary task. It might be as simple as studying other people's behavior or as complex as "overthrowing" the staff.) When the group approved the request of two women to go out as delegates to other groups, Ken spread-eagled himself in the doorway, literally barring them from leaving. He felt, he said, that the group had not defined the women's mission sufficiently. The group then talked until it had produced a better definition, and Ken let the women out. But nobody said a word about a man's using his body, his physical power, to prevent two women from exercising the authority the group had given them. I was fascinated that in a group like this, denial was so strong.

Later in that same group, it was my turn to suggest a mission to other groups. The group agreed and chose me as ambassador. Mindful of the equality of men and women at the conference, I pleaded for a woman to go with me. Evelyn Pratt,* one of three women in the group who had asserted leadership and one whom I had thought friendly to me, responded to my use of the word "plead" by saying, half jokingly, "Why don't you go down on your knees?" I looked to left and to right and after a moment crashed to my knees. It was a moment of process, half intellectual and half emotional, in which I realized that I was, I had to be, capable of a gesture that would make "real" my professions that women deserve equal power with men; that the symbolic gesture, so full of meaning, would not deprive me of any power I had that I cared about, because it would also testify to my strength; and that therefore the mere making of the gesture would deprive it of some of the load of negative overtones that made other men hate it or feel incapable of it. But I didn't understand that until later. At the time I was conscious only of an audible gasp from the other members of the group, followed by a few seconds of silence—the first since the session had started. Evelyn flushed, moved quickly toward me, and we left on our mission, saying to each other that the group would surely spend a lot of time and energy discussing my making a gesture of giving up power to a woman. When we came back half an hour later, we both were astonished to learn that not one word had been said about it. The group was avoiding an uncomfortable reality, a physical departure from the norms of male power, almost as thoroughly as Jack had.

Men and women alike took part in those two examples of denial that responded to change in the distribution of power between the sexes. This is one more bit of evidence that denial is an important mechanism in human psychology, regardless of sex, but it does not diminish the importance of denial as one of men's main responses to changes sought by women. Since men usually dominate group discussion and the shaping of open and hidden group agendas, it's possible that the men's need to deny elicited or encouraged the women's denial.

HOSTILITY, CRUDE AND SUBTLE

Hostility is more familiar than denial as a consequence of men's feelings about women and power, a result clearly connected to our rage and anger. It turned up in crude form at an A. K. Rice conference that was supposedly a gathering of subtle intellects.

At the second of my two A. K. Rice conferences, a woman named Natalie Finestone* spoke so intelligently and forcefully that she became a leader despite her youth (she was twenty-six). We readily gave the leadership she took; I was one of the members of a group who voted to make her chairman for a period. But I was one of many participants who perceived her as controlled and controlling, almost manipulative. "Abrasive" was an inaccurate metaphor, but her psychological shape didn't fit the jigsaw puzzle of the group; it did not so much irritate us as penetrate deep into the wells of sexual antagonism. I found myself in a fantasy of beating her up. That disturbed me because I had not laid a hand in anger on anyone, male or female, in more than thirty years. I mentioned the fantasy to another man, a mild Presbyterian minister who was one of the few men in the conference older than I. He grinned sheepishly and said, "That's nothing. She affects me the same way. I fantasized raping her. Anally." In other words, the only way this kindly Connecticut Yankee could deal with this kind of powerful woman in his mind was by the grossest kind of violence—and by turning her, not even into a man, but into a boy, a person of less power who was to be penetrated in the most humiliating of ways. I was appalled by the way he and I both translated the issues from competence and leadership into anger expressed in sex and physical power.

Some women have told me there is nothing new in a man's desire to rape a woman who departs from tradition by taking power or doing other things. I think it highly unusual for men who are incapable of rape in real life (and I believe there are such men, because I am one) to acknowledge a rape fantasy in this context, which was not an exercise in collecting imaginary sexual scenarios. So many rapes are committed on total strangers or on women met by accident, in the course of a burglary, say, on the one hand, or on acquaintances, wives, and lovers on the other hand, that I think it is also highly unusual for an actual rape to be committed on a woman *because* she has gained power.

That did happen in New York in 1980, however. A bartender had worked for a few years in the bar of a hotel owned by a large company. He had some hopes of promotion. But a woman of twenty-four, who had worked there for a shorter time than he had, was promoted over his head and became manager. He was Hispanic, which may explain some of his attitudes and may have evoked prejudice against him on the part of his employer, though there is no clear evidence on either score. He had told his friends that he would never work for a woman. And after she was named manager, he waited for her in an alley and raped her, confirming in his own mind and in the crudest way the superiority he wanted to feel in himself, the superiority his employer had not seen or had refused to ratify.

TRANSFORMATION

The third negative consequence of men's feelings about women, work, and power that I've mentioned is the compulsion to transform women from peers and powers into such familiar roles as wife, lover, mother, daughter, whore, or nun. This is a powerful psychological force, but it has a sociological aspect much plainer than any in denial and hostility. Sociologically it is a dominant's imposition of a role on a subordinate, in this case a man's distortion of an individual woman's characteristics to make her fit preexisting generalizations.

Rosabeth Moss Kanter, in *Men and Women of the Corporation*, calls this "role encapsulation" and says it is particularly likely to happen in an organization where women in professional positions are tokens, fewer than 15 percent of the total. The dominants use the traditional ways men expect to treat women to keep the tokens "out of the mainstream of interaction where the uncertainties they arouse might be more difficult to handle."[5] My research suggests that men transform women in this way even where there are enough women to take them out of the token category. That means that the process is more frequent and more important, and also more complex, than can be explained by analysis of role and structure alone.

For many men it is terrifying to see a woman as both a peer and a potential lover, as both an independent, critical, task-oriented actor and a fully sexual being. We fear a woman who can destroy us—on the one hand as we feared the destructive Terrible Mother, on the other hand as we fantasy destroying business rivals—instead of or in addition to nurturing us. So we use transformations to deny either her competence or her sexuality.

If we expect our sexual partners to be submissive, we may act as though a competent and assertive women cannot be sexual. If a woman seems both capable and dedicated to an organization's goals and rules, a man may cast her as a nun, respectfully. If a woman resists all the stereotyped roles, freezes sexual innuendos, but shows strength in displaying her competence and in claiming her rights, men may cast her as an iron maiden, disparagingly.

Transformation of a woman peer into a wife or mother is also, ironically, a way of denying her sexuality. The male executive who calls his woman boss by his wife's name while arguing that she should reverse a decision is blotting out her sexual as well as her professional independence.

Men's transformation of women into roles that deny their sexuality is less common than the transformation of peers into sexual partners, however. The latter is a classic much older than the contemporary movement of women into "male" occupations. It underlies the charge that men often made when the rare woman rose in an organization in the old days—that she was sleeping her way to the top. Even as a fantasy that denies women's competence and entitlement to power much more than transforming her into a mother does.

An ugly transformation of colleague into sexual hunter, less a denial of competence than a declaration of war, came to light at an A. K. Rice conference.

It started when two self-proclaimed older women (one in her fifties, the other in her forties) expressed a desire to perform a conference task with two younger men. Back home they had never had the experience of working with younger men as peers. Anne Norton,* a business school professor of the same generation, said she would try to find young co-workers for them in the Institutional Event groups. She discovered that all but one of the men under thirty-two at the conference were, by accident or conscious choice, in the same Institutional Event group, as were three of the younger women. Anne, acting as broker, gave them the older women's proposal.

The young men responded by calling her a pimp. They found her request outrageous, they said, because she had remarked in the Large Group that morning that she had found it rewarding to sit next to a young man there and wanted more—meaning more association with young men, but taken in the new context to mean more of that particular young man. They said that they had no desire to "screw around with" older women. Anne returned to her own group, feeling bruised.

Later I asked two of the young men why they had behaved that way. Neither acknowledged that they were fleeing from their own unconscious perceptions of older women as fearsome or powerful. One denied any sexual aspect, insisting that he had turned Anne down only in order to keep his own group at work, intact, on its task. The other acknowledged the sexual side of the incident, confessing his own difficulties in relation to older women and adding, "If we had given you two young men, that would have left space for your older men to come in and take our younger women." I was again appalled, because I had seldom heard the substitution of sexuality for competence and the treatment of women as objects made so explicit back home, even though I knew it happened all the time.

Then I remembered the woman scientist, someone with plenty of anger from her own experience of the way men denied her competence at work, who teased me when I remarked that over the years all the women I had seriously pursued had had careers, most of them in my own field. "Maybe," she said with a smile, "you have to conquer us in order to accept us." I did a double take. She was not seriously indicting me, but the needle slipped neatly under my skin, and I've been checking on my own transformations ever since.

Every one of the next five chapters gives examples of similar transformations in the real-life workplace, which often injure a woman's work or her career, or show how the men who do the transforming are unconsciously fighting her. Sometimes, however, they become ways for men to work their way through to support of and association with the woman who is the object of the transformation. The work chapters also deal with everyday examples of the denial and hostility that were so vivid at the A. K. Rice conferences—and with other positive male acts and feelings about women demanding equality at work.

Three chapters on personal life, on marriage, parenting, and sex, deal with other genres of real-life denial and hostility—and more frequent real-life examples of acceptance, support, and association. These negatives and positives are shown again in different lights in two chapters on the men's movement, significant despite its tiny size and its many flaws. They are seen in other perspectives in a chapter that examines how men have dealt with the issues of women's independence and power in literature and the arts, and in chapters on the dividing lines of race, region, age, and sexual preference and on the current historical moment. These last two and a chapter on conclusions bring reality and theory back together in a final effort to show that the revolution is indeed possible, and worth the cost.

Part Two

HOW MEN FEEL ABOUT WOMEN IN "A MAN'S JOB"

Chapter 4
THE ARMY

Wooden cabins, four sets of bleachers, a couple of trucks perch in a clearing in the piney woods of northeastern Alabama. It could be a campground, or a back-country ballpark. But a line of soldiers staggers out of one of the cabins, crying, retching, gasping for breath. The clearing is a corner of Fort McClellan where the U.S. Army gives basic training in nuclear, biological, and chemical warfare. Inside the cabin a tin-can candelabrum blows rings of tear gas in a foggy room. A squad of soldiers enters, wearing gas masks. A noncom, his voice loud yet hollow, a claustrophobic echo under his mask, tells them to think of the gas as lethal. "If your equipment wasn't working properly, you'd be dead. By now." To learn the difference between the security of a properly sealed mask and the corrosive reality of the gas, each soldier must yank the mask off and recite name, rank, and Social Security number before plunging out. Almost everyone breathes deep, by reflex, before the words can get out, and starts to choke. Many panic and must be forced to finish.

It's familiar terror and triumph to millions of men who served in the Army during World War II, the Korean War, or the Vietnam conflict. But on this day, one in every four of the trainees who stumble out of the cabin has a young woman's lips and eyes and sometimes hair falling to the shoulders. Otherwise, the uniform of steel pot, fatigue jacket, and field trousers effectively hides gender. At the foot of a tall pine twenty feet away, a noncom barks at a trainee who couldn't recite his lesson on what to do in case of nuclear attack: "Get your head out of the commode, Bradstreet, you're pissing me off." In this case, only the words belie the noncom's gender. The crisp creases in her fatigues do not hide but accentuate the curve of breasts and hips, and she wears the Aussie-style hat, brim flipped up on one side, that is the mark of the female drill sergeant.

A PARADIGM OF CHANGE

The scene is one of many that make an army with women, the United States Army, a paradigm of what this book is about. If you think of the Army simply as an occupation, women soldiers are taking over what is traditionally the most masculine of all jobs. But it goes much deeper. Women soldiers challenge many aspects of traditional manhood. One is the assumption that men are stronger than women and that it matters; army men insist endlessly that women can't lift, or march, or endure, in all the ways that military life demands. Another is the belief that it is men's instinct, or men's duty, to protect women. Army men talk about the way men's morale would plummet if they saw women maimed or killed. They talk about the way male warriors would be so busy helping female comrades-in-arms that they would neglect their own military mission. Women soldiers challenge the myth that women are pure, which many men still believe, or want to believe. Some army men think women are too pure to share battlefield sleeping and sanitation arrangements with men; others, in contrast, think any woman willing to join the Army must be either immoral or perverted. The women in the Army have won some of these challenges. Even where they haven't—there are many physical fitness tests where most men do indeed outdo most women—they have still shown that many women make good soldiers.

The challenges that men experience when women become soldiers all relate to combat. The law bars women from combat in the Air Force and the Navy. In the Army, it is not law but policy that bars women from combat arms such as infantry and armor and from any unit in which "they would routinely participate in close combat." When President Carter proposed in February 1980 that women register for a possible draft, he promised that they would not see combat, and the fear that women might have to fight was precisely the reason that Congress defied the President and refused to make them register. The Reagan administration has tried to reduce the Army's reliance on women in general and the chance of its using women in combat in particular.

All the same, women are still everywhere in the Army down to brigade level. If there is a war, women will certainly be in combat. From sergeant to general, soldiers talk about the seven Soviet airborne divisions designed to be dropped to the rear of frontline Western elements. They will jump into areas where units with a full complement of women will have to defend themselves. And every soldier with command training knows that in the kind of war we fought in Vietnam or may have to fight in the Middle East, "there is no such thing as a front line any more."

The Army knows this, but it still doesn't know how to deal with it. During the invasion of Grenada, military police supply battalions were ordered into action from Fort Bragg, North Carolina. Four female MPs were stopped at the loading ramp and sent back to their barracks three times before they were finally allowed to depart. They arrived on Grenada four days after the invasion only to be ordered back to Fort Bragg while the Pentagon dithered. Three days later they were allowed to return to the island and take up duties, among them searching female prisoners and assisting the Caribbean police. One narrowly missed being caught in a sniper attack in her first night there.

It would be easy to treat the Army's ambivalence as slapstick comedy, but going into combat compels women soldiers to cross two of the fundamental divides in Western, in most human, culture. One is a matter of power: women soldiers violate the male attempt to monopolize licensed killing. This challenges men's power in society. As Simone de Beauvoir wrote, "It is not in giving life but in risking life that man is raised above the animal; that is why superiority has been accorded in humanity not to the sex that brings forth but to that which kills."[1] The challenge is also to men's power in the Army. So long as women are kept out of jobs that require them to kill or stand ready to be killed, they cannot rise to high command in the Army, whose leaders generally come up through the combat arms.[2]

The other divide is a matter of biology, of reproduction of the species: women are the beings who bring men to life, and war plunges them into death. In almost every society—even those, de Beauvoir to the contrary, that value the power to give life as highly as the power to take it away—there is a basic conceptual symmetry in which the female's biological monopoly of the power to give birth is balanced by a male monopoly of the power to kill. Underlying this symmetry is an obvious but profound truth that Peggy Sanday restated: "If women willingly embraced mass slaughter, there would be no social body to preserve."[3] Conservatives in America take up this idea as though women had no other function than giving birth, as though "army" and "combat" were synonymous and coterminous. They have voiced their belief more often and more loudly, in ordinary life, in politics and in the Army, since Ronald Reagan became President. But even men who are prepared to acknowledge masculine and feminine equality in every other respect become uneasy when it is extended to war. In them, the belief that women's raison d'être is to give birth may be silent, but it is still real and still powerful.*

Most army men can't talk about these fundamentals. Power is so basic that it's almost unmentionable, and the idea that women might wield power is even more so. Many men at Fort McClellan spoke highly of Major General Mary E. Clarke when she commanded there, but most of them breathed a sigh of relief when she was promoted to the Pentagon and replaced by a man. Reproduction is more mentionable, but embarrassing. It is spoken of mostly in complaints that pregnancy keeps women soldiers from doing their jobs. Six weeks visiting army camps convinced me that most men can't talk easily about something that they recognize more clearly and feel more strongly about than power, something that masks or subsumes the fundamentals. This

---

* A three-judge federal court defied the power of that belief when it declared the Selective Service Act unconstitutional because it excluded women (though the court never said it was unconstitutional to keep women out of combat). The Supreme Court, perhaps unconsciously, showed unease at the idea of extending sexual equality to war and reaffirmed millennia of respect for the idea that women should not fight when it overruled the lower court and ruled that it was *not* unconstitutional to exclude women from the draft.

is the danger they feel women pose to the male bond—that emotional tie rooted in millennia of hunt, work, and war, which reaches its most intense form in the military—and to the passage to manhood. We used to believe, and most of us still believe, that war turns boys into men. So, by extension, does peacetime military life, whether it be the ordinary rigors of basic training or the exalted tests of West Point. Many men feel that if women can survive the same rites of passage, their manhood is emptied of its meaning. In consequence, they insist that women can never be good soldiers.

WARRIORS' COMMUNION

The best clue I could find to this tangle of male fears in military minds was in Philip Caputo's book, *A Rumor of War,* which describes the barbarity that took place in Vietnam. Caputo was a Marine infantry lieutenant there in 1965; in the 1970s he was a war correspondent in Israel, Cyprus, Vietnam, Lebanon, and Ethiopia. In infantry battalions, Caputo writes,

> The communion between men is as profound as any between lovers. Actually, it is more so. It does not demand for its sustenance the reciprocity, the pledges of affection, the endless reassurances required by the love of men and women. It is, unlike marriage, a bond that cannot be broken by a word, by boredom or divorce, or by anything other than death. Sometimes that is not strong enough. Two friends of mine died trying to save the corpses of their men from the battlefield. Such devotion, simple and selfless, the sentiment of belonging to each other, was the one decent thing we found in a conflict otherwise notable for its monstrosities.
>
> And yet, it was a tenderness that would have been impossible had the war been significantly less brutal. . . . It was as if in comradeship we found an affirmation of life and the means to preserve at least a vestige of our humanity.[4]

In another passage Caputo calls courage the urge to rid oneself of fear "by eliminating the source of it. This inner, emotional war produces a tension almost sexual in its intensity. It is too painful to endure for long."

These descriptions of the communion and tensions of combat made me realize that men might find them literally impossible to share with women, with anyone with whom one might have sexual communion. Or sharing them with women might multiply the intensity beyond bearing even for the moment that Caputo experienced. In his book Caputo says nothing about women. But when I interviewed him, he articulated the underlying fears about women in the Army more completely than anyone on active duty with whom I spoke:

I have an old-fashioned, chivalrous attitude toward women. You could call it primitive. They kept out of wars because they were the means by which the race is propagated. Men, at least I, look with a kind of awe on women and women's bodies. The thought of women being shot up I find appalling. I also think that war and armies even in peacetime vulgarize and brutalize people. In this century, perhaps the bloodiest in all history, I'd like to think something would not be touched by this brutality and vulgarity. Up to now, it's been women.

On what he called a more pragmatic level, Caputo was not concerned about questions that many men raised, like a woman's ability to carry a seventy-pound pack through miles of mud or to survive a month without a shower. He feared, rather, that women lack "the endurance, the violence, the ferocity necessary to survive a battle." If they did, that might itself bar them from battlefield communion. But something else was more important to Caputo:

The emotion of camaraderie, which I think is a basically male trait going back to earliest history, is of its nature chaste. It may be more intense than what happens between male and female lovers, but it has to be nonsexual. It's not just women. Warriors can't be homosexual lovers either. The emotional shock of losing a physical lover would be detrimental to the effectiveness of the Army.

The only women with combat experience comparable to Caputo's are Vietcong veterans who have not expressed their views to Westerners. But American army women, acknowledging that they have not been through combat, disagree with him. They don't think they need or should be seen primarily as potential lovers. I asked Second Lieutenant Donna Woodard, then an adjutant in a signal battalion at Fort Campbell, Kentucky, how she felt about Caputo's ideas. She said:

That emotional intensity happens. You feel it even when you're in the field for thirty days. But being a woman does not prevent that kind of bond with men. It may enhance it. It's easier for some women to talk to the guys, so being a woman might be an advantage. Women understand feelings, women have learned to accept vulnerability.

I thought she had a point; men's difficulty acknowledging vulnerability is one of the things that makes them crack under tensions. All the same, feelings like Caputo's underlie the complaints of many army men about women soldiers.

THE ARMY CAN'T DO ITS JOB WITHOUT WOMEN

But whatever the men say and whatever they fear, the reality is that the Army is going to remain dependent on its women so long as there is no draft. Without women, the all-volunteer Army would not have enough volunteers to function. Most women are in traditional administrative and medical jobs or such almost traditional work as supply, food service, and data processing. These are comparable to the jobs of the old Women's Army Corps, abolished in 1978, but many more such jobs have to be filled in order to support each combat specialty today. And many women are in the nontraditional jobs that the Army labels "combat support," such as military police, signal, missile artillery and air defense, transport and weapons repair.

Reagan and Caspar Weinberger, conservative here as in many other areas, sought ways to limit the Army's dependence on women. They abandoned a 1980 plan to increase the proportion of women in the Army from 8 to 12.5 percent and, despite their military buildup, ordered a cut in the number of women allowed to enlist. They closed more career specialties to women, transferred women out of many combat support specialties, and had the Army set up groups to study "the problem of women."* The civilians at the top of the Pentagon were backed by army men who wanted to revive the draft and who felt that reliance on women was a proof that the all-volunteer force had failed. The seriousness of the change was attested by a letter that General Mary Clarke felt compelled to write *Army Times* on her way to retirement in the fall of 1981. Long known as a loyal member of the army team, she still protested the decision of the top men to suspend the planned increase in the proportion of female troops, which she said "appears to be a retreat from the army's commitment to the fullest possible participation by women." In the end, however, it was the administration that retreated before a combination of female, congressional, and economic forces. The number of women on active duty reached a record high of seventy-seven thousand in 1985, 10 percent of the total—an improvement on the old figure of 8 percent though still short of the 12.5 percent goal.

Whatever men fear, the Army also has two traditions that force it to modify its hostility to women and even to accept them. One is the tradition of making the best use of available resources. The other is the tradition of following orders—and the orders, reflecting in different degrees under different

* Eight percent of all military occupational specialties (MOSs) were then closed to women because they were combat slots, but they accounted for 42 percent of peacetime army jobs. The proportion of MOSs closed to women has gone up to 14.6 percent under Reagan, less than the Pentagon wanted but enough to close a much higher percentage of peacetime army jobs to women. (The Army claims it no longer keeps track of these percentages except by specialty, from 100 percent in the infantry and armor specialties to a mere 9 percent in the adjutant general's department and finance.)

presidents the changing views of society on the equality of women, are that the Army will make good use of women and give them equal treatment in the noncombat specialties open to them.

The fears and the countervailing traditions are both reflected in Lieutenant General David E. Grange, Jr. When I interviewed him, he was commander of Fort Benning, Georgia, home of the Infantry School, which is still closed to women except for its airborne department, the famous Jump School (which graduated more than a thousand women along with fifty thousand men in a five-year period). Grange, now retired, was a rarity among generals: he fought as a private first class in World War II and commanded at every level from squad to brigade in combat. He agreed devoutly with the army policy that bars women from frontline combat. He said the rifleman's basic mission, "to close with and destroy the enemy," is too grueling for women, and he elaborated on "grueling" in terms of weeks in a foxhole under enemy fire that made me feel the strains.

Later this career warrior said, "War is hideous and obscene, the worst damn thing you can participate in. I wouldn't want my daughter to be exposed to that as a steady fare." Yet he was proud that his son served in Vietnam, where he almost lost an arm. When I asked him to account for the difference, he could say only, "It somehow bothers me that our country might let our women do that. Maybe I am a traditionalist, I don't know. I just think that is a man's job." Grange halted for only a second and then said, "I never wanted my wife to work." I was fascinated by the jump and asked if Mrs. Grange were working now that their children were grown. He answered, "No," and then added, "I am not against women working, of course. I just— maybe I am old-fashioned. And there are just too many young men around, good men. We have got great youngsters in the Army."

But General Grange knows the realities. He was the first soldier I interviewed to mention the Soviet airborne divisions and the likely disappearance of the front line. "If there is a war," he acknowledged, "women will be exposed to combat. You have to know how to fire a weapon, throw a grenade, and do things to protect yourself, to protect your installation." He was genuinely proud of the five hundred women he commanded in the Second Division in Korea, who "made a great contribution." He particularly mentioned the signal teams he used there. They were usually one man and two women or two men and one woman who flew with a package of gear by helicopter to mountain posts when they went on alert. They served for days at a time in situations where they would have been prime targets for an enemy—and as Grange said, "You can't get any closer to the enemy anywhere in the world than in Korea." When I asked him about battlefield communion, the general was only half in agreement with Caputo:

There's a connection that develops between frontline soldiers and—certainly there is nothing quite like it in anything else we do. Would it develop if there were women? I really don't know how to answer that question. If you go through the danger of privation with anybody, with either sex, it has to enhance the relationship, it would seem to me.

THE PROBLEMS

General Grange's experience with women soldiers made him sound sincere when he said, despite his opposition to sending females into combat, "I don't see any problems with women in the Army." One who did see problems was Colonel J. Ross Franklin, who was Grange's deputy commander for readiness and training at Fort Benning. Franklin was a thirty-five-year veteran, a bald-headed maverick who boasted of his Russian immigrant father. He voiced gut feelings for half an hour. In one stretch, he said:

> Our business is killing people. We train to kill people here. And look at where our women are. We have got them in helicopters as door gunners. Anybody who has ever seen a combat assault and seen those soldiers coming off those slicks, seen choppers blow up, I don't think they really want women in those door wells. I don't think we want women as we have right now in all these medical ambulances. They can't physically muck it. I was out in the field yesterday, they were just loading litters [with bodies] into ambulances and they just couldn't do it. And as they told me the men and women have the same military occupational specialty and the women can't meet certain tasks or requirements so they send a man in and it just makes a bigger requirement on the man. They have got women ammunition handlers around here. They can't physically do it. . . . [And] even if you get around the physical we don't bring up our women to do the things that people do in war. We don't even begin to understand what is going to happen with men and women under stress in units. We have never had that.

The fear that female casualties would damage male morale is not just fantasy. Lieutenant Colonel Eugene E. Bouley, Jr., was at Cam Ranh Bay in Vietnam when a shell blew a nurse's head off. "It aroused more fuss, more horrified reactions than the same thing happening to a man," he recalled, "but in telling it now, it seems just as horrible to think of a man being decapitated." The Israelis root the fear even more firmly in reality. It is one of the main reasons they have kept women out of combat after allowing them to fight during the war of independence in 1948. Women did serve on the Suez Canal during the war of attrition in the late 1960s, and when a female lost an arm or a leg to an Egyptian shell, it sent the unit's morale down much further than the same casualty suffered by a man, according to Israeli army psychologists.[5]

Israelis and Americans both link horror over female casualties to what some call the male instinct to protect or help women. It's more likely to be a cultural factor than an inherited instinct, but I saw it operating in noncom and officer training. Soldiers of both sexes and all ranks said the protective urge was likely to abort military missions. They feared that men would see a woman as weaker or ill-prepared for combat. The men would then spend so much time and energy protecting her that they would not engage the enemy as they should. Admiral Elmo Zumwalt, the retired Chief of Naval Operations, disagreed. He pointed out that the 1 percent of American warriors who win medals for bravery often show their heroism in acts that say, in effect, "I am not going to let my buddy get killed." With women in the service, he thought, the proportion of men who qualify for a badge of honor might go up to 10 percent.

If the protective urge looks like a psychological reality, problems of strength and athletic skill are questions of physical reality. Every man in the Army has a favorite combat task that he thinks a woman cannot do. For an infantryman, it's carrying a seventy-pound pack, for a helicopter pilot it's changing an eighty-pound battery, and so on down an endless list.

Under President Carter the Army began to ask how many soldiers really need to do those things. A Pentagon study showed that only 10 percent of all military jobs require infantry duty. The experts gave up on their effort to estimate the strength needed for every MOS ("How much muscle does it take to launch an ICBM?"). Particular tasks were too complex to be measured by the ability to lift so many pounds so many feet in the air, they found, and soldiers who couldn't meet certain fitness tests sometimes turned out to be able to do heavy jobs all the same. The Reagan army reversed that stand and claimed in 1982 that 76 percent of army jobs required the ability to lift one hundred pounds, which the Army said that only 11 percent of female soldiers could do. The Pentagon had to retreat a little there too; in 1983 it adopted a test dividing recruits into those who can lift forty to eighty pounds and those who can lift more than eighty pounds (20 percent of female soldiers). It also claimed that no one would be barred from a specialty requiring heavy lifting, unless it were a combat job. But the Army "counsels" those who cannot lift more than eighty pounds about the effects on their career if they choose a heavy-lifting MOS.

Physical training standards were revised in 1980 so that men and women would do the same exercises with different minimums. Until then, some training programs allowed women to do push-ups with their knees down and sit-ups with their arms extended, both easier than the male version. In other programs, men and women were supposed to do identical numbers of the same physical exercises. Sergeant First Class James Batten was one of many male drill sergeants who said the numbers were propaganda, not reality. Women trainees, he said, were supposed to do twenty-two push-ups, "but out of the thirty-two I have right now, I dare say only five could do twenty-two push-ups, good and accurate push-ups." About 35 percent of the women in his company's previous training cycle failed the physical training test, but the Army found ways to graduate them. Batten was pleased because the new standards set lower minimums for women. He called this "realistic." Yet I noticed that almost every time a basic training company split into a fast and a slow group, there were some women in the fast group, presumably meeting male standards, and a proportionately larger number of men in the slow group, presumably failing to meet them. These physical training standards were one Carter change that the Reagan administration kept.

Men who see women as lagging in physical fitness also insist that women can't or shouldn't face field conditions as tough as the men's. Women have done well in field exercises that last a few days, General Grange said, but have never faced the test of months of living in the open, sleeping in foxholes, meeting recurrent enemy attack. At one level the worry is like Caputo's: women should not be brutalized, and the field is brutal. At another level the worry is rooted in male mystification about female bodies and their functions. There is a myth, for instance, that "female plumbing rots faster than ours." Yet Caputo himself testifies in grimly precise, anal detail why men, too, get filthy and funky if they can't shower for a month. Women aver from experience that a menstrual period in the field, as one put it, "was uncomfortable and it was, you know, ugh, but it wasn't impossible." Colonel Edward M. Johnson, a gynecologist who was commanding officer of the army hospital at Fort McClellan, snorted, smiled, and said, "The vagina is a self-cleansing organ. There's no difference between males and females in the field. If there's no bath, they'll both have problems."

Some men feel that women will be hopelessly degraded if they have to dig a latrine for themselves or share a latrine with men. Army women are doing both without any resultant outrage to discipline.

Similar concern about sleeping arrangements starts from the assumption that the only relations between men and women are sexual. Sometimes the worry is about public relations rather than private—don't let civilians know that soldiers sleep together. When men and women went through basic training together, women were assigned two to a pup tent for their five days of bivouac, in a group of tents separated from the men's. Some line outfits billet women separately even if it means an extra tent; if that takes too much time or work, others let two men, say, and two women share a tent, with or without a poncho hung down the middle in imitation of Clark Gable and Claudette Colbert in *It Happened One Night.*

Not all combat veterans wrinkle up their noses at such innovations. Colonel David J. White, then commanding officer of the Second Infantry Brigade at Fort Campbell, laughed when I asked him if either sleeping or sanitation was a problem with women in the field. "Sure it is," he said. "If you go outside the tent to take a leak, you've got to look around first." He called the obsession of some army men with billets and latrines "pole-vaulting over a mouse turd." White has the infantry's aversion to women's "going out to seek the enemy, to kill him. That's a male job." But when I asked him what would happen to battlefield communion and battlefield effectiveness if women were in combat alongside men, he offered an honest "I don't know" where others were quick to predict disaster. And he gave high marks to the women in his brigade headquarters units—particularly intelligence, aviation, and supply—who would be no more than three miles from the front, if there was a front in their next war.

DEALING WITH THE FEARS

White's jokes and his serious comments both showed that some military men are overcoming fears about women in the service. The ability to do so can be as impressive as the fears. Admiral Zumwalt, the retired Chief of Naval Operations, knows the fears are deep-seated but says he has never felt them. He is a conservative on military preparedness and foreign policy, but he sounded liberal or even radical when he talked about racial and sexual integration of the armed forces. Both, he said, are required to achieve a goal that obsesses him—a goal that he calls half justice, half efficiency. Zumwalt in fact ignored both racial and sexual discrimination in the forces until the numbers of blacks and women became so large that he no longer could. When he went to Vietnam, he found the Navy, like the other services, in racial trouble. He set about sparking its racial integration—a generation late, by his own account. When he was named Chief of Naval Operations, he became an advocate of sexual integration in all the services. He said:

It took a hundred years to do it for race and it may take another hundred to do it for women. The fascinating thing for me is that it was a tougher battle to get flag officers and generals to be truly objective about sexual integration than it was about racial integration. There is a greater bias toward male chauvinism than there is toward racism. It goes back a million years.

The admiral found reasons in recent and not-so-recent history to discard the million-year-old pattern:

The most ruthless, vicious, cunning enemy I ever had to fight were the Vietcong women who had the stamina to keep up with their men in the jungles and plod through the marshes and who were very capable of suckling their babies by the roadside and then dropping the baby and picking up a rifle and shooting a sailor in the back. Those of us in this country who have that protect-mother complex forget that our great-great-grandmothers fought the Indians right alongside their husbands. . . . I have an eighty-seven-year-old first cousin who remembers hearing our great-great-grandmother tell about their having greater fear of women being scalped than of men being scalped. Yet they marched together. Nobody refused to give the women guns when the Indians were attacking.

Zumwalt's most important reasons for wanting women in the services, including the combat arms, had nothing to do with history, real or mythical, however. First, the Army finds a disproportionate number of its volunteers in Category IV, the lowest mental-aptitude level it will accept (though the number went down in the early 1980s as economic conditions drove more higher-level men to enlist). "We are literally enlisting idiots," Zumwalt said in 1980. "We will be better defended if we draft intelligent women than idiot men. They give you much greater deterrent capability. You might make a case that with the outbreak of war, with the public reading about this woman losing a leg and that woman being decapitated, it might turn the public off. My own hunch is that it wouldn't be nearly as significant as the general concern about win or loss casualties overall."

Second in Zumwalt's mind was the possibility that women in war councils might change military measures of cost effectiveness when the cost is human lives.

> In a management situation, the presence of women brings out a better product in men. . . . I can't document this, but my instincts have been that [when you have] the same discussions without women and another time with women—I've participated on a couple or three occasions in the Pentagon—the presence of a woman almost subconsciously seems to make the man approach a problem in a more idealistic vein. It's almost as though the presence of a woman reminds the male that the species needs to be preserved. . . . For example, you remember the famous Hamburger Hill in Vietnam. I think it was legitimate to ask, should that particular campaign have been carried out? I had to make many specific tactical decisions in Vietnam that were going to get people killed. One of the things I constantly tried to force my staff to keep in mind was the need to evaluate potential cost versus potential reward. The presence of women may just help to bring that characteristic out more among men.

Experience may change stereotypes, not only for officers like Colonel White, but for noncommissioned officers, the backbone of the Army and the class most hostile to women soldiers. Sergeant First Class Bobby Hopper, a drill sergeant with the training company I saw at the Fort McClellan gas-chamber site, said, "I'm infantry, so I might be prejudiced. We don't need women at the front in category one. But I've seen females run, crying every step of the way, knowing I'm not going to give them any slack. They don't want to quit. Some women right here in this company can outshoot men. They'll do all right in combat. They should be able to handle rear areas as well as any male. Hell, even farther back than rear areas you can be wounded or killed. I was an Eleven-B [the basic infantry MOS] in Vietnam. I cried when my best buddy got hit. Wouldn't I with women?"

Sergeant First Class Oscar Cunningham, a black from Georgia and an Airborne Ranger, still believes that women don't belong in combat and that female physiology and female psychology are ill-suited to field conditions. But he has changed a lot since he first came into the Army in 1966:

> I think the reason why a lot of people think about not having females in the Army is because each and every one of us sitting here knows that the female always has been known to belong in the house, and now here we are working side by side with you and you doing the same job that a man has always done. It sort of makes the man to feel like—I'm not really the man I thought I was, I've got a female who can do the same job.
>
> When the females first came into the airborne field I was totally against it. I thought the standards would be lowered when females came into the course. Then I became an instructor and saw that some of them could outdo the men. Really. Right now, I think I accept a woman in the Airborne just as I do a man, because they have shown that they can help the situation.

One of the women that Cunningham saw literally outrun the men was Elizabeth Dunlop. He married her. When I interviewed them, she was a sergeant, one of three female instructors in the Airborne Department at Fort Benning, teaching men and women how to jump from a tower before they learned to jump from a plane, while he was a Ranger instructor. His acceptance of women in the Airborne did not extend to the Rangers because he still believed that women cannot meet combat and field conditions.

Marriage to Beth also made Ham one of the minority of NCOs who depart from the patriarchal norms that most army men still try to put into practice at home. They have separate savings accounts, for instance, and two checking accounts, one joint and one in her name. He pays for housing and fresh food from the joint account (which was originally his alone) and she pays for utilities and groceries from her checking account. She tries to educate her women friends on the need to establish their own credit, still not the usual practice at Benning or its symbiotic host, Columbus, Georgia. He backs her up with a soldier's concern: "For example, if I go out there and get killed or something, she has an account that establishes herself." Each of them does the housework in turn when off-duty hours come in the daytime, though Beth says not when she has one of her rare days off during the week. They make decisions together but joke that at home she outranks him—Beth saying, while he smiles agreement, "I'm the sergeant major at home, he's the drill sergeant in the field."

Even men who have been unable to give up their traditional macho views have learned in the Army to change some of their behavior. Drill Sergeant Batten told me, in between barking orders on a twelve-mile march, that 95 percent of army women know nothing about combat and won't make it in battle because their training lowers army standards. I asked him if he meant that women really impair the Army's combat effectiveness. By then we were on a break, and he came unconsciously to attention as he replied, "Affirmative, sir."

Yet Mary Coleman, the female drill sergeant in his company, had told me that he and the other male drills had given her all the support she needed, after a bit of initial hazing, and women trainees testified to the impartiality of the male drills. I asked Batten how he could help Coleman in integrated training if he felt as he did about women in the Army. He replied, with the barest trace of a grin, "I have to, sir. It's my job."

EQUAL OPPORTUNITY

At every level of the Army, I found the same thing: men obeying orders and making a maximum effort to achieve something they don't believe in—following one army tradition to defy another. There is plenty of serious sexual discrimination in the Army, and even more sexual harassment. It seemed to me that even so, there was less male sabotage of female noncoms and officers than I have found of female factory supervisors or management executives in civilian life. Most army women I talked to felt the same way.

This seemed terribly important to me because behavior that gives women real equality may eventually modify the values held by most army men. It won't be easy, since the traditionalist majority is so large and the values are so ancient and so deeply held. The Reagan army is closing rather than opening new opportunities to women as the Carter army did. But a change in values is possible. I don't think the Army needs so many of the old values to fight effectively. And I think it's good for the country that women bring the Army into closer touch with the normal world of civilian values—the real world. One way that army women do this is by insisting on their right to traditionally masculine jobs and by doing those jobs as well as men, without losing their femininity.

Today's Army can't escape the touch of the civilian world because it is more than just a fighting machine. It is a major employer. Neither men nor women join the Army clamoring for combat. Both sexes enlist for many reasons, the most common being a steady job in an economy that provides too few. They also join because the Army promises education, travel, a chance to meet people—reasons for many career choices regardless of the work involved. Even the work can be comparable. The vast majority of peacetime army jobs are nine-to-five equivalents of clerk and mechanic jobs in the civilian economy.

But the Army is a different kind of employer because of its combat function —the familiarity with violence and the monopoly of force, shared only in limited ways with the police, which put the Army on the edge of the traditional division between men and women in labor and sex roles. The combat function is dear to career army men but often ignored by army women, unless they are the daughters of military men; many women come to the Army because their fathers were in the service. But the combat function explains other differences between army and civilian work that are more obvious: the overwhelmingly male labor force, the emphasis on physical fitness, the hierarchy of ranks.

The Army is also different from other groups in being simultaneously a refuge for the underskilled and the disadvantaged, and a social pioneer in advancement for minorities and now for women. The women I met felt that the Army, unlike civilian employers, really does provide them with equal pay for equal rank, which usually means for equal work, and an even chance for promotion with men, at least through the grades of staff sergeant for enlisted personnel and major for officers. The Army claims that women have been promoted to the higher grades of first sergeant, lieutenant colonel, and colonel at rates equal to or higher than the army average. And the Army gives women opportunities to do things, from flying helicopters to running police departments, that they seldom find in civilian life. The women I met also felt that army men, like men anywhere, frequently denied them opportunities, treated them as less than equal, and tried to transform them into sexual objects or partners in order not to have to treat them as peers. They frequently came to feel they didn't like what the Army does to human beings, male or female. Whether positive or negative, the women's experiences and their emotions cast light on what men feel, what men do, and what it costs both sexes to change the ancient idea that military occupations should be male.

HOW ARMY WOMEN FEEL

Since army men so often emphasized their fears about women in combat, it seemed significant that most women are not combat-minded. The average army woman, if asked about combat, would probably echo Private First Class Veronica Lyday, whom I met in military police training while she was guarding a missile site against an "aggressor" attacking behind clouds of simulated gas and colored smoke. The scene only reinforced Lyday's reservations: "I don't feel qualified to go up against anybody's bullets. I don't believe I'll be in combat; my mind will not allow that." Lyday is a black graduate of Michigan State University, which puts her well above the Army's educational average. She joined the military police because she couldn't find a civilian job where she could use her psychology degree and because she needed to get away from family conflicts.

I met a few women who were eager to fight, but most of those who could imagine themselves in combat spoke of it as something they would do if they had to, because it was part of their job or because they felt the pull of patriotism. "Just because I'm a female, am I less patriotic than a man? I don't *want* to go into combat, to see a bloody mess or die. But if there's a war, if I join the service to fight for freedom, do I have to sit behind a desk?" Sergeant Terri Heggs was the drill sergeant whom I heard chewing out a male recruit at the gas-mask training site at Fort McClellan. She didn't seem aware that her rhetorical questions aroused echoes of the famous speech in which Sojourner Truth recited the many kinds of hard, "masculine" work she had done, setting each item to the refrain, "And ain't I a woman?"

Heggs was twenty-three when we met, from Longmont, Colorado, a veteran of five years' service. She had a determined chin and a gaze that was intense whether it was directed at a miscreant trainee or an abstract question about a woman's place in the Army. When she enlisted she wanted to join the infantry, but that was barred to her because it's a combat arm. She tried for the military police but was told she was too short. She then asked for a weapons specialty, was sent to learn tank turret repair, and ran into the male chauvinism of the Ordnance Corps, which of all the army branches that must take women is probably the most resistant to them. As Heggs told it, a teacher at Aberdeen Proving Ground deliberately omitted some of the required curriculum in one of her courses "because he didn't like females in leadership." She flunked a test and fell from first to eleventh in her class before working her way back up to sixth place when the course ended. Heggs changed her MOS from tank repair to equal opportunity NCO after she left drill sergeant status, in order to combat such incidents. She said the Army resembles the outside world in discriminating against women but differs in making discrimination easier to fight.

Paulette Loris had a slightly happier time of it. When I met her she was twenty-six, a five-year veteran from East Hampton, New York, with fine bones and the calm that comes from knowing your own capacities and being pleased with them. She was in charge of a male platoon, and fairly strong authority over fifty men is something the civilian world seldom gives a woman. She found the men easier to handle than a platoon of women. "They respond more," she said. "I don't have to put in half the gruffness, getting on cases. They want to please a female sergeant, just the way the females want to please a male drill."

Loris had a Signal Corps MOS in multichannel communications, but she had never worked it. The Army, in one of its resemblances to the civilian world, put her behind a desk. But unlike most civilian employers, the Army saw her leadership potential after she had sat behind a typewriter for a year and moved her into noncom positions normally held by men. She was an administrative supervisor at the 9th Infantry Division headquarters at Fort Lewis, Washington, and then became assistant noncommissioned officer in charge of the plans office, known as G-3. The job normally calls for an infantry MOS, but when no infantryman was available and Loris proved able to do the job, they gave it to her. If the division, part of the new rapid deployment force, had been sent into combat, she would have deployed with it.

For drill sergeants like Heggs and Loris, the most important thing that made the Army different from anything else they'd ever known was not the agony of combat, which they had yet to encounter, or the agony of small weapons and large machines. What was important was the Hat—the symbol of drill sergeant status, an Aussie-style hat for women, a pre–World War II campaign hat for men—and the authority that goes with it. The Hat carries authority to keep the trainees up to snuff in physical training and military skills, to counsel them on everything from whom to salute to their sex lives. That's not yet authority in combat, but it's on the same spectrum. With Heggs and Loris, the Hat seemed to sit as naturally on their heads as did their own hair.

WOMEN OFFICERS

It was not a hat but the pistol and the law that made the Army different for Major Sharon Best. She was serving as adjutant of the reception center at Fort Lewis in 1972 when she went on a weekend fishing trip with a man who kept pushing her to take potshots at beer cans with his .22 pistol. She didn't hit a can until she threw a rock, but she liked the feel of the gun and decided to use her duty hours—empty because the reception center was idling as the draft ended—to go out for the Fort Lewis pistol team. Best became a good marksman, she said, because she knew nothing about pistols, had no bad habits, and listened to her instructors more carefully than did men who thought they already knew how to shoot. (Some male noncoms told me they'd had similar experiences with women trainees, while others insisted that men shoot better than women because they're more familiar with guns.) She moved from Fort Lewis to Fort Ord, California, and the Sixth Army pistol team, then to Fort Benning and the U.S. Army Marksmanship Unit. In 1974 she was a member of the U.S. team that earned a silver medal in the world shooting championship, and she herself was rated "distinguished international shooter." "I wasn't number one in the world, so I had something to shoot for," she said. "I still could be, but . . ."

The "but" was a sign of the pistol's failure to challenge her mind. When the Army offered her a chance to go to law school, she took it. She chose the University of Florida because she thought Gainesville would provide a place for her to shoot in her spare time. But she gave up pistols "because I was scared to death I'd flunk law school. The Army had paid all this money for me to go, so I worked my tail off and my time was utterly filled." Best finished in the top 10 percent of her class at the University of Florida and was editor in chief of the law review. She also broke off an engagement to an army officer who had asked her to resign from the Army and let him pay for her law school. That sounds like an offer of patriarchal benevolence, and he was an "older man." That is, he was old for his rank of captain because he had served for years as an enlisted man and was only two years away from retirement in his forties. In his own eyes, he was not traditionalist but modern: when she finished law school at his expense, he wanted her to support him while he went to law school himself after retiring. But Sharon saw him as wanting leverage over her that he would lose if the Army paid for her legal education and she remained in the service. It was another case of the Army's providing a woman with independence. He lost more leverage in his own eyes when he was passed over for promotion the very week she made the team for the world pistol championships. He was promoted to major on his next and last chance and retired in that rank, still feeling friendly toward Sharon Best. But I couldn't escape the feeling that his respect for her and his regret over losing her were both tempered by a sensation of confusion—and of relief that he would not have to keep up with her.

Best's first assignment in the Judge Advocate General's Corps (JAG) was in Panama, which had never seen a woman JAG officer. Her record made her look "like I walked on water," so she felt she had to work twice as hard to prove herself truly superior as lawyer and as officer. That meant she had to forgo the pistols once more. She also had to do physical training for the first time. She ran with the men, doing a mile in eight minutes, and went on a route march in combat boots. At the halfway rest period, the general drove up and asked if she had fallen out. The men with her said no. But when Best took her boots off, the blisters bled. The general offered her a jeep ride back to the base. She told him she'd take it only if she needed it. Then she let a sergeant bandage her feet and marched back, conscious both of the men's pride that she had refused the ride and of the threat of subtle harassment if she hadn't. The general told her later, at a command performance cocktail party, that he was proud of her. And Sharon Best, a woman who went on special assignment from her Pentagon job to recruit women law school graduates for JAG, told this story as one more proof that she is an achiever. In the Army, that often seems to mean achieving things "a man's way"—the hard way.

Sometimes the man's way is the soft way. In the helicopter school at Fort Rucker, Alabama, a female cadet complained that Captain Deborah Gilbert, an instructor pilot, was harder on her than the male instructors were. Gilbert refused to help the student fly a chopper with its hydraulics turned off. Every student must master this arduous task, comparable to driving a car designed for power steering without power steering. The student claimed that male instructors helped her if she asked. Gilbert was tough on little things too. I first met her when she was chewing out a female cadet who had her hair in a single braid that ran down inside her uniform collar. Regulations say that hair may not be worn below the collar or so that it interferes with military headgear. Male instructors, susceptible to the sight of a woman's long hair even when it disappears into a fatigue jacket, had ignored the violation.

Gilbert was stricter than the men, one of her male colleagues said, because she was only the second woman in army history to become an instructor pilot and felt she had to prove she could handle the task. Many army women complain that they must constantly prove themselves where men would be accepted automatically—a trait the Army shares with the civilian world. Gilbert was one of the few women I met who believed women should be drafted and serve in combat, which she considered a matter of equal responsibilities as much as equal rights.

She may get her chance to fight. Of nearly fifteen thousand army officers rated as aviators, fewer than a hundred are women, and the rules say women may not be pilots or mechanics on attack copters. Most male aviators resist the idea that women can fly. But some copter men do not seem to have the same problems with the idea of women in combat that infantry men do. Colonel Teddy Allen, commander of the 101st Aviation Group at Fort Campbell, said the infantry lagged because "they haven't trained men and women together as we have. At Fort Rucker the training is very rigorous, and women gain respect from their male counterparts. When they get to a unit like mine they show they're as good as the next." Allen insisted that the intensity of combat and of communion is as strong in helicopter flight as it is on the battlefield. "I had three tours in Nam," he said, "and after ninety-eight holes in my copter I stopped counting." He added, in response to a question, "I don't see where a female crew chief or aviator would be a distraction. I'd take my crew chief or those two female pilots into Nam every time."

Allen's pilots were chief warrant officers Ruth Wilson and Linda Sullivan. Wilson described flying a helicopter as more difficult than driving a car, but not as hard as driving a semitractor. She had done many missions successfully but said, "If any hadn't worked out, I would have heard about it. If something goes wrong, they say it's because you're female, not that it's wind shear or something like that."

That was one example of the way an army woman's life is more heavily and obviously conditioned by what men think, do, and feel than it would be in the civilian world. Most of the women don't talk about this in terms of combat or philosophy or psychoanalytical factors. They talk about concrete or flesh-and-blood problems—which often reflect or embody those loftier notions.

Wilson, for instance, kept a Frederick's of Hollywood ad for male underwear under the glass on her desktop and a copy of *Playgirl* magazine, with its male centerfolds, in the desk drawer. Linda Sullivan joked that "it's our equal opportunity." Both enjoyed the vestigial male embarrassment over the pictures, which proved that between peers teasing works both ways. Both felt that sexual harassment, though it certainly exists in the Army, is overemphasized. Both were married to helicopter pilots who liked their wives' careers.

But Sullivan felt emphatically that one kind of discrimination ought to be ended. She was pregnant when she arrived at Fort Campbell and was grounded twelve weeks into her pregnancy because flight surgeons feared that metal vibration, safety belts, and the possibility of accidents endangered the baby. They never consulted army gynecologists, who know better but sound as though they would defer to flight surgeons' position in aviation. Civilian gynecologists say that a woman pilot in good health, with no history of hemorrhage or spontaneous miscarriage and with no complications in her pregnancy, can fly a helicopter well into her eighth month without danger—just as ordinary women drive cars and experienced equestriennes ride horseback until it becomes uncomfortable.

Sullivan had her baby, a boy, by the Lamaze method of natural childbirth, with a midwife instead of a doctor and her husband as monitor of her rhythmic breathing and exercise. Many army hospitals encourage use of the Lamaze system and discourage anesthesia and cesarean sections—progressive attitudes by the standards of the women's health movement. It was also a step forward when the Army changed pregnancy from grounds for compulsory discharge to "temporary physical disability," like a broken leg. A pregnant woman is assigned to limited duty, like clerical work, and can get up to six weeks' paid maternity leave.

But as Sullivan found, army attitudes about pregnancy are still rooted in a male psychology that venerates women as mothers of the race and belittles their ability to do anything else. About 15 percent of army women were pregnant in 1980, half of them unmarried. Army men accused them of immorality, of seeking an easy way out (a pregnant woman can still be released from service immediately), and of ignoring the Army's manpower needs. I met a male helicopter mechanic who swore that at his previous post, in Hawaii, three of the four women on his seven-person team had become pregnant at the same time. They couldn't be transferred to other units and replaced because it was only a temporary disability, but they couldn't carry toolboxes, do in-flight maintenance, or clamber up on top of the choppers. That is, the flight surgeons said they couldn't. Some women's pleas that they could were ignored. As far as the NCO in charge of the team was concerned, he had to operate without 40 percent of his "manpower." Such stories have proliferated into the status of myth; scores of men tell about being in units that had dozens of pregnancies at once, "and that's a lot of morning sickness." Men seldom talk about one nonmythical happening. Passage of the Hyde Amendment stopped free abortions in army hospitals, and the pregnancy rate soared.

The Army worries not only about pregnancy but also about single parents. They must sign statements that they have arranged for legal guardians to care for their children if they are sent into action. Just as there is an endless flow of stories about heavily pregnant units, there is a cycle of tales about women who have missed maneuvers because they couldn't find baby-sitters, or who have brought their children on maneuvers with them. Some are true. In 1982 the Reagan army tried to restrict enlistment of single women or parents with a spouse already in the Army; it had to retreat there, too, at least so far as formal policy is concerned.[6]

Some women who want to make the Army a career complain that it provides far too few day-care centers, especially for people working shifts other than nine-to-five. This hurts not only single parents but also women who are married, as most army women are, to army men whose duties prevent them from playing a significant role in the daily care of their children. Other army women think day care is beside the point; some of the female soldiers who have done the most to refute male stereotypes about women's abilities feel there is something incompatible between the military life and motherhood, and they plan to leave the service when they have babies.

THE SEXUAL MYSTIQUE

Pregnancy and parenthood are important policy matters to an army that needs women soldiers to fulfill its mission. But the Army's concern is not merely functional. It is part of the military man's mystique about women, which almost always translates into a mystique about sex, on the pedestal or in the pits. Women soldiers and women reporters covering the Army told me how surprised they were to discover "how sexual the Army is."

The Army has probably become more sexual as it has enlisted more women, but old soldiers have always thought there was only one thing to do with a woman. Some, to be sure, are confused when they feel fleshly desire for a body wearing a uniform. In the old days they dealt with their confusion by classifying all female soldiers as either "whores" or "lesbians." In the new army they have added a third category, "husband hunters," which angers women only a little less than the first two.*

Old soldiers also worry that if a man and a woman ever land in a foxhole together, they'll be more interested in fornicating than in fighting. I think this is ridiculous, and so do many men who've been under fire. But the fear feeds on the way new soldiers, male and female, find basic training a time of sexual opportunity despite strict rules prohibiting what the Army calls "fraternization" between trainees. "They spend more time thinking about sex than about training," said Drill Sergeant Loris, "with more possibilities than they ever

---

* There are lesbians in the Army, of course, but most civilian observers think the proportion is no greater than in the general population. There are also male homosexuals in the Army in proportions similar to the general population. Officially the Army bars them and can discharge them. Practically they pose problems to commanders only if their private lives prevent them from performing their duties—just like heterosexuals.

had at home just one door away." Men and women sleep in separate rooms, "but they make out in the stairwells, in the mail rooms, in the post beer halls, in the bushes."

For soldiers barely out of adolescence, this only multiplies the problems they would have encountered at home. I remember a beautiful trainee, eighteen years old, whose camouflage could not conceal her fantastic eyelashes. She said she had joined the Army to achieve self-discipline, and the noncoms described her as a model soldier whom they sent back to her hometown to recruit other women.

Perhaps it was part of her recruiting line when she told me, "You keep pushing yourself here to do things, you build up your confidence. The drill sergeants can't hug you and kiss you, so they're hard on you. The guys like to have their fun, but they don't harass us. They tease us. They think it's easy to compete with women, 'cause physically we have a handicap, but mentally we're struggling right ahead of them." I wondered about her, however, when she talked about how lonely life in basic training can be, how in civilian life you can quit a job and move on, while in the Army "you're obligated, and that can make you cry." She turned out to be a frequent off-duty drunk, and she let other girls in the company drag her into weekend motel crawls where each would go through, or be gone through by, enough men to make up an infantry squad. She would wake up in tears Sunday morning and cry on the shoulders of older women trainees, saying she didn't understand why the Army treated women that way. The Army—the men in the Army—had made her a recruiter because she was pretty, because she was proof that it was possible to be a soldier and to be feminine at the same time, not because she was a good soldier. The Army—the men in the Army—had provided her with no more discipline than civilian life.

Fraternization rules go beyond the bar to romance between trainees in the company area. More important are regulations that forbid dating between noncoms and lower ranks in the same unit, or between officers and enlisted personnel even in different units. Many women say their difficulties in adjusting to the rigid military hierarchy often start with an inability to understand why they can't date an attractive man of higher rank. Ironically, the Army here is trying to limit the impact of power on sexual relations, and some women see it as a denial of freedom. In a reverse irony, marriage may be allowed where dating isn't; I met one female major married to a male master sergeant. Whatever the rank, most army women prefer to go out with army men, who understand their hours and their language. But some complain that a soldier seldom stays in the same place more than two or three years and prefer a civilian whom they will be able to find when they come back again.

Fraternization rules are also the Army's main weapon against sexual harassment, an old problem that received new media attention in 1980. Harassment starts with such "normal" acts as whistling on the street and making raucous comment in the mess hall. It may be half-unconscious, like the moment when a major said in a staff meeting that a particular situation "gives me a hard-on," evoking nods from the men around the table but startled confusion when a woman lieutenant said, "Funny, it doesn't have that effect on me."

More serious harassment, well-documented, occurs when soldiers make assaults just short of rape on females they encounter in a barracks, or when a superior demands sexual favors from an inferior in return for leave, promotion, easier duty, or some other benefit. It isn't always a male predator and a female prey, as old army men love to point out. One of the celebrated 1980 cases involved a woman on a woman, and the *Army Times* almost seemed to be chuckling when it reported the case of a woman who was reduced in rank, fined a month's pay, and sentenced to a month's confinement for placing her hand on a man's penis, uninvited, and squeezing. The two were American soldiers in a bar in Germany; the *Army Times* did not report, as other sources did, that the man protected himself by saying to the woman, "Back off, you scumbag."

Acknowledging the fact of harassment or even the idea of harassment is often seen as a violation of camaraderie. It may be the comradeship of all soldiers; of people of the same gender; or of soldiers of the same rank, regardless of sex. The first was barely discernible when a sergeant on a rifle range said he never lets a woman get within three feet of him on duty lest she decide to trump up charges. The second was painfully clear when Staff Sergeant Stephen J. Heinrich, a fifteen-year veteran, told Phil Donahue on network television that he had received an efficiency report with less than half the average rating for his grade because of his "outspokenness"—though the only thing he had spoken out about was sexual harassment, violating the camaraderie of males.

Drill Sergeant Terri Heggs violated the comradeship of rank when she turned in two male drills in her company for sleeping with female trainees. She said she had warned the offenders to stop during an earlier training cycle. Then two members of her platoon complained that two other girls were "messing around" with these particular sergeants, going openly to the company day room after bed check to do so, and the whole platoon was jealous and upset. The witnesses wrote out statements and Heggs took them to the company commander; the offenders "had their hats lifted." That is, they lost their drill sergeant status and its hundred-dollar-a-month extra pay, and returned to regular duty. Male and female noncoms alike criticized Heggs in this case.

Sergeant Loris had the reverse problem: not a superior but a subordinate, a male trainee who "came on" to her. The first time it happened, she had his drill sergeant "counsel" him. ("Counseling," in new army parlance, means what "chewing out" did in the old more often than it means advice and guidance.) That kept the trainee in hand for a few weeks. When he started up again, she put down a veto and it worked. Not only was a sergeant giving him an order, but a woman was saying no, and the latter, as a decently brought up boy, he had to accept.

Such a well-behaved ending to an adolescent crush may seem a long way from the Army's problem in fulfilling its combat mission. But both happy and unhappy outcomes of sexual harassment cases are part of the recurring counterpoint of sex and combat, sex and physical training, sex and soldiering; and that counterpoint is one of the things that reveals the fear I discovered in talking to army men. It is the fear that if women get to the heart of the Army, they will destroy the identity between military and masculine that lies so deep in our culture.

THE PARADIGM DEEPENS

It's an ancient identity and a profound fear. The fear is one of the things that makes the Army, as I've noted, a paradigm of what this book is about. It rolls many fears into one: the fear that women might combine the power to give birth with the power to inflict death, the fear that men might therefore lose their power in society, the fear that the male bond might perish as women invade the quintessentially masculine occupation. When the fear is not articulated, it often turns into anger or anxiety. As this chapter has shown, it frequently produces denial and hostility, and a narrow breed of transformation that most often turns women who choose this work into degraded sexual partners.

The question of women in the military also shows how far-reaching the women's revolution can be in our society and how men respond to it, cope with it, and sometimes support it ("I have to, sir. It's my job"). The identity of male and military could make America a country exclusively of missiles and machine guns. I don't want that. Nor do I want the identity modified only to make America a country of brass bands, push-ups, jockstraps, and jogging bras in the service of national security. I think the military/masculine identity can and should be more profoundly reshaped. That means ending or at least loosening the male monopoly on licensed killing, an immensely difficult change. I don't think women need equal freedom or equal compulsion to kill in order to achieve full equality in our society; I'd much rather reduce men's drive to kill. But I do believe women should have and do have the right to fight and to kill, if they must—to protect their own lives or to fulfill their responsibilities in a military life that they have freely chosen.

Apart from the right to kill, women keep the military in touch with the real world—in serious ways, for example, by their insistence on their right to jobs that army men forgetfully deny them even while proclaiming the Army a pioneer in putting women in traditionally masculine tasks. But there may be just as much significance in gentler or teasing symbols of the way that women tie the new army to the new world outside.

Captain Susan Sensel provided one. She was the first woman to come in first in an ordnance training course—and the first to be denied the traditional plaque on the ground that the award was too competitive, though it was revived in the next training cycle when a man won. As executive officer of a training battalion whom several Vietnam veterans said they would cheerfully follow into combat, she created a delightful symbol: she "suggested" that every man in her headquarters, from battalion commander to buck private, take turns cooking Wednesday lunch for the battalion staff. Chili, lasagne, beef burgundy, and fried chicken flowed in turn—and nobody thought himself any less of a soldier (which he would still translate as any less of a man) when the bugler blew retreat on Wednesday night.

Chapter 5
BLUE-COLLAR WORKERS

In 1971 the women office workers at Solidarity House, the Detroit headquarters of the United Auto Workers, went on strike against the union for higher pay and benefits. Emil Mazey, the UAW secretary-treasurer and a veteran of the violent days of organizing in the auto industry, blew up. The Detroit *News* reported that he charged the women with "premeditated greed and selfishness." An eyewitness told me Mazey had said much more than the newspaper thought fit to print. He went into a harangue when he had to cross a picket line of his own employees. It culminated in a blue-collar version of Freud's famous question: "What do you fucking bitches want, anyway?"[1]

Mazey's hostility was unmistakable—hostility to women who by striking against his union were invading his world of work, even though they were clerks and secretaries and not women from an assembly line. His feelings were typical of blue-collar men, who in general have a harder time accepting women as equals on the job than men in other kinds of work. I don't mean that the percentage who fight the presence of women is higher than the percentage in other categories; there is plenty of male hostility to women in higher-status fields.[2] But the blue-collar men I've interviewed express their anger and their fear more bluntly, show their hostility and denial more plainly than men in other occupations. "I don't think that working-class men are more conservative than middle-class or upper-class men," a woman dockworker told me. "I just think they're more honest about it."

The female invasion of blue-collar occupations is real. Women today hold more than 18 percent of the thirty million blue-collar jobs and 8.5 percent of skilled craft jobs. Their rate of increase since 1972 is faster than the men's, with some exceptions during recessions.[3]

The men's resistance to this invasion takes many forms. It may be no more than extra or extra-loud complaints. It may mean denying women the technical know-how they need to do a job, which experienced men usually give freely to male newcomers. It may mean sabotage, as in the case of a woman who left her machine loose and lubricated every night and every morning found parts screwed so tight that she needed male help and precious time before she could start work. Sometimes hostility goes as far as rape and attempts to kill.

Such acts testify to the strength of negative feelings about women in the blue-collar workplace. Even where women workers describe the environment as positive and relationships as good, men typically express reluctance, skepticism, doubt about women on the job—especially the first women. When these reservations evaporate, blue-collar men still express positive emotions like admiration for and identification with nontraditional women less often and less easily than other men do.

But some blue-collar men do support women on the job. It's more important that there are such men than that there are so few of them. Some younger men have freed themselves from the old chains around their feelings, or have seen their stereotypes soften under the impact of the women's movement. It is a few middle-aged men, however, who accept women the most openly and completely. They show that in the blue-collar world as in most others, the man who feels sure of his own masculinity and his place in the world is more easily supportive than the insecure and the immature. Men whose wives work, even in traditional jobs like secretary and teacher, accept women next to them on the assembly line more easily than men whose wives stay at home. They have learned that women take jobs for the same reasons men do: first for the money they earn, then for other satisfactions—productivity and accomplishment; challenge; recognition and feedback; well-being, psychological and especially physical; and autonomy, some form of control over the pacing and sequence of work and some freedom from supervision.[4]

Neither that kind of autonomy nor freedom in the broader sense is common in most blue-collar jobs. Women who talk about such goals are skilled craft workers, who may find those satisfactions more often than people on assembly lines. But it is also true that many jobs that men see as routine and alienating offer a sense of challenge and reward to new generations of women workers, who find even tiresome blue-collar labor a happy alternative to the traditional and equally tiresome tasks of the (unpaid) housewife and the (lower-paid) pink-collar worker.

This irony is significant, because the most important reason for the reluctance of blue-collar men to accept women as equals on the job is their sense of the powerlessness of workers and the degradation of their labor. The men seldom talk in those terms, except for a few like the auto workers who speak about the plant as a "circle of Hell" or the hatred that workers have for manufacturers who they feel treat them as serfs.[5] Not all blue-collar work is degrading, but even automation, which is supposed to improve the worker's lot, can worsen it. Automated production is one of several kinds of technological advance, like the increasing use of computers in office work, that often seem to require less and less skill in the use of the worker's hands, eyes, and judgment, and more and more obedience to company rules and computer instructions. This is often translated as meaning that the work has become suitable for women, which injures both sexes in different ways.

The men acknowledge their lack of power and glory by trying to refute it. They assert that their characteristics are still those that once made the blue-collar worker emblematic of the American male:[6] his work depends on his strength, on the contortion of his body and the strain on his muscle, on the skill of his hands with different tools and materials. They identify both this strength and this skill with their sexuality. Strength is what blue-collar men mention most often when I ask about women in their kind of work—the physical strength they have, and the strength they fear women lack. Their talk moves quickly from strength to competence, to knowledge of certain tools and familiarity with the etiquette of the workplace—how to set the pace of work, how to deal with the boss. These kinds of knowledge are again qualities they have and fear women lack. They are also quick to talk about family and their fear that the woman who leaves home to work is damaging hers. And they talk about language almost as much as about strength. The plaint sounds shallow, but it voices a deep pathos: "With a woman on the job, I can't talk the way I want to."

Strength, skill, language, work etiquette, the need to keep the family at home, which is to say elsewhere: these things constitute a common culture that makes blue-collar work a man's world. When women come into this world for the first time, they seldom share this culture or the male emotions that bind it in place.

MALE BONDING

Blue-collar men don't talk in so many words about male bonding, that powerful drive that interlaces with all the other forces moving in them. But almost everything they say is imbued with the feeling that blue-collar work is indeed defined by this bond.

Male bonding is the tendency of some males to form relationships that exclude other males and all females. It goes back thousands of years, perhaps almost a million, to the time when human males began to cooperate in the hunt. Lionel Tiger, the anthropologist who first popularized the concept, sees bonding as a phenomenon that has become part of the genetic code, and he says the male-male bond is "of the same biological order for defense, food-gathering and maintaining social order as the male-female bond is for reproduction."[7] Tiger in fact offers no scientific proof of the genetic nature of the bond. I doubt that it has become part of our biological heritage. Its persistence for millennia has made it immensely powerful in both human psychology and human sociology, however—and immensely difficult to change or restrict.

Tiger adds, "Males bond in a variety of situations involving power, force, crucial or dangerous work, and relations with their gods. They consciously and emotionally *exclude* females from these bonds." (Tiger's italics.)[8] The connection with work is important, and it need not always be dangerous work. The power of the bond starts in the occupational sphere. In almost all of the 186 societies in the Standard Cross-Cultural Sample studied by anthropologists George P. Murdock and Caterina Provost, men monopolize fourteen of fifty work activities. Most of them fall into two categories: hunting and butchering (recalling the primeval all-male hunting band); and the processing of hard or tough raw materials, particularly metalworking and metal mining, and working bone, horn, and shell.[9] The male monopoly also includes the manufacture of weapons and most tools, which presumably originated in metalworking. No technological activities are exclusively female, though food preparation and the manufacture and repair of clothing come close.

Men might think that these monopolies are matters of size and strength or of activities incompatible with bearing and raising children, as blue-collar men and soldiers, architects and doctors, all describe their occupations today. But women often do things like mining and working stone or carrying huge burdens, which refutes the claim that strength is male. Marxists might claim that the men dominate the means of production and the economically most rewarding tasks, and it's true that few of these are controlled by women. But there is no evidence that this is a cause of the basic division of labor in human development. Men keep to themselves the manufacture of musical instruments, neither economically important nor physically demanding nor incompatible with mothering; I suspect this has to do with a connection between music and religious ritual that men want to keep to themselves.

On a simpler level, it may be a consequence of the way the male bond is related to male work. Tiger suggests that when they can, males choose their workmates in processes analogous to sexual selection; that the bond they establish generates considerable emotion and important satisfactions; and that the sexual division of labor is a consequence of males' wishes to preserve their male-male bonds and not simply a result of physical or temperamental differences with females.[10]

Even though I doubt the biological nature of the bond, I think Tiger is right in suggesting its emotional nature. It gains much of its strength from something Tiger does not mention—the pattern of psychic development in which males feel betrayed by the mother who "abandons" them, and therefore fear and exclude females from the craving for connection with another that helps form the bond. We also crave connection with females, of course, but the bond reinforces the human tendency to polarize work, where the bond operates, and love, where by definition, at least for heterosexuals, it cannot operate.

The male bond, then, remains the likeliest and most important cause of male occupational monopolies. It underlies the division of labor that is the first attempt to restrict women to the private parts of human activity (see

Chapter 2). It may also go beyond the occupational to the political, excluding women from other forms of public life. Tiger calls the bond the spinal column from which "communities derive their intra-dependence, their structure, their social coherence, and in good part their continuity through the past to the future."[11]

The link between the male bond and occupations is not restricted to "primitive" cultures. The modern equivalents of their hunting and metalworking are male domains to this day, and the dislike that blue-collar men feel for women on "their" assembly lines goes back for ages. When the industrial revolution took most work out of the home and into the factory, the tendency of men to bond and to maintain the division of labor excluded females from some occupations; in compensation, others, usually rated lower and paid less, were reserved for females. Even today when women have invaded so many traditionally masculine jobs, the negative side of the male bond—men's refusal to do certain jobs—helps keep many fields still feminine: both pink-collar jobs like cashier, clerk, and elementary school teacher, and blue-collar jobs like textile worker and electronic panel assembler.

WOMEN AND HIERARCHY

However strong the male bond, it has not been able to keep women out of the workplace. They even serve a purpose for blue-collar men. Focusing on women in any sense—talking about them, talking to them, harassing them, even supporting them—takes a man's mind off power and glory and their opposites. Individual militancy and verbal harassment become habits that shift easily from one target to another. Men often focus hostility on foremen and superintendents, which diffuses it from the company and the line. Women do not personify authority in the same way, but men sometimes see their presence in the workplace as a plague that authority has visited on the male world ("They're only here 'cause the company is trying to keep in good with the government" was a constant theme with variations), and directing anger at them can be a form of rebellion, like directing it at bosses.

Yet hostility to women at work, paradoxically, may come out of its lair deep in the individual or collective psyche only after the women have been taught that they are at the bottom of the hierarchy. Working men often feel, want to feel, need to feel that somebody has even less power and does less satisfying work than they do. If that somebody rises to do their kind of work, they feel their labor is devalued. Once the somebody was black. Today she is at least as often a female. If a woman can do a man's job, he may feel less than a man, emasculated. Sometimes this need to assert superiority is oppressive. Sometimes—toward women, though rarely toward blacks—the need to be on top is expressed by protectiveness, a desire to keep women unsullied and unhurt by the things that damage men (like Caputo's desire to keep them unsullied by war). If a woman sees blue-collar work as more rewarding than brutalizing, that only makes things worse.

Lucy Gwin didn't accept her place as "bottom dog" in a hierarchy when she worked as a deckhand on the boats that serve the offshore oil rigs in the Gulf of Mexico. She was a woman in a "man's job," and she talked back. Some men supported her, some harassed her, and two, one a captain and the other a shipowner, tried to kill her.[12] It's rare for the male response to go as far as death threats, but physical intimidation is common. It may be seen as a matter of strength, of masculine competition that creates an informal hierarchy, intimidating men as well as women. In the mines, for instance, it's common horseplay to tape a male newcomer—to strip him and bind him in heavy electrical tape, leaving him untended until someone happens to come his way later. It's common to grease him—to remove his pants and slather thick engine grease between his legs. In at least one case, reported by a woman, the greasers drew a smiling face on the head of the victim's penis. That made such hazing a kind of sexual harassment, as it always is when the victim is female. But when the physical danger is great, the community may have less tolerance than it has shown for other kinds of sexual harassment. A woman miner in Kentucky came down with a vaginal infection after a greasing. She sued the man who did it and was awarded several thousand dollars by a local jury.

All sexual harassment may be classed as intimidation, but women in several different blue-collar jobs made a common distinction. They said that a male worker who does things like shoving a woman against a wall while "talking dirty," or laying heavy hands on her rather than using the equally offensive pinch or tweak, is engaged less in sex play than in frightening her with his strength. A Southern metalworker admitted, after several beers, that he sometimes acted like that:

> Sure, it's nice to squeeze a little tit. It's nice to feel something softer and warmer than a cold chisel. But who wants to go into a ventilator shaft to screw? Sometimes, if I lean on a girl, I'm not thinking about getting ass. I'm just scaring her a little. Especially if she's the kind who works extra hard and talks like she wants extra credit for it, I don't mind showing her who's really stronger. I don't do no real harm. I'm just reminding her where she fits.

The sense of hierarchy was unmistakable in his last comment. It is harder to see, but still present, when the action shifts from this kind of intimidation to horseplay that may still border on sexual harassment but has a lighter spirit, an adolescent sense of humor. Like focusing on women, it is yet another way to relieve the frustrations at the bottom of the power system. Bob Selden* is an assembly line worker at a Midwest heavy equipment factory, a man who seems like a character out of a Larry Woiwode novel, clean-living and thoughtful, with a sense of the world beyond his own limits. He said:

Nothing on this line goes through right every day. There's no such thing as a perfect day. You work on this floor. I don't care who you are, when you get off at night they tell you not to run, but you're keyed up, you feel in the back of your head you're kind of tense and tight, so you're kind of moving fast out of here—you rush home, and it takes a little time to calm you down. On the line, you either blend into it or it will drive you crazy. Sometimes the guys go in for horseplay or stuff like that; it breaks the monotony. If you're not in a good mood and they do this, it sort of ticks you off. There's a guy on this line they call "Preacher." He'll grab your ass one day and preach a sermon on hellfire the next. Or Barry, he's always lying down on the floor pretending to have a fit, then he'll ask you how's your rope [gesturing toward his penis]. I don't like it when they do that, and it really offends me in front of the women.

Grabbing ass is something that men do to men in the factory as on the football field, one of a range of gestures like putting an arm around a shoulder, hitting someone on the back, tapping him on the chest, pulling at a nipple. Beneath the adolescent humor are serious currents—competitive masculinity and hierarchical challenge twinned with a need for physical intimacy, perhaps even for reassurance, and a completely unconscious trace of homosexuality. If a man does this kind of horseplay with a woman, it is another form of sexual harassment—and another demonstration that he, no matter how powerless vis à vis the foreman or the company, is more powerful than she.

Most supervisors, most companies, and most unions discourage physical contact between men and women on the job, whether intimidation, horseplay, or sex. Most of the men I talked to would not admit to such harassment, those who did it seldom showed as much insight into themselves as either Selden or the metalworker. But the need to keep women lower on some hierarchy, whether it followed or violated the conventional seniority ladder, was a common theme. In the same heavy equipment factory, Ed Hubbell* was a shop steward in the section that prepared engines for shipping. He said the men worried that women couldn't do the heavy work and complained if they were given light jobs:

They bitch when women are favored, and I believe a lot of them have been favored on the [neighboring assembly] line. Most of them come out and get a good sweeping job [the lowest category of factory work], and that's okay. If a woman came into shipping we'd expect her to start at the bottom, on the saw or building skids. I'm sure it would stir up trouble if guys who had been here longer and deserved easier jobs didn't get them. And it would cause some friction if they had to carry her or do her work on a tough job.

Many men, of course, want to move up the hierarchy. They particularly want to escape jobs where, as a cannery worker said, "I never have to use my brain, goddamnit, I only have to do what they tell me." They want to move up to jobs that make them "feel good as a man," to jobs that allow some autonomy in the work—like construction worker and skilled mechanic. As women invade both the lower blue-collar ranks and the skilled craft jobs, men complain that they are competing for the good slots and reducing the men's chances.

Underlying this complaint is a historical fact: if women move into a field in large numbers, it usually loses status and often pay, like clerical workers and elementary school teachers in this country. This tendency is reinforced by the trend of technological advance to demand less skill and impose more routine, often tedious, painstaking routine. The need is for more "reliability"—for "workers who appear punctually and regularly, who work hard, who don't sabotage the line, and who see their own interests as identical with the welfare of the company."[13] These are the characteristics that men traditionally expect from women clerks, electronic assemblers, and the like. Male managers do not try to hide what happens. Most technological changes in one factory "were of a type that would tend to increase the percent of women. For example, we have broken down the alignment of components and simplified [the] job and as the jobs called for less skill, they became women's work."[14] That was one New Jersey executive quoted in a study that cited many more.

Working men seldom leap to describe historical trends, but they know this one. It makes real the feeling that if a woman can do a man's work, the job is devalued in his eyes and his employer's. It's one of the unspoken axioms that intensifies the need to keep women down the ladder of power as it raises men's consciousness of their own powerlessness. In fact, it's not always unspoken. A middle-aged machinist in Chicago said, "I've seen it happen more than once. Work gets simple enough and they turn it over to the girls." A colleague young enough to be his son said, "That's why I don't want to see too many girls here. Just encourages the computer jocks to screw around with our specialties." The older man shook his head and turned to me with a weary smile that seemed to say, "It doesn't need girls in the shop to make the engineers go to work on us."

GENDER, SEX, AND COMPETENCE

The overlap between the degradation and the feminization of labor makes blue-collar men, like the young machinist, fear and hate the idea of women in the workplace all the more. They fight back with a simple strategy: assert that males are the only workers with the strength and competence needed for a particular job. They charge, or at least worry, that women are not strong enough to lift machine parts, to push pallets of packed cartons, to pull a

ship's lines. They talk about this weakness and the fear that they will have to
do the women's work as well as their own even while some women are doing
the very things they are worrying about—and even while some men are failing to do them without help.

Concern about strength, as I've noted, moves often and quickly to concern
about competence, particularly the kind of technical knowledge that grows
out of familiarity with machines and tools. I saw this unconscious strategy
most clearly in one of the first interviews for this book, when I was talking to
Barry Brock,* the young assembly-line worker in the heavy equipment plant
whom Bob Selden described as quick with the horseplay. Barry put on his
most serious face when I started asking questions; that combined with his
stocking cap and his granny glasses to give him the look of a student, though
he was in his thirties and had not finished high school. He said:

> Out there on the line where I work, they're all the same number [i.e. job
> classification] and they're all supposed to be able to do any job out there,
> and some of them women cannot do it. Some of them flywheels out there
> weigh 180, 190 pounds [an exaggeration], I can lift 'em, but some women
> can't.

The union contract in that plant specified that the company provide a mechanical hoist to lift such weights. Barry disdained it because it was slower
than using bare hands, so without the hoist you might be able to take a few
minutes' worth of extra break on each shift. He went into a litany of "jobs out
there that women can't do": putting on front covers, putting on engine heads,
taking the engine off the line, and others. Some of these tasks required the use
of a crane:

> I don't know if you ever worked with a crane when it's got a weight on it,
> how it swings. Sometimes it's kind of rough to get the object where you
> want it. You have to balance weights, your own weight against the machine
> weight. Sometimes you get the head over the engine and it will drop right
> down on it. Sometimes we have a heck of a time getting it on there.

As he said this, he went through the motions required, half shadow boxer,
half ballet student at the barre. The cumulative effect of his recital and the
counterpoint of tone and gesture made me realize that what he was really
saying was that he did all this flywheel lifting and crane balancing with his
penis, so of course a woman couldn't do it.

Bob Selden didn't agree with Barry. "I don't think there's a job on the line
that a woman can't handle," he said. "If you say that's so heavy that she can't
lift it up, that's idiotic, because there's hoists and cranes and air lifts." But it
is true that the average woman can't lift as much as the average man. I heard
auto workers, coal miners, construction workers, dockers, garage mechanics,
machinists and oil refinery foremen express worry about this in "rational"
terms. I would guess that a large majority of blue-collar men would do so. I

would also guess that at least half of that majority would go on to let an emotion like Barry's subconscious penis pride (it is somehow the opposite of penis envy) become visible behind their rational concern if they talked about it long enough.

While skills with tools and techniques are also gender-connected for many men, most are not so quick to disparage women's competence as they are to question female strength. Many acknowledge women's talents as a way of protecting their pride in their own strength. Ed Hubbell, the shop steward in the shipping section, asked me what women wanted in the factory. "A chance to use their brains, for one thing," I told him. "Hell, let them do brainwork, right here in the plant, push a couple of buttons on the computer," he replied. "But the jobs that require manual labor, they're not really qualified to do." Other men spoke of one woman or another who didn't know how to use a wrench or a plane or a drill or a lathe. Or they cited a woman who took longer to learn than a male apprentice because she didn't have the aptitudes they expected to find in young men, or the training that boys still pick up more than girls do, in school shops or under their cars.

Consciously or unconsciously, men often deny women the chance to become competent. They are reluctant to share their know-how with women peers. One study reported that in one company 70 percent of the men went to other workers when they had a technical question about the job, while 85 percent of the women went to the foreman.[15] Much of that vast difference is explained by the male bond, which shuts out women particularly from informal communication like the socializing over lunch or over drinks at the end of the day, where much information and training is traded in blue-collar and other worlds. Other factors may also be at work, of course, like the tendency of men to defy authority at the foreman level and the tendency of women to defer to authority when they are not making more profound rebellions.

Blue-collar men usually do meet responsibilities to give women formal training if the company spells them out. Even then, it may not be easy. Jim Chatham* is a journeyman electrician at the heavy equipment plant who had to work hard to overcome the disturbance he felt at having to train Ginny Meinecke,* a woman who would formally become his peer when she completed four years of apprentice training. Chatham's wife had gone to college at thirty-two and completed her Ph.D. at forty-two and become a teacher, only to lose her job when the school board had to cut back. She then went to work in private industry as a receptionist. Chatham liked the idea of her working and bringing in a second paycheck, remembering how he had worked two jobs while she was raising their children. He professed to have no problems with a wife who was better educated and sometimes earned more money than he did. He liked the idea of women working in general. But he did not like the idea of women entering his blue-collar world and mastering his trade. "I made up my mind that I will accept Ginny because she's in the apprentice program," he said—sounding like an army man obeying orders. But when I asked how well she had done, he would only say:

> Ginny hasn't been up here long enough for me to make a good judgment. But I have strong feelings that a woman doesn't belong in all fields of a man's world. My experience so far with Ginny has been that she has done some good work and that she's smart, but she lacks the common sense that the average man has about how to go about doing things.

Chatham's first example of her lack of male "sense" was the old question of strength, her inability to lift a sixty-pound box to her shoulder and walk up a flight of steps. (She made a point of carrying such weights as she could manage on her hip, "which I'm built to do.") He refused to appraise her knowledge of electricity and her ability to wire a machine—in a way that suggested that she was competent but that he wasn't going to say so until she had passed every formally set test. He spoke wistfully about the need to watch his language and stop the horseplay when she was around, adding, "You just sort of got to change your curriculum in little ways. I think maybe that's the biggest problem, you don't like to change your habits." Then the rational side washed over him and Chatham abandoned his emotions about male bonding and added, "But I have no objection to her being down there. I can't blame them for wanting to make a decent wage and support themselves."

Sometimes the problem is seen as one of attitude rather than aptitude, of productivity rather than capability. An oil refinery foreman recalled that in the early 1970s, when the first women came into the refinery:

> Our question was "What the hell are you going to be able to do here?" We wondered, have they ever done it, do they know anything about it, can I rely on them to do it or is my best defense to put them off in some corner where a helper will do all their work and they will be perhaps tool cleaners or parts washers.
>
> There were women who came in here and traded on the fact that they were women. They didn't have any more idea of coming out here and becoming a producer. . . . They knew that if they got with the right person he would protect them, protect them in quotation marks. He just didn't want to get them involved in his work for fear of their not being able to accomplish, or that it would take a longer time. So he shunted them aside, to some corner, like I said. . . .
>
> But I hired a woman who possessed a dedication, a wide open avenue of wanting to learn. She was very excited about getting this job and she put in the effort. . . . I saw her go over to that plate and try to do that job. She wasn't able to set it up properly and I had to get down and show her how

to do it. But Joe Blow here, I had to ask did he even make that type of attempt or was he content to stand there and wonder, what am I going to do, is somebody going to come along and bail me out?

That foreman believed that he, and many other refinery workers, had become more able to accept women on the job in the previous decade. Even the shift in concerns from strength to competence and productivity was a move toward acceptance in his eyes. Other men in the same refinery still questioned the basic competence of women workers. Overall, I would guess that the proportion of men who think males are more competent than females is smaller than the majority who think that men are stronger than women and that it matters. And I'd guess that perhaps half of the smaller group, too, is masking penis pride behind its "rational discussion" of the issue.

SEXUALITY IN THE WORKPLACE

That is just one way that the issues of strength and competence are linked to the issue of sexuality. Blue-collar men seldom *do* sex at work, but they think it and talk it—to relieve the frustrations of the workplace, to proclaim their own masculinity, to reinforce the male bond. When women come in, men may try to exclude them, to intimidate them, to keep them in their place. Raising the issue of sexuality is another way of keeping them in their place, returning them to the primary relationship between males and females.

In the blue-collar world, men do this most often by making women sexual targets. It may be as crude as rape, as tasteless as displaying pornography, or as silly as talking dirty. Most women find even the lesser acts offensive and may see them as forms of intimidation.

Rape is certainly an act of power and intimidation, a crime of aggression and violence. But it is committed with a sexual weapon, and when it is attempted in the workplace, it usually grows out of a sexual context: the belief of many men that a woman on the job is making herself sexually available. Lesser or noncriminal sexual aggression also grows out of this context. The belief is partly a matter of sex-role stereotypes: the woman has departed from what is seen as her proper place at home taking care of her husband and children. It is partly a matter of male bonding and the division of labor: women who do not know the language and etiquette of the supposedly all-male world of work are relegated to the conventional male-female scenario. This happens all the faster because men in an all-male world of work expect to meet women only out of that world, in places where the main purpose is play or pleasure—or love. When women come to the workplace, men assume them to be licensing those pursuits and turn either to truly sexual behavior or to sexual varieties of aggression. Most women make it very plain that they did *not* come to work to seek play or pleasure or love. Many men take a long time to get the message. They have been socialized to think that women are meant for those things. And often, men who do exhausting and dirty work with the hardest of hard objects also feel a desperate need for someone who is not only sexual but also soft and gentle, someone who can be both pillow and anchor. This need is not always met at home or at play. When it surfaces in the workplace, it sometimes does lead to love or pleasure. But all too often it is perverted into acts of brutality or insult that violate the very feelings it seeks.

Something else is important in both rape and other acts of sexual aggression in blue-collar work. The offender is seldom in a position of authority, a man who can trade sex for favors or make it a condition of employment, as is so often the case when sexual harassment occurs in the white-collar world. He has no power over the victim except that of his body. (Some blue-collar foremen and supervisors of blue-collar workers do commit quid-pro-quo sexual harassment, of course; the point is that in this world, it is peers who often and explicitly become threateningly sexual. This happens less often in the white-collar world, where physical power counts for much less than hierarchical power.)

One estimate says that twenty-one thousand women a year face rape or attempted rape or assault connected with work. The documented cases I've come across are blue-collar more often than white, in coal mining and construction. The Coal Employment Project, for instance, selected fifty-nine women in the mines at random for a survey; 76 percent said they had been propositioned by men they worked with, 53 percent said they had been propositioned by their male bosses, and 17 percent said they had been physically attacked.[16]

Darla Baker, a miner at Consolidation Coal Company's Shoemaker mine in Benwood, West Virginia, fought off a rough rape attempt by another miner. He followed. She kicked him in the crotch in front of his workmates, who laughed. He still came back later to the site she was working on, the site where he too should have been at work, fondled his penis, and said, "Gee, I'd like to see you in a black negligee." She protested to one supervisor who laughed at her and to another who grew angry at the offender and made sure he never worked with her again. There was no other punishment and no investigation. But later, Baker's car was damaged in the company parking lot, rumors spread that she kept a bed hidden in the mine for prostitution, and graffiti saying "Deep Throat Darla, the blow job miner" were found on the mine elevator and vehicles. When she brought this to the attention of the senior personnel man, he told her, "Now don't start no shit, Darla, or you'll be blackballed out of coal mining, where women don't belong anyway."[17]

Later, Baker joined eight other women miners in suing Consol for permitting the operation of a peephole in the women's shower room at Shoemaker for more than a year. While the peephole was open, graffiti began to appear proclaiming details, real or imagined, of the women's anatomy: so-and-so "has inverted nipples"; a vehicle used by a woman who supposedly had protruding vaginal lips was labeled "low lip express." The women regarded this as sexual harassment; one called it "torture." The men charged that the women knew about the peephole and "paraded" in front of it "to turn us on."[18] Consol ultimately settled after the case went to court but before it went to the jury, paying the women an amount of money that their lawyer said "we could live with." The court kept it secret. In a similar case involving the Pittston mine in Beckley, West Virginia, in 1984, the jury denied the women money damages, but Judge Elizabeth V. Hallanan ruled that the company and the men had discriminated against them, violating Title VII of the 1964 Civil Rights Act. She ordered that the company post notices at the mine forbidding sexual harassment, conduct training for men to prevent harassment, and provide assertiveness training for women to train them to defend themselves against it.

Clearly the use of the peepholes was both intimidation and an example of the male belief that women at work are sexually available, a belief that persists despite a flood of evidence to the contrary. So was the remark of the miner who told one of the Shoemaker women that she didn't need to work underground to support her children because she could turn prostitute— "You're sitting on a gold mine." So were the many sexual invitations.

For the women miners, the rape attempts, the peepholes, the graffiti, and the propositions were all of a piece, and rightly so. They were all ways of making the women sexual targets. But the distinction between violent crime and lesser, nonphysical acts is one of the important lines that civilization draws. Blue-collar men sometimes draw this boundary themselves. It smacks of self-justification in many cases, but it can also show a sincere effort to put limits on how far they will go to keep a woman "in her place." A woman might feel that even one step is too far, but a man with an idea of limits may be educable.

At the heavy equipment plant, a young woman in a cooperative training program for college engineering students came to work one day in white jeans and a white sweatshirt. The younger men on her assembly line noticed what happened when she leaned up against the machines and maneuvered her into positions that put spots akin to black handprints on her breasts and behind. That provoked further remarks by the men. An older worker took her aside to give her a lesson on protecting herself from this kind of horseplay; he also asked a woman manager to reinforce his suggestion. The men on the line insisted that they had not threatened her and would never have gone beyond the teasing. They said they had no desire to injure or frighten the girl and underlined that during the tease they had gone on giving her the on-the-job training she was supposed to get.

The young men never propositioned the engineering student, but her blue-collar supervisor invited her to dinner. She accepted after considerable internal debate, partly because she feared for her job if she said no. When he drove her to a restaurant in a hotel forty miles away and asked her to go to bed with him, she did say no, assuming that it meant her job. It didn't. Her boss didn't take the harassment he had committed as seriously as the women in the company who learned about it, but he made two points to his friends: he would never have forced her sexually once she said no, and though he admitted using his leverage as her boss to get her to go out with him, he would not and did not try to penalize her on the job when she turned down his proposition. In other cases, a turndown by a woman can lead to loss of her job or other penalties. Or it can lead men to ignore her, in effect to exclude her from the group—the basic form of denial.

None of the men I interviewed admitted touching women sexually on the job or making sexual propositions in the workplace with serious intent. Surveys of blue-collar women, however, report that such behavior is widespread. Some of the denials are obviously men's attempts to protect themselves, but it's important that many men sincerely believe they are joking (except for those like the Southern metalworker who knew he was intimidating the women he "leaned on"). They don't count it as a proposition if they say something and the woman turns them down in a way they can laugh off. Longshoremen, for instance, agreed with a woman dockworker's description of their behavior but not with her interpretation:

> When you work on a truck with one or two other people, and the truck is very dark, someone will say half jokingly, "What are you doing in that truck, what are you doing in the dark there?" The women who work in the trucks are very serious and are there to work, but some of the men really believe something could happen. Sometimes the guy in the truck will say, "Do you want to go out with me?" or "What would happen if I made love to you?"

Some men really say "make love," she insisted, but then she admitted with an embarrassed laugh that some use four-letter words in their propositions. One man from another dock, when I repeated her story, said, "Sure, that will happen." His mate said, "I haven't been taken up on it yet, and most of the time I don't even say it, but it's all just a game." The two thought that if a woman said, "Great, let's fuck," they might have a go on a coffee bag—but more important to them, that such ploys, if offered in the right spirit, were *not* meant to intimidate or assert hierarchy.

Sometimes sex play on the job appears to be something between equals and not a matter of hierarchy. Men say it is certainly an affair of equals when a woman starts it (though that often makes them hostile to the woman because she is "not a lady"). A foreman on the night shift in the equipment plant felt that way:

> There's a little bit of grab-ass in the wee hours. It's probably put and take, she's probably making the initial movement half the time. A couple of

weeks ago, one guy was bent over applying a decal, one of the gals had some cold coffee. She saw the moon shining and reached over and poured the coffee on him. The guy reached around, took a broom handle and pushed it to her where the sun never shines. That was the end of that—I took them both to task about it, said that's horseplay and we're not going to have that. But that's acceptability [of a woman on the job]. Crude as it is, it's real.

Sometimes sex play may be a matter of even more basic mutual interest. Women in the equipment plant saw couples disappear on night-shift lunch breaks with mattresses under the arms. They said it was mutual attraction rather than male harassment at least half the time. Genuine sexual attraction creates a tension on the job that upsets men as much as women—an irony both bitter and sweet because it derives from the profound belief that the boundary between the worlds of work and play should be well marked and well fended, yet blue-collar men are constantly fudging that boundary in the kinds of sexual play and sexual harassment that we're looking at. A young man working his way through a four-year apprenticeship as an electrician said he had "let myself" pay attention to one woman in the apprentice program.

It got me to work on time every day [with an embarrassed laugh]. That week I terminated 150 wires, and every single one of them was terminated on the wrong sides. That was when I first started and I didn't really know what I was doing.

But a journeyman in the same program, attracted to one of those young women, admitted with his own embarrassed laugh that he had propositioned her something like 1,630 times in a four-month period. That made it a game rather than a serious invitation or a harassment, but he was genuinely worried that it had interfered with the quality of his teaching. He admitted that his upset would have been much greater if the woman apprentice had ever said yes to one of his propositions. She was young enough to be his daughter, and he had both wife and daughter of his own.

It is neither a game nor a way of ignoring women when men display centerfold crotch shots and harder-core porn photos, but it is an almost universal practice. Men mentioned this in every blue-collar place that I visited, whether they were admitting with a snigger that they did it or piously blaming others for it. Both types knew it was harassment intended to put the women symbolically in their place, in the primary male-female relationship seen in its most vulgar images. They often sounded, however, as though it were a natural thing for men to do in our society. It was certainly a predictable thing.

On the docks it is only foremen who have the power to put the pictures up and the walls on which to put them. In other places it's more "democratic": every man has the power. As a result, in some shops, garages, and parts rooms, the small offices will be wall-to-wall "pink." In the oil refinery and the heavy equipment plant, the male workers put pictures in the tool lockers that they can flip open as women workers walk by. Women foremen (the phrase used in the equipment plant) were also targets. These were women on the lowest rung of management in the company's terms, bosses working on peculiar terms of intimacy with blue-collar men. One named Betty Ballard* told me:

> There were people out in the shop daily, like my boss, who saw the pictures of the naked women on the men's desks and did nothing. Rather than make a big issue out of it, I chose to ignore it. One day I was off, perhaps I was sick, and my boss was out there not as my supervisor but in my place as foreman. He was out there daily and nothing was done. But the day that he was boss for the day and I was gone, all the pictures were ordered to be removed. But they were fine as long as I was there.

A machinist whose wife had played it cool when confronted with a sexy poster in her workplace expressed surprise at the kind of picture the men selected. "If I wanted to embarrass a woman," he said, "I'd put up a picture of some big stud hanging out, instead of a crotch shot. If a guy were really casting for a reaction, I'd think that's what he'd put up, not something of a female." Of course, the men are not casting for a sexual reaction at all. They are only showing a woman what they want to reduce her to. And most men, it seems, don't identify with a picture of "some big stud hanging out." They feel competitive and insecure. Or so Martha Baird* found when she decided the best tactic was not to play it cool or ignore the porn. She was technically the men's peer when she faced the issue, but she was a woman in her forties who later became a shop steward and then a foreman, someone who could not be intimidated. She said:

> The men's cabinets were open. They had naked women. They wouldn't put the doors shut. After a week or two, I went out and bought me a *Playgirl* magazine with the naked men. I had never done that before. I opened the cabinet and pasted the men on the inside. I left the doors open. The men shut them. I went to the foreman and said, "If they can leave theirs open, I want these open." It wasn't too long until theirs came down.

Talking dirty is much more universal than exhibiting crotch shots. It's part of male culture and part of blue-collar language, as men recognize even or especially when they choose to clean up their lives or their words. When women arrive in the workplace, talking dirty may continue as a habit so ingrained it is almost unconscious. It may become a conscious test or act of intimidation.

It may also be abandoned as men try to act on the belief that a woman may be a lady even if she is doing blue-collar work.

"Talking dirty" covers a multitude of sins and a variety of vulgarities. It may have a high sexual charge, like one man's challenge to another's sexual accomplishments *(Why don't you take me over to your house and let your wife meet a real man?)* or an appraisal of a woman, whether seen on a TV screen or a factory floor *(Her tits are too big for your hands, but those legs really go up to her waist.).* Or it may simply be conventional profanity without true sexual intent or content, in which any one of a surprising range of people, objects, and actions shits, fucks, or sucks.

Sexually charged talk in the presence of women has a more obvious testing or frightening purpose than the mindless use of four-letter words. Men who admit that they have foul tongues seldom confess an intent to test or frighten women; the mere admission is usually part of the plaint that they can't talk the way they want to. But men who have cleaned up their own acts often see such an intent in other men. Dick York,* a foreman at the heavy equipment plant, heard a shop steward making sexual remarks to Elaine Stanley,* a woman foreman whose desk stood a few feet away from his. He said:

> I found myself racing like a knight in shining armor to protect her. He's by nature a little bit of an abrasive character, and he was really trying her on to see "how far can I push." I saw her redden, but she very quietly and methodically sent him back to his workplace. She eliminated any reference to what he said, to his vulgarity. She could have fired him for some of the things he said. He did make some reference to the two of them. That got my hackles up a little bit. Elaine handled it quite well.

I was amused when both Elaine and the shop steward corrected the white knight's story. The steward said to her, "I'd like to get in your pants," and Elaine, far from eliminating all reference to his vulgarity, replied with the classical line, "I think one asshole in there is enough." The steward later became one of her warmest supporters.

Two crane operators at that plant who worked for Martha Baird when she was a foreman reported that a male colleague had been anything but a knight in shining armor. One said:

> There's one other foreman who don't like her, I imagine because she's a woman. He'll talk just as dirty around her, and that's not right. She went down on the floor and could match every word he said. She come back so mad and said, "That son of a gun, he stood there and said, 'Fuck fuck fuck fuck fuck.' " She wanted to say it but she didn't want him to hear her.

His mate joined in:

> If she come up with cussing, we'd go right in and cuss. But she's already in the shop. If I know she's there, I ain't gonna do it.

They believed she was a lady, in other words, because she didn't talk dirty and disliked it when they did. Their belief was stronger because they knew that she knew all the dirty words, could use them if she had to, and still chose not to, other things being equal. In the equipment plant, in the oil refinery, and on the docks there was a common pattern: a woman who talked the same four-letter language as the men risked their contempt and further harassment. The refinery foreman with the sense of history reported that when a woman tried to match the men word for word:

They'd call her bitch, or whore. By her trying to become part of the group of peers, if language is a way to startle, to surprise, to see the reaction in a man, she lost. She'd go through, they'd say behind her back, "She's a filthy mouth." She didn't gain any stature whatever.

But a woman gains stature in the men's eyes when she acts like a lady. The first thing that means is inspiring the men to watch their tongues; if she's enough of a lady, she doesn't have to ask explicitly. The next thing is watching her morals. That usually means behaving chastely, but it too can be a matter of words. Among the men on one assembly line, a divorcée who had been to bed with one fellow worker was ranked a shade higher than a married woman who complained to the men that during her menstrual period she was "bleeding like a stuck pig" and asked one man if he had spent the weekend playing "hide the weenie" with his wife.

Being a lady, to the men, is not only a matter of morals. It also means being feminine. The refinery foreman remembered:

It was somewhat of a shock to see some woman crawling out of a tower after having been in there for hours soaking wet. Maybe while she was in there laying in whatever position she had to unloosen her bra, and when she came out it would be bouncing around in the wind. Seeing a woman come out covered from top to bottom with grease and dirt and scale, it was very startling if you'd always seen women in offices or in the home.

What was important, in the foreman's memory, was one woman who "would not back off any job like that."

But at four in the afternoon, after the work day was over, you could never tell that she would get into a tower and roll around in the dirt with the best of them. She was operating in two worlds. She might sweat in the tower, but she was a lady when she came to work, she was a lady when she went home, her nails were well manicured, her hair was curled, and she never lost her identity as far as her femininity was concerned. To the men, she was a very accepted person. She had more accolades from the people. They could accept her as a laborer cleaning out a tower and pay her respect for maintaining her femininity when she wasn't engaged in a work activity. They liked that.

WORK VS. FAMILY

Finally a woman proves to blue-collar men that she is a lady by showing deference to her husband, if she has one. The refinery worker was liked because when she left work every day she was making herself look good for her husband, and making sure they knew it. Her fellow workers would have felt threatened if she had sounded as though her work were a way of either defying or giving orders to the man of the family. She was showing respect for her family, and family is tremendously important to blue-collar people.

That importance is reflected in surveys showing that less educated people are much likelier than the more educated to say that marriage is the bond of a couple rather than the coexistence of two separate individuals, and that parenthood defines their social validity more than work or being a spouse.[19]

The importance of family to blue-collar men is reflected in a different way in their answers to questions about women on the job. After strength and language, the idea they mention most often is family, particularly the fear that when a woman goes to work she damages her family and threatens all families, including the men's own.

The first form this fear takes is the idea that it is wrong for a woman, especially a married woman, to take a job that an unemployed man might use to provide for his family. The idea is that it damages the family if the man is not the main breadwinner, so no family should have two jobs while any family—that is, any male who provides for a family—is without a job. The feeling shows that being a good provider is not only an economic function but also one that fulfills an ancient sex role in our culture. The men are also expressing a largely unconscious belief that I think just as important as the sex role: that being a good provider is a way of claiming power and the satisfactions of work in a society that so often denies them.

The men accept divorcées and widows in their kinds of work more easily than other women, recognizing that in today's world it is often women who must provide for others. But they worry that these women's children may be neglected while the mothers work. Then they criticize women who take time from the job to call home and check on their families.

Ed Hubbell, the shipping department shop steward whom I quoted on the hierarchy of light and heavy work, expressed the thoughts of the majority of blue-collar men whom I interviewed in an era of recessions:

We've got two hundred people, men and women, applying for jobs here every week. If a woman is beating a man out of a job just because she wants to show she's got a place out here, I can't say that's good, with the economy the way it is.

Don't a lot of families need two jobs just to stay alive?

> Not if they work at this company. A man with a good job here can make twenty-five thousand dollars. Depends on the style of living you want to do. There just wouldn't be any jobs if everyone's wife went to work or tried to go to work. An injured or disabled man could do sweeping, but there's a married woman doing the job that he could do and it's hurting things. I don't know how they do their hiring. If a widow or a divorcée was looking for a job she'd have every right in the world. But if any woman putting an application in had a husband working for good money, I can't see why they'd want to hire her.

That was the majority view. A large minority of the blue-collar men I spoke to disagreed, however. The main reason they departed from tradition was economic. Tad Rucker,* a crane operator in the section next to Hubbell's, was one of many men in different industries who recognized that the "two-income family in this day and age is a necessity." The strength of the stereotype that kept this a minority view impressed me, if only because it showed that psychology and culture do sometimes shape economic behavior. But the large size of that minority was itself an important sign of change. Some men were in painful conflict between economic need and the demands of the stereotype, but most of those who recognized economic necessity seemed to think it was legitimate, or even a good idea, for the wife to be out earning. Rucker said his attitude was "Why shouldn't she bring home some money too." He claimed that men with his views tended to be younger than the traditionalists (he had just turned forty-one and Hubbell was forty-four; not much of a difference, but I think he was right). Rucker was pragmatic about the benefits of women working:

> I say give a woman her due. If she doesn't have a particular job skill and she's oriented to the household chores and motherhood, fine, let her do it and you worry about bringing the bread home. But any woman who can combine any kind of a home life and even a part-time career is fine with me. If a woman has the ability to perform a job function and add to your total income and derive a fifty percent share or whatever you gain in a working situation, that's fine, too, that's great. As long as it doesn't take too much away from the home life. The family life, I don't think there's anything greater than that.

Rucker appeared to have no trouble accepting a woman in his department. He said he would accept a woman working in his specialty as a crane operator, but none had qualified for the job in that factory.

He moved, significantly, from the pragmatic to the ambivalent when the question was having a woman not as his peer but as his boss. He filed a request for transfer when Elaine Stanley came in as foreman over him. One reason he thought he wanted out was the old question of language:

Communications between the men and the supervisors are always out in the open, and when you communicate around here you use salty language. That does have a partial bearing on my attitude toward the change in the sexes. I'm not inhibited when I speak to a woman, but I'm enough of the old time to give them their due, they're ladies basically until proven otherwise. I would be more prone to go in and tell my superintendent what I thought of him [though a superintendent ranks higher than a foreman] than stand here and talk to a woman and have the same conversation with her.

Rucker also couldn't believe that Elaine was qualified:

I don't want to work for anyone when the scuttlebutt is out that the people aren't qualified for the particular work in question. It was no personal thing between her and I, a one-to-one shoot-out, but I wasn't just too fond of the idea that a woman could come in and tell me where to and when to, short of qualifications or any knowledge of the job. I can see a vicious cycle of unqualified people, particularly blacks or ladies, coming in to look for jobs.

But Rucker, unlike some men, was able to see the difference between his biased expectation and the reality:

She's got a good attitude. I'm surprised. I'm really surprised. She's a good bit more intelligent than I was led to believe. She is making her own judgments as she goes along. She has been in error in one particular instance and she said, "Okay, I made a misjudgment, I'll try not to do it again." But the jury's still out in this particular instance.

Rucker never withdrew his transfer request officially, but he agreed to Stanley's suggestion that she not put it through the personnel mill until he had had a chance to see what she was like as a boss, and he was still working for her a year later when she decided she no longer wanted to be a shop manager in that company (for reasons that had nothing to do with him or her other subordinates) and went back to office administration.

Hubbell's wife had never worked, and he liked it that way. Rucker's wife had worked for fifteen years—in office jobs for a finance company. The two men exemplified a pattern I've already mentioned, which I found at every blue-collar site I visited: men whose wives work, whether in traditional or nontraditional jobs, are more likely to accept women in blue-collar work than men whose wives stay at home. That doesn't always mean they want their own wives in shop jobs. Several men with good records of support for women working alongside them and for the idea of women working said they didn't want their wives doing that kind of work. Their reasons might be the roughness of the work or the sexual attitudes of their fellow workers or the less explicit feeling that they didn't want their wives doing the same kind of work they did. If other women insisted on showing that they could do a man's job, that was their right and these men would help them, but they would be happier if their own wives didn't try it, thank you.

Hubbell didn't know it, but he talked like an archetype of the traditionalists. I asked him if his wife agreed with him, and he said:

We've never really talked. She likes staying at home, doing her housework, watching her TV shows. I feel a woman's got an easy life at home. . . . They got no gripe coming so long as I bring in a paycheck every week. I think where they really belong is at home. I don't know why women feel they've got to come out in a man's world and work.

What about the uses for that second income?

I'd just as soon keep her at home dependent on me rather than be dependent on her bringing in so much a week. People get in over their head that way, and if one of them loses their job, then what are they going to do? They get in trouble. Like I'm working a lot of overtime, but we can't go out and buy something for that overtime pay because you never know when it's going to stop.

What do you mean about her dependence?

If women work and they're married, they get too independent. Before long there's trouble at home. I'd say that three quarters of the women working, within a few years they're going to be divorced because they're too independent, they don't depend on their husband as much as they used to to bring in the paycheck, and she's bringing in one too, so what does she really need him for?

In his last comment, Hubbell was voicing the second version of the fear that a woman damages her family when she goes to work: a woman who works will cease being a willing subordinate to her husband, and if she doesn't need his paycheck, she won't want to take wifely care of him. (This feeling is articulated in feminist analyses more often than it's expressed in men's own words.) Hubbell's prediction of divorce was also an example of the way this fear unfolds into the idea that a wife who is economically independent and psychologically insubordinate will soon be sexually unfaithful. It's one more way of saying that a woman who works for pay is making herself sexually available.

Blue-collar men have yet a third version of the fear that the family is damaged when a woman goes to work. It centers on the children. Unlike the other versions, this fear is widely shared by men in other kinds of work, most explicitly by professional men like doctors and architects who work long hours. Blue-collar men may feel it more sharply, since more of them find their social validity in parenthood than men in other classes. And blue-collar families can neither find nor afford the kind of nursemaids or well-endowed child care centers that ease the consciences of two-career executive or professional families. The working men I interviewed had a plethora of Ronald Reagan-like anecdotes, always involving people they knew well, like the Southern metalworker who said:

> It's pretty important when a kid gets off the school bus at night that he see Mama, even if he only says "Hi!" and runs out to play with the neighbor kids. He's got that feeling that Mama is there in case he needs her. I recall a neighbor of mine who quit her job. She said she went home one night, they were leaving her boy with the baby-sitter and found him calling the sitter "Mommy." That really hit her. She quit; she said the extra income wasn't worth it.

Many workers, including some of the women who thought working with their hands was a cheerful change from domestic chores, dealt with this problem by insisting that mothers wait until their youngest child was in school before taking a paying job. The women saw no inconsistency in combining this traditional concern with their liking for nontraditional work, and many husbands found the nontraditional aspect much easier to accept when their traditional anxieties about their children had been eased in this way.

Some blue-collar men were still disturbed by the feeling that worries about children were being thrown onto the job floor. In the past ten years it has become common in the blue-collar workplace for a woman worker to take time off to phone home and make sure the kids are all right. Some employers adjust to this as a matter of course. One of the oil refinery foremen thought it was normal to let a divorcée off to fetch her son if the school called and said he was sick. Dick York, on the other hand, the equipment-plant foreman who charged off like a white knight to save a female peer from vulgar language, thought it could become a serious problem:

> As far as pulling their weight, 95 percent of them were eager to stand alongside a guy and prove they could do an equal amount of work, or more. But one characteristic that stood out, doggone it, a lot of them were either divorcées or engaged to remarry, trying to work up a new life, and it was a situation of "I got to use the phone every night, boss, because I got to check on the kids." Some of them were good about it but many of them abused it all to pieces.

How much productivity do you lose from a couple of five-minute telephone calls?

> It's not so much the productivity that the woman loses by making one call, but it becomes an ongoing thing, maybe a temporary problem becomes a long-standing problem, and the darn thing mushrooms. The guys say if she can call her boyfriend or check on the kids, we ought to get the same

consideration. If you try to be a nice guy and be reciprocal, all of a sudden you get several employees saying if she can do it, I ought to be able to do it, and if you say no you're almost into charges of reverse discrimination.

It seemed ironic that York should be worrying about this problem because he himself did more than the usual amount of child care for a midwestern, blue-collar father. His wife worked—running her own beauty salon—and their family included five children, two girls from his first marriage and three boys from hers. The youngest was already ten years old, however, so emergencies were less likely to interrupt work.

TRANSFORMATIONS

Blue-collar men seem to subject women workers to a smaller repertoire of transformations than men in white-collar occupations do. The reasons are connected both to their concern about family and to their readiness to bring sexuality into the workplace (violating their own taboo, but in response to women who they think break the taboo by merely being there). All men (see Chapter 2) tend to transform women in their fantasies and in their symbolic behavior from peers into madonnas and whores, wives and mothers, daughters and lovers, and other roles. Blue-collar men find it just as difficult as others, or perhaps even more so, to treat a woman as a peer. But sometimes, in what would be whore or lover transformations in other men, they commit so explicit an act of sexual aggression or propositioning, or just clustering around an attractive woman and offering to help her, that it can hardly be called acting out a metaphor.

But blue-collar men do make some transformations. One extraordinary one was voiced by the workers at a Bethlehem Steel plant near Los Angeles. The company shut the mill down. The men, struggling to keep the union going and expressing their feelings in community theater work, call the plant Lady Beth and talk about her as a lover who has rejected them, who can be addressed as "whore" or "bitch," or as a bad mother and evil grandmother. It's rare to see such an identity of class and sexual hostility.

Factory workers also transform women colleagues into daughters and sisters and mothers, putting them back into the family situations that they often see as women's place when they're not defining that place as sexual. Ginny, the apprentice electrician, felt that Jim Chatham and several other journeymen treated her like a daughter:

They can handle thinking about me if they think of me like a girl. They can't handle thinking about me if they think of me as a weakling, and they can't think of me as an equal. It weakens them, they feel like they're weakening themselves to consider a woman their equal. And thinking of me as a daughter saves them from danger, from the sexual danger they see in me, if the guy is middle-aged. Some of the younger guys, especially the ones I went through a year of classes with, treated me like a sister. Most of them were married and I wouldn't go out with them, so I was their sister.

Chatham agreed that he treated her like a daughter, but not on the reasons. His own daughter and Ginny were the same age, twenty-two.

I told her she reminded me a lot of my daughter, she's got a good head on her shoulders.

Does it make it easier to deal with her if you treat her like a daughter?

In a certain sense. Her folks are divorced, and she wants to be more independent so she can take care of herself, and I like helping her do that.

If Ginny becomes a journeyman, your daughter will be your equal. How do you feel about that?

It's my first experience, so I can't very well say. Well, it has bothered me, but not to the extent that I can't perform my job. It bothers me because we put a woman on a pedestal at home or think of her as a secretary type or a schoolteacher type, and when they infringe on your domain a little bit, naturally it might make you feel a little bit insecure, that a woman could replace us on the job. That my daughter could replace me.

Fathers through the ages have had to struggle with the thought that their sons might replace them. If they transform women workers into daughters, they may have to repeat the struggle in a way they didn't expect.

Younger men, on the other hand, sometimes learn to accept women on the job by transforming them into mothers—especially older women in shop steward and foreman positions. I saw enough of this to make me believe that many blue-collar men can accept a woman as a boss, a low-level, first-line boss, more easily than as a peer. Men of all classes have trouble treating women as equals. Men in service jobs and business also have trouble accepting women even as first-line bosses. Blue-collar men can accept women as foremen, I suspect, for two reasons. One is that it's a job whose occupant can take care of her subordinates as a mother or teacher takes care of her children. Her presence still violates the male bond of the workplace, but the role relationship is a familiar one. Perhaps that is the very reason that male foremen so seldom take care of their workers that way.

The other reason for acceptance is that workers see very clearly that a foreman has very little power, so a woman in the job is not as threatening as she might be at higher, more truly powerful levels. This mocks the mystique of places like the heavy equipment factory, part of a company where about 85 percent of the top six ranks have once been foremen, and 98 percent of all executives, from foreman to chairman of the board, are men. Management in that company sees the position of foreman as the first rung on the ladder to real executive power. That makes it a sacred male preserve in which females are an alien presence, though it is neither fashionable nor legal to say such things aloud. Mothering can translate the alien into the familiar.

Martha Baird was a prime example of a foreman in that plant whose mothering helped her win acceptance. She was the woman who turned off the porn flow by putting up a male centerfold. Later the men chose her to be a shop steward; she won so many grievances that the company made her a foreman and turned her energy and her drive to take care of people to management use. The men who worked for her, in a section that checked the proper assembly of engines, were company veterans in their thirties and forties. She did not use the word "mothering" to describe her style. Neither did her boss, even when I put the word into play. But his description of what happened came as close to an idealization of the mother function as it did to an idealization of the manager:

> Those men are really strong and set in their ways. They've taken on every foreman who's ever moved over there. They try the same old techniques, and they're testing. If they find a strong foreman, they go back and do nothing. If they find some weak foreman they go ahead and do something. They don't respect him. They tried that with Martha. She took them right on and they threatened to do some things that they hadn't done for years around here. Then they cut back and stopped the nonsense. Why they cut back I don't really know, but I suspicion it's respect. She hasn't been on the assembly line, she doesn't have the mechanical knowledge, but she knows how to talk to people, tell them what she wants, how to earn their day's pay. So she gets their agreement to start with. I think they respect her. She's got the authority, but that means nothing if you can't convert it to respect.

Two of the older men who worked for Martha confirmed the respect but couldn't see it as mothering because they had known her in high school. One had gone hunting with her husband. They were able to acknowledge her as a peer, not so much at first from the relationship on the job as from earlier relationships. That meant they didn't see her as a mother. But a mechanic who was thirty-one years old saw the maternal element very clearly:

> She has a different style than a man would. A lot of times it's pretty hectic here. . . . Being she hasn't been on the job too long, she gets kind of mixed up once in a while. We try to help her out, and in turn we expect her to help us if we have a problem. Sometimes with a man you're just expected to do your job and if you have a problem, sometimes you might get help and sometimes you might not. She tries to the best of her ability to see that we have everything we need to do the job well. She takes care of us.

How would you feel if I said that's like being a mother? She's a little older than you. Is that ridiculous?

No. I often thought about that myself, maybe it's her motherly instinct. To say someone is motherly doesn't mean she's not taking care of business. When we go to Martha for help, we're asking her to be mother, and she keeps business where it belongs.

Elaine Stanley, the woman foreman in the shipping section who persuaded Tad Rucker not to put his transfer through, said that on one of her shifts, the workers' average age was twenty-five to her thirty-seven, and "it was easy to mother them. Some. In a couple of cases I really did." Dick York, the "white knight" who had tried to save her from a worker's dirty language, agreed on Elaine's mothering: "I got the impression that a number of eighteen-, nineteen-, and twenty-year-old kids really appreciated some of the direction she was giving them. I think that had a lot to do with the respect that she was able to get from her people. The older guys saw that she was taking the time to try to develop some of these younger fellows, and they were able to tune in on that."

ELAINE STANLEY'S STORY

The men who worked for her confirmed that they liked Elaine and thought she did the foreman's job well. They said she brought some knowledge of management and mechanics to the job and learned more after she got there. They also said she went to bat for her employees.

Their comments fit the impression Stanley had made when she started as a foreman. Management, workers, and her husband, Mick, who had worked his way up the blue-collar ladder to the post of scheduling supervisor at another company, all agreed: she was smart, she was energetic, she liked challenges. She had what it would take to break through the barrier at the heavy equipment company.

Yet after little more than a year as a foreman, Elaine Stanley cried "Enough!" and went back to office administration. Most of her workers and all but one of the executives who worked with her said she was a better-than-average foreman. Yet she became the twelfth woman foreman in eleven years in that division who failed to make the breakthrough. No woman stayed in a foreman slot more than two years. None rose to the next higher level of management (which Elaine had aspired to). They all either left the company or, like Elaine, went back to office work—often at no loss in pay, but with a definite loss in status in company eyes.

This merely proved something obvious: the company was a classic male operation. Most of its executives and most of its workers had no desire to bring women into nontraditional jobs. They were compelled to open new possibilities to women in order to comply with the law and win government contracts, but if they could show that women had tried and failed, they had met the obligation without having to shoulder the consequences. That made them happy, sometimes consciously so. Some managers and a few workers did want women to succeed, but they had no idea what had to be changed or how to change it—how to change the feelings and behavior of the men in the company in order to make it possible for women to succeed.

Elaine's reasons for quitting might have made either an equal opportunity case or a business school case history. Not all of them reflect the things discussed in this chapter. Her first reason, for instance, was that her boss, Ben Maitland,* was a terrible supervisor, a weak man and a weak manager who overworked his staff and his foremen and gave them no backing vis à vis other bosses, the union, or their own workers. This was confirmed by everyone I spoke to in the division. Maitland was neither reprimanded nor removed, however; he was putting in three more years before retirement, managing a relatively unimportant section, and even at higher levels nobody wanted to rock his boat.

Elaine's second reason for quitting was her feeling that she was being shortchanged on her pay. She started and ended at the minimum for the job; she received several raises, but the minimum rose as her pay rose and she never moved above it. She felt that was unfair, especially since Maitland gave her excellent efficiency ratings. He insisted that her raises exceeded company norms for maximum increases. She griped that male foremen with lower ratings and less seniority in the company were getting more than she was; Maitland said they had come into the job at higher pay levels and had more time on the job if not in the company. Here standard operating procedures concealed, or betrayed, a male inability or a male unwillingness to see how important it was to treat a woman as an equal in money terms—a problem not only for blue-collar men but for all classes.

The third reason that Elaine quit was another example of bad management that hit a woman harder than a man. She was supervising thirty-nine workers, 75 percent of them new hires unfamiliar with the work. She felt that was far too many for one foreman of either sex. No man in the job had ever complained. Perhaps she felt the burden more than the men. Perhaps she was more willing to rebel, to refuse the settlement the men had accepted. She did refuse, and Maitland was forced to agree. He asked the company to split the job in two, but only when she left and he had to replace her. Higher management said no.

Elaine's remaining reasons for quitting as foreman were more directly connected to the questions in this chapter. Most of all, she grew tired of working not eight but nine or ten hours a day, not five but six days a week and sometimes seven. The company often demanded such schedules of this level of "manager." Maitland did it more than most superintendents; he worked many hours of overtime himself, because he was a bad manager and because he hated going home to his wife, and he wanted his subordinates to do the same. The men complied, and their wives learned to take it as an unhappy fact of life. Elaine Stanley did it for a while and then gave up. She wanted to have more time for her family, her studies (she was going to a community college at night to complete the schooling she had stopped in her teens, and she was also trying to qualify for a real estate license), and herself. Her husband, Mick, thought she was absolutely right. But Maitland didn't see the schedule as inhumane or Elaine's desire to have time for her own life as legitimate. He saw it only as a woman's letting family interfere with work because work was interfering with her family. It was not a work problem, it was a woman's problem:

I still feel a woman can do a job as good as a man, with one exception. Women still have their domestic responsibilities at home. Elaine worked many Saturdays and a few Sundays. When I, or any other man, work those hours we can usually go home and sit down to a table with a cooked meal, whereas she's got to carry on her own domestic responsibilities. On top of that she has a foreman's paper duties to take care of, so I can see where it would be rather harder for her [than for a man] to put this all into one package in the total week. With that in mind, I feel that placing women out in the shop on some of these jobs is asking a lot of them, and I told Elaine that.

Maitland's view of a woman's difficulty in meeting both job and domestic responsibilities was inseparable from his belief that her family life affected her decisions about her work much more than it would a man's. Stanley turned down the foreman's job the first time it was offered, then took it when her husband was about to lose his job because his company was closing its plant in that town, where he had worked for seventeen years. Mick went to work for the heavy equipment company nine months later—three months before Elaine gave up the foreman's job. Maitland and several other men, foremen, and executives felt that when she no longer had to be the breadwinner, Elaine lost her main reason for shouldering the challenge of the foreman's job. Mick and Elaine both denied this vehemently. Her new office job paid only a couple of dollars a week less than the foreman slot, so it was nonsense to suggest that her husband's new paycheck "enabled" her to give up the foreman's pay. Mick said:

My getting off unemployment had nothing to do with it. It was the way she felt. You remember I told you last year our sex life had always been positive. Fulfilling. While she was on days, it was still that way. When she was on nights and working all that overtime, it wasn't noticeable at first, but probably the last four months, zip. Nothing. Tired, run down, lost weight, grouchy. I'd come in the house at night and say hello to her and she'd tell me to shut my damn mouth. She'd get up [from sleeping during the day-light hours], fix a little supper, hit the couch, get up, fix herself up, and go to work, that's where my life went those four months. . . . Coming home tired is one thing. Coming home tired and defeated, feeling like you never accomplished a goddamn thing, or you're not getting any support when you feel it's needed, day after day, it affects you mentally as well as physi-cally. . . . We didn't get anything from one another, let alone friends or family.

Mick's picture of a person exhausted by work and management responsibil-ity used to be a commonplace portrait of a man, a husband, and a father. Finding a woman, wife, and mother as the model might seem like a mirror-image role reversal. But Elaine was not ordinarily a woman whose work exhausted her, and Mick was not ordinarily a man who complained about his wife's work. Indeed, his feelings about her work were anything but conven-tional. A year earlier, when she had just started the foreman's job, he said:

We couldn't have gotten married if she weren't working. [When they met, she was a secretary in the same company.] She owed money to the people who took care of her kids, and I owed money because of my divorce and child support. My feelings haven't changed in the seven years since. She wouldn't be happy if she wasn't working, even if we didn't need the money.

I was struck by the differences between Mick and men like Ed Hubbell, who hated the thought of women, and especially of their wives, working at a man's job. Mick Stanley differed from Hubbell in having been divorced and in having two more years' education (a high school graduate compared with tenth grade), but they were in the same age group (early forties), had both grown up in Midwest farm country, and had comparable work experience (over twenty years in factories). No sociological data alone could explain their differences. I asked Mick what he thought the explanation might be. He replied:

I don't know. I've always been accused of being different in the thought process. I've got my own thoughts on everything. I believe you just have to understand your mate. If Elaine weren't working, she might be satisfied for a week or two, but after that it would be no good. She's energetic and she likes to be around people, she likes challenges, she likes to do different things. Before she started as a foreman, she had an office job in sales with a boss who treated women like servants. He really said, "You're here to serve." She was ready to do anything to get away from him, even go down to file clerk. I said, "You've worked too hard for too damn long to let one guy beat you down like that. Your ambitions are to better yourself. Some-body in that company has to be smart enough and interested enough to prevent you from taking a downgrade. By God, you hang in there." And then they offered her to be foreman. But when Maitland treated her and everyone else like donkeys, and I saw they were never going to let her move higher up, I told her, "You tell Maitland to shove it up his ass, you've proven to me and to anyone with eyes to see that you're capable of doing it." Then she did give it up.

Mick's attitude toward Elaine's job and the factory had had an impact on management's appraisal of her before she quit. It was a tiny incident, but I thought it was a revealing illustration of the way men's feelings affect their treatment of a woman at work. One Friday night, three of Elaine's men didn't show up for work. That was payday, and their checks were delivered to Elaine. According to the book, she should have turned them over to a cashier or duty secretary to be given to the men when they next reported. Elaine forgot the rule and took the paychecks home with her when the shift ended at 8 A.M., expecting to give them to the men the next night, Saturday, when they were all working a sixth day.

One worker came into the plant on Saturday morning just to pick up his check so his wife could go to market. When he couldn't find it, he complained all the way up to the plant manager. A secretary called Elaine at home at 9 A.M.; she acknowledged that she had the checks and said Mick would bring them to the plant an hour later. Meanwhile, the plant manager had chewed out Maitland because one of his foremen had taken paychecks out of the shop. Maitland didn't ask and didn't learn that the mistake was in the process of being corrected. He simply called Elaine himself, an hour after the secretary had and a few minutes before Mick was leaving to bring the checks in. Mick refused to let him talk to Elaine because she had gone to sleep and the problem had been resolved. It was the first time that anyone at the plant could remember that a spouse had refused to connect a supervisor with a subordinate at home. Certainly no man had ever been in the position of being shielded by *his* spouse. The memory affected judgments of Elaine Stanley's performance even for men who thought she had been a good foreman.

In Elaine's final handful of reasons for giving up the foreman's job, one that stood out was a series of obscene phone calls. There were five in all, on five separate nights while she was working the midnight to 8 A.M. shift. They started when she had been on the job for almost a year, just a few weeks before she finally quit. Elaine, who had been quick to respond with the ass-hole wisecrack when a worker she knew said he'd like to get in her pants, was unable to repeat the caller's words aloud to Maitland. Eventually she made herself write them down for him. Mick told me that one night the caller had said, "We're going to fuck tonight, baby, whether you want to or not, if you don't quit fucking with me." Maitland described this to me by saying, "Some of it was highly suggestive."

Elaine, usually a woman with a lot of nerve, was frightened. Maitland, she felt, handled it too casually, talking about tapping the phone or keeping a log of the calls but doing nothing. Other management men took a similar line, taking it seriously as a matter of form but in tones that made it clear they thought they were humoring a scared child. With one exception: she and Maitland both said that he had asked her if she had provoked the calls by her own behavior, or given the caller "even indirectly" any reason to think she might be sexually available. Elaine said this did not anger her. Mick interrupted, "It ticked me off so damn bad I threatened to go over and talk to him myself about it." His tone left no doubt about the terms in which he would have talked to Maitland, but Elaine was getting ready to quit and stopped him.

UNION MEN AND UNION MAIDS

As a foreman, Elaine was management and could not ask the union for support. The union at the heavy equipment plant was the United Auto Workers (UAW), an international that officially was very supportive of women and named its first female vice president in 1966. But five years later, UAW official Emil Mazey, confronted with women striking against his own union, could still ask the question that started this chapter. Many of the UAW members at the plant shared his hostility to women who played radical roles or took unions too seriously. The supportive attitudes of Solidarity House never percolated down to the local there. Martha Baird, recalling her days as a shop steward, said:

> The local president—I went to those meetings almost every time—if you had something to say and raised your hand, he'd look right at you and bypass you for a man. The men stewards say the union's not prejudiced. I say the union's more prejudiced than the company will ever be. As a shop steward, I was fighting two battles, one with the management to win my grievances and one with the union to put them through, because I knew they were good. A bad grievance I didn't write up. But the union didn't trust a woman to write a grievance properly.

Other women have found similar resistance in other locals and other unions serving other industries. Few of the more than fifty thousand locals in the country have put women in the key positions of president, organizer, or grievance chair. Yet women *have* been elected presidents of locals by men as hostile to the idea of women in the workplace as coal miners and steel workers.

That preceded and seems more important to me than the appointment of the first women members of the Executive Council of the American Federation of Labor and Congress of Industrial Organizations (AFL-CIO), though male resistance there is certainly significant. Joyce Dannen Miller, a vice president of the Amalgamated Clothing and Textile Workers, was the first woman appointed to the council. She was named under a special rule on August 21, 1980, and Lane Kirkland, the AFL-CIO president, said he hoped the time would soon come when women as well as minorities would gain election to the presidencies of international unions and make special rules unnecessary. Barbara Hutchinson of the American Federation of Government Employees joined Miller on the council by another special appointment in 1981, but Kirkland's hope had still not been fulfilled by 1985. Linda Puchala, president of the Association of Flight Attendants, ran for one of four vacant places on the council that year and lost. Union officials who wanted the AFL-CIO to broaden its appeal to the growing female work force called it a setback.[20]

Women stewards and local officers are elected for many reasons reflecting politics in the locals, just as men are, but men's feelings about women occasionally come into play. The men are sometimes motivated by thoughts like Ed Hubbell's about putting the women's brains to use. For example, United Mine Workers Local 1971 in Rum Creek, West Virginia, was the first UMW local to elect a woman president. Bill Stratton, the local's mine chairman, said Mary Maynard had "a high school education, two years in college and she goes to the local union meetings. She's as good as anybody we could get. We're supposed to have women's lib now, anyhow."[21] Other miners' locals have elected women presidents, and Sandy Dorsey, one of the women who brought suit in the Shoemaker peephole case, was later elected financial secretary of the local at that mine.

Several of the men I talked to suggested that the same mothering qualities that sometimes help make a woman a good foreman also lead men to elect her to local union office. "She takes care of us, she fights for safety in the shop. And she campaigns to keep the union democratic," a Chicago steelworker said of Alice Peurala, the first woman to head a steelworker local.

Union men also are beginning to see their own interest in some of the changes women want. The United Mine Workers of America (UMWA) voted in 1983 to make unpaid parental (not maternal) leave for the birth, adoption or serious illness of a child a bargaining issue; members' insistence on the matter surprised the leaders. Stephen F. Webber, a member of the UMWA international board, said two years later, "It caused us to realize that the whole issue of parenting is not just from the women's perspective. There are more and more men that want to take part in that."[22] The leaders weren't ready to make it a bedrock demand in negotiating the 1984 national contract, but they pursued it and won the coal operators' agreement to study the issue. Moving even this far, in discussions that make the point that men will benefit as much as women, is a significant step forward.

FEMINISM AND CHANGE IN MEN

The role of unions was one of three important questions about the feelings of blue-collar men that came up in different ways in my workplace interviews. The second was male workers' feelings about feminism, as distinct from their feelings about women. Even the men who like to see women at work don't like to hear ideological or theological rhetoric from the women's movement as a rule (which is also true of men in other classes, according to public opinion polls). One woman dockworker said she encountered more hostility from the longshoremen than many of her sisters because she was the most vocal about her feminism. One of the most supportive of the men at the heavy equipment plant responded this way to a question about the women's movement:

> I think some of it is ridiculous. The most part of them being equal would be all right. A lot of these women are trying to prove that they're equal. I'd say that 80 or 90 percent are my equal. They can do just about everything I can do. But a lot of them get carried away with themselves, it's just like any kind of movement, they've got radicals and conservatives, they go back and forth about a lot of things and what they have the right to do. I don't much care for having a woman come up and ask me if I want to go out. Myself, I'd rather do the picking. That's the way I've always been. It might be different in the next generation. So I can't cheer when these women say they can do the asking. They can work the line or be shop stewards or foremen and I can imagine voting for one for the legislature or for Congress. But they make me nervous when they go to big meetings, national conferences, and foreign conferences, and talk big about women's rights.

The third question was whether men are changing as the contemporary wave of the women's movement approaches its twentieth year. When I visited the heavy equipment plant for the second time, several men said they felt acceptance was much greater than at the time of my first visit a year earlier. A male foreman predicted that as more women moved into worker and supervisor positions and stayed in them longer, more men would learn to accept it, even if it meant significant changes in the male bond.

I think it can happen and will happen, but it hasn't happened yet at that factory. Altering the ways we deal with women in our psychology and our culture is an immense burden for blue-collar men and for all classes; doing it when the economy is in trouble makes the costs even higher, and most of us aren't ready to pay. There were fewer women foremen at the heavy equipment plant in 1982 and 1985 than there had been in 1978, and fewer women in the shops; women were the least senior and the first to be laid off when the company had to cut thousands from the payroll. Few men there thought there was anything wrong with that. The old personnel executives had retired and the new managers thought it was a bygone issue in an era of Reagan and recession and cutbacks to meet heavy international competition. The anger and the fear that are so plain to see in this chapter because both workers and executives showed them in good times were even stronger when they were buffeted by economic forces. Envy, shame, and guilt were seldom visible.

Individuals certainly do change, like Kenneth McCann (see Chapter 13). He was a community organizer who at first opposed a feminist attempt at organizing the women in lower-class Detroit in the 1960s. But he was deeply shocked when the men he worked with started beating up their wives and neighbors to stop the women's newly displayed militance. He is now a psychotherapist helping some working-class men control their own violence and helping others who try to integrate feminist values into their own lives. This chapter has shown some men moving from opposition and ambivalence to pragmatism, like the miners who voted to study parental leave, like the oil refinery foreman and Ed Hubbell. Men like Mick Stanley have grown even stronger in their support of women who claim independence and equality. Some of us are learning.

Chapter 6
SERVICE OCCUPATIONS

"Women don't belong on police patrol. They're not aggressive enough and they can't do the job physically, and I don't have a very high opinion of one who even wants to try. I don't think she belongs in a job where she'll confront to all the violence and the blood. Half the time I think a woman should be in a palace, maybe, and half the time I think she should be in the bedroom or the kitchen. That doesn't make too much sense, I'll admit. But I know she shouldn't be on the street." The speaker is a big-city police man whom I asked what he thought about women officers.

"I'd rather work with Maria than any of the guys," says another police man in another large city. "She's aggressive. She won't back down for anything. But aggressive isn't all she is. She can cool things down when trouble is brewing, and she can give people warmth when that's what they need. My feeling is that basically, the public believes female officers are more sympathetic, they're more attentive, they're more thorough than male officers, they care when the public calls for service."

Police men, in fact, reject the idea of women in their work far more often than they welcome it. But those two comments are typical of the combination of acceptance of and resistance to women shown not only by police officers but by men in almost every occupation that belongs, like police work, in the service category. In computers and data processing, for instance, some men will talk about how good women are at computer language and solving systems problems as though this were a new discovery befitting a new occupation, while others—and sometimes the same man in the next breath—will say in the most time-worn terms that women can't be trusted to service huge mainframe systems because they're thinking about clothes, sex, and marriage when they should be worrying about million-dollar deals.

"Service" is a label that covers a wide variety of jobs. I use it to cover not only such occupations as police officer, bartender, nurse, and computer programmer—linked together in government lists—but also most white-collar jobs that are neither executive nor professional. Any work that does not involve making a product is a service occupation. About 70 percent of the 107 million people in the labor force in America work in service industries, which also provide nearly 95 percent of the 25 million new jobs created since 1969. Hence the idea that we have evolved from an "industrial" to a "service" economy.

Some service jobs are traditionally masculine, like police work. Others are too new for a traditional gender but are at supposedly masculine locations in the hierarchy, like information supervisors, or they require supposedly masculine skills in math or technology, like computer analysts. Women entering these occupations pose the same challenges and encounter the same reactions that they do in other "masculine" fields.

Traditionally feminine service jobs are also important to this book. To some eyes they look like anything but feminist breeding grounds, but they had a lot to do with the rebirth of the women's movement in the 1960s. They are also significant today because men are entering them in increasing numbers.

Some of these jobs are "pink-collar," a term coined by Louise Kapp Howe for low-status occupations populated overwhelmingly by women who are paid relatively little and seldom move up from those jobs to careers that can develop. Examples are waitresses, beauticians, retail sales clerks, and a whole array of office workers—secretaries, bookkeepers, key punch operators, word processors, and so on.[1]

Pink-collar office work, much of it later retitled "information processing," expanded rapidly after World War II. So did "people-processing" jobs, which either have traditionally been predominantly female, like nurses and elementary school teachers, or have recently become so, like social workers. Expansion in all these fields provided jobs for millions of women, including married women and mothers, who began to enter the labor force in the 1950s.

Their primary motives were originally to help meet their own rising expectations for clothing, furniture, and appliances in a newly affluent society, and later to help keep up with inflation.[2] At least those economic pressures were apparent before women began to voice loud dissatisfaction with the boredom of being a housewife and before feminist ideas were established.

But the movement of those millions of women into the workplace, even the pink-collar workplace, helped start the changes in marriage and parenting and the perception of women's place that in turn helped crystallize the ideas of the women's movement and the subsequent invasion of traditionally masculine occupations. The pink-collar world was thus one of the motherworlds of the women's movement.

Men have not had to respond to change here, however, as much as in other service fields. They seldom stay in pink-collar occupations except as managers, and the change that they respond to most often is the rise of the female supervisor. (That produced the classical example of male hostility described in Chapter 3, when a bartender was so angry that a woman was named manager of his saloon—promoted over his head, as he saw it—that he lay in wait for her in an alley and raped her.)

The majority of service jobs resemble older categories of work, blue-collar or white-collar, and the men who hold them react to women in ways that usually resemble those of men in the other categories. Some service jobs, for instance, can be called blue-collar because they depend on physical strength and manual skills and traditionally recruit from the working class or the lower middle class. These traits are common to such apparently disparate occupations as police officers, truck drivers, and telephone linesmen. Men in these fields tend to resist the invasion of women as sharply as men in factories, and sometimes—notably in the case of police and fire men—even more so.

Some white-collar service jobs are administrative: low-level managers, and positions in specialties like accounting, credit, customer service, marketing, office management, and personnel. Others are partly technological or almost professional: airline pilots, computer programmers, health technicians, and social workers, among others. Negative male responses in these areas resemble those in business and the professions—more denial, more subtle resentment, less overt hostility or physically explicit sexual aggression than many blue-collar men show.

But there are also significant differences between men in both blue-collar and white-collar service occupations and those in the older categories. The most important is that there are more positive responses, even if the proportion is still small, and that positive feelings are easier to see. On the blue-collar side, while most police men and truck drivers resist the invasion of women even more strongly than factory workers, a minority still offers more examples of significant acceptance. On the white-collar side, acceptance also seems greater than in the business and professional worlds, but the difference is fuzzy.

Those at least were my impressions from interviews in a dozen service occupations, which showed the patterns I mentioned combining acceptance and resistance in sets of men reacting to the same women, and sometimes in the same man. A Department of Labor study of ten public utilities produced similar findings.[3] It first identified target women, those in jobs that would have been unusual for a woman to hold five or ten years earlier. Most of the white-collar target women were in jobs I would classify as service. The researchers interviewed male supervisors and peers of these women, and subordinates of both sexes. About 75 percent of the white-collar male peers expressed "generally positive" or "very positive" views of the women, compared to 35 percent of the blue-collar men.

Significantly, only 41 percent of the white-collar peers thought others of their group had positive attitudes about women. This suggests to me that the men expressed warmer feelings about their women peers to the interviewers than they did to one another. This may reflect political sophistry, to make a man reporting his own acceptance look like a warm supporter of equal opportunity policies. Perhaps, however, the prevarication ran the other way: some men may have told the interviewers the truth but lied or distorted their views to one another in order to maintain the male bond and the male sex role. Of the ninety-one women involved, thirty-six—not quite 40 percent—reported that their male colleagues "definitely" accepted them. Another twelve reported at least a form of acceptance because of the company's equal opportunity policy. The total is far below the 75 percent of men who reported positive views of the women, and the total number of answers made plain that many women reported both acceptance and resentment in the same men.

The resentments are hardly surprising. The important thing is still that there are more positive reactions to women in service jobs than in other kinds of work. One reason is that the dynamics of power are diffused, sometimes subtler and sometimes merely weaker than the more obvious physical power of the blue-collar man or the money, command, and prestige power of the physician or the corporate executive. Men in many service occupations express less anxiety about powerlessness and the degradation of labor than do factory workers. They recognize and enjoy, even if unconsciously, the authority ascribed to the police officer, the enterprise and adventure shown by the truck driver, the power that the teacher and the social worker exercise over pupil and client. I suspect that this small advantage over outsiders makes men in many of these jobs less likely to feel that female colleagues are challenging their male power. So does the idea, held in all but the blue-collar variety of service jobs, that service is what our culture has traditionally demanded of women and that men in a service occupation must therefore expect to find women in it.

That expectation is linked to another reason that men react better to women in service jobs: there are more women in them than in blue-collar or business management or most professional fields. This is obvious in pink-collar jobs, where women form an overwhelming majority. In some nontraditional service jobs (police work in a few cities, for instance) and in some new ones (personnel management or computer analysis) the proportion of women is either approaching the token barrier or has moved past it. The barrier is the 15 percent line below which any minority is treated as tokens whose contrast to the dominant group is exaggerated and feared. As the proportion rises, the numerically dominant tend to harass the tokens less. Men, in this case, treat women a little less as stereotypes and a little more as individuals, as members of a minority who are significant to the balance of the group as a whole. One of my favorite examples is a field where the number of women is still probably no more than 5 percent, but they clump together in highly visible groups at a few locations—women truck drivers on routes where truck-stop operators have found it profitable to install women's rest rooms, showers, and dressing rooms complete with rentable blow dryers for the freeway coiffure.

Bigger numbers of women do not always mean better reactions from men, however. In many companies, resistance and discrimination continue long after women pass the 15 percent level (see Chapter 7). Many service jobs also illustrate the old observation that when women invade an occupation it loses status and pay, and men who work in it lose self-esteem as well. I believe that the women's movement has slowed the frequency with which this happens, partly by campaigning for equal opportunity and equal pay and partly by loosening sex roles to the point where more men—only a few, but more— enter fields where women are numerically dominant or increasingly in supervisory positions. In these fields, however, men sometimes develop new resentments as well as positive feelings, resentments focused on what seems to some like a loss of masculine status and to others like a perverse or ironic denial of equal opportunity.

POLICE WORK

The combination of acceptance and resentment that appeared during my interviews was particularly fascinating in police men. Police work is traditionally a man's job, and police have fought the arrival of women in the workplace more strongly than any other working men except fire fighters. They have harassed women officers and discriminated against them in ways as petty as making them clean out the precinct house (including the men's rest room) while on duty and as serious as charging them unjustly with cowardice. Yet I found, interviewing officers in large cities and small, that positive feelings kept turning up. I suspect that they have grown even as the number of women police officers has grown—from 1.5 percent of the national total in 1972 to 7.7 percent in 1984, while the number of women on patrol has increased eightfold.[4] In some cities like Atlanta and Detroit, the proportion of women officers is over 10 percent.

Large cities have more crimes and more violence than do small towns, but they're not very different in the feelings of their cops. In every size of community, police work seems masculine because police risk death and injury and because the force is organized on military lines to deal with that danger. The police have a monopoly of legitimate force in civil life, they embody authority, and they fight crime—three roles with a masculine ring in our culture.

In addition, police officers regard the public as hostile, or potentially hostile. They feel that their work sets them apart from the larger world, which they see as always likely to spew up a criminal or break down its precarious order. That hostility and the recurring danger make them feel intensely dependent on one another; patrol partners often achieve a closeness akin to battlefield communion. But they operate under rules that are more detailed and restrictive than a soldier's, and they frequently feel compelled to violate those rules in order to prosper or even to survive. They have a code of silence about such sins that is linked to a group loyalty far stronger than most workers feel. All these things intensify the already-strong male bond among police men.

Yet the society in whose name they act is challenging these facts and these ideas. The women's movement stimulated the community to pass equal opportunity laws opening the police, as well as other occupations, to women. The economy changed so that more women, including young mothers, had to work, and the movement helped legitimize that work. That put many more women into the labor force who meet police recruiting standards and who find police salaries attractive.

The nature of police work is also changing. The crime rate is rising, increasing the need for police officers regardless of sex. The proportion of crime committed by juveniles and women is rising much faster than the crime rate overall, and women often deal better with these offenders. The same public that wants to fight crime also wants to end police brutality, which means putting bounds to some "masculine" behavior. And the public wants more and better service. Police forces are increasingly used to maintain order and to do the work of social agencies rather than to fight crime, which is already down to 10.3 percent of police work.[5] Order and service involve functions that America has traditionally classed as feminine, such as understanding individuals' emotional states and persuading people to behave rather than issuing orders or using force.

But fighting crime, however small a part of police work, is the part that police men care about most. Their concern leads them to focus on some of the same things as their brothers in the Army and the factory: the ability to fight, competence at "masculine" tasks, physical strength, and women's supposed need for protection. Those things lead them to think that women make bad cops. But there's a central problem beneath those specifics that is the same in police work as in all traditionally masculine occupations: the women are both police officers, expected to follow the rules of the games that peers play, and women, expected to play the games that women play with men. In the world that cops live in, those male-female games usually make men dominant and invoke the problems of sexuality that the other game's rules say you ought to repress at work. Police men treat female officers of every kind as women far more often than they do as peers. Susan Martin talks about the problem in *Breaking and Entering,* the best book yet written on what happens to women in big-city police work.[6] Her characterization reproduces what I found among soldiers and blue-collar workers:

> The men are caught in a bind: they want a partner who will be "tough," fight, and back them up and whom, in turn, they are willing to back up. But women are not supposed to fight, be tough, or protect a man. The more a female partner acts like a police officer, the less she behaves like a woman. On the other hand, the more she behaves like a woman, the less protection she provides, the less adequate she is as a partner—although such behavior

preserves the man's sense of masculinity. The way out of the bind is simple: keep women out of patrol work.

Many of Martin's Washington, D.C. police men clearly hated the idea of women on patrol. Some put their reasons starkly. One said:

Women can't hold up their own end in fights. I'm no baby-sitter. Equal pay means an equal amount of work. No woman performs the same way or amount as a male. Women are physically inadequate. . . . not mentally but physically and this job is both mental and physical.

Another male officer shifted the threat from himself to the male citizens with whom police must deal:

Any man I've talked to doesn't like being told what to do by a woman so this may lead to a bad situation, especially a hot-tempered woman who tries to exercise more authority than she has. . . . She's an insult to his manhood.

THE STORY OF BONNIE BERGEN

These Washington officers were echoed by police men I interviewed in both large cities and small towns. A small Southern city I'll call Gantry is half redneck community and half wealthy suburb of a commercial center. In five years of repeated visits, a period when the town had neither a rape nor a murder, I found the same varieties of male reaction to female police as those in a crime-ridden metropolis, though they were often expressed in more personal terms. After my last visit, I wasn't sure whether I was more surprised by the enduring resistance of some male officers or the marked acceptance by others. The force never had more than two women among its fifteen officers, so there were never enough to overcome the token barrier. But some men learned to like the idea of a female cop as they learned over the years to know Bonnie Bergen.*

Bonnie grew up in a small town two hundred miles south of Gantry, with one brother who was a police officer and another who was an FBI agent and uncles and cousins who worked for long periods and short as police men and deputy sheriffs. She came to know the work, but she never thought she might do it because everybody knew it was a man's job. Instead, she married at fifteen, bore her first child at seventeen, and had three more kids before separating from her first husband—"just like any good old girl," as she put it when I first met her.

When her marriage broke up, Bonnie took a business course and then held a variety of office jobs. She found a new husband, Bernhard Bergen,* a millwright turned paperhanger. She quit work when their daughter, her fifth child, was born. But she still had energy to burn and kept busy, first as a Girl

Scout leader, then as a school-crossing guard. That was almost like police work. It reminded her that the idea of policing was familiar, and that was important when she started rethinking her life after recovering from a bout of serious surgery. It was 1974; changes in federal law and state rules were opening up new jobs, and Bonnie Bergen—a tall, good-looking woman with long brown hair and blue eyes and a strong chin, who had just become a grandmother at the age of thirty-five—decided that she wanted to make a career in her brother's field.

When she told Bernhard that she wanted to become a cop, he threatened at first to leave her. "I was very negative, I guess you could say chauvinist," he said two years later. He found it hard to explain why he had changed. He started looking at his life and what he valued in his marriage. A little psychotherapy showed him that his possessiveness was not really aimed at Bonnie but at his mother, and he was able to let go a bit. He recognized and started to enjoy a wildness in himself, a tendency to dissent from some middle-class values, a nonconformity that embraced Bonnie and her cause but went far beyond them. Events later brought him to more common forms of feminist consciousness-raising. "You're raised traditionally, but deep inside, you know it's wrong" was the way he summed it up. "It disturbs me that it took me thirty-eight years to find that out." At some point a few months into the struggle, he told Bonnie that he would accept her joining the police because "you weren't made to live my life, and I wasn't made to live yours."

Bernhard's support for Bonnie was mild when it was only a question of reexamining himself. It turned downright fierce when she made her first effort to get a police job and ran into trouble. She applied for the local county force, the largest police department in the area. She passed all the tests and was told she was accepted—until a man already on the force accused her of sexual promiscuity that would make her unfit. Bonnie denied the charge but refused to answer questions about how many men she had slept with. She asked to face her accuser and to take a polygraph test. The county refused the first and denied the second unless she would answer the offensive detailed questions. Bernhard backed her completely. It was he who called the local office of the National Organization for Women (NOW) (which he joined, dragging Bonnie in with him); it was he who learned how Bonnie could file charges with the Equal Employment Opportunity Commission (EEOC). "I thought, 'Somebody will show them what a Bergen is,' " he told me. "I don't know whether it was pride, or revenge, or what it was. Now I'm happy as hell." That was when Bonnie had been on the Gantry police force for a year. The county by then had hired eight or ten women (it now has twenty-seven out of a hundred police officers), and the EEOC charges were moot.

Bonnie attributed the county officer's accusations to his wife's jealousy of a prospective woman partner on patrol—a common problem on big-city forces too. But men repeatedly translated their resistance to her being a police officer into sexual fantasies of their own. When we talked on my first visit to

Gantry, a patrol officer named Larry Munck* combined sexuality with every other reason a police man rejects women on his force.

Munck started with the need he saw for physical confrontation and women's unsuitability for it:

> When I first met Bonnie [in a police academy course at a local junior college], I couldn't stand her. She was the most outspoken of the group. She could not comprehend the fact that you cannot talk a drunk into a car all the time. You're going to have to whip somebody's ass somewhere along the line. They had been taught that in police work you could coax somebody into this or that, you were always respected. The thing we tried to get across to them was that no, you could not. Fifty percent of the time, people aren't going to pay any attention to you whatsoever.

That was the reason, Munck said, that

> I just can't picture a woman in police work. I cannot picture a woman taking down a drunk, outrunning a man, running a man down like we have to do. I guess it's more the physical aspects than the mental. When it comes to women, I realize that they're as mentally capable as any man. I'm not saying more superior, I'll never say that.

The question of superiority bothered Munck a lot. Later in the conversation, he said:

> If Bonnie was my superior officer, I don't know if I could swallow it. I'd have to, but it wouldn't be too tasteful, I don't think. It just has to do with the way I've been raised. I sound like every other redneck, but my parents were German. I was always brought up under the impression that the man did the work. I always pictured the woman as being subhuman, physically. I always thought a woman's interests had to do with home and sewing.

Interspersed with his remarks about the need for toughness in a police officer were Munck's thoughts about the male bond, its language, and its mixture of sex and hunt.

> She asked me point-blank one day, "How do you feel about me being a police officer?" And I said, "I don't think you should have anything to do with it." I just couldn't imagine myself being in the position of riding with a woman officer. You know, the guys ride around in a car, we cuss and cut up and raise hell and look at the women.

But Bonnie was hired full-time and was assigned to ride patrol.

> She told me to go ahead and cuss, say whatever you want to say, and I just couldn't do it. For some unknown reason I didn't want to cuss, I wouldn't look at the women, you couldn't have your regular conversations.

Eventually, things loosened up a little.

The thing that broke the ice the most, we were riding down the road one day, there was a man and a woman walking. She whistled, like that. I said, "She don't look that good," and Bonnie said, "Yeah, but he does." It took me a minute to get over it, but I finally figured the situation and from then on it was pretty good.

In Munck's mind, it soon moved from liberated conversation to something more explicitly sexual.

We didn't get all downright nasty. But one day she says, "Boy, I'm horny." Of course I'd never heard that from a woman [though he was married]. It got to be a game watching people's reactions to me having a woman police officer as a partner. You get stared at enough when you go in some place [with a male partner] to eat dinner. When they see me and her together, I know the first thing they're thinking is, "I wonder if he's screwing her." The women took to her real well. I guess she's a symbol of their freedom.

But sexual feelings about a woman officer were not only in the realm of fantasy, Munck said:

The sexual thing comes into it a hell of a lot more than anybody thinks. Sometimes we come in, the guys will hug each other. But with her, you start thinking it's just another uniform, but you hug her and she acts like a woman would act. It strikes me as strange sometimes because I catch myself hugging her, kissing her, feeling her out, because she's a woman, and then I think, "Shit, she's wearing a uniform and doing the same job I'm doing." It's confusing, you see her go out and cuss like the rest of us, talk about kicking ass, then you turn around and hug her and treat her like a woman.

I don't know how much it was kidding. There was a lot of seriousness in it at some point. Riding around late, at 4:30 or 5:30 in the morning, you get horny as hell for some reason. You get a hard-on riding around. One night we rode down this dirt road. There's a little lake down there, we got up to it and the moon was on the lake. It was a perfect setup. If I'd gone down that road with a male officer, it would have been just to check, we'd proba-bly talk about fishing. But with her, I says, "I guess we better leave," and she says, "Yeah, or something might happen." I just don't know, I can't really put it into words how you explain something like that. Her as a police officer, riding with me, doing the same job, and I'm sitting there thinking about trying to get into her pants.

Munck knew that according to the old rules, he wasn't supposed to desire a body that wore a police uniform. It put him in a state of total confusion when he found himself actually lusting after one. Bonnie said she never took the sexual possibility as seriously as Munck, but she admitted she might have chosen a womanly phrase rather than police language to defuse the situation. That inadvertently reinforced rather than reduced his confusion.

Munck never did learn how to handle work and sex in combination. For a period, he combined police work with a career as one of Gantry's better known Don Juans—usually off duty, but easily recognizable by his fellow cops (who caught him in flagrante in a car more than once) and his wife. She eventually threw him out, and he moved to the next state with a woman who had worked for the Gantry force as a radio dispatcher and had then become a police officer in a neighboring town. He left before Bonnie rose to sergeant and then to lieutenant, so he never had to face his nightmare of a female superior officer.

Other Gantry police men didn't admit to fantasizing about Bonnie in their own right but kept accusing her of affairs with someone else and interpreting every one of her meetings as sexual. By the time of my last visit, she was a six-year veteran who had risen to be one of three lieutenants on the force. She knew the community well and police on both Gantry and county forces frequently discussed common professional problems with her, usually over a cup of coffee in some very public place—which provided others with grounds for explicit complaint and behind-the-badge gossip. A man who accused her of sleeping with someone else even though he never claimed her as his own conquest was being prudent—avoiding the confrontation that might have arisen if he had boasted on his own behalf. But he was still putting her down —asserting superiority over a woman by categorizing her sexually even though she not only did the same kind of macho work he did but also out-ranked him.

Sexual fantasies about police women return them to a traditional dimension where certain fears don't operate. For many men, when women emerge from that dimension, they give new force to the old fears of death and injury. In big cities and in small towns alike, police men talk about the need for a cop to be physically large and fighting tough, to be good with guns and fists, to be clever at paramilitary thinking. If a cop lacks these qualities, they say, the criminal will have an advantage—and they fear that women police will add to that advantage by their physical weakness, which increases the risk of defeat, injury, and death and which invites police men to protect them instead of pursuing perpetrators.

In Gantry, the chief of police, Harry Higbee,* was an ex-Marine and an ex-big-city cop. He started as an opponent of women on his force when Bonnie was the only woman. (He was appointed during her third year on the force.) Later he became one of her strongest backers and mentors. Yet even then he admitted:

I prefer large husky individuals. If a woman can fit into that category, she's better equipped to handle a job as a police officer. Bonnie's size in at least one instance has created a problem. She was placed in a position where she almost had to shoot a perpetrator. She would have shot him had not a couple of my larger officers arrived.

Luther van Dusen* was senior to Bonnie, but by the time I met him, they were both serving as lieutenants, she on the morning and he on the evening (3 P.M.-11 P.M.) shift. He was shorter than Bonnie, which may be why he talked less about size than about competence. He saw rank incompetence in the policy that Bonnie followed and Chief Higbee adopted, a policy of caution in using force and weapons. He claimed to recognize Bonnie's talents but still felt that she lacked things he considered essential:

When I get into a fight I'm going to have to look after her because she's a woman. In a fight it's every man for himself. Every person, I'm sorry, I didn't mean to say that. Every individual. With Bonnie as a person rather than as a representative of women, she has a lot of physical problems, back problems and all that kind of stuff. If I were going on a call and I knew when I got there I was going to have trouble and Bonnie was my only back-up person, I would worry. . . . We're going to have some PT tests coming up here, and she is not physically capable of taking those tests. And an area that I'm really shocked about, Bonnie seems to strive toward excelling in other areas, but she always cries about the handling of her weapon. I'm a firearms instructor, and Bonnie's shooting score has never gotten any better by even two points. She's still one of the worst shots in the entire department.

At the same time that van Dusen saw Bonnie as physically weak and a bad shot, he blamed her for being "overly assertive, overly aggressive, domineering. She's touchy to show she's as good as the guys, and she has a tendency to go overboard, to overcompensate." Yet he had begun his discussion by saying:

You know why people get in this business to begin with? It's the John Wayne syndrome. A lot of cops are cops because they used to watch John Wayne. They really get off on kicking people's asses. They feel, they assume, that close to that gun they are God, whether male or female. And the people on the street, male and female, agree.

Perhaps it was the same John Wayne syndrome that made van Dusen back up Dan Marvin,* a hulking patrolman on Bonnie's shift who kept coming to him with tales of her "incompetence." Bonnie eventually charged the two with violating the chain of command. Chief Higbee backed her up. Van Dusen kept talking back—and talking about the likelihood that Marvin and others would walk out if Bonnie retained her command. Finally, Chief Higbee suspended him for ten days—for insubordination.

One particular incident revolved around Marvin's and Bonnie's coming to a church building at night and finding a Sunday School door open. Marvin wanted them to go in as a pair of buddies with guns drawn. Bonnie ordered otherwise:

> I maintained there was no sign of forced entry, nothing to indicate anyone had been in the building who wasn't supposed to be there. The church was a maze; if we had gone in together on the buddy system anyone who had been in there could have doubled back on us. I didn't feel it called for having my gun out. Unsnapped and ready, yes, but not out. This officer who wanted to go in with guns drawn, he had been with the county [police force], and one time then he was checking a building with another officer and he shot himself in a mirror. When this Marvin and van Dusen talked to Harry Higbee, that seemed like a relevant example. He and Luther both maintained that he saw a gun [in the mirror] and that was all that mattered, he shot the gun. The chief said, "No, you shot a police officer."

The officer, of course, was Marvin himself. Higbee ruled that Bonnie had been right, and denied Marvin's and van Dusen's appeal for a rule that guns automatically be drawn in such cases.

The whole van Dusen-Marvin story, with its John Wayne echoes, sent me back to a comment by another of Bonnie's colleagues five years earlier when she was still a beginner. Gabriel Taylor* had said:

> I personally feel that it's not that the men honestly think women can't do the job. It's that their masculinity is threatened. A woman will prove that a police man's job is a pansy job and that it doesn't take a big man to do it.

Police men, like men in other occupations classified as service jobs, are more able than most factory workers to talk about the threats to masculinity and to family life that they see when women work in their fields—the result both of better education in general and of greater exposure to psychology and the therapeutic subculture. Of the four men who were Bonnie Bergen's peers and superiors, three had John Wayne notions about the ideal police officer, three departed from traditional family norms, and three came to accept Bonnie in particular and the idea of women in general as police officers. What was striking was that none of the threesomes was the same.

Harry Higbee, the Gantry chief; Stanley Wyatt,* a former Gantry captain who transferred to the county as a patrolman; and Luther van Dusen, the insubordinate lieutenant, were the men with John Wayne ideas. Gabriel Taylor,* who like Bonnie and van Dusen rose from patrol officer to lieutenant in five years, claimed he never felt that way "because I'm not very stout myself." (In this part of the South, "stout" retains the older meaning of "strong," of "large" rather than "fat.")

Wyatt was the only one of the four with a completely traditional marriage and family. Higbee departed from stereotype in his obsessive devotion to his three-year-old son; he spent hours with the boy every week, almost every day, in the house and on the farm. He conformed to the norm, however, in not doing the diaper-changing kind of primary care, and he virtually ignored his daughter, two years younger than his son. Despite his support of Bonnie's career, he believed that a mother should stay home, keep house, and raise her children rather than leave them to the tender mercies of day care, where he felt children are "either not developing or they're not learning how to behave right."

Taylor's wife was a schoolteacher. He had entered the marriage with the traditional expectation that his wife would do all the housework and cooking, but he had learned that he could not have Higbee's attitude and still have a happy marriage.

It's not fair for her to work forty hours a week and me to work forty hours a week and come home and sit down and watch television while she does all the housework. It's not right. I have four days off every other week and three days every week. I can spend three hours on one of those days and get all the housework done. Kathy cooks more than I do, but I cook out in the summer, and we do the dishes together every night.

That was before their daughter was born. Four years later Taylor added:

The chief says that I should make arrangements for Kathy to quit teaching so she could take care of the baby. But if she quit work we wouldn't have enough money for her to be able to play tennis and go to the spa and run around shopping all the time. She'd have to sit at home, and she'd go crazy. Her mother's already crazy from that kind of life. All the same, a lot of people find it really surprising that I do take care of the baby. On my schedule now, every Monday, Tuesday, and alternating Wednesdays, from the time she wakes up until the time she goes to bed, she's mine. I don't take her to a baby-sitter. From day one I learned how to change a diaper and bathe her and feed her and all that stuff. And now she's Daddy's girl; she won't go to her mommy. It can get to be a pain when you're trying to cook or trying to work in the garage or something, and she's pulling on your britches leg, constantly wanting.

I was touched to hear Taylor leaven his pride in his parenting with a housewifelike complaint about the pain that goes with it.

It was easy to see Taylor as an example of a man who had learned to accept women in "masculine" jobs because his own wife had a career. It was ironic, since he sometimes cared for his daughter when she was sick, that he complained about the amount of time Bonnie took off from duty when her mother or one of her own children was ill. And it took Taylor several years before he became consistent in his support for Bonnie Bergen—years before he could overcome his tendency to resist when his superiors resisted and accept when they leaned toward tolerance. But the important thing was that his acceptance of her did become wholehearted.

Luther van Dusen, however, took equal prominence as an example of a man whose dual-career marriage had not enabled him to accept women on the force. His wife was a middle-management corporate executive with a large department store chain. She made more than twice his salary as a Gantry police lieutenant. When I asked how he felt about that, he said, "I love it. I love it. Get that on the tape twice." But he added:

If we were in comparable jobs and she was making twice as much money, that might upset me. The fact that I'm in police work, and she's out there in the business world, it's taken for granted that she's going to make twice as much money as I. There's no way you can make any money in this business and be straight. . . . We do have one guy that works here, a patrolman, his wife works for a corporation and makes more money than he does, considerably more, and it bothers the hell out of him. He doesn't feel very pure. It comes close to breaking him.

Despite van Dusen's claim that he loved his wife's career (and that he loved being an active, nurturing father to his young children), I could not escape the feeling that his hostility to Bonnie was at least in part the product of a dislike of his wife's career that he could not admit to himself. He was clearly the one man of the four who could least accept the female lieutenant as a peer.

Stanley Wyatt's acceptance grew out of Bonnie's performance. He had had some troubles in his own mind about her when he was captain and she first joined the Gantry force, but he tried to keep his mind open because officers under him who had gone to police school with her told him good things about her. He said:

I've had to apologize to Bonnie a lot. I didn't think she'd make it. I guess I was like a lot of men when I was first introduced to the idea of women in the uniformed divisions, particularly on the morning watch. I just couldn't accept the fact that they can make it, that they do have a place. I was one of them that didn't want to be shown. Bonnie proved me wrong.

What do you think made it possible for you to overcome those first doubts and fears?

I think she had a lot to do with it, her performance. That would be the key thing. I had to accept the fact that a woman could do it. Being honest, I have to admit she's made it. I haven't heard of any other female officers making it in the smaller departments here in this county. None of them is going to be given the chance. . . . Now, the county has been altogether a different experience. We have twenty-seven women now. Women have rode a number of months with a male officer. There are so many more police vehicles within a given area to support her or help her need if she's in trouble. And in the city of Gantry you have city hazards. I don't worry about it in the county. I wouldn't hesitate a minute to expect a woman that's on my beat or in my area to back me on a call, just like a man. And I think I have learned to control my feelings more with them, to accept what they can do, and accept what I'm expected to do.

A lot of women would be glad to know that someone starting out like you can learn to feel that way.

I didn't like having to admit I was wrong. That was difficult. [And he gave something between an embarrassed giggle and a secure chuckle in his nasal baritone.]

Harry Higbee was in some ways a more sophisticated version of Stanley Wyatt. He introduced himself with a smile as a "male chauvinist pig" and made his first point his doubts that women had the size or strength needed for police work. But he had noticed Bonnie's performance and potential, and he had gone out of his way to push her to qualify for lieutenant. She actually came in fourth on the exam. The top scorer was made lieutenant in the detective division, and the next two turned down the promotion—encouraged to do so by Higbee, according to several men—because it would have meant going on the morning watch. Bonnie became a lieutenant and Higbee made her his confidante, consulting her more than anyone else on the problems of the police in Gantry—to the dismay and derision of van Dusen and his friends. Higbee said:

If I were king of this country, things might be a little different. Right now, though, I'm forced by federal laws and state laws against discrimination to work with female officers. I'm a little extreme. I'm going to abide by all the rules and regulations, and I mean all. As long as she's the one with the most experience, and size has nothing to do with being a lieutenant. They all have the same responsibilities. She's more capable than anybody else I've got here in exhibiting leadership. . . . I think the world of Bonnie; I think she's a fine officer. The other female officer I have I think is great, too. I brought her down from the city; she's a great administrator. But I know very well that if circumstances arise where she has to make a difficult arrest, she's going to call in a male officer. Bonnie, she'll tackle anything.

Then Higbee qualified his enthusiasm a little.

I'm happy to have Bonnie here, but basically I feel there are always going to be problems. But I think women should be utilized. I'm just as opposed to having men handle rape cases. Some things men are better suited for and some women are.

Even that was a change from the way Higbee had felt five years earlier. He no longer felt threatened. He couldn't say he had learned there was nothing to be threatened by, but maybe I'm more mature now than I was five years ago. I probably wasn't aware at the time that I was feeling threatened. All I knew was there were women there and I was opposed to it. Maybe it was my macho that was threatened, but now I know I'm still a man even if there's a woman wearing a police uniform.

I think something important happened when I got married. I didn't get married until I was thirty-one. Before that I couldn't relate professionally to a woman. Every time I had a relationship with a woman, no matter what basis it was, I always saw her as a female. And back when I was a bachelor I was a moving bachelor. So I saw a female first and whatever she was second. Now I'm a happily married person. I can deal with females on other than a sexual basis. That's a big help in taking my extreme position on obeying the rules.

I was fascinated that a small-town, suburban police chief should say—spontaneously, without questions that might suggest the nature of the response—that a general maturing process, his own marriage, and women's performance on the job were all forces that moved him from opposition to acceptance of women on his police force. It made me feel hopeful. Then I remembered van Dusen, unable or unwilling to make the same journey even when touched by the same forces, always in danger of doing figuratively what his friend Marvin had done literally—of getting lost in the maze and shooting himself in the mirror. Even as I labeled him both wrong and silly, I knew I was still capable of getting lost in that maze myself.

OTHER CONTRADICTORY COMBINATIONS

The patterns of acceptance and resistance that were so striking in police men were just as interesting, sometimes in more subtle ways, in other bands of the service spectrum—in office, health, and computer jobs, for instance. In traditional service occupations I found classical hostility to women combined with modern recognition of their abilities. Where more men are entering predominantly female fields, I found new kinds of resentment combining with self-proclaimed liberation from sex-role stereotypes and positive attitudes about women at work combining with traditional feelings about family. In new occupations like computer sales and data processing I found old stereotypes about women losing a yard here, gaining a foot there, in a perpetual struggle with the de facto presence of women and occasional moments of liberation in men. My explorations uncovered a few of the endless array of permutations.

I call one example of hostility "classical" because it involves a good ole boy from a southern town and a job involving money—a macho hero in what has usually been a male preserve. Tom Welby* runs his own garage, which makes him both blue-collar worker and businessman in the service world. It took a lot of conversation before he admitted that women could do "maybe half the work" of an automobile mechanic, but once he had gone that far, he revealed both his intellectual perception and his gut fear:

> Women ought to be allowed to do anything [where] they're capable of doing a satisfactory job. If they can do it better than a man, as long as I'm not that man, let them do it.

When I teased him about being unwilling to compete with women, he talked about the five years in the 1970s that he worked for a finance company, another kind of service business.

> At first I was assistant manager. An assistant manager in the finance business is nothing but a chase boy, a collection man. We had a secretary; she was much better; she could collect more in one day on the telephone than I could collect in a week.

Did it bother you that she could collect more than you?

> It really did. If I had had my way about it, I'd have fired her. She was very vindictive, she made me know that she was better than me, every day. She despised the fact that she had been there twelve years and was still secretary-receptionist and a guy who didn't know nothing about it was hired in as her assistant manager.

Why didn't they make her an assistant manager?

> It took them fifteen years and they finally did. She took my place as assistant manager when I moved up to manager of another office, and she's manager now. She overcame all their resistance to women in management. But she was very underhanded about the way she did it. She'd call the home office and say, "I've got this much done and I want to do this much and I ain't sure the manager's going to let me, will it be okay with you all? I think I can collect from these people, but he don't think I can." It worked. She should have been a manager.

But you would have fired her.

> I would have. There's a chain of command in any business. But I couldn't fire her. I did not have the authority. Instead, I accepted a transfer, a promotion transfer, to get away from her. I was made a manager and had two chase men and six women working for me. I had one lady who had been in the business as long as the first one and was as good as she was, but wasn't as overpowering. She's still a secretary-receptionist after twenty years, and the woman who was so overpowering became a manager.

Why didn't you try to promote her?

I could have promoted her to assistant manager. It's a better title but not as good a job, and no real raise in her salary. As receptionist-secretary her salary was higher than any assistant manager would have got. But the truth was I didn't want to lose her. She was too good.

I was struck by two things in Tom Welby's comments. One was his failure to name either of the women whose capabilities at work he was recognizing, though he named all three of his wives and eight of his girlfriends in telling me about his life. The other was that even if he didn't want to give these women the individuality of a name, he was still able to recognize that they could do and had done better than he. Most men find it very hard to admit that a woman is able to do a better job than they can—and even harder to admit that she has done so. Welby made the admissions, yet he refused to do anything on his own responsibility to help the women.

Arnold Zimmer* exemplifies a different, relatively new kind of negative reaction. Born in 1946, he was a member of the generation of the sixties that was shaped by so many wars of liberation, including women's. He dropped out of college and went into clerical work, moving from pink-collar to slightly higher-level office service jobs. (He was not alone in this progress. The number of male secretaries, stenographers, and typists rose more than 300 percent, from 26,700 in 1972 to 112,700 in 1984—from 0.9 to 2.3 percent of all workers in this category. But male secretaries advance into the managerial ranks much faster than their female peers.[7]) Zimmer welcomed attacks on the old sex-role stereotypes and never thought less of himself for working in a female world. But he came to see himself as a victim of female power.

I've worked in the medical profession around male nurses, I've worked in educational institutions around male teachers, and I've worked in clerical positions. Sexual discrimination by women against men I've seen firsthand in all these fields. Female bosses have screwed me out of seniority and promotion.

When I met him, Arnold was working in the career planning office of one of the California universities, matching up college seniors with employers who came on campus to interview them—setting up 23,000 student interviews with 650 employers over a year's time. He was an administrative assistant, supervising between six and eight part-time clerical people. And he was the only male among fourteen peers whose boss was a woman and a former Navy commander.

There was a conflict on how my unit was to be run, and rather than letting me run it, she sought to interfere. She proceeded to dictate to me how to run the unit. But whenever mistakes would happen, I was blamed, because then she would change caps and say, "You're to administer this unit." So if anything went wrong, I caught heck for it.

Of course there are male bosses who act the same way.

Yes, but I felt there was sort of a sexist attitude on her part. She has been there for fifteen or twenty years and she's never pulled this on anyone else. I don't think she ever had a male in such a position before. . . . She eventually demoted me to a typist-clerk position, three levels down. I went on leave and filed a grievance.

Zimmer said he had had a similar experience earlier, at another university, where a woman boss had refused to promote him from the clerical job he had held for three years. He had been doing the work of an administrative assistant, a higher position that was vacant.

When she finally listed that position as open, I applied for it and she didn't even interview me for it, much less offer me the job. She screwed me out of seniority and hired a woman she knew.

As far as Zimmer was concerned, he was a victim of reverse discrimination —the same kind that women are quick to complain about when they are the victims. I thought the situations he described included both the problem of tokenism—the pressures that the numerically dominant usually put on the token, in this case the one male in a female organization—and the problem of (probably unconscious) revenge, a woman's treating a male subordinate in a way that compensated for all the times she had felt mistreated by male superiors. I couldn't tell how much of those situations was the result of personality conflicts that might be independent of gender-class conflict, or at least distinguishable from it. Nor could I tell if Zimmer might have been genuinely incompetent for the jobs he was denied. But when I admitted that as a logical possibility, I thought how indignant many women had been when men had raised the same possibility about females who claimed discrimination. They asked if the men could recognize competence in a female. I thought Arnold was entitled to ask the same question. He was quite certain that he knew discrimination when he saw it.

I felt discrimination of that nature a long time before other men did. But now men in executive positions are getting screwed over because they need to hire a woman to fill their quota. So men who wield more power and a louder voice than I do as a clerk in an educational or medical institution are now experiencing it.

What we really want, and I hollered as loud as anyone else for it in the early sixties, is equality. . . . I don't think we correct history by discriminating in favor of someone because their ancestors were discriminated against a hundred years ago. If we want equality now, then what we have to do is assure that everybody starts at the beginning line and runs a clean race.

As the conversation ranged over several different jobs he had held, Zimmer talked about another kind of equality and showed how questions of physical strength can be as significant for white-collar workers as for blue-collar men.

There's a whole stereotype about physical labor. It's okay if a man gets ruptured because he's a man, but you wouldn't ask a woman to carry your typewriter across the office or move a file cabinet. Working in clerical jobs, I have been approached many times by people doing the same work I am, saying, "Would you move this desk over here, that file cabinet over there." For several years I took it, and then a few years ago I started liberating myself and saying, "No. Last time I had to move my file cabinet I did it, now it's time to move yours, you do it." I got a lot of flak on that at first, people thought I was being an asshole or a sexist. Because I wanted equality, I was called a sexist.

In Arnold's view such stands are not trivial. He regards himself as truly liberated and is a member of two men's rap groups whose members feel they are struggling for equality in both their personal and professional lives (see Chapter 13).

Paul Roth* is also a man in a predominantly female field, but his experiences have been very different from Arnold Zimmer's. He is a male nurse who likes working for and with women. When I met him he was medical director of a community health clinic serving Mexican-Americans, an unusual situation because it made him not only an Anglo male who took orders from a Chicana woman executive director and a predominantly female board, but also a nurse who sometimes gave orders to doctors. (The doctors, all male, said they liked having someone else do the administration so they could concentrate on their medicine.)

In nursing school and in a year of hospital nursing, however, Roth had been in a contrasting position—that of all nurses, subordinate to doctors and others in authority, and that of members of any tiny minority, subject to pressures from the majority. But he came to nursing in the 1970s and never felt the low self-esteem that was typical of men in that overwhelmingly female field in the days before the women's movement. (Men constituted less than 1 percent of American nurses in 1970. They had the same objective rank as female nurses, but both men and women felt that the men's subjective status was lower.[8]) The number of male registered nurses rose more than 200 percent from 1972 to 1980—from 14,625 to 45,060, or from 1.6 to 2.7 percent of the 1980 total of 1.7 million. Some male nurses foresee a rise to 30 or 40 percent of the total—and see men as improving the status of the job.[9]

I asked Roth how he felt as a male nurse. He answered:

Very strange. I'm not really a believer in this, but it almost seems like karma that I've experienced a lot of things that most males don't. Being in a minority, experiencing what that's like. In my class of one hundred there were fifteen men, and that's just huge compared to most. Sometimes I felt as though I was being praised just because I was a member of a minority. And there were lots of times when I was hassled because I was different. But most of the time I felt I was treated fairly, even if the women and I could never ignore the difference.

I asked Roth if the men in nursing school or the hospital where he had worked had moved ahead faster than the women, as some female nurses complain. His answer, despite his own rise to a high-level job, was "I've never experienced that." Then he added, "It could happen. But in my school of nursing, all the powerful people, the dean of the school and all the faculty, were women. All the secretaries were men."

After his year in the hospital, Roth worked for a heart association and a family-planning clinic and then went to public health school before moving on to the Chicano clinic. The family-planning center wanted him because he was a qualified male who could reach out for male clients.

In a family-planning clinic there's a feeling that says, "Men are never here, those bastards." So if a male walks into a clinic he gets a dirty look from everybody. The ambience of a family-planning clinic is like a beauty parlor. It's got the women's magazines. So a male feels totally uncomfortable and out of place. He gets nasty looks, and he leaves. My job was to change that. I would go out into the parking lot and tell the guys, "Quit waiting out here, come inside and be with your partners." That was really a great feeling. We would show them a film about the male role in birth control that was made for high school students. There's a girl in it who says, "My boyfriend calls me up every day and reminds me to take the pill, he really cares." Another says her boyfriend came with her when she got her IUD. Another says, "I've got one who helps me insert my diaphragm." I felt I was making a contribution in that job, to men and women.

Roth liked working with the women who staffed the family-planning clinic. He also liked working with the Mexican-American women who occupied most of the policy-making and department-chief jobs at the Chicano clinic. The unusual power dynamic there had them frequently confronting the doctors, all but one of whom were Anglo males. The confrontations, equally unusually, tended to be resolved happily. At the heart association, Roth had worked primarily with men.

Working with men, even when you can get closer, there's still this tension, this competitiveness—kind of a mutual fear and respect. There's a tension. That's especially true when you don't know the people, but even when you get close it's always there, the need to prove yourself, to compete, to be better, to cover yourself. Working with women, a lot of that's not there, and it's really nice. There's far more cooperation.

At that point, Margie Gonzalez,* one of Paul's Chicana colleagues, interrupted with a derisive snort and said, "I'm surprised to hear that. I think some of the women are very competitive. Is it possible that they show that to one another and not to you?" I followed up with a related question: Are they showing you that even if they compete with one another, they are not competing with you because you're a man, or are they acting like male subordinates who compete but want to show their boss they're not out for his job? Paul replied:

> That's possible. All of those things are possible. I know there's things that I don't see. Other people will say, "God, this person is really very competitive," and I have to say that I haven't seen that, they haven't been that way with me. But mostly it's just a feeling of more cooperation; things are more at the emotional level and less—less circling each other.

When you say "emotional," is that a negative judgment?

> No, it's positive. I like that warmth and I think it's good for the clinic. The negative aspect is that I think our culture makes women have a difficult time making decisions. They have a hard time being maybe authoritarian. They're afraid of being wrong, afraid of having to compete. They back off a little bit. At the clinic I like it when they're not crazy gung ho to do the job like men, but there are times when I think we all wish people felt better about making decisions.

One decision that frequently troubled Roth was the working woman's decision to have a baby. Almost all the women who worked at the clinic were in their childbearing years, and he estimated that more than 20 percent of the staff was pregnant at any given moment. One executive director had been hired when she was six months pregnant and had been given a contract allowing her not only to take some maternity leave but also to bring her baby to work with her for a specified period while she was nursing. In the end, she left the job, feeling that she was cheating both her baby and the job by trying to take care of both at the same time. That posed the problem of finding and breaking in a new boss.

Many of the women on the clinic staff brought their babies to work; there was a child care center and Roth welcomed the infants so long as they were not near patients and did not interfere with their mothers' work. But other clinic workers put their babies in child care or brought in a grandmother to care for them, and Roth thought that was tragic.

He turned out to have a combination of very liberated and very traditional ideas about parenting, part philosophy and part emotions about his own son, fourteen months old when I met him. The traditional side made an ironic contrast with his supportiveness of women at work. He was a very involved, active father, who found it "really painful to leave in the morning and realize that I'm not going to be spending the majority of my waking hours with

David." Yet he and his wife had decided that she should give up her own career as a nurse to take care of David at least until he was old enough for nursery school. I asked why Paul didn't bring David to the clinic while he worked, as so many of the women did.

> I run around too much. I guess I could, because he stopped breast-feeding when he was one year old. But it just wouldn't be good or practical for me to do that. I wouldn't want to be like the executive director who had to quit. My wife was going to go back to work after six months, but she decided not to. It's hard for me to understand on the emotional or the rational level how anyone could plan to have a child and not plan to spend considerable amounts of time with it, one parent or both parents. It almost seems criminal to me to put a baby in child care—those early years are so important.

Roth's sense of realism about his colleagues' economic needs had led him to accept a child care facility at the clinic despite these feelings, even though the feelings made him think that close friends of the parents were likely to provide better care for an infant than a child care center would.

Roth also criticized the women's movement for moving from the idea that women should be able to make a choice about career and parenting and not have child care forced on them to the idea that a woman without a career deserved little respect. This was the feeling he said he met almost everywhere he went, whether for social or professional gatherings. He had little sympathy for women who complained that being locked into child care was so boring that their brains atrophied, because "my wife thinks it's the most exciting thing she's done in her whole life."

When I asked if he and his wife couldn't have split the responsibility of caring for David, Paul talked, accurately enough, of society's unreadiness to make that easier with programs like job sharing. But he was not aware that more and more men in mainstream jobs are resisting demands that they give their whole lives to the corporation that employs them and neglect their children accordingly. And he never came up with an answer when I kept asking why, if sharing were economically impossible, it had to be his wife who gave up her career temporarily rather than he himself.

Roth went back to nontraditional attitudes when we returned from the plight of the baby in the two-career family to what happens to men in women-dominated health services. He had served under two women executive directors in the Chicano clinic, and during his career he had had both male and female bosses. Despite his wish for quicker and sharper decisions by his female colleagues, he said:

> In many ways it's far more pleasant, less intimidating, to have a woman boss. Men think in terms of power plays, let's-crush-you military maneu-

vers. Since women haven't been exposed to that, they don't use that kind of power play. It's much more on a collegial basis. Or being more sensitive.

Some people say a woman can't be as good a boss as a man if she hasn't been exposed to power playing.

Some of *the* most effective executives are the nonpower men, and women. I've been as intimidated by a female boss as by a male, but I think they do it as needed. Men do it all the time, whereas women can be selective, and it's very effective.

I thought it important to say, "The clinic is in a sense a self-selecting body. Women who play hard power games are not going to come to work here. Neither is the kind of man who is very insecure, very macho, or ethnically unsure of himself." Margie commented, "And the salary is not very attractive. That tells you something about what society does to women." Paul added, "Or what it does to service organizations. Which are mostly handled by women."

THE COMPUTER INDUSTRY

Many service organizations, of course, are part of the business world and are not "handled" by women in the sense that Roth meant. The computer industry and the information sciences, for example, are new occupations with a strong technological side that are often considered more open to women than are older fields. But they are still run by men, and "men are the same everywhere, even in the computer business." That at least was the view of a woman who had just moved from marketing support, a heavily female specialty, to sales, still 95 percent male, in the company for which she had worked for ten years.

It is unquestionably important that women went into computers and data processing early and in large numbers, quickly passing the token barrier. Women moved from 19.9 percent of the country's computer programmers in 1972 to 35.4 percent in 1984, and from 10.8 percent of computer systems analysts to 30 percent.[10] Until economic troubles hit computer manufacturers in 1985, the electronics industries were undergoing what one executive called a "cosmic expansion," which entails such keen competition to fill the labor shortage "that the question as to whether a candidate is a woman or not doesn't even arise."[11] The expansion will continue in the long run. This creates possibilities for women to achieve equality with men that have not yet opened in other fields.

But it is just as important that women have been promoted to managerial positions in the computer world only half as often as men—better than traditional areas, but suggesting that new fields produce old attitudes in attenuated form. (They constitute 14 percent of managers and 17 percent of professionals in California's Silicon Valley.[12]) One sociologist who specializes in computer occupations believes it is very likely that the historical pattern will repeat itself there "with women serving as assistants, while men have the jobs with real responsibility."[13]

That certainly is what Mike Modzelewski* has found. He is a data-processing manager for one of the big automakers. It happens that he has been personally dedicated to the cause of equal opportunity for women from the moment he discovered that his twelve-year-old daughter thought her only career choices were nursing and teaching (see Chapter 7). But he hasn't been able to make as much difference as he'd like in his employer's practices.

> The field is wide open. Of the people we've hired this year, 70 percent have been women, young girls right out of college. But for some reason we just don't seem to be able to promote them into supervisory or management-level positions. Not that they're not talented. Not that they're not capable.

Only two of the forty-six people in management-level positions in Mike's division were female. When I asked why women weren't promoted in greater numbers and to higher levels, he replied:

> So many times I've seen people who were proficient as programmers or analysts be promoted to managers because of their proficiency in the technical aspects, yet when they were promoted they didn't have the skills or the training or the inclination even to be a manager. When they promote into management-level positions based on the technical skills, there seems to be a conflict.

I suggested that men, too, often fail to make the jump from technical to management proficiency. Mike agreed but repeated his belief that this was an important reason women failed to rise. Neither society nor company, he felt, had trained women to be managers or made them want to be managers, as it does men. This can also work against women who are eager and qualified, he said.

> Maybe our management is just too chauvinistic. They are concerned that the women are going to go out and get pregnant and have children and leave. I had a case here where I wanted to promote a gal who was working for me to the next higher grade, which would put her just one step short of management level. My boss asked, "Is she capable of being promoted to management level?" I said, "Yes, in my opinion she certainly is." It just so happens that her husband also works in our division. In another building, but nonetheless in the same organization. The manager said, "Well, we'd have a problem trying to promote her to management level if her husband was working in the same department."
>
> I said, "Maybe that's true, but maybe what we should do is to promote

her out to another division. You certainly did that to the last *guy* who was in here who got promoted to management level whose wife also worked in the department." My boss kind of winced. Maybe he gets pressures from his bosses not to promote too many women. But he said, "Well, you're right, okay." He put his approval on it and she was promoted.

Of course, Mike is in the auto industry, still a traditional male business grouping many macho occupations. Bill Segura* is a marketing support executive for a computer maker—a specialty that involves programming and systems analysis and is heavily populated by women in an industry that is, as we have seen, very open to women. Bill likes to talk about how well women do in his company and in the industry as a whole. When he talks about his thirty years in the business, however, he reveals a fairly complete set of traditional attitudes. Listening to him, I couldn't decide whether it was more interesting that such a conventional man could be so genuinely supportive of women or that such a supportive man could hold to so many stereotyped beliefs. Either way, Bill Segura embodied both the hopes and the frustrations that men in the computer industry offer women.

Bill explained to me that women did well in the industry because it had evolved to a point where it needed their skills. The first programmers had to be men, he said, because the programs of that epoch were so close to the machine:

You had to understand how the machine handled everything. It's electronic, it's logic, but it's almost mechanical. It was manipulation by making the machine work the way you wanted it to work by moving wires around [in the days before single silicon chips]. You could get in there and by changing one instruction you could wildly change the throughput, the response to that system. It's like tuning a car, it's more a guy's kind of thing. It was too close to the machine for women to be trusted with hardware like that. And at that time there were no computer science courses. Anywhere. The logical people to do the programs in assembly language were the men who designed the computer and serviced it.

Eventually computer scientists came up with higher-level languages like Cobol, Pascal, and Basic. That made a vital difference, Segura said.

All of a sudden you removed that interface between you and the machine, you didn't have to understand how the goddamned machine worked anymore. You reduce the whole thing to saying, "This is the problem, I need the solution using this language to solve my problem."

Then, as Segura saw it, women could come in and make a difference.

You had two things. You had syntax, and I think women were always better at language than men were, so the syntax of computer languages was simple for them to learn. And they like rules. You'll find that women don't ask why as much as guys do. Guys seem to want to know why something is happening. If you tell a gal this is the way you solve this equation, fine, she doesn't ask why, she remembers it, done.

I noted, but didn't say, that this made one of women's talents in the new computer field a matter of old stereotypes. As it turned out, so was the second.

The second thing was you had to solve problems. The solution to a problem is first finding out what kind of problem it is. That means talking to the people who have the problem, and women are people-oriented. The only things that computer systems do is perform tasks. Those tasks are not necessarily complex scientific algorithms. You're doing accounting problems, you're doing payrolls, you're possibly working on inventory problems, you're doing sales analysis, very plain simple tasks that have got to be done.

The problem is that now so many people are using computers for these tasks. . . . Women are people-oriented, and the computer industry right now had better be people-oriented, because you have a whole raft of entry-level users coming in now on these personal computers. Everybody in the world is going to have one. You're looking at solving problems involving an awful lot of people who aren't familiar with computers.

Women were particularly good at that kind of problem, Segura said. Women had always operated and installed the old mechanical bookkeeping devices, and they installed the computers that took their place:

They do install better than men. There's a case that they operate keyboards better than I do, but just in people skills and teaching skills they do better than men do. They're more patient, they're not as intimidating. And there was a natural evolution from installing it to making some slight changes in the racks to make it operate a little differently.

This acceptance of women on small machines did not always extend to the big mainframe computers, Segura said, only half realizing how stereotyped the reasons were.

There's resistance on big projects. You get a guy who's in there fifteen years or something, with a multimillion dollar system to bring in, he's very nervous about a gal if she's young and she's pretty—because, where is her mind really at? Is she just putting in time here and thinking about what she's going to wear? Or she's going to get married, she's going to get pregnant. With the pill, a lot of that changed, but there's still a fair amount of it around.

Segura made plain that he did not share that worry, that he had supported the promotion of women to selling mainframe accounts. But he talked about a different traditional feeling that he had. His marketing support function means servicing the client's machines whenever they have a problem or breakdown. A customer with a massive system running twenty-four hours a day must have service right away because "they'll lose 150 man-hours for every hour they're down." That means going in to solve a problem at three in the morning, or being away from home without notice for a couple of days of round-the-clock work. He said:

> For the most part, I have a problem with women on accounts where they might have to do twenty-four-hour work. I don't like them coming from their houses to an account. Eight or nine o'clock at night I don't really mind, but I don't like the idea of women being there twenty-four hours or at five o'clock in the morning. I feel very uncomfortable with it. I try to keep them out of those accounts. If I have to put a woman in one, I usually try to see that I have another systems engineer with her, on whatever pretext.

Bill moved from such traditional attitudes to modern ones in the course of a few minutes while trying to answer another question—does the increasing number of women in the computer industry mean a rise in office romances or sexual tensions, and if it does, is it good or bad for business? At first he said it was probably bad, not because it lowers productivity, but because it adds a risk to the high turnover in the business. People move from one company to another every two or three years to learn new designs, new techniques, new equipment, new languages. If two employees of one company were sexually involved, and one moved to another company, he asked, what would happen?

> I wouldn't like to have somebody in bed with someone that's working for another company and expose him intimately to what's going on in our accounts, what accounts are we trying to crack. He or she is into a problem that's jeopardizing the account, and there's somebody who's working for a competitor, and they're bedding down together. That's a very uncomfortable situation. In the past it was always assumed that they would talk, that there would be a total exchange.

As we talked, Bill moved from that "old" idea to two new ones. On the one hand, he continued to drink and to play racquetball with men who used to work with him and now worked for competitors. "I've maintained my relationship with them, and yet never disclosed anything that would hurt the company, and they've done the same with me." And on the other hand:

> With today's rules and today's society, I'm not sure that two people bedding down with each other means that they share secrets with each other any more, any more than two guys going down for a drink. . . . The whole thing of sex has been liberated to the point where it isn't as deep or as needy as it used to be. I think a lot of gals and a lot of guys are looking

at it as "Hey, he's a nice guy, I respect him, we have a lot of fun when we're together, why not?" I don't really think it's that emotional an experience. I don't like it, I'm incapable of having that kind of relationship, but it's all over, and I'm not really ready to condemn it. And if it is that casual, am I kidding myself that all this heavy exchanging of mutual secrets takes place?

I interjected an "Alas!" when Bill said sex has become so liberated it isn't deep or needy anymore, but I was fascinated that this conventional man should have developed the idea that casual sex might lead to mutual respect and better friendships between men and women.

He had also developed the ability to accept a woman as his boss in a way that many conventional men find hard to do. For a year he had reported to a woman. He still didn't like it when a woman tried to pick up the check for a business lunch, but he had no problems working for this particular woman. When I asked him why, he said, "She's smarter than I am." I said I had met many men who hate to admit that a woman may be smarter than they are. He replied, "No. Their ability, I'm not talking management ability, but their ability to find solutions, it's so clean-cut. You can't sit back and ignore the fact that when they're good, they're good. When a solution is presented that is a solution, I don't see how anybody can say no. You can't argue with results. In that respect, I don't have any problem."

Other men, regional managers like Bill, did have problems reporting to that woman, the director of marketing support. He commented:

The other guys resented her. They were regional managers before she was. But she was a very ambitious gal, she took on more work, more duties in the marketing organization. We got into things we shouldn't be involved with. No, not "shouldn't be," but hadn't been involved with before.

The unhappy managers would have hated a male director who tried to acquire new responsibilities, but they hated her twice as much because she was a female empire builder. Yet there was not too much they could do about it. The culture of the company and the industry and the nature of the work did not permit them to try the kind of sabotage that men use in factories. They could only complain.

It was always, "What the hell is she bucking for, why doesn't she do what she gets paid to do?" When they got back to their own regional directors, they would pop her that way, possibly in front of meetings; instead of following good management practices and saying, "We," they would say, "She, you know how she is." It would be a subtle type of thing. They would not defend the position that she would take. And they'd make remarks every time she named a gal to a position. [She had promoted one woman out of her division and added two at managerial level within it.] I don't think she went overboard. Of the women she's got in there, they're not the same type she is, but they're good. They're not taking a free ride. They're good and they're tough. [She also promoted a homosexual from a staff job at company headquarters to a management position.] She took a lot of ribbing about that. The guys said two physicals, one logical. I think the men resented that it was a woman pushing them to do all those additional things, saddling them with that extra responsibility.

But did they do it in the end?

Oh yeah. They fought, kicking and dragging, but they did it. And she was promoted [one level, to a higher grade of director], now she's in charge of market support for a whole new kind of system.

It seemed equally important to me that the vaunted computer industry, supposedly so open to women, was so full of classical male reactions, and that the woman executive had still won a promotion despite them. Bill emphasized the heights she had reached, moving from two levels down from a vice presidency up to one level below. He ignored her relatively low position in the top management hierarchy, four levels down from chief executive. I thought it might be a long while before she made vice president, and even longer in that company before a woman moved to national management in any area outside marketing. With all his support for women in his own specialty, Bill Segura never even envisaged the possibility. And he was only middle management after thirty years. The men who build new companies and design new computers, often much younger than Bill, are seldom as willing and able to acknowledge the talents of women as he is.

Still, the computer industry emphatically demonstrates the combination of acceptance and resistance to women, of positive responses on the one hand and denial or subtle resentment on the other, that I believe is much more visible in service jobs than in blue-collar, executive, or professional work. The service sector offers a multitude of the low-paying jobs that women traditionally sink into, and which increasing numbers of men, especially young men, find themselves trapped in. That may produce a kind of equality between the sexes that nobody really wants.[14] At the same time, service occupations offer more of the new high-technology, high-paying jobs that will be established by the end of this century than any other kind of work, jobs that will provide women with new opportunities to win independence and equality and men with more opportunities to transcend the hostility, denial, and transformation that so often are tied to traditional kinds of work. Higher-paying, higher-status occupations in business and the professions may provide women with more dramatic challenges and (I hope) achievements, but service jobs from police to paralegal, from filing to computer analysis, will provide more of the real test of the women's revolution in American society.

Chapter 7
BUSINESS MANAGEMENT

The story of Bill and Mary began only a few years ago, but it has already taken on the quality of a grim fairy tale in the business world. William Agee was the chairman of the Bendix Corporation, aggressive and unorthodox, in many eyes a young hero challenging the giants of the business establishment. Mary Cunningham—whom the media insisted on describing as a princess with golden hair—was a Harvard Business School graduate who became Agee's executive assistant and needed only fifteen months to rise to the position of vice president for strategic planning at Bendix, at the age of twenty-nine. Many officers, employees, and shareholders of Bendix responded to Cunningham's rise like the sisters in the original Grimm who spewed toads and snakes from their mouths when they tried to speak. They claimed that she had made her way up the Bendix tower by romancing her boss, Bill Agee.

After some personal and corporate agony, Cunningham resigned from Bendix; later she became an executive vice president of Seagram Corporation. Agee went on a quest he and Cunningham had shaped—to divest Bendix of unprofitable or unpromising subsidiaries and to use the cash thus realized to take over companies that would enable Bendix, primarily a maker of automobile parts and jet engine controls, to move into high technology. His corporate adversaries repeatedly used his relationship with Cunningham as a psychological-warfare weapon to demonstrate that he was no parfit, gentil knight. They kept it up even after Bill and Mary got married. Agee tried to take over Martin Marietta and failed, after much costly, internecine corporate warfare; instead, Bendix was taken over by Allied Corporation. It was supposed to be a friendly rescue, but Agee was ultimately fired (with a six-figure "golden parachute" contract) rather than kept as number two at Allied. Cunningham eventually left Seagram so she and Agee could form a venture capital and strategic consulting firm.

The Bill-and-Mary tale does not prove that the business world will cripple every woman who reaches for the top, or drip the acid of sexual innuendo on her and her male sponsor. It does show that that sometimes happens. Perhaps more importantly, it illustrates in an unusually stark and public way how seldom men or women know how to mix work and love when they meet as equals and the prize is power. And power is what is at stake when women invade the executive suite. Some men have it; many men have a chance at it; some women want it, or at least the same chance at it. People moving up in the business world can reach for real power unknown to people in blue-collar and service occupations—at the top, power over thousands of workers, over billion-dollar efforts to produce or to serve.

Being close to real power sometimes makes male executives even more vulnerable than other men to illusions of power: if they fail to achieve the reality, they may need the pretense even more desperately than men at the bottom whose powerlessness is more obvious and more oppressive. They seldom say so openly, but I believe they often feel subconsciously that sharing with women dilutes the reality and shatters the pretense.

At this level, power is usually more important than getting any particular work done. But executives, like other men, often feel that work as well as power loses some of its magic if women participate in it as peers, whether the work is commanding administration, running production, handling finance, or any other function at the top of a corporation. They talk less about it, but they find it just as hard as men in other occupations to mix equality in work with sexuality or family. And, like other men, they find it hard to meet women in the workplace without expecting business and pleasure to mix.

The presence of women also compels them to reexamine the myth of male success. When men and women managers can be compared, they turn out to have many of the same qualities rather than significantly different ones—high needs for power and achievement and high self-esteem, among others. Men also seem to have many of the same problems that women do. In career development, for instance, both sexes do too little to measure their own strengths and weaknesses, to ensure the flow of information they need, to learn how to deal with supervisors unwilling or unable to train them for promotion. Both sexes seem equally prone to fear of success, once thought a predominantly female trait. Women's achievements and problems are often compared to the myth of male success rather than to the male reality—which is much closer to the female than business men like to admit.[1]

So executives may punish a man who tries too hard or too obviously to share power with women, who compounds the confusion of the boundary between business and sexuality or business and family, who opens the male myth to comparison with reality. They punished Bill Agee when he shared too much with Mary Cunningham. Yet the Bill-and-Mary story also shows that some executives know more than men in blue-collar and service jobs about the way American society is changing. Some, like Agee—not a lot, but more than a few—support the changes women are making more openly than do men in other occupations, as a matter of moral right and as a matter of personal and corporate interest.

The legend of Bill and Mary illuminates these important points no matter how the corporate world ultimately rates Mary Cunningham. Allan Sloan interviewed many people who knew her and had worked with her, and he reported "an almost unanimous portrait of a person lacking in both practical business experience and emotional maturity." They described someone of great energy, a synthesist who would take other people's ideas and make them into her own, a person who found it hard to make decisions.[2] Gail Sheehy wrote a favorable series about Cunningham in the New York *Daily News* but later said Cunningham had lied to her and added, "I think that she's been a disaster for well-intentioned, bright, honest, hard-working women in management. . . . Mainly, I think, because she is what most women fear being thought of as."[3] Agee and others still describe her as a brilliant corporate strategist.

Whichever she is, nobody evaluated her corporate competence while both the general media and the business press were making Agee and Cunningham a major story. They looked at her only as a woman, usually mentioning her blond hair, blue eyes, and shapely figure. I believe the coverage unquestionably reflected the feelings, conscious or unconscious, of the male executives and stock analysts who were the media's primary sources and of the male editors and reporters who wrote most of the stories, though most of them would deny any bias.

But Cunningham and Agee's supporters as well as their critics think they handled their public and their corporate relations badly—or at best with astonishing naïveté for two people high in the business world. Perhaps the first in a long series of corporate strains came when Cunningham moved into an office next to Agee's, which some people saw as a threat to his "monogamous" relationship with the woman previously cast as his office wife—his secretary.[4] On the public side, while Cunningham was still Agee's rising young executive, they appeared together at places like the U.S. Open tennis tournament and the Republican national convention. If they had both been men, they might have been just corporate buddies. But one of them was a woman, both were still legally married to other people, and gossip flowed.

As it began to flow, two top Bendix executives left. One was President William Panny, who was fired. His macho, four-letter-word management style was incompatible with Agee's, but he told Allan Sloan that Agee fired him "because we had arguments over the girl. I told him she was a disruptive influence, and I talked to some of the directors about it."[5] The other was corporate planner Jerome Jacobson, who had lost his real power to Cunningham. Jacobson's departure was particularly important because his policies had represented security to executives who felt threatened by the divestiture strategy identified with Cunningham. After Jacobson left, anonymous letters started reaching board members asking that the Agee-Cunningham relationship be investigated; many of them reportedly came not from men but from women in middle management.

Agee's practice was to hold an annual meeting of employees from corporate headquarters where he sought to know what was causing discord or anxiety. At the September 1980 meeting he acknowledged the existence of the gossip and said, "It is true that we are very, very close friends, and she's a very close friend of the family. But that has nothing to do with the way that I and others in this company evaluate performance. Her rapid promotions are totally justified." The Detroit *Free Press* made it a front-page story and the wire services made it a national story.

In the next few days Cunningham offered to take a leave of absence. The Bendix board refused and gave her a vote of confidence. But she and at least some board members came to feel she ought to resign, and on October 9, she did.

A few months later she went to Seagram. As she tells it, her relationship to Agee changed. By 1982 they were engaged to be married and she welcomed publicity. She acknowledged that she had had foes not only because of her sex but because of her youth, since corporate management is usually a world of people who are middle-aged as well as male. She said the Bendix experience had been one in which "I was mentally raped, and that's no exaggeration." But she attributed a lot of the 1980 Bendix gossip to "individuals who were being hurt" by Agee's strategy for the company. And she charged that three or four individuals "who really spearheaded this media event . . . were jealous of Bill. It wasn't me they were after, it was Bill. Most people realize that."[6]

When Agee went off to fight takeover battles, it appeared that the corporate warriors were still after him—and still using Cunningham as a weapon. His first target was RCA; in March 1982, Bendix announced that it had acquired 7.3 percent of RCA's stock and might buy up to 9.9 percent. RCA defended itself by attacking—that is, by issuing a release in the name of its chairman, Thornton Bradshaw, which said, "Mr. Agee has not demonstrated a capacity to manage his own affairs, let alone someone else's." Readers did not have to be feminists to think that the word "affairs" was not chosen by accident.

Bradshaw may have been acting out of character. In his previous job, as president of Atlantic Richfield, he had shaped corporate policies giving women more opportunity than they had found at any other major oil company. A few days after the press release, Cunningham met Bradshaw in the receiving line when she was inducted into the Economic Club of New York. He said to her, "Mary, I am so sorry for the way that was repeated in the press. I would never have wanted to say something like that. That was the advice I was being given." Cunningham told him icily that it had been beneath his dignity. Later he apologized to Agee too.[7]

But the damage continued. Before Agee became Cunningham's sponsor or her husband, the press had labeled him "brash," "egotistical," "aggressive"— words whose macho tone made them compliments rather than insults in the business world. Once his connection with her became public, he was seen as "weak" and "easily influenced." Agee claimed that, before and after, he was a businessman who valued good advice, whatever the sex of the adviser.[8]

Bill and Mary got married in June 1982, and Agee announced Bendix's intention to acquire Martin Marietta in August. The business press immediately revived the Bill-and-Mary story. Cunningham was doing her high-level job at Seagram, but she took time to give Agee advice on all the choices of tactics and strategy that he faced, advice that he called "invaluable." Marietta fought back by bidding in turn to gobble up Bendix. Each side brought in huge corporate allies to help—United Technologies for Marietta, Allied for Bendix. Cunningham took a four-day vacation from Seagram in September 1982 to help her husband in his final negotiations with Thomas Pownall, the Marietta chairman, and his lieutenants. Reports differ as to how conciliatory Agee's position was, but Pownall rejected Bendix's final terms.

Agee made a number of strategic mistakes in his attempt to take over Marietta—misjudging the personalities of the men who ran the target company, its financial reserves, the damage it would do Bendix to buy 70 percent of the Marietta stock. He also made what others interpreted as a tactical error —bringing in his wife as part of the Bendix team. The New York *Times,* the Washington *Post,* and *The Wall Street Journal* all reported that Cunningham's role as a consultant to Agee had been a significant factor in the failure to bring Bendix and Marietta together on a friendly basis. The *Journal* reported: "The fact that Mr. Agee brought Miss Cunningham to the session as an adviser 'infuriated the guys at Marietta,' according to a Wall Street banker who later spoke to Marietta directors. 'Just the thought of losing their company to a guy who is being advised or guided by Mary Cunningham was more than they could stand,' the banker says."[9] *Newsweek* quoted an unnamed "Marietta man" as saying, "What in hell did he bring his wife down for? I don't care if he wants to consult with her, but this is a conservative business . . . where wives are left at home."[10]

Agee was furious, and the Marietta executives said it wasn't so. A letter to the Washington *Post* said that Cunningham's presence "was not an irritant to Martin Marietta and her presence, alongside her husband, Mr. Agee, the Bendix chairman, did not contribute in any manner to the failure of Bendix and Martin Marietta to reach agreement at that time or subsequently. . . . Everyone present on both sides behaved professionally, with total propriety and civility. It was apparent that Mr. Agee took some comfort from his wife's presence, but not then or later did any of us find that to be irritating or curious."[11]

There was no doubt that the Marietta directors wanted to present themselves in public as gentlemen so far as Mary Cunningham was concerned. On another level, however, their letter was (and was seen as) a put-down of Agee and Cunningham. Bendix, in another of Agee's surprising public relations gambits, saw only the gentlemanly disclaimer and sent the letter out as a news release. It had little effect. Four months later, the New York *Times* was still reporting that Cunningham's presence at the negotiations "amazed and angered a number of the participants." Three years afterward, *The Wall Street Journal* again quoted the banker who spoke to some of the Marietta directors during the Agee-Cunningham visit. The *Journal* said he quoted them as saying, "We'll burn this company to the ground before we let that [woman] have it." "[Woman]" was presumably the *Journal*'s substitute for an expletive deleted.[12]

MEN VS. WOMEN AT THE TOP

William Agee was a chief executive officer who wanted to open the top management of his company to women who could do the job. He and Mary Cunningham found out the hard way that there were a lot of men at Bendix who were not ready to open the company that wide. The same thing happens all the time at other companies. Thornton Bradshaw made Atlantic Richfield an oil industry leader in the employment of women (18 percent of its total payroll when he headed the company). But during his regime an ARCO publication on its social responsibilities carried, in addition to expectable doses of self-congratulation, the verdict of Kirk O. Hanson, a Stanford Business School lecturer:

> Atlantic Richfield has made some progress integrating women into lower levels of hourly and professional employment, but lags badly in moving women into higher levels of management. . . . With only two exceptions, top corporate management is all male and all white. More distressing, I found a surprising lack of urgency about women's employment, and an unexpected number of managers whose language is consistently "sexist."[13]

I wonder why Hanson thought these things were "surprising" and "unexpected." To me, they were neither. Such predictable behavior shows how many men at management levels as well as lower down in the hierarchy feel about the arrival of women in their workplace. It is what they do and not the noble pronouncements of the chief executive officer that determine the fate of most women in their corporation. Their feelings and their behavior have both a social and a corporate cost, as ARCO recognized by including Hanson's analysis in its report on its social actions.

Similar recognition came from a new vice president installed near the top of a Midwest-based retail chain by the conglomerate that had just taken it over. He told his assembled managers that they were losing customers because market surveys showed they were perceived as a company run entirely by WASP males. He sent out a letter telling the managers they would hire and promote women and blacks—or else. The white male managers "were taking that letter and throwing it in the garbage, or ripping it to shreds," said one of the few black men who had stayed with the company over the five-year period before the takeover. "I could feel the tension. People were staring at me, and I go into the washroom and a guy says to me, 'Oh, you gonna be my boss now?' And I have a few friends here who are white women, and they said, 'You think it's bad for you? What about me, too? I get all those lousy wisecracks too.' We were all damn nervous and worried was anything really going to change."

In that company, things did change. The men who bitched in the bars and the men's rooms started promoting women and blacks, because the vice president said he would fire them if they didn't. They learned how serious the corporate cost was.

But that kind of follow-through seldom happens. Back in 1970 the chairman of the board of the company that owned the heavy equipment factory described in Chapter 5 made a videotape that was shown to every person in the company's management. He said on the tape that they were going to have women and minorities in the shop and in management. They were making the change because it was "legally required, morally right, economically sound, and we owe it to the community." And the chairman added that if anyone looking at the tape thought he would have trouble handling the change, "he has the choice of resigning."

Ten years later women still accounted for less than 10 percent of the shop employees—and less than 5 percent of management. The highest-ranking woman was a section chief eight levels down from the top. A division personnel chief who described himself as eager to promote women in management said, "It's hard. For us, management is like a men's club. Look at my boss and me. We're typical. We've been here a long time. We're white, male, in our fifties. We're both over six feet tall. It's hard for us to believe a woman could do the physical things in the shop that you have to do to work up to our level. It's hard for us to watch our language when women are around. You could say this company has a male chauvinist tradition."

In that company such attitudes two to six levels down from the top determined the real corporate policy and practices. They also fit the true feelings of higher management, the spirit revealed in the company's practice rather than in the pronouncements of the board chairman. The same thing might be said in a different sense of a very different company, a diversified conglomerate that has done better than average with women at entry and middle-management levels; women now account for 20 percent of all managers there. It has a tradition that is not male chauvinist, but the gender equivalent of white liberal.

Roger Mortimer* is at the top of middle management there, an East Coast Ivy Leaguer transplanted to California, a lawyer with experience in multinational operations translated to marketing. He said:

Marketers tend to be looked upon as slightly wild people, out wining and dining customers and the like, and there's concern about whether they're obeying all of the rules and regulations with regard to how they talk to their dealers. . . . But the fact is, they're the most conservative bunch of people I have ever run across in my life. Essentially they're very traditional in terms of morality and mores. They're not used to dealing with women in business and they're somewhat reluctant to do it, they're somewhat uncomfortable doing it. They don't want to go out on a limb to be someone who hires the first woman or promotes the first woman. It's not a thing that is encouraged. It's rather like sitting in a bar with men telling dirty jokes. Having women with you there, or having women out selling, or even in an office meeting, it's a little uncomfortable.

Now, that being said, we've hired a lot more women in marketing than we ever did before, very bright, very well educated women. There are an awful lot of women who are MBAs these days. Perhaps because they're women, perhaps because they're bright, perhaps because they're both, they're unusual. Like anyone unusual, they may get a little extra attention, and if they're good, they get promoted. . . . But if you ask, most of us would probably say we prefer men because it's easier, we understand them better, we know how to deal with them.

Roger excluded himself from that preference with a word and a smile—a gentleman's acknowledgment of a change, in part in himself, in part in the world, springing from feminism. His ambivalence and his company's ambivalence were a far cry from the company that owned the heavy-equipment factory. The chief executive officer and other senior management in his conglomerate wanted to open up much more for women than the heavy-equipment chiefs—without unduly disturbing the marketing men Roger described, or the even more macho production executives. But the ambivalence in his account illustrated the same truism as the low statistics in the heavy-equipment company: managers tend to do what the boss wants, and the ability to distinguish his real desires from his pious rhetoric is important. Without it, a manager can't effectively protect his own interests. With it, doing what the boss wants can become a reason for the continuing resistance to women in business—or for the gradual erosion of that resistance. It's distinct from men's genuine emotions about women, but it reinforces them.

RESISTANCE

Many people thought that sex bias and resistance to women in business would diminish as more and more women came into the management world. Once they passed a certain proportion of the total, they would cease to be mere tokens, and discrimination would change and then start to disappear. The barrier was assumed to lie somewhere between 15 percent, where women (or any outgroup) are still tokens, and 35 percent, where they are seen as a minority—but a minority whose members are full participants in the executive community. In some cases, women have become full members when their number crossed that boundary. But in many more, even where there are enough women so they can no longer be regarded as tokens, resistance and discrimination continue.[14]

One reason for this is economic. Men's responses to the arrival of women in every masculine workplace, but even more in management than most others, are shaped by economics as well as by psychological and sociological forces. It may be the economy as a whole: it is always easier to bring women (or racial minorities) into nontraditional occupations in a time of economic growth, when new jobs are being created, than in a recession, when jobs are disappearing.

At the same time it may be a question of company or individual economics. It will cost corporations money to close the wage gap, for instance, and pay women equally instead of sixty-two cents for every dollar earned by men—for the same jobs and especially for different jobs requiring comparable education, skills, and experience, if the principle of comparable worth is ever firmly established.[15] It will cost men money, or seem to, if they see themselves as a group losing jobs or promotions to women. At the very least it will limit men's economic opportunities if they have to compete with women for jobs that used to be predominantly male. The odds against any individual's receiving a promotion will remain the same if he competes against the same number of peers. But he may not perceive that, or may ignore it, if he sees that half of those peers are women—which would double the odds against any man's receiving the promotion. (Women, of course, have always felt the odds were multiplied against any woman's being promoted.) These costs are likely to reinforce male resistance or sex bias against women in management.

Resistance may also be greater when change is large and rapid, which increases the sense of threat. Anne Harlan and Carol Weiss of the Wellesley College Center for Research on Women observed one company where the number of women in management increased 46 percent in five years, from 1974 to 1979. That brought the proportion past the token barrier, from 13 to 19 percent, in a short time. They found women reporting more bias there than in another company, where the proportion of women increased only 20 percent in the same period, from 5 to 6 percent of the total—a smaller increase, to a new high that was still a smaller, less visible proportion than in the first company, and well below the 15 percent token level.[16]

The higher bias in the first company also reflected the economic context of the period that Harlan and Weiss studied. The company went through a high growth phase followed by a slowdown as economic recession took hold. That combined with the change in the proportion of women managers to increase ambiguity and uncertainty about promotion for many male managers. The second company did not grow in the period under study; it did suffer a decline in the recession that limited opportunity for managers, male or female, but they did not undergo either of the marked changes, in growth and in the number of women managers, that affected the first.[17] The economic factors gave rise to uncertainty and change, which in turn induced frustration and fear in the executives. Every stage of the process strengthened the psychological and sociological forces that promote sexist behavior in the best of times.

Business people mention two of these forces in particular. Both are felt not only by managers but by men in all classes and occupations, but they take different forms in different kinds of work.

One force is psychological: men's fear of women. It may be fear of female talent and energy. On a deeper level it is fear of the combination of competence and sexuality; many men (and women too) see a real and painful conflict between them. At its most basic, it is fear of female rage and of the threat of emasculation that men sense in that rage. Many men attribute such rage to at least some of the women who have reached high management levels—particularly the women who have shown what are seen as masculine kinds of aggression in the quest for or the exercise of power. All these fears, of course, are fears of female power.

The other force is sociological. Male executives, like men in blue-collar and service occupations, are socialized to feel they are superior to women. (Most people, men or women, need someone to look down on to prove that they have power.) In business that translates into the belief that we belong above women at any level of any hierarchy. That makes it very difficult for some men to accept women as peers, and even harder to accept women as bosses.

Both forces are visible on Wall Street, where women make up a quarter of all professionals and from 9 to 19 percent of vice presidents of selected investment banking firms but hold only seven of the six hundred positions of partner or managing director.[18] Fear of the combination of competence and sexuality is manifest crudely in the Goldman Sachs recruiter who asked women at Stanford University if they would have an abortion rather than jeopardize their career, and a trifle more subtly in the merger and acquisitions specialist who growled, "Listen, the business is tough enough without having to deal with a woman's life-style." The notion of male superiority is clear in instructions from one firm that a man sign letters to clients that were drafted by a woman trader; in the relegation of women to specialties like retailing and cosmetics, which were deemed "natural" for them, or to public finance, considered "a place for also-rans"; and in the statement of a senior partner in a small banking house:

> There's been a reluctance on the part of the partners to allow women to develop more than a secondary role. The feeling is, having a woman as the first line of contact might not be the best. A backup role would be preferred.[19]

Fear of women makes itself felt even in men who support women's demands for equality. Carl Woodman* is a real estate developer turned theatrical producer, with a good record for treating women as true peers. He said:

I have this abiding suspicion that in a lot of areas, women are essentially more capable than men. Maybe part of that is because they're trying harder, because we've had it our way for so long. But in most of the fields I see women in, they really have more on the ball than most of the guys. I'm thinking about real estate, some lawyers, some accountants, some bankers. I only comment on it because I think it's part of what scares men. Whether it's their wife or their girlfriend or their colleague, they fear "I may find out that she is more capable than I am, perhaps she'll end up earning more than I earn." They don't want this to happen, and as a result, behind the artifice of support, they lay all sorts of traps that keep it from happening.

And they see all kinds of threats. If you go to parties, most business types sit around going "Glug, argh"; they're extremely nonverbal. Most of their wives, and most of their female colleagues, are much more verbal. I think that frightens them, the notion that all that communicating energy might suddenly explode and be used in ways other than arranging social functions. There are a million threats that surround men all the time.

And we react. I react myself. Whenever I run across a woman I think is tremendously competent, I tend to develop all sorts of adjectives to describe her behavior that are pejorative. "Pushy," "overaggressive," all the rest of it. I find myself doing it frequently enough to know that it's a way I deal with that problem, so I'm able to laugh about it a little bit. Women in a lot of fields who really tend to succeed have precisely the attributes that men are willing to put up with from other men but not from women. To succeed, you've got to be pushy, you've got to be aggressive, you've got to be hard, focused. Some guys when they run up against a woman like that say she wants to cut their balls off. At least I've never caught myself thinking like that, but maybe it's what's underneath all those adjectives I use.

The assumption of male superiority is seldom stated so clearly, but it crops up in almost every conversation about women in business. "Most men just don't like reporting to women because a woman's a woman," said a male manager quoted by Harlan and Weiss. "It's an insult to their intelligence."[20] "Intelligence" isn't the word I would use, but the important word is "insult."

The psychological and sociological forces to which such men give voice are more than the sex-role stereotypes to which we often reduce them. The stereotypes are easy to observe, however, and are the obvious link between those forces and sexist behavior. By questioning people in their two companies, Harlan and Weiss found that, despite the marked similarity between men and women managers, the indirect effects of sex bias accounted for more than 15 percent of the difference in the performance appraisal of men and women and about 5 percent of the promotability ratings.[21]

Increased age, for instance, produced more favorable appraisal of female managers and less favorable ratings of male managers. Longer job and company tenure also produced more favorable ratings for women than for men. I have no doubt that this reflected the old stereotype about younger women being less committed to a career than men and more likely to leave it for marriage or babies. Supervisors who saw a subordinate's potential as high did not reflect it in their evaluations of a woman's performance but did so for men. Supervisors of men whose traits fit senior management's picture of executive capability saw them as highly competent and recommended them for promotion more than they did women who fit that picture. All these patterns surely reflected stereotypes about women's supposed lack of interest in advancement; I suspect they also reflected awareness of the true probability of promotion for women in those companies.

Another study of nearly eight thousand male executives showed "exceedingly high" overall acceptance of women in managerial roles—49.4 percent. But the researchers noted that many answers were "so positively skewed toward women as to cast doubt on their truthfulness." They saw it as progress that men should give what they thought were the right answers rather than the old stereotypes. But they also found many men still agreeing with such statements as "Generally women are not as career-oriented as men" or "A man is better suited for handling executive responsibilities than a woman." They constructed a matrix measuring men's attitudes toward women's abilities (responding to stereotyped statements like those quoted) and toward relationships at work (agreeing or disagreeing with statements like "male subordinates feel inferior when their superiors are female"). They gave no figures but seemed to suggest that few male managers showed true acceptance on both scales.[22]

These stereotypes reflect massive denial. For instance, despite the myth that women do not pursue careers, studies show that in many industries, women in technical, professional, supervisory, and managerial positions turn over at the same rate as men or lower.[23] Male managers often are simply unable to see this; they deny the reality in front of them. They recognize the reality, in contrast, when a woman is aggressive in seeking responsibility. But like Woodman, they often see it as female "pushiness," and they deny that it's a reason for recommending promotion even when they consider it so for men.

TRANSFORMATION

Hostility and denial are ways in which men try to keep women out of a male workplace, to push them out again after they have entered, to limit their achievements, or at the very least to control their activities. In the executive suite overt hostility is constrained compared to the blue-collar world, and denial keeps bumping into reality and into a variety of pressures—from women, from society at large, and from the need to make the best use of "manpower" regardless of gender.

Transformation then becomes even more important here than in lower levels of the work hierarchy as a way to avoid confronting female power, female talent, and female energy in their starkest forms. If we can transform a woman peer or power wielder into wife or mother, whore or nun, into something we "know" how to deal with, we can do two things. We can deal with our fundamental fear of female power by denying that a woman is simultaneously competent and sexual, and thus cushion her and ourselves against our fears and angers. And even though we have not kept her out of the workplace, we can keep her out of the "mainstream of interaction" where we find her difficult to handle. Or we can at least pretend, we can fantasize that we are keeping her out.

This was clearly a major element in the treatment of Mary Cunningham as lover, at a time when there was no evidence she really was Agee's lover, and as wife, at a moment when she was functioning not as wife but as strategist. It is a major element in less dramatic transformations. Some put the women not into domestic or sexual roles, for instance, but into business roles—the old familiar kind. Rosabeth Moss Kanter cites two.[24] One is status leveling—treating an unusual woman like the perceived usual or average woman, particularly treating a professional woman like a secretary. Magazines like *Ms.* and *Savvy* have a constant supply of anecdotes about the vice president or lawyer who is asked to take notes or get coffee. Another is less obviously a transformation, but it has the same effect—establishing a woman's slot, even on managerial and professional levels. Certain personnel jobs, frequently powerless, are familiar examples. So are affirmative action jobs.

Kanter, who uses the term "role encapsulation" rather than "transformation," moves from business roles to "stereotypical roles." One is mother. In training groups in her pseudonymous Industrial Supply Corporation, token women did laundry and sewed on buttons for men—something it is hard to imagine the readers of *Ms.* or *Savvy* doing. Men may also make the "mother" in a work situation an emotional specialist, whom they reward for service but try to keep in her place as a noncritical Good Mother. This prevents her from winning the rewards men give one another for "rational," task-oriented work.

I have been struck as much by the way men transform women into daughters as into mothers, particularly younger female subordinates. "I see enough of that for it to bother the hell out of me," William Trask* told me. He is executive vice president for employee relations of the same conglomerate where I found Roger Mortimer. Trask said:

> I had a senior vice president who was both forced and seduced into hiring a female to be in charge of real estate management for his division. He got to

like her, and he would insist on taking her everywhere with him, treating her like his daughter, like his spoiled daughter. When they went on the golf course one afternoon, he had to have her in his foursome so he could look after her and play father. He was full of paternalistic attitudes. If it distorted his evaluations of her, I don't think it was serious. But it might have affected her career development anyway. She was so concerned about what it was doing to all the other people who were watching it happen. And it might have prevented him from giving her some of the tough tests a subordinate must pass in order to grow.

Men turn peers into wives as well as daughters and mothers, just as they traditionally turned secretaries into office wives, who did everything from buying presents for their "real" wives to doing their laundry. And women may turn male colleagues into husbands. A manager in Trask's conglomerate spoke with amusement about an unmarried female colleague who called him and other male peers repeatedly to do the husband's traditional jobs around her house.

One of the best-known transformations tries to turn a woman peer into a lover. This is not an office affair, happy or unhappy, but a fantasy, whether of man as seducer or of woman as seductress. This fantasy is much older than the contemporary movement of women into men's occupations. It underlies the old charge that the woman who rises is screwing her way to the top. In another version of the fantasy, the man of high status becomes the figurative "protector" of the seductress—in Kanter's words, "gaining through masking his own sexual interest what the other men could not gain by declaring theirs." If he buys her a drink to talk about the problems their male peers give her, for instance, he preserves her role as sex object. The other men may then resent the protector for winning the female prize, or resent the woman for her ability to move close to the protector that they, as men, cannot have. In the guise of helping a woman, a protector may actually put up barriers to her acceptance or advance by making himself an insulator between her and the rest of the group. Even as a fantasy, that particular transformation denies women's competence and entitlement to power much more than transforming her into a mother does. In the opposite or mirror-image transformation, a woman who declines either the fantasy or the real sexual proposition may be cast as an "iron maiden," frigid or repressed, denying not her competence but her sexuality.

Today sexual transformations take new forms that may even admit some competence. A Texas purchasing agent, for instance, does buy from saleswomen, sometimes, but he says he won't take a saleswoman to lunch or even shut his office door when one calls on him, as he does with a salesman. Other men adopt similar tactics. None could really make it clear whether he was imputing uncontrollable sexual aggressiveness to himself or to the women.

In some cases it is the woman who first transforms a work or power relationship into something else. Many do it on male terms, in response to male expectations. I suspect that women who make transformations on their own terms do it less often than men but more aggressively, while men do it more often and more defensively. Women who play this game skillfully are amazed at the ability of their male colleagues to subsist on fantasy.[25] A woman suggests by hint and innuendo, for instance, that she is attracted to a male colleague and would like nothing better than to fall into bed with him—but somehow, something always interferes with every possible opportunity to fall. Next time, she always says with a soulful look and a warm touch, it will certainly happen. But it never does. If the pseudoseduction truly makes the work relationship more effective, the transformation in the male mind is at worst harmless and at best productive. But even then it probably forces the man to underrate the woman's competence by making her as much lover as peer. That may be why most women of real ability today are unwilling to act out the pseudoseduction fantasy and seldom even perceive it as a possibility.

Women executives in the old days seldom cooperated in real or fantasied seductions. The women who had risen to the highest positions in American firms in the 1960s tended to have neither marriages nor long-term relationships with men until they stopped and reassessed their positions when they reached a job plateau about the age of thirty-five. Then those surveyed by Margaret Hennig discovered that they could be women and managers.[26] Half of them married between the ages of thirty-five and forty and the rest remained open to the idea of marriage even in their fifties. Those who married chose older men, all of them fathers, all widowed or divorced, all with earned income more than double their wives'. The husbands saw no clash between career and femininity and were delighted when their wives rose on the corporate ladder.

The husbands' success—and perhaps some guilt from their earlier days— enabled them to transcend the anger, fear, anxiety, and shame that individual men feel at the conjunction of career and gender, the combination of competence and sexuality in the same beings. They also transcended the collective belief that society cannot exist without the traditional division of labor. Today's executives feel these difficulties even more strongly as more and more women enter their workplace. The difficulties are something managers have in common with men in other classes and other kinds of work, but both the problems and the consequences are magnified because managers tell other men what to do. The husbands of Hennig's women managers showed that it is possible to overcome the difficulties. Some of the women's colleagues, though most had not achieved as much success as the husbands, were also secure enough to overcome. They did not use either of the traditional ways of dealing with the conflict.

One is to escape it by transformation. Our fantasies may transform women from peers into seductresses. That removes the conflict by removing their competence and making them totally sexual. Other fantasies may deny women's sexuality just as completely, which happens not only when we turn them into iron maidens, but also when we turn them into mothers, often when we turn them into daughters, and sometimes, ironically, when we turn them into wives. Transforming women into such nonsexual beings seldom leaves them supremely competent at work in our fantasy worlds, however.

The other traditional way of dealing with the conflict is to deny sexuality in real life. Some people do this by making it a commandment never to have an office affair—or never even to shut the office door when they're with a woman peer. Others reject the idea of sex between office peers by calling attractive women unfit for management. Tests of business students and managers show that both men and women rate attractive men and unattractive women high for managerial jobs. Attractive women receive only small percentages of the top rankings and are seen as having less competence and integrity. Madeline Heilman and Melanie Stopeck cite research showing that an attractive man is seen as more masculine and an attractive woman as more feminine. Top jobs are believed to require "uniquely masculine skills and talents for success," so people with feminine attributes are thought to be unqualified. "Simply put," the researchers say, "they were most often believed to have gotten where they were for reasons other than their skill and/or talent."[27] This denies not the sexuality of the attractive women but any justification for their bringing it into an executive suite.

Men can also learn to develop nonsexual relationships with sexually attractive women peers without denying their sexuality entirely. This disentangles competence from sexuality rather than denying the possibility of or insisting on the danger of the combination. It is neither easy nor traditional, but often a difficult, painful change. But more and more men are learning how to do it.

SEXUALITY IN THE OFFICE

Not all real-life conduct is based on a refusal to let competence and sexuality combine. A few of us love discovering that the two really can come together. Others are neutral on competence but welcome serious or casual romance with women at work.[28] Still others may exploit women at work sexually, or harass them, which is as much a demonstration of power as a matter of sex.

But whichever of these things we do, we usually cannot help but see women as sexual. We are constantly finding ourselves forced to respond to a mixture of sexuality and work that we have barely begun to learn to deal with. Our responses usually show that in this situation the baggage of anger, fear, and other negative feelings that we carry outweighs our pride, identification, and other positive feelings.

Jack Mason* is a young corporate president, a man who runs his own electric products company in New York City. When we talked about sex and management, he said, "An attractive woman is very threatening to a middle-aged executive sitting behind a desk." I asked him why, and he said:

Because she has control. All of the props that men use traditionally, the bigger desk, the large office, the big chair, all those things are to impose authority and control of a situation. Now an attractive woman walks in to do business and crosses her legs, and the guy's reacting, right? Who's in control? She's in control. And that's very threatening to a lot of people.

Mason's awareness of negative feelings in the threat did not lead inevitably, in his view, to negative behavior. A story from his own recent experience showed how consciousness of sexuality might work both for and against sexual activity.

People make a mistake when they deny their sexuality. You can't deny that there's a pull, that there's a hormonal thing going on. That doesn't mean you sleep with everybody you deal with, but you have to understand that you're going to have these feelings. A rep called on me about a year ago to sell me some printing, an attractive lady. There is no question that sexuality was present, that she used that. First she invited me to lunch, a business lunch. She picked me up in the corridor and I said, "Well, let's go to the diner down the block and not to the fancy Italian restaurant," because I wasn't going to let her do this with things still in the bid stage. We went to the diner and I said, "Look, let's get this on the table right now. You're obviously attractive and obviously I'd like to go to bed with you. But I'm not going to. We can't deny the level of sexuality, but we're not going to play the game because there's too much money involved here, and it's very hard to deal with you on business when there's so much sex hanging in the air. I just want you to know that." And you know, she said, "You're making it a lot easier for me."

Mason added, "Afterward, I screwed her. After the whole thing was over. We were sexually attracted, and when there was no longer any chance of the sex interfering with the business, we went to bed." For him that crude effort to disentangle competence from sexuality was part of *not* denying the sexuality. Mason's life history had made him conscious of his and his women colleagues' sexuality and explicit in his thinking and his conversation about them. (He had blue-collar Jewish parents; he had served in the Navy and gone to a state university before making money; he was divorced and had been through several years of psychotherapy.) I doubt that he realized that some women might find his words graceless and angry.

Roger Mortimer, the Ivy Leaguer transplanted to California in the service of William Trask's conglomerate, seemed more typical of the large-corporation executive in his very ambivalence, his being conscious of sexuality at work without being as explicit as Mason. That is, Mortimer used either polite or business language to talk about sexuality where Mason used sexual language.

As more women come into the work force, sexual tensions undoubtedly start, they undoubtedly make it a little more difficult at first, they undoubtedly make it a little bit more interesting as things go along. I think they probably don't interfere. If one doesn't like a particular woman, the emotion isn't that powerful and they don't interfere. If one does like her, it would interfere only if it went to the point of wanting to actuate it somehow and one was frustrated in progressing with the relationship. Or else the relationship would progress and become a romance.

Mason was quick to see that sexual tensions might interfere with work, while Mortimer thought they would not. Phil Randall,* a Chicago management consultant, was one of several men who saw sexual tensions as carrying more positive possibilities. "There's something exciting about working with a person of the opposite sex when the work is going well," he said. "I'm talking about a situation where a man and woman are professional peers, so the man does not really have more power. On some occasions for some men it can be more exciting than doing the same kind of work with a man."

A retail chain buyer saw sexual tensions as exciting and possibly bad for productivity at the same time. He was friends but not lovers with a woman merchandiser, and he liked the extra dimensions that the friendship gave his work, particularly the insights she had as a woman on the business world, which he found "enriching." But he said, "It can be bad for business because it takes your eye off the ball." It was his job as a buyer to select a vendor for a product, and hers to make sure he and the vendor got that product to the right stores on a schedule that fit the marketing campaign. He felt that sometimes her liking for him had made her "less insistent on nudging me and the vendor to get the merchandise shipped than she should be."

Sexual tensions are one band of a spectrum that includes relationships of many kinds with fellow workers, from use of the office as singles bar to true love; both low and high have often been included under the rubric, "office romance." Most men and most companies, I suspect, don't trust either the personal or the professional effects of these romances. One recent study of 130 romances found that 90 percent of them lowered job performance and productivity. Co-workers were jealous and resentful. Robert Quinn, a management specialist, saw men using the most serious relationships for ego gratification while women used them for power and said, "That's really explosive." In 10 percent of his cases, one romantic partner was fired—and it was the woman twice as often as the man.[29]

From the company's point of view, firing someone may be necessary in far more than 10 percent of the cases. That at least was Eliza Collins's recommendation in a 1983 article in the *Harvard Business Review* that received much media attention.[30] Collins took the position that when two high-level managers are in the most serious kind of love, it is almost inevitably in conflict with the company's interests. They form, or are thought to form, a coalition against other executives. If their departments often conflict, or ought to, their love for each other as people may make them unable to deal with it. Their equality as lovers may contradict their rank in the hierarchy. Collins recommends that the chief executive fire at least one of the lovers—the "least essential" to the company, who she regrets will usually be the woman, since even in the 1980s, the woman usually ranks lower and has less experience than the man. She also urges the chief to help the fired executive to find a new and perhaps better job, and in her four examples, the women did find jobs as good as or better than the old ones and the lovers eventually married. (The media, trumpeting the recommendation to fire the women, overlooked the happy endings Collins reported.)

I don't believe that love and work *always* conflict in the ways that Collins describes. I was both sad and angry that she recommended no changes in the corporate culture to make the conflict less common, to make it less necessary to fire a managerial lover. I can't believe it's inevitable that relationships between managers and departments be so neurotic, so destructively competitive. I think it's possible to hire an A, B, and C who won't speedily become insecure or even paranoid when colleagues X and Y fall in love—as Collins describes them doing, and as they did in the Agee-Cunningham story.

Women executives furnish one proof that the world no longer works only in the fashion Collins depicts. *Savvy* magazine published a survey in 1985 in which 55 percent of female executives (median income, $39,000) said they had had sexual encounters with co-workers without any heavy penalty to their careers.[31] That was two years after Collins published her article, perhaps enough time to allow for major changes in the corporate culture. But several male executives I interviewed before her article appeared recognized that things had already changed. Phil Randall, the Chicago consultant, said:

> The fact that people who work together can have affairs is something that companies have to allow for. They have to get it into their managers' heads not to prejudge people automatically, not to penalize them. . . . Of course, you can have someone of either sex whose love affairs even outside the company can undermine his work. A corporation should deal with any relationship that lowers productivity in a way that could be called "responsible," case by case, without legislating against all relationships. And I hope they'll look carefully at teams of men and women whose love—or whatever relationship outside the office—makes them more creative at work. I've seen some and I know they exist.

The spectrum of office sexuality also includes the infra and ultra of harassment. It still happens. But one significant change is that more and more male executives admit it happens, even while accused offenders still deny it almost universally. More and more governments and corporations have issued rules to control and punish it, and more and more victims are willing to protest.

Many people still think of the primary offender in harassment cases as the male boss who tries to exploit his female subordinates, particularly secretaries and clerks. That still happens, of course. But a survey of harassment in the federal work force shows that co-workers and other employees now outnumber supervisors among identified offenders.[32] My research suggests this is also true in many corporations. The reason is obvious: the arrival of women in traditionally masculine jobs and levels of work has enabled the man who must harass women at work to find peers to pick on. When he does, he is acting like the blue-collar man, using his sexual aggressiveness to replace the power over women that he can no longer claim hierarchically.

Another change shows more and more men claiming to be victims of sexual harassment. (In the federal survey, 42 percent of all women and 15 percent of all men reported being sexually harassed.) Some of this is homosexual contact. Some is conflicting perception: a woman may see a touch of her hand as nurturing and a man may see it as sexual (though women often charge a man with sexual harassment when he thinks he is only trying to communicate through touch). But part of the male charge of harassment certainly reflects both women's liberation and sexual liberation—the increasing readiness of women to take a sexual initiative.

It may seem hard to believe the fat, bald, fifty-six-year-old manager of a retail store who claims that his female employees harass him sexually. But Working Women's Institute defines harassment as "any attention of a sexual nature in the context of the work situation which has the effect of making a woman uncomfortable on the job, impeding her ability to do her work or interfering with her employment opportunities." By extension, it can be any attention that makes a man uncomfortable, even a young woman's invitation to an older man for an evening out that ends in a motel room, or another's suggestion that older men prefer blowjobs. The Chicago manager who complained was perfectly aware that it was his power as an employer and not his body that made up most of his sex appeal (which made him consistent with Quinn's study of office romances). He insisted that he did not exploit that power. He was both plaintive and indignant when he told a newspaper columnist, "It's not fair for women to complain about the same thing they've always done themselves. If a man does it, it's harassment. If a woman does it, it's just exerting her freedom."[33]

In a classic case of male harassment, David Huebschen of the Wisconsin Department of Health and Social Services won $196,500 in compensatory and punitive damages in 1982 from both his former supervisor, Jacquelyn Rader, and her boss, Bernard Stumbras. Huebschen claimed Rader demoted him after he rejected her advances, though she had earlier praised his work in a written evaluation and recommended him for a pay raise. He charged Stumbras with "callous indifference" to his complaint. The amount was a record, and Isabelle Pinzler of the American Civil Liberties Union commented, "Sexual harassment is a pervasive problem for women, not for men, yet you don't see this kind of award for women." Women in fact have won several six-figure sexual harassment awards. The federal court jury in the Huebschen case was five women and one man, so the award could hardly be described as an example of male backlash. But it was certainly a commentary on the newly recognized (if in this case traditionally styled) power of the woman boss. The amount of the reward was reduced on appeal to $35,000 for back pay and attorney's fees, but the verdict and the implicit commentary were sustained.

THE WOMAN BOSS

Every aspect of male response to women's arrival in the management workplace is reinforced or intensified when men are dealing with a woman boss. The fear of female talent, female energy, and female rage is subsumed in the fear of female power, which combines reaction to the familiar power of a boss with response to a female power that is strange to adults but familiar to the unconscious memory of infancy. The habit of assuming male superiority is forced to confront a hierarchically superior female. All the other problems of human beings in organizations, from the tendency of policy to weaken as it filters down to the transformation of women into other guises, make themselves felt more sharply when the boss is a woman.

This makes basic male hostility to a female boss unsurprising. Yet we often hide from it or deny it, and that in turn may make us find it remarkable when we have to face it. Two magazines covering women as bosses emphasized the same classic case of the seven male vice presidents of Butterick and Vogue Patterns. They met at the all-male New York Athletic Club in 1974 to consider what to do about their new boss, Jane Evans, a woman then only thirty. Most wanted to resign en masse, but one man with four children to support persuaded the others to adopt this idea: "We'll give her three months and if she doesn't shape up, then we'll resign." Evans learned about the meeting, called them in, and told them they had more to prove to her as their boss than she had to prove to them. "That came as a bit of a shock to them, for up to that point, they had looked at me as a woman—not as their boss." The story also shows that male resistance can be overcome. Evans made the men a bet that they would find her the easiest boss they had ever had. A year later, five of them (one had been fired and one had died) paid off in roses and a check for fifty dollars. Evans later went on to top-level jobs in two other companies where the men presumably either were less hostile or hid their feelings in a more sophisticated manner.[34]

Nick Stabler* is a vice president of a consumer goods company who reports to a senior vice president who happens to be a woman. He has worked with her for four years, moving up one level in tandem with her (but not as mentor and protégé since she is two years younger than he and has spent fewer years with the company). He says:

When I first started reporting to Alison, I wondered whether she was strong enough to be a good boss. It didn't take me three months to find out that she was. But that made me listen to a lot of guys who reported to her or to women in a couple of other companies. They'd gripe about how much this broad or that one was working them twice as hard to prove to her bosses that she was as strong as a man. Then they'd bitch about how their company still didn't give this woman any credibility or any clout, so they'd suffer from working for a weak boss. Or they'd say some other woman who was pushing them still didn't know how to manage or to delegate. It was a real double bind. And two or three could never admit that any woman knew how to manage, even if she had ten years as an executive or a Harvard MBA.

Talk about the inadequacies of a woman boss may seem silly, but it often has consequences that are serious. Bob Bannister* works in one of the federal bureaucracies that regulates business. His boss for many years, Jim, was a branch chief, "a very traditional man" who had a lot of trouble reporting to a woman who was assistant director over him.

He could not cope at all. He used to try to make fun of her, belittle her. He was also afraid of her. He didn't try to sabotage the work, because that would have come back on him. But he'd sabotage her authority, verbally, behind her back. It affected our work, the work of the staff under him. We were put into a constant position of opposition to her. Jim's whole attitude was, "It's us versus her." That wasn't the case.

I put sufficient pressure on so they'd move me and I wouldn't have to deal with the problems that resulted. I went into another branch where the branch chief was again a man, still under the same woman. His attitude was "Let's go see Julie and see if we can work it out." Jim's reaction was "We've got to go see Julie because we've got a problem." He'd go down and present the problem and let you take the heat, because he was afraid of her. Seldom if ever was she wrong. She was an accountant and I think she probably forgot more about our regulations than he would ever know. It got so that nobody in the branch would go down with him without taking at least half an hour to go over whatever it was so they'd be prepared. That was a real cost in productivity, if you admit that there's ever productivity in government.

Robert Schrank, then of the Ford Foundation, wrote an unusual and unusually moving confession of male sabotage of a female boss, which he published in a journal that might be thought unusual for either that confession or those emotions—again, the *Harvard Business Review*.[35] It described two women and three men on an Outward Bound raft trip through many rapids down the Rogue River in Oregon. All the tasks of outdoor survival kept bringing out macho stereotypes for both sexes even as the people of Raft No. 4 showed "a *real* concern for each other as mutually suffering humans." When one of the women was helmsperson and cried out, "I can't do it," the men (except for one, John, who was an Outward Bound guide) tried to convince her that she could—but in half hearted and infantilizing ways. Schrank reported:

> As the days wore on, Bill and I proceeded subtly but surely to take charge. The teamwork was unraveling. When we approached a tongue, if either Marlene or Helen were helmsperson, Bill and I would look at each other, and with very slight headaches and grimaces we would indicate agreement that things were not going well at all. Once we had established that things were not going well, we then felt free to take our own corrective measures, such as trying to steer the raft from our forward paddle positions. . . . The unaware helmsperson is then totally out of control. When that would happen . . . Bill's and my disgust would mount.

On the fifth day, in a fast-moving chute, Marlene froze and gave no command, the raft slid up on a boulder and flipped over, and five people had a narrow escape from death by water. Schrank analyzed what had happened:

> When one of the other two men was in charge I was comfortable, supportive, and worked to help him be a better helmsperson. When a woman was at the helm, I seemed to direct my activity at getting her replaced rapidly by one of the men.
>
> A most revealing part of the raft experience . . . [was] how Bill and I unconsciously or automatically responded to protect our power from female encroachment. When the trip started I knew that I might have some difficulty accepting a woman at the helm, but I did not realize that the threat would be so great that I would actually desire to see her fail. On that trip I did something new: I actively tried to sabotage Marlene's and Helen's efforts to lead.

Schrank went on to compare his raft trip with organizational life. "There," he said, "the male need to be in charge in the presence of females may be subtle, which may make it harder to identify than on a raft on a swift-flowing river." But he believed that "what happened on Raft No. 4, Inc. occurs in most organizations when women enter positions of leadership." And he suspected that a woman boss faces not just one man who withholds support, but others who reinforce that withholding, that nonsupport that rapidly becomes opposition. This kind of sabotage, Schrank says, "is a collective activity. . . . Women trying to navigate most organizations may find them more complex than the Rogue, but they need to look for similar hazards. The sleepers and chutes will be vested groups of men, who, when their power is threatened, will pull any woman down for tinkering with their interests."

Some men, of course, are exceptions to Schrank's generalization. I interviewed several men who reported that they had less trouble adjusting to a female boss than to a female peer. Some of them found it natural, consciously or unconsciously, to take orders from a woman. In some cases that may have revealed something about their relations with their wives or lovers. But if the woman was older, said New York communications executive Matt Friedman,* ready acceptance of her as boss

> was probably because we were used to taking orders from mother. My first job was working for a woman who was very motherly, very much a giver of instructions, very possessive. At one point I went away for a week's vacation that I had earned. I didn't tell her where I was going. When I came back, she was so enraged at my vanishing act that she fired me. How motherly was that? Sometimes I think it was very motherly.

Later he spent twelve years working for another woman who was seventeen years older than he was.

> Elizabeth was brilliant and knowledgeable and she really became my mentor. That was very unusual. I loved working for her, and she taught me everything about the business. Then I became president of the company and she was one of my subordinates. That was very complex. Partly because things fell apart at that company. I tried to buy it and failed. She got disgusted and quit and later wound up as chief planning officer in a firm that had never had a female executive. But that all happened at the same time that I moved into my mid-life crisis and had to get away from my mentor. When she had to work for me, she never weakened or became dependent. But the younger person can take over without the older collapsing. Later, when my own parents moved into a retirement community— not a nursing home, a retirement community—I wondered if there wasn't some of that in my relations with Elizabeth, if I hadn't unconsciously seen her as a parent who had been forced to acknowledge her child as the responsible person in the family.

Some men, unlike Matt, have major problems with the boss as mother. They have never truly resolved their conflicts with their own mothers, and their problems return when they have to face a woman in authority anew, even or especially as adults.[36]

They are sometimes among the men who transform a woman boss into a lover rather than a mother, especially if she is younger than her male subordinates. It's significant, as all folklore is culturally significant, that the sex letters in *Penthouse* have begun to "describe" sex with the boss, though usually on a low level of the hierarchy. This transformation also occurs in real life, as John Tedesco,* a sales executive in the fashion industry, saw in 1980 when he worked for a woman president.

She was young, brilliant, single, and very attractive. A couple of men were afraid she'd cut their balls off. I gathered that a couple of others had made passes at her. I never saw that she punished the guys who made passes. But one left the company while she was still there, and the other never earned the bonuses he had expected. The only reason I didn't make a pass was that I didn't know what the rules were in that situation. But I realized afterward that I was just like the others. None of us really knew how to have a nonsexual relationship with a woman. I learned for the first time, reporting to her, that such a thing was possible for me. Maybe it was the first time I realized that such a thing even existed.

HOW THINGS ARE CHANGING

Many men are learning, as Tedesco did, that it is indeed possible to have a nonsexual relationship with a woman, especially a woman peer, without denying her sexuality entirely. This realization has grown as American society has absorbed both the women's movement and the therapeutic subculture. It is one reason that things *are* changing, sometimes slowly, sometimes suffering backlash or reversal. They are changing faster in the business world than in the blue-collar world and many service occupations.

Things are changing as men look at the morality of the issue and as they look at personal and corporate interests. Businessmen in small but growing numbers have modified some of their negative feelings, some of their stereotyped attitudes and some of their sexist behavior. Sometimes this is the result of conscious effort; more often, I suspect, it's the result of unconscious processes flowing from women's achievements or their mere presence. Often this kind of change makes a counterpoint with continuing sexist behavior even in the same men. But even then it opens possibilities for the use of both men's and women's talent and energy that would otherwise be wasted.

One of the major reasons men are changing is their sudden but long-overdue realization that there is a huge pool of talent out there that was, and all too often still is, wasted because it happened to be female. Mike Modzelewski,* the data-processing executive in the auto industry (see Chapter 6), said:

> It drives me up the wall when men act as though women are not as intelligent and persevering and hungry to achieve as they are. I hated it when I realized that not only in our organization but in general women just weren't being utilized. I thought it was a crime, a tremendous shame, that there was that much talent available, that we simply didn't make use of it. I put myself in the male category and said, for whatever reasons of fear and insecurity, we've developed this attitude. It was just very difficult for me to sit back and let it happen.

Mike used to be like the men who drive him up the wall, with a full complement of traditional attitudes. Two things made him change. One was running head on into his department head's prejudices against women who were already in the workplace, which Mike could see was lowering both actual and potential productivity. The other, more important event came in 1975, when his daughter, then twelve years old, came home from school one day and started talking as though nursing and teaching were the only things that girls could do.

It really upset me to realize that here I was going to have a truly close, firsthand example of an enormous talent going to waste. It was incredible for me to realize that at her early age she was already conditioned to this kind of situation. It just blew my mind. I said, "Well, Karen, you really don't have to limit yourself to those kinds of professions." She said, "What else can I be?" I said, off the top of my head, "Well, you could be a lawyer." And she replied, "But Uncle Dick is a lawyer, I can't be a lawyer." And this was already 1975. I told her that Uncle Dick's being a lawyer didn't mean she couldn't be. We would talk about it from then on, not on a regular basis, but the topic would come up. . . . I wrote a paper shortly after that, in a course I was taking for a master's, on America's greatest wasted resource. It was women.

The talk with Karen and the paper he wrote brought home to Mike what all the women's agitation for equality and choice was about. He still has doubts about the Equal Rights Amendment and the men's movement, but he wants women to be able to do anything they want. Today Karen is a college sophomore taking sophisticated math and philosophy courses and aiming at either law or business school. When Mike's wife wanted to reenter the world of work, he encouraged her to do it at the professional rather than the secretarial level. He doesn't feel he's done as much to change his own work world as he has to change his family, but he has helped three women to win promotion, and he keeps trying.

Many executives have found themselves compelled by numbers to recognize the size and quality of the female talent pool. The proportion of women in all executive, administrative, and managerial jobs, including entry- and middle-level posts, has gone up from 19.6 percent in 1972 to 33.6 percent in 1984, rising steadily even in the Reagan era.[37] Women account for more than 30 percent of MBAs and law school graduates. The men who deal with these women often emphasize something they had not expected to see: the ability of women to do "masculine" work as well as, or the same way as, men do.

Roger Mortimer, for instance, thought his conglomerate had changed since the influx of women MBAs started. He saw them and many of his women peers as aggressive in a productive way:

A woman in a senior category, her aggressiveness tends not to be deployed against the company or against oneself as the boss. Her aggressiveness makes her want more and more responsibility, to be given broader scope. Those women can be dealt with easily because they tend to be strong people that one can rely on, in which case they're a help and a support.

Other managers prize women for doing "masculine" jobs better than men do. Carl Woodman saw women as more capable than men in many fields, though he spoke of it in connection with men's fears rather than their joys. Marvin Rutman,* a California purchasing director, saw women, like new immigrants and ethnic minorities, as the heirs of an old American standard:

When I was growing up, it was part of the work ethic to be enthusiastic, develop your skills, and work harder than the next guy and you'll get ahead. With young people today, the males don't have that work ethic and all of a sudden the females do. I generally hire three or four women for every guy I pick. And so far, I've seen six of the women I hired go from very junior levels to senior buyers and above. They're the ones with the ambition and the guts and the willingness to sacrifice for the future.

Some men said women were valuable in business because they *don't* do things the same way men do. They often put the differences in stereotypical terms but remodeled them into advantages. Phil Randall, the management consultant, said he had often seen women enrich business discussions because their minds and ideas are different from men's. Some of his clients had developed a desire to suspend the "rational" thinking that businessmen prize in themselves, as people learned that other mental processes also produce results —"women's intuition," presumed sensitivity, and right-brain thinking (the latter also found in artists) among them. Randall also offered as one example what he saw as the female tendency to shift from pure task orientation to a concern with what made people feel better, which he said often improved employee morale and therefore productivity. He gave women in management as much credit as the lobbying of the women's movement for a few corporations' adoption of policies that ease conflicts between work and family, such as full-time fringe benefits for part-time employees, flextime working hours, job sharing, and paternity leave. Nick Stabler spoke of women lawyers who persuaded their boss to abolish hierarchical titles in a corporate law department where all professionals were equal. In the retail chain I visited, after their new boss told them the company had to change its WASP male image or die, executives started voicing the thought that women executives provided better understanding than men of female employees and customers.

All these changes in male consciousness and corporate behavior provide an important contrast to what I have been emphasizing, men's resistance to the arrival of women in management. They add up to a sign of a happier future.

Yet in business as in other worlds, many women see their hopes of change as having been set back in the Reagan era. Women have been laid off even on the executive level for lack of seniority. Male managers have felt freer than they did in the 1970s to voice their old fears and prejudices, to suggest that the answer to the discomfort they feel with women peers is to bar or minimize the presence of women in the executive workplace, to discriminate. Others recognize that it's both more moral and more efficient to remove not the women but the causes of discomfort in men. But that in itself may be uncomfortable; a lot of hostility, denial, and transformation is expressed in both processes.

This makes it all the more important to say that the executive suite is one of many places where I think the revolution is irreversible. True, it has made only small gains. Whatever the proportion of all managers, only eight of every thousand employed women hold high-level executive or managerial jobs, and women occupy only 3 percent of the sixteen thousand seats on the boards of the thousand largest corporations.[38] Women are seldom treated as true equals; victory, whether on traditional masculine terms or on new, still-to-be-defined terms, is still a long way away. But small clues are significant. *Savvy* found twenty-two corporations in the 1980s that were well-managed, profitable organizations "where women would find people eager to help them succeed and programs designed to ensure that success."[39] The number of corporations that give women this kind of opportunity is small, and I have interviewed men in some of these very companies who still show much more anger, fear, and anxiety than relief, admiration, or pleasure, who still flee from women peers into hostility, denial, and transformation. They raise the cost of change. But they will eventually conform to the wishes of top managements that make sure their commitment to opportunity for women filters down. Not all, probably not even a majority, but still many of their middle-management colleagues are already changing their minds—some out of a Pauline conversion, some out of self-interest. Companies like American Telephone & Telegraph and Equitable Life train managers to overcome bias and reward supervisors who advance women and minorities; as a result, AT&T quadrupled the number of women in upper-level jobs over eight years, while Equitable had fifty-five women officers and four women on its board of directors in 1984.[40] Citicorp had women in 35.6 percent of its managerial positions in 1983 (the last year it released such a figure), and that will probably be as important in the long run as its having only one woman on its policy committee as late as 1985. Procter & Gamble has raised the percentage of women among its officials, managers, and professionals from 3.7 percent in 1973 to 18.5 percent in 1985. That makes a curious contrast with its ridiculously traditional toilet paper commercials and soap operas (in the 1980s no woman has yet been able to have both a career and a happy marriage on "Another World"), but it suggests that even a bastion of provincial stereotype has recognized reality. That kind of suggestion makes me feel the odds are good against reversing the tide of change.

Chapter 8
PROFESSIONS

Phyllis Wolf* was chief of infectious medicine in a Boston hospital. That meant she worked, in effect, as a consultant. A resident or attending physician would call her in and say, "This patient has a fever that his illness doesn't explain; would you see if he has an infectious problem?" She sometimes discovered that the patient had not only an infection but a cardiac problem or a kidney problem that the doctor in charge was not managing well. She was very conscious of the need to find tactful, diplomatic ways to deal with such situations, and ready to admit that she did not always succeed. Her boss, the chief of medicine, called her in once and said, "Phyllis, you're doing a very nice job and teaching very well, but—well, a lot of the residents complain that you're too acrid, you're too blunt with them, you embarrass them. Couldn't you please handle it in a better way?" She said she kept trying to do it better—but she resented his not giving a similar lecture to equally blunt and acrid male specialists.

Residents once resisted her, and her bluntness, with a combination of denial and hostility that was so clear it reached the point of transparence. "These doctors asked me to consult, and I found they really had botched it," she said. "They really should have known better. But I was in a terrific mood, and I was feeling magnanimous, and I said to myself, 'I will not attack them, I will just control myself and not tell them what schmucks they are.' I was very nice about it and said, 'Don't you think you might have diagnosed such-and-such for the following reasons.' I was really very happy."

Phyllis went off on vacation with that sense of satisfaction. When she returned, she discovered that the doctors had not followed her advice, or reported her diagnosis as the rules required, or changed their own. Instead, they had presented the case to the chief of medicine as if she had supported their original incorrect diagnosis and course of treatment, when she had in fact done just the opposite. When she learned this, she called a conference at which the doctors had to present the case again before the whole staff; their mistake, her correct diagnosis, and their misrepresentation of it came out. She made the offenders uncomfortable, taught them a lesson in medicine and ethics, and showed the house staff the right way to handle that medical problem.

I asked Ben Sherman,* the doctor who had misrepresented things, if he had been responding to her being a woman in power in his professional field. "Certainly not" was his first reply. Would he then lie to anyone in authority to protect himself? "Never. Absolutely not. You can look at my record. No other chief, no male chief of service has ever accused me of that." I suggested that his use of the word "male," combined with his denial of the facts of the consultation in his report to the chief of medicine while Phyllis was on vacation, showed his hostility to her as a woman of power. Eventually he admitted that he might have been affected by the fact that the person who had caught him in a serious error was a woman. "I went to medical school before girls started to take so many of the places there," he said. "When I grew up, there was something unnatural about a woman having the power I saw in a doctor. And I grew up with the feeling that becoming a doctor was like preparing for knighthood." In his mind the rituals for entry into pre-med, medical school, and residency could be attained only by "great sacrifice by a man and his family." He spoke constantly but not always consciously in terms of male deeds, male competence, and male stamina—of brotherhood. It was clear that a woman, though he did not say this in so many words, simply did not belong in a body that combined ritual, sacrifice, and act.

MALE ELITES, MEN'S WORK

Dr. Sherman's reluctant answer illustrated a number of feelings that men in the professions have about women in their work—not only in medicine, but in law, architecture, science, engineering, academia, and the clergy. People in these occupations think of themselves as members of elites. These elites can be entered only after training that is sometimes scientific, always arduous, and—most important of all—possessed of a sacramental character. Few other occupations demand such training (though the rise of business schools and the MBA degree makes some executives professional in this sense). Professionals still think and speak of themselves as though they were independent and self-employed, another mark of an elite in our mythology, although in fact they are increasingly becoming employees or at least working in organizations (like hospitals, law firms, and universities). Whether independent or organizational, they are proud of the sixty- or seventy-hour weeks that many of them work; long hours are an elite badge they like to show off.

Law and medicine are also elites in terms of earnings and status, with other professions close behind (though the highest level of corporate executives, entertainers, and athletes make more and the clergy earn less than other professionals). Most professions are elites in terms of power over society (like lawyers in both politics and the economy), or over individuals (like doctors with nurses and patients). Even the elites that seem least powerful connect with power; academics train leaders or do research that produces tools for leaders, while clergy mediate between people and God, still the ultimate power in many minds. Members of these professions control standards of performance by the kind of monitoring that has become known as peer review, and recruitment by a process that sociologists call gatekeeping—both phrases with overtones from the age of chivalry, when men were men and male roles were male roles. Such elites keep their numbers small for economic as well as social and psychological reasons to make sure that incomes stay high and that the market is not glutted by large numbers of people who claim they can do the difficult work.

The economic interest reinforces each elite's behavior and sense of itself as a community whose members define themselves as insiders with particular differences from the large group of outsiders. The important thing here is that men always see women as "others." The characteristics of long hours, higher earnings, and power also have a masculine stamp for many, probably most, Americans. These qualities combine to make these elites very special examples of the male bond, something few social scientists have noticed. At least they were examples of the bond in years gone by. (It was a white male bond, of course, and blacks were also excluded or confined to a few entry points.) The arrival of women in large numbers in law and medical schools in the past decade makes it hard to maintain the bond in those professions; it seems stronger in architecture, engineering, and the "hard" sciences, and its strength is one reason that fewer women make the effort to enter those fields. Yet the numbers there are also rising; if more women tried those professions, they might further erode the bond and some of the other forces that block them as they have in law and medicine.

But in all these elites in the 1980s, either an active male bond or the residues left after it starts to wither still generate important feelings in men that affect the way they treat women who claim to be their peers. These emotions make it harder for professional men than any other group except factory workers to accept sexuality and competence in the same person, or to take orders from a woman. As members of elites, they have class interests in common with business executives, but their psychology is at least as close to that of blue-collar men (something I may be the first to have seen).

At the same time, many Americans, again probably most, have come to recognize the right and the ability of women to qualify for professional elites. And many members of these professions present themselves as modern and liberal—as educated people often think they should be. This makes many professional men eager to welcome women into their elites, once they make the discovery (which sometimes surprises them) that women have been excluded. When their old male emotions meet their new intellectual ideals, professionals become highly ambivalent, more ambivalent than men in other fields of work, in an effort to accept women without giving up the subconscious notion of the professional elite as a brotherhood.

These characteristics give law, medicine, and architecture an immense amount in common in the way they deal with women who demand to be treated as the equals of men in those professions. All three kept women in token status, at best, until the mid-1970s and are now admitting women in roughly the same proportions as they apply after finishing professional school.* All three are slow to promote women to positions of power in the same proportions; women still tend to be restricted, or in lower positions than men, in specialties, income, and place in a hierarchy.

Men in all three professions speak about their work as man's work. They are quick to add that this is a notion from the past that is rapidly disappearing, that they don't really mean women are *incapable* of the tasks. But many go on to voice ideas or feelings from that past, and a majority in my interviews spoke of one thing that makes their jobs man's work—the long hours of labor, especially in the years before becoming a partner in a law firm, finishing a medical residency, or getting an architect's license. Men in the sciences, particularly those where significant discoveries are being made, speak about the necessity of long hours in the same way. This is another way in which professionals resemble blue-collar men, who also speak of long hours of work and the years needed to learn a craft. Some men in both groups feel women can't work this hard, some feel that women don't want to, and a large majority feel the hours and years are incompatible with motherhood—with what they see as the woman's job of not only bearing but also caring for her children.

The similarities among the professions seem more important to me than the differences, but the differences are real. Law and medicine have admitted a greater proportion of women than architecture. In my interviews, lawyers expressed more acceptance of women than did members of the other professions. (A 1973 survey showed lawyers seeing more discrimination in their own field than doctors or architects did, but I suspect this only means that lawyers deny less and are aware of discrimination more than people in the other professions.[3]) The law was indeed even more of a men's club than medicine was before the 1960s, perhaps because it focused on such "masculine" activities as crime, finance, and politics, while some parts of medicine seemed to fit "feminine" nurturing capacity. But the bar is closer than other

* The proportion of women among lawyers rose from 4.7 percent in 1970 to 16.1 percent in 1984. The proportion of women in law school rose from 8.5 to 37.7 percent. The proportion of women among physicians rose from 8 percent in 1970 to 16 percent in 1984, while the proportion in medical school rose from 9.6 to 30.7 percent. The percentage of women among architects rose from 3 percent in 1972 to 10.8 percent in 1984, and the percentage in architecture schools from 5 to 27 percent.[1] The increase of women going into business and the higher-status professions has "drained away" many of the brightest women who used to go into the teaching profession, however, and is a major cause of the "alarming" drop in the quality of new teachers.[2]

professions to the changes in the law that aim at equal opportunity, and it feels them more quickly and more deeply. Physicians seldom say so explicitly, but they acknowledge indirectly that they have more problems accepting women than lawyers do because they are dealing not only with female doctors who have invaded their turf but also to challenges to their power from nurses, midwives, and patients, particularly in the women's health movement. Architects have had fewer female challenges, which means fewer opportunities to jump or be pushed into acceptance.

Thinking of professional work as man's work can be a metaphor for acceptance of women as well as rejection or discrimination or inhospitability. Ruth Rybov* remembered getting an A on her first project in her second semester in architecture school. "My professor looked at my project," she said, "slammed his fist down, and said, 'Yesterday you were a girl, today you are a man.' I had no idea what it meant then, but it stuck with me for years. He was taking me seriously for the first time, and he always did after that."

Usually, however, the idea of a profession as man's work raises challenges to women. Sometimes the issue is real. Both male and female lawyers wonder, for example, if society has allowed as many women as men to develop the aggressive self-confidence, the ability to give orders and take responsibility and enjoy it, that is needed in Wall Street law firms and their equivalents across the country. Traditional sex roles make this unlikely—one way that the past imbues the present. Another manifests itself less in reality than in mythology. Chicago architect Herbert Hodes* has hired women and fired women, but when I asked about women in his profession, his first comment was, "Architecture, although traditionally a gentleman's art, also had something to do with brick and mortar and toilets and the kind of thing you didn't talk to women about. So we just thought it was too rough an art for women to participate in. The Medicis and the da Vincis talked to each other, but I suspect they didn't discuss even with their wives how large a closet they needed."

Today Hodes is one of the professionals who recognize that women can master the technicalities of their work. Yet the idea that architecture is a rough art also makes him one of many architects who still prefer not to send a woman to a job site (because she will have to deal with contractors and their blue-collar men as well as brick and mortar) or to have her sell a major design or discuss a major budget (because society hasn't trained her, he says, to deal with the big picture or big money). Architects who do this are acting on stereotypes—like the many doctors who still say that women's emotions make them unsuitable for specialties requiring quick, hard decisions or exposing them to large amounts of blood and death. But few doctors admitted to me something that Hodes recognized: the belief that a profession is man's work has put men in his office who have been trained not to work with women, but rather to denigrate their suggestions and make peer collaboration difficult if not impossible. This hurt the achievement and advancement of the women he hired, as he acknowledged. This also happens in hospital medicine, even though most doctors I interviewed were unable to see it—a clear example of denial. Those who saw it blamed society, as Hodes did, not themselves or other men.

LONG HOURS: WORK VS. MOTHERHOOD

The conflict between long hours of work and family needs, men's or women's, is another problem that exists in both reality and mythology. Many women say it's a real agony for those who want a professional career but feel either the desire or the obligation to care for small children—or older ones or husbands or for a family of any kind. Professional men, however, often see a problem even when women don't feel it. In my interviews, they returned to this again and again. Their explicit emphasis contrasted with corporate executives, who hardly ever talked about the problems of the working mother even though they know that some female executives quit and the morale of others sinks because they find it hard to give hours needed to both career and children. (Most husbands seldom even try to share the burden.) Their training is thus wasted, in whole or in part.

Some professional men speak of this in terms of concern for the welfare of children that they say only a mother can provide. But architect Zachary Rowan* made his feelings even clearer for being quite the contrary. He had formed a partnership with two women. He said:

> Architects traditionally work long hours. Like lawyers. It's extraordinary. I do that. I was at work at seven this morning and I left at eight tonight. My partners couldn't do that because they had to think about their children, and our profession did not generate enough money for them to have a full-time baby-sitter or housekeeper, whereas a banker or a lawyer would have that kind of cash. . . . That was something I didn't accept very gracefully, because I don't like children. I could see no real value in the whole situation. They would leave earlier, and they would get in later, and that's why we're no longer partners. Not because of morals but because of money. One of them was an extraordinarily hard worker who couldn't bring in a dime's worth of business in a year. The other had a lot of contacts over the three years we were partners, but in fact she didn't bring much in. Because of the hours they worked, they couldn't do both the design work and the marketing. So I found myself receiving only a third of the income in a firm in which I was producing two thirds of the money coming in. I offered them a partnership in which the profits would be divided in proportion to business brought in. They didn't accept because they were older than I and could not see themselves being financially subordinate.

Rowan kept repeating that "the partnership did not fall down because they were women. It would have been the same if men had not worked a full day." Yet he was equally sure that those particular partners were "unable to work an architect's hours" because they had children. They were both divorced, so they did not have two-income families that might have made paid child care easier.

Several other architects I interviewed expressed even stronger feelings about any married woman, not just single mothers: women in architecture shouldn't have families because a husband or children interfere with work. Ruth Rybov, the architect who moved from girlhood to "manhood," said they were just projecting, because in a seven-day, round-the-clock profession,

> you need a support system. The men need wives to come home to, they can't take the responsibility for the kids. It's an incredible threat to be faced with one more responsibility, to share responsibility for children. If they told women it was okay to have children and still work as architects, it would mean they would have to share responsibility for their own children. Suppose their wife died, what would they do with the kids? That would be their worst nightmare.

The doctors I interviewed also regarded their endurance as a test of fitness, particularly in medical school and internship. They did not put the problem in terms of hours so much as of years of sacramental training. They were angry over what they saw as profanation of the sacrament by women who went to medical school and then dropped out of the profession to care for their families. One gynecologist expressed the common view more explicitly and more intensely than most. He said:

> I happen to be a very liberal person, but I'm against women doctors. Over and over again my experience has been that women never utilize their training. In a sense it seems to be cheating the public, cheating somebody. They got all that expensive training but were never really serious about practice in the traditional sense, or serving the public. . . . Women have a natural function in life, which is to produce children. Most women doctors in my experience have gotten married and become encumbered.

Feelings like that reinforce the reluctance of hospital chiefs to put women in authoritative positions. Yet the gynecologist's impression "from experience," echoed by many other doctors, is one more denial of the prevailing reality. Six studies from 1881 to 1965, when the odds were higher against women in medicine than they are now, show little variation in the number of years that male and female doctors practice.[4]

Worry about the conflict between work and motherhood is most striking in male lawyers just because law now seems to accept women more easily than does architecture or medicine. In the Wall Street type of law firm that to many represents the top of the profession, corporate work often requires twelve-hour or longer working days for young lawyers ambitious to become partners. Here again, women say the conflict can be real. And here too there is a lot of mythology. Most lawyers say at first that they work those hours to meet their clients' expectations, but there is evidence that court or client deadlines do not always create the need. (On some of the rare occasions when a management consultant is invited to look at a law firm's management practices, they seem irrational or inefficient to those not entrapped in the mystique.) Late in the nineteenth century attorneys created work rituals that demanded endurance. Endurance is a form of strength, and the rituals tested and attested their masculinity. It was an era when men hardly ever thought about women in the profession, to be sure. Male lawyers simply hired young men as a matter of course—young men patterned on their own model, who would be tested by years of "masculine" hard work; the best would then become partners, and the lesser would find jobs in other, often lower-ranking, firms. Later, I suspect, both lawyers and clients felt even more masculine when the long hours created problems for female attorneys—in reality or in the men's imagination. Male partners certainly used to deny women the same opportunity as the male associates to work overtime, whether they assumed that women had families to care for or that women would not become partners in any case and therefore had no need to work overtime. Women whose firms worked on the latter assumption had little motive to work long hours.[5]

PROMOTION

Today law firms know they can't afford either assumption. As a partner in one firm, a man in his forties, said, "About a quarter of law school graduates now are women. We'd be dopes if we cut ourselves off from a quarter of the top talent by being sexist." (I thought his sentiment was admirable, but I wondered why his figure was low by 8 percentage points.) Women associates who want to work overtime are usually given the chance. Equally with the men they can, like Jacob, labor seven years for the prize—not of marriage, but of partnership.

This is a matter not of admission to the practice of law but of ability to earn promotion, to succeed. Men of law have given promotion to a slowly increasing number of women. The number of women partners in Wall Street firms rose from three in 1968 to forty-one in 1980, when a quarter of the large firms still had no women partners. That's a little over 2 percent of all Wall Street partners. The figure was up to 3.5 percent in 1983 and is growing faster as the statistical bulge in women law school graduates reaches the years of partnership decisions for the first time.[6] But women are not yet making partner in the same proportion as men. For example, 61 percent of the women who graduated from Harvard Law School in 1974 went into private practice with established firms, compared to 58 percent of the men. But 60 percent of those women had left private practice nine years later, and none of the men had. Sixty-three percent of the women in private practice in 1982 had made partner, compared to 73 percent of the men.[7]

Male partners frequently insist that a candidate's being female never affects their decision on whether to promote her. They also insist, sometimes in the same breath, that they welcome the idea of women partners. They seem to regard each as proof of the other. The men want to believe they are considering only a woman's talent and her commitment to the job. In fact, her gender is almost always a consideration. A firm may agree to a woman's request to work part-time, or a fixed eight-hour day, only to have the partners say they haven't seen enough of her work over six to eight years to evaluate her. Similarly, it may assign a woman to the kind of detail work that buries her in obscurity, so that partners say they can't assess her (as it has always assigned men who lack some indefinable element of partnership appeal). Some men talk about women who "smile too much" to make partner, which apparently means they are not serious about their work. A woman's tears, fact or male fear, are equally disqualifying; they are taken to mean the weeper is not tough enough to deal with the challenges of the lawyer's job.

Those are all largely unconscious transactions. There are conscious ones as well. Elizabeth Anderson Hishon was an associate with the Atlanta law firm of King & Spalding (one of whose partners is former attorney general Griffin Bell). The firm denied her partnership and she sued, charging it with sex discrimination. King & Spalding claimed law firms were partnerships not subject to the federal law she invoked. The Supreme Court ruled in 1984 that partnerships must indeed comply with federal law prohibiting discrimination in employment—a decision that also applies to advertising, accounting, architecture, and engineering firms—and sent Hishon's case back for trial on the merits.

There are also positive conscious transactions. Men know that the number of women who work for a firm and the number eligible for partnership are both increasing. Some want to make sure the firm elects women partners, some lean over backward to make their judgments gender-blind (and a few even succeed). One male partner said, "A few firms have been forced to think about gender by consent decrees or other bias settlements, and the rest of us have certainly been affected by our knowledge of those settlements."

I talked to members of a New York law firm that is relatively liberal on hours and years. It departed from precedent in the mid-1970s and elected to partnership a woman who had taken time off to have children and had then worked part-time before returning to full-time work on a partnership track. She therefore came to partnership years later than usual, also a significant departure for men who resist change in a profession that resists change. Even in that firm, however, young male partners who sound sincere in expressing pleasure at women's joining their ranks wonder how many women will survive the test. One partner there, Quentin Hays,* was unusual among his peers because his mother had had a full-time teaching career and his wife had a career in finance that she maintained even when her children were small. He described himself as both more familiar and happier than his associates with the idea of working mothers. Yet he too saw difficulties in months or years off and part-time or fixed eight-hour days. He said:

> What we've realized, and had to point out, is that with most of the work we do, time off and shorter days mean you'll have less career development and less responsibility because the person can't be depended on to be there. . . . When I get a call on New Year's Eve that something has come up and somebody has to do a real estate deal, it's just my problem if I'm on the phone making business calls all over the country, to a quarter of eleven at night at the start of a holiday weekend. . . . A key aspect in the way we do work is the psychological distinction of whose problem it is, and we love associates who make the problem their problem. They're not helping you with your problem, in their mind, they are working on their problem. What I found when I was working with a woman who worked only from ten to five was that the problem was always my problem, because there was no guarantee that she would be there when it was necessary to go beyond that time. And it was therefore very very difficult to think of her as showing partnership capacity.

And it is usually a "she" whose partnership possibilities are affected. Although many younger men have joined the demand for less overtime in big law firms, the people who actually ask to work part-time or fixed hours are almost always women.

Hays is typical of those who welcome the idea of women partners but add that it is up to each woman to decide if the partnership endurance test is compatible with her own feelings about wife- and motherhood. Many women say it isn't, and some very eligible candidates take leave or withdraw from the partnership race because they have decided to have babies. The men insist that this is why the proportion of women who become partners in the next few years is unlikely to match the proportion hired out of law school. Most men feel no obligation to ask if or how they could change the nature of their business to make it easier for women to be both mothers and partners. Nor do they feel any need to find ways to obtain qualified women partners sooner. Jim Calvin,* a male partner who felt his firm was quite welcoming to women, acknowledged:

> I did go out with a woman last year who knew something about the firm. She heard we had only one woman partner, in the easier specialty of estates and trusts, and that it might be three years before we had more women as partners, and she felt that that was fairly indicative of our lack of interest in women as a separate group entitled to affirmative action. That was one further indication to me that there are many different ways of looking at a

problem. She thought we were not doing enough, but to me partnership decisions were perfectly consistent with our standards—the rate women came into the firm and stayed or left and our general unwillingness to take in people from the outside. But I must admit that in the past year we've taken in two men from the outside. . . . I think it's fair to say that none of the male partners thought that it was sufficiently important that we have a woman partner to go out and find a qualified woman.

Many men have attitudes like Calvin's. They seem to me to rest on the unconscious assumption that a profession is still a ritual brotherhood—for which women can now qualify, but only on fraternal terms. Those terms emphasize the difficulty of combining child care (which the men seldom distinguish from motherhood) and work, and they usually insist that work take priority over child care. The terms may also include promotion of women and people from racial minorities to new grades of partnership, with less power, influence, and income than older partners had even when they were younger. The men know they have refined their hierarchies, but rarely agree with the suspicion that one reason was to find places for outsiders. Women voice the suspicion fairly often.

Similar problems arise when men consider women trying to qualify for an architectural partnership or a hospital department chieftaincy. These professions have not promoted women as consistently as the law, and the difficulties women face after admission to a male elite are if anything more visible, though the timing is not so fixed as it is in law and the law firms' policy of "up or out" not so rigorously followed. Lawyers say, for instance, that women have the option of trying to combine child care and full-time practice, if they can give the latter the necessary priority; many architects and doctors raise the barrier much higher when they insist the two are completely incompatible.

The difficulties can be seen when architects—who, unlike Wall Street lawyers, often want partners who can function in more than one specialty—talk about the tasks they think women can't or don't do well, whether it's bringing in business or dealing with contractor personnel on a job site. They can be seen when hospital doctors, who like lawyers emphasize a single specialty, find it hard to give women higher places in the specialty or hospital hierarchy as a matter of course. When women are the logical contenders, men often name them "acting" rather than full heads of departments, appoint them research assistants rather than professors in teaching hospitals, or leave them at a salary lower than usual for the post to which they've been promoted. The decision makers seldom treat men that way in the promotion process.

I asked several why they do this. Some denied that they in particular or hospitals in general put women doctors at a disadvantage. Some claimed the women had fewer years of experience than the positions demanded. Some spoke of tight budgets. Lewis Berliner,* a young New York internist who is not yet in a high position, laughed and said:

I'd hate to have to decide whether control is more important to doctors or to lawyers, but doctors surely do believe in control. They want to keep the women doctors under control, just the way they want to keep female nurses and female patients under control. Look at the way they tried to put those nurse-midwives out of business down in Tennessee when they tried to practice independently instead of being subordinate to some doctor. The hospitals wouldn't give them the right to admit and care for their own patients. An insurance company that some doctors owned canceled the malpractice insurance for the doctor they hired as their obstetrical consultant. Imagine, those women employed a male doctor! No wonder it took the Federal Trade Commission to force the insurance company not to discriminate against doctors who did that. That was nurses. Sometimes we know we need them. Patients can bug us even worse. Look at the way the medical establishment resisted the women's health movement. They had the nerve to look at their own cervixes, to ask for birthing stools instead of being thrown on their backs with their feet in stirrups. It seems so down to earth you could call it trivial. But they were challenging the idea of the doctor as a male deity who could treat women in whatever way was convenient for him. They were challenging the man's control.

USING FEMALE TALENT

The difference between law and the other professions in acceptance and promotion is important, but I think it's more important that all three professions are failing to do as much as they can to make use of the huge pool of talent that happens to be female. If the problem were as much childbirth and child care as the men believe, the firms would have to provide child care assistance, make part-time work a "normal" option, and stop holding to the rigid six-to-eight year climb to partnership.

Proof that this is already possible comes from firms that can't believe they're exceptional because it seems so much a matter of common sense. One of these firms is Kutak, Rock and Huie of Omaha, one of the fifty largest law firms in the country, which in 1983 had eight women and three blacks among its eighty-nine partners and twenty-seven women and four blacks among its sixty-nine associates. If a woman takes a six-month maternity leave during her six and a half years before partnership is decided, nobody says he doesn't know her work and no special considerations are necessary; she is still up for selection with her "class." When I asked what happens to a woman lawyer's cases when she goes on maternity leave, senior partner Dean Pohlenz said, "Why, the same thing that happens when a man is off on a month's business trip or a month's vacation. People cover for each other." Two of the women partners work part-time so they can care for their children, though one is a litigator and works full-time when she has a trial going. Kutak does not provide child care; women with children make their own arrangements when they have to travel on business, and none of the men considers it a problem. Pohlenz insisted that "we never said we wanted to be on the cutting edge of things, we don't consider ourselves on a crusade. It just sort of happened. When we recruit, we don't say 40 or 50 percent of our new associates will be women. We look at all the best lawyers. Frequently today they are women." Lindsey Miller-Lerman, the three-day-a-week litigator, attributed part of the firm's attitude to the late Robert Kutak, a founding partner whom she described as "a work is joy person" who understood "that there are also other important things in life." She also thought that the critical event at Kutak, Rock was getting hired—"that if you are good enough to get in the firm you are good enough to move up, and most people do."[8]

Full use of female talent also demands that the professions not turn certain specialties into female ghettos. Male partners in my "liberal" law firm made a point of mentioning that the woman they elected to partnership in 1982 (their second) was a litigator, once considered a very masculine field. The next class of candidates there includes some women in corporate work, once also classed as even more man's work than the law in general. This is not the only progressive firm; almost half of the women partners on Wall Street are in corporate work and litigation.[9] (Some women litigators, however, are told they're so good at writing briefs that they can't be spared to do the courtroom jousting.) Big law firms used to encourage women to go into either family law, "blue sky" work (keeping up with changes in securities laws), or estates and trusts (which accounted for six of Wall Street's female partners in 1980). Male partners say that these became female specialties because they were the least likely to demand overtime work, and many women agree that they found them attractive for that reason. But some men acknowledge, if questioned, that these fields were also seen either as appropriate for women (letting the homemaker and conductor of family emotions deal with family failure) or less challenging, less combative (presumably the men in estates and trusts took over when heirs fought each other or a will).

Women have also tended to congregate in a few specialties in other professions, encouraged and sometimes compelled by men who think they belong in anything with a domestic or feminine flavor, like interior design in architecture and pediatrics in medicine. Dr. Francis Lovell,* an Atlanta cardiologist, said to me, "Of course women go in for pediatrics. They're good with children. I don't know if it's good that they've gone in for obstetrics and gynecology, but it's natural. But women in surgery? I'd need years to develop trust in them. And what about a woman urologist? Would you be at ease letting her examine you?" I asked why a woman should feel comfortable taking her

clothes off for him; he knit his brows in a frown that said he had heard that
before from women—and perhaps that I had lost status in his eyes by repeating it. But he gave me no answer in words.

Many men express their feelings that some specialties are feminine in subtler ways. Herbert Hodes, the Chicago architect, put it this way:

> Women emerge as being peculiarly suitable in certain aspects of architec-
> ture. We do not say that we hire women in this office for a specific role, we
> rather examine what they have chosen for themselves as their role. Take
> Lily. She has a particular aptitude for the organization of relationships—
> human relationships, which in architecture boil down to spatial relation-
> ships. There are many architects here who can do spectacular designs for a
> façade and couldn't care less about the way spaces are organized behind
> that façade, or the human elements that affect the shapes and relationships
> of those spaces. We're used to that, we're accustomed to it in men. In
> women we have to dig very hard to say this is a field in which you have
> special skill and therefore instead of being a kind of donkey in the office,
> doing draftsman's tasks or design tasks, we want you to go out and be
> creative, in addition to whatever else you'd like to do, we want you to be
> creative in these tasks.

Many women in architecture insist that the "donkey work" of drafting is one
of the things they must do to be true peers of the men. Lily Poulenc,* the
architect whom Hodes mentioned, was a specialist in hospital design who
expressed pride in the talents he attributed to her. But she also wanted to sell
whole designs and budgets in client meetings, which he felt most women
couldn't do. She left his firm because she felt he was unwilling to tolerate her
moments of disagreement with him. He described her motives to me by saying, "We wanted her to do work she didn't want to do." A man would have
done such a job even if he didn't want it or like it, Hodes said, as a normal
part of working for somebody else. For Lily, "It came back to her feeling that
in a male society, she wasn't being recognized." Hodes insisted that he did
recognize her. I thought he recognized some of her talents but not others—
because he could not accept what he saw as her refusal to play by male rules.

HOSTILITY, DENIAL, AND TRANSFORMATION

At every level in a professional career—admission, specialization, and promotion—men behave toward women in the same patterns I have described in
other fields of work. Hostility and denial are more modulated, however, and
transformations less frequent or less obvious than in the business world. One
reason, I suspect, is that organizations with elaborate hierarchical structures,
which provide the playing fields for those actions, are less important or less
all-embracing in the professions. Another is that the threat embodied in the

arrival of women in the professional workplace is often less obvious. They are coopted into the male elite and adopt its approach to power, usually subtler than in corporations. Hostility, denials, and transformations are most visible when the threat is most clearly felt—at the entry gate of the professional school, for instance. When the threat is subtler, it invites more ambivalent responses. The ambivalence that seems so much stronger in the professions than in other kinds of work belongs in the same spectrum because it often combines the other patterns.

Hostility is often a survival from the past. A 1963 survey, for instance, showed that in selecting new recruits, 430 law firms saw being female as the least desirable characteristic in a candidate—worse than being black, than being from a blue-collar family, than being in the lower half of the law school class.[10] The feelings of that era are still alive in many lawyers. The profession is certainly trying to overcome them, but the residues of such hostility may well explain the inhospitable treatment that many firms still give the women they are officially proud to hire.

Hostility today seems clearer to me in medicine than in any other profession. This may be accidental; my sample was small and I may have happened to choose hostile doctors. But it seems just as probable to me that doctors, further from changes in law than lawyers and more accustomed than architects to giving orders to others, may actually resist change with stronger or sharper feelings. Dr. Mary Howell, then a Harvard Medical School administrator, did a survey of women medical students in 1973 that elicited a number of horror stories. In one case, a histology professor demonstrating the digestive system asked for two women to help. He added hydrochloric acid to some food and showed the class one of the end products in the beaker—which he labeled "shit." He told the women to clean up the "shit" and said, "That's the place of women in medicine!" The men laughed.[11] Today, no doubt, few medical school lecturers still strike such a note. But that happened when the women's movement had already begun to affect the professions, and the doctors trained by such men are still young, still developing their skills, still affecting the way the profession treats women.

Walt Sokol,* the gynecologist quoted earlier, was the right age to have had that kind of training. He spoke in 1981 of women doctors who were "castrating" and women doctors who responded "hysterically" to pressure. He mentioned a woman doctor who committed suicide three days after she helped him with a cesarean section that had turned into a disaster and a woman with whom he had done an operation just before I interviewed him who "was one of the worst technical surgeons I've ever seen. She couldn't even do the cutting and sewing women are supposed to do." He repeatedly acknowledged that men had done equally bad work, but every time I asked for an example or an anecdote the men had done things right and the women had messed up.

Sokol claimed women were incompetent. Sometimes hostility is a response to female competence, and even more often, to female aggressiveness. A man who is aggressive in his work usually draws admiration, "but a woman doing the exact same thing is really looked down on," California attorney Joseph Linwood* said, and linked aggressiveness to competence:

> If she's aggressive you'll feel she's nasty, or not what you want in a woman, not feminine. If she does a better job than you do, you'll be worried. If she's your adversary, it may be worse, especially if she beats you. I've heard men say the woman who beat them is a bitch, a heartless bitch. There was a woman in the U.S. Attorney's office who used to win all the time. We used to say she had more balls than her boss. That was saying something about how we didn't like her as a woman. And it was a way of saying you can't mess with her, she doesn't have any judgment. We didn't trust her. But a guy who won all the time would be greatly admired. He'd have a macho image.

Denial in professional schools is related to the often-noticed tendency of men to dominate any group. Teachers and male students treat women much more nearly as equals than they did ten years ago, but there are still many cases in law, medical, and architecture school where women complain that they are somehow invisible to a professor looking for raised hands to answer questions, or that a woman will be ignored when she says something, only to see the same point become the subject of eager debate when a man makes it later on.

In professional practice, denial may be abstract. In medicine, I've already cited doctors' denial that men are trained not to work with women, and Sokol's denial of facts about women doctors' working as many years as men do. In law firms, it tends to be denial of "sins" like being conscious of gender in selecting partners or assigning associates to specialties.

But denial can also be concrete. Arthur Morton,* a New York architect, liked to use women for program analysis and design presentation. The latter was a public relations process that involved making delicate drawings and wining and dining clients. Ruth Rybov said that when she asked to leave those fields and do the working drawings that an architect must be able to make, Morton responded, "You probably can't do it. I give you caviar and you want turnips." She insisted, and Morton switched her to turnips, but "he ignored me for the three months I was doing working drawings. He would pass me in the hallways, and it was excruciating because we had had this friendship. Finally it was finished, and he accepted the fact that I was able to do those drawings. But he said, 'Now can I put you back on design?' And I said no, I wanted to do the technical drawings on a major project, and I did. He made me job captain. Normally the next step would be site supervision, but he gave that to the man who'd been job captain on the planning side. That's when he told me, 'You don't send blacks or women to job sites.' I made sure that was in the paper two days later." Twelve years later, after having had several women doing technical work and site supervision, Morton's first impulse was to deny that he had ever felt that way or ignored Rybov. Then he smiled and said it had been delightful to have her "push me in the closet and slam the door and leave me in there." He admitted that it was still difficult to avoid unconscious stereotypes, but he insisted that he had learned to enjoy it when women showed competence.

Transformations in the professions, as in other occupations, diffuse the threat that men feel in the arrival of women without the explicit damage that hostility and denial do to human relationships. In the past decade, as changes in the culture have made overt hostility less acceptable, transformation has become more common in professional schools, the entry places into the chosen elite where men are most likely to see women as a threat. Lewis Berliner, the New York internist, and Joe Linwood, the California lawyer, said that when they were in medical and law school in the mid-1970s they had seen students turn women colleagues into playmates, lovers, and wives. In response to my questions, they added daughters and mothers. "The women didn't like it if they felt the men were being condescending," Berliner said. "That happened when it was playmates and sometimes daughters. But it was easier for some guys to treat a woman as an equal if they could think of her as a wife or lover rather than as just another student competitor."

In all three professions the most common transformation that people spoke of was colleague-into-daughter. Older doctors used it to "justify" to themselves the desire to welcome women into nontraditional specialties. Lawyers and architects said it was the most common transformation because they seldom work with colleagues of the same age; partners and senior associates, both still predominantly male, work with junior associates, the class which still includes most women. They did not always distinguish, in their own minds, between the father-daughter transformation and genuine mentoring. When they heard women's objections to being made daughters, it sometimes helped them to see that the transformation ran the danger of blocking a woman's career development while mentoring promoted it.

Sometimes transformation was a matter not of colleagues but of clients and contractors. Ruth Rybov talked about the contractor she used most often:

Sometimes he's a little boy and I have to protect him. Sometimes I'm a little girl, doing things that are stupid, or I need his protection and I will turn to him as a father. That's when I need something done. I don't have the power that a man has on the site. And the lover idea, I can see that, because the contractors always come on to me. They're always glad when I slide out and talk about their wives, but it looks like the first way they think of to deal with a woman.

ACCEPTANCE VS. EXCLUSION

Ambivalence about women in the workplace is the product of men's efforts, conscious or unconscious, to reconcile two conflicting forces. One is acceptance of women, which they have come to think morally right or socially approved. The other is the desire to exclude women, which combines feelings that start early in life with ideas and acts from the cultures of the society as a whole and of the particular profession. The feelings and the cultural practices "cement the brotherhood of men [and] at the same time reinforce the outsider role of women."[12] This happens in every kind of occupation, but the forces demanding acceptance of women are stronger in the professions. The near equality of the two forces makes it difficult for professional men to do things that roughly exclude women or affirmatively accept them. They therefore talk more than men in other fields about countervailing forces, about the conflicts they see between women's roles as women and as workers.

The negative side of the resulting ambivalence is still full of hostility, denial, or transformation. Walt Sokol, for instance, alternated his obvious anger at women doctors with statements like "A midwife can take care of a pregnant woman just as well as I can," or "I honestly feel there's no difference between men and women." Architect Ryan Barber* went from anecdotes about how he welcomed aggressive female colleagues (he refused a client's request that he fire one who had pushed too hard for her firm's solution to a problem) to stories of how they made him feel uncomfortable (starting with one about a woman who had used the men's toilet in a building that had none nearby for women).

Subtler forms of ambivalence are harder than obvious ones to recognize and change, so they may keep women longer in their place as outsiders on the inside. That certainly happens with surgeons who at first sound as though they think it's great to train the first women entering their specialties but then complain that women are indecisive (if they change their minds about the specialty) or too emotional (if they express their feelings about losing a patient).[13]

When acceptance of women is greater, the subtler kind of ambivalence may show a positive face that sometimes brings the outsiders in. Jim Calvin, the lawyer who saw that women had a different perspective from men on the same problem, talked about a time when

> I found myself acting in a way that was contrary to my professed beliefs. I caught it only after I had done it. A young woman associate was doing some work for me on a short-term basis while someone else was away. She seemed very anxious to take on a lot of work, but I was afraid she might be taking on too much. She was talking with the partner who makes work

assignments. I got a call from him after I had told her what I wanted her to do. He said she was with him, and I said, "Oh, is she in tears?" I was thinking to myself, "Oh God, I've given her too much work to do and she's got too many things to do and she didn't tell me, but she's going off to him and crying on his shoulder, saying she can't handle all the work she has." He unfortunately didn't think quickly and repeated my comment aloud, saying, "Tears? No, she's here looking for more work." Later I apologized to her, because as soon as I had said it and as soon as he repeated it, I knew I had made a loaded remark.

My first thought when I heard Calvin say that was "Great. Here's another 'liberated man' who hears the click that reminds him that he can still say or do something unliberated." Then he continued, "But I certainly have found that tears flow more easily from women than they do from men in a work situation." That made me start to change my mind, to think he might be trapped in a stereotype where he would always expect water no matter how often it might turn out that he was dealing with a female stone. I had to change again when he went on to talk about another woman associate, to whom he had been adviser rather than supervisor.

She was doing some work that she didn't really want to do. She had a strong emotional reaction to work on a particular theme. She was trying to be a good soldier, to cope with it, but she found herself so emotionally at odds with it that she came and talked to me and wound up crying.

Calvin's discomfort at the tears was overcome by her following the rules of the law firm's game. When she came to him, it "removed the tears from work to a personal situation because she wasn't with the man she was working with." Neither his discomfort at her crying nor the woman's subsequent leave of absence to have a baby prevented Calvin from describing her as a strong candidate for partnership, so the positive side of his ambivalence was winning out.

SEXUALITY AT WORK

Men have trouble dealing with the idea of sex in the workplace in the professions just as they do in other occupations, but professional men do not put the same emphasis on it as corporate executives or factory workers. My interviews made me think that a greater proportion of professionals succeeds in making sure sex does not become a reality in the office. Others minimize or deny the problem rather than voice fears of its effects as many executives do, or act out their fantasies as many blue-collar men do.

Professional women recognize the presence of the problem more clearly. Past experience keeps them alert for men who tread the boundaries between sexual transformations and sexual harassment. An architect in the days of miniskirts was given a drafting table in the front rank so the men could look at her as she bent over her drawings. A doctor recalled complaining about a colleague who kept putting his hand on her knee while they discussed a patient. The women say there has been less of this in recent years, but they are quicker than the men to say that sexual attractions do occur and are sometimes fulfilled. They are certainly more aware than men that many women doctors and architects (but fewer lawyers) marry men in the same professions.

Many professional women, however, agree with the men who say that the long hours of work apparently deprive people of more opportunities than they create, to say nothing of the energy needed for a sexual relationship. The tendency of professionals to work together as senior and junior, which sometimes encourages father-daughter transformations, may also narrow the field for sex in every profession's equivalents of the Wall Street law firms, but it may create more opportunities where the senior males are less conscious of the morals and the etiquette of power. I suspect there is more opportunity for sex in the office in medium-sized law and architectural firms and shared primary-care medical offices than in the giant firms and hospitals. Many men and some women assume that business travel, being away from home in two senses, makes it easier to try sex with a colleague.

Even or especially in the puritan atmosphere of the larger firms, men remain conscious of what they see as the dangers of mixing work and sex. Jim Calvin recalled:

> By the time I was divorced, I was also a partner, and I felt that getting involved with an associate could only mean trouble. I was never really tested because no associate ever came along who appealed to me enough to run the risk. Only once do I remember, at four one morning, a very bright woman was working with me on a very difficult problem. She had done a very good first draft of something and was just bristling with ideas. She also had a bad image of herself. She felt the work was no good, she didn't really go with it, she couldn't improve it. At four in the morning when we were discussing all this, there was a feeling on my part to comfort her by putting my arm around her. I decided fairly quickly that it wasn't such a sound idea. It could have led to something else or it might have demanded the kind of explanation that would have been bad for the work relationship. She was a good example of a very bright person, but terribly neurotic, hung up on her personal problems.

For Calvin, even a comradely touch raised the specter of sex when the colleague in need of help happened to be female. He was quick to add that it could have been a man who needed reassurance, but "however I might have tried to reassure a man I wouldn't have felt the danger of its being taken for another kind of emotion."

WORKING WIVES

If professional people talked less about sex than business people did in their interviews, they mentioned their spouses more often. In both kinds of work, most women with husbands in the same field mentioned the support their spouses gave them in their work while voicing their despair, already almost a cliché, over their own need for a "wife," for the kind of support that a traditional wife gave her husband. But two professional women spoke of men, a husband in one case and several lovers in the other, who had been unhappy at the demands of their jobs and had ultimately asked them to choose, "Your work or me." Both had chosen to continue their professional careers.

Professional men whose wives had careers were more likely than men in traditional marriages to be genuinely supportive of women peers in their own offices as well as of their wives. Here, too, professional men resembled blue-collar men, and here, too, the men with career wives were usually younger than the traditionalists. The number of men who marry women in their own profession is increasing, though the proportion is easier to measure by looking at the women. Perhaps 70 percent of women doctors marry other doctors, for instance. The majority of women architects who marry choose other architects. Spouses in the same occupation understand the professional problems and the mystique of long hours better than partners in some other field, but they are more likely to compete with each other, to find it hard to get appointments in their first-choice specialties in the same city, and to discover problems in deciding who will raise any children.[14]

Whether or not their wives are in their own profession, professional men with working wives often told me what they learned from their wives about their own work relationships. Quentin Hays, the lawyer whose wife and mother both worked, was one of these. He said:

> My wife educated me at a time when I was working with a woman who was working very hard. She had a young son and a husband with a nine-to-five job. I came home and commented that I felt bad that she was working so hard that she wasn't seeing her child. My wife pointed out that maybe I would be thinking of that less if it were a man and that I shouldn't be adjusting my behavior [to her being a woman]. I thought this was an interesting point. My wife made me see that that kind of adjustment would be unfair to the woman. It was up to her to decide whether she wanted to go all out or not, and I shouldn't take her out of the game by sending her home to be with her child.

I asked Hays if his wife had suggested that it was also up to the men who worked for him to decide if they wanted to go all out or to take time off with their children. She had not, and the question surprised him.

Long hours for lawyers are a fact of life. The question is whether we were going to vary it for women. My wife was suggesting that we shouldn't, and I think she was right. I was glad she made me see that you have to watch your attitudes on things like that, making assumptions for people.

HOW THINGS ARE CHANGING

When men begin to watch or change the attitude that says they have the right to make assumptions for women, it's significant. The arrival of women has done no more to change the general practices of professions than it has in business, but the first changes, however few, provide some reason to hope for others. Men in law, medicine, and architecture agreed that women were forcing the professions to make their work less of "a be-all and end-all in comparison to the family. It's a humanizing of the practice," as lawyer Jim Calvin put it. I asked if he thought this humanization was good for the profession. He replied:

It's got to be a good thing. What would be nice would be if the clients would go along with it and adapt to the new situation. The pressures really come from competitive firms and from the internal makeup of many lawyers who seem to be obsessive and compulsive and unhappy when they're not working hard.

I asked what form the humanization took. Calvin replied:

I'm not sure I have a good answer. Women are readier than men to talk about their own feelings and the way the personal counterpoints with the professional, and without them men might be shyer than they have become in talking about families and things. Having women as lawyers is making us communicate better.

In architecture too, men believe that women improve communication. Herbert Hodes worried that women might lower the productivity of an office by increasing its sexual tensions, but he added, "There are compensations for it, or I wouldn't hire them. They see things that men don't see, or they see the same things in different ways. Some of the time, at least. There's an interplay, be it ideas or relaxation or emotions or sex, when there are women in the office. I think we have a much richer exchange of ideas. Who wants a monastical society?"

One of the more obvious of the humanizing changes deals with the long hours that men see as holy ritual or at least as symbols of their elite status. Some women's determination to work the long hours has compelled men to change their preconceptions about women's ability to do the job. Others are reinforcing the demand for shorter hours. A woman who was her law firm's first female partner said, "Most women tend not to view the law with the all-consuming dedication that you get among some very ambitious men. From my perspective that's great, because life is too short and you're all dead in the end, and who wants to practice law twenty-six hours a day for all your life?"

She and other women in many firms have reinforced a challenge that began in the 1960s to the mystique of the long legal working day. That was before women lawyers were numerous enough to be a significant factor. An older lawyer in a Louis Auchincloss story laid the challenge to an important change in young associates' thinking. They did not, like his generation, see the law as fun or as fulfillment but as work. For pleasure or for emotional needs they went home to wives or lovers.[15] That already gave indirect credit or blame to women, and some real-life attorneys made that point too.

Most of the male lawyers I interviewed attributed the new increases in the demand for shorter hours to "the younger generation." But questions revealed that the views of the new younger generation are shaped even more by women than those of the preceding younger generation. Women are making demands for their own time both as lawyers in their own firms and as the wives of lawyers, the latter often fueled by their own careers. These demands are making the challenge to the twenty-six-hour day more effective.

The demands have not yet made as great an impact on architecture, where the earnings are lower, or in medicine, where the mystique of the hospital is geared to the round-the-clock cycle of emergency and death that in fact touches only a small part of medical practice. But even in those professions, women are making sure the demand for shorter hours is heard.

The campaigns for humanization and shorter hours are quiet rebellions against existing authority in the professions—authority that, like most authority in Western society, happens to be male. In medicine, women have mounted a more profound rebellion. The women's health movement has challenged the authority of male doctors to set the terms for treatment of women peers, women subordinates like nurses, and women patients. Some women doctors have joined in the challenge and others have not, but there is no question that the combination of consumer and professional forces has compelled male physicians to react to women's demands for changes in medical treatment. And changes have taken place—some as simple as the presence of fathers in delivery rooms for childbirth, some as complex as the testing of new drugs for birth control and women's diseases. Simon Lublin,* an older surgeon, said, "The increase in the number of young women doctors makes some of my friends fight harder against what they see as radical feminist ideas. But it makes a few of us take what both the doctors and the patients say more seriously." Jim Riley,* a small-town pediatrician, linked the increase in the number of women doctors to a more general challenge, "a new movement among nurses, male and female, that says doctors are no longer God. They think if there's a bad practice going on, they have a right to tell the doctor to stop. I grudgingly accept this. I don't fight it. I know that when a nurse anesthetist is anesthetizing a child, she knows a hell of a lot more about it than I do."

Authority is more than a target of rebellion. It is the right to exercise power, and as women play larger roles in work and in society at large, they must be able to exercise authority. Jim Calvin commented:

> A lawyer is an authority figure. Some people wonder, if women in law are going to express emotion or show vulnerability, can they be as authoritative as lawyers are supposed to be. I wonder if they can recognize authority when they see it. I'm a senior partner and I put myself very low on the kind of authoritative scale that demands confrontation. I don't relish confrontational scenes. Of course, other lawyers in the firm are quite different. And some women are coming along who are very authoritative indeed. When they make partner, I wouldn't be at all surprised if they frighten some of the older partners.

I wouldn't be surprised either, since fear is so frequent a male emotion in the confrontation with women who claim authority or any other aspect of power. Authority is indeed a quality of lawyers—and of all professionals in one form or another. It is also an attribute claimed by elites. Calvin clearly recognizes that some women have the quality and therefore qualify for the elite to which he belongs. All the remarks quoted from my interviews with him show him working through the ambivalence I found so frequent among professional men, dispelling much of his anger, fear, and anxiety, until his supportive feelings win out. As more male professionals do that, there will be fewer obstacles to women's passage through the elite's sacramental training, the well-kept gates of entry, the ritual of peer review. But it will be a constant process of challenge by both sexes and resistance by both sexes, and it will be a long time before it becomes easy.

Part Three

HOW MEN FEEL ABOUT CHANGES IN PERSONAL LIFE

Chapter 9
MARRIAGE AND FAMILY

Vic Lawson* and his wife, Barbara,* live with their two sons and one daughter in a San Francisco suburb. Those bare facts could describe a stereotypical nuclear family, and most of the Lawsons' neighbors indeed fit the stereotype. In deeper fact, however, Vic and Barbara show how much the nuclear family has changed. Barbara, far from being a full-time homemaker, has just moved from terminal manager to a headquarters position in a trucking company. Vic is a middle manager for a shipping line. "When we got together, we started penniless," Vic said. "We both went to work and that's all I've known for the last ten years." They didn't become a two-career family just to survive; their suburb is a wealthy one, and their life includes occasional luxuries like a twenty-five-hundred-dollar trip to a Superbowl weekend. Vic added, "If we weren't both working, we wouldn't be in this neighborhood, we wouldn't be in this house, we wouldn't have what we have now."

The boys are from her first marriage, the girl from his, all born in the 1960s. Barbara's employer forced her to leave work in the seventh month of each pregnancy and gave no maternity leave. She went back to work when her children were three months and six weeks old, respectively, because she needed the money to support them. Barbara has no intention of using the paid maternity leave that's now standard, but she sounds both satisfied and gratified that it's now a legal requirement.

In this family Barbara keeps the checkbook and makes most of the decisions on major purchases that traditionally were a male prerogative. She always discusses the decision with Vic, but he normally says, "If you like it, buy it." "I make decisions all day," he explained. "This is one less that I've got to worry about."

Vic does most of the housework, something very few husbands do even today, and fewer still with good humor. Barbara hates it and refuses to do it. She said, "If it's worth it to him, he'll spend whatever," (a reference to the Superbowl extravagance) "but if he doesn't think it's worth it—he couldn't bring himself to pay somebody to do housework when it's so easy to do. It's not unpleasant enough for him to pay somebody else to do it." Vic said, "I don't think anybody really loves to do housework. But when Barbara said we could get a maid, basically I'm probably too damn cheap to get a maid."

Another way Vic differs from stereotype is in liking the effects of Barbara's work on the family. "Our businesses kind of overlap," he observed. "We have a lot to converse about. I enjoy knowing her friends more than a lot of guys like their wives' friends, but of course most of her friends are men that she works with. If she weren't working she'd be miserable and that would make me miserable even if we had no money problems." It doesn't come out in a neat sentence, but it's obvious that beyond these sentiments, Vic is also proud of Barbara's steady promotions and achievements at work.

THE FAMILY CHANGES

Vic and Barbara are just one example of the way marriage, family, and all the ties between men and women are changing shape and structure. The traditional picture shows a man engaged in work and public life who dominates even as he depends on the woman who takes care of emotions and relationships—usually a father who is the sole wage earner, a mother who is primarily a homemaker, and their children. That image still colors the feelings and values of most Americans. But today only a tiny minority of American households conform to the image—10.7 percent. Almost three times as many, 30.5 percent, are two-earner families, and more than half of them (17.5 percent of all households) are two-earner families in full bloom—father and mother who both work for pay with one or more children living at home. Another 32.5 percent of all households consist of married couples with no children, or none living at home.[1]

I believe the rise in two-earner marriage is the most important of the changes in the family over the past fifteen years. Most of these changes, like those at work, are moving relations between men and women toward new balances of power and new divisions of labor that bring the participants closer to equality. The movement of women into the workplace has given them a new measure of economic power. Many have ended the traditional dominance of husband or lover in some households and modified it in others. Many are ceasing to be psychologically dependent on a man in the same way or the same degree that the culture has long demanded.

This is difficult and painful for both women and men. Men are full of conflict. We grow angry over threats to our power and we fear for our identity even as we feel pleasure when the women we know enrich their lives and ours. We think we're independent, but it's not easy for us to reduce our real dependence on women—to understand that to stand on one's own feet emotionally is neither to be alone nor to be lost.

Before looking more closely at those feelings, I find it helpful to glance at the whole array of changes in the family and their causes. Fewer and fewer people are thinking of marriage as a permanent relationship, or one to be entered as soon as possible, or the best of all possible states. But these changes have not destroyed marriage and family as institutions or sent them into irreversible decline, as many social scientists suggest. The institutions show surprising strength even as their weakness increases.

Changes, strength, and weakness are all visible in the statistics. On the impermanence of marriage: the divorce rate more than doubled from 1961 to 1981, when it stood at 5.3 per thousand people. In 1982 the number and rate started going down for the first time in twenty years (it reached 4.9 percent in 1984), but the basic trend continues at a high level.*[3] It is more significant that women instigate an increasing proportion of marital breakups, in effect abandoning their husbands. (A few studies suggest that this proportion has reached a majority of divorces, but the samples are too small to generalize from.[4] The important thing is the increase compared to the past, when women were more socially and economically vulnerable in divorce than they are today.) They are also leaving their children with their husbands more than they used to.

On the erosion of the dominant status of marriage: about 23 percent of all households consist of one person living alone, a large increase from a generation ago.[5] The Census Bureau says that if the trend continues, half the households in the country will be single-person by 1990. Both for older people, often widowed, and for younger ones, not yet married or between marriages or determined never to marry, these one-person households often provide both scenes and actors for dramas of the new relations between men and women.

In addition, two million unmarried couples of the opposite sex were living together in 1984—4 percent of all couples, an increase of 25 percent over 1980 and almost four times as many as in 1970.[6] This testifies to both the lower popularity of marriage and the survival of the institution of the family. An unmarried couple is both a family and an institution, though the notion may distress those pairs who remain unmarried on principle.

One other set of figures shows an important weakness in the family: 25.7 percent of the 33.2 million families with children under eighteen were single-parent families in 1984, up from 12.9 percent in 1970. About 940,000—2.8 percent of families with children under eighteen—were headed by the father alone, still more theaters in which men play new roles.[7] The rest were headed by a woman, usually mother or grandmother.

On the continuing attractions of marriage, despite the changes: the number

* The significance of a high divorce rate looks different when it is seen as part of the rate of marital dissolution, marriages ending in death and divorce combined. This has risen very little in a century, from 34.5 per thousand marriages in the 1860s to 40.5 today.[2] In the old days, many marriages ended in the early death of the wife, so the couple's ability to live together for decades was not tested. Today people live longer, women in particular. Increasing divorce may be in part a male reaction to that new female equality (as well as a female reaction to longer male domination).

of marriages has risen steadily since 1958, except for 1974 and 1975, and reached successive record highs in 1982, 1983, and 1984.[8] This is partly because the total population is increasing, partly because more than two thirds of all divorced people remarry. (Remarriage has produced an increasing formation of step-families, currently estimated at 475,000 a year; many have more than three children, running counter to the national trend toward smaller families, and in many the father is a newly active figure.) A smaller share of Americans remain single their entire lives; about 6 percent of women aged sixty-five and over had never married in 1984, compared to 9 percent in 1950.

THE CAUSES OF CHANGE

These figures form a constellation whose center is one simple, overwhelming fact: 53.5 percent of all women aged twenty and over were in the labor force in 1983. Proportions were much higher in important demographic categories —69.9 percent of women aged twenty-five to forty-four, for instance, and 68.2 percent of mothers of school-age children.[9] Women go to work primarily because the economy no longer fits the myth of the male wage earner; a family needs more than one income to live on middle-class terms, and many need more than one just to survive. Looked at another way, a woman needs her own income to survive; married or single, few can afford to be economically dependent on a man.

Women also go to work for another reason: the quest for equality, autonomy, and choice—the desire to be a fuller person. The need for money and the drive for what some feminists call "personhood" are both reasons that an increasing number of women do not merely work outside the home, but leave traditionally feminine jobs to enter supposedly masculine occupations and pursue the supposedly masculine goal of career. The quest for autonomy has also affected millions of women who have not gone to work outside the home.*

Women's going to work and women's quest for autonomy are not the only causes of the current changes in their relations with men. Another important

---

* Some middle-class white women consciously pursue personal sovereignty by going to work or entering "masculine" occupations. Poor women may not get their heads above the economic quicksand long enough to think of themselves as involved in such a quest. Black women have worked so long, also originally for economic reasons, that they seldom see going to work as liberating. Many Latin women, traditionally tied even more tightly than Anglos to their domestic functions, share with Anglo women the notion that work for pay can be liberating. But in American society, work creates either a degree of autonomy and power or a desire for them, no matter how much it is economic need that sends a woman, or a man, to work—or how little work is seen as a liberating choice. In a New York *Times* poll in 1983, the majority of women said they would rather work than stay home even if they didn't need the money—except for blue-collar women, half of whom said that given the option, they would rather stay home.[10]

one is a little-recognized desire in men to shed the burdens of the family-wage economy and the breadwinner ethic. In *The Hearts of Men,* Barbara Ehrenreich is the first to trace the evolution of this idea, which she sees as an historical force that antedates the current renaissance of the women's movement.[11] It goes back to the years just after World War II, when adulthood was seen almost entirely in terms of finding an occupation, selecting a mate, and rearing children. (Ehrenreich does not mention that this view was in part a reflection of earlier crises in the family-wage system—the Great Depression, which deprived many breadwinners of their jobs, and the War, which took men away from their families and put many women in war-factory jobs.) A succession of male rebels began with gray-flannel dissidents against conformity in the novels of Richard Yates and the sociology of David Riesman. They were followed, in Ehrenreich's analysis, by Hugh Hefner and the men who followed his *Playboy* philosophy; the Beats of Jack Kerouac's time; cardiologists who related the traditional provider function to the Type A personality, whose hypertension and work obsession could be fatal (seldom thought of as rebels); the psychologists of growth; the counterculture, and the men's movement. I would add fathers possessed of the new impulse toward active parenting, which is being socialized not only by the men who do it but also by mothers, obstetricians, pediatricians, and some men's and women's organizations.

Ehrenreich is right in calling attention to the ways in which men have rebelled against the traditional family and its economic base. One of her recurring ideas may profit by being repeated even more explicitly: despite that rebellion, we have seldom initiated demands for independence or equality between the sexes. In most of the movements she charted, we were usually trying to have it both ways, privilege but no burden; we were also fleeing intimacy and responsibility.

But her appraisal is distorted in two respects. First, she ignores a force that is a contradiction or a counterpoint to her thesis—the many men who regard their labors at intrinsically unsatisfying jobs as a gift or sacrifice they make to their wives and children. Perhaps their growing recognition of the unrewarding nature of those labors was a reason for the rebellion she describes against the traditional family and the breadwinner role. Second (and ironically, since she is a feminist and calls herself a radical), she is reluctant to give women and the women's movement credit for their role in changing the traditional family. The reluctance springs from her determination to show that feminism has not made war on the *idea* of marriage. She's right, but she overlooks an important fact: women *have* challenged the system, in and out of the women's movement. All but one of the forces she describes preceded that challenge and helped shape male responses to it; the exception was the men's movement, which is one of the responses those forces shaped (see Chapter 12). So is active fathering.

A third cause of change is the sexual revolution in which first men and then women threw off the legacy of Victorian morality which was part of the upbringing of the vast majority of Americans now over the age of forty. This was more than just a *Playboy* phenomenon. In the beginning it was simultaneously part of both a new male exploitation of women ("Come on, baby, you don't have to say no anymore.") and a new sensitivity to women ("Have you come yet?"). Later, when large numbers of women started expressing their own desires and taking the sexual initiative, or having their own extramarital affairs, it began to delight or frighten and anger men in new ways—another paradox that complicated the male response to the female and the feminist challenge.

CHANGE, EMOTIONS, CONFLICT

These changes in relations between men and women involve pain and struggle for both. Men who see the changes as things that women have demanded or designed sometimes think the trauma is all on our side. In truth, even the women who have engineered change feel the pain because the old ways are so deeply rooted in psyche and culture. Yet men often feel heavier pain and longer, because we were usually the beneficiaries of privilege and sometimes of power under the old system. We are anxious lest change deprive us of the nurturing care and the part of our identity that we get from women in the traditional relations between the sexes. We fear that change will give women power, and the traditional system is based on our buried fear of female power.

But those emotions are not all that we feel. We are full of conflict, much stronger than the ambivalence I mentioned in the chapters on the workplace. We hate the very idea of change—and at the same time many of us want change in our personal relationships with women, and more of us think we should want it. Our professions of acceptance are often disguises or denials of our hatred and refusal. But they are not only denials. Most of us truly want the women in our lives to be happy. Many of us have come to realize this means they must have personal autonomy, including economic freedom. Some of us want to overcome our fear of female power. Some of us want relief from traditional masculine burdens. We therefore struggle to welcome change.

These new emotions are just as real as the old familiar feelings that attach us to the traditional system and make us shriek, at least figuratively, when the tie is broken. But the new feelings are usually weaker than the traditional ones, whose inherent strength reinforces and is reinforced by the many ways society is organized around them. We don't want to give up real privilege or power even when we become conscious of the burdens that come with them; we don't want to give up the fantasy of power that hides real powerlessness. The old feelings and the old system are still so strong that we can usually accept the changes in marriage and family only when they stop well short of revolution. We start to fight these changes when they threaten to tear the roots of our feelings. The battle becomes bitter when it challenges our perceptions of our power, which sometimes precedes and sometimes follows threats to the reality of that power—or both, as often happens when a wife earns more than her husband.

The conflict between change and tradition, then, between our old and new emotions, is intense. But most of us accept the changing balance of power in our personal lives more easily than we adjust to finding women as peers or bosses at work, judging by my interviews and several surveys of middle-class America.[12] We love our wives or lovers, we can be proud of them, admire them, identify with them. On a lower level we often like the things the family can do with the money they bring in when they work for pay. Those emotions help balance the basic fears of female power, especially when we retain an edge in the power struggle. We seldom have positive feelings about women at work, however. There, we deny or balance our fear by putting women "in their place" in what was once a male hierarchy of another kind of power. Traditionally they were subordinates. Today they are also peers, competitors, and superiors; subconsciously we see them as combining the power of women with the power of work, the power to reshape the external world. That is frightening in itself and makes it much clearer than it is at home that real change involves heavy costs that might end male control of the system. As a consequence, even in the few cases where we do love or identify with female colleagues, or in the many cases where we sleep with them, we find it harder to accept changes that approach equality at work than at home. We show this in the kind of hostility, denial, and transformation described in the chapters on work, and in the material discrimination against women in pay and promotion documented in this book and many others.

While most men accept change at home more easily than in the workplace, private life is also the arena in which some of us feel our strongest anger and deepest hurt from women's quest for equality.* We feel betrayed because we discover that the women we love and who love us are also hostile to us in ways that go beyond the hates we always knew went with love. We feel betrayed because we are forced to recognize that the women in our lives were often deceiving us (and perhaps themselves) when they made us believe they

* William J. Goode, whose insights into the sociology of men's reactions to the women's movement illuminate the subject with unusual clarity, believes that the most important change that men experience is "a loss of centrality, a decline in the extent to which they are the center of attention." He emphasizes that we feel this particularly in "informal relations" with women, though it also may happen in the workplace. I would reply that the truth of this loss and our resentment of it conflict with our accepting change that benefits the women we love. So do the betrayals and rejections that hurt and anger us. That does not mean they prevent us from accepting change; conflict simply makes it more difficult. And Goode notes that we do see ourselves bound in coalition with our wives and daughters. This may, as he says, explain much of our resistance to feminism, which tries to break or reshape that coalition, but it also explains much of our acceptance of change at home. We would rather reshape the bond than give it up.[13]

were happy in the traditional system. Particularly in marriage, some of us feel outraged because women are rejecting the gifts of the breadwinner that we labored for, that we thought showed our love and would win their admiration.

SINGLE AND DIVORCED

Heterosexual men tend to feel the entire array of emotions about change, from betrayal and anger to love and identification, whether we are married or single. (Homosexual men feel comparable stresses, but that's beyond the compass of this book.) I did most of my interviews with people in dual-career marriages, but I found that the range of male feelings were shared by men in all the single categories (living with a woman, divorced, or never married) if they had any form of sustained or intimate relationship with women who work outside the home or seek autonomy in other ways. (Men in traditional marriages feel anger, fear, and anxiety even more sharply and are more likely to resist change.)*

The tendency of more and more people to live alone is important, however, because it's one more thing that is changing the balance of power between men and women. Not all of the increase is a rise in the number of single people; many unmarrieds used to live with their families, but a greater proportion are now on their own.

The number of unmarried people is growing, however. One reason for this trend can be found in the population statistics: there are fewer men than women in every age group over thirty, and the problem for women is greater both over and under thirty because men usually choose women who are younger than they are. The problem is probably worse for those women who postpone marriage while they rise in position and income in "male" occupations. There are too few unattached men above them for many to fulfill women's traditional desire to marry "up." The culture makes it hard to choose "down," and even if they do, men are likely to be leery of relationships with women who outearn or outrank them.

Increasing numbers of people also stay single by choice. They see marriage and family as limiting freedom to change roles or careers, to move, to grow, to develop networks of friends, to find new sexual partners. (There are, of course, counterpart reasons for people who would like to move from the

---

* It's important to distinguish between two-career and traditional marriages. Philip Blumstein and Pepper Schwartz, the authors of *American Couples,* did not. But their statistical survey on comparable questions reported different responses from couples who were married and couples who were living together.[14] Comparing my own interviews with their more extensive study, I found few significant differences among cohabiting couples, single people with experience of long relationships with working women, and couples in two-career marriages.

single to the married state, which helps to explain the increase in the number of marriages.)[15]

For some people these are merely reasons to be happy about being single, or to remain single longer, before or after marriage. They still think of the married state as at least temporarily desirable. But both sexes talk as though being single is preferable to marrying the wrong person or the wrong kind of person, and women often seem to be setting tougher standards than men. Or perhaps only newer ones. "There are few models for men who want to [meet women's demands that they] be both strong and tender, vulnerable without being weak, attentive and loving as fathers, husbands or lovers while at the same time reasonably successful in their working lives," William Novak reported after doing research on single people.[16] One of the men he interviewed complained, "They seem to be searching for some kind of androgynous man, a man who has all the qualities and sensitivities of a woman. I think they want some new kind of species that hasn't evolved yet." Some men voice much stronger resentments.

For others, reasons for remaining single are not transitory. They refuse the married state on the grounds that it injures the self, the selves of both partners. This refusal may rise from the shallowest narcissism or the deepest philosophical recognition of the loneliness of existence, but at every point on the spectrum, those who refuse feel that marriage contradicts the reality of their lives.[17] This tendency pleases men who—in a modern, "adult" version of the male infant's need to separate—don't want to commit themselves. It often terrifies men who hunger either for some deeper connection, egalitarian or dependent, or for someone programmed to let them dominate. Sometimes these are the same men who refuse commitment, unable to see that only commitment can give them what they long for.

Whatever the combination of psychological causes and effects, those who choose not to marry create a situation in which men and women must do things for themselves—clean house and nurture the body and the self, or maintain the car and cope with the outside world, among many examples— that they used to get from partners in traditional relationships. That changes the balance between them. Men who equate the single state with freedom or reject marriage for narcissistic reasons are not necessarily happy with the new balance, however. They often dislike taking care of themselves, and may find it hard as bachelors or later as benedicts to be supportive of women's claim to equality and independence.

The balance also changes in the alternatives to traditional marriage and family that small but increasing numbers of single people are trying. The most obvious leads two people to live together without marrying, which to my mind is hardly being single. Martin Marty, the Catholic theologian, said years ago it was the only revolution of the sixties that took hold among young people. He thought it undermined the intimate bonding needed to maintain society. That may be true of couples who stay together only for a few weeks or months. I can say from my interviews and from my own recent experience, however, that people who live together for long periods are usually making a commitment, even if it is not the lifetime commitment that is at least the hope of marriage. They often make as much effort as a married couple to be faithful to their partners, to create an intimate bond. They then create an institution intended to endure; its nature and structure are different from those of marriage, but still support an institution. It's one that is adaptable to change: individuals who live together are consciously resisting powerful social traditions and are likelier than conventional people to depart from traditional sex roles and male dominance as well.

Among other alternatives to marriage are "apartner" relationships in which two people commit themselves to each other but live apart and share few responsibilities of daily life. Some people share houses or apartments with people of the opposite sex without forming attachments. Some develop a "family of choice," sharing living quarters or not but relying on each other as people used to rely on families for the sharing of joy or sorrow. All these alternatives require men to share power and transcend traditional sex roles to some extent. Men who try them claim to like them—if they stay in them for any time.

Many of the people who choose the new reasons for being single are under forty. The young can spend years staying single by choice or professing high and narrow standards for a spouse and still have time to change their minds or discover a mate and marry. Alternatives like living together, apartners, and families of choice also appeal to many people over forty, however, many of whom claim to be single by choice after they divorce, though some of them make that choice only until they remarry.

Divorce is another area where men react to the changes that women are making. Sometimes change and reaction are both stark. Gideon Gordon* is a California lawyer in his fifties. He was and is in good shape from swimming and handball, but when he talked in 1977 about the end of his second marriage two years earlier, his athletic aura evaporated, his voice took on the melodic intensity of his Talmudist grandfather, and he grimaced so that his beard, shaped to make him look like Zeus, or at least like Ulysses, became rabbinical too. He said:

Four or five years ago my wife's friends started to leave their husbands. Not because the man was an alcoholic or beat her or was a poor provider. In every case the guy was reasonably decent. They all had at least one child. In every case it was a wish for fulfillment. "I want to be me," on feminist terms. When the number reached four, I said to my wife, "Thank God, that's four horsewomen of the Apocalypse." We were the fifth. The feminist make-your-own-space, be-me mystique had something to say about my marriage. I think it was a bad thing to break up my marriage. I don't think that either she or I have grown as a result.

Gordon displaced his anger from Natalie, who was his second wife, twenty years younger than he, to other women who had, he thought, shaped events. They had certainly made him see that marriage and work intersect:

Everyone saw Natalie as a slave. We had kids right away. A women's studies professor said to me, "Why don't you stay home and take care of the kids and let Natalie go out and work? After all, you've tried a hundred jury cases already, you don't need to litigate anymore." She had no sense of what a continuing life is about. And Natalie did get a master's degree while we were married, and had a job. We had enough money for a full-time housekeeper for the kids, and the feminists said, "You're hiring a woman slave."

Gordon claimed that one woman in his ex-wife's circle had incited trouble in all the marriages that ended. "She makes it with women," he said, voicing what might have been a fact but certainly fit a common male myth about the women's movement. "She's been putting pressure on her husband to find a man to make love with, to show solidarity with his own sex. She puts her sons in skirts. She's an obscene feminist. But their marriage survived, damnit."

Four years later Gordon's anger had subsided. He said of himself, "I've put my life together. I've not settled with one woman yet. I'm a little bewildered by my own reactions. I have too many, but I'm satisfied." He still believed the friend who incited their split "felt triumphant when my marriage ended." But his anger at Natalie had become something between sympathy and pity. He admired her ability to stand up to her boss, but felt that in her personal life she had become dependent on a series of men, which he saw as an ironic comment on her feminist motives for ending the marriage.

His anger had also been tempered by his enjoyment of the children of both his marriages. He was an enthusiastic father of the youngsters he had had with Natalie, grateful that she gave him wide access to them, and happy that her "feminist" desire for her own space and time reinforced her willingness to do so. He was also friends with his grown daughters; he applauded the independence of the older, exemplified in her career and her marriage, while having some doubts about the younger's involvement with a man whom he saw as inferior to her and who certainly earned less than she did. He acknowledged that the self-reliance of both women was an example of the good effects of feminism. After four more years he is even mellower, though he still has not embraced female self-reliance enough to marry again.

Some men see more validity than Gordon did in their wives' desire to plunge into autonomy or develop an identity that they feel marriage denied them. Eric Skjei and Richard Rabkin, writing about the "male ordeal," quoted one man who said he felt "victimized" and "manipulated" when his wife left him, but who came to understand that for her,

> it's a gut-level drive, like nothing can get in her way, nothing can stop her. It's like a survival drive. It's life and death. Like she's saying, "I'll die, I'll die, I'll actually physically die," if she has to stay in the marriage. She'll somehow vanish, be annihilated.
>
> I don't think men are really quite aware, generally, that there is this kind of desperate strength of determination going on in many, many women. . . . I know I was in disbelief, and I know that lots of men I know are getting the shock of their lives, every day, from their wives. . . .[18]

Even sadder than that man or angrier than Gideon Gordon are men whose wives have left them for another woman. Giving up heterosexual marriage for a homosexual relationship involves dramatic change in both women's and men's autonomy. Attention went first to women who left their husbands for a lesbian love, especially in the early 1970s when it seemed as much political as visceral, an extreme form of separatist feminism; later it became clear that men also were leaving their wives because they had newly discovered or newly acknowledged that they were gay. A handful of interviews suggests that the abandoned partner in these cases is much angrier than one who has been left for the traditional other man or other woman; there is no way to win the lost love back, to compete or compensate.

Women's demands for independence and equality have also affected conventional divorce. One result is more equitable division of property, including the homemaker's contribution in thirty-one states. Most men accept this but still resist the idea that a wife who supports her husband through professional school is entitled to compensation that may include a share of his future earnings, now being fought out in conflicting court decisions. Another result relates support or maintenance to a spouse's ability to support herself—or himself, since some courts have ordered support paid to men whose wives earn more than they do. Decisions on children are moving away from the automatic award of custody to the mother, particularly in the spread of joint custody. But many men complain bitterly that the system does not give fathers equal rights. Women complain just as bitterly that men seldom pay child support, and measures to compel payment have become matters of state and federal legislation. Passions in this area have become a major element in the development of the men's movement and its occasional conflict with the women's movement (see Chapter 12).

THE TWO-EARNER FAMILY

The two-earner relationship is the reality for most Americans. In many families, especially the growing proportion that can be called two-career rather than two-job, men are accepting more and more of the changes that grow up around the fact. Men respect their wives for developing skills and earning money. Men feel relief at not having to shoulder the economic burdens of the family alone. Men and women say they understand each other better because their worlds are less foreign to each other.

Yet the force of the traditional image is still so strong that men cannot always recognize the significance of their new emotions, so strong that the values that people profess do not yet match the reality. As I noted above, 52 percent of American women work. But Philip Blumstein and Pepper Schwartz, the authors of *American Couples,* surveying more than six thousand married, unmarried, and gay couples, found that among the married people (again lumping traditional and two-career marriages together) the proportion who believe both partners in a marriage *should* work was much smaller.* This study also found, however, that 74 percent of women and 66 percent of men who cohabit think both partners should work.[19] I believe that is likely to be the minimum level for dual-career married couples as well—but there, both partners are working in 100 percent of the cases!

The difference between the reality percentage and the "shoulds" proves there is conflict over change in American men but says nothing about what really happens in our souls when we are in a two-career marriage, or in the marriage as a functioning, dynamic system. Many of the things that happen are good, like the respect, identification, relief, and communication that I've mentioned. A large minority of the men I interviewed found pleasures like those I described in myself in Chapter 1, pleasures in the achievements of women colleagues and the women we've loved. It was hard for most of them to admit, as it was hard for me to recognize, that we also feel many of the emotions that complicate or damage relationships, or that these feelings are often stronger than the pleasures.

The first thing we feel, in our personal lives as in the workplace, is anxiety over this new mixture of work and love, because it blurs one of the fundamental boundaries by which we orient ourselves. Even the most liberated of us has somewhere in his head the idea that it is we who work and deal with the external world—and that it is women who bring us into the inner world of relationships, of sex and love, nurture and feelings. We worry that a woman who works, especially a woman who takes her work seriously, will change into a being who will not want or not be able to love us, to take care of us. We

---

* The figures: 39 percent of wives and 31 percent of husbands believe both partners in a marriage should work; 36 percent and 35 percent, respectively, were neutral, and 25 percent of wives and 34 percent of husbands do not believe both should work. The last figures go up to 60 and 64 percent when there are small children.

The authors reported no significant differences between younger and older people. They claimed to have interviewed couples at all income levels but made no distinctions between classes. My interviews suggest that a higher percentage of blue-collar men and women would vote for the traditional male breadwinner system.

would then have to face the fact that we are often more dependent than women are, a fact that traditional relationships protect us from because they are built on the assumption that women will be the caretakers.[20] We also worry that we ourselves will not want or not be able or (perhaps the worst of all) not have to provide for our women as a "real man" should. We worry that if we learn to express our own emotions, we will be less able to achieve things at work. We worry, in short, that in a two-earner family both man and woman may lose the sexual identity that we tie to work and love.† Neither blue-collar men nor high-income, educated men often express this anxiety in so many words, but we reveal it when we talk about many of the other problems that it underlies.

We certainly reveal it when we show fear that a woman's work will end our dominance, or the shade of advantage that we like to feel even when we have given up any thought of being lord and master in a relationship. I'm not talking here about the rare man whose wife makes twice as much money as he does. I'm not even talking about the more frequent cases when both partners hold professional, traditionally male jobs, though one study shows the chance of divorce in such marriages is twice as high as it is when the wife holds a traditionally female job, even if she's a nurse or teacher who earns more than her husband.[21]

The male fear of losing advantage shows up on such basic levels as the widespread assumption that it is up to the husband to "let" his wife work, even in a supposedly female job. It can take subtler forms. Carl Woodman,* the real estate developer and theatrical producer whom I quoted in Chapter 7, had helped his wife, Wendy, start an art gallery. I remarked that lots of men did not see that their wives needed help. Carl agreed and said many did not know how or did not want to help: "The guys who don't help, the obvious thing is their desire to maintain the edge. Large numbers of men are not comfortable unless they can maintain some sort of traditional advantage over their wives." Of course, sometimes helping a woman can be a way a man keeps that edge, a matter of patronage or paternalism. Carl felt that was not true in his own case because Wendy had gone from her initial dependence on his money and management skills to complete independence as a profit-making executive in her own right, and then to putting together investment and management teams for some of his ventures.

Carl Woodman put his finger on another fear that reveals our anxiety that working women may erase our (and their) identities. A woman at work, especially a woman with a career, is exploring worlds where the man in her life has no important or active role. He may fear that she will find a world

---

† For many people this fear operates in marriage but not outside it, which may be one explanation for the growing numbers of couples, both members earning, who live together without marrying.

that he cannot enter at all. (Lillian Rubin, the California social scientist and psychotherapist, spoke of a man who had said, "My wife is crossing over a bridge, and I am going to be left behind."[22]) Carl met a friend on a jet en route to their college reunion. The friend said his wife had written a book whose reviews and sales had been so good that they were both surprised.

I asked how that made him feel, and he said, "Well, I'm having some real problems with it. She's begun to travel around with writers and I'm a business guy and I can't penetrate that world. I get along in a lot of worlds that are unrelated to what I do, but the world of literary people seems particularly impervious to me. They don't really give a shit about what I'm doing. I try to care in a social way about what they're doing, but I find it difficult, and she's very much attracted to that world, and we've had some strain over it." A few weeks later, she left him. Obviously a lot more was happening there than he told me that time, but her success gave him real concern long before he discovered that.

He rang a bell with me because I was very worried that I might not be able to enter the art gallery world in which Wendy was operating. I was the same way my friend felt with writers. The art world is a very incestuous world, and I remember thinking there was no entry point for me in terms of being able to stay involved with what Wendy was doing, and I felt threatened by that. I was afraid. I worried she might have some private thing that would be inaccessible to me. In the end, I was able to see that she did want her own world—but it wasn't a world that would keep me out, just one she found for herself.

COMPETITION

There are many problems in a two-career marriage besides (but often related to) those fears of loss of dominance and inability to enter a woman's new world. I think one is more corrosive to the soul than all the others: competition between partners in love. Yet this problem is only beginning to get attention from sociologists and psychologists.

Competition, like aggression, is part of the psychological development of every human but seems stronger in males. It is not clear how much it is a product of aggressiveness and how much of socialization, but it is most clearly visible in traditionally masculine sports and occupations. In many of these competitiveness is an element of the constructive side of aggression: the drive to achieve a goal, to get work done that changes the external world, in a context that gives rewards for doing it before or better than someone else. It can also be harnessed to the destructive forms of aggression.

Psychoanalysis sees the paradigm of human competition in the son's oedipal rivalry with his father for the love of his mother, a struggle the boy always loses. If he wins any competition with his father, he weakens or destroys the model on which he is building much of his own identity; if he loses, he weakens the self he is trying to build. Therefore he represses his bond to his mother and his rivalry with his father and plunges himself into tension and insecurity. The father feels the rivalry and is hostile to his son, fearing the virility he bequeaths him. The boy fears castration, which generates new insecurity. Both as part of the oedipal rivalry and in contradiction to it, the boy attempts to develop a masculine self by identifying with his father, but the father is usually absent at work and alien in his authority and repressed emotions. This subjects the boy to yet another kind of tension. To resolve all these insecurities, to bolster his identity, he searches for reassurance, recognition, and reward. In school and sports and work, these have traditionally been won in competitive struggle. In the identification process, the boy may replace the absent father with cultural images of masculinity and with other men, both frequently figures from competitive worlds. In addition to his struggles with his father, he may experience sibling rivalry, competition of another kind for the mother's love. Competition is the constant companion of his growing up.[23]

The insecurities of growing up may also make girls competitive. A girl competes with her mother for the love of her father, and she experiences the competitions of sibling rivalry as much as her brother does. In today's changing world, girls and women in growing numbers also learn to develop and assert their strengths at school and work. At any age a female who does this may be identifying with her father, an ambivalent process in itself. She may be elaborating a new stage of identification with her mother if her mother works outside the home, a stage that may contradict her earlier identification with her mother as nurturer. Any of these paths is likely to plunge her into insecurity not only because of its inherent ambivalences but also because it conflicts with traditional female roles, and insecurity increases her compulsive drive for recognition and reward just as it does a man's.

Traditionally for men, and today for both sexes, this psychological process is reinforced by the scarcity of reward in Western culture and economy; feudalism, capitalism, and existing forms of socialism all make most paths to achievement, wealth, or power competitive.

Ironically, jealousy and envy, the emotions that return so destructively in competition in marriage, begin in competition for a reward that is not in short supply—in competition, whether with father or with siblings, for mother love. The mother's time and energy are always limited compared to the child's desire for her attention, and all the more so today when mother is likely to work outside the home. The child may perceive this as meaning that her love, too, is limited. This is the root of jealousy. Originally jealousy is the feeling that the rival is getting more of the parental affection than you are. Later it can be of two kinds. One fears the loss of an object of desire or love to someone else. The other sees someone else as already having what we want.

This jealousy can grow, or decay, into envy. Willard Gaylin differentiates these two by defining envy as independent of your relationship to the people you envy. To feel envy, you must feel that you are denied something you want; that somebody else, with whom you compare yourself, has it; that you are powerless to repair the disparity; and that you do not have what you want *because* the other has it. Envy makes you convert noncompetitive situations into false competitions, as you do when you find yourself unhappy at a friend's success even though it costs you nothing and deprives you of nothing.[24]

Women traditionally experience envy and jealousy as much and as sharply as men, or more. They too must therefore be competitive. But traditionally they competed against one another, not against men and not in the world of work, so men did not associate the idea or even the word "competition" with them. And competition still retains its male aroma in an age when women *are* competing with men for achievement, wealth, and power.

I am not sure that men today are still significantly more competitive than women, but my interviews suggest that in marriage it is usually the man who is the first or likelier to feel competitive. Often, however, it is the woman who makes the matter a conscious one—like the wives who say they are careful not to earn more than their husbands, though the husbands have never brought the matter up. Women still are socialized not to compete with men, and apparently this persists longer in relation to their husbands than it does in relation to peers at work.

Competition is certainly much more frequent in two-earner than in traditional marriages.[25] When both men and women work for pay, both play roles that used to be considered male, whether breadwinning in general or holding "masculine" jobs in particular. Competition can pit mates against each other in terms of who works harder, who makes more money, who gets more attention at a work-related party or more publicity in the media, who has higher status within his or her occupation, who has greater authority. They act as though the victory of one partner in the outside world of work can only come at the expense of the other in the marriage. Often this is tragic nonsense, but sometimes it is real. I interviewed three men who are happy with their wives' achievements even when the women earn more in higher-ranking jobs—but who don't want to work directly for their wives. Two said that would put the difference in authority on the line and create a relationship contradicting the reality of struggle for egalitarian balance at home; I inferred that for the third, it would contradict his fantasy of male dominance despite the wife's status.

The man with that fantasy was one of those men who see competition with their wives or lovers as a woman's challenge to male advantage (a matter of fearful jealousy). They compete to reassert or recapture that margin, to win. Some men see competition as a woman's way of denying the man the femi-

nine care that was once both a prime need and a reward for competing
against other males (a matter of potential envy). They compete to punish her
and compensate themselves. Other men, more secure in themselves and in
their masculine identity, do not see it that way. But they too may be socialized to compete as a matter of course against "anyone who does the same
thing I do."

Both partners in two-career families are also apt to play traditionally female roles as the man does a greater share of the housekeeping and child care,
and that too may lead to competition: who does more housework in a given
week, say, or who cooks or cleans better.

The clearest picture of destructive competition in my research was, to my
sorrow, my own marriage to Susan Jacoby. In some ways we were made for a
worst-case example. We were in the same profession. We were both ambitious
and competitive before we ever knew each other. I was a husband thirteen
years older than his wife, so that our life cycles were likely to go out of kilter
in ways that would increase both the competition itself and many of the other
strains of married life likely to intensify competition.

When we married, I was a star foreign correspondent and Susan was a
young reporter. Marrying me turned out (to our shock) to mean Susan's
giving up her career with the Washington *Post,* first when she took a leave to
go with me to Moscow and then when I was reassigned to New York, where
there was no job for her (see Chapter 1). Her anger at the deformation of her
career and at the insult of being treated in both Moscow and Washington as a
wife rather than a journalist made her more competitive than I was in the first
four years of our marriage.

But having no daily journalism to do in Moscow gave her the opportunity,
or compelled her, to put together material for two excellent books about the
Soviet Union that were published in our first years in New York. I had not
organized my coverage to make the traditional *tour d'horizon* of the Soviet
Union easy, and my attempts to market a book about Soviet science found no
publisher. I was jealous of what I saw as her achievement in "my" field, and I
became more competitive with her; in adults as in children, jealousy grows
out of competition and vice versa. This was intensified and jealousy turned to
envy when she won assignments to write about two Soviet figures for the New
York *Times Magazine,* though the first came while I was still with the Washington *Post* and could not possibly have sought or accepted a commission
from a competitor. (Susan remembered in 1985 that I had voiced my envy at
the time. She thought it had been expectable and something we were, or
should have been, able to handle.)

Our competition sharpened further when Susan made her free-lance breakthrough with a *Times Magazine* article about blue-collar feminists in 1973.
Her career was visibly going up just as mine seemed to be going down (as I
thought when the *Post* in effect forced me to quit). The same achievements

that fed my love and admiration fed my envy; in adults as in children, insecurity feeds the wrong kind of competitiveness. It took Susan years to master the insecurities, economic and professional, that are inescapable in a freelance existence, and that made her more competitive; she didn't believe she was as successful as I thought she was. For years I felt she was insufficiently grateful for the help I had given her by making editorial suggestions or by introducing her to people who gave her assignments or advice or pointed her toward grants. Whatever the objective facts, I felt that her failure to acknowledge the help I had given was a failure to acknowledge my "superior" position in our competition. That made it impossible for me to feel, as she did, that this was the kind of help any professional gives friends and even acquaintances. Later I could agree that my demand for expressions of gratitude was comparable to a husband's expectation of praise from his wife for scrubbing a kitchen floor.

But I still felt that colleagues who are also spouses are both closer and likely to be more bitterly competitive than either colleagues or spouses. Our professional competition and our personal problems fed on each other in a destructive synergy. We argued about abstruse subjects with a heat fueled by our rivalry as writers as well as by our quarrels over housekeeping, money, sex, and all the other things that married couples fight about. Our mutual hostility might never have reached a level that made the marriage impossible if we had been able to master our competition.

MONEY AND POWER

Money is a source of competition and conflict between men and women, and also of mutual support. It plays a major part in determining relative power in both two-earner and traditional marriages, and indeed in almost all relationships in our society. At least men tend to use money to assess a person's identity and power. Women traditionally see money as a matter of security; today they also associate it with autonomy, which is only a short step from power. As women become more familiar with the world of work for pay, they become more and more willing to make money the measure of power and to do the measuring themselves. That produces new anxieties in many men. Women's readiness to use money as a yardstick increases as their earnings rise, and men increasingly combine anxiety with anger and fear. The male emotions proliferate and intensify further when a woman consistently earns more money than her man, making him feel he has lost the male edge.

Blumstein and Schwartz found that in their mixture of traditional and two-earner married couples, both husband and wife see the man's income as determining the couple's place in the world. Cohabitors are more likely to make satisfaction a matter of individual economic success, but male cohabitors are like the husbands in that study in ignoring their partners' income in measuring their own well-being.[26] In contrast, the two-earner couples I interviewed tend to take both incomes into account in measuring the family's place in society; most regard their households as joint enterprises in a much truer sense than traditional families. But I suspect it is easier for the men to take this seemingly egalitarian view because they retain the male edge by making more money than their wives. Two men whose wives earn more than they do are less willing to measure their social standing by combining the two incomes. That would translate their economic disadvantage into a degree of dependence they couldn't acknowledge.

Most of the men I talked with earn more than their wives do (as the man does in most two-earner couples), welcome their wives' contribution to the family exchequer, and acknowledge that this has changed the balance of power. Many are even happy with the idea that the woman has more power and the man less than they used to—so long as they still have the usually unvoiced feeling of male advantage.

Ed Dudkiewicz* is this kind of pragmatist. He is a high school graduate from a blue-collar family of Polish descent, not a background that makes departure from tradition easy. But he asked his wife, Elizabeth,* to go to work because his job as an auto mechanic didn't produce enough money for the life they wanted in a lower-middle-class suburb of New York. The only job she could find was working as a waitress. His brother was making money as the owner-driver of a taxicab, so Ed decided to quit his job as a mechanic and buy his own cab. After driving for a while, he thought that Liz, who was a good driver, could produce more by sharing the taxi driving than by waiting tables. When I met them, they jointly owned the business—in which the taxi itself was less important than the medallion that allowed it to operate in New York City, which was then worth forty-three thousand dollars. It was not a matter of equal rights in Ed's eyes, but of saving money; if Liz had not been an owner, she'd have been an employee, and Ed would have had to pay her employee benefits. He said:

> I want Liz to work so that we can live better. Buy the boat we want—twenty-eight feet—have a decent house, go out to a good restaurant if we want to. My best friend and my brother-in-law won't let their wives work, but it doesn't bother me if someone says my wife works, or even that my wife *has* to work. I like the money she makes. . . . Between us we gross five hundred to a thousand dollars a week. It depends on whether we work every other day or each work a twelve-hour shift the same day. It's a lot for her and for me too, but I like the money part of it.

Ed is the kind of man who has no use for "women's lib" even though he brings some of its ideas to life. "I don't look at that at all," he added. "I look at the money part of it. To me, it keeps her better than staying home and getting fat."

Ed and Liz pool their earnings in a joint bank account, like the majority of American couples. Pooling seems appropriate for two-earner couples at first glance, but it's also the system of traditional, male-dominant marriage, and it often conceals traditional values. Caroline Bird, analyzing a survey of five thousand self-selected couples, found that partners see the joint account as a symbol of mutuality but that pooling in fact does not assure equality or even joint participation in spending decisions.[27] Even at combined income levels as high as ninety thousand dollars, in couples that pool earnings, the men usually make the major financial decisions.[28]

In my interviews I found fewer husbands in pooling couples openly making the major decisions. But several husbands in this group are disturbed or angry because their wives refuse to pool everything. The men put all their earnings into "our" account and feel their wives have always had partial control of that money—but are now denying them equivalent control of the money the women earn. The women feel that the men really control the joint accounts, even in some couples where both partners say they share spending decisions. More wives than husbands prefer separate accounts so they can control their own money. Some of these husbands have agreed, but voice resentment.

Ten of the thirty-eight two-earner couples I interviewed were what Bird calls "bargainer couples," where both husband and wife agree that a paycheck belongs to the person who earns it and divide household expenses either fifty-fifty or in proportion to their incomes. They maintain separate bank accounts, though seven of my ten also have a joint account to which each contributes for mortgage or rent, food, children's needs, and other common expenses. This combination of separate and joint accounts seems to produce the fewest fights. I thought at first it was of value mainly for those with upper-middle and higher incomes, but the factory worker wife of a farmer had to switch her unemployment checks from their joint checking account to a savings account in her own name before she could persuade her husband to listen to her suggestions on how it should be spent.[29] Joint accounts, whether pooled or "bargainer," work better when there's good communication between the partners and work best for people with similar financial outlooks. A free spender and a tidy saver have to do a lot of work to avoid battle over what happens to the joint money.

Bird also analyzed two other ways of dealing with money in two-earner marriages. In "pin money couples" the husband tells the wife to keep her money and use it for whatever she likes, so that he won't have the pain of seeing the money or acknowledging that they need it. I met no one following this traditional line. "Earmarker couples" designate the wife's earnings for particulars so they can pretend that they are living on the husband's pay but that she helps him. Two of my couples fell in this category.

When I asked who controlled spending, I was surprised at the number who said both partners shared equally, regardless of the way they managed money (twenty-seven husbands and twenty-four wives in thirty-eight couples; *American Couples* similarly found that 63 percent of married couples claimed that husbands and wives participated equally in spending on furniture.[30]) Some of these answers were sincere, the result of explicit acknowledgment that money is a matter of power and of conscious effort to share that power. Others had the ring of people saying what they thought I wanted to hear, or what they thought their spouses wanted to hear. Some of the men in the latter group were disguising the advantage they thought they still had; some of the women were disguising the fact that their men didn't have it.

The men who did not claim equal voices in spending decisions were engaged in other kinds of denial. Some asserted a right to veto major purchasing decisions like a house or a car but seldom exercised it. Others said they delegated responsibility to the wife in a way that suggested relegating her to the traditional role of buyer and bill payer for the family. It seems to me that they were imagining male money power that they seldom had in fact; if the wife of such a husband earns more than a third of the family income, she has more power in the family balance than he recognizes.

The situation that most clearly links money to power, and most sharply contradicts the traditional image of marriage, is the one in which the woman makes more money than the man. In 1983 there were 7.1 million wives who earned more than their husbands—14.2 percent of the 50 million couples with both partners present.[31]

Psychology Today, analyzing data from a December 1980 survey, reported that husbands who earned less than their wives fantasized and worried about money more than other husbands, and had lower self-esteem. In one third of the cases where the husband earned less, he said his love for his spouse was greater than her love for him or was unrequited. The men were less happy with their marriages in general and reported their sex lives in worse shape than men who earned more than their wives. The husbands' combined perception of themselves as more loving and their sex lives as bad implies that the men felt their wives didn't want sex with husbands who earned less, or were too busy making big money to bother with bed. But Isaiah M. Zimmerman, a Washington, D.C. therapist, says that in couples among his patients where the wife earns more, the husband often withdraws sexually. "He claims fatigue or demands of work. He not only loses sexual interest but becomes anxious if his wife approaches him sexually or makes an attempt to seduce him in a straightforward way." This suggests that the husbands fear being dominated in bed as they feel they are in the checkbook.[32]

Wives who earned more than their husbands (not necessarily the wives of the men surveyed) agreed that they were less likely to return their husbands' love and had sexual intercourse less often than women who earned less, *Psychology Today* reported. These women argued about money more often than other wives and, like the husbands who earned less, were more obsessed with it. But perhaps because they earned so much, they were more satisfied with their finances and had higher self-esteem than other wives.

In another survey of men in comparable situations, Carlton Hornung and Claire McCullough of the University of South Carolina studied Kentucky men who were underachievers (their education was greater than their occupational status) married to women who were overachievers. They found that about 80 percent were likely to be victims of "psychological abuse" by their wives. Hornung did another study in which he found that among underachieving men between forty and fifty married to overachieving women the death rate from ischemic heart disease is eleven times higher than the norm.[33] Alcoholism and depression are also often associated with a husband's economic dependence on a wife, though it's not always clear which is cause and which is effect.[34]

The truth of these observations only emphasizes their echo of women's many accounts of the way their economic dependency on men has withered them. Our society, however, still tends to find dependency expectable in women and alarming or contemptible in men, so the increase in men's economic dependency on women is a change to which it is extremely hard to adjust.† But it doesn't always have to be dependency. Some women find that the removal of traditional male financial dominance frees the partners to mesh their needs and their gifts, their weaknesses and strengths in ways that are not based on gender, or at least not on sex-role stereotypes.[36] I suspect this happens more easily in cases where the woman does not assert dominance just because she earns more money, but even then the man may have trouble feeling good about the economic reality.

I interviewed eight men who earned significantly less than their wives. All but two claimed they had adjusted to their situation. Three said their economic situation had helped their marriages become more egalitarian, but they were among the five who admitted that acceptance came only with considerable difficulty. In many cases I heard overtones suggesting that the acceptance was still less and the difficulty still greater than the men were admitting. Even where the man seemed as happy as he claimed, I found the testimony of pain important.

Jim Calabrese* and his wife became parents early in their marriage and originally planned to alternate primary responsibility for income earning and child care. But Ruth* rose faster and further as a magazine editor than he could as a teacher, and he has spent seven years as househusband, Ph.D.

† In this context it is no surprise that typical American millionaires, not figures from "Dynasty" or *Town and Country* but men who have built up small businesses like a string of dry cleaning stores or hamburger franchises, men who are and expect to be dominant in marriage, have wives whom one researcher described as "airheads about money; a lot of them can't balance a checkbook." Four out of ten of these wives work, but their average pay is only ten thousand dollars a year. The marriages last for many years.[35]

candidate, and part-time college instructor while she earned most of the money. He enjoys this role reversal and takes pride in its results:

> It's rare to find a real man with both masculine and feminine sides developed. Living this way brought forth parts of my feminine nature that I never would have discovered otherwise. I'll be out in the room preparing a lecture, and I'll have to go do the dishes. That's slipping out of the male gear in which all things progress and into cyclic things that women associate with the seasons.

Jim's pleasure in this aspect of his life made it all the more poignant when he said:

> You know, my background is Italian. A man who lives by a woman, the Italians say he's a gigolo. There are times when I have to fight off despondency because by traditional standards, I don't make it. I'm a part-time teacher and by money standards alone, teachers are shit. So I work like a son of a bitch trying to prove that even though I'm a failure by that standard, I'm not lazy, I'm working. I'm going crazy, putting twice as much into my lectures as some teachers do and doing twice as much work as most men do, with the teaching and the housework.

OVERLOAD AND CONFLICT

The balance of money and power, like competition, is clearly a major problem in two-career marriages. Other problems seem less profound at first glance but in fact are far from trivial. Over the long run they can erode a relationship as deeply as the others.

One of these problems is overload, the strains on both partners in trying to find enough time in the day or the week for their jobs, their housekeeping, their children, and their connection to each other—the last three being things for which the woman was responsible in traditional relationships, but that the man must share in a two-earner family.

Another problem is conflict between the two partners' careers and between careers and family.[37] If one partner accepts a series of transfers involving promotion, it may abort the other's career. If one is in a profession that demands heavy overtime, the other may have to choose work that allows more time at home. The timing of children always affects a mother's career and often the father's, too. There may be another conflict of timing if one partner is much older than the other. It's usually the male who is heading for retirement while the female's career is entering its peak period. A third problem is conflict between the partners and their respective families, their neighbors, or the community, any or all of which may still follow traditional norms. There are still many people, prime among them parents, who make fun of a man who doesn't do most of the breadwinning or who does a serious amount of housework and child care.

People in different classes deal with these problems in different ways; usually, the higher the income, the easier it is to find a solution. A book publisher married to a television executive will not feel the same strains of overload as a factory hand and a beautician; they can afford a nanny and a maid even in an era when servants are scarce, and neither has to work a night shift to make sure someone is there to care for small children. But upper-income people do have problems in certain jobs, particularly in business management, and in younger age groups. I interviewed an international banker who postponed transfer abroad several times to allow his wife to pursue her work as a hospital management consultant; he finally took a post in Europe when she was ready to suspend her career long enough to have a couple of children.

For men and women in every class, however, these conflicts in love are painful. In most cases it's still the woman who makes the sacrifice and feels the pain of frustration in the development of her career or her quest for equality and autonomy.[38] Some men never feel their wives' pain. Many do, but cannot stand the pain that they themselves would feel from an equal sacrifice that would erode their traditional dominance or traditional signs of sexual identity. To reduce overload, for instance, a man may have to give up some of the extra hours he works. To give his wife's career equal opportunity to develop, he may have to forgo a transfer that would mean promotion for him but would force her to change jobs. Working long hours and uprooting the home in a transfer are both burdens, but they help advance his career, increasing his strength and authority vis à vis others (his wife among them), and are seen as signs of maleness. For some men, giving up the burden is easier than giving up the symbols.

Today more and more men are trying to resolve these conflicts in ways that approach the egalitarian. Some two-career couples alternate or refuse all transfers or try commuter marriages so both can hold better jobs, but in different cities. Some take joint responsibility for housework and child care and find friends who support their departures from tradition. It's seldom easy because the traditional image is so strong. Most women feel the cost is worth the achievement and the independence they were once denied. Most men have moments when they feel they are giving up something that was once important to them, and they wonder if the result is really worth the price. Of course, many men believe it is. A growing minority are thoughtful, cheerful, even enthusiastic about living so their wives' work and their own are equally important. But it's still a struggle and it still can hurt.

Commuter marriage is a compelling example of spouses' efforts to make both careers equal. Nobody knows how many of the 26.1 million two-career marriages are trying the commuter option; guesses range from 500,000 to 2 million, and the sociologists who have studied it most closely are sure the number is increasing. The couples tend to be white, middle or upper-middle class, and well educated; many are academics. A five-year study of 121 commuter couples found that they are angry at having to be apart and feel they have made more sacrifices for their marriage than most couples do. They reported fewer trivial conflicts and some spoke of "rediscovery" or "transformation" of the marriage in their periodic reunions. They all had problems in housework and child care. About a third of the commuter spouses had extramarital affairs, but the proportion is the same or higher for all married couples, and timing and motivation suggested that the commuting was not the cause for the couples in the study.[39] Couples in other studies reported ambivalence among their friends and employers about their choice of marital structure. A minority ultimately get divorced. Many revert to normal one-household marriage when they can find jobs in the same city, but that too can require compromise and sacrifice, as Paul and Cynthia Wallach* discovered.

Paul is a research chemist; his wife, Cynthia, teaches the history of science. He's thirty-four, she thirty-one. When they married in 1979, he had a job with one of the top companies in his industry, doing work he liked, with good prospects for rising income and authority. She was working for her Ph.D. When she finished, she was offered a teaching job as attractive to her as Paul's was to him—but in a city 250 miles away. They tried commuter marriage, hardly ever more than a temporary expedient for any couple, and found they both hated being apart. "I'd only do it for love," Paul said, "but I didn't feel good about a love that allowed me to be with the person I loved for only two days every two or three weeks." It cost them money to maintain two homes and two cars, even though Cynthia took a roommate. Paul disliked doing all his own housework even though he cheerfully took responsibility for half of it when they lived together; he had more problems resisting the temptation to have extramarital affairs than Cynthia did and worried more about her temptations than she did about his.

After a year of commuting, they decided it was not something they could live with. Paul thought Cynthia would be able to find an acceptable job within reach of his workplace. She couldn't. By the end of the second year, they settled for a move from northern to southern California, to a combination of company for him and college for her that each rated acceptable but that neither found as desirable as their original jobs. Cynthia said, "I'm not crazy about it, but it was the best compromise we could find, and compromise is something you have to expect when two people try to deal with conflicts of interest in marriage." Paul agreed that it's expectable but had a harder time accepting it. When he talked about it, he bent his tall frame as he sat so that he was looking down at the floor; he has a high forehead, glasses, fair skin, and blond curly hair, and his face flushed as he said:

> I was brought up so that I wanted to be not the world champion, but in the
> top class in whatever I did. And there are times when I realize it wasn't just

that I wanted to be one of the best, I had it in my head that a man is supposed to be the best he can. Well, in this company I'll never be a world-class chemist, and sometimes I wonder, am I being as much of a man as I can be? Am I being as much of a man as I want to be? Did I really have to give that up in order to give Cyn equal opportunity? I know that when you make a real commitment to total equality, every step is a certain compromise. But I still have moments when I ask myself, couldn't one of us have a top job, did we both have to take second-rank jobs?

And then I wonder, suppose it was Cyn who was offered a top job, could I take a third-rank job, would I be willing to, if that was all there was in some place where Cyn could teach in a first-class university? I'm not sure I could compromise that far. Thinking like that makes me angry sometimes, or it can depress me. Maybe that's why I don't make as much effort to go to Cyn's faculty parties as she does to go to my company shindigs. Then I feel guilty because I make so much effort to keep this marriage an equality. I want it that way and I'm happier that way, so why do I get angry or depressed or feel guilty? Sometimes I talk to Cyn about it, but sometimes I can't. She's great to talk to and lots of times she's helped me figure it out, but she reminds me that we talked a lot before we got married about how hard it was to try for an equal marriage, and I feel as though she's saying, "I never promised you a rose garden."

I asked Paul whether the reactions of the Wallachs' friends or family or of the community made any difference. He replied:

Cynthia's mother has some problems, I think, that I'm not taking proper care of her daughter. . . . All of our friends are in marriages or relationships with both people working, but I feel as though I never hear them talk about this. I know for some of them, if there's a real crunch, the man's career takes priority. I've seen articles about taking turns, or refusing to move unless both people can find satisfactory jobs in the new place, lots of things like that. It's all very nice and rational and can even help people plan. But nothing I've seen tells you how hard it really is, how hard it is for a man and a woman to take their work equally seriously. It's hard for both of them, but I think it's harder for the man to put his wife's work first.

Paul came back to my question later in the interview:

It really pisses me off that our society still expects a wife to help her husband when she has a job or a career of her own. How many companies do anything to help a spouse find a job when they want you to transfer? How many do anything to give a father time off when his wife has a baby or so he can take care of a child? Not very fucking many.* I'm an instinc-

---

* In 1985 more than 1,800 American employers were providing some form of child care assistance to their employees, compared with 600 in 1982.[40] But the nation has 5 million employers. Catalyst, a nonprofit organization that works to prevent gender from being a factor in the careers

tive Republican, but I want the government to do something to make employers get on the stick. So far as I can tell, this kind of thing has gotten worse under Reagan, but I don't see either party paying much attention to it despite all the talk about the gender gap.

ROLE CHANGE AND HOUSEWORK

Paul Wallach knew that when Cynthia pursued her career, she was changing a major sex role: she was biting into the part of the breadwinner. He was happy with that, but not with a change that expected him to do all the housework. At every level of society, shifts in other sex-role tasks and particularly in housework have been slower and smaller than changes in the wage-earning role. This lag illustrates anew how great resistance is to change in both men and women, how strong the classic sex roles are.* Men in particular are reluctant to give up the aspect of dominance in which housework, child care, and all the business of ensuring the survival of the species are menial female labor, to be hidden like females in private as they have been since early times. We tend to dismiss the issue as trivial, but it can be deadly serious. Many of us quite literally cannot feed ourselves or wash or even buy our own clothes. We need a woman to help us or do it for us. Our inability to take care of our bodily needs is, like our difficulties expressing our emotional needs, one of the main causes of male violence.

We often talk as though we were not reluctant to give up our exemption from housework, as though we were ready to accept change here too, but we seldom practice what we preach. In my interviews, twenty-four of the thirty-eight two-career husbands claimed they were either willing or obligated to do at least half the housework. But checking their own recollections of what they actually did, and their wives' perceptions, only ten turned out to live up to their principles. One claimant to equal time turned out to make Sunday breakfast. Another had agreed to do the dishes every night his wife cooked, but after an hour of conversation he admitted that at least three nights in the week he was "too tired from work" to fulfill his contract, and that he seldom made beds and never vacuumed.

---

of men or women, reports that in 1984, 119 companies, 36 percent of corporations responding to a survey, offered men paternity leave, usually unpaid—a rise from 8.6 percent in 1980. Very few men take such leave. Catalyst also estimates that 20 to 25 percent of all companies have formal policies offering placement help to "trailing spouses" when their own employees were transferred. Many more offer informal assistance. Both formal and informal programs use third parties who begin by offering relocating families assistance in buying and selling houses and go on to helping spouses find jobs.[41]

* Some sociologists used to think that men do less housework and child care than women because they spend so much time and energy on their paid work. Joseph Pleck has reviewed several studies of husbands' and wives' family work. He finds that the demands of paid jobs are important but less significant in determining how much family work husbands and wives do than the roles, expectations, and behaviors created by individual, family, and culture.[42]

Broader surveys show similar results. Gayle Kimball summarizes thirty-four studies of the division of family work between spouses. Several show men with egalitarian beliefs, but not a single one shows husbands *doing* as much as wives. The closest is Kimball's own research into seventy-one couples where both partners have egalitarian attitudes; the women average 32.5 hours a week on housework and child care and the men 29.4 hours.[43] I like the specifics in one advertising poll that is not on her list. It shows 64 percent of men saying that washing dishes is equally appropriate for husband and wife, but only 39 percent doing half of the dish washing. Comparable figures for vacuuming are 53 percent and 27 percent, for cooking 44 percent and 22 percent, and for doing laundry 33 percent and 16 percent.[44] In high-income couples, too, with household earnings of more than eighty thousand dollars a year, the women put in many more hours per week on housework and child care than did the men.[45]

There are some signs that things are getting better. Joseph Pleck, collating several studies, concluded that wives spend less time and husbands more time in family work than they did twenty years ago—that their levels are converging. He also found that employed wives' overload relative to that of their husbands was disappearing—not that they were doing less family work, but that their total of time in family and paid work was almost exactly equal to their husbands' total. And he found that social sentiment that husbands should do more family work was increasing.[46]

But the two major studies that Pleck reviewed still showed wives doing about twice as much family work as their husbands, even with the convergence. It is not at all clear that "new" or "emerging" egalitarian values will be adopted by a majority of men, or that if they are, performance will catch up with attitudes. There is further room for doubt because some observers are discovering that egalitarian behavior does not necessarily increase people's happiness. While many men exaggerate their contribution to household tasks, others do them but don't boast about them and indeed feel bad about them. I will never forget one of the first men I talked to for this book, a gray-faced man shifting a load of laundry from washer to dryer in a gray-walled apartment basement laundry room. He was a retired air force officer who had gone into the advertising business and married an assertive woman. He did half the chores, but he told me that his wife's demand that he do them and the admission of women to the Air Force Academy were both examples of "the weakening of the national fabric." I thought of him when I read Blumstein's and Schwartz's report that the more housework married men do, the more they fight with their wives about it.[47]

Yet Pleck found that in two-earner families, the husband adjusts better as he puts in more total time in paid work or family work or the two combined. The wife's adjustment worsens as she works more total time in every category except child care, which is positively related to family adjustment for both sexes.[48] A Michigan researcher, analyzing traditional and "modern" men in two-earner couples, came to the conclusion that a modern man may feel damaged by housework if he feels he is doing it at the expense of his "real" work. But he can be happy about doing it (perhaps as an achievement of his own, perhaps as a contribution to his wife's or the family's well-being) when it goes along with good work in the kind of job that he likes and that attests to his competence and his masculinity.[49] For most men, however, doing more housework and child care means being less productive, less ambitious, and earning less in their paid work.

There may be room for a grain of hope. Men usually do not learn to love housework by doing it, but the experience sometimes makes them realize they can no longer expect their wives to find fulfillment in it. Mike McGrady became a househusband for a year and concluded in a humorous book, "This is a job that should not be done by any one person for love or for money."[50] Vic Lawson, the shipping manager with whom this chapter began, would never describe himself as "progressive" or "pro-feminist," but he knew from the beginning that his wife wouldn't do it because she hates it. He therefore does the housework himself: "I'm probably too damn cheap to get a maid." In fact, he decided to take on the housework when his youngest child was old enough for nursery school and he and Barbara could not afford both that and a maid to replace the housekeeper who had just quit. Vic does the laundry and the vacuuming once a week.

Barbara's boss, a trucker who rose into management, shows what hope is up against when it comes to housework. He was astonished when she told him that Vic ironed his own shirts. "I thought he was going to jump right over the desk and kill me," she recalled with a smile. "He literally was horrified. He said, 'You don't make that man do the ironing, you can't be serious!' I said, 'I don't make him iron his own shirts, he can wear them wrinkled or take them down to the cleaners, I don't give a damn what he does with them, but I'm not going to iron them!' And to this day he cannot believe that. He is absolutely horrified at the thought that any man would be willing to do such woman's work."

Cooking does no better than other "woman's work" in the surveys that compare what men say with what they do, but for an increasing number of men, cooking is different. Other chores seem repetitive and mindless efforts that yield no positive products but only hold off the tides of dirt and decay. Cooking yields products that can be enjoyed, if only briefly. Men have learned that cooking can be an art, or a technique of seduction. In both cases, they are using a traditionally female skill for traditionally male functions. Cooking can also be an experience of nurturing, using a female skill for a traditionally female function, but one in which a man can find validation of his existence (see story of Sidney Miller in Chapter 13).

Cooking is another subject on which I want to offer my own testimony. I made dinner a few years ago for my first wife, Gail Potter Neale. She smiled as we finished the main course. I asked why, and she said, "We've known each other for twenty-five years and it's the first time you've ever made dinner for me." I was not really surprised at her memory, which I knew to be accurate. But I was a bit startled because it reminded me that I had cooked seldom in my second marriage as well as in my first. Both my wives are superb cooks, so it was easy for me to depend on them. Only when Gail spoke did I acknowledge to myself that I had been sticking to sex-role stereotype despite what I thought of as a slightly raised consciousness during my first marriage and a higher one in my second. But I became a decent cook in the seven years between marriages, and it was startling to realize that in my second I had not only denied Susan the pleasure of being served regularly, I had also denied myself what I now know to be a pleasure.

Cooking makes me feel good. I feel good because I can indulge my own delight in the joy of eating. I feel good because cooking makes me feel competent, both in the display of an artistic skill and in taking care of myself instead of depending on someone else, usually a woman. I also feel good because this competence enables me to take care of others, women among them. Cooking has become one of the few places where I am sure I live up to my own egalitarian goals.

Because cooking has a nurturing aspect, I feel when I cook for someone I love that I am, at least for a short time, taking care of the relationship. Traditionally women did this. It was women who put more time and energy into love and living together than into work and career. Today women are still more likely than men to put relationships before work, but more and more men are putting more and more time and energy into the relationship or the family than they used to, just as an increasing number of women are putting work first.[1]

THE GOOD SIDE

That more men are learning to put time and energy into their relationships just as more women are learning to put time and energy into their work seems to me to be a wonderful thing. It is one of many good things flowing from the changes in power and sex roles, in two-earner marriages and in all relationships. I've been dwelling on the difficulties, the pain, the stress, and the cost because I want to emphasize that neither gentle change nor dramatic revolution is easy. But there are also benefits that I want to come back to.

First is the relief that men feel from learning that the women in our lives can bring in the money that we need to live well in today's strained economy. If we recognized and acknowledged this relief from the burden of the old breadwinner role, more of us might be able to deal with the strains we feel from "failing" in that antiquated part. Beyond buying basic needs and luxuries, two incomes can enable one partner to follow a career that entails risks in free-lancing or entrepreneuring while the other earns steady money. I mentioned this as a conflict if the latter partner feels compelled to maintain steady employment, but if it meets his or her inner tastes, it can be a reassurance and a gift to the risk taker.

Second is the respect we feel for the women we love who develop skills and earning power. Ed Dudkiewicz said:

It made me feel good when I saw Liz tackle some of the things a taxicab driver has to do, and if I see another woman driver, that turns me on a little bit. Once I was waiting in the taxi line at the airport. There was this girl driver in front of me. It was a hot summer day, so we all got out on the grass and were talking. Then we had to get in our cabs and move up. This guy came up to her cab with a big suitcase. She opened the trunk, and he put the bag down. If I was him, I would have lifted it up. But she took the thing—she had to really hustle to get it up there—and flopped it in the trunk. And that made me feel good, that she did it, and I knew Liz could do it if she had to.

Blumstein and Schwartz developed an interesting index for a man's respect for his partner. They asked heterosexual men if their partners were the sort of persons they themselves would like to be. When the woman was employed full-time, 35 percent of the men said no. When she was a full-time homemaker, 47 percent said no, a significant difference. They also asked the men how often they and their partners had a significant exchange of ideas. Sixty-nine percent of the men with employed partners said at least three or four times a week, but only 47 percent of the men whose partners were full-time homemakers.[52]

The third happy effect of two-earner relationships is the way the partners can fill each other's needs and interests. This can make men feel gratified rather than threatened by the new system. In their latest book on dual career families, Rhona and Robert Rapoport offer several examples. One was a sales manager with an easygoing persona that hid his drive and determination, characteristics that his wife expressed for him in her career, starting as a scientist and rising to run a laboratory. Another woman's work as a theater director expressed an interest of her husband's that he was unable to follow as he established his career as an architect.[53]

A fourth benefit, related both to respect and to the fulfillment of the partners' interests, is the sense of being colleagues. This may be merely an ability to exchange ideas or talk about work and family to each other instead of boring each other, as the work-centered husband and the full-time homemaker often do. Or it may be the more active help that comes when one partner can edit another's writing or make specific suggestions for the other's work, manual, clerical, managerial, or professional.

Sam Tarshis* is the man who probably tries harder for an egalitarian marriage and achieves more of its good effects than anyone else I know. He and his wife, Marion,* share a college job teaching history. They are therefore a two-earner but not a two-income family. Sam gets some relief from the single breadwinner role, but the two get no benefit of two salaries. Sharing a job makes it easier for both of them to limit work time and spend more time on family, he believes; different kinds of jobs demanding different amounts of time and paying different amounts of money would make equality harder, and the reach for equality is important to him and Marion both. He said:

It's obvious that the traditional relations between the sexes are too unequal. The question is, how much equality do you strive for? There are many different answers, but each one is a compromise. The only philosophically clean answer is complete, absolute equality in everything. Marion made a very clear demand that we go as far as possible toward equality. That actually creates a certain amount of security. There is no time when I face the question, should I make this decision? Because I don't make decisions by myself. We make all these decisions together. There is no question in my mind what my role should be. My role is no different from her role. We've eliminated the gray area by going as far as possible. I'm convinced I moved to that extreme to a great extent in response to the demands that Marion set out.

Sam is shorter than average, with wavy hair, an olive complexion, a beard a bit longer than the usual academic adornment. His face has the repose of a man who has knit his thoughts and feelings together more completely than most, a quality I also found in what he said. He mentioned that despite his conscious efforts at equality, Marion still regarded him with suspicion on occasion. I asked what made that happen. He replied:

Her experience of other men, to start. She rightly regards most men, I think, as not willing to provide total equality. She developed a certain reluctance to believe that men would actually come through on certain promises, before she met me. And when we first met, there were some things in me that aroused suspicion on her part. My ideas were not as oriented toward full equality as they are now. This means she wants to be sure that in a new situation I'm going to react as I have recently rather than as I did previously. There really are a whole host of reactions that I was taught as part of a male role over my first twenty-five years, reactions that were not equal. They still can come up at certain moments. Marion misinterprets some of this as being willful, trying to evade equal responsibility. I don't feel that way. My intentions are good, but I'm constantly dredging up ready-made answers out of my past, which I then have to confront and decide whether I want to accept. For example, when I first thought about children, I really wondered if there weren't some truth to the idea that women would have an easier time with children than men. That being a mother really was different from being a father, that there was a certain ease in relating to a child that mothers had and fathers didn't. It seemed to me that that might be true and therefore I would have some extra difficulties dealing with children. I don't think that that's true anymore, but it's taken me a couple of years of thinking about it, confronting it as a myth.

Marion was pregnant when I first interviewed the Tarshises. By the time their son was two years old, she had lost much of her suspicion because Sam was doing literally half the work of taking care of Ben. He has kept it up with the birth of their second child, Sara.

I wondered what sharing a job in the same field did to their independence at work, as teachers and scholars. Sam said:

It's important that even though we share one job in college, and we both have to be evaluated favorably if they're going to keep us on, we are separate. I teach my class and Marion teaches hers. I have my tasks in the department and she has hers. And outside the college we are completely independent experts and teachers. Nobody thinks of my work in relation to anything that she does. For others in our field, it's much more important what each of us writes, what she says and what I say, what she thinks and what I think.

I asked Sam whether competitiveness was ever a problem for him and Marion. He said it could be:

Neither one of us is competitive in the sense of one of us trying to get ahead of the other. But even without trying, you can resent the fact that someone else is ahead, doing better than you. I'm publishing more things than Marion is. That could be a difficulty. If one of us was perceived over the years as a significantly better teacher, that could be a problem. I don't think it will happen. I think we will both do well. And in teaching we have each developed certain specialties that will take us out of identical fields and perhaps make us less competitive.

And it also helps that we work together. We're each other's major critic. We both recognize that our first or second or fifth drafts are eminently criticizable. It's important that we be each other's critics because the college is fairly isolated, there are very few other people who know the field as well as we do. And we push each other. Sometimes I think I have to encourage her to promote her own career more actively. I suggest that she be more active in looking for ways to publish or to give papers, I suggest that she write people and try to meet some people who are important. She's a little bit reluctant sometimes, more reluctant than I think she should be. So I encourage her to do that more than she encourages me. But she also does it with me.

Sam and Marion have confronted the pain and difficulties of the two-career and egalitarian relationship more than any other couple I interviewed, and they haven't been defeated by them. As I complete this study, I'm impressed with how exceptional they are among those 26.1 million two-earner couples. But they and Jim and Ruth Calabrese and Ed and Liz Dudkiewicz make me believe there will be more men and women like them in the future.

Chapter 10

THE NEW FATHERING

Jim Calabrese* did most of the work of raising his son, Eric. That gave him pride in the way the feminine side of his nature flourished, which he spoke of in the previous chapter. But he was still a former college football player from an Italian-American family who grew up in the relatively wild west culture of Montana, and raising Eric was no easier for him than learning to accept that his wife earned more money than he did. He was a graduate student when Eric was a baby, doing four courses a quarter, reading stacks of books, writing papers. Nine years later, he remembered that disciplined study "was a male world for me, a shaped world. I had the mastery of the son of a bitch, I was good, I just had to read my books and do this stuff. But in this shaped world I had, there was this little wandering presence, crying at the wrong time. He was the shapeless element that didn't fit. There was a sense of great frustration. I would say in fantasy, 'Why didn't you cry when I got the test over with, why did you start doing it this afternoon?' But it was my responsibility, this life that was growing. It wasn't a higher mark on a test, it wasn't a bigger paycheck, it was a growing human life."

Jim's life as a father included toilet training Eric in what he thought was

probably a very peculiar male way. He had the inevitable big one where he dropped it in the john, and wow, we celebrated. And then he backslid, shit in his pants again. I'm trying, the male instinct is to goddamn make him, but you can't do that. He's got to have a sense about it. All these things were very new to me. I don't know how it differed from the traditional way, but I know for sure my own feelings, I felt this was foreign to me. What happened was that one day he came out with a big load again and I brought him over to the diaper pail, and I pointed to him and I pointed down there that he was going to be the one to get this off, I didn't care how much shit landed on the floor, he was going to help in this process, or he could go take it to the john. It took a little while after that, but he got the point. He got the point that a little bit of his own self-interest was involved there. When he dumped in the john for the second time, we had ice cream, it was a big deal.

The ends of Jim's dark blond mustache drooped over his laugh at the memory.

He also enjoyed fathering a nine year old. Ruth slept past the hour when Eric had to get up and go to school because she didn't leave for her editing job until after 9 A.M. Jim made his breakfast and the lunch he took with him. "In my experience, I'm in my mother's role," he said, "but it's a male world in the morning. I have this great sense of pride, this special relationship with him. Ruth and I laugh uproariously at times, saying, 'My God, what if he turns out to be a Poppa's Boy.' We imagine him forty-five years old, telling his wife, 'Shit, my father didn't make macaroni like that, you don't boil weenies like my father used to make.' "

THE CHANGES

Jim Calabrese is an example of the shift to active fathering, which may turn out to be the most profound of all the changes in men that reflect the changes women have been making. So far, there are two major developments. One is that increasing numbers of men are feeling and expressing the pain and joy of their emotional ties to their children more than traditional sex-roles allowed them to do. The other—the distinction is important—is that smaller but also increasing numbers of men are sharing in the work of child raising. Many do an important proportion of the tasks, and a few (but more than formerly) do something of even more significance: they actually assume part of the responsibility, first in taking charge of the work and then emotionally.*

My interviews make me think that middle-class men share the work more often than do men at upper or blue-collar levels.† High-income fathers often claim to do equal parenting, and may indeed do as much as their wives, but most of the daily, dirty work of their child raising is done by nurse, maid, or nanny, almost always a woman. Working-class fathers share in chores more often than they used to do and more often than middle-class observers believe. But they shoulder responsibility less often than middle-class men do and have more trouble accepting or enjoying their own departures from stereotype.

Bob Sayers of Larkspur, California, one of the leaders of the "fathering movement" that encourages men to play greater roles in their children's lives, cautions that rhetoric about active fathering is much greater than the reality. Men pay lip service to the idea but often are not there when it comes to the

---

* Two studies show that since 1970 there has been a 15 to 20 percent increase in the amount of time that men spend with their children. Another study estimates that 10 to 12 percent of today's fathers are "substantially more involved" in their family's lives than the typical father is or used to be.[1]
† Most surveys say income and education has no effect on child care; the remainder contradict each other on whether the more educated and higher-income fathers do more or less.[2]

real work. Sex-role stereotypes still work powerfully against the idea of the nurturing father.* The rhetoric remains important, however, whether it's word of mouth or word of media. Men are sharing fathering not only in the different classes of the real world but also in the superclass of magazine articles, television shows, movies like *Kramer vs. Kramer* and *Ordinary People,* and novels like *Mother's Day* and *The World According to Garp.* This helps keep the idea and the imagery of the change alive even in periods of backlash like the Reagan era.

These changes have many causes. Chief among them are the same two forces that changed the balance of power in marriage—women's going to work in ever larger numbers, and women's demands for independence, equality, and personal sovereignty. Some women have made explicit demands on their husbands to share or take over certain chores or so many hours a week of child care. Some have ended their marriages and left their children with the husbands. Those are extreme cases, but even in families evolving on gentler curves, more mothers are away at work for more hours per week, and more fathers are putting in more hours on child care. Even in families that are still mainstream in spirit, feminist ideas are changing both the collective culture and individual values and attitudes. Both external reality and internal ideology draw fathers into more active roles and more direct work and play with their children.

Another psychological or ideological shift that brings men to active fathering is a new interest in expressing emotion, in overturning the stereotype that says it is not masculine to show feeling. This new male openness to emotions has been stimulated by three related social forces. Again, one is the women's movement, which makes a moral demand that we change the way we live in families at the same time that it exposes us to the emotional process of consciousness-raising.

The second is the therapy subculture, which tries to make us aware of our feelings and often makes us focus in new ways on our parents, our spouses, and our children. In men's meetings I have been struck by the pathos and the passion with which men talk about compensating for a father's sins in their relations with their own children, sometimes for the wounds inflicted but more often for the emotional absence during their childhoods. I have not heard men talk as clearly about being active fathers in order to make sure their children don't reproduce their dependence on the good mother or their anger at the bad mother in their own mothers. But there are hints that this too is a motive.

The third element in the new male openness to emotions is the search for

---

* The strength of those stereotypes was shown (among many other places) in tests of college students in Utah and of rural men in North Carolina. Both groups were shown a nurturing father who hugged his child, rubbed his back, and sang to him, and a father who refused to do those things. They rated the first as more feminine, less active, less potent, and less likely to succeed than the second.[3]

self-fulfillment, which some observers see as an historical force in its own right.[4] This is a movement away from old systems that alienated people from their work and created an impersonal, instrumental, industrial society. Many men, struggling toward the sacred and expressive and finding it harder and harder to reach satisfaction in their work, turn instead to their families and find new kinds of fulfillment in new relations with their children. (Others move into narcissism, seeking so hard to gratify the self that they refuse or postpone having children, who so often compel self-sacrifice.)

More pervasive divorce is paradoxically another tendency that can encourage active fathering. Many divorced fathers move away from their children, literally or figuratively, to take a new job, to avoid conflict with their former wives, to avoid feelings of guilt about the divorce or of marginality in their children's lives.[5] A national survey of teenage children of divorce found that only one out of six had seen the father once a week or more in the previous five years. But other men react very differently. The stress of divorce hits many former husbands even harder than former wives in the first year. The men feel they do not know who they are, that they have neither roots nor home nor structure in their lives. Then they feel a great sense of loss, of a dependency they had not known was in them. Resolving these anxieties may make them discover new dimensions in their love for their children. Twenty percent of men in one study reported that their relationships with their children had improved after a divorce. Men who have not been active fathers in marriage often become more active in divorce. Some men who have been active feel even more fear of loss than those who have not, and do even more fathering to compensate. Some in both groups seek exclusive or joint custody; if they get it, they are compelled to be active fathers—a consequence that some do not understand until they are in the middle of the fact.

Men who do not pay child support after divorce may seem anything but caring fathers at first glance. Many failed to provide for their children in the traditional manner when they were still married, and they are completing that failure after divorce for one or many of the reasons just mentioned. They feel economically as well as psychologically vulnerable, especially if they have remarried, and are protecting themselves in that vulnerability. They are often showing hatred of their former wives. They contribute to their children's suffering. Recent federal legislation set standards for states to compel payment of court-ordered child support, with measures including seizing state income tax refunds and withholding wages from people who fall too far behind in their payments. At least twenty-one states have passed laws complying with the federal requirements, and Washington will help them collect support money. I believe these measures are justified. But the system should recognize that some men who don't pay do feel their fatherhood. The law should recognize that fathers are entitled to full access to their children, which some divorced wives deny. And individuals and organizations should recognize that a significant minority of nonpaying fathers are not showing indifference to their children but repressing pain over their loss.

THEORY AND RESEARCH DISCOVER FATHERS

The new fatherhood surprises us because we didn't know it was even possible. Psychological and sociological theory long neglected fathers, giving them only limited or indirect roles in the raising of children and the development of personality, especially in the early years. Freud gave fathers prominence only as objects in the oedipal stage of a child's development, but said little about the father's acts or feelings and their effects on the child. John Bowlby, an English ethologist a generation later, saw the mother as the first and most important object of the infant's attachment. Such theories reinforced society's assumption that "a biological bond between mother and child made fathers less able, less interested and less important than mothers in caring for children."[6] Theory and society both subordinated the male urge to create life to the woman's ability to give birth. Society transformed her biological ability into a parental function and then used that function to subordinate her in the polity and the economy. It also subordinated her in the arts, a form of creation that men tried to keep for themselves.

This began to change in the 1960s, when the women's movement focused new attention on Margaret Mead's old reports of societies in which men cared for children. Milton Kotelchuk did the first direct laboratory research on fathers and children in 1970. Benjamin Spock revised his bible of child care to give fathers more place and more of the burden in 1974.

Later in the 1970s thinkers who happened to be women reformulated the theory and analysis of infant development to focus on the importance of mothering for social structures and relationships. This opened up both the possibility and the necessity of a greater role for fathers if the changes that women are making are to come to fruition. A look at the new formulation is thus essential to understanding the new fathering.*

In this analysis, the infant makes the female the object of first need, first love, first fear, and first rage. The baby experiences the female as having the power to destroy as well as create. This happens because the mother whose breast gives the child its first nourishment, its first sensual satisfaction, is also "the first to stop the flow of milk and of unconditional acceptance, to forbid sexual activities and impose restrictions, as in toilet training."[7] It is she who fosters or forbids, who regulates, the first steps toward autonomous activity—

---

* For the ideas in this section, I am profoundly indebted to Nancy Chodorow's *The Reproduction of Mothering,* Dorothy Dinnerstein's *The Mermaid and the Minotaur,* and Lillian B. Rubin's *Intimate Strangers.* It seems significant that men have done little of the innovative thinking in this area.

the activity that later becomes the enterprise that is part of being human.[8] If it is not the biological mother who does these things, in our culture the person who does them, who raises the child, is usually female.

(The development of the infant thus recapitulates primitive man's belief that if woman could give life, she could also take it away. The belief produced myths and practices in every culture to deal with the giving, nurturing Good Mother and the aggressive, devouring Terrible Mother. These still resonate in life today because society has transmitted them down the ages and because the infant develops in this way. They are the wellspring of male fear of women.)

The infant's experience of the mother's power is also deepened by intense anxiety over separation from the mother. Separation breaks the symbiotic bond that is the child's first experience of life, but it is necessary for survival, the first step toward individuation and growth. Men's responses to the changes that women are making—and women's responses too—are shaped by the way adult relationships between them repeat, in highly attenuated form, the early struggles around separation from and unity with the mother.[9]

The child's rebellion against maternal authority feeds on the unconscious memory from infancy of the mother as the contact with the world out there, the center of the nonself that the child labors to discover. It's a long time before the infant can perceive her as a person with a subjectivity of her own.[10]

The perception of the mother as a nonperson has as corollary the idea that to be human is to be male, and to be female is to be other. (When feminists insist on their equal humanity, many men say, "Of course," and criticize them for belaboring the obvious. But I keep bumping into the idea that humanity is male as an unspoken, often unconscious assumption in society, in other men, and in myself.) From these perceptions flow most forms of the devaluation of women, which in turn reinforce (and are reinforced by) the division of labor that makes women the primary parents and repress the ability to nurture in men.

The child's rebellion is difficult because of a paradox: the first independent acts require an audience to recognize them and therefore reaffirm dependency on others, usually the mother. The child resolves the conflict by imagining that it can become independent without recognizing the mother as equally free; it feels, "She belongs to me, I control and possess her." In doing this, the boy denies his likeness to his mother, separating completely and turning her into an object he believes he can manipulate. This leads males more often than females into dominance, the adult repetition of the failure to recognize the other person as like oneself, but separate and autonomous.[11]

In forming his gender identity, the boy must protect himself against the pain of loss of his mother and the sense of betrayal by her that he feels because he cannot understand that it is he who has severed himself from the adult he loves. He therefore builds firm boundaries that separate self from other and constrict his connection to his inner emotions. These defenses reinforce his natural aggressiveness. Both processes are part of his seeking a deeper identification with his father.

For a girl, gender identity requires no break with mother, so she builds fewer defenses and develops more permeable ego boundaries than a boy does. As she grows, she retains her internalized mother and internalizes her father as well. She has two characters besides herself in her psychic structure, so her inner life becomes triangular. A man has banished his mother, and no matter how much his adult life recapitulates a search for her, his inner life remains dyadic. This has immense importance for the differences in the way men and women see the world—especially since in our society it is men who define the world, usually in bipolar terms.[12]

The male child's identification with his mother, the need to renounce her, and the secondary identification with the father all make him doubtful and obsessive about his masculinity. This produces another set of fears that make men angry about women, work, and power—fears about the penis. The fear most frequently described derives from the Freudian assumption that a woman envies a man his penis. It is the fear that women who claim equality with men are stealing our penises, the organ with which we commit the primary aggressive act of penetrating women and the organ with which we often identify our work and our power. I am skeptical that penis envy and castration fear operate, even in their transmuted adult forms, as often or as readily as some psychiatrists think. The Freudian theory could have been applied to women's professional ambitions only in a society that confined them to the roles of wife and mother. An anxiety described by Karen Horney seems more real, more frequent, and less likely to be ethnocentric. Horney suggests that the boy's anxiety that his penis is too small to fit his mother's vagina produces a dread of being rejected and derided that is a major element in the male psyche.[13]

Whichever fears are operating, there is no escape from penis metaphors in dealing with money, with machinery, with weapons, or with power. (Such metaphors work both ways, as when we speak of giving either a competitor or a woman "the business.") And the penis is a symbol of our power that women may envy even if they care nothing about the organ itself. I do not doubt that the theft or transplant or even duplication of a penis, when our unconscious perceives that to be happening, evokes and intensifies both our anger and our fear.

This anger and this fear are just one set of consequences of the dominance of mother in infancy. As I noted in Chapter 2, the way to dispel these emotions and to change men's responses to the challenges posed by women is to have men take an equal share of primary parenting responsibilities from the moment of birth. Boys and girls alike would then have both male and female figures to attach to, identify with, rebel against, and separate from. For boys, the connection to a male self would be defined positively, by primary identification with a father figure rather than negatively by renunciation of the mother. Men might then be less obsessive about their masculinity and less compulsive about devaluing women. Since the mother whom boys must relinquish would not be the only loved other of infancy, they would not have to develop rigid defenses against their own vulnerability and dependency, as they do when they are raised by women alone. The subconscious fear of women that is really fear of maternal omnipotence would diminish. Men would then have less need to exclude women from public life or deprive them of public power. For girls, separation would entail less conflict in childhood, and there would be fewer problems in developing a well-bounded and autonomous sense of self in adulthood. All this would constitute a profound change, painful and costly, but it can be done. The newly active fathers are taking the first steps toward it.

The scientists doing the current research on fathers, mostly men, virtually ignore this view of infant development and the possibilities it opens. It's just a theory, of course. The new experts on fatherhood don't even pay much attention to the fact of the two-earner family, however, and seem to assume that most families still fit the traditional pattern in which the father interacts with the child mostly when he returns from work and the outside world, and the mother is entirely responsible for the early years that are crucial to development of the individual psyche. They also tend, like their predecessors, to make the boy's development the norm (once more, humanity is male), though they are beginning to see girls as different rather than deviant.

Despite these blind spots, the new experts make a number of important points, which in principle apply to both old- and new-style fathers. The first is that fathers are indeed interested in their newborn babies. They are just as nurturant as mothers if given the chance, and are capable and competent in caretaking tasks. In traditional families, fathers engage less in caretaking than mothers do but play more with babies and have different styles of play from mothers.[14] Dual-career fathers and mothers usually describe themselves as more equal in both play and care giving, but one study of the actual behavior of dual-career families shows that mothers play more with babies than fathers do. They apparently need to engage the baby after being away and perhaps to compensate for substitute care or to assuage their guilt; they seem to crowd the fathers out, so the men interact less with the infants, and care is less egalitarian—contrary to expectation and to what parents say and believe.[15]

The father also affects the child's development in significant ways even when he does not do literally half the work of child raising. In the classic pattern he offers both boy and girl infants their first counterpoints to the mother, the first means to separate from her and develop an independent personality. Ideally he offers a warmth and security that help the child deal with its anger at and fear of the mother. His play, particularly roughhousing or tossing a toddler in the air, encourages the baby to explore the space around it and develop a sense of "body self." In the traditional family all these functions align the father with reality, which the child must try to conquer.[16] I believe that as the family changes, father and mother may trade or share some functions, but the child will always need both. Learning to relate to two different parents, whether or not they are classical father and classical mother, is vital in helping the child consolidate the idea of self and other.

Whether traditional or new-style, the father helps form the child's gender identity. He touches and vocalizes more with a boy than with a girl baby, for instance, but holds a girl more snugly.[17] He offers the boy the first figure with whom he identifies as he differentiates himself from his mother. He offers the girl the first male to whom she relates in a different way from her attachment to her mother, as early as the second year—long before the oedipal period. He feels hostility and rivalry toward his children, in different ways for boys and girls. There is no simple relationship between the father's masculinity and the son's; the boy's masculinity seems to be related to the father's nurturance, dominance, and participation in the son's care.[18] Later in childhood, the father seems to do more than the mother to modulate or control aggressive drives in both sexes.[19] When the children reach adolescence, his relations with his daughter affect the way she prepares for and assumes womanhood, while he offers his son new kinds of stimulation and guidance into manhood.[20] Perhaps as sex roles and ideas about parenting change he will begin to challenge a daughter as much as a son; there is already evidence that this happens in many men whose firstborn is a girl or who have only daughters.

In traditional families the father is the family's main contact with the outside world. That makes him important to the child's intellectual development, though the mother usually is the one who starts the child's learning process. It gives him primary responsibility for the transmission of social mores and values, which in turn is the main reason he is responsible for discipline—for preventing others from doing what they want or from violating basic rules, depending on the point of view.*

The patterns that spring from paternal authority often persist even as dual-earner families become the norm and the balance of power in the family shifts. We are a long way from the day when men will participate as fully as women in the initiation of infants into humanity. When that day comes, it will make things so vastly different that it's hard to imagine what it will be like. But Jane Lazarre, a writer, describes an early example of a girl's differentiation from a nurturing father. Her mother died when she was a young child, leaving her father with two daughters:

* Women have always made children scapegoats for their impotence and anger. Letty Cottin Pogrebin suggests that men may go even further in times when the revolt of women combines with economic stress, when their own feelings of worthlessness and powerlessness may impel them to transform needed discipline into physical punishment and then into violence against children, the remaining subordinate class.[21]

He had many of the characteristics of the traditional mother: physical affectionateness, excessive anxiety concerning the development of his children, extreme identification with his children (though girls) as continuous verifications of his own ego. . . . Not being a man of fanatic virility, he learned to cook, clean, wipe our behinds, and temper his worldly ambitions. . . . For close to 20 years, he acted as much like a "mother" as a "father."

Like most girls with their mothers, I grew up angry at my father for a thousand nameable things; I hated him for his continual concern; I was frightened that no matter how hard I tried for psychological independence, I would always be just like him; I was tied to him for life. When I had my first child, I treated my father like the grandmother he was, calling upon his baby-sitting services indiscriminately, fighting with him about how to change diapers correctly, how to bring up a burp.[22]

HOW FATHERHOOD AFFECTS MEN

I am sorry Jane Lazarre's father died before I could ask him what the process of fathering had done to him. Theories of child development tend to skimp on how it affects parents because they concentrate on the ways that parents affect the child. But child raising of course affects the father and mother and influences not only their effects on the child they raise, but also their relations with other people and with society in general.

The first effect on a father is getting hooked on the bond with his newborn —his intense absorption in the infant, his desire to look at it, hold it, and touch it. Bob Sayers, Ross Parke of the University of Illinois, and others think the bond is closer if the father is present at birth. This certainly leads to a more positive birth experience for the mother, but some studies of men who were there show they are not all equally or highly involved in the care of their infants. I suspect that the father's expressing of his emotions, holding the baby, and caring for it in the first few hours of life may be more important in forming the bond than being present at the moment of birth, though that surely makes the emotions around the bond even stronger.

Martin Greenberg and Norman Morris, who wrote the first clinical description of the father's absorption in the newborn, labeled the process "engrossment." They noted, "The derivation of the word *engross* means *to make large*. When the father is engrossed in his individual infant, the infant has assumed larger proportions for him. In addition, it is suggested that the father feels bigger, and that he feels an increased sense of self-esteem and worth when he is engrossed in his infant."[23]

An important strand in the father's enlarged self-esteem is the feeling that the newborn child gives him immortality, or the chance for immortality—a quest that is either more intense in the male or unique in the male, who cannot feel the immortality of the body that he sees in the woman who actually bears the child. Religion, history, anthropology, and our own family life all provide ample evidence that in most societies the father's search for immortality runs particularly through his sons, on whom he projects his own aspirations and his hopes for self-realization.[24] This may be a matter of hope —that children, especially boys (with whom the father identifies more easily in our culture), will somehow renew or repair the aging parental body, for instance, or fulfill the goals the father has failed to achieve. But fatherhood also offers corresponding fears that children growing into their own adult-hood will somehow surpass the father's achievements and hasten the death that can no longer be denied.

That fear is one of many ways besides engrossment that the experience of being a father influences the evolution of the adult personality.[25] It offers a man the opportunity to integrate childhood wishes to become like his own father, and adolescent wishes to complete rebellion against that father, to be unlike him in important aspects. The father may feel, particularly about his son, a hate and helplessness like those he felt as a small boy in relation to his father. He may feel for his daughter an unrealizable sexual desire like that he felt for his mother. He must learn to deal with such emotions in order to give both sons and daughters the support they need to complete their separation and emerge as independent sexual adults. His feminine side can take on new dimensions during his children's adolescence and early adulthood, enabling him to be more generative with them, their mates, other members of their generation, and eventually, his own grandchildren. Many men have gone through this to a tenderness with their grandchildren they never showed their own children.[26] It will be interesting to see what happens to the growing number of fathers who do show tenderness to their own offspring, when they become grandfathers.

DISCOVERING THE BURDEN

Mothers have always gone through parallel processes. As women grow old in the external world of the workplace and men grow old as active fathers, both will share specific pains and pleasures of parenthood more fully. Being the responsible parent is already leading some men to what seems to them like a discovery: the deeper pains and joys of parenting are intimately interlaced, first with the practical and often menial tasks of being a parent, and then with the responsibility that makes those tasks an inescapable cumulative burden. A woman with her first child also feels the sense of revelation that comes with an experience that cannot be imagined fully beforehand, yet she has a sense of familiarity, of déjà vu, because it is something that mothers have always known. Women have begun speaking of this ancient burden in new ways since the current wave of the women's movement began in the 1960s; now men are feeling it and talking about it too.†

The central core of the burden is time. Active parents spend time with their children. Not "quality time," but time. Traditional fathers and traditional sons knew this, whether they honored it in the breach or in the observance. A few of the men I interviewed were happy in the memory of their fathers. None had had a father like one county judge of sixty years ago, who spent every afternoon from the end of school to bedtime with his four children, discussing the day's happenings, reviewing each child's problems, accomplishments, and hopes, giving advice, approval, or reprimand.[27] But all these happy few voiced feelings like one who said, "My father was certainly *there*. He went to work every day and he sometimes had two jobs, so there were lots of days when I didn't see much of him. When he came home he wasn't all that demonstrative. But he knew what I was doing in school, he talked to me and listened to me at breakfast and when he was home for dinner. I knew when he was proud of me and I knew when he was angry at me. I knew that when I needed him he would be there." Apart from that small number, some men complained that their fathers had been too much there, authoritarian or competitive, but more of the men I interviewed wished they had had a father who was there. They complained that their fathers were either silent or absent when they were growing up, and they intended to be there for the raising of their children.[28]

Neither they nor those whose fathers had indeed been there imagined spending time with children the way mothers spent time, however. The discovery of the burden of time and task and the emotions tied to it was made by new-style fathers. This burden is heaviest in the years before the children are old enough for school. Mike Clary wrote a book about his life as a full-time father for his daughter Annie's first two years, while his wife Lillian worked as a college counselor. He said:

As I became familiar with diaper rash and fits of colic and finger food and water play, I would learn to get out of bed like a robot; to cope with my estrangement from men and my difference from women; to conquer my resentment of Lillian's job and her freedom to leave the house each day for the office. In caring for a child, I would see, there is no woman's work and no man's work. There is just work, and responsibility, and bad hours, and small rewards that appear like sudden snowflakes and then quickly go glimmering by.[29]

Ted Osgood* spoke of the way the burden continued after infancy. He did 80 or 90 percent of the work of child care for three children, earning part-

† Most of the mothers and fathers who talk about the burden, about the conflicts between child raising and love life or intellectual life or career, are middle-class. People who can hire full-time help don't feel the burden. Working-class people talk about it less and don't measure it in the same way, but my interviews suggest that they too feel its weight.

time pay as teacher, editor, and church organist while his wife rose in the advertising business. He went on:

The menial side is what every mother goes through. Some of that is just the grubby and grungy things, especially with a baby. It's a bit different making sure a two year old doesn't destroy herself as she learns to explore stairways and electrical outlets. Or with more than one kid. When you have Liza who's two and doesn't respond to your command to cross the street *now*, or dillydallies in the middle of the road, and you've got the baby in one hand and a bag of groceries in the other, it's untenable.

But the menial aspect of child care is its constancy more than any single action. And that's something you feel infinitely more when you're responsible and not just helping out your wife. Maybe she'll help you, or you'll get a baby-sitter for a short time, but you know you can't escape for long because you're responsible. You have no time to do anything on the spur of the moment, to have a beer with a friend, to read a book for the sheer pleasure of it, no time to goof off.

Active fathers soon discover that the feelings to which the burden is tied in an infinity of knots are not all rosy and affectionate. Joseph F. Riener, a Washington psychotherapist, describes this dark side of parental feelings:

How can my kids make me feel so bad? I love them a lot. The turmoil they evoke inside me is confusing, baffling, and often leaves me unhappy. How can it be that my five-year-old son and my two-year-old daughter cause such ambivalent and painful feelings?

I hated having my life disrupted. Before having children, my wife and I had worked out a fairly harmonious way of living together. Our first baby ripped that apart. Shouting at each other at three in the morning while our infant son screamed, my wife and I saw each other's ugliness as never before.

Our family has known much sweetness: bringing our new babies home, watching them crawl, then toddle, then run. Our house has echoed with much laughter. Yet in the moments when their needs exhaust me, I become bitter, angry, wishing only to be left alone.

Being a parent has often made me very unhappy. It's no fun seeing how selfish, or angry, or limited I am. The happiness I experience in being with my children gives me the resolve to go through these hard times. But it's a piece of work, being a parent.[30]

Many fathers' burden-anger grows out of their discovery that it is next to impossible to combine serious child care with serious work at home in their vocations or paying professions. Raising children takes so much time and energy there is seldom enough left for the work of the career. Ted Osgood remarked:

Your responsibility and your kids' constant demands make it hard to do anything else that you really want to do. If you've got two children whining at you, there's no way you're going to get the other thing done. All you are is frustrated. That makes you angry with the children, and either you explode or you get depressed. Or you realize all of a sudden that you shouldn't be angry, that you'd better just put the work off until later. Nothing goes with child care except puttering.

You can try to put the children out of the way for a while, but that doesn't work very well. You worry about what they're up to. Or you start to think about all the lessons you haven't prepared, or the music you haven't practiced, and you resent the kids even when they're not there. Or you get so tired that you can't do anything well enough to be proud of even after they're in bed.

In addition to burden-anger and mother-hate, there's another discovery that surprises active fathers: their children can rebel against them and even hate them. Like mother-hate, this child-hatred contradicts but need not conquer love. In traditional families the father is the target of adolescent rebellion against tyranny or weakness, real or imagined. In sharing families the father may be the target of separation agonies of the kind younger children have always directed against mothers, or of the anger that many kids feel against the custodial parent in divorce. George Grossman,* the divorced father of two sons of ten and eight, was happy to have custody and thought the boys loved him and liked their lives with him. He was still frequently depressed because they blamed him for their mother's departure from the household. They cried more often than he thought necessary, often refused to do their homework, refused to welcome the new women in his life (though he was careful not to have any women spend the night for the first two years after the divorce), and every three or four weeks would get into a fight with each other and with him that would end with their putting their hatred into words. "It's frightening," Grossman said. "Sometimes I feel like I'm in a tank of acid. Sometimes I feel I'm in a desert. When they start fighting me or hating me or refusing to use their own brains and talents, I have to work to remember the times when I know they love me. But when they take me out to play softball, or cook me some pasta and vegetables, I know there are still green places in my world."

JOYS AND STRAINS

The searing quality of a father's first experience of "mother-hate" amid the burdens of active parenthood has the force of revelation, but hate and anger and anxiety are hardly a father's only feelings. Most of the caring fathers I interviewed, including those who emphasized the exhausting weight of the burden, agreed with Kenneth Pitchford: "The hours of shitwork that go into even one moment of 'reward'—that flash of unique understanding between infant and parent, as when the child says a new, unprompted word for the first time—are worth it."[31] The men I listened to conveyed the joys of being a parent without ever using the word "joy"—in the intensity of their tone, the warmth of their glances at their children, their mention of a first kiss or a new adventure shared or merely heard about.

Fred Farina* is a blue-collar man who makes his living as an electrician and flea market vendor. He was a househusband and became a single father after a difficult divorce in which his wife left him for another man. Like most single fathers, he feels everything about his children more intensely than most married men, even househusbands, because he has no other intimate with whom he connects emotionally. He is as involved in his children's lives as Jane Lazarre's father was in his. His joy in giving care shines from every memory of his life as a father, from the period when he had to insert his finger in his baby son's anus to relieve the infant's constipation to the time he won compliments on his daughter's record in her schoolwork. Her teachers asked him to congratulate his wife, assuming both parents were involved in Laura's care because she did so well in class and was so well adjusted, unlike most of her schoolmates from divorced families. He told the teachers her mother seldom saw her, but he loved the unwitting testimony that he really was both mother and father to her.

That gave him pride and joy, but he was frequently in agony because the old sex-role stereotypes of man as provider and woman as homemaker were so strong in him. The conflict was clear in his memory of a conversation with his ex-wife as they argued their separation, with his voice shifting as he reenacted each part:

I said, "What about the kids?"
She said, "They'll survive."
"What do you mean they'll survive? I want those kids, they're part of me."
"Well, you'll always be their father."
"I wanna be more than just the father image. I wanna be involved in the raising of those kids. I wanna see them, day after day, I wanna see them mature, I wanna see the cutting of their hair, the whole thing."
[He shifted suddenly from reenacting to remembering.] It was tearing me up, I mean it was emotionally eating me up inside. Then I'd come there and pick them up on the weekends, and that wasn't good enough for me. It didn't fulfill what I really wanted to do.

But at virtually the same moment that he had that gut feeling, Farina was gripped by the powerful traditional belief:

I thought that as a man you couldn't raise children. It never came to my mind that children could be raised by their father and live with their father. I always thought it was a natural thing for kids to be raised by their mother.

Farina was, like many caring fathers, a living example of what the sociologists call role strain and role incompatibility—the conflicts between the expectation of one role and the reality of another, or between two roles that the same person must play. He had no role model and was full of the fear and uncertainty that every person feels who creates a new role that doesn't fit easily into society's script. Yet he had been creating such a role for himself since his early teens, when he had made his own lunch, ironed his own clothes, and done more than half the work of caring for his much younger sisters. His mother wasn't there to do it because she was out working for pay after she divorced his father.

That was probably the most important preparation he had for taking custody of his own children, but instead of strengthening him it made him vulnerable to doubts about his masculinity. One rose as an unintended consequence of his cooking for the kids. Farina was tired of canned spaghetti and sauce in a jar, and asked his uncle, who worked in an Italian restaurant, how to make meatballs and Italian sauce from the ground up, cooking for five or six hours.

This particular day, I was doing it on my own. I was proud of myself. [His voice rose several notes on "proud."] I did everything my uncle said, I'm following the recipe to a T. My wife happens to show up with her aunt to get the kids because my wife's grandmother and grandfather asked for them. So while they was sittin' there, I says to myself, "Hey, maybe I can impress the two of them with my sauce making." That day I felt proud, I did something I never thought I would be able to do. She's lookin' at me with a weird look, and I'm sayin', "I bet she thinks I'm some kind of weirdo because I'm makin' sauce." The aunt says, "Mm, that smells good." I was happy. Now I can see they were being sarcastic, because she never brought the kids back, they stayed with the aunt, I had to take Laura physically away from the aunt. Some time later my wife and I got into a discussion, she started yellin' and screamin' at me and says to me, "And you, you faggot, stirrin' the tomato sauce." It was really a long time later, and she's callin' me a faggot because I was stirring tomato sauce.

Farina consulted a psychiatric social worker about that incident and others centering on remarks by his ex-wife. He said she reassured him by telling him that many divorced men question their masculinity. She also told him, "You're more of a man than you realize you are." But she left him confused because she added, "What man would put aside his own personal life to raise two children? You're making a sacrifice. There's not too many men that would do that."

STRUGGLING AGAINST STEREOTYPES

Not every active father, not even every househusband, suffers from role strain or role reversal as acutely as Farina. Mike Sammler* gave up his job as a finance company manager after his son was born in 1976. His wife, Eileen, was more interested in her office job than she was in staying home with their son and her son by her first marriage. She took care of the new baby for nine months. Mike's company was then bought by a conglomerate and his office closed. He could accept a transfer to an office in another city, which meant either a one-hour commute each way or moving to that city from the New York neighborhood where he had grown up and still lived—or he could stay home and raise Justin while Eileen went back to work. They decided the househusband choice would be best, but conversations with both of them made clear that his voice had carried more weight than hers in the mutual decision. Mike feels less role strain because even as he nurtures Justin "like a woman" he still has a psychology that fits the traditional male sex role: belief in the importance of his own work and a tendency to give orders, for instance. He also has what I see as a male tendency to deny problems related to role reversal, the twin of men's denial when women come into traditionally masculine jobs.

Mike pushed Eileen to move up from secretarial to managerial work in her office—and described her work as higher-level management than it really was (she turned out to be one level up from the bottom and to have just one subordinate, which she said suited her). Mike told Eileen she should spend time with Justin at breakfast or sit next to him at dinner, and sometimes she resented it. He described the process clearly:

> I'll say, "Gee, why don't you read a book with him," and she'll say, "Why don't you let it come naturally from me, why do you tell him when I'm home at night time that I should read a book with him? You're dictating," she says, "you're telling me what to do."

When Justin was admitted to a kindergarten gifted-child program, Mike felt a sense of achievement about this that he insisted had nothing to do with any genes he had contributed. He sounded "male" to me even though he was talking about doing something that most people think of as female:

> I don't feel that the giftedness was osmosis. You may say that it's genetic and it would have happened anyway. My feeling is that every child that's born is the raw material to work with. I don't think any child is born dumb, except for a few special cases. I think it's the nurturing that's done

in those first few months, the first year, the second year, the third year. In 99 percent of the cases it's the mother that does the work. But in this case, I did it.

Sammler insisted that neither the mothers he met at playground and school nor his and Eileen's friends had belittled him for being the house spouse. Only neighbors, he said, had harassed him. I was interested, because most caring fathers talk about lack of support from friends and suspicion from "other" mothers. I began to think Mike was denying, however, when Eileen told me that in fact there had been a noticeable degree of discomfort and ridicule. She said several of their friends had spoken to Mike in ways that suggested they thought he was effeminate. She also said that Mike liked spending time with the mothers more than he had told me, "telling them what to do or analyzing and criticizing what they do."

Sammler said he was trying to bring Justin up free of sex-role stereotypes. At first this surprised me because I thought he had "male" attitudes in what society considers a "female" role and in his views about housework. Then I saw that those attitudes in that context could be taken as a departure from stereotype. He was one of only three fathers who spontaneously mentioned that they were trying to avoid traditional sexism with the help of books like Letty Cottin Pogrebin's *Growing Up Free*. (Three more said in response to a question that they had read it or a book like it.) When I told him Pogrebin was a friend, he said, "Tell her I love her. The ideas she puts forward in that book, I think she's hitting the target right on the head."

Justin was not yet old enough for Mike Sammler to have made him a partner in the housework, but I was sure he would in a few years. The active fathers I interviewed, both single and married, seemed readier to enlist children in housework duties than most mothers are; at least, many of them perceived their readiness as a significant difference between men and women, and mothers talked more than fathers about the difficulties of getting teenagers to share chores. Harry Mowe,* a divorced father with joint custody of his two sons, lives half a mile from his ex-wife, so the boys spend alternate weeks with him and with her. He said:

A lot of the friction in my marriage was coming from the difference in our parenting styles. Mine was to let the children have as much responsibility as they are capable of assuming and exercising at the earliest possible age. I'll give you a mundane example. I insisted that my children start making their own lunches to take to school when they were about seven years old. I saw that it didn't take much more than a seven-year-old brain to figure out how to pack a lunch. I don't know any woman who stopped making lunches for the children at seven years old. I think there's a difference between male and female parenting style based on a man's greater willingness to allow children to assume responsibility at an earlier age.

I suggested that men were less willing than women to do all the dirty work of child care and more eager to share the burden, as many other fathers had recognized. Mowe said it was more a matter of women's reluctance to give up chores that are part of mothering and therefore essential to female identity. Yet he acknowledged that sharing housework with children is a way for caring fathers to feel more secure about their departure from sex-role stereotypes.

Mowe was unable to see that some women are ready to break down their own stereotypes. Single mothers and mothers in two-earner families are beginning to share domestic chores more than traditional mothers do, including cooking and having kids of eleven or twelve buy their own clothes. They accept that this may mean lowering housekeeping standards from the perfect-mother level. Some of these mothers are quicker than most men to talk about sharing responsibilities rather than merely sharing chores, which reflects their longer experience with the burden.

Sharing responsibilities is one way that both men and women in divorce treat their children more nearly as equals. They also turn to them for companionship and emotional support. This can be a burden, with tragic consequences later on, if the parent becomes dependent on the child in a reversal of the usual relationship. But if not overdone, it can be rewarding for both. Fathers seem more impressed by the wonder of this than do mothers, especially if they had not known how to reveal their emotions to their ex-wives. Martin Menzies,* an Atlanta public relations executive who is the father of a boy of fourteen and a girl of eleven, said:

I didn't know how to show my wife what I was feeling or sense what she was feeling except maybe in bed, and not all the time there. I changed after I got custody of the kids. I began to open up more to them than I had to her, more than I think I would to any adult I might live with. I talk to them about my money problems and my work and my wanting to feel that my soul is well-seated in my body. They seem to understand, and I think they talk to me more about their own lives than they did when their mother and I were together. When I was married I never thought this much companionship was possible with anyone. I never had it with my wife or with a lover or a male friend. I've learned more from my kids than I ever thought I would from any human being.

PARENTS NEED SOCIETY'S HELP

Fathers who share the pains and the joys of active parenting soon learn that society—government, corporations, institutions, friends, neighbors, family—does little to help men who are primary or equal parents. Two failures are at work here, separately and reinforcing each other. Neither institutions nor ordinary people know what to do with men who reverse or even modify only slightly the traditional roles of provider and child carer. And child care gets a low priority from government, business, and unions. It has always been a woman's job; making it harder has become one of the many forms of discrimination against women in the workplace.

On the first score, single fathers, househusbands, and active fathers in two-earner marriages agree that colleagues, relatives, friends, and other men in general are embarrassed by a man who takes time from work to care for children. Parents and in-laws take dim views of men who "are not good providers." Few employers are sympathetic to a man who wants time off to see a child in a school play. Schools often make a father feel unwelcome among the mothers on a school trip or a parent-in-classroom program.

Active fathers often express a need or a wish to meet other men in the same situation. In some places they have started networks or newsletters. Schools and service organizations are providing resources for men—and for boys. The Fatherhood Project at the Bank Street College of Education in New York has assembled a list of more than four hundred programs around the country in a guide called *Fatherhood U.S.A.*[32] Among them are classes that teach infant-care skills to eleven- and twelve-year-old boys, classes on co-parenting, step-parenting, and single-parenting, play groups for fathers and small children, health and family law services, and support networks.

Some fathers see their connection with America's failure to help care for children in general, and particularly the children of women who work for pay. "It's unbelievable," Martin Menzies said. "The majority of mothers are in the labor force and America isn't doing a damn thing to make sure their kids are okay. And it's doing even less for fathers like me."

The lag between need and action is long. In the spring of 1984, Congress began to consider the first federal support of child care since 1972, when President Nixon vetoed a bill that conservatives said would "Sovietize" American children. The House passed a bill to help local groups set up child care centers, and a House Select Committee on Children, Youth and Families started a major effort that produced a legislative package in 1985. It authorizes $300 million for child care services—demonstration programs, upgrading state standards, grants to nonprofit organizations to set up demonstration programs in partnership with for-profit businesses, training child care personnel, and other programs. Significantly, the committee was not only led by a liberal, George Miller, a Democrat from California, but also energized by a conservative, Dan Marriott, a Republican from Utah. More than half the women in that conservative state, which has the highest birthrate in the United States, work outside the home, and Marriott recognized their need. Families there can afford to spend 10 percent of their budget on child care, and families with more than one child—more plentiful in Utah than most other states—would have to pay 25 to 50 percent of their budget for child care. Marriott introduced a bill that would have given employers a tax credit for up to half of a $1,200 contribution to an employee's child care costs. Unfortunately it did not survive in the committee's legislation.

Marriott's bill and the program to put nonprofit organizations and businesses in partnership both recognized the need to get corporations involved. They prefer not to face their employees' conflict between jobs and child care. Only 1,800 of the nation's 6 million employers offered any kind of child care assistance in 1985, of which at least 400 were hospitals. Only 120 offered the most obvious kind of assistance, on-site day care.[33] (A comparable survey showed that 48 percent of American companies support alcohol-abuse counseling and 42 percent emotional counseling, which says something about priorities.[34]) Marie Oser, a pioneer on working-parent issues who founded the Texas Institute for Families and worked as a technical adviser to the private sector office of the Reagan White House, says there are many other ways besides on-site care centers to create a work environment that acknowledges that an employee is also a parent and supports that role. She suggests financial assistance to public and private child care centers away from the workplace; flexible sick leave policies that allow an employee to take days off to care for a sick child; flextime, which allows employees to choose their own hours of work so long as they work a full day; part-time work and job sharing with partial or full fringe benefits; adequate maternity and paternity leave; voluntary shift and relocation changes; personal days off; community information and referral, and workplace seminars on family well-being and time and stress management.[35]

Many of these ideas—paternity leave, flexible sick leave, flextime, job sharing, and seminars, among others—would benefit active fathers as well as working mothers. But they must be accompanied by a real change of heart in the corporate culture and the men who carry it. Few men now take advantage of paternity leave in the handful of companies that offer it. Most such leaves are unpaid, for one thing. And paid or unpaid, the men are afraid that if they take such leave they will be marked as people who don't want to advance in their careers. *The Wall Street Journal* showed why such fears spread in an article about Don Demers, a Dayton, Ohio, industrial engineer who quit his job as an industrial engineer to care for his children while his wife finished medical school. When he started looking for a new job after two years as a househusband, he told the *Journal*, "I'm black and blue from being fended off by personnel managers with 10-foot poles" who don't know "that changing diapers doesn't cause leprosy." After five months' effort and only one job, at half his old pay, he gave up and went back to full-time fathering.[36] Society has not yet made child care a matter for parents of both sexes.

FATHERING SONS AND DAUGHTERS

There is another sense in which a father's child raising is a matter for both sexes. He affects boys and girls differently. This is true even if, like Martin Menzies, he makes a conscious effort to be as warm and giving with his son as with his daughter, as encouraging to the girl's drive to achieve as to the boy's. Active fathers are more deliberate than many traditional men in their efforts to be equally loving with both sexes. But nobody can treat boys and girls identically, and some can't even try for emotional equity. Some men are interested only in their daughters, but many more follow the classical pattern of identifying far more strongly with their sons in the ancient quest for immortality. The strength of old feelings was startlingly clear in a piece that Edward Tivnan wrote in 1984, long after feminist ideas had begun to color social values and long after the new fathering had taken root, mourning that though he had two daughters he would never have a son." He expressed happiness over social changes that allow women to ride into space or sit on the Supreme Court, which he said deprived him of any reason to pity daughters as he once had. But he still felt grief that he would never know "the joys and secrets and conflicts between a father and a son" as had his own father, a very close and active parent. I could empathize with that, if only because I had such ties to my own father, an important presence in my own childhood, which I had not been able to reproduce with my own sons. But I was shocked and saddened that he thought only a son could have provided him with the kind of friendship for life that his wife felt she had already found with their three-year-old daughter. I know men whose daughters have given them equivalent joys and secrets, conflicts and friendships. I want to believe that men who become active fathers might spread and strengthen changes in sex roles and parenting as they and their sons identify with each other. I didn't find ground for hope in Tivnan's piece.

Active fathers do things that should, or at least may, free their sons from stereotypes in housekeeping, cooking, and expressing physical affection. This does not mean they ignore all the traditional links between fathers and sons, though the combination of old and new styles sometimes seems odd—as it did to a group of divorced fathers who moved from a soccer game with their sons to the home of one father, where the boys raced around the living room in the familiar style of nine and ten year olds while the fathers gathered in less familiar style in the kitchen to discuss the host's restaurant-style stove and exchange recipes, giving a completely different meaning to the phrase *nouvelle cuisine*.

Jim Calabrese, whom I've quoted on his discovery of his feminine side while being the caretaking parent, is a new-style father who did not want his son to grow up without some of the old masculine ways. When his son, Eric, was on the brink of adolescence, Calabrese had an idea:

> As a rite of passage, for his birthday this year, we decided to send him to Montana, to my father, his grandfather's, for three weeks. He went up there age twelve and came back age thirteen. I wanted my father to teach Eric to shoot a rifle, to take him fishing, and above all to tell him all the stories he had told me that I loved. . . . So sure enough, he told Eric all these stories. The first night he was home Eric said, "I'm going to tell you one of these stories." He didn't know I had sort of planted this, that I knew these stories already. He told us a story, mimicking my father, and he was ingenious, he's a good mime. If I had closed my eyes, it would have taken me a couple of seconds to realize it wasn't my own father, the pauses, the cadences were right. And Eric cooked for him. My father was the old tradition, a first-generation American. I don't know what he thought, but I think Eric fed him some of my lines about a man being able to care for himself. One night they had hot dogs, and Eric fixed them and brought hot dog buns; and Grandpa had only one plate and Eric had to wash the thing. The two styles came together there.

Whether their attitudes were traditional or new, the active fathers of sons whom I interviewed seldom seemed to question their ability to raise the boys, their instincts, or the ideas and information about parenting that they'd acquired. I interviewed thirty-five fathers whose children had been born in 1968 or later. Fifteen had sons, ten had daughters, and ten had both. I had the impression that all twenty-five with sons gave the boys messages that put work before love. This is the traditional male priority, but they were not the traditional messages. All the men seemed to tell their sons that they should find satisfaction in their work, but only ten or twelve gave the old masculine injunction to succeed. More than half the twenty-five also gave messages that said love is important and should be expressed in words and body language, including physical embraces—ideas and feelings supposedly silent in the traditional socialization of boys. The toughness of the old male culture made it hard for fathers and sons to express their love for each other, but young men in particular are trying to be different.[38]

Six of my ten fathers with children of both sexes recognized that they spent more time with their sons than with their daughters, as one study shows many fathers do. Another study concludes that fathers are more likely to express approval when sons and daughters play with traditionally "appropriate" toys and to disapprove when boys play with dolls or pots and pans. I didn't ask questions that would produce a comparison, but nine of my thirty-five fathers expressed similar views in our conversations.[39]

The fathers of daughters in my small sample frequently expressed doubts and fears as well as hopes and confidence. Most of the doubts and fears centered on questions of love and sexuality, reflecting new ideas about the way fathers have always shaped daughters' development, which I mentioned earlier in this chapter. A girl develops with less emphatic individuation than a boy, more continuity with her mother and other psychological "objects." She adds her father to this world; he helps her separate from the mother and gives her her first relationship with a man, which becomes a model for the relationships she will usually make primary in the bundle she will keep tying all her life.[40] Father-daughter love is a dream love, and like any dream its perfection does not match and may even contradict reality. A father may be generous or abusive, seductive or rejecting. Extremes in either direction may leave a daughter desperately searching for a self; a loving middle path leaves her secure in her identity. Whatever its quality, the father-daughter relationship has a high erotic charge, before and after as well as during the classical oedipal period. Some fathers give their daughters the "desexualized affection" that the girls need to develop confidence in their femininity; some disapprove of the daughters' growing sexuality; some come on far too strong.[41] This last can be as grave as incest or as light as a kiss on the lips of a teenager who can accept it from her boyfriend but not from her father.

No matter which of the three patterns they followed, traditional fathers often didn't see how important they were in their daughters' sexual growth.* A few of my new-style fathers were familiar with the new ideas about their roles in giving their daughters the ability to form relationships that our society makes a fundamental part of a woman's identity. Many had some vague impression of those ideas, and none of them could repress feelings as thoroughly as earlier generations of fathers had. As a result most found themselves conscious of problems about love and sexuality that may have been ancient but still surprised them.

Single fathers lamented their difficulties in preparing daughters to deal serenely with first menstruation or the other body changes of puberty. Fred Farina felt that way, yet he and his daughter were well prepared:

> That's why I say I have to stick with women, I could never ask men about menstruation. What do I do? I talked it over with this woman I made friends with. She says, "There's nothing to panic about, you go out and buy a little Kotex, a little Tampax, whatever, a little pad, when that day comes you just give me a call, we'll go and get it." She put it all in a little cigar box for her daughter. Then she wrapped it up and put a bow on it and said, "This is for you." I wanna do that for Laura. But I'm going to do one more thing—buy a split of champagne and drink it with her when that happens. Anyway, I think Laura knows what it is; I talk about sex with her, and

---

* Fathers who take an active role in holding, feeding, and diapering their daughters in their first three years of life are less likely to abuse them sexually in later years, according to a significant study by Seymour and Hilda Parker of the University of Utah. Thirty of the fifty-four abusing fathers in their study had no contact with their daughters in the children's first three years.[42]

they already had movies in school about it, one for the girls with Marlo
Thomas, and one for the boys with Ken Howard, the guy that was the
basketball coach on "White Shadow." I think the boys should see the girls'
movie and vice versa.

That was a problem with a pragmatic solution. Some problems ran deeper.
Many fathers, for instance, single and married, were more conscious than
men used to be that they were finding their daughters sexually attractive, and
it disturbed them. Several mentioned telling teenagers to put clothes on when
they let themselves be seen naked or half-dressed—which can be an expression of disapproval of the girl's sexuality, or simultaneous testimony to her
attractiveness and establishment of limits, depending on the words and the
tone. One father was horrified when he found himself with an erection when
his five year old climbed on his lap. He eased her off and had to do a lot of
talking with his wife and with other men before he learned that he could
continue to hug and kiss his daughter without feeling embarrassed or being in
danger of sliding into incest. (More than half the fathers of daughters whom I
spoke to were aware of incest as a danger or an issue—a reflection of feminist
and media attention to something that happens often but is often unmentionable even today.) He said he wished his wife had been able to make him laugh
about it instead of turning it into a therapy lesson, but she and one male
friend were able to lead him into accepting the idea that sexual feelings were
part of his love for his daughter.

David Carlin* knew himself so well he didn't feel surprised or need lessons.
He is a lawyer and his wife an English professor. When I interviewed him,
their daughter, Cathy,* was twelve, a champion swimmer in her age group,
tops in both math and art classes, pretty with dark eyes and a mouth already
promising wit and sexuality, tall for her age but her figure still chunky with
baby fat. He said:

I get a charge out of seeing her in a swimming match. Some of the girls
have no sex appeal, too scrawny or too pudgy or too short. She's one of a
few who men look at and even fantasize about. I've seen other men doing it
and I do it, even though I'm her father. I can look at her and think, "What
nice long legs." I don't tell her that. God forbid. I remember how embarrassed she was one night when she was warm and her mother started to
take her sweater off over her head in a way that pulled her T-shirt up and
left her breasts bare. I think that was the first time I noticed how sweet
they were. I loved her embarrassment, because it was the first time she
knew she was old enough to need to be modest. But she knows when I look
at her in new clothes that I think she looks terrific, and I've never seen her
embarrassed by that. I think she'd tell her mother if she was, but she hasn't
so far, and I hope she never does. She's quite capable of flirting with me
over her soda and my wine, but I've never heard her call it flirting. She's
still so innocent she doesn't know that what she does could be called sexual

play. But I don't confuse fantasy with reality. One evening some friends were dancing here, and she got up on the couch so our faces would be at the same height and threw both arms around my neck and her legs around my waist so we could dance cheek to cheek. Part of me wanted to shout at her to get down, but another part of me wanted to keep hold of her, and I did. I just had to remind myself consciously not to grab her by the ass to keep her in place, but there was never any danger of my touching her in a way that would be too much for her or for me. I want her to know that I think it's great that she's a sexual female, and that all the same, I'm safe. I want to give her what she needs to grow up right. That means not denying that my love for her has a sexual thread running through it.

If the doubts centered on sex, the hopes were clearest on the question of endeavor: all of the twenty men with daughters said they tried to show the girls that they valued their achievements; fourteen claimed to encourage them to look for new kinds of work in school and new adventures. I couldn't be sure how many lived up to their intentions, but I thought most probably did. All six of the daughters I met seemed happy in their enterprising drive.

David Carlin had introduced Cathy to architecture as a subject in books and museums because she was good in both math and art. He and his wife had both taken her to their workplaces and encouraged her to feel at home in them, and I thought she was in the ideal situation—the daughter of a two-career marriage who could identify with both her mother and her father. For Fred Farina, it was a question not only of a career for his daughter but of upward mobility for his children. At the age of ten, Laura was already talking about being a lawyer first and then a mother. He was suffused with joy about both ambitions, especially when she looked at the marriage vows in a book and said, "When I become a mother, I'm not going to do what my mother did. When you marry a man, you're supposed to take him for better or worse, till death do you part."

Farina liked Laura's putting career ahead of marriage and motherhood in her timetable. All the new-style fathers recognized that daughters as well as sons are human beings who by definition need both love and work, which I am sure was an effect of the women's movement on our culture. But the messages Farina gave her made love equal in importance to work, or more important. So did the messages given their daughters by all but two or three of these twenty fathers who consciously tried to encourage achievement. They were still saying, in effect, that a woman needs a man to define herself. They wanted their daughters to achieve, sometimes with a very strong desire indeed, but not at the expense of a femininity that was often expressed in conventional terms. Even those who encouraged their sons to love and to express love did not make a woman part of the definition of a man. They did not see a son's achievement as a threat to his masculinity.

The wish to see a daughter relate to a man shows the strength of old ideas

and old feelings in the struggle with new feelings about women's independence and equality and careers that the fathers were acquiring, sometimes
painfully. The wish is also related to another risk that fathers run when they
are determined to be warm and loving rather than rejecting. Some experts
warn that fathers trap their daughters into one form or another of immaturity
by being too kind and generous far more often than they warp them by
hostility or rejection.[43] The daughters in my post-1968 sample were too young
for an analyst to tell if this would happen to them, but I was inclined to doubt
it would be the fate of many. I didn't think many of the men I interviewed
showed signs of the kind of benevolent tyranny that demands adoration from
a daughter. And the new ideas about active fathering and women's work and
independence were often strong enough to give men a conscious desire to
avoid adoration, especially the kind of adoration of a father that often used to
be transformed into the wish to serve of traditional wives or secretaries or
assistants to a strong male figure.

In fact, many more of the men I interviewed, in and out of the post-1968
sample, had been awakened to women's demands for equality by their daughters' experiences than by their wives' or colleagues'. They were like Mike
Modzelewski,* the data-processing executive who describes in Chapter 7 how
he found his twelve-year-old daughter thinking about her choice of careers in
stereotyped terms and was moved to a vision of women as America's greatest
wasted resource.

OLDER FATHERS

Modzelewski was one of several men I interviewed who were older than those
in the sample I've been describing. Most, like him, had had children before
1968 and were closer to traditional than to activist fatherhood. The changes
in fathering have given them perspective or led them to ask themselves questions about what they had done. Did they spend enough time with their kids?
Enjoy them fully? Hardly any said yes to those questions. Did they overem-
phasize sports or learning to play a musical instrument? Did they put too
much or too little emphasis on grades, college, well-paying jobs? Did they
succeed or fail in keeping their kids off drugs? The answers they gave themselves varied, but the ones who were most sensitive to women's demands or to
the changes in male sex roles took pleasure in realizing that they had mat-
tered to their children, had had some positive effects on the children's lives.
Several of those old enough to be grandfathers were, as predicted, being
tenderer with their grandchildren than they had been with their own. That
might be a result of their reaching a particular season in life rather than of
changes in roles or in the sexual balance of power. But I believe the men were
feeling the effects of those changes when they found themselves doing as

much or more with their grandchildren as were their wives, the grandmothers, or enjoying being surrogates for sons who were active fathers.

Other "older" men have married younger women and fathered children, usually but not always second families, in their late forties and fifties. The changes in work and family life of the past twenty years affected their wives' decisions on when to have children and influenced their dedication in principle to equality in child raising. The few I interviewed, like those in other studies, often spend time with their children that they did not spend with their first families, because they no longer have the same need to work long hours, are financially more secure and better able to decide on priorities. I think it's important to note that they are usually people with high incomes who hire caretakers, almost always women, for the burdensome part of child care. Researchers also cite problems with older fathers: they have decreasing stamina, are likely to face illness or die while their children are still young, and meet with social disapproval often enough for it to be noticeable.[44]

The new ideas and the cultural changes have also had an effect on other middle-aged men—fathers who played relatively small roles in their children's lives. I was such a father, for reasons I still do not entirely understand. Most fathers at least live with their young children; my father was a constant presence in my life; I was absent from too much of my sons' lives. Sometimes I think of it as a sin, sometimes as a mistake.

I started thinking that way only after I started work on this book. It crystallized when my older son, Owen, graduated from Dartmouth in 1978. I took pride and pleasure in seeing him get his diploma, summa cum laude. When I watched him drive off to begin a master's program in teaching, I imagined the joy my father would have felt had he lived long enough to see his grandson finish college and enter his own profession. I was surprised to find tears in my eyes after the last goodbye—less because a child had left the nest than because I knew with terrible certainty that it was too late to repair the wrong I had done.

Their mother, Gail Potter Neale, and I separated when Owen was five and Josh was three years old. I lived overseas without them, except for two summer visits, for seven of the next ten years. At first I was continuing the work I had started in the American foreign aid program, training Africans to use communications media in their economic development programs. I was also refusing to digest what had happened in my first marriage, but I returned to the States when Gail remarried so I would not be obliterated in my children's minds. Later I was fulfilling a career imperative, a long-held ambition to be a foreign correspondent. I never asked how much I might regret suppressing my nurturing instincts, being away during the years when the boys' minds and characters were taking shape.

As it happened, their minds and characters took splendid shape. Contradicting conventional wisdom, my children, grown, seem little damaged by their father's absence—thanks to luck, the care that others gave them, and their own strengths. I came to feel that the person whom I damaged most by being away when they were growing up was me. (Daniel Levinson notes that the difficulties between parents and children are usually studied from the viewpoint of the children. Parents, too, have growing pains, he saw.[45] I can add that they may be self-inflicted.) I let my nurturing impulse dry up. I denied the possibility of doing something good for myself, something Gail did and nourished herself on while having a fine career—learning from my children and connecting with their love and energy. I frustrated even the fundamental, selfish desire to transcend my own mortality by putting my stamp on the next generation of my own flesh and blood. (I know that nobody really succeeds in stamping his offspring, and when he tries too hard the results may be hideous. But the desire needs to be worked out, not ignored.)

When I began to realize how I had hurt myself, I also saw that it was not only as a member of a small, dramatic minority of absentee fathers. There was also a large, unhappy majority of fathers who, even if they live with their children, play relatively small roles in the children's upbringing. Fatherhood may be terribly important to them, but they act as though child care were exclusively a mother's job, while the father's function is to support the family by working outside the home. I hate to admit that I have anything in common with the conventional, hardworking, long-married father who sees his children at dinner or on their way to bed and spends time with them only on selected weekends. But in terms of the effects he has on his children and the effects they have on him, he is not much different from the divorced father in a distant city or a glamorous foreign job. We all give the children less than they need.

Many of us in this majority, when we reach our forties—the period that we are now told is our "mid-life crisis"—find ourselves reaching out for our children in the same way, whether we were absent or present in earlier years. We reach out for them just as they begin to want distance between themselves and their parents, just as they come able to live their own lives. Our children are in their teens or twenties and we dream of the response we might have elicited ten years earlier, but it no longer comes. I started doing this when I came back from Moscow in 1971, and began to accept that it was too late only when my tears surprised me after I said goodbye to Owen.

The desire to nurture has a variety of effects on men in this once-silent majority. Some form bonds with fathers doing just the opposite of what we did, being primary or truly equal parents of the kind I have been describing. We sympathize with men who learn by experience about the burden of child care and mother-hate because, though we have done very different things, we have both left behind commonplace fatherhood. Some become mentors to young men and women, elaborating the parental impulse. Like parenting, this role benefits the mentor as well as the protégés. He makes productive use of his knowledge and skills, he learns in new ways, he connects to the youthful energy of others and himself. Some men develop mentorial relations with their own grown children. (Active fathers may also become mentors when they reach a generative stage of life after their children are grown.)

Whatever absentees have in common with ordinary fathers and active fathers, however, we have some characteristics of our own. We devote an extra intensity to assessing our children's condition and apportioning responsibility, fearing that all is ours and that none is ours. I've been lucky on the assessment. Owen and Josh both did well in school. Neither went in for the kind of behavior that makes parents want to wring their hands, or their children's necks. Both have learned some of the art of living with other people and both have shown themselves capable of love.

On the apportionment, most of the credit goes to their mother, who demurs and says it is due to the boys themselves. My mother played a role, and I'd like to believe my letters, the two summers the boys spent with me in Africa and Russia, the weekends during the years when I was in this country, all helped. I feel it's particularly important, however, for me to recognize the credit due the men who were there when I was not—my father, until he died in 1974, and Dick Potter, a stepfather who honorably kept my image alive while he functioned as a father in daily life. They provided my children with a surplus rather than a shortage of father figures.

Gail later added another father figure, her third husband, Bob Neale, a clergyman whom Josh asked to perform the wedding ceremony when he married in 1983. At moments at the wedding it was painful for me to acknowledge that I was only one of three living father figures in Josh's life, a fact emphasized by the way the pictures and the boutonnières gave me exactly equal standing with the two stepfathers. I wanted more recognition of my unique genetic contribution to the making of my son, of both my intelligent and handsome sons. I wanted recognition that despite my profound absence when Josh was young, I had given him something in love and care and intellectual guidance that was different from what everyone else gave him. But I also wanted people to recognize reality and celebrate the truth. At the rehearsal dinner most of the toasts equated Josh's family with Gail's or held up the hope that he and Barbara would emulate the lifelong marriages of both sets of Barbara's grandparents. I toasted that hope and what I have always felt was Gail's wonderful mothering, and then offered a toast to Josh's wealth of father figures, the three present at the dinner and my father, present in spirit.

That was an act of remembrance as well as celebration. An absentee father necessarily has fewer memories of his children's growing up than does a father who was there in the midst of it—though he may well remember a higher proportion of the smaller number of moments that he was part of. It's hardly surprising that my favorite picture of my sons is one I took when they were two and four years old and we were all living together. Or that they and I all remember their long summer stays with me in Nairobi in 1968 and

Moscow in 1970 more warmly than most of their later weekends in New York.

A resident father learns to doubt that his children share the experiences that are most meaningful to him; it's a normal part of the generation gap. An absentee father has even greater doubts because he has less time to absorb his children's reactions. I remember Owen and Josh mocking the lecture I gave them on the statues in the Medici Chapel in Florence, when we were in Italy on vacation from Moscow, but I don't know if they saw the beauty that the pedantry was meant to illuminate. On the other hand, when there is some evidence of sharing, it may be more warming than usual. Owen and Josh often seemed uncomprehending of, or hostile to, my interest in the women's movement. But they grew up with a group of boys and girls whose communal activities made it unlikely that they would adopt traditional sex roles, and their comments and behavior as adults—including equal partnership with women in cooking and housekeeping—show an unwillingness to adopt the usual male blinders that warms me.

Finally, an absentee father looks harder than a conventional father for moments in which it is clear that his children resemble him, and moments that show that he has had some influence on them, moments that ordinary fathers take for granted. I'd gotten into the habit of thinking that my sons look more like their mother than like me, and I was used to seeing their faces in conversation. So I was startled at more than one moment in the past few years to see Josh silent, in profile, with his glasses on, looking very much like me. I was even more so when I caught Owen, waiting for his commencement procession to start, with one of my more equine expressions on his face. It's one that people mistake for arrogance when it's really paying equally careful attention to the world in one's head and the world outside at the same time. I took more than usual paternal pleasure in seeing Josh play Lucio in a Yale production of Shakespeare's *Measure for Measure,* because he unconsciously used the same gestures and grimaces that I had used in the same role thirteen years earlier. I took a longer-range satisfaction in Owen's telling me that I had given him two of the five books that had made him want to become a teacher.

Some resemblances would give pause to any father, ordinary or active, resident or absentee. One thing that Owen and Josh have in common with me is that neither they nor I rebelled sharply against parental authority before we reached the age of twenty. The theorists of adult development say they'll have to complete the process of separation at a later stage, and probably more painfully. I know from experience that the theorists are right. My separation from my children was part of my separation from my parents. When I compare myself to the men who complain their fathers were never *there* when they were growing up, while I enjoyed my father's presence so much, I wonder how I could have been willing not to be there for my sons. One answer: I left the major portion of the father's role because I was unconsciously afraid I would not be as good a father to them as mine was to me.

That's apt to be a self-fulfilling fear. My absence made improbable the resemblance I'd like most from my sons: some indication that they think of me as I think of my father—indeed as *they* think of my father: as a man whose stories were always worth hearing, a man whose mastery of his craft was illuminating, a man whose wisdom was always available, a man whose love could always be relied on.

The last might seem especially unlikely. Owen used to fantasize about it. Shortly before his graduation he found a story he had written in the second grade, about a fisherman who catches a magic fish but lets it go in exchange for wishes—wishes for a swimming pool, a bicycle, and for a father who was always there to play catch with his sons. But filial feelings do develop. My sons seem aware in adulthood that a father can be a mentor. When I told Josh I was wondering if I'd had some effect on him, he said, "Some, and not all in the past, either." If I hadn't been studying new-style fathers, I might never have had the courage to ask.

Chapter 11

SEXUALITY

Michael Castleman, a San Francisco sex counselor, tells the story of a client he calls Henry.* Henry was a computer designer whose wife, a teacher, died of cancer when they were both forty. He prided himself on their egalitarian relationship, and before she died she asked him not to mourn her too long. After her death, her friends suggested that he start dating. He met a woman who asked him out. He accepted. She asked him out again and he accepted again. He also said yes when she asked him to bed. He was ambivalent about the love-making and about the possibility of a relationship, but he had never said no to a woman.

Soon he developed the first erection problems he had ever had. That upset them both. The woman, very liberated by her own and other accounts, suggested that despite the public egalitarianism of his marriage, Henry might not be able to deal with strong women. Perhaps he was a "closet male chauvinist." He went to Castleman for help, worrying that her remark might be true. He said, "When my wife was alive, I did the housework, I was good to her, she had a career. Now my girlfriend says I can't deal with assertive women, my dick doesn't work, and I feel as though my life is ruined. Maybe I am a male chauvinist. Maybe I've been fooling myself all these years. Since this thing started, I'm not sure of anything anymore."

In counseling, Castleman asked Henry if he masturbated. He did, frequently, fantasizing not about his new lover but about his dead wife. Castleman was able to show him that the problem had nothing to do with assertive women. It was simply that he and his penis were both still mourning his wife. Henry decided not to date until he felt his bereavement had ended.[1]

He learned, in other words, to say no when he didn't feel like making love. Women are taught they can say no from an early age and used to be taught that they *should* say no. Most American men don't know that we too are entitled to say no. We are learning now that we can and sometimes should, that like women we are entitled to choose rather than be the ever-ready studs of our own mythology.

This is one of many changes in sexual relations growing out of women's quest for independence, equality, and choice. Women have climbed off their sexual pedestal. They are thinking and feeling for themselves about their own sexuality, discovering what they want and don't want, and telling their partners about it—far more often than they used to and far more often than men do. They take the initiative in sex sometimes, which confronts us with the need to say no sometimes. They are asserting their right to be free of anyone else's control of their emotions and their bodily functions, which includes their right to have abortions (in law) and to commit adultery (in practice). Men are only beginning to make comparable discoveries in comparable numbers, to learn what women want—and what we ourselves want, which sometimes surprises us even more.

Many of us find it hard to give up the old manners, the old rules, the old games. We find it hard to get rid of the notion that it's the male function to take the initiative, which we take to mean it should be a male monopoly. We find it hard to give up the idea of ourselves as sex machines that are always ready to function when given the least opportunity, the idea that men never say no. We've been socialized to act in these ways for centuries, with particular variations in the twentieth century. Jack Litewka called it socializing the penis.[2] He saw it as a process that leads males to turn females into objects, "others" without individual desires and often without individual qualities; to divide a female body up and fixate on the breasts, sometimes the buttocks, later "that hidden unknown quantity, the vagina"; and to conquer the female objects by turning those parts into tactical targets, establishing maleness with every conquest.

Men, and women, often speak of this entirely in sexual terms, but like everything else in this book, it's a matter of power. Litewka didn't see this at first. He started analyzing the question after three instances when he failed to get erections, each with a different woman whom he knew and liked (though with other women he had no problem). He said:

> Because I knew them as whole beings, I couldn't objectify them, and consequently couldn't fixate on (though I tried) or conquer them. And they didn't put pressure on me to do that (as women can, and do, for a variety of reasons). So, I didn't play my role and they didn't play theirs. No roles; no seduction, no Objectification/Fixation/Conquest—ergo, no erection. . . .[3]

Litewka then went on to quote a woman friend who put a very different interpretation on what had happened. She said he had accepted the three women as equals on all levels except the sexual. There (speaking as though in his voice),

> I still had to deal with them on an objectify, fixate, and conquer basis. But since I couldn't objectify them, I rejected these women rather than give up my last heirloom of maleness. . . . [The women] could not understand that I was in fact forestalling my own liberation because I lacked the courage or the knowledge necessary for the last step. What the women

would feel is that I have rejected them. . . . that there is something wrong with them, some way in which they are lacking, if they can't arouse me. So . . . I have in fact turned the tables and made them feel inadequate in relation to me. . . .[4]

Litewka's woman friend summed it up by putting these words in his mouth: "By preventing my penis from getting into gear, I ironically preserved my male superiority in the situation."

MALE SEXUALITY, MALE DOMINANCE

Few men have acknowledged so plainly the connection of male sexuality and male superiority, male hegemony, male dominance. We don't see the political or sociological link so clearly, while women make the connection frequently, from the highest theoretical to the lowest colloquial levels. Yet male dominance is visible in the idea of man as initiator, man as hunter that is still in the minds of many of the men I've interviewed. It is palpable in the words of prophets like Sigmund Freud and D. H. Lawrence, who were vastly different but who both defined male sexuality in terms of aggressiveness and female sexuality in terms of passivity, of attraction to the very dominance of the male. On a lower level, Henry Kissinger translated this back into the political in his explanation of his supposed success with women, "Power is the ultimate aphrodisiac."[5]

Male dominance is manifest in a feeling that most men have—our sense of ownership of a woman's body. Many of us find it hard to give this up even though few of us admit we ever had it. The sense of ownership has two roots. One is the myth of the male sex drive that once triggered cannot be stopped and overrides a woman's emotions or morals. It is often accompanied by a companion myth that women have no significant sex drive of their own, but it is also found even among people who see the female as the fount of sexuality. The other is the traditional male control of money, security, status, and power in our society. Women of all classes learned to trade their sex for access to those needed things.* Men then constructed a compelling logic: "Women have the sexual commodity we want. Therefore it's women who are sexual. But women are our social inferiors because they lack money and power—if they're within our class and even more if they are women of lower classes. Sexuality is therefore a matter of social inferiority." This led them to reserve love for women of higher class and lesser sexuality.[6] It seems to me that this logic of class distinction reinforced Christian teachings that sex is sinful and

* This profound social and historical experience survives in its basic form in many parts of our society. It also survives in the issue of who pays for a date, sometimes classed as trivial but still a subject of deep concern and passionate debate between men and women individually, in couples, and in groups.

that the woman Eve inflicted the sin on man, but it contradicted the idea that it is men who possess the unstoppable sex drive. Perhaps men used their class dominance to deny, or compensate for, their lower animal nature. And the assertion of class dominance, however much based on the truths that men are more aggressive than women and have more money and power than women, helped disguise the truth that most men are powerless (even if most of the few with power are men).

Rape is also an act of male power and aggression, committed with a sexual weapon, that tries to disguise a comparable truth: it is often committed by men with little economic or social power. It seems important to emphasize here that sexual dominance and aggressiveness in men are not *identical* with rape or other violence against women, even though one can lead to the other. In this chapter, I am talking about sexual relations that at best are loving and consensual, at worst matters of economic or power bargaining, but not shaped or determined by physical violence.

It's also important to note that men who love rape victims—fathers, husbands, lovers, brothers, friends—unconsciously confirm that what is usually labeled a sexual crime is a matter of power. The first confirmation comes when these "secondary victims" become angry, as they often do when they learn of the rape. They want to seek revenge against the rapist and often commit new violence in miniature, like tearing up the furniture in a room, if they can't lay hands on him. This makes the matter a power duel between the rapist and the man connected with the victim and shifts attention from her needs to his. A second confirmation comes if the man concentrates on the sexual aspects of the rape rather than the violent assault, making it a matter of his own shame or dishonor or implying that the woman may have invited, cooperated in, or enjoyed the rape. This asserts his power over the woman and his desire to show power vis à vis the rapist because it suggests in another way that the woman, particularly her body, is somehow the man's property, which the rapist has damaged.[7]

Male dominance in sexual relations is not only a matter of male hegemony in society or male potential for violence. It also grows out of the prevalence of dominance and subordination in erotic fantasy—in some form, open or disguised, vigorous or attenuated, permanent or momentary—in most relationships, although the dominant person is not always male and the relationship is not always heterosexual.

Jessica Benjamin has shown how erotic domination reflects and repeats the process of differentiation, the process by which a child becomes an individual.[8] The child's first independent acts require an audience to recognize them and therefore reaffirm its dependency on others, usually the mother. The conflict in this paradox tempts the child to imagine that it can become independent without recognizing the other person as an equally autonomous agent, to feel, "She belongs to me, I control and possess her." In doing this, the male child denies his likeness to his mother, separating completely and making her an object, while the female remains in relationship or continuity with her.

Domination is ultimately an adult repetition of this failure to recognize the other person as like oneself, but separate. In the Freudian model and the Hegelian master-slave model, the self discovers that if it completely controls the other, it cannot get the true recognition it wants. But it gives up the desire to control unwillingly, with an unconscious wish to fulfill the old fantasy of omnipotence. Benjamin sees in this a truth: acknowledging dependency is painful and denying recognition to others because of this pain leads to domination.[9] In our minds acknowledging dependency threatens the death of the self. So does the merger of selves, the loss of differentiation and of boundaries, in love and particularly in the sex act. (This psychic death is often misperceived as equating sex and death. In truth the erotic breaks the taboo between love and death. This profound metaphor combines with the literal, physical shriveling of the penis after ejaculation to produce the idea of lovemaking as *le petite mort*, the little death.) In most cases the male sees the female as imposing the pain of dependency and threatening the death of his independent self, echoing his sharper separation from his mother. He goes into domination to avoid that dependency, and domination sometimes—too often—gives license to male violence. But the relationship of self and other does not always develop this way, so actual men and women may play opposite roles.

True differentiation produces a mature self that does not need to turn the other into an object but can recognize her or him as independent. It maintains "the essential tension of the contradictory impulses to assert the self and respect the other."[10] This tension is in fact hard to maintain over every moment of waking life, and the most egalitarian of relationships is likely to have moments when dominance and submission manifest themselves again—perhaps most frequently in sex.

WHAT CHANGED THE SEXUAL BALANCE

The tradition of the male as the dominant aggressor in sex is probably even stronger than the tradition of male power at work and in the family, but here as in the other arenas, a number of events have changed and challenged the balance of power between men and women. In rough chronological order, they were women's working for pay in increasing numbers; the invention of the birth control pill and other high-assurance contraceptive techniques that enabled women to end the fear of unwanted pregnancy; the sexual revolution, and the women's movement.

Women who worked for pay, even in low-paying pink-collar and other stereotyped jobs, had less need for men as suppliers of the money and status for which they traded their sex. So did women who seized the new ability to escape or control the burden of bearing children. Often these forces allowed men to escape their responsibility for the support of women and children more easily.[11] But sometimes contraceptive freedom reduced men's need to control women in order to control progeny and family property—though at other times or for other men, it increased the need to control. With or without the pill, it was still the woman who became pregnant, and men seldom found it necessary to take responsibility for contraception themselves.*

By separating intercourse from reproduction, the pill had two profound effects. It made possible the sexual revolution, and it enabled women to discover their own sexuality and seek their own sexual pleasure on a new basis.

The sexual revolution began before the pill, of course. I think its major prophet was Alfred C. Kinsey, who made people aware as early as 1948 that their fellow citizens were doing quite a lot of things, sexually—that sex wasn't only or even primarily for reproductive purposes in marriage. (I'll never forget how relieved I was at the age of sixteen to discover I was not the only boy who regularly petted to a climax with his girlfriend.) But the numbers of men and women who pursued sex as a source of pleasure, abandoning both religious and class obsession with female purity, multiplied only when it became possible to separate sex from pregnancy (and also to separate the moment of contraception from the moment of sex).

The sexual revolution was a genuine attempt to cast off the sexual repression that had become associated with the nuclear family and the economic system built around it. It was one wave in a broader tide of rebellion against the system and outlasted most of the others. Indeed, it changed the nuclear family; where Kinsey showed married men under thirty-five having sex about twice a week, using data collected from 1938 to 1949, Morton Hunt put the figure from three to three and a half times a week in a 1972 survey. Blumstein and Schwartz reported a majority of married and cohabiting couples in the late seventies having sex once a week or more, with emphasis on the more. Forty-six percent of their couples married two to ten years had sex between one and three times a week, for instance, and 27 percent three times a week or more. Another survey reported that 89 percent of two-earner parents and 87 percent of childless couples engaged in sex at least once a week but only 67 percent of traditional couples.[13]

Some impulses of the sexual revolution were genuinely idealistic. But the idea that sexual relations created happiness in themselves and that they could

* This may be changing. The combination of new technology and the sexual revolution has made vasectomy popular, giving men a third choice besides withdrawal and the condom. Women can choose among eleven contraceptives. Many feminists and some population planners hope that growing male concern for their partners' health and family happiness will speed research on male contraceptives and encourage more men to share responsibility for birth control. The World Health Organization estimates that it will take twenty years before a new male contraceptive is marketable, however. The lag in developing a male birth control has many causes: technological difficulty, the preference of women and birth control advocates for female contraceptives, and the reluctance of scientific researchers, mostly male, to tamper with male physiology.[12]

be conducted without regard to the partners' identities or characters was false psychologically; the idea that they took place without regard to the partners' positions in the dynamics of power and economics was false politically.[14]

These fallacies had several causes. One important one was the revolution's being at first another male-dominated process. *Playboy* led a consumer rebellion against the producer standard that nice girls don't; the counterculture rebelled against consumer, producer, and all bourgeois standards. Despite the differences, in both rebellions it was men who said, as the pill spread in the 1960s, "To hell with female purity, let's all be sexual animals together." There was an illusion of independence and equality because the woman took the initiative of going on the pill, but it was the man who took most of the subsequent initiatives from inviting her to bed to deciding what to do there. The liberated man was one who worried whether he had brought his partner to orgasm—usually whether he had lasted long enough to bring her to orgasm in intercourse.

In this revolution men may have thought (subconsciously, of course) that they were depriving women of their advantage in the old bargaining process, the scarcity of sex. They certainly assumed they no longer had to exchange the economic security of marriage for the scarce sexual commodity, because women, working, no longer found economic security so scarce. Some also assumed this freed them from the need to offer any emotional involvement. Few realized that to the extent these assumptions were true they undermined one of the main bases of male dominance.

Soon the women's movement, while fighting that dominance in the sexual revolution, reinforced the basic rebellion against sexual repression that had spread throughout the culture. At least, some parts of the movement, some women, did. Ellen Willis spoke for many when she said:

> My idea of feminism is that society has set up a polarity of masculine and feminine, which is an artificial and oppressive political construct. In the feminine construct, women are denied the right to express lust, and by repressing our sexuality, our humanity is denied. The split between sex and affection is also an artificial product of sexism for many men. Fighting this sexual repression was really a motivating factor for my joining the Women's Movement.
>
> The opposite position, which I call cultural feminism, accepts the polarity as reality. . . . Men are seen as predators: women as good, sweet, nice, not really interested in sexuality. This continues the problems women have with sexuality and is a poor answer to male violence—which I think is a function of repression and power. We need a movement to change the institutions that create this, but cultural feminism just puts the sexual rage into a moral crusade against male vice.[15]

Men are not always happy with women who enjoy expressing their own lusts, especially when they combine that drive with feminist ideology and challenge male dominance in bed. But if men think about feminism at all in connection with sex, they probably identify it more often with what Willis calls cultural feminists, some of whom sound as though they are against sex when they make war on rape and pornography, as though sex were inextricable from those things.

Women who learned to express their lusts were empowered and energized by the new contraception. They made the search for their own sexuality part of their quest for independence and equality. That was a leap in philosophy that owed a great deal to the next great jump in the study of sex after Kinsey —the work of William H. Masters and Virginia E. Johnson, whose research on human sexual response demonstrated the importance of the clitoris in female orgasm. That led to new techniques, and new emphasis on old techniques, which made orgasm easier and more frequent for women than the sexual culture had expected. Some men paid less attention to that than to Masters' and Johnson's skill in curing premature ejaculation and other male dysfunctions, but feminists, sex researchers, and therapists kept the clitoris in focus in talk and in print, and women everywhere soon learned to do the same thing in bed.

Masters and Johnson also emphasized the importance of "sensate focus" and "pleasuring" in their therapy—touching, caressing, and kissing all parts of the body without intercourse or orgasm. Feminists and other therapists found that most women had more interest in sensual play over the whole body than did most men, whose sexuality was more narrowly genital. They started urging men to broaden their sexual horizons. Men often used to complain that women were not responsive in bed. Those who acted on the new focus on the clitoris and the new perception that the whole body was a field for sexual play had much less to complain about. Both the fact and the male-generated myth of female frigidity shrank to manageable proportions. In this whole process, the women's movement added dimensions to the sexual revolution. One of the most important was that women could take sexual initiatives.

HOW MEN RESPOND

The combination of sexual liberation and women's liberation has produced responses not only in bed but in politics. The old feelings and the old ideas about sex provide much of the fuel for the right-wing attacks on sex-related issues in the 1980s. Both men and women make these attacks, distorting the effects of pornography, opposing abortion and sex education, trying to limit family planning and contraception, fighting homosexual rights. Consciously or unconsciously, but quite correctly, they see both the sexual revolution and the feminist revolution as enemies of the classic combination of male dominance and female dependence that underlay the old morality and the old family. Women who oppose sex-related changes fear they will lose their emotional and economic security. Many men, probably more men than women, also oppose these changes. They fear they will lose an important part of their power, real and mythical—and will become vulnerable to a female power all the greater for its newly liberated sexual energy.

Those fears also operate in the bedroom. I suspect that most men feel them. But judging by my interviews and by the handful of surveys of male views on sex, most men do not want to fall victim to those fears. They want to be independent, to feel confident of their power, but not to assert that power and diminish women's by returning to the old ways of repression and the double standard.† They want to integrate the two revolutions into their lives, and particularly to join forces with the women who have discovered their own sexuality and actively seek the kind of sex life they want. At best this becomes mutual exchange and accommodation between men and women in the effort to assert the self and at the same time respect the other's independence. That's vastly different from doing things by the old rules, which usually meant by the male book, and fears about male and female power still complicate men's efforts to do things differently.

The idea of mutual exchange is what makes some men like women's new knowledge and openness about their own sexuality. "I think that sexuality is a kind of emotional expressiveness," said Graham Goring,* a California high school teacher. "To share feelings, whether it's conversationally or sexually, is something a lot of us lost growing up and becoming men. A lot of men are learning to do this from the women in their lives."

Sharing feelings about sex requires a degree of trust in the partner, in both the man's and the woman's ability to be open and not to be defensive, that usually takes time to build up. Even men who have trouble expressing feelings or hearing about them say they like communication from women about sexual specifics, especially in positive terms: "Do this," or "I like it when you do that." Several men I interviewed said they wanted their partners to tell them, or show them, if they had reached orgasm (though others were sure they knew without any signals).

Some men, however, dislike what one called "a woman acting like a traffic cop in bed." This reflection of the old tradition of male dominance turned up

---

† Of the surveys I've seen, *Beyond the Male Myth,* by Anthony Pietropinto and Jacqueline Simenauer, had the fewest statistical flaws, but not necessarily the best questions. Still, it was striking that when 4,066 men were asked, "How do you feel about today's women?" only 23.3 percent said, "They are too independent"—but that was still the most frequent answer. Only 11.4 percent said, "They expect too much from men." Over 22 percent said, "They are better company," and 16.9 percent said, "They've become more loving and giving." Over 57 percent of the responses to six questions were positive.[16]

in perhaps one in five of my interviews about sex.† Kenneth McCann,* labor organizer turned therapist, said:

> If your lady turns around in the middle of this wonderful, intuitive sex act and says, "Hey, don't rub it that way, rub it the other way," that causes you to lose spontaneity and maybe your erection. Men don't want to deny her the right to say that kind of thing, but it sure puts them off. It takes a period of learning to allow that. They think a man is supposed to administer this wonderful orgasm to the woman, and all of a sudden in the middle of it she proves that he's not such a good technician, it's like your boss telling you that your work is no good. And these men identify with their work as much as with their pricks.

Women's openness, in other words, can increase the old male anxiety about sexual performance. The fear is often worse when it moves away from a woman's specific traffic directions to her demand for orgasm, and then to broader judgments. A woman who demands performance from her sexual partner is transposing and taking over the very emphasis on achievement that was thought to be a male trait. Blaming the lover for failure to achieve is not exactly the same thing as mutual effort. Four or five of the single men I interviewed and three or four of the married men had had partners who demanded and blamed. They all expressed anger at those women, or felt threatened by them. Some sex therapists think the true proportions are even larger. It's even worse when men encounter women who use openness as an excuse to compare lovers, as men have always done, especially if they do it in a way likely to make the current lover miserable. It doesn't have to be explicit. Bernie Zilbergeld, the California sex therapist, told me, "Men see women as informed consumers, in contrast to the perception of their past ignorance. They can tell the good from the bad, the real from the false. For some men this is very scary, and even if the women say nothing, the fright softens their erections."

That is likeliest to happen where there is little trust between partners and little self-confidence in the man. Where there is more faith, men are learning to communicate their own desires, just as women are. Pietropinto and Simenauer asked the men they surveyed, "Do you tell the woman you have sex with what you'd like her to do?" Almost 48 percent said they don't. That divided into 25.3 percent who said, "No, I do what she seems to enjoy"; 19.6 percent who said, "No, I just do what I enjoy"; and 3 percent who said, "No, I'd be too inhibited or embarrassed." But the significant thing was that the majority of men said they can and do tell their partners what they'd like in bed.[19]

† But Pietropinto and Simenauer found only 5.8 percent of their respondents listing the woman's making demands as the most unpleasant aspect of sex.[17] And Lonnie Barbach and Linda Levine reported that *none* of the women they interviewed received a negative response from her partner once she was able to talk about sex with him.[18]

DEEPER SEXUALITY

Fewer men are able to move from talk about immediate specifics with their own lovers or their psychotherapists to deeper grasp of their own sexuality. Dr. François Alouf, director of the human sexuality program at Northwestern University, told me that more men are interested in their own sexuality now than ten years ago. But only a small minority of men know their own feelings well enough, and are used to expressing them freely enough, to discuss sexuality in the fashion that is routine in feminist writings or women's rap groups. Dr. Alouf's observation agreed with my own: in all my interviews and scores of other conversations with men, only four brought up deep sexual subjects of their own volition, before I asked any questions.

Men almost always link the question of a woman's openness about sex to her sexual assertiveness as well as her readiness to say what she wants or doesn't want. We are concerned with who initiates sex within an established relationship, who makes a sexual advance to a stranger, and who gives directions and how. Some of us like it but many of us have trouble when the woman takes the lead in sex—another reflection of male dominance, of the belief under our skins that we are the aggressors who must take the initiative. Goring said, "One of the most difficult things for me and for men that I've talked to in groups is being able to receive sexually, to be passive, to be loved." Several men I interviewed said they wanted the woman to make the first advance, but then didn't like it when she did. One of these said, "I told my lover I'd like it if she was more aggressive, but when she tried it, I didn't like it. You could say it almost turned me off. I love it when she goes down on me when we're making love, but one night, about two minutes after I got to her place, she stepped back from a hug and looked me in the eye and said, 'I want to suck you off,' with a lot of soul in her smile, and I backed away. I couldn't take it. It really bothered me that I couldn't, but I couldn't."

He was clearly a man who saw taking the sexual initiative as a sign of power in a relationship. This is very much related to the problem that began this chapter—to our not knowing how to say no. We have only recently begun to learn that the ability to say no also carries power. It can be power over oneself, as Henry learned. It can be power over a sexual partner if the one who refuses transforms the initiator into a supplicant. Blumstein and Schwartz note this. They say that among cohabitors, the woman is more likely to refuse sex when she is more powerful and the man when he is more powerful, and I suspect that here as in money matters, cohabitors strongly resemble two-earner couples. But they also make a point that I think is much more important: couples in which both partners initiate and refuse sex with equality have more frequent sex and are happier with their sex lives and their whole relationships than couples that do not achieve this equality. (In their survey, if a couple goes beyond equality to what may be seen as role reversal, with the woman doing much more of the initiating than the man, the partners "become troubled."[20])

I interviewed twenty men who were married or in a serious committed relationship; sixteen said they liked it most of the time when their partners made an advance, but even they had occasional problems. But those who knew we have the right to say no seemed to enjoy it more when a woman took the initiative than did men who still think we must always be ready for sex. Marvin Rutman, the California purchasing director who saw women as the modern practitioners of the work ethic, was one (see Chapter 7). He said:

I had two big problems with women. One was that I didn't know how to say no, the other was that I didn't want to say no to anything. I hadn't become that selective. Those two problems combined got me into a lot of trouble because any woman that made an advance to me, I picked up on it, for the game of it, the fun of it, the flirtation, the ego. Sometimes I ended up in situations I was sorry I created, where I didn't really like the woman, or the sex was all work and no play. Eventually I learned how to say no. I even went through a stage where I would say on the telephone when a woman would call me, "Well, thank you very much, but I'm busy this weekend." Because when I was young, that's what a woman would say to me. But the women didn't know the signals, so they'd call again, just the way I had. [He laughed here.] Sometimes I got intimidated by it, but not very often. I learned to deal with it. I like an aggressive woman, but sometimes it's embarrassing. You're driving a car with a woman you're intimate with, and she'll reach over and be aggressive, and you may not be in the mood. I've found it hard to say I'm not in the mood. That's another learning process for me. Even now I sometimes say, "Not now, babe," but if she persists, I usually get in the mood.

Another of the men I interviewed, Michael Wald,* a New York sociologist, described a relationship that showed a woman's openness and assertiveness and what I took to be a fair equality:

The woman I'm currently involved with certainly tells me unmistakably and often very explicitly when she wants sex, and I'm glad that she does, even if at that moment I'm not horny. She expresses herself very creatively through sex. I think she's very good at it. She likes being active as well as passive. That educated me in some of the pleasures of being passive, so that I could lie back and let her do some of the work. Some of that is subtle and delicate, and some of it is when she gets on top and fucks me. She's the first woman I've known who loves to suck my cock as much as I love to eat her. But this woman gets just as turned on when I'm active as when she is. I'm thinking of the way she likes it when I enter her from behind, there's a real moment of dominance there. She certainly tells me if I'm doing something

she doesn't like, but she's never made me feel stupid in bed. Making love
with her, I find myself using sexual words more than I did with anyone
before. She didn't teach me or persuade me to do that; if anything, I taught
her, but then she was more verbal than anybody else I had ever known, and
I think her openness encouraged me to be expressive. And it's not only
words. I make more noises when we fuck instead of holding them back,
and I think hearing her cries enabled me to do that. It's expressing something too, letting myself out more.

When it's a question of a woman taking a sexual initiative with a man she
doesn't yet know, a few men like it even when it verges on the crude. A
participant in one of Dr. Alouf's sexuality workshops said, "The woman I
ended up marrying was a woman I met at the swimming pool. She came up
and said, 'Looking at you in your bathing suit, you must have the largest pair
of balls, and that made me want to meet you.' I liked that and I married her."

Unlike the man in the pool, however, many men don't like a first advance
from a new female acquaintance. Dr. Alouf said some men dislike it when a
woman says, "I'm attracted to you," because they liked the old game of
outguessing the prey and using what they saw as their capacity to talk a
woman into it. "Some men feel somewhat deprived," he added, "because
nowadays you don't have to talk them into it. It's like the old story of the
Turkish merchant who wouldn't sell to a customer who tried to pay his
asking price, without bargaining. His joy was in the haggling."

I asked twenty-three unattached men hypothetical questions about crude
and subtle advances from a woman they had just met. All but one disliked the
idea of a crude advance—a woman you meet at a party putting her hand on
your belt and saying, "Let's go home and fuck"—but only two had ever had
an experience of that kind. One was Gideon Gordon, the lawyer quoted in
Chapter 9 about divorce. He said:

I love it when a woman indicates quite clearly that she wants me. If she's
attractive to me. If she's not, I'm just turned off. If she's really aggressive
about it, I react the way a woman does to a man who says, "Let's go fuck."
Most women get angry or disgusted. But sometimes you can't tell what will
turn you off. I brought one woman home, a woman from Argentina. I
didn't know who was going to seduce whom, but I thought she was attractive. Until she took her clothes off, got on the bed, stuck her ass in the air,
and said, "I want you to fuck me in the ass." That's not a genuine invitation. That's hostility. I got my driver's license out to prove to her I was too
old for that kind of thing.

Only four of the twenty-three men disliked the idea of a subtle advance—a
new female acquaintance putting her hand on your arm and saying, "I really
like you." Fourteen, however, said they would have trouble if a woman they

already knew took an initiative to turn a friendship into a sexual relationship before they at least signaled readiness, and nine had had that experience.

One change that can be considered a particular form of female sexual initiative, and one that some men find startling when they first encounter it, is the growth of infidelity among women. Kinsey found that about half of all men and a quarter of all women had had extramarital experiences. Today, a *Playboy* survey showed, 48 percent of men and 38 percent of women have been unfaithful at least once.[21] Under the age of thirty, unfaithful women outnumbered men, 33 percent to 25. A *Cosmopolitan* survey put the proportion of women who had had at least one extramarital experience at 54 percent.[22]

This is more of a break with the old double standard than a break with the ideal of sexual fidelity, which indeed may be making a comeback in the 1980s. Women as well as men turn to infidelity because their marriages are bad, whether for neurotic reasons or because they didn't know how to choose a spouse. Women as well as men turn to lovers outside marriage because their spouses leave them sexually deprived or frustrated. Or out of emotional or sexual boredom, which is not the same thing as long-term deprivation. Or in a quest for self-fulfillment that they think demands either simple sexual variety or some kind of sexual experience, presumably joyous, that they don't find at home. But women more than men turn to lovers who can communicate, who can give them a sense of intimacy they don't get with their "inexpressive" spouses.[23]

Some men think women's new readiness to be unfaithful is only fair play or equal rights. Some are happy to exploit it. Others, I suspect a large minority of all men and a majority of married men, welcome the premarital break with the double standard but find it hard to live with the extramarital break. It brings home the truth, in a particularly painful way, that they do not own their wives. Some men learn the hurt their own infidelity causes this way. Some find confirmation of their fears of their own inadequacy, economic, emotional, or sexual. Others, surer of their strengths, turn the feeling of betrayal into new insights into the challenge of being self-reliant. That can lead to false domination, the denial of dependence. Or it can lead, either in the marriage where the infidelity took place or in the next one, to the effort I keep mentioning, the effort to assert the self and at the same time respect the other's independence—which sometimes means acknowledging mutual dependence.

SEX AND WORK

The rise in female infidelity, like most of the recent sexual shifts, is often connected to women's joining the labor force in increasing numbers. Traditional men, particularly blue-collar men, often feared that their wives would be seduced or compelled to be unfaithful by the men they met at work, and made that an additional reason to try to keep them home. That fear grows out of the old view of women as passive on the one hand and sexually charged but inferior on the other. Women who would sneer at that view recognize, however, that a woman who goes to work outside the home does meet more men than she ever did as a housewife, which creates opportunity. She can risk divorce more easily because she is more able to support herself (especially if she is middle-class and has found a job with reasonable pay), which removes a barrier. Most important, she finds out things about herself that she may not have known before, which may create the desire for a new connection.[24]

Not all the connections between work and sex mean more or better sex, however. Working women and their men, single or living together or in dual-career marriages, colleagues or working for different companies or in different fields, may find any or all of the problems mentioned in Chapter 9 turning up in bed. The simplest problem is finding time to make love when both partners work long hours, especially if there are children who also demand time. Even if there is time, one partner may run out of energy, or be troubled in bed by problems at work. It used to be the sixty-hour-a-week male executive more often than his wife or lover. Today it's just as often the woman who works so hard or so late that she can't manage dinner and a show and a bout in bed in one evening and still get up for work the next day. Men in every kind of work agree with the lawyer whose wife was a banker, who said, "When my wife's work goes badly, she turns off on sex." Mick Stanley, the supportive husband of the woman foreman in Chapter 5, thought that overall their sex life had improved as her career developed. But in her last year as foreman, "she was very unhappy with the way the factory was handling her and women in general. I heard this many times. And our sex life took a turn for the worse."

Competition between men and women, always likelier and often sharper when the woman has a professional life of her own, can also take place in bed. Lovers or spouses may compete to see who can have the most orgasms or produce the most orgasms in the other, and the devil take the new statistics on women's propensity to have more orgasms than men. They may compete to see who can discover the most new positions, have the most partners outside of the marriage. None of these is terribly good for love, according to the sex counselors.

The juncture of work and sex is a place where even without competition it is very easy to bring out the conflicts between a woman's claim to equality or her professional status and both reality and myth of male sexual dominance. The most obvious example is a fact cited in Chapter 9: married couples in which the wives make more money than their husbands have sexual intercourse less often than other couples. Several of the men I interviewed mentioned the Faye Dunaway character in the 1976 movie *Network*, who took the sexual initiative with vulnerable, middle-aged but sexy William Holden, insisted on being literally on top in bed, and had orgasms only while talking about how she was winning at the office. She was a caricature of the problem who evoked real fears; none of the men had actually met a woman like her but all were sure she existed. The problem can also work in the opposite way. A woman who likes being submissive in bed may have to fight all the harder for equal status with the same man in housework and social life, or for his recognition of her professional standing.

Sometimes men confuse their perceptions of a woman's attitude toward her work with their expectations about her attitude about sex. A journalist told me how she had talked and flirted with a man for several weeks before they finally fell into bed. After that he didn't call her. Eventually she called him and said, "I thought our relationship had changed." He replied, "Wait a minute. I thought you were sure of yourself. You're high powered, you have an important job, you make as much money as I do. I thought you'd be as casual about sex as I am." She added wryly, "He wasn't the greatest lover I've ever had, either."

Arnie Hyder* had a different set of expectations. He and his wife, Lisa, are both truck drivers. She was a pioneer in a traditionally masculine occupation both as driver and as union activist. He showed both support of and association with her invasion of a male workplace. He obviously loved her and worked hard at treating her as an equal. But he wanted her to be liberated and equal in the bedroom as well as in the truck cab. Arnie said:

As liberated as Lisa is as a woman, she's so goddamn puritanical when it comes to sex, it's a paradox. It's not just that she doesn't want me to play around. Most of the time she expects me to make the first move. When we go to bed and try to make love, I want some more active participation outa her and yet I can't get it. It's sort of a passive thing with her. Like I told you the other night, I would love for a damn woman to attack me. Not all the goddamn time, but every now and then. They expect us to come over there and kiss them and love them and this and that and put the make on them. I'd like to be aroused myself, and I guess that's part of equal rights. But Lisa always expects that I'll start it.

Here I am feeling she should make the advance, but being male, you get to the point where you can no longer hold out. Then you make that advance and you hate yourself for it. I did. Because I thought I should have held on. I guess it's searching for some kind of approval or proof that she really cares. Then I made up my mind that, goddamnit, I am not going to do it. A while ago, for something like a month and a half I did nothing, and then she'd say she was wondering what the hell is wrong with me.

Hyder wanted Lisa to show her sexual liberation not only by making the sexual advance now and then, but also by learning to like some sexual specifics that were still foreign to her.

One of Lisa's big hang-ups is oral sex. She won't reciprocate. I just feel like I am entitled to some gratification also. In the thirteen years we've been married she's probably done it three or four times at the most, and I had to have a rubber on. I don't know why anyone would want to suck a mouthful of rubber, but she says it don't taste as bad as a peter does. Lisa was very naïve sexually to begin with. It took about three or four years for her to be able to have an orgasm when I went down on her. She has come a long way but I don't think she'll go any further than that. I guess she tends to enjoy the lovemaking so much that she completely forgets about me. I feel that I can't be expected to perform without any foreplay by her.

SOME SEXUAL SPECIFICS

Hyder was a man voicing what is usually presented as a woman's complaint —the partner who forgets about her sexual satisfaction and thinks she can be ready for intercourse without foreplay. The number of women who forget about their partner's needs has probably shrunk since the women's movement and the sexual revolution converged, yet a man's ability to make the complaint when he finds such a woman has probably increased.

Oral sex has certainly become much more common since the 1940s. According to one comparison of two slightly different age groups, Kinsey found that 33 percent of young Americans had experienced fellatio a generation ago, and Morton Hunt reported a figure of 72 percent in the 1970s. Comparable figures for cunnilingus were 14 and 69 percent, respectively.[25]

There's no statistical evidence that women have demanded or refused either one more than men have, but the anecdotal evidence sometimes contradicts the folklore. Men used to talk about cunnilingus as something both exciting and shameful, that women demanded more than men wanted to do it. And men used to assume that most women would be like Lisa Hyder, reluctant to try fellatio. Many women report that men who offer cunnilingus do so in a way that makes them feel the men don't really enjoy it, but are only doing it as a quid pro quo or because they think the women expect it. In truth, many women don't. François Alouf says that when oral sex is discussed in the Northwestern workshops, "What comes up is not so much to do it or not to do it, it's almost a given that everybody does it. It's simply a kind of imbalance in the situation. Women are much more willing to go down on men but are uncomfortable with men going down on them." This usually reflects women's traditional shame about their own genitals, the feeling that the vulva is neither clean nor beautiful; today several observers find this feeling more prevalent among working-class than middle-class women. Feminists often blame men for this emotion (assuming that men created the myth of Medusa, the sight of whose grotesque face, surmounted by snaky hair, turned men to stone), but it's possible that in many sectors in this era women feel it more than men.* Alouf says that it seems to be diminishing over time, with fewer women expressing the feeling in recent workshops than in earlier ones. The change probably reflects the teachings of those feminists who want women to be able to express their lusts, which starts with liking one's body.

Men have sometimes treated fellatio as a metaphor for male dominance, and some women have responded negatively. For other women or at other moments it has become an expression of lust, of love for a particular man, and sometimes of female assertiveness. (The ancient Romans had different words for a sexual act with the mouth as passive recipient and one with the mouth as active sexual aggressor.) The question of whether or not to swallow the semen is not only one of taste; men usually hope the woman will swallow, experiencing refusal as a rejection and sometimes making it a matter of dominance.

Women who have explored their own sexuality have often discovered joys in caressing themselves and in using vibrators even when they're with a lover. Several sex therapists say that many men dislike seeing a woman caress herself; it's a minority who turn on more at the sight of her hand on her crotch and want to get in on the act, and an even smaller minority that feels that way about a vibrator. The woman who caresses herself is taking responsibility for her own excitement, and that disturbs a man. It makes him feel inadequate, or that she is telling him he can't understand what she wants. He has to get past that before he can see that he can learn something about where and how to touch her by looking at the way she caresses herself.

For many men, the woman who takes care of her own needs that way is another version of the traffic cop in bed. She's telling him what to do when he thinks he knows what to do. Men who have trouble taking direction offer an infinity of traffic cop examples, sometimes within a very small range. The most common may be a woman's request that a man not put his fingers in her vagina, or that he soften the pressure of his fingers anywhere in her vulva. Men find it hard to believe that a woman who masturbates or who likes clitoral stimulation can really be so hostile to fingers with good intentions. Michael Wald recalled a problem in his marriage, which ended before he met the woman he talked about earlier:

My wife would ask me to take my fingers away from the entrance to her vagina, or soften my pressure. I wanted to do what she wanted, and I frequently didn't use my fingers. But I had to admit later that I often did use them because I thought she had once liked it and I knew other women liked it. Years later she told me she had never liked it in the early days but had been afraid to tell me for a long time. This all came out when we got to

* Blumstein and Schwartz contradict Alouf: their survey reveals that women do not perform oral sex on men as often as men perform it on them. They report that men who receive and perform oral sex are happier with their sex lives and their overall relationships than men who do not. They also note that more liberated women and career women are more likely to enjoy receiving oral sex, which I think confirms the idea that feminist discussion has made a difference.[26]

talking about the way some men don't like it when women assert themselves in sex. She accused me of being that way myself, and I got mad because I thought I did like it when a woman said what she wanted. But she felt I was rejecting her directions when she finally developed enough courage to tell me she didn't like what I did with my fingers. I thought I was trying to do it her way, but she thought I was ignoring her. When she told me, we were certainly communicating in words. But I didn't perceive that I wasn't paying enough attention, and I think she didn't perceive that I was trying. There was some failure in emotional communication, I guess. And we never got clinically precise enough to help because that wasn't our taste. I guess we thought we shouldn't need to be clinical if we loved each other. By the time she said I was one of the men who didn't like sexually aggressive women, she had come to like my fingers in her cunt, still without any clinical talk. She said I was doing it differently, and I didn't even know how I had changed, but by then we were on the verge of divorce for lots of reasons besides sex.

Sometimes men don't resent a woman's sexual request, they merely feel surprised. Garrison Bell,* brought up to believe he had to last long enough to make a woman reach orgasm during intercourse and later educated to a high regard for the clitoris, found it very hard to believe when his partner told him she was indifferent to penetration and put a low priority on clitoral stimulation, manual or oral. What she liked was pressure on her pubic area, from his hand or the weight of his own pubis. She also taught him a lesson later repeated by other women, that a woman may want the same pressure in the same rhythm over a long time, rather than the frequent changes of pace that some men think make for a refined technique. Bell was grateful for both lessons and regarded them as part of his continuing education in feminist sexuality. But in 1979, two years after that encounter, he said, "She didn't capture my erotic imagination the way women did who liked both good old-fashioned fucking and oral sex."

His reaction made a point that in one sense is so obvious it belongs in a "Dear Abby" column but is still often overlooked by both men and women when they discuss sex as a field of power. Bell's voice showed genuine feeling, a mixture of anger and slow revelation, when he followed up his story by saying:

Women are refusing to do things they dislike in bed just because a man asks them to or tells them to. Fine, I accept that. But I've met more than one woman who always wants something a man dislikes or never wants to do something the man likes. She's not just saying something about equal rights or sexual freedom. She's also saying something about their compatibility as human beings. Women took orders for far too long, but I think they need to learn just as much as men do that in sex, if it's going to be anything more than the crudest kind of getting your rocks off, people have to find things to do that they both like.

Or as psychotherapists and sex counselors say, a relationship has to be mutually fulfilling. It may be a question of truly equal rights for both the man and the woman, or it may be a very different question: are they the right people for each other, sexually (or emotionally or intellectually).

For the men I interviewed, questions about women's quest for equality and power in bed usually translated into talk about women's and men's desires for sexual acts other than classical intercourse. This made me feel almost surprised when I found Blumstein and Schwartz reporting that intercourse was more essential for women than for men in their survey. They also found that the less power a woman has in a relationship, the more likely it is that the couple's intercourse will be performed in the missionary position.[27] Presumably, the less power the woman has, the more traditional the man, and the less likely he is to want to try exotic positions in making love.

MISPERCEPTIONS AND MYTHS

Men today face not only the challenges posed by women's discovery of their own sexuality, but also the classical sexual problems and sexual situations that we have confronted for years, or for millennia. It's very easy for us to confuse the former with the latter, and to blame women's new openness and assertiveness for old familiar troubles. These changes may be responsible for some of the problems, may be involved with some only in very different ways from the ones we perceive, and may have nothing at all to do with others. It's important to look at some misperceptions and some myths.

One set of confusions surrounds sexually transmitted diseases like herpes. *Time* blamed the sexual revolution for the current epidemic of herpes (since displaced from the headlines by acquired immune deficiency syndrome or AIDS, but still epidemic), and there can be no doubt that an increase in sexual intercourse outside of monogamous relationships increases the opportunity for STDs to spread. Some men, including two whom I interviewed, tend to blame the sexual liberation of women for the herpes phenomenon. (Burroughs Wellcome, the drug company that makes the first oral medicine that relieves herpes outbreaks, reinforces the idea in its ads in medical magazines for Zovirax. They feature a naked woman breaking out of a transparent sphere that has broken out in cylindrical excrescences.) Middle-class men used to associate syphilis and gonorrhea with lower-class women and prostitutes, rightly or wrongly; herpes from the start was the "nice girl's venereal disease." Or the nice guy's, but the men looking for someone to blame seldom see it that way. If the nice girl hadn't learned to express her lust, these men seem to think, there would be less herpes.

There's also the question of what you do if you get herpes. People with the disease have learned that there is still sex after herpes, but those who have thought the matter through are careful not to make love while they are having an active episode. This leads rapidly to the question of whether you tell a new partner that you have it. If you don't, you have to tell some fancy lies about why you can't make love for a week or two, and you raise doubts about your respect for your partner. Therapists who specialize in the problem usually urge patients with herpes to tell fairly early in the game.

Joel Cort* had the disease for four years and gave it to two women before he realized either the need to be scrupulously careful or the moral imperative of telling a lover or prospective lover that he had it. He said:

> After one woman got angry with me, I began to feel I had to tell. She said my failure to reveal to her that I had it was typical male defensiveness, a man refusing to be vulnerable. I began to see it as a feminist commandment, one that I agreed with. Telling was one aspect of being open about sex that I associated with women. I think the general idea that someone with herpes should tell a new lover owes something to the women's movement. So I was surprised when I joined a consciousness-raising group of men and women with herpes and discovered that there were women who didn't tell. There was one who made a point of not telling if she knew she was not active and thought it was going to be only a one-night stand. I liked her, I even went to bed with her, but I told her she ought to tell anyone she went to bed with.

Other women didn't tell, Cort added, because they were ashamed of the disease or the stigma, or because they could not imagine themselves departing from monogamy or celibacy—human reasons beneath or beyond the changes of the past fifteen years. But he recognized that he was disturbed to find a woman who was sexually venturesome and remained silent about herpes in order to complete a sexual score, "just like a man."

A man reaches another junction of an old problem and new attitudes about sex if he can't ejaculate, or has a hard time reaching ejaculation. Some causes of nonejaculation are physical, but some are emotional patterns. In one, a man reacts as a sexual adult to a mother who was seductive, overprotective, or cruelly dominant. In another, a man chooses a partner "who is or becomes an arsenal of grievances all aimed at him. She may direct the artillery of her woes—her difficulties with sex, self-assertion, identity, monogamy—upon him so continually that his angry and helpless response may take many forms, including orgasmic failure."[28] It's easy to see how a man in this position may feel that he is reacting to what he considers feminist demands. He may feel the same way if he is suppressing anger at a lover, another common cause of nonejaculation. Presumably he won't put it in terms of a feminist context if he is simply going to extremes in an effort not to make his partner pregnant, or if he is preoccupied with work or family life so that he can't give undivided attention to making love. But he might if he is dealing with other emotions like fear of disappointing the woman or fear of abandonment.[29]

One physical process that can cause problems with ejaculation is simple and inevitable: aging. This underlies many male fears and resentments of women's sexual demands. Many of the women who make such demands are in their thirties or forties, often coupled with older men who are making their first discoveries of the effects that aging can have on their sex lives. In their late forties, most men find it takes them longer to become erect, and longer to become ready for a second time. Later, they may find they don't ejaculate as readily or as often. Even when a woman is not demanding, these events are very likely to affect a man's self-confidence and to coincide with other anxieties, at work, for instance, that also erode his self-assurance. Anxiety usually causes a drop in his testosterone level, making the problem worse. A man may drink more or quarrel with his partner to hide his sexual doubts or choose younger, supposedly less experienced lovers who he assumes will judge him less harshly. Any or all of these "remedies" are likely to make matters worse again.

The answer is obviously for both partners to be loving and mutually supportive, and for both to give up some of their sexual stereotypes. For men, this has to be part of discovering their own evolving sexuality as so many women have done. Six of the men I interviewed about sex were over fifty, and four of them found that hard to do. They couldn't abandon their belief in the importance of the instant-rigid penis and the total orgasm. They had been told that a man can still bring a woman to orgasm with his mouth, his fingers, and his penis, even if his erections are no longer those of a boy of eighteen. They had been told a woman can give her lover vast pleasure with her mouth and fingers and her genitals even if he doesn't come—and she hasn't failed if he doesn't ejaculate. But they hadn't been able to bring that information to life in their own lives, and they were not happy in their sexual relationships. Garrison Bell was one of the two who were happy. He was fifty-three when I interviewed him again in 1983, and he had begun to have the experience of aging sexually. He said:

I'm still having trouble learning to get away from the old classic ideas like making a woman come by fucking her good and hard and long. The woman I'm with now is ten years younger than I am, and she still has trouble getting over the idea that there's something wrong with her if I don't come, or if I don't get erect in the first three minutes, or if I want to use a little body oil on my cock. But because we love each other and because we like to use everything we've got, we get more out of our sex life than I did with most of the lovers I had when I was younger and supposedly better. What did you tell me Masters and Johnson said? [They called intercourse once or twice a week regularly for many years the best defense against sexual aging.[30]] I'm for that.

One of the great myths about the consequences of women's new sexual demands is that they are producing a vast new wave of male impotence. I call this a myth for two reasons. One is that there are no statistics on impotence in earlier times that would provide a basis for saying there is more now. The other is that the U.S. Patent Office granted ninety-six patents for inventions touching the genitals from 1887 to 1975. The vast majority through the 1950s were intended to create or maintain erections—prima facie evidence that impotence was a serious problem in this country a century before women became sexually assertive.

François Alouf and Bernie Zilbergeld share my skepticism. Alouf sees plenty of impotence, but said: "It's very hard for me to say, 'Yes, you can clearly relate it to the fact that women are more aggressive and more demanding, therefore the man is losing his potency.' I've seen this happen under certain conditions, yes. I've also seen the opposite happen, where the woman's openness, open sexuality, has been extremely encouraging for the male. And there are so many other external circumstances now affecting sexual behavior. There are so many people on drugs, which was not true in the old days. Lots of people drink, lots of people taking medication that they don't even know about, that did not exist years back. These have a tremendous effect on man's sexual capacity. But they have nothing to do with women's new sexual assertiveness."

One thing that is new is that more men are willing to talk about their impotence. Zilbergeld told me, "There are no good statistics from the past, and as far as I'm concerned, there are no good statistics from the present. But now there's a combination of pressure and opportunity to do something. We've all been persuaded that sex is a highly important part of life. So there are more cases looking for help. That doesn't mean there are more cases."

Some doctors estimate that ten million American men, about one out of eleven, suffer from chronic impotence. Impotents Anonymous groups, patterned on Alcoholics Anonymous, have been formed, though they tend to concentrate on the 50 percent of chronic cases that have physical or medical rather than psychological causes.[31]

And despite the skeptics, many therapists insist that there is a new impotence—if not a statistical increase, at least new sources of impotence. Avodah Offitt offers the most convincing analysis I have seen. Some of her male patients have become impotent in the face of female aggressiveness. So have men who were merely changing partners, but whose new partners pose challenges of age, income, or sexual desires departing from the men's familiar routines. Men who are themselves heavily aggressive, who must both fight and win all the time, are prime targets for impotence. So are men who are compulsive controllers. (The two types are created often by the sex-role stereotypes of our culture.) Anything that threatens their total dominance may cause impotence. The threat can take surprising forms. It may be understanding and tenderness undermining the aggressive man, or sweet disorder and spontaneity confusing the compulsive one.[32] This was true long before women developed new approaches to sexuality, but it may be true much more often as women learn the joys of being active and being free.

Another myth about the effects of the new female sexuality on men is that it has increased the incidence of homosexuality. This is vastly harder to prove than the claim that there are increases in impotence. Many gay men, and a disproportionately large number of gay activists, say the honesty and bravery of the women's movement helped them gain the courage to come out of the closet. The militancy of the women's movement inspired the gay rights movement, and women's openness about sex encouraged gay men to be open about their sex lives, first in the gay world and in the long run in media that also reached straight audiences. (It was not the women's movement but the sexual revolution among straight people, whose peak coincided with the birth of the gay rights movement, that encouraged gay men to be open about the promiscuity that had always characterized a large segment of the homosexual community.) But only one of all the men I interviewed said he had been straight and had turned to other men in anger at what he felt was mistreatment by a woman, mirroring the motives of some lesbians.

A few men, turned on by their support of feminism and their experience of male consciousness-raising, have tried same-sex lovemaking for political reasons, as many women have done. Zeb Barna,* a veteran of many of the revolutions of the sixties, went through this process. He sought intimacy with some men by having sex before he got to know them—a mistake men make constantly with women. He also developed real intimacy with some to the point of lying in bed with them, hugging, cuddling, and sleeping together. With one or two, he added genital sex. He discovered "that for me to get turned on to another man's genitals takes a great deal of effort. There was a period when I felt I had to learn to enjoy sucking somebody's cock. If I didn't, I wasn't fully liberated. Now, I've gotten to the place where I know my gut feeling. I enjoy sucking pussy and I don't enjoy sucking cock." In other words, he had learned how to say no.

Myths like these and all the senses in which men miss "the way things used to be" produce anger and confusion, the only sexual results some men are willing to attribute to feminism. I believe that this confusion has large elements of fear, anxiety, envy, and shame. Both anger and confusion would probably evaporate if more men, like Mike Wald and Garrison Bell, explored their own sexuality as thoroughly as women have begun to do. They might, like Wald and Bell, discover feelings of relief and admiration and identification with women in bed—and pleasure beyond the usual meaning of sexual pleasure.

We might dispel anger and confusion most of all if we learned how to say no—and how to do a better job of saying yes at the right moments. We would then come back to what the women's movement is all about and what men can learn from it, what some men have already learned from it: the right of every human being to independence and to choice, the right to decide for one's self when to say no and when to say yes. Only then would we make deep and genuine a further change that students of sex and society think men and women have begun to want, a return to fundamental values of love, trust, intimacy, and commitment.

Part Four

THE MEN'S MOVEMENT

Chapter 12
THE MOVEMENT

The women's movement has touched the lives of millions—by its impact on public opinion and social policy, but even more by its spur to women's quests for equality and choice in the workplace and in the family, quests that pose a myriad of challenges to men.

The men's movement has touched the lives of only a few thousands.[1] The men's movement? Most Americans don't know there is a men's movement. Yet there are men who want, like women, to change the boundaries of their lives and reshape sex roles, so men can spend fewer hours at work and more time caring for their wives, their children, and themselves, for instance. Some men, like women, claim rights they feel they are denied—like equity for divorced fathers in custody cases. A few men feel deep concerns about injustice and the inequality of power between the sexes. As both a participant in the drama of change and an observer fascinated by its theater, I believe that the small groups these men have formed are important. They constitute the clearest response to the women's movement on its own terms. They are now combining into national organizations, and they may even begin to affect public policy in the 1980s.

Unfortunately, men usually do this without facing the tough issues in the relations between men and women in our society. It's easy to see why the women's movement is large and the men's movement small. Women respond to their movement because they know firsthand the injustices it wants to erase. They feel a passion to change a system that denies them true equality with men in access to power, economic opportunity, family life, personal autonomy. If the men's movement were fueled by (or merely pretended to) the same kind of outrage, even fewer men would join it. Most of us are the beneficiaries of existing political, social, and economic systems—in fact or in our own mythology. We are privileged compared to women, whom we often treat as an underclass. We see them as central to our lives only at home and in bed.

That is probably why the men's movement is *not* driven by a passion to change the system. It started in the early 1970s with consciousness-raising groups for men trying to respond to the changes women, particularly their wives or lovers, were going through. At first many of those men said they wanted to give up "illegitimate power over women," as one C-R veteran put it, but the meetings soon became "get-togethers to talk about the things that matter in men's lives"—which in men's eyes often had little to do with either women or power. Many shifted their focus to sex roles (as though sex roles were not affected by power), particularly the damage that the traditional male sex role does to men by making their emotions a field of drought.[2] Today, while many men in the movement lament the oppression of women or of men or of both, according to taste, few act like revolutionaries who want to shift the huge forces underlying the social order. That might sometimes mean joining women and sometimes fighting them, perish the thought either way. Instead, after a decade of local, regional, and national meetings, most of the men in the movement worry about three things, singly or in combination: relationships with other men, the male sex role, and "the way women keep changing the rules of the game." (The men who want to change the divorce and custody system may be partial exceptions.) The vast majority of men prefer to deal with these things at home if they deal with them at all, and the movement remains small.

All this makes it tempting to say that speaking of a men's movement is false advertising, since a movement is a group of people organizing around a common passion for change.[3] The conscious desire to solve political or social problems often conceals other motives for joining a movement, however. One is the need for emotional support, for the company of people who share the same opinions. Another is the need for new roles and for status. A movement may offer any or all of these things to people who do not find them easily in more orthodox groups. The men's movement does offer them.[4] At a men's meeting, for instance, men often find themselves undergoing the same experience as the women who discovered sisterhood ten or fifteen years ago. That is, they too discover that there are a lot of people out there whom they didn't know, who have the same grievances they do and the same need to share them.

That similarity between the women's and men's movements cannot obscure the differences. The second reason they differ may help explain the first. The women's movement began in the era of movements, the 1960s of the civil rights movement, the antiwar movement, the new left movement. Indeed many leading feminists rebelled not only against the system but also against the male dominance of those other movements that called for liberation from the system. The men's movement, in contrast, began in the 1970s, when the era of passionate intensity was already giving way to a period of conservatism, malaise, and narcissism, the "Me Decade." Men had no moment of revelation comparable to what some women found in Betty Friedan's *The Feminine Mystique* and others in Kate Millett's *Sexual Politics.* We had no accumulation of brilliance, energy, intellect, and emotion like the feminists'. We had just a trickle of books and meetings. Some groups triggered changes

in the lives of a few participants, but none excited people to collective action
that affected the whole society, as many women's gatherings did.

Despite this low voltage, the men's movement had enough energy to form
three different currents. The first was pro-feminist—the one I've mentioned
that began about 1970 with consciousness-raising groups and soon shifted
most of its attention from men's power and privilege vis-à-vis women to sex
roles and other problems. This shift was emphasized even more when a few of
the men from C-R groups came together in regional and national meetings,
though they continued to support women's movement demands. The second
and third currents, which started a few years later, also fed on the obsession
with sex roles. I call one the no-guilt stream because it insists that men have
nothing to feel guilty about in their relations with women. It emphasizes
men's angers and fears and the feeling that men as well as women are victims
—of sex roles and of feminist-inspired social changes. The third stream concentrates on divorce and child custody. This is one of the few areas where
women sometimes have real advantages over men (though the men in this
part of the movement tend either to ignore statistics that show how few men
actually pay alimony and child support or to oppose legislation to enforce
payment). It is also one of the rare areas in which men feel intense emotion
about a matter of public policy, the combination necessary for a movement
that meets the full definition of the word. The no-guilt stream and the divorce
reformers came together in a national organization in 1981 that is already
quarreling with itself. The pro-feminists launched their national organization
in 1983. Men in both organizations tend to say theirs is *the* movement and to
deny that it might be a faction or fraction of a larger movement.

THE PRO-FEMINISTS

Nobody can say with certainty when the first men's C-R group met, so the
start of the men's movement is usually pegged to two events in 1970: the first
men's center opened in Berkeley, California, and *Liberation* magazine published Jack Sawyer's article, "On Male Liberation." Sawyer was, and is, pro-
feminist. He said, "That one-half of the human race should be dominant and
the other half submissive is incompatible with a nation of freedom," and he
talked about the burdens of dominance—specifically men's dominance over
women in social relations and over other men at work. That kind of language,
spoken when the spirit of the sixties still lived, seemed revolutionary to many
of the men who read it, and even now they like to think of the men's movement as revolutionary. But Sawyer made plain in the article that he saw male
dominance primarily as a product of sex-role stereotypes and the purpose of
male liberation primarily as a help in destroying those stereotypes.[3] To me, if
it doesn't deal with power, it can't make a revolution.

Gene Marine published the first book that achieved a mass audience, *A*

Male Guide to Women's Liberation, in 1972. It gave many men their first exposure to a man who had positive things to say about the women's movement, but its strength was that it quoted the main feminist thinkers so that men could not only understand their ideas but also feel their anger, their pain, and their hopes.[6] In 1974—a year when one kind of unliberated male, Gerald Ford, replaced another, Richard Nixon, in the White House—three books appeared that became basic reading for the pro-feminists: *The Liberated Man* by Warren Farrell, *The Male Machine* by Marc Feigen Fasteau, and *Men and Masculinity,* an anthology edited by Joseph Pleck and Jack Sawyer. All three were important because they told men that we could change the way we did things if we really wanted to, and because they offered some ideas on how to make those changes. But all three seemed to me to fail in important ways when they were published, and they still seemed that way when I reread them years later.

None of the three books, for instance, looked closely at the "impossible contradiction on which our social order rests": that men and women are class enemies, but enemies who make love as well as war with each other.[7] None of the 1974 authors, almost all white, middle-class males, examined the way this contradiction relates to other kinds of class conflict. None dwelt on the oppression of women as their critics in other streams of the men's movement later accused them of doing. Indeed, all three books began to develop the ideas later championed by some of those critics—that "masculine values" and traditional sex roles damage men as well as women. All three deplored the requirement of the masculine mystique in America that a man conceal his emotions, and in all three the authors (except for a few of the writers in *Men and Masculinity)* concealed the struggle they presumably went through to reach liberation. All three touched on political issues, like the way presidential habits of thinking in sexual metaphors affected the Vietnam war; on economic questions, like the male domination of the world of work; on psychosocial problems, like the way boys are brought up or the chauvinist piggishness of male sports. But all virtually ignored the way these forces help shape the dynamics and the institutions of economic and political power. All ignored the possibility of collective action to remake public policy. Instead, they called for consciousness-raising as the generator of behavioral change. So had many feminists, of course, but the women then asked how to move from individual to institutional or societal behavior. The men did not.[8]

Some of the things these pioneers omitted were provided later by writers on the left of the pro-feminist wing. Jon Snodgrass, for example, edited *For Men Against Sexism,* an anthology published in 1977, whose authors provided things so notably absent from the first books: intimate revelations of their own lives, examination of their own sexuality, and accounts of working-class and racial minority experience. Other writers produced books expressing sharper political or philosophical views of "men's issues" than the pioneers, or developed related concepts in social psychology.[9]

The ideas in these books imbued the pro-feminist side of the men's movement as it grew from consciousness-raising groups and local men's centers to regional and national meetings. The first National Conference on Men and Masculinity was held in Knoxville, Tennessee, in 1975. It has become almost an annual event; the tenth met in St. Louis in 1985, and starting with the eighth, in Ann Arbor, Michigan, in 1983, the conferences have been held jointly with meetings of the new National Organization for Changing Men (NOCM).[10]

Every Men and Masculinity (M&M) conference has combined the personal and the political—the concern for personal growth, new experience with other men, and emotional support on the one hand, and the concern for forming a national men's organization and for seeking changes in the system on the other. In one perspective, each national conference has been more political than the previous one—the perspective that includes the theme chosen by the organizers; the workshops; the plenary sessions and resolutions and since 1983 the task-force efforts of NOCM, and the conversations and interactions outside the "formal" meetings. But every conference spends most of its energies on workshops (there were 104 scheduled at the tenth meeting, for example), where political subjects have always been outnumbered by sex roles, gay issues, and personal-growth topics.*[11] Every conference has also included sessions on fathering, sexuality, and rape and violence against women. Several have had workshops on education and, in recent years, on "men's studies" as an academic discipline. Most have included sessions on massage, awareness of the body, theater, and music or poetry.

Some of these workshops were attempts to get men to reveal or acknowledge feelings they would ordinarily conceal or hide from. I remember one on emotions about wives, where a man complained that he had been cuckolded by his wife's feminism. A year later, over a beer at another M&M conference, he said he had changed his diagnosis: he had been cuckolded by her sexism. He said he had worked to support them both while she completed her nursing studies, but she didn't want to support him through three years of unemployment while he tried to work out a new philosophy of life. When he complained about her feminism, he thought he heard her say she wouldn't slave for a man; when he complained about her sexism, he felt she was trying to lock him into the male provider role. Another workshop, on fathering, pro-

---

* Examples of sex-role workshops: "The 'Strengths' of the Traditional Male Role"; "The Legacy of Spock"—referring to the unemotional scientist hero of "Star Trek," not the sage of child care; "Growing Up Male," a slide show by Perry Kaufman. Political subjects might be as subtle as "The Intimacy of Equality: sexuality and sexual politics in loving relationships between nonsexist women and men," or as plain as "Male Privilege: what it is and how to give it up." The gay category might include "Gay Men—About Sex," for gay men only, and "Differing Perspectives and Common Areas: for gay, bisexual, and straight men." In personal growth, two of my favorites were "Toward a Radical Faggot Identity" and "Toward a Positive Heterosexual Identity," both held in Boston in 1981.

duced two revelations that were memorable to the men who uttered and the men who heard them. One man had been shocked to find himself getting an erection when his five-year-old daughter sat on his lap; other men then confessed to similar discoveries, and eventually agreed that the ability to look at it consciously and to talk about it, to friends or to therapists, would keep them out of the incest quicksands (see Chapter 10). Another, a single father, spoke of his feeling an emotion that Jane Lazarre called "mother-hate," that companion to mother love, when he found that he *had* to do, and to limit his world by doing, the "shitwork" that he had previously seen as something only women got mired in.[12]

Other workshops followed the seminar model, for better or worse. In one on male privilege, we tried to distinguish privilege from power and oppression (privilege is a condition, the others are dynamic processes); to decide whether it could be earned (most said no, a few said yes); to produce ideas for reducing it (behave on the street so a woman alone will not feel a threat of rape; try consciously to avoid dominating meetings that include women). In one on rape, several men insisted in breast-beating tones that they sometimes called women "chicks" or "broads" and that this was only a step, or maybe two steps, away from rape. I grew sharp in my insistence that the line between an offensive word and a vicious act is one of the boundaries of civilization.

In addition to the workshops, every M&M conference has held plenary sessions; from the fourth through the eighth, every one passed resolutions, and in 1984 questions of principles and program shifted from the conference as a whole to the NOCM meetings. Among the pre-NOCM resolutions were votes against sexism and in favor of the Equal Rights Amendment, free choice for women on abortion, and the twenty-six resolutions adopted by the National Women's Conference for International Women's Year in Houston in 1977. Many resolutions dealt with gay rights. A few dealt with fathering, child care, and the need to draw men into the movement who are not white and middle-class. Two supported androgyny as an ideal.

Despite the political nature of many of these resolutions and the principles that NOCM later elaborated, participants have done little politically once a conference was over. Barry Shapiro of San Francisco started an organization called Men Allied Nationally for the ERA, which lobbied in several states and helped organize men's participation in the ERA March on Washington in 1978. Groups formed in several cities to prevent rape and to counsel men who batter women, like RAVEN (Rape and Violence End Now) in St. Louis, whose founders met at the fourth M&M conference in that city in 1977. Some individuals joined in feminist projects like Take Back the Night marches (against pornography). The California Anti-Sexist Mens Political Caucus (CAMP) encourages men to join or support grassroots efforts, from C-R and study groups to abortion clinics and lobbying programs. Such projects are useful and sometimes noble—RAVEN is a model for thousands of groups around the country that deal with men who batter women—but very few are political in the sense that women's organizations pursue political goals on local, state, and federal levels.

The most obvious reason for the lack of political action was the failure for many years to form a national organization. At every M&M conference starting with the third, there was some effort to organize. At every conference it had to fight strong, emotional opposition. Some men felt the movement was for personal growth, which they thought would be inhibited by organization. Some distrusted any effort at organizing and any kind of leadership, either from unhappy experience in other movements or from the feeling that they lead inevitably to the kind of hierarchy and structure associated with the hated masculine stereotypes. In 1977 and 1978 other men opposed organization from fear that anti-feminists would take over, or men who deny guilt; later, when they were sure the organization would have a pro-feminist spirit, they favored going ahead. At every conference those who favored organization seemed to win, though votes were seldom taken. And every time little happened; the opposition was strong enough to prevent the accumulation of the consensus needed to fuel an organization. Over the years, however, the activists formulated principles and kept on organizing.

Then at the seventh M&M conference, in Boston in 1981, about thirty of the six hundred participants decided the time had come. They put together a national organization over the next year and launched it, still unnamed, at a press conference in New York in March 1983. It held its first national meeting combined with the eighth Men and Masculinity conference in Ann Arbor in August 1983. By the time the conference ended, it had about five hundred members from thirty-nine states, and it has fluctuated around that level since. Members decided to call it the National Organization for Men but had to change the name when an anti-feminist man in New York incorporated under that title. It became the National Organization for Changing Men.

NOCM's 1985 draft statement of principles calls for pride in such traditionally masculine qualities as independence and courage and for changes in such traits as "excessive involvement with work, isolation from our children, discomfort in expressing emotions, lack of close friendships, excessive competitiveness and aggressiveness." It also supports women's struggle for equality and "the creation of a gay-affirmative society," opposes a variety of injustices, and says, "Our goal is to change not just ourselves or other men as individuals, but the society as a whole."

Some NOCM leaders emphasize the need for ideological purity in support of these principles, while others want to attract as many members as possible, presumably educating them to the organization's purposes in the process. It is not at all clear whether NOCM is going to pursue political goals in the broadest sense.

The men's movement, of course, like all movements, cannot be defined solely in terms of organization, resolutions, or workshops. The whole first conference at Knoxville was called "a playshop" and many sessions at later conferences were called playshops to show that men were moving away from the traditional masculine focus on instrumental work and intellectual debate. The dominant flavors at an M&M conference, like the ham and mushrooms in a quiche, are psychotherapy and legacy of the counterculture. Most participants wear jeans and T-shirts or sport shirts; a necktie is hard to find. Every conference includes not only playshops but also films, dancing—often men discovering a joy in dancing with other men that is not free of the frissons of shocking the bourgeois spectators—and rituals intended to free people from uptight traditions of masculinity. One is an almost compulsive determination to hug other men as a sign of brotherhood. Another is holding ceremonies in which men form circles to sing, move, and otherwise express the joys of being different.

One ideological point frequently expressed in work and play at these conferences says that competition and the drive to achieve are macho, or at least part of the stereotyped sex roles that the participants want to shed. This seems to me to fit the men who attend M&M conferences. Nobody has compiled accurate data on them; merely asking about occupations and income levels would be suspect, if not grounds for tar and feathers. But I would guess, from the conferences I attended and from cross-checking with participants in others, that between two thirds and three quarters of the people at any M&M meeting are counselors, therapists, social workers, psychologists, teachers, and graduate students. The last two are usually in psychology, sociology, and the helping professions, with a disproportionate number part-time and few from the country's leading universities. There are few managers and few doctors or lawyers, though the number has increased slightly since 1983 —partly because the number of men over fifty has also risen. The sprinkling of blue-collar workers usually includes more people who have moved into factories after some college education than people born into the working class. I would guess that the median income of participants was no higher than the national average and quite possibly lower.

Local consciousness-raising groups, in contrast, often include doctors, lawyers, corporate executives, accountants, and scientists as well as men like those who go to M&M conferences. Alan Gross believes that most men in C-R groups give priority to personal growth and developing a support network, goals that a C-R group fulfills and a national conference, in their eyes, does not. Gross also suggests that those members of C-R groups who strive for strength and independence may be using the groups as cover. They presumably would be disturbed by the connotations of weakness that would arise if they joined a therapy or growth group, and therefore find it more legitimate and more "male" to join a men's C-R group that offers vague hope of freedom from restrictive sex roles.[13] I take this to mean that the members of a C-R group who are more "successful," the doctors, lawyers, and businessmen, are likely to be more interested in personal growth and emotional support than in changing the system that has given them material rewards. They are therefore the least likely to go to a national conference or join a true men's movement.

Many of those who do go to national meetings, and many in C-R groups as well, are "men who fear they won't make it," Ted Noland* said. He started as a male member of his wife's NOW chapter. They both went to law school and worked as army lawyers overseas. In 1979 Ted was a struggling lawyer and a member of an East Coast men's group that was interested in the possibility of political action. He is now a businessman in a southern city. The men's group helped him come to terms with his desire to be masculine without falling into rigid sex-role traps, yet left him full of doubt. "In effect," he added, "the men say, 'I'll join a men's group that has lots of rationalizations. If I don't make it in the world, I can always say I'm liberated.' "

Terry Dokukin* put it more positively, saying that many of those involved in local men's groups and national conferences are men "for whom the traditional system hasn't worked well. They say, 'Competition isn't a positive value for me; I don't like what it does to my relations with other men.' " Dokukin hopes that a national men's movement will balance such men with those who do achieve. He himself has accomplished things without becoming entangled in destructive forms of competition. He took a year out of his public relations career to serve on the commission for sex equity of a city government and is happily married to a feminist. He is also a veteran of many M&M conferences, one of the men who have put years of effort into struggle for sexual equality in their own lives and in society.

The men who attend national M&M conferences also include a high proportion of homosexuals—at least 30 percent, compared to 10 percent for the general population.[14] For the straight men, the point is to deal with homophobia, which they see as a major force in establishing traditional sex roles, particularly the male tendency to repress emotion and deny weakness. They also recognize that gays are men who are more oppressed than they are. Both points are underscored when others suggest that attendance at a men's meeting or concern with sexual equality implies homosexuality. At the 1979 conference, held on the University of Wisconsin campus in Milwaukee, some students made jeeringly plain their belief that the men who were not openly gay were just afraid to come out of the closet. This kind of happening at a meeting mirrors events in daily life. Dokukin said that when he switched from public relations to sex equity, he found that many colleagues perceived him as a gay activist. He remembered one man who seemed fascinated by Terry's remarks and then said, "You know, what I think you really want is a sex change." That kind of reaction strengthens Terry's belief in gay rights as a men's movement cause—and his belief in the need for workshops on positive heterosexual identity.

For gays, attendance at M&M conferences provides a chance to work against homophobia and against the narrow conceptions of sex roles that reinforce gay oppression. It also provides a chance to meet other gay men, a sexual reinforcement of the social function of all groups, comparable to the way straight singles meet at political gatherings in large cities. Few of the gays who have taken leading roles at M&M conferences are also active in gay rights organizations. One reason may be that they like the opportunities for dialogue between gay and straight men that M&M meetings provide but that are as rare at gay conferences as they would be at American Legion conventions. It is also possible, as Gross suggests, that attendance at M&M meetings gives gays a chance to speak out about topics of passionate concern without revealing their sexual preferences to employers or casual friends as they would if they became gay activists.[15]

When I try to analyze the pro-feminists, my vision is colored by the emotions I felt at the meetings I've attended—one more example of the way the personal is political. At every conference I went through three stages, starting with the detachment of an observer collecting material for a book. That detachment was dispelled by surges of hope and joy—when men actually departed from the old male sex role instead of talking about it; when they faced questions of power instead of talking around them, or when, as I did at every conference, I found a few men whose feelings drew my sympathy and whose minds compelled my respect, men whom I wanted to be my friends. These feelings gave way in turn to disappointment, dissatisfaction, and sometimes anger when I felt the meetings were failing to address the very wrongs that had brought the movement into being, the wrongs that men and women do each other. I felt more hope, less dissatisfaction, and little anger at Ann Arbor in 1983 and St. Louis in 1985, when this part of the men's movement seemed to me to be moving in the right direction.

Some of my discontents can be dismissed as the result of personality conflict, or the kind of difference of opinion that makes horse races (a sport patronized by few M&M participants, because it produces winners and losers). Such differences made it hard for me to be a wholehearted participant in many M&M rituals and ceremonies. I wanted to laugh at some of the songs whose words imitated those of labor, the old left, and the 1960s protest singers, though I liked some of the country and western numbers and some of the sophisticated piano comedy at the concerts of the 1983 and 1985 conferences. I was annoyed at having to hug men I didn't like, and I didn't believe that a meaningless hug makes it easier to touch a good friend or tell him that he's important to me. Yet I found myself applauding Jeff Beane, the keynote speaker at Milwaukee, when he urged men to play as well as work during the conference by citing a popular version of a thought from Emma Goldman: "If there's no dancing at the Revolution, I'm not coming!"[16]

My disappointment and anger also had other, stronger roots. One was the perception that these men were unlikely to form a movement that would win a mass following or change society as the women's movement had. One was the belief that many of their ideas and programs, if put into action, would make people just as unhappy as society does now.

Strongest of all was the feeling I've mentioned—that their activities for many years seldom addressed the wrongs that men and women do each other. I was repeatedly struck, for instance, by the small number of workshops in explicitly pro-feminist conferences that dealt with relations between men and women apart from rape and violence (1 out of 35 at the regional conference at Pemberton, New Jersey, in 1976; 6 out of 82 at Milwaukee in 1979). This reflected the desire to learn about and experience relations between men and men. I shared the desire, but I didn't think it forced us to ignore the relations between men and women. The people who planned the Ann Arbor conference in 1983 apparently felt the same way, and 29 out of 92 workshops, some personal and some political (including six on rape and violence), dealt with issues between men and women. The figure was 26 out of 104 workshops at St. Louis in 1985. This was one reason I began to think NOCM might be moving in the right direction.

That feeling was reinforced by changes in two other areas where I had previously thought that M&M conferences reinforced or reflected failure to focus clearly on relations between men and women. One was gay rights and gay problems. I understood that homophobia is a foundation for injustice and repressive sex roles, and I welcomed the chance to talk to gay men in ways my ordinary life seldom makes possible. But I didn't like it when concern for gay issues overshadowed concern for problems between women and men. I didn't like it when a workshop on intimacy—a subject about which I needed to learn a great deal, as most men do—turned into a gay cruising ground, as did many areas of many M&M conferences. At Ann Arbor and St. Louis, I felt that concern for gay issues went hand in hand with concern for male-female issues and that neither gay nor straight men were confusing their need to communicate with each other with a search for new partners.

At the last three M&M conferences there was also little emphasis on the second subject that had disturbed me at earlier meetings: androgyny.

In the late 1960s and early 1970s, psychologists applied the word to the discovery that masculinity and femininity are not opposite poles of the same dimension but separate and independent dimensions in the process of sex-typing or building a sex-role identity. They found, in other words, that an individual can have both masculine and feminine traits and attitudes at the same time. Some offered evidence that androgynous men and women were better adjusted than either traditionally masculine men or traditionally feminine women. Later this came to be seen less as a matter of inner identity, which some psychologists insist on regarding as hypothetical, and more as a matter of adaptation to the demands of given situations or social roles. More and more situations require people to employ both masculine and feminine skills. Androgynous people cope with such situations better than those who score high in masculinity and low in femininity or vice versa.[17]

This important discovery was first simplified and then taken to extremes. If androgyny is merely being "assertive *and* yielding, independent *and* dependent, job- *and* people-oriented, strong *and* gentle, in short both 'masculine' *and* 'feminine,' " as Fasteau put it,[18] it means no more than the old "Tough, but oh! so gentle" spark plug ads. This is fatuity. To say, "It is not enough for us to broaden our concepts of masculinity and femininity. We need to conceptualize a new personal identity and life-style called androgyny," as one of the M&M resolutions did, goes far beyond the ideas of the developmental psychologists. I thought that if taken seriously, this might start to erase boundaries on which our culture and perhaps our sanity depend. My fear was reinforced by a later resolution that equated gender identification with sexism and said, "For androgynous persons, genders are irrelevant and claim no rule of force or meaning." I can't speak for androgynous persons, but I know that genders will never be irrelevant to the human race.[19]

Daniel Levinson's eloquent generalization is much closer to the truth: a man grows when he learns to find and recognize the feminine in himself and to integrate it into his personality.[20] Levinson says this happens most often in mid-life, a stage most M&M participants have not yet reached. Perhaps that is why they used to speak of androgyny in ways that made it sound repellent. But many M&M veterans are now close to or over forty. That fact and the higher proportion of older men among the newcomers at the past three meetings may explain why there now seems to be less distortion of the subject.

I grew angry again over another failure to address a central issue: what happens at work. I believe that work is one of the activities that defines and, at its rare best, fulfills humanity—and that it is one of the primary areas where men react to the changes that women are making. The men at M&M conferences often sound as though they believe work is nothing more than a curse that descends on men as part of their sex-role training. That was certainly the emphasis of workshops on work—which before 1984 came to a grand total of three out of the hundreds at all the M&M conferences put together. I feel compelled to say that I too am aware that the rat race, the compulsion to succeed, the overidentification with work are evils that in our society afflict men more than women. I too want men to be able to demand less of themselves, to work fewer hours, to let themselves enjoy all the things from emotional expressiveness through nurturing to sexual passivity that our culture has long labeled as feminine and that we think are incompatible with a man's work. But I do not believe that this compels us to give up skill, achievement, the healthful kinds of competition, the satisfying kinds of work. I do not think competition and achievement must always be oppressive or force men to deny their emotions.[21] I believe men can and should have both satisfying work lives, which is to say public lives, and satisfying private lives. I believe women can and should have them too. NOCM now has a task force on work and job satisfaction, and the St. Louis meeting ended the tradition of ignoring the subject. Many participants in the task force and workshops come from the new group of older men whose retirement, actual or prospective, gives them a new interest in what's wrong with the work system. But with the exception of one or two members, the emphasis is still on what happens to one's self at work and not on what men can do for women—or for other men, straight or gay.

The obsession with the evils of the work ethic persists in men's movement thinking despite the new task force. It probably begins with the desire to end oppression—to stop men from being the worst kind of bosses or the saddest kind of tenant farmers or assembly-line workers. This obsession has become a form of tragic denial. One of the most important ways that men oppress women—and other men—is by barring their path to achievement. Saying "Down with achievement!" denies this by shifting attention from the evil of the blockade to the supposed undesirability of the goal. One of the most important ways that most men are like most women is in their both being denied the satisfactions of achievement. Saying "Achievement is worth nothing!" denies the common condition by again denying the desirability of the goal, which in turn invalidates the frustration of finding it barred to both sexes.

Another kind of denial is even more tragic—the avoidance of power, the myth that because powerful men have created oppressive systems we too must become oppressors or at least soil our hands if we touch power, or if we even think too much about it. This suggests that the men in the movement feel they have no power, as might be expected of those "for whom the traditional system hasn't worked well." That is only partially true. The men in the movement, ironically, share an important disability with the men in the majority, with Middle America. We can't tell when we have power and when we do not. Few can admit the truth of the Janeway analysis that I quote at the beginning of this book—that compared to the real rulers, male though they usually are, most of us belong with women in the category of the powerless, the weak. Our male privilege is often compensation for our powerlessness and is equally often based on our fantasies of identification with the powerful. Most of the men in the movement would insist that they know they are powerless, that they do not identify with the powerful. This only makes it harder for them to recognize their own moments as oppressors and their complicity in their own oppression. They are like the rest of us, like almost all men: we seldom admit our position, strong or weak, in the dynamics of power. If we recognize that we are caught up in those dynamics, we might be able to change our part in them. We, especially we the powerless, we the weak, could take power—at least some power. We could change the way power is exercised. If we refuse to do this, we will only continue to be oppressed by others and therefore to oppress others.

Believing this, I grew angry at the men who wanted the men's movement to avoid power structures and power processes. I grew angry at men who even as they endorsed the Equal Rights Amendment seemed only too ready to repress their knowledge of what men do to women—and to gays and to men of other races. When people who wanted to start a national organization came to the Milwaukee conference in 1979 with a statement of principles carefully drafted to unite the personal-growth enthusiasts and the more political people, the word "oppress" did not appear in the draft and there was no recognition that heterosexual men hold most of the positions of power in our society. I lost my observer cool and voiced the loudest of an earful of protests. In response, the organizers amended the statement by adding these words, composed by committee: "All men, by virtue of their gender, have certain powers over women. Not all men have the same power. Many men—and women—are denied power because of their race or their class. We pledge to find ways to share power equitably."

The National Organization for Changing Men has been less evasive than the M&M meetings from which it sprang; its statements voice support for "the fight for full social, legal, and economic equality for women" and mention the need "to change the unjust patriarchal system, and to escape from the sex roles and power imbalances that have so often made women and men view each other as enemies." The 1985 draft principles oppose "the unequal distribution of power." But NOCM still does not make the question of power a priority issue or address it directly.

Yet the members of the NOCM and the people who attend Men and Masculinity conferences, however little they do politically, do read books and join C-R groups and attend meetings whose subtexts all recognize, at least with a glance, that in our society men have more power than women. It may be in the small group of rulers who are almost all male, or in the masses of men who treat women as an even lower class, but the imbalance is real and the men of the movement know it. They may feel only a vague pricking of conscience about their own complicity in the imbalance, or they may openly acknowledge that men as a class (which does not mean all men) oppress women as a class (which does not mean all women). In either case, what they feel is guilt.

But they don't always recognize it as guilt or admit that they feel guilt. They resent the accusation from the other side of the men's movement that they proclaim guilt. Men who feel defensive about guilt overlook its potential for liberation. Guilt is not always a repressive burden. It can free us from failure to live up to our ideals (which means it can free us from sex-role stereotypes). Guilt can be the key to acting on our need to love and care for others—the key, as Willard Gaylin says, to fusion between individual pleasure needs; it is one of the emotions that bind us to those we need for our own survival (see Chapter 2). Sidney Miller, one of the wisest profeminists, a man who helped start a dozen consciousness-raising groups in New Jersey in the 1970s, knows how productive guilt can be from his own experience. When I interviewed him, he said:

One of the most positive things in the world is to feel guilty when there's a reason to feel guilty. . . . I felt guilty when the time came, when I thought about the consequences of my behavior toward my wife, toward my daughter, toward women in general. I had every reason to feel guilty, because I had been indulging in destructive behavior to other human beings. When I began to change that, and began to be a little more accountable for what I did and said, I didn't have any more trouble with guilt then. . . . Not only didn't I have guilt, but I began to get love and support from these very people.

Expressing anger can also be liberating, if we can make good use of the energy it furnishes. Denial of anger at women makes it harder to love the target of that anger, to love the "class enemy," to love the people we must love to keep our selves and our society going. The pro-feminists tend to deny anger at women. Yet such anger is constantly voiced in men's C-R groups. Arnold Zimmer,* a California critic of the pro-feminists, said:

I'm involved with two men's groups right now. In talking with men, I find a lot of anger and a lot of resentment. I don't find men saying, "Yes, that's how I feel"—unless I divulge how I feel and make myself vulnerable, to the point where I say that I get pissed off because I am stereotyped by women and by men because of being a man. Once I divulge that, other men say, "You know, I feel that way too." And I know it's there. I really know it's there. The male feminists I meet, who are not even addressing men's anger and resentment, are not going to be able to help these guys reveal it. As a matter of fact, I think they intensify it.

The people at M&M meetings do voice some anger at the system, the stereotype of the male as competitive overworker and provider, and the oppression of gays. But they are reluctant to look at their anger at women in their own lives and in society. At three M&M conferences, organizers rejected workshops on anger at women proposed by a very angry man. The first national conference workshop on the subject was not held until the seventh meeting in Boston in 1981. That was carefully channeled to have one man at a time talk about anger at one woman in his life history. This was in keeping with the psychological axiom that men are angriest at their wives and mothers—but it did not look at the way men project their anger onto other women in other contexts, or other forms of male anger at women in public settings. Apart from a few men like Sid Miller, the pro-feminists seem to me to do too little with their guilt and even less with their anger to move very far toward men's liberation.

THE NO-GUILT WING

The second wing of the men's movement denies guilt almost completely. It denies the difference in power between men and women and the oppression from which male guilt springs. It labels guilt induced by feminists or occasionally expressed by pro-feminists as self-hate, and it tells men to get rid of it. Sid Miller commented, "It sort of gets me a little mad when these guys say people are 'into feeling guilt.' If you can't own it, you can't leave it." But you can even deny that you're denying it, as I think Washington writer Dan Logan does when he objects to the "no-guilt" label and says he prefers to speak of "no-fault liberation." The men in the no-guilt wing of the men's movement are very good at expressing anger, however. They often sound anti-feminist and sometimes antifemale. Some of their small-group meetings simply ignore women.[22] Local groups often hold public meetings with women panelists and many women in the audience, however, drawn by the advertised hope of solving problems between men and women.

The philosophy of the no-guilt wing is expressed most clearly by Herb Goldberg, a Los Angeles psychotherapist, and Richard Haddad, a Maryland human resources manager. Goldberg's first book, published in 1976, was called *The Hazards of Being Male: Surviving the Myth of Masculine Privilege.* Like Farrell and Fasteau (whom he often seemed to follow without giving them credit), Goldberg deplored the damage that traditional sex roles do to men. He also deplored male guilt at not living up to the destructive stereotypes. But he told men they had no reason to feel guilty about privilege and domination, which he called illusions. In *Hazards,* he urged men to follow the feminist example, to find their energy in anger and outrage, even or especially at women. The male will not change, he said, until "he experiences his underlying rage toward the endless, impossible binds under which he lives, the rigid definitions of his role, the endless pressure to be all things to all people, and the guilt-oriented, self-denying way he has traditionally related to women, to his feelings, and to his needs." He also denounced the pro-feminist wing of the men's movement and said that because its spirit is "one of self-accusation, self-hate, and a repetition of feminist assertions, I believe it is doomed to failure in its present form."[23]

When Goldberg published *Hazards,* he was himself angry, emerging from a painful divorce. By the time he wrote *The New Male,* published in 1979, he had mellowed enough to entitle one chapter, "The Feminist Movement Can Save Your Life." In it he reduced feminism to "an insistence by women that they function as whole people, rather than feminine gender stereotypes."[24] After a new marriage and the birth of his first child, Goldberg wrote *The New Male-Female Relationship,* in which his view of feminism had evolved enough for him to say, "Women's consciousness seems to be arriving at a broadened awareness that both sexes have been locked into a mutually reinforcing dance in which there are really no victims or victimizers, only the illusions of such."[25] None of these books deals with politics or power. When Goldberg speaks publicly, he states frankly that he says nothing about power in his books because "I'm pretty naive in that area" or "I'm politically stupid."

Goldberg's philosophy and psychology are also open to question. In *The New Male*, he told the male reader "what feminism *could* mean to him, i.e. no longer having to take responsibility for the woman. Furthermore, he could now also expect from her as much as he gave to her." He deplored a picture of "men's lib" as that of a

harried man rushing home from work to help with household chores such as vacuuming, washing dishes and cleaning or baby care. While there is nothing inherently wrong in the man's sharing of these responsibilities, compare that image of liberation with that of a woman emerging as an independent, assertive, sexual person who is redefining her role and her life to meet her needs for growth. In other words, while women's liberation has been depicted as a joyful, energetic freeing up and casting off of sex stereo-types and the onerous responsibilities that accompany them, "men's lib" has been depicted as the *addition* of responsibilities and onerous tasks to an already laden and pressured life and little else. No wonder the average man has resisted and reacted defensively.

. . . What has been commonly described as "men's lib" is not liberation at all, but merely accommodation to women's changes. *What this means is that once again he is playing daddy, only this time, unlike in the traditional relationship where he got nurturance and support, the payoffs are almost non-existent.* [Goldberg's italics.][26]

Goldberg seems completely unaware that there is a contradiction between his rejection of "onerous tasks" and his declaration, only two paragraphs later, that liberation for a man should mean "a reentry into the world of playfulness, intimacy, trusting relationships, emotions and caring." A man cannot take more than one step into that world with a woman (or indeed with any other person) unless he is willing and able to share the onerous tasks that are part of caring, among them household chores and child care. (I was fascinated that a chapter on parenting in *The New Male-Female Relationship*, included after the birth of the daughter with whom he has the "purest" relationship Goldberg has ever known, still said not one word about "onerous tasks.") Goldberg obliterates the connection by equating man's "reentry" into that world—after exile imposed by a flaming sword?—with "a priority on fulfillment of *his* needs and *his* growth."

That priority, that incantation of "his," tells men to ignore others (with woman, of course, the primal other) and concentrate on the liberation of the self, as though that were possible without the freedom of others. It thus reflects the culture of narcissism, of a society that encourages the individual either to ignore the external world, to incorporate it into himself, or to project himself onto it, as though it had no function but to be his mirror. Goldberg's books are repellingly clear examples of the way the culture of narcissism deforms the desire to improve one's self and one's relations with others into what goes by the misshapen name of "human-potential movement."

The Hazards of Being Male inspired Richard Haddad to become one of the four founders and the principal theoretician of Free Men, originally a group in Columbia, Maryland, and now split up into a handful of chapters in different places. Haddad has the political mind that Goldberg lacks: he acknowledges that men have more political and economic power than women—and says it should be shared. But he thinks that women have equivalents of that political and economic power.[27] One is domestic power—the role of the woman in passing on the values of society to children. The other is sexual power, by which he means a woman's ability to deny a man sex until he does what she wants. "If she wants you home at eleven o'clock and you come home at five past, you don't get laid that night." After giving this example in the interview, Haddad added that women do not do this consciously or evilly, "but because they're conditioned to do it." He does not talk about men's manipulating women this way; he seems to believe, like Phyllis Schlafly, that women either have a much weaker sex drive than men or much stronger control over it.

In his analysis of "power," Haddad sounds like a Jeremiah of the forties or fifties. Yet these are the views he has come to in reaction against the feminism of the sixties and seventies. If feminists say that their aim is to break down the very stereotypes he objects to, he replies that they have not achieved it—and accuses them not so much of failure as of hypocrisy. If feminism coincides and coexists with women's transmission of traditional values to children or with their sexual manipulation of men, that too is female hypocrisy rather than the tragicomedy of cultural change.

Haddad's equation between political and economic power on one side and domestic and sexual power on the other leads him to the explicit conclusion that men as a class do not oppress women as a class but are similarly victims. I asked where he felt men had been victims as feminists have shown women to be. He replied, "I have trouble simply choosing. Let's take the draft, there's one. Divorce and custody, there's a second. Arrest and conviction, where 96 percent of inmates of prisons are men, there's a third."

I thought these replies were important because the issues are real and the pro-feminists virtually ignore them. But Haddad himself seemed determined to ignore important things about them. It is the men of the Congress and the Supreme Court who have barred women from the draft. It is predominantly male judges who until recently have almost automatically given wives custody of children in divorce cases. (The father retained custody in the rare divorce cases up to roughly a century ago. Then men helped shift custody to the divorced mother as part of the shifts in differentiation of sex roles after the Civil War. The woman's role has undergone several changes in the past century, but until the 1970s each of the transformations assumed that women would be the child raisers, which Haddad himself angrily makes a proof of female power.[28]) It is predominantly male officers of the criminal justice system who prosecute, convict, and imprison women in smaller proportions than male offenders. This of course testifies to the continuing power of sex-role stereotypes, but that too is changing as the number of reports of offenses by women continues to grow. Haddad did not mention that more than 80 percent of all crimes are committed by men, which makes the high percentage of men in prison slightly less outrageous.

The issues are important whether it is men as a class or society as a whole that is responsible for the injustices involved. Many draft-age men talk of refusing to register if women are not also subject to the draft. The continuing propensity to give mothers sole custody of children in divorce produces genuine grievances that men are organizing to protest. In talking about such problems, the no-guilt wing of the men's movement is closer than the pro-feminists to the political concerns of mainstream America. It may also be more interested in acting on the possibility of change. Haddad's sometime ally, Fredric Hayward, for instance, once a leader of the Boston offshoot of Free Men and now the proprietor of his own Men's Rights (MR) Inc., boasts of his lobbying the state of Massachusetts to end higher automobile insurance rates for men and "happy hours" in which bars offer drinks at lower prices to women. In some areas where it seeks change, like the drive for joint custody of children in divorce, the no-guilt wing meets women's organizations head on; in others, like unisex insurance, it joins in uneasy coalition with them in principle but is seldom as visible or audible as Hayward was in Massachusetts.

Apart from such peripheral activism, the no-guilt stream wins a momentary audience. Goldberg's books have outsold Farrell and Fasteau, neither of whom had the pop-psychology, self-help-for-narcissists approach that boosts sales. Some Free Men chapters have garnered a share of media attention and large crowds at occasional meetings; their ability to voice anger attracts new waves of recruits. Others, however, have been unable to draw enough men to survive. The Columbia group of Free Men that Haddad helped found no longer meets. He and some of his colleagues attributed the decline of that group to burnout after more than three years of activity; fatigue among the few with the administrative skills to keep an organization going, and discouragement with the election of the Reagan administration and a Senate capable of serious consideration for a Family Protection Act that attempts to revive the sex-role stereotypes they hate. A number of Free Men have come to find Haddad's harsh polemics embarrassing, though they still espouse many of the same views in gentler form. Many no-guilt men, failing to form their own coherent organization, have tried to combine with another force—the men whose prime motivation is winning custody of their children in divorce cases.

THE DIVORCE REFORMERS

In the early seventies, men who were stunned by the impact of their divorce proceedings began to come together with others in the same plight in their home cities. They were a small minority of all divorced men, but they had strong feelings. They were outraged by what they saw as the propensity of divorce lawyers to create or exacerbate adversary relationships between divorcing spouses. They were outraged by the amount of money they had to pay in alimony and child support. (They usually ignored statistics showing that the courts award alimony to only 14 percent of divorced women, and that only 46 percent of them collect it regularly. The courts award child support to only 44 percent of divorced mothers, and only 47 percent of these collect it regularly.[29])

The men were outraged most of all by limitation or denial of their access to their children. When a bulky Michigan salesman rose at a meeting to voice simultaneous anger and grief at the people and the system that had prevented him from seeing his children for five and a half years, I thought, "This is the first time I've heard a man express the kind of passion that fueled the women's movement." Of course, beneath these authentic grievances, some men may also be outraged by the loss of male control that they expected, at least subconsciously, to find in marriage, but I don't think that invalidates their passion. So far as the issue of parenthood goes—the important one for both feminists and the men's movement—nobody knows how many of these men had been doing a significant share of the child care before their marriages ended. It was probably very few. But some certainly had, and their indignation over being relegated to the role of provider rather than child nurturer colored and reinforced the feelings of men who had been less intimately involved with their children.

These men formed local organizations, frequently with names like Fathers United for Equal Rights or U.S. Divorce Reform. Sometimes they had names like Coalition Organized for Parental Equality (COPE) or Divorced American Men Unite (DAMU, pronounced "damn you"). Some of the organizations have only one or two members and serve simply to increase effectiveness in legislative lobbying or making expenses tax deductible. Others have many members, with a constant flow of veterans leaving as they win change or adjust to their lot, while new recruits come in with their first sufferings. These groups provide two things: emotional support networks, and help in dealing with legal issues and with coping. The legal help may be basic information about fathers' rights and local divorce courts; it may be referrals to "good" divorce lawyers (which may mean less adversary types or, in contrast, what one man called "killer sharks" to counter the ex-wife's legal counsel); it may be advice or seminars in fighting divorce proceedings *pro se,* for oneself and without either kind of lawyer. The coping help is less common: lectures or discussions on how to care for children of different ages, how to cope with both menial and delightful sides of raising kids.

After a few years the divorce groups began to multiply and exchange ideas and information. Men from these groups sometimes spoke to pro-feminist or no-guilt groups; the latter adopted custody reform as one of their causes. Some of the divorce-reform experts began to find regional and national markets for their newsletters, though the men in the divorce groups were not the kind who follow a guru. No book in this field has had the impact that Warren Farrell and Herb Goldberg had on their respective audiences. Most of the half dozen volumes that these groups talk about are handbooks for wringing paternal or joint custody out of the legal system, with little of the philosophy or psychologizing of the writers who have influenced the other wings of the men's movement.[30]

The local divorce-reform groups bring together men of different classes, with blue-collar and clerical workers and the poor seeking help from the lawyers, doctors, and businessmen who have been through the same embittering experiences. These men from different levels have in common a sense of being losers in marriage. But they have yet to form an effective alliance for either politics or consciousness-raising, and it is usually the better-educated men with higher incomes who have spent money and time lobbying for changes in divorce laws and trying to form a national organization.

Three efforts to organize nationally failed in the sixties and seventies because participants from different places couldn't agree on means or ends. Then people from several groups met in Houston in June 1981 and formed the National Congress for Men (NCM). All but a dozen of the 101 people who registered were from divorce-reform groups. (I counted six no-guilt men and three who called for a return to one form or another of male dominance.) The planners emphasized the idea of delegates representing local groups and said the 101, from twenty-one states, the District of Columbia and Canada, represented 7,000 to 8,000 people. This was unlikely because so many of the groups were one-man paper organizations, as James Cook, the first president of the NCM, acknowledged in an interview. (Cook is a Los Angeles lawyer who helped lobby for California's recently passed joint custody law.) The majority of the men at the meeting wore ties and jackets, not jeans and T-shirts, to most sessions. There were doctors, lawyers, scientists, stockbrokers, and other mainstream occupations galore; I would guess that the median income of participants was in the top 25 percent nationally. They were not all from the world of success, however. I was impressed by the emotional intensity of one man who said he had put his blood, sweat, tears, and money into organizing the Congress and that it had to succeed because nothing else would pay for his failures—his failure to get custody of his two sons, and his failure to make the living he had expected, which had led both to his being jailed for nonpayment of child support and to the professional disaster of having his office phone cut off.

Divorce-reform meetings hold relatively few subsidiary sessions compared to M&M conferences, and few are called workshops. At Houston two working groups dealt with the main issues on the divorce-reform agenda—discrimination in custody and men and the law. Three were on topics that M&M workshops often deal with: networking, how the sexes differ and why, and traditional male roles and the cultural portrayal of the male. The two legal groups and networking attracted the most participants. The networking meetings, indeed, drew so many people they had to be moved to a larger room —one more case of men discovering brotherhood as feminists used to discover sisterhood.

That discovery of brotherhood is one thing the divorce reformers have in common with both the no-guilt and the pro-feminist streams of the men's movement. It is connected with something else they have in common: the sense of grievance, of being victims or losers, among many of the participants. In some cases that sense operates in terms of the socioeconomic system, in some in terms of sex roles or marriage or relations with women in general, in some in terms of relations with other men. But the widespread feeling of being at least a sometime loser is unmistakable. It contradicts the fact and the feeling that men are privileged, which we all grew up with. It contradicts the material success of many of the divorce reformers. It forces us to recognize that most men are powerless, even if the powerful are male. The recognition can be profoundly unsettling.

This shows that the divorce reformers have something else in common with the other currents of the men's movement. They too are responding to the women's movement, which is often the origin of their awareness of privilege and sometimes of their sense of grievance. Most of the men in this wing don't realize this; they are too early in their consciousness-raising, too much aware of their opposition to some women's groups on proposals for joint custody and government-enforced child-support payments, too obsessed by their individual situations and too hostile to their former wives. But when I asked how much they thought fathers' demands for equal rights were related to women's demands for equality, a few said the correlation was very high and called men's new claim to custody the same kind of change as women's claim to traditionally masculine jobs.

One of the products of the recognition of powerlessness, and of the sense of grievance in which it is rooted, is anger. I believe it was the sense of grievance and the anger that brought the divorce activists and the no-guilt men together in Houston. The pro-feminists were unlikely partners because they feel less anger and look so little at the anger they do feel. The no-guilt men provided the ideological or philosophical building blocks that the divorce reformers lacked. That may well be why, after the second meeting in Detroit in 1982, people from the no-guilt stream took four of the seventeen places on the

NCM board of directors—a much higher proportion than their share of the membership.

Some NCM members, including some of the founders, were uncomfortable with the ideology. A significant minority boycotted the third meeting in Los Angeles in 1983, because they wanted to concentrate on family law and exclude all other men's issues "such as AGENT ORANGE, PRISON SODOMY, and PENSION PLAN PAYMENTS," to quote a letter sent out by the dissidents. Discussion in a divorce-reform magazine, in the corridors of the meeting, and at the plenary session made it fairly plain, however, that the real targets of their protests were resolutions proposed by Fredric Hayward and NCM members from Free Men groups supporting gay rights.

The protests were hardly surprising. No gays had been visible at any NCM meeting. Several men at Houston, including some of the leaders, took the line of "I wouldn't care personally if homosexuals joined, but I know a lot of the men here don't want a lot of gays to come in." A few expressed alarm that some of the no-guilt men hugged other men, M&M style. James Cook proposed an alternative resolution in Los Angeles saying that "NCM neither opposes or disparages, nor aggressively promotes or campaigns for, the cause of gay or homosexual rights." Cook had never heard of Richard Haddad, but he was unknowingly reflecting Haddad's basic view: that gay rights is not a men's issue but a civil rights issue; that the population is 90 percent heterosexual and 90 percent of that is homophobic as well, so "you lose nine out of every ten prospective converts by waving the gay flag." But at Los Angeles, Cook lost. After considerable debate, the meeting adopted two resolutions on the subject. One declared that "all people, regardless of race, color, creed, religion, national origin, sex, or sexual preference are equal before the NCM. The Congress is composed of a cross-section of our population and is therefore concerned with the rights of all." The other urged that all "private sexual acts between consenting adults be decriminalized." The word "sexual" was substituted as an amendment for the original "homosexual."

The gay rights supporters won that battle, but two years later they seemed to be losing the war. The resolutions were too much for the men who provided the money and energy of the National Congress. The members were also divided by power struggles between two leading personalities, Cook and Alan Lebow of Michigan, who had been more sympathetic to the no-guilt ideas. The Congress and its resolutions were moribund by May 1985. Fifty-six activists from NCM and other organizations, including both Cook and Lebow, met then in Gaithersburg, Maryland, to form a new organization dedicated first and foremost to divorce reform and fathers' rights. Some of the no-guilt leaders were there, and the group agreed to pay lip service to equal rights and the fight against sexism. But Peter Cyr, a dentist from Portland, Maine, who had been secretary of NCM and was elected chairman of the new organization's planning committee, told me, "We will make no gesture toward gay rights. A lot of the support for divorce reform comes from men on the conservative right in the Midwest, California, Texas, places like that. These men are homophobic, they don't want to deal with gay rights."

These developments have interrupted the attempts of some no-guilt and fathers'-rights leaders to unite in what I thought would become a single wing of the men's movement. Some men are trying to continue in that direction, even with the newly reinforced priority for divorce reform. It seems important to me that before gay rights became a divisive issue, the no-guilt men and the more sophisticated of their allies among the divorce reformers had given this nascent wing a significant handful of ideological points in common with the pro-feminists. The first meeting of the National Congress for Men adopted nine resolutions on societal goals. At least five of the nine could have been adopted in slightly different form at an M&M meeting: those supporting equal rights and the Equal Rights Amendment; deploring stereotyped sex roles in the media; encouraging employers to allow flextime, parental leave, job sharing, and other programs to allow working parents more time to participate in their children's lives; and encouraging both men and women to choose from a full range of behavioral options rather than gender stereotypes. NOCM has moved in the direction of Congress resolutions on family law and family relations by saying in its draft statement of principles, "We also support reform of policies that may affect men unfairly, such as child custody laws." The Congress, of course, was more specific, endorsing an end to adversary proceedings in divorce, the concept of joint custody, and frequent contact between children and both parents after divorce.

I do not mean to belittle the differences between the two sides of the men's movement, quite apart from the question of support for gay rights. Some are differences in socioeconomics and psychology. The M&M conferences, with their counterculture flavor and their helping-profession orientation, do have a different "feel" from the National Congress and its successor, and from local Free Men and divorce-reform groups, with their businesslike approaches and their higher-income professions. The pro-feminists mistrust or despise hierarchy and link destructive sex roles to the culture of the corporation; Richard Haddad uses words like "hierarchy" and "establishment" to describe members of Free Men and when the Columbia group started, he incorporated it. M&M meetings operate in terms of participation, process, and consensus, while the divorce reformers have credentials for different classes of delegate, a palpable sense of parliamentary procedure, and a readiness to count votes.

Some of the differences show important political and philosophical disagreements. The M&M conferences hesitated to move to national organization lest power corrupt even the powerless, and they hesitated to court media publicity lest they be subjected to glamorized misunderstanding. The National Congress decided as a matter of course at its first meeting to set up a national organization and won CBS, NBC, National Public Radio, New York *Times,* and Washington *Post* coverage—all steps toward getting a finger on the levers of power, that is, changing the divorce laws in as many states as possible. (The New York *Times* sent a Style page reporter to the opening press conference of NOCM and then refused to run the story she wrote, on the pretext that the *Times* doesn't cover embryonic organizations; nobody thought of that when the Houston correspondent sent a news story on the first meeting of the National Congress for Men to the national desk in 1981.)

The M&M people believe in equal rights as a matter of justice for women, and for gays and racial minorities, as much as or more than for straight white men. The 1981 NCM resolutions on equal rights were worded to insist on equal enforcement for men and women, as though existing laws are enforced and the proposed amendment would be enforced mainly for the benefit of women. The no-guilt participants in NCM meetings, who shape most of these resolutions, struck the anti-feminist chord in a more genteel way than some of the angry divorce reformers. (Overall I was surprised at how little rather than how much antiwoman feeling was expressed in Houston and Los Angeles. Still, Fredric Hayward won applause for the passage in his Houston keynote address in which he said, "I do not want to stop women from going out and finding high-paying jobs—I want to DEMAND that women go out and find high-paying jobs. I am tired of being their wallet."[31] A little of that goes a long way.)

Similarly, on abortion the pro-feminist wing of the movement is unequivo-cally for free choice and the woman's right to control her own body. The Houston organizer who wanted to translate his failures into movement suc-cess replied to a question on abortion by saying, "If you spread your legs for me and you get pregnant, I expect to have some say in what happens to the kid." Others "explained" that the man in that case is not forcing the mother to use her body for a purpose she does not want, he is only asserting the right of "an unborn child that belongs to two people." But the no-guilt men do not seek to ban abortions. Indeed, they argue that if a woman makes the free choice to carry to term a fetus that the father would like to abort, the father should not be obliged to pay child support.

Such views might be expected to make the divorce reformers anathema to the women's movement. The NCM found itself opposed to at least two state chapters of the National Organization for Women on joint custody (men for, women against, making it an alternative that must be considered) and to many women's groups on government enforcement of child-support orders (women for, men against). But the divorce reformers sometimes work in alliance with women's groups, and ironically, before 1983 the NCM received more expressions of support from women than the M&M meetings, perhaps because it sought them and won more publicity for itself. In 1983 feminists began to show new signs of interest in the pro-feminist wing.

Both sides of the men's movement are certainly aware of their philosophi-cal differences and sometimes translate them into hostile acts that would recall the Bolshevik-Menshevik struggles to an observer who took the new revolution seriously. The divorce reformers' campaign against gay rights was one example. Peter Cyr, the de facto leader of their new organization, says the NOCM members "are very feminist-oriented. I can't talk with those people. They want to protect women, support them, no matter what they do." Robert Brannon, the first chairperson of NOCM, has written polemics against Herb Goldberg, Free Men, and others whom he sees as anti-feminist. Fred Hayward was invited by a minority of organizers to speak at a panel discussion at the 1981 M&M meeting in Boston—and was then "disinvited" because many M&M veterans said they would not come if such an anti-feminist spoke at their meeting. The organizers of the 1983 M&M conference turned down his request to hold a workshop in Ann Arbor.

The hope of alliance and the dream of unity remain alive, however. After barring Hayward from Ann Arbor, the National Organization Council decided to call a cease-fire. It appointed Alan Gross, a council member and historian of the men's movement, as liaison to other men's groups and sent him to the Los Angeles meeting of the National Congress a few days later. He spoke at the final lunch there and emphasized the common views of the two groups without denying their differences. He also attended the 1985 meeting of the divorce reformers in Gaithersburg. Dan Logan, one of the leaders of the Washington group of Free Men and a participant in both the first meeting of the National Congress and the Gaithersburg meeting, has become a member of NOCM and was one of four men invited to present different viewpoints at a workshop on "Perspectives of the Men's Movement" at the St. Louis conference.

WHY THE MOVEMENT MATTERS

The men's movement is concerned with change at a moment of history that does not seem encouraging. The two attempts to start national organizations began in 1981, the first year of the Reagan era and its backlash against feminism. But the same trends that seem to strengthen sexism carry with them forces that can bolster the struggle against it (see Chapter 16). The National Organization for Women added members fearful of Gipper-style machismo in 1981, just as the American Civil Liberties Union enrolled people fearful of the Reaganites' redefinition of freedom. Since then the backing in both wings of the men's movement for more active, nurturing roles for men in the family seems likely to match both a new feminist expression of interest in the importance of the family and the old feminist interest in sharing power in the home with men. The National Congress of Men was full of Reagan supporters demanding change in "historic" divorce laws.

That's a long way from revolution, but it's the start of an effort to focus on the real issues—the laws, practices, and prejudices that embody sexism at home and at work. The men's movement may be small and ineffective compared to the women's movement, and it may not aspire to the dramatic changes in society that "real" movements dream of and others fear. But it remains part of a social drive that reflects happenings in individual lives. It provides channels where some men can exchange thoughts and feelings about those happenings, where they can work on the angers and fears and guilts that some shout and others don't admit feeling. It's a source of ideas for change that may reach the mainstream, and a source of energies that even in tiny sparks can be applied to shift the course of the mainstream a trifle. These channels, these ideas, these energies testify to the importance of the men's movement, however small it seems, however exasperating its shortcomings. With all its limitations, the movement will help give a new shape to the society in which our children and our grandchildren grow up.

Chapter 13
THE MEN OF
THE MOVEMENT

Sidney Miller and Phil Stein* came to the men's movement because their wives demanded that they change. In the early days most of the heterosexual participants were drawn into the movement by their wives or the women in their lives.[1] That testifies to a fundamental fact of those lives that's usually obscured by the collective characteristics of the movement, however much a social drive reflects happenings in individual lives: there is no escape, not even in a raised consciousness, from the contradiction of love and war, continual and simultaneous, between men and women—"the contradiction on which our social order rests."

PROFILES OF FOUR PRO-FEMINISTS

Most of the men (though I suspect it's a very small majority) who entered the movement because of their wives are still in the same marriages. Sid and Sylvia Miller learned to deal with their angers and their marriage stayed together. But many saw their marriages end in divorce, as Phil Stein did (see page 321); war defeated love.

Sid Miller was unusual among men in consciousness-raising groups and at national conferences because he was older (fifty-two when he first faced the need for change, sixty-seven in 1985) and because he was born and grew up blue-collar. He was the son of immigrants. He never finished high school, was a Communist Party member as a youth, and made his living as a window dresser. That made it hard at first for him to deal with college-educated men, but in the end it gave him an authenticity and an ability to relate to main-stream people that many men in the movement lack.

Sylvia had read *The Feminine Mystique* when it first came out in 1963, and in 1970 she joined an early C-R group that met in an old loft in a nondescript part of Manhattan, north of Union Square. It was not a safe neighborhood at night and Sid would pick her up after the meetings. He knew something important was happening because

for the first time in our married life I got so to speak a cold shoulder. We had always communicated about everything. So I began to feel curious and in some way shut out. This went on until we had a serious talk and Sylvia sort of told me, "The relationship can't go on any longer in the way it has." She would be willing to reassess things and maybe start on a different basis, but she was seriously thinking, if there wouldn't be any changes, of leaving.

Sid took that very seriously indeed; they had been married for thirty years. He found out that Sylvia was objecting to

the fact that I never took her seriously when she spoke. I never really listened to what she said. And I was not accountable for what I did, to anyone. I sort of took it for granted that I was the planet and everybody else was satellites around this planet.

Sid also discovered that he had alienated his daughter, then a student at Bennington College and active in the women's movement there. He was astonished and overwhelmed.

I felt like I was walking down an alley and being attacked from the back. I just couldn't understand what it was all about. My God, I'd been breaking my ass all these years, trying to get money to take care of these people, like many other men.

Sidney understood quickly that he was going to have to change. His first example was as piercing as only something small and homely can be. Susan, his daughter, was doing some work at Radcliffe and the Millers went up to Boston to see her.

We took a motel room. Sylvia wanted to go back to the motel. We were in Harvard Square and Susan and I were going to do something. So Sylvia said, "Give me the key to the room." And for some reason, I had this terrible problem giving her the key. She asked me again. Finally I came up with the key in a very reluctant manner. You're not going to believe this, but I said, "How are you going to find the room?" She exploded at that point, and my daughter, they both looked at me, and I realized, this is proof that I love you, I'm going to make you so distraught that you won't be able to find the number on the door when you have your key in your hand. I realized that I was trying to cripple her so she would rely on me. I needed to be responsible for her, which was a very destructive thing to be. Men do this all the time.

Sid found that he was treating his daughter, like his wife, as though she were not a person in her own right—but in a very different way.

> We went up to Bennington very often. I would talk with Susan about intellectual issues, about books, *War and Peace,* Dostoyevsky. I never asked what she was feeling about her life up there. It was like an ego thing for me that my daughter went to Bennington. . . . She had a tremendous amount of anger. She wanted more than me asking her what this or that course was like. She had a life but I was not related to that, anything emotional I steered away from; I was not available, there was nobody at home.

The emotional field was not the only one from which Sidney was absent. Bennington students had to write a thesis on which their graduation depended. Sid, who discussed Tolstoy and Dostoyevsky with Susan, never talked to her about the subject of her thesis, the poet Charles Olson. He never even asked to look at it. He failed to make an intellectual connection just as he failed to make the emotional connection.

"I was just proud of her," he said. "She was like an object." I was fascinated. Woman as sex object is a truth that has become almost a cliché of the women's and men's movements and the whole therapeutic subculture. Sid had learned that he was turning his daughter into a pride object. The pride he felt then was not true delight in the accomplishment or independence of a beloved that is one of the positive emotions men can feel about women who have changed. It was pride in a possession that a man can use to validate his masculinity or symbolize his power, a crystal-clear example of Joseph Pleck's hypothesis (see Chapter 2). I asked Sid about this and he said, "I think that's true, I think that's what happened."

For Sidney Miller, reading was the first step out of the trouble he was in— reading the feminist literature that Sylvia had plunged into, from John Stuart Mill to Kate Millett.

> I realized that I was indeed guilty of what was being said. At the same time I was feeling mad. There was a tremendous resentment at this time of my life to be faced with all of this. I thought about it and I figured, there have got to be some other guys who are having a similar experience. I have to find some people.

Soon he read a piece in the New York *Times* that he remembers as describing Warren Farrell as a male feminist who warned about the price men pay for repressing emotion. Farrell was an officer of NOW, but women at the New York chapter of NOW did not make it easy for men to find another man. Finally Sid did reach Farrell, who put him through a telephone quiz on the feminist literature he had read and eventually invited him to join one of the first men's consciousness-raising groups.

That group lasted eight years, a long life that few C-R groups have attained. Sid said it tried to be "hard-minded" about the question of how men treat women, as few other groups have done. After five years the members brought in the women they were married to or living with. Sid said that until then the men had been hiding the real truth from one another, and that the women forced them to be honest. The men got even closer to one another, to their wives or lovers, and to the other women. Few C-R groups last long after including both sexes, and in most that try, the opposite happens: people begin to be less honest, to play games to impress the opposite sex, to compete with members of their own sex.

In Sid's group a few of the marriages dissolved. He feels that consciousness-raising does not spoil any marriage that is strong enough to weather storms. His own marriage came out stronger for the experience.

The group opened up a whole lot of things for me about the issues in my relationship with Sylvia. I began to see how not only had I been very domineering as far as she was concerned, but even as far as the issues in the world were concerned, the things we shared about music, about painting, about writing, things where I respected her opinion. I had to learn to show my respect. And in some way I examined my whole life, not just my relationship with her. . . . I learned that as long as one is alive one has to examine and think about the consequences of what you say and do. . . . You can't be busy with it twenty-four hours a day, but if you hurt someone or someone hurts you, the big thing is to develop a directness, to have an agreement with the other person—let's be direct.

One change in Sid's life grew out of the new directness when he began to come home early, working shorter hours as he headed from self-employment to retirement, while Sylvia was still working full-time.

I'd come home, there'd be nobody here, I had this feeling I had lost something. I was very uncomfortable. Then there was no food ready. Sylvia said to me, "Listen, if you want to eat, you'd better do the shopping and cook. You have more time and I work regular hours."

Sid took over the shopping and cooking in 1974 and came to feel it produced a new and healthier kind of validation than using women as symbols of male power.

To me there's nothing more enjoyable than to cook something and make people happy when they eat it. In some way that's an experience of nurturing for me. Sylvia had a women's group and everyone in it had a marriage busted up; they were mad at men and I don't blame them. I invited them here and made all this delicious food, I nurtured them all, and it was a way I could be validated. I need that. I want to be validated.

Cooking at home, of course, is traditionally a woman's task in our society. It is also a sexual stereotype that has been broken down more often than most, but seldom for reasons like Sid's. It seemed important to me that he was finding validation as a man not only by doing a woman's task, but also by doing it to serve a group of women, which in our society is almost taboo for men.

Sid tried therapy for a short period and was glad he did, but he felt he owed the survival of his marriage, his improved relationship with his daughter, and his own greater happiness to his C-R group.

> The group became supportive of me, and I began to realize there were people who loved me and thought very highly of me, and that in some way I had earned that. That gave me a confidence in myself that I'd never had before. Behind all my blustering and the intellectual fireworks was a tremendous insecurity. I owed a debt. Not in a corny sense, but I felt that I wanted to help. I felt that I had given myself, with the help of other people, a second chance, and I wanted to help other people in the same way. And maybe because I had this old political indoctrination from the thirties, maybe that made me want to spread the word.

Sid put an ad in the newsletter of northern New Jersey NOW, offering help in forming men's C-R groups, and over four years he started thirteen groups with a total of 108 male members. He would attend one or two meetings, find a facilitator for each group, and then just step away from it.

Sid Miller does not think that consciousness-raising is a panacea. Few men in the groups that he helped start got the benefits he had found in his own group, or so he discovered when he tried to follow up in the late 1970s. The C-R groups did help some men take their first steps—away from their fear of other men, away from their oppression of women.

> I don't think anyone got hurt in a C-R group and it might have opened other possibilities for a number of these men. But you can't go to three C-R meetings where everybody's being impersonal or even where a lot of guys outwardly profess good feelings, and get up to say, "I feel this way." You've got to work for those things, you've got to share for those things. . . . When you grow up in a society and in a world that has taught you for your own survival to fear other men, and there is something to be afraid of, it's not just a made-up thing, and it's also taught you not to tell anybody this, you're afraid or you feel a failure if you tell that to another man. It's unrealistic to expect consciousness-raising to handle this problem. What the world needs is a culture that permits men to learn that the reality of life is that other men can be brothers to them.

However distant that culture may be, Sid made me feel, America is closer to it today than twenty years ago, and consciousness-raising is one of the things that helped bring us closer.

Sid Miller's C-R adventures led him to other experiences that made his life different. He went to Men and Masculinity conferences to meet other men concerned with the same issues—first a regional one, then a national one at State College, Pennsylvania (where the conference was held in a Holiday Inn when the university withdrew its sponsorship in fear of gay and political demonstrations). The national conference announcement included an invitation to bring original songs, poems, and stories to share at an open reading. The night before the meeting, Sidney wrote his first poem. He read it at the gathering. The men grew increasingly silent and attentive as he read, and when he finished, they burst into shouts and applause: a man, one of their own, had given form to his feelings and theirs, had put emotion into art in a way they didn't know a man like them could do. That poem, written to Sylvia, was about growing old and still wanting to live. Sid has also written about men and women, marriage, and things he knows and loves in American culture, things the men of the movement seldom admit they care about, like professional football and the jazz of Billie Holiday and Lester Young. He is now as active in the world of poetry readings as he is in the men's movement.

Sid Miller is a man whose experiences with both women's and men's movements have left him happier. Ever since I first met Phil Stein in 1977, he has seemed to me a fascinating example of a man who came the hard way to the men's movement and stayed with it for years despite wave after wave of troubles. When I met him he was a psychology instructor with training in biology and mathematics, a man going through an unpleasant divorce from his wife, Ellie, and trying to maintain joint custody of his nine-year-old son, Ben. About the early part of his marriage, Phil said:

> Our relationship had really been stereotypic. I was trained as a kid, I knew all my strengths, the West Point book of etiquette—rules for men were different and I knew them all. I had a job, she didn't have a job, therefore it was her job to take care of the kid—Ben was about a year old—and my job was to bring in the money.

But one day in 1970 Ellie joined a consciousness-raising group.

> I remember the day she came home from her second time at the C-R group. She was sitting on the couch, the same couch you're sitting on, but she was sitting like this [Phil lay back, only his neck and head up], all pissed energy, radiating power, and hostility. She was just getting in touch with all the rage.

Phil said that for Ellie the main point of rage at the start, and of her feminist analysis of marriage and society, was the question of who would take care of their son.[2] In those days, in their city in Middle America, nobody had heard of a man really sharing child care. Phil agreed, after much resistance, to take care of Ben one half-day per week, feeling it was a major sacrifice because he had research, teaching, and committee work to do. Ellie insisted that half a day was not enough. She had to drag Phil, and he had to drag himself, to a point where he could take care of Ben two half-days and then three half-days. When Ellie wanted him to take care of the child two full days, and do 50 percent of the housework, he felt he couldn't do it. He was working eighty hours a week, constructing every lecture at the beginning of his teaching career.

When Phil remembered these things seven years later, he was conscious of ironies that had been little consolation at the time. Ellie had had a hard time in childbirth and had been sick for the first weeks of Ben's life, so Phil had had to be the nurturing father much more than most men. And he came to the marriage with a full set of housekeeping skills from childhood chores, caring for an invalid mother, and living alone before he married Ellie. He taught her how to cook, "but it was like teaching somebody who really knows how to be an athlete how to play tennis. Ellie has a feeling for cooking that I never had."

Child care, housekeeping, and cooking were not the only points on which Phil's change of direction hinged. Ellie started talking about sexism on those points and went on to others. From the very first day, Phil recalled:

I believed in the justice of what she said. At first I could not deal with it in terms of the way my life had been structured, but I thought it was just. She had to drag me, true, but she was never dragging against a person who said, "What you're asking for is unfair." I was always saying it was fair, but.

At one point the dragging and the "but" turned into a crisis, triggered by a column in the local paper that offered advice to teenagers and the lovelorn.

One day they had run something really sexist. Ellie wrote them a protest letter and it was really obscene, all sorts of swear words in it, calling them "you shits." I said, "You can't send that." She said, "Oh yes I can." I said, "I can go to jail if you send that. This is a state where the husband is responsible for his wife's acts." I understood that I could take it and tear it up, but I also understood that she could get pen and paper and write a new one. She took me by the hand while I argued with her, sealed the envelope, walked me to the mailbox, and threw the envelope into the box. I could not handle that, that she would do something so offensive to me. I went to my C-R group and we talked about it. What came out was my realization that it was perfectly all right for me to agree with Ellie or disagree. I could write my own letter, but I had no business talking about what Ellie wrote. It fit. It was a way to think that clicked into place.

Later the Steins moved to California. Phil found a job flexible enough to let him organize two and a half days' worth of daytime hours to take care of Ben and fulfill Ellie's demand that he do half the child care, which by then he wanted to do for his and Ben's own sakes. The new university also agreed to let him do more teaching and less research, to allow him to give up the specialty he had come to dislike in his old job. Eventually he started studying masculine roles, giving talks on masculinity and forming men's groups.

I offered to be a speaker on consciousness-raising, women, masculinity. I got a call every few days. [This was in 1974.] A lot of people wanted to hear about men's liberation, but what they really wanted to hear was how fucked the women's movement was. So I'd ask if they had had a speaker from the women's movement before me. If they hadn't, they'd have to ask a woman to speak before I came.

Phil's conversion to feminism had little effect on Ellie's anger, however.

Other men are more aware than I am, less sexist than I am. But in terms of degree of change from where I began to where I finished, I've changed more than any man I know. And no matter how much I changed, I never got the strokes, I never got the goodies out of that, from her. Other people, yes, from her, never. That never changed. She was never able to do anything except dump anger on me. I never got any joy out of the relationship.

Despite this joylessness, Phil said, he spent years thinking he could not separate from Ellie because if he did, he would be interrupting her anger, and "I as a man have no right to interrupt the anger of a woman. Because she's oppressed." At first he felt that if he were indeed an oppressor, he was obliged to listen. But then he saw that he and Ellie both had feminist values that enabled, or compelled, them to see "the male scripting that was oppressive in the situation. But only one person had male scripting. Therefore I always lost, from the strict feminist point of view. At the end it would always be me that felt guilty. I began to say, 'I don't think that's right, I don't think it's always me who's doing something wrong.'"

He didn't want to separate at first because "we were the last feminist couple in our circle that was still together. I felt I owed it to the community to show them it could work." But Ellie's anger continued, and Phil finally decided "that I have no right to interrupt her anger, but I sure as hell don't have to put up with the kind of anger that she puts out. I'm entitled not to have to live through that stuff." Another reason he gave up, Phil said in our second interview in 1981, was that the anger and the marriage had become violent.

Ellie and I used to hit each other, but I never hit her first. She always hit me first. She hit me for a long time, and for a long time what I would do is hit her back. She used to threaten me with putting razor blades in my shoes, and I would check my shoes every day. . . . Toward the end, I suddenly realized I didn't have to hit her back, I didn't have to defend myself. When she hit me, I was just going to leave. I began doing that. And once, just a couple of weeks before the end, she hit me once while I was naked because she figured I wouldn't be able to leave. I walked right out of the house stark naked and walked around the yard for a while. It was evening, it was cold out. The last thing that Ellie ever did to me, I was getting in the car to drive away from the house, and she grabbed a shoe I was carrying and hit me with it.

Ellie's anger and her violence never led Phil to think feminism was wrong. He remained active in the pro-feminist wing of the men's movement. In particular, he involved himself in a local project to counsel men who batter women, usually their wives. One reason he became concerned with violence was undoubtedly his experience with Ellie. Another was his feeling that helping the victims of male violence was an obligation that grew out of his feminism. But shelters for battered women, he felt, were a Band-Aid: "Half the women go back to their husbands and get beaten up again. And most women don't get there, and even when they do, the man is still out there; he finds another woman and beats *her* up. The problem is the man's, not the woman's."

Phil had a third, even more powerful reason for getting involved with men who beat women:

I realized that I identified men as "the other," instead of identifying women as "the other" in the traditional way. When I talked about men, I talked about *them,* and when I talked about women I talked about *us.* The violence project was an attempt to say, "Men hit women. I don't like men who hit women. I want to work with men who hit women so I can start to accept those men as human beings and deal with their behavior as a separate issue. I want to start thinking of men as *us* again." That worked. That was very helpful. I do like the men I work with. I detest their violence, and I have kicked out men who continued to be violent, but I like the men, most of them. And now I'm beginning to identify with men.

In the four years between our first and second interviews, Phil not only started to counsel wife beaters, he also married again. And divorced again. He said that when he and Dee started dating, she insisted on paying her own way and doing half the driving, "all the standard feminist stuff." When they married, she paid a proportionate share of the rent and bought her own food. But she also borrowed money from Phil. "She'd give me the money," he recalled, "and that would be her feminist statement, and then she'd borrow the money back. We've kept track of the debt, but now she's going off with some other guy and she's not going to pay me back. And under California community property law, I'm going to wind up paying her two thousand dollars because I bought my car and paid it off during our marriage, and my retirement fund increased in equity. It galls me that she will walk away from our marriage with more money than I do." Phil also feels that Dee ripped him off by making his violence project the subject of her academic papers but denying him credit even as a junior collaborator. So Phil, although he disagrees with their psychology and their philosophy, has acquired some understanding of the men whose primary concern is not feminism but the injustice of the divorce laws.

Today Phil is in the difficult paradox of remaining pro-feminist while being angry with women because of his own experiences in marriage. He is also unhappy when his anger makes him sound as though he is putting down his wives, an intention he denies. Ellie told a psychiatrist during a legal battle over custody of Ben that she thought Phil was unhappy because she was succeeding in her career.

I don't know if she really believes that or if she was just saying it as a ploy. I didn't believe that and I still don't believe it. I'm pleased whenever she's successful, because every success that she has makes Ben's life a little easier. As far as my second wife is concerned, I encouraged her at every point to be successful. I need strength, I need competence. My mother worked hard and was successful. It doesn't bother me when a woman is successful.

I asked Phil if he saw a connection between his feminism and his choice of wives who made him angry. He replied:

I would phrase it differently. I chose women who were attractive and "strong." I mean strength of opinion, willingness to be assertive. My ideal is a woman who will be assertive and still take care of me, and I guess I haven't chosen well. I talk feminism, and I mean it. But what kind of feminist was it—and both my wives despite their differences were both feminists—who was very unhappy about the fact that I was "unsuccessful," teaching at a second-rate university that has no respect for my work on sex roles, without hope of promotion.

Shortly after our second interview, Phil Stein left his "unsuccessful" academic position and went to work for a computer software company at twice the salary. The last time I talked with him by phone, he had full custody of Ben and he still talked feminism, but the violence project had petered out because neither he nor anyone else had had sufficient energy to keep it going. Nor did Phil any longer have the interest or the energy for men's movement meetings, though he swore his ideology had not changed.

For Phil Stein, as for many men in the pro-feminist stream of the men's movement, ideology was a set of axioms about sex roles, with a couple of postulates about the imbalance of power. Barry Shapiro and Kenneth McCann* were exceptions to that kind of pattern. They saw that there was a political struggle involved, and they fought in it.

Barry was one of the many men on the student barricades in the 1960s— and one of the few who later found sexism a worthy enemy. He became a men's-movement activist partly out of flesh-and-blood feelings about himself, his ex-wife, their son, other women in his life. But he also moved partly out of a passion for justice that was as genuine as it was abstract. (He was surprised, but only a little, when I said he reminded me of Admiral Zumwalt, who had become a crusader for women in the Navy when his passion for justice and his passion for efficiency had synergized each other, as I describe in Chapter 4.)

Barry was one of the men who discovered that feminists regarded men on their side with suspicion, just as blacks had come to regard whites in the civil rights movement and as many working-class people had come to regard their middle-class "allies." When people asked their allies, when women asked men, "What's in it for you?" Barry found it "despicable because it had no margin for moral vision." Yet he believed that it *is* in men's own interest to combat sexism.

There are two angles. One is that men ought to be involved in the women's movement because it's the right thing to do. You morally have to do that. Most people reject that. Or ignore it. Second is that men are going to be involved in the struggle for women's rights because it's in men's best interests. To the first motivation, women say [here Barry's voice rose to a mimic shriek], "Out! I don't want you involved unless you show me it's in your interest." To the second claim, women say, "What! It's in your interest! I thought it was in my interest. You fuckers win all the time, no matter what we do, it's always in your interest. Heads you win, tails you win, everything you win. I don't want to be involved."

Barry thought that this double-edged rejection was at work when two different women's organizations turned down his request for small amounts of money to organize men in support of the Equal Rights Amendment. He was told that one nationally known woman leader said, "If he can't raise his own money, fuck him, what good is he." A state fund-raiser told him, "I'm not going to share my resources with you. You're competitive with me, you'll go to the same people I'm raising money from."

At first that kind of response infuriated Barry. Later he moved from anger and despair to exhaustion. He told me:

I don't feel like putting out for feminism anymore. I don't feel good about putting out for a group that constantly rebuffs me. Five years I've been working real hard, despite insults, despite indifference, despite no support. Men and a lot of women say, "Why work with them. Why take on the responsibility of transforming the world when the women involved in it seem to be fucking it up so badly. You don't have a chance to win anyhow." That set me on my heels. But I'm feeling as though I don't have to continue the struggle as if I had an obligation to be a martyr.

Barry later said he was relieved not to be in a day in, day out struggle with feminist separatists and other "antagonistic political people." But despite the moments of anger and exhaustion, he never stopped being an antisexist activist. Two years after giving up the "obligation to be a martyr," he was one of the people who launched the National Organization for Changing Men, which proclaimed itself pro-feminist. He was no longer exhausted because he had found paying work, in addition to his teaching in community colleges, as a management consultant on affirmative action and sexual harassment for local governments and corporations. Significantly, it was women who had seen him do training who prevailed on male officials to hire him for his first consultant work. Now he promotes his services as someone who can get his message across to other men because he is a male whose message comes across as sympathetic rather than accusatory.

So Barry is still involved in the effort to create a united front of men and women against sexism. "Men had something to gain from it," he said. "Women had something to gain from it, obviously. But the two not working together spelled disaster for the success of the movement."

Kenneth McCann saw the conflict between men and women in labor and community organizing (described in Chapter 6). He seemed important to me because his passage through the men's movement helped him escape conventional ideas (in the sense that even a movement dedicated to change is burdened by its own conventions) and shape new insights of his own, with enough philosophical or psychological force to change his attitudes and his behavior.

Kenneth is a Scot who came here at the end of the 1950s. After fifteen years of activity on the American Left, he became interested in the personal relationships that underlie class and power relationships—a dimension that few of his comrades explore systematically. He worked with Claude Steiner, the founder of radical therapy, who tried to combine Eric Beirne's transactional analysis with an understanding of the social-power relationships between couples and between men and women. Then Kenneth violated the principles of radical therapy by going to work in an institution—a mental hospital.

His work in the mental hospital led Kenneth to his two beliefs: that sexism is one of the main forces that drive people crazy, and that male violence is the fuel of sexism and of all politics. He derives the first from the idea that the infant hates being socialized into sex roles. "Most people find ways to succumb, to accept sex roles; those who can't, who refuse to let society destroy their vital drive to avoid sex roles, may go crazy." Kenneth's second belief grew out of his work with working-class men who were violent. He saw them as both victims and carriers of the insanity of sexism. There were plenty of them in the mental hospital. During periods classified as "psychomotor seizures," they terrorized the place, the more so because that hospital did not believe in drugging patients or putting them into straitjackets. But in between seizures, they were "charming people," relieved by being able to talk about their violence.

The way these men talked about their plight and their problems led Kenneth to see sexism not as a narrowly defined matter of men oppressing women, though that is one of its main results. He saw sexism primarily as the ordering of sex roles and gender power so that they interfere with men's and women's creativity, with property and the ability to produce, with the very ability to survive in nature. As a leftist, he blames this on the existing economic order. "To me," he said, "one of the things wrong with capitalism is that the owners not only own the means of production, they own the ability to imagine what can be produced." I objected that while capitalists may own or manufacture and sell us most of what we use to project our imaginations, they can't control the human mind and its ability to fantasize. But I had to admit that few of us develop much capacity to imagine. Kenneth attributed this to the determination of "the rulers" to absorb all the ability to imagine the future. I said this described the rulers of the Soviet Union even more than the rulers of the United States; he replied that the Left almost everywhere is patriarchal in its refusal to imagine a society that is open and free, a society that it labels "utopian."

Kenneth insisted that it is male violence that proscribes creativity and imagination, with a simple syllogism: "Creativity springs from senses and emotions. Violence is a product of sensory and emotional deprivation. And it's a male ethic to be sensorily deprived and emotionally immune." Later he added another deprivation that produces male violence: men's inability to take care of our own basic bodily needs—to feed ourselves, clothe ourselves, keep house. He had a clear vision of the significance of housework tasks so often dismissed as trivial. His insistence that men must learn to take care of themselves and nurture themselves led him to oppose the whole idea of couples as oppressive. He knew that humans need to pair by sexual and emotional definition, "but the social view is that we need to live in couples because the man is incompetent to take care of himself, because he's incapable of self-nurturing and needs a mate to be a nurturer." So he thought couples had become producers of male violence by encouraging the basic deprivations of the male.

In the mental hospital McCann did both fantasy work and body work with psychotics to deal with those deprivations. He said, "We were the only people I know of who got a ticket from the state hospital inspectors for indiscriminate hugging. It was wrapped in among the 365 other citations for a dirty lavatory here, a broken window there."

In his counseling practice, he does workshops in which men start by simulating emotions they are not used to expressing, like being sad and being hurt. The first response is usually, "What? Sit down and cry?" The participants can then talk about what's wrong with crying, what's the value of crying, and they usually go fairly directly to talk about the experience of brutality and its function as an expression of male supremacy. Kenneth's description rang much truer to me than most men's movement hugs and most C-R group talk about the value of tears, which usually omits the firsthand male experience of brutality.

PROFILES OF TWO NO-GUILT BELIEVERS

The wing of the men's movement that combines no-guilt and divorce-reform tendencies might seem to have more potential members than the pro-feminists, but many of the men in it feel like pioneers, lonely and brave. Lou Malespina,* for instance, was thirty-two when I interviewed him, a young man from an Italian working-class background who had been working for ten years as a clerk in the Boston financial district and had then reached a salary of $225 a week. He was and is single, which is unusual for a man of his background, but he has uncles who never married, so his family has not made a fuss. He said:

> From high school, I was always hung up about my image—was I macho enough, strong enough, competent enough, everything that young boys are taught to be. . . . I always felt somehow that there was something in me lacking. I wasn't into sports as much as other boys were. In parochial school I did play basketball, but I never scored any baskets. I still don't know beans about baseball. . . . I'm very into running now. . . . I always used to feel kind of embarrassed about it. I wear contact lenses anyway. I'm nearsighted. When I was a boy, I used to be the proverbial bookworm. I always felt kind of vulnerable, the focus was always on wiseacres, boys a little on the wild side. I guess it's kind of stuck in my mind. [By this time, Lou was mumbling so his words were difficult to transcribe.] I wanted to be more competent. I wanted to be myself more.

When he saw a newspaper article about Warren Farrell in 1975, Lou said, "My eyes lit up, I thought, wow, somebody's speaking out for men. Here was a man telling you you didn't have to be like John Wayne or James Bond." Lou went into and out of two men's center C-R groups and flirted with the politically active side of the pro-feminists before finding more congenial company in a no-guilt group, a chapter of Free Men. His group is more liberal than Haddad sounds, and Lou himself professes the belief that "women's liberation goes along with men's liberation. You can't have one without the other." He also believes that "feminists say all men oppress all women, that all men are the enemy. Which isn't true, it's stereotyping men in general." When I asked him about power in our society, Lou said, "There will always be an edge which men have over women. They're somewhat more aggressive. But a lot of assertive, aggressive women have encouraged themselves, have been encouraged, to be like the men; they're going against the grain of the traditional male."

The group is giving Lou more than these ideas, more than either his old friends or his psychotherapy have given him: support and a feeling of belonging.

I feel as though I have become part of something. I reach out to other men. Even women, because my group has women come to our meetings, mostly married, some single. We encourage women because we're trying to get women to see men's problems through men's eyes, not how women perceive men's problems. . . . We are going to have future workshops on men and their relationships to women.

I was struck when I heard that by the group's interest in problems I felt the pro-feminists neglected. I was struck even more by Lou's recognition that politics is personal. He said he is afraid of the way the Reagan administration and the conservatives in Congress reflect traditional stereotypes.

What I feel threatening is that someone will turn the clock back to traditional roles and there'll be no other way. What we're trying to do is give options, and all I see is diminishing choice. If a man wants to live a traditional role, say, like a couple of my friends, fine. But just give me the chance to—let's say, maybe if I want to be a househusband or do something that's not considered macho—not to be put down for being less than a man. That's what I'm asking. . . . Men shouldn't be typecast so they have to be a certain way all the time. That bothers the hell out of me. It makes me feel trapped. If I can't live up to that ideal, automatically I'm branded as a loser.

In his men's group Lou Malespina feels the possibility of being a winner without either oppressing or being heavily dependent on a woman. But he still feels that he is a member of a meager and courageous band.

So does Arnold Zimmer,* a member of a no-guilt C-R group in the San Francisco Bay area, whose testimony on men's anger I quoted earlier. He often feels like a member of a beleaguered minority because he thinks too many Americans—he doesn't say a majority—have adopted a "fish-eye view of our society where feminists and men who agree with them take all the bad points in society and say that's what men have done and take all the great things in society and say that's what women have done." I don't know anyone who talks like that, feminist or otherwise, and my experience of the world is so different from Arnold's that I had to restrain the impulse to interrupt him with arguments that would have prevented me from hearing what he had to say. In the end, I didn't like Arnold's weltanschauung, but I was impressed that he had one—a worldview that the men's movement helped him form, which combines intellectual perceptions and emotions of an almost religious intensity. Arnold believes that men suffer at least as much as women in our society and perhaps more. So do many other men in the no-guilt stream, but unlike them, Arnold is convinced that this is not only a matter of sex roles, but also of the dynamics of power in work and in love.

Arnold has worked for ten years in offices run and staffed largely by women; he feels many of them, especially his female bosses, have discriminated against him (see Chapter 6). He felt himself just as much the victim of female power when the woman he loved, whom he had seen five or six nights a week for two years, made two important decisions without consulting him: to have herself sterilized and to move into a cooperative building with two other women. She and Arnold broke up as a result. Such experiences have long been part of the human comedy, or tragedy, but the men's movement puts them in a new context. I asked Arnold if he felt he had gone through what feminists might call a classic woman's experience in being discriminated against at work and shut out of major decisions by someone he loved. He didn't see it that way.

I have thought about it, but not in those terms. I'm very resistant to labels. Since at least ten years ago, when feminists started labeling me as having certain characteristics because I'm a man. I really took issue with that and it has sort of snowballed until now I'm almost adamant about it. I don't consider myself as being in a feminine bag because I've gone through all these difficulties. I think that they are human difficulties. I don't think that men are immune to them at all.

Arnold considers himself a true egalitarian. "What we really want, and I hollered as loud as anyone else for it in the early sixties, was equality. I think we hollered too loud, what we got was a reversal, and discrimination is discrimination no matter who's doing it to whom." He opposed the Equal Rights Amendment at first "because I felt I would be losing rights by it. But after I analyzed it and really got to talking to people, I found out that it was as much for me, as much for men as for women. When you approach it that way a lot of guys I've seen turn around and support it also." He believes that the ERA would compel equal rights for men in traditionally female job fields like clerical work and social work. He thinks affirmative action can go only so far to correct historical discrimination. Otherwise, he says—and it's hard to tell how much he's being sarcastic and how much he might really mean it—

Men have been discriminated against in child custody, so let's have some affirmative action on that. Give men custody from now on in all cases until everything is balanced again. If we apply the concept of affirmative action to the draft, our country is two hundred years old, and up to now only men have been drafted, so for the next two hundred years, only women would be drafted, right?

Arnold knows that only the tiniest minority would agree that affirmative action is that bad, but he says that a growing number of men share his basic feelings. He and a friend from his C-R group had to spin off a second group to accommodate all the men who wanted to join; the second group includes at least one other man who thinks the women at his workplace (a photographic agency) discriminate against him, and several single men who charge that their social life is in upheaval because women demand new rules and then refuse to play by them.

PROFILE OF A DIVORCE REFORMER

Jim Riley* became active in the National Congress for Men in the hope that other men might be able to profit from his experience. In his case, unlike Phil Stein's, the divorce came before the anger or the men's movement. Jim was an Irish boy from upstate New York who worked his way through college and medical school and became a small-town pediatrician. He married an Italian girl whom he described as old-fashioned, meaning that she stayed at home raising their two children and did not work for pay. Yet when he reviewed the history of their marriage, he spoke of power struggles in the last few years— an idea that an old-fashioned consciousness is reluctant to raise. She would speak her mind at length and not listen to his side at all. "When she was upset, there was no talking to her," he said, "only listening. . . . She was an extremely domineering person. She knew always what was best for you." Yet in the last few months of their ten years together, "My wife was obviously getting discouraged, feeling like a lot of women feel, like a second-class citizen. I got all the plaudits and she got nothing."

She started talking about a separation, and he listened and tried to speak his mind. He was still astonished when he came home from work at the hospital one day and found no wife, no children, no car, no checkbook, no bankbook. "I never so much as looked at another woman," he recounted. "I don't drink, I'm not a drug addict, I'm not a homosexual. Our sex life varied from average to good." He had called her a loud-mouthed bitch during a quarrel, but he felt he deserved points for never using a sexual obscenity. And he was shocked that she took the children because he felt that his daughter, nine at the time of the split, was closer to him than to her mother.

In the months that followed, Jim Riley learned how the adversary system of divorce works. In the end he had to pay his ex-wife twelve thousand dollars a year in child support when he was grossing forty thousand and netting twenty-seven thousand after taxes and office expenses. He also had his children with him 135 days a year. He knew that was unusual when the mother is awarded sole custody, but he felt injured that he was paying her even for the time the children were with him and he was buying their food and clothes. And his right to be the loving father to his children had become so important to him that he went through agonies every time there was a new legal action, every time there was a new psychiatric examination to see where the children would be better off.

Even if Jim's story of the marriage and divorce is discounted by 50 percent and his ex-wife's version given equal weight, the changes in his consciousness seem important. I met him at the Houston meeting of the National Congress for Men. He told me that in the bus from the airport to the hotel another man who was not attending the Congress had heard his story and said, "I'm amazed. You have this potential, but you're not living. If I were you I'd be screwing the belly button off all sorts of women. Why don't you go where there's life and make a hundred thousand dollars a year? Why don't you give up what has happened to you, stop being upset by injustice?" But giving up injustice would mean giving up the children, and that was impossible for Jim. In any case, Jim said, he was not interested in the *"Playboy* stereotype of women and wine racks." Instead, he was working on the knowledge that "statistics are starting to show that the average divorced man is a devastated being whose sexuality has been all screwed up, as mine certainly has been, whose whole outlook is not appreciated. He's a man who loses his home, his family, his emotional stability—and money, thousands of dollars."

Many of the divorce-reform men at the Houston meeting would have echoed his words and gone off complaining about their ex-wives in particular and women in general. Jim had done a little of that and gone beyond it. He had found a magazine called *Single Dad's Lifestyle,* published in Scottsdale, Arizona, by Bob Hirschfeld. It deals much more with divorce and custody problems than with what single fathers actually do with their children, but eventually it put Jim Riley on a list of resource people, and father's rights groups began to ask him to lecture on noncustodial parenthood. This repeated exposure to the men's movement gave him a new sympathy to the women's movement. As he put it, "I am disliking it less and less with every passing month. I am violently antiabortion. But that aside, on sex stereotypes I think they're right."

I asked Jim if he had reached this position by seeing himself in the position of a mother. He replied:

When I'm home with my children, cooking, cleaning up, washing their clothes—I feel like a human being when I'm fathering [he quickly corrected himself and said], when I'm parenting. The fact that I have not been recognized as a better parent than my wife, which I clearly am, and I have not been so recognized because of sex stereotyping, has raised my consciousness to the fact that women as well as men have been sex-stereotyped to a crippling extent. It's come to me slowly. I didn't read ERA literature, women's literature. It has to come from inside. Then I realized these broads over there that I've been thinking ill of are really saying some things that I agree with. Fathers for Equal Rights in my state *don't* say women are all shits, men should have sole custody. We say fairness should prevail, we should have joint custody, women as well as men deserve to parent and love their children. We're pro-ERA, we want to move forward with them and not against them. . . . I have a feeling anti-my-wife, anti-sex stereotypes. I do not have an antiwoman, anti-mother feeling. Remember, I'm a pediatrician, I see hundreds of women a week in my office, and they're all mothers.

Jim Riley also makes a point of encouraging fathers to be the parents who bring their children to the pediatrician, or to come in with their wives. It seemed natural to me that he believed Houston "should not be a session for us to pour out our griefs, to bitch bitch bitch. It's a session to say, Where are the solutions?"

There are no easy solutions, and the determination of a few men to look for them does not lessen the odds against immediate or dramatic change in our society, built on that contradiction of love for a class enemy. But the testimony of men like Jim Riley shows that more and more mainstream men are seeing the connection between the political and the personal, between the ways men and women relate to each other in public and in private. More and more are sensing injustice to women as a result of feeling injustice against themselves. Their anger and fear are leading them to forms of admiration for and identification with women. The thirst for change that these men feel is as compelling as the political analyses and the statistics that remind us, correctly, how hard it is to change our society, our economy and our culture.

Part Five
CONTEXT AND CONCLUSIONS

Chapter 14
THE CULTURE GAP

Victor Grant is a lady-killer. Not metaphorically, literally. His wife, Samantha, leaves him after raising her consciousness in a women's rap group, and he murders three feminists whom he considers responsible for her departure and for threatening the male order in general. He kills one by stuffing fruit, most memorably testicle-shaped plums, down her throat; he stabs the second at the end of an incident in which she tries to bite off his penis; and the third, a woman whom he recognizes as his equal, impales herself on his knife while he is trying to talk her into stopping their battle. He regrets this last death.

Victor justifies his behavior by talking about the working man who has no money, no power, no status, only his masculine pride "to maintain the boundaries of his self against any incursion that would diminish him. Fine. And he has a life-and-death need to reconstitute himself by an act of revenge against whatever offense may chip away at him." Victor identifies himself with this archetypal worker by saying, "Everybody is a working man in relation to the society around him and the cosmos around it. Everybody has a motive for revenge by virtue of the mere fact that he is somebody."

In the end he mellows a bit, digests some of his hostility, and begins to show some signs of respect for women. Samantha returns to him and he admits that he himself gave her cause to leave him, not the women he murdered. She treats Victor as a sex object and he finds the fact, unlike the fantasy, demoralizing. She writes a column "for women" in the small town to which they move and prepares to run for town supervisor. One can imagine two faint feminist cheers, or more likely, two faint male cheers for feminism. But Samantha also gets pregnant, becomes expert in "domestic crafts," and seems to join in a female bond that mirrors the traditional male bond. Those cheers seem to echo on a patriarchal playing field. Is it Victor's consciousness that has been raised, or only the nature of his revenge?

I never expected to meet a man who expressed as clearly as Victor did, in word and act, the hostility I had found in so many men about changes in the dynamic of power between men and women. Fortunately I didn't meet him in real life. Victor Grant is the protagonist of a novel by George Stade, published in 1979, called *Confessions of a Lady-Killer.*[1] Stade is a professor of

English at Columbia University, a man with a wife and four daughters. He says in a recent essay, "One of the many good things about literature is that it stimulates you to do in your imagination what for good reasons you will not allow yourself to do in the flesh."[2]

Victor, in Stade's imagination and the reader's, is a fierce, sometimes funny, often grotesque portrayal of masculine anger against women after ten years of the contemporary women's movement. He is thus a prime example of another sphere in which men and women struggle with changes in the relations between men and women. It is not only at work and at home that we act and react, positively and negatively. We also show how we feel in literature, theater, films, the media, advertising, and all the other realms that constitute our culture.

We have wrestled with the combination of love and war between men and women in plays and poems and stories since culture began. *Medea, Antigone,* and *Lysistrata, As You Like It, Macbeth,* and *The Duchess of Malfi* are all examples of classics by men that deal with women who challenge male authority.

Men haven't written so much or so well about such challenges in the past twenty years, however—years when the challenges proliferated and women produced a torrent of stories, novels, poems, and plays about their condition and their revolution. Our failure to produce more is revealing. When we ignore these changes, it's usually another example of male denial of the female claim to power, another denial that testifies to the importance of what is being ignored.

Not every failure to be explicit is denial, of course. Many artists work on political matters without seeming to address them. Men who work in words and images often deal with the issues between men and women, no matter how far such subjects may be from our conscious design. We can't escape them because women have made so many changes in American culture over the past two decades, taking some of what used to be a male power, the power to name and define. These changes often rewind men's as well as women's concepts and vocabulary around feminist armatures, or impel us to rebel against sex-role stereotypes even when we can't see the women or their revolution.

In art as in life, when we do deal explicitly with women's claim to independence and equality, we show little support and less association. We seldom even show a determination to struggle with the basic contradiction, because we seldom recognize that the person we love is someone from the enemy class unless she opens our eyes, painfully. The few works in which we face the issues reveal the same feelings that I found in my interviews, with anger, fear, anxiety, envy, shame, and guilt again outweighing relief, pride, admiration, identification, and pleasure.

That observation leads to two important judgments. First, negative feelings and behavior are genuine male responses to female challenge. They do not always brand an author as misogynist, a word some feminist critics are too quick to use (though I think it does fit authors like the Stade who wrote *Confessions of a Lady-Killer*). They may be signs of struggle that will lead some readers (and perhaps even the author) to acceptance or support.

Second, our positive emotions often produce works that seem to dilute or render safe ideas that once had radical energy, as though the male-run establishment were coopting the women's revolution. This is particularly likely if the works are commercially successful, like such recent films as *Tootsie* and *Tightrope*. I'm often sorry when one of the radical notions I like is softened in this way, but I also think it brings true change a small step closer; incorporating revolutionary ideas into the established system is probably the only way to bring about meaningful change in this society.

FICTION

Negative feelings took root in the novel in the nineteenth century in America, in the works of the great male writers whose heroes flee or fight against "civilization" and its threat to feminize them (though I don't think they ever use a word like "feminize").[3] Among the writers whose heroes run away are James Fenimore Cooper in all his works, Herman Melville in *Moby Dick*, Edgar Allan Poe in *The Narrative of Arthur Gordon Pym*, Mark Twain in *Huckleberry Finn*, Stephen Crane in *The Red Badge of Courage*.[4] Nathaniel Hawthorne's heroes do not leave home in the same sense as the others', and he creates major female characters as the others do not, but in his novels, Hawthorne rebels as much as or more than the others against dominating or assertive women.

The important male writers of the twentieth century, Faulkner, Hemingway, Mailer, Bellow, sometimes sound the same theme. Some (not all) of their men, too, run from their women, or attack them, or—a contemporary innovation—kill them. So do some heroes of popular fiction, no longer so broadly opposed to high culture as a century ago. The early Travis McGee starts traveling whenever feminizing civilization grabs hold too firmly. Sam Spade and Mike Hammer fight rather than flee villains whose evil is the greater because they are women—women the men also love, or at least make love to. Spade jails and Hammer kills women who depart from a cultural norm, which marks them as "independent" in some senses. These popular heroes, of course, wouldn't be caught dead in a novel that explicitly addresses women's demands. George Stade creates Victor Grant from the same gene pool as the private eyes, but makes him an intellectual and plunges him into a world full of women who demand equality. Victor catches them dead, without hesitating. His hostility is more intense and more explicitly articulated than Spade's or Hammer's.

A few other male writers, whose characters show more anxiety than anger or fear, acknowledge that a world exists in which women demand equality but do not really cross its boundaries. Philip Roth seems to many feminists a writer who denies this world much more than he recognizes it, and it's true that these issues are not his main concern, but he knows the world is there. The novel in which he deals most directly with the question of power between men and women, *My Life as a Man,* is preliberation: the hero is a novelist whose two wives vary from the passive to the pathological, showing strength only in the ability to survive and in rage. He dominates them in different ways. Both free him through death, the fictional Lydia by killing herself, the "real" Maureen by dying in a car accident after surviving a beating he gives her. Peter Tarnopol in *My Life* shows an abundance of anger and fear, but not because his women claim independence and equality, only because they have made him commit himself to them.

Tarnopol is like almost all Roth's men: they are so concerned with themselves that they can hardly treat a woman as an equal. Nonetheless, several of his heroes encounter women who assert a claim to respect and respond with anxiety. Even Alex Portnoy, that obsessive womanizer, confronts such a woman in Mary Jane Reed, the Monkey who seems at first glance like nothing more than a prime victim. He abandons her (quite literally, as she threatens suicide on the balcony of an Athens hotel) because he is so completely unable to fulfill her demand, but Roth has her make it very clearly. Nathan Zuckerman in *The Anatomy Lesson* meets women who take sexual initiatives, who proclaim their independence of him and other men, who make careers that enable them to reject male imperatives, emotional, economic, or intellectual. Presenting himself as a pornographer, he tells Ricky, the chauffeur who drives him around Chicago, that she won't work for him "because you are a God damn feminist." The key to her long reply is, "No, I don't find you unacceptable because I'm a God damn feminist. It's because I'm a human being."[5] Zuckerman comes back with a reply that is almost a parody of Herb Goldberg, about the *power* (Roth's italics) over men held by the women in the porn films that he is only pretending to make. Neither Zuckerman nor Roth ever resolves the issue because it's not central to a novel about a writer trying to "unchain himself from a future as a man apart and escape the corpus that was his," but both author and hero are certainly aware that there is a world in which the issue lives.

C. D. B. Bryan, much less of a novelist than Roth, gets a bit closer to the world in which women claim equality in *Beautiful Women; Ugly Scenes.*[6] This is a story of a man in mid-life crisis as his marriage falls apart in the 1970s. The nameless narrator/hero is curiously passive, the glad receiver of many women's sexual advances and the sad object of their social decisions and emotional brutality. In the latter cases he resembles some of Sinclair Lewis's heroes, and he can hardly be called a product of feminism, but overall, it's impossible to imagine him in a novel of the twenties or the forties. One major reason for the collapse of his marriage is his wife's anger at being left to do all the housework, cooking, and coping with two adolescent children. Crises of housekeeping and family relations also trigger conversations in which other men say, "Any man with even the minimum degree of sensitivity realizes the essential validity of women's rights," and "The women's movement has already had enormous impact on men's consciousness." Housework and child care can be matters of major passions and moral choice, but neither Bryan nor his hero ever lifts them out of the trivial. The narrator and his new love eventually achieve something close to an egalitarian relationship, but none of the women achieve true independence of men, emotional or economic. Bryan shows no visceral appreciation of what really happens in this world. It's as though he were describing a country he had heard much about but never actually seen.

Leonard Michaels moves a step closer to this country in *The Men's Club,* but doesn't actually set foot in it.[7] This novel tells the story of seven men who decide to form a club as a defense against a world in which, as another nameless narrator says, it is women who talk about "anger, identity, politics, rights, wrongs. I envied them. It seemed attractive to be deprived in our society. Deprivation gives you something to fight for, it makes you morally superior, it makes you serious. What was left for men these days? They already had everything. Did they need clubs?" At their first and perhaps only meeting, the men show a hunger for friendship that we seldom expressed so clearly before we grew envious of women's friendships, which we saw in a new light as a result of the women's movement.

They decide to tell the stories of their lives, but the stories they tell are all about women. They live through women, in single state and marriage and adultery, in anger, anxiety, and the rest, with little relief or identification or pleasure other than the sexual. One man who boasts of his open marriage tells of the one time he feels jealous: he and his wife trade partners with another couple, and he hears her "moaning with love." He loses his erection with his swap mate and goes outdoors; his wife comes out to ask what's wrong, he hits her, she starts crying, his erection comes back, she hits him, and they make love. Many of the men's adventures involve women and food, in a perverse array of nurture metaphors. One, a basketball player turned university official, picks up a woman who notices how much he is buying in a supermarket, goes home to bed with her, leaves, and then realizes he doesn't know her name or address or phone number, so he can't find her again. Another, a doctor, drops a woman when she takes a bite of his rich dessert at a gourmet dinner, literally never sees her again, and still mourns for her ten years later. The seven collectively "rape" the host's refrigerator of the elaborate food his wife has prepared for a women's meeting the next day. She comes home close to dawn while the men are still there, sees the mess, and hits her husband on the head with an iron pot. The men leave their new friend to his bleeding marriage and drive off to breakfast together. This is not a story of men who leap onto a field of change and take joy in the battle, but of men who fail to deal effectively with an enemy they have identified in a war they know damn well is out there.

John Updike goes further and actually enters a world of independent females in *The Witches of Eastwick.*[8] He told an interviewer that his novel and witchcraft "are both about female power, a power that patriarchal societies have denied while they try to retain the 'wonderful male power' of killing people."[9] Yet in Updike's fantasy world, women become witches only as their marriages end, lose their magic powers as soon as they have used them to capture new husbands, and employ those powers mostly to hurt or kill other women, primarily to punish them for mistreating or even acquiring husbands whom one witch or another also loves. *Eastwick* would be a fascinating example of male fear of women, except that Updike seems to like and enjoy his three witches and to have such a good time telling their story. The book is a tour de force in which a male author actually creates three-dimensional female characters—a rare achievement (as it is for a woman writer to create three-dimensional men), even if female critics object that he is not accurate in every detail, like how it feels for a woman to pee. There are men in the book as the women's husbands and lovers and colleagues, but the only independent male character is Darryl van Horne, who no matter what his human traits is clearly the devil of the witches' sabbats, down to his desire to have his ass kissed and the icy coldness of his semen. This devil Darryl has a more highly raised consciousness than any man in the Roth, Bryan, and Michaels books. He envies a woman's ability to make a baby and then make milk to feed it, he tells the three witch divorcées that the whole European witchcraft scare started as an attempt by the new class of male doctors to take childbirth out of the hands of midwives, and he talks about his love for women. In the end, however, he runs off with a young man, raising the devil in a way the witches did not foresee and opening Updike to the interpretation that he is declaring the futility of heterosexual love and war in a way he may not have intended.

A few other male writers, of varying levels of skill and reputation, explore the world of changing relations between men and women more deeply than Updike. Alan Saperstein's first novel tells the story of a man who comes home to find that his wife has killed herself and their two sons to escape from the prison of sex-role stereotypes.[10] His chief emotion is guilt. He enters a fantasy dialogue with his dead seven year old: "The truth is that Mommy hated being a mother. The truth is I did not know how to be a father . . . She did not like the time and space and energy it took. She resented having to spend her days and nights with you . . . As for me . . . The whole time, in seven years, I never even gave you a bath." *Mom Kills Kids and Self* includes several encounters between men and women in which the narrator is discomfited by his own sex's ability to dominate. His one significant extramarital affair is with a business colleague who takes the sexual initiative in a way that astonishes him, but once in bed, she too seems to shrink and grow weak, to act like a baby and tremble like a virgin. He thinks about these things while trying to deal with his catastrophe; in the end he goes crazy and tries to convince the police that he killed his wife and sons, taking all the blame on himself, though the police know that he was at his office when the three died and could not have done it. The book combines real emotion and hype in a way that fits the "Me Decade" and its media consciousness.

Two other novels of the seventies attracted more attention than Saperstein's. They rode the flood tide of public consciousness of women's demands for change. Indeed, they accepted one kind of change: their authors didn't voice a woman's view but made their heroes claim a woman's role, the role of mother. One was Avery Corman's *Kramer versus Kramer*, the other was Robert Miner's *Mother's Day*. [11] Each tells the story of a man who takes over the care of his small children when his wife leaves "to be her own person," and who then is battered by the cumulative storms of work, money needs, housekeeping and cooking, day care, their own daily child care in sickness and in health, their children's interference with their sparse sex lives. *Kramer* was a tearjerker both as book and as movie; I saw it with my younger son, then twenty-one years old compared to Billy Kramer's four, and I still wept. I felt good, as many men and women did, about Ted Kramer and his struggle with the problems of being a middle-class father, and I was glad when his wife, after making a bid to regain custody of Billy, decided she couldn't take the boy from his loving father. I thought some feminists were unfair when they complained that this was one more case of a man's outdoing a woman in her own function and putting her down in the process; hadn't they celebrated the reversal of tradition when women left both husbands and children to learn how to be independent? But I never felt Ted Kramer's passion in my guts the way I did Matthew Vole's.

Matthew is the hero of *Mother's Day*. He discovers that being a mother can drive you mad, that mothers not only love their children with fine and beautiful passions, they also hate them with broad and ugly passions. He learns, and tells, what it feels like to have those winds of work and child care batter endlessly, tirelessly, on his head, belly, groin, and skin. The accumulation is more than most real-life mothers or single fathers or Ted Kramers have to bear; the kids are more obnoxious, Matt more violent, the house more slovenly than the norms we fix in our heads to preserve our own sanity. Matt is crazier than we are. He does things we don't want to accept. When Keturah, his infant daughter, sleeping in his bed because she is quieter that way, gropes for the nipple that in Matthew is only "perfunctory," he gives her his penis to suck for a few seconds—until he starts to stiffen and pulls her to his chest, "suddenly protective, as if someone had meant her harm." He fantasizes teenagers castrating his two-and-a-half-year-old son, Thomas, when his burdens force him to let the boy go into a public toilet by himself. He fantasizes both children's deaths. He really does abuse them once or twice, and comes close to drowning Thomas.

I found myself accepting Matt's unacceptable "secrets," not despite but because of my exasperation at his inability to use some common sense. It makes him real. So does his obsession with food and shit and clothes, an obsession he shares with real-life fathers much less crazy than he is. So does the humor with which Miner makes Matt tell about his small calamities. So do his moments of grace. Some are simply times when his love for his children overcomes the tides of anger. Some are stages of his own growth to adulthood.

Some moments of grace are part of the effect that Matthew's role reversal has on his sexuality. He finds himself having "lesbian alliances with some women. This is no androgyne surrender, understand, no shift to the platonic. More a kind of license, an abandon. A thaw . . . In the way men often find themselves attracted to the tomboy, . . . certain child-bearing women are attracted to me, a mother." The change is not only lesbian, it is incestuous, as when Matthew winds up in bed with Joanne, his best friend's girl, while the three adults and Matt's two children are sharing a New York apartment: "For Joanne, I began to discover, such sisterly intimacy with a man urged her into sexual explorations she might never have tried—confident, I guess, that I wouldn't use her as a man might. For me, Joanne's increasing physical abandonment led me deeper into emotional intimacies I'd never known with anyone, man or woman. Both of us arose from such encounters giddy with possibility but confused and scared at our new vulnerability." This seems to me to say more about some of the ways we modify gender than mountains of pseudoscience or ideology.

Mother's Day has a full share of faults. None of the characters comes to life except Matthew. It's impossible to decide whether the ending, in which Matt lets his ex-wife and her new husband take the children, is adult recognition of the need for two parents or a cop-out. But the novel always conveys its emotions directly, without falsification or insulation. It's a powerful picture of a man in struggle with a kind of equality with women that most of us seldom see, much less portray.

Miner drew attention with *Mother's Day*, but the book didn't sell. John Irving has written two bestsellers about men who struggle with feminist issues that go beyond the domestic horizon. He is an "old-fashioned storyteller" who writes fast-paced novels with fat, contrived, and improbable plots, thin characters possessed of more sentimentality than emotion, and a sort of fake Dickensian flavor. These traits explain his popularity but make it hard to take his work seriously as literature. Still, *The World According to Garp* deals seriously with rape, and *The Cider House Rules* with abortion.[12]

Garp is the story of a writer's life, but it tells more than incidentally of three rapes and the way the rapists are punished. In the first, two men rape a child named Ellen James and cut her tongue out so she can't identify them, but she describes them in writing, they are convicted, and murdered in jail. In the second, the rapist only gets his teeth knocked out. In the third, which takes place in a novel that Garp writes within the novel, the woman kills the rapist while he is in the act; Ellen James reads the novel eight times because this book by a man is the best book she has ever found about rape.

Garp's mother, Jenny, is a feminist heroine who gets a job, lives alone, and has a baby without sharing her life with a man—in the 1940s, when it isn't fashionable. She is murdered at a 1970s political rally by a traditional man, the New England version of a good ole boy. Garp's wife, Helen, is his intellectual superior, a woman able to judge his writing, a person of high self-esteem, his equal even in adultery. Garp himself is the child raiser in the family, active, overprotective, a cook who bakes bread and has a stockpot always simmering on the stove. His mother's and his best friend is Roberta Muldoon, a professional football wide receiver who undergoes a sex-change operation and becomes a woman. *Garp* seems to me to show many kinds of equality and many changes in the dynamics of power between men and women, right down to the satire on the women's movement that made many feminists dislike it: the Ellen James Society of women who have their own tongues removed to show their solidarity with the rape victim, women whom Ellen James herself comes to despise as much as Garp does.

The Cider House Rules tells the story of two men. Wilbur Larch is a doctor who does abortions at a Maine orphanage over several generations from 1890 to 1950, when abortions are illegal. He does this because he thinks a woman has a right to choose, even if the choice is no more than orphan (the child she bears and gives up) or abortion. Homer Wells is one of the orphans, who never finds an adoptive home and who Larch hopes will succeed him as the giver of choice. Homer too believes women must be able to choose, but he comes to feel that the fetus has a soul, so abortion is taking life and he does not choose to do it. In the end he finds himself forced to do an abortion to save the young woman his son loves from bearing the baby her own father has fathered on her. (She murders her father, who contrives while he is dying to make it look like suicide.) He then decides to go back and take over when Larch dies, because he does not want to deny women their right to choice. Homer also works as an equal in a crew of women at the apple orchard where half the action takes place, and like Garp is a natural father who loves babies and loves to take care of them.

There are two important female characters, neither of them truly independent in her soul. Melony embodies anger, fueled by her hatred of the mother who abandoned her to the orphanage and by her largely frustrated love for Homer; eventually she takes another woman as her lover. Candy is a superwoman in the making, beautiful and intelligent, though her career is limited to running the family apple orchard. She embodies love; her conscious choice is not to choose between the two men she loves—Homer, who loves her and whose child she bears, and his best friend, Wally Worthington, whom she knew first and whom she marries when he comes back paralyzed from World War II.

Critics, some feminist and some very traditional male, condemn Irving on the assumption that he chooses such subjects as rape and abortion because they are "sexy" or "controversial" or media favorites—in other words, because they are almost guaranteed to sell. Perhaps he does, though if the critics are right it's strange that other male writers don't make the same choice. But *The Cider House Rules* is still important, precisely because it's a book by a man that shows some of the truths and passions on both sides of the abortion issue. It may be a caricature of a novel, but it makes plain that a woman left to have an illegal abortion by herself feels like a victim of a man and of society, and it declares in so many words that women must be able to choose. John Irving may choose subjects because they sell, but he is also and unquestionably a male writer who chooses to spin novels out of matters that society and women both label "women's issues."

Two other men have written novels about the archetype of female challenge to male authority—an army of women. The very concept gives a fevered vision of the idea that the sexes are class enemies; it almost has to be done as satirical fantasy because the idea that warriors are male is so deepseated in our culture. The authors have indeed portrayed female armies with a large dose of such fantasy, one negatively and one sympathetically. In Thomas Berger's *Regiment of Women,* women rule through military force, and the dictatorship is as onerous as any male tyranny known in history. In Lawrence Sanders's *The Passion of Molly T.,* American women form an urban guerrilla vigilante force, the Women's Defense Corps—who win public support from both sexes and eventually see their leader elected vice president. The novel was published just after Geraldine Ferraro won the 1984 Democratic nomination; Sanders may have hoped to capitalize on events, but his picture of militant women is supportive.[13]

Few other men have chosen to write creatively about women's issues. Many novelists who broke both literary and political convention as they shaped the tastes of the past twenty years hardly ever dealt with these questions, though they were writing throughout a period when the issues were inescapable in daily life and produced books that have a vision of society with breadth and depth. I am thinking of men like Kurt Vonnegut, Thomas Pynchon, Donald Barthelme, and John Barth. Ken Kesey did make a powerful woman the evil figure in *One Flew Over the Cuckoo's Nest,* but he was looking at a different issue and did not deal directly with women's claim to legitimate power.

Younger authors like Frederick Barthelme and Raymond Carver have none of the political consciousness of their predecessors. They write about relationships between people who lead lives without meaning in places without meaning, with no true connection with, and no broad perception of, culture, power, society, or history. I'd like to believe that's why they tend to ignore the questions of women's independence and equality. But then how explain the identical failure of the earlier writers?[14] Frederick Barthelme does create impassive male characters who frequently must deal with assertive, energetic, even manic women. They respond with a very low level of anxiety. On the rare occasion when someone confronts them with a specific issue, they have absolutely no idea what to do except retreat into their loneliness. Other young writers do connect, of course, like Robert Ward, whose *Red Baker* tells the story of an unemployed steelworker. One of the hero's agonies is that when he's laid off his wife makes more money than he does, an increasingly frequent element in real-life changes between men and women.

A writer who never turns his back on the issues between the sexes is one of our oldest—Isaac Bashevis Singer. Many of his women, consumed by sexual desire that makes them subservient to men, or willing accomplices of male rule in *stetl* and urban Jewish quarter, will never be feminist heroines. Yentl, the woman yeshiva student, however, in the novel of the same name, struggles with men and society to achieve her own goals, as do some of Singer's other female characters. His men are not oblivious. The narrator in one of Singer's latest stories, "A Telephone Call on Yom Kippur," says, "I'm not an anti-feminist. All I can say about women is that they are neither better nor worse than men." A man from a long tradition of male dominance in an oppressed society could hardly bear clearer witness to sexual equality.

POETRY

That makes ten novelists who have either skirted the subject of changes between the sexes or made it the center of some of their work. I know there are more, but whatever the total, it's still a small number. It's just as hard to find poets and even harder to find playwrights concerned with these changes in the past twenty years. This seems strange and sad in a tradition that goes back in the theater to Shakespeare, Webster, Ford, Congreve, Wycherly, and Sheridan, in poetry to Chaucer, Crashaw, and Pope, all of whom wrote about women of power, some with hatred or disdain but some with surprising sympathy. There are fewer names in this tradition in the nineteenth century; perhaps we started turning our backs on the problem then. But there are Byron, Hardy, the Wagner who created Brunnhilde and Isolde (going outside the English language, but his operas were certainly known in England and America), and Shaw. There are poems and plays with weak or tormented male heroes, certainly part of changes in the sexual power equation—in Poe and Strindberg, for example.

In talking about poets in this context, I'm forced to say nothing about rhythm, rhyme, and metaphor, the things that count most in poetry, and to concentrate on content—the poet's choice of word and image to show he sees a woman as an equal or a person of strength and independence, to show his own vulnerability, to make the reader see some connection between man and woman and the world or love between class enemies. I hope Erato and the other muses of poetry, all female, will forgive me.

Of the great twentieth-century male poets, the two whose verse sings most to me about men and women are William Butler Yeats and William Carlos Williams. Yeats was traditional about love but celebrated the power of women in scores of poems. I love those in which Crazy Jane defies the Bishop and cherishes rather than regrets the memory of Jack the Journeyman. I love the spirit of the man who could write, in "No Second Troy":

> What could have made her peaceful with a mind
> That nobleness made simple as a fire,
> With beauty like a tightened bow, a kind
> That is not natural in an age like this,
> Being high and solitary and most stern?
> Why, what could she have done, being what
>   she is?
> Was there another Troy for her to burn?[15]

Williams was a more modern spirit than Yeats, yet also traditional in many aspects of his view of women. Sometimes he addressed the subject directly, as in "Chanson" and "The Monstrous Marriage"; sometimes he simply showed something that can be called feminine in his seemingly masculine poetry. He anticipated the contemporary version of the theme of enemies in love in many poems, including these lines from "The Ivy Crown":

> The business of love is cruelty which,
>   by our wills,
>   we transform
>   to live together.[16]

John Crowe Ransom, of the same generation as Williams, was a poet of old familiar scenes, but I think he anticipated contemporary male feelings even more explicitly than the poet of modern cities. Ransom wrote many poems showing respect for the intellect and power of women, though he emphasized their beauty and spirit as might be expected of such a traditional gentleman and scholar. "Eclogue" is a dialogue between two lovers who are emphatically equals. "Judith of Bethulia" voices both awe and fear of female power. "The First Travels of Max" shows a boy's encounter with a sexual witch. "To the Scholars of Harvard," the 1939 Phi Beta Kappa poem, takes Sarah Pierrepont as seriously as Jonathan Edwards.[17]

Robert Lowell was celebrated more for other things, but he was the only important poet of the two generations after Ransom whose work treated women as equals.[18] His poems of the seventies to his mother, his different wives, and his daughter are all examples. He is not afraid to acknowledge either the fear or the pleasure he finds in strong women. From "Jean Stafford, a Letter":

> You did miracles I blushed to acknowledge,
> outlines for novels more salable than my
>   poems,
> my ambiguities lost seven cities down. . . .
>
> You have spoken so many words and well,
> being a woman and you . . . someone must still
>   hear
> whatever I have forgotten
> or never heard, being a man.

From poem 5 of "Mermaid":

> Will money drown you? Poverty, though now
> in fashion, debases women as much as wealth.
> You use no scent, dab brow and lash with
>   shoeblack,
> willing to face the world without more face.
> I've searched the rough black ocean for you,
> and saw the turbulence drop dead for you,
> always lovely, even for those who had you,
> Rough Slitherer in your grotto of haphazard.
> I lack manhood to finish the fishing trip.
> Glad to escape beguilement and the storm,
> I thank the ocean that hides the fearful
>   mermaid—
> like God, I almost doubt if you exist.

It's hard to find a male poet younger than Lowell who writes so often about the issues between men and women. The majority of men ignore the questions here as they do in fiction. Certainly no man is as explicitly dedicated to the dynamics of gender as Adrienne Rich or as consistently rooted in them as Marilyn Hacker. But several, including some unexpected ones, do occasionally illuminate feelings about women who show some independence, equality, or power.

Allen Ginsberg, for example, gay and beat, does this with irony in "The Archetype Poem" and "The Affair," two poems of 1950, and with love in "Aunt Rose" (1958) and "Kaddish" (1957–59).[19] Charles Bukowski appears to be macho, a poet of the streets who is rough on women, but I think that the women in his poems are as strong and as independent as he is (or at least no more bound by the world), that he recognizes that and loves them and knows he is loving the class enemy. He shows that with bemusement in "the lady poet," and in "making it" he writes:

> I wasn't good at war with women
> I was too serious and they were
> too good at it.
> they were smarter than I was
> and I felt worse and worse.
> the more I fucked them and fought
> with them
> the worse I felt.[20]

Richard Hugo's "Invasion North" tells the story of a man who thinks he is the sole survivor of an invasion by an army of women, and several poems by Ronald Koertge describe more figurative battles between men and women who love each other. William Stafford writes about "admirable" women, John Beecher about women caught in race and class wars.[21] Mark Strand shows a man's consciousness of the ironies in his relationships with women— a lover in "Courtship"; mother, wife, and daughter who all treat him as a toy in "My Life"; and a daughter whom he wants to protect in "For Jessica, My Daughter."[22]

Gary Snyder and Robert Bly both are men whose poems and essays are concerned with the feminine in the cosmos, in nature, in mythology and psychology. Both are also men in whose poems real women showing or claiming power, or men facing such women, are hard to find. Snyder has written at least two: "The Bath," which gives a lovely scene of a man recognizing his wife's beauty and strength as they bathe their son, and "To Hell With Your Fertility Cult," in which a woman refutes a man's commitment to a myth of motherhood that abuses her.[23]

Bly is a poet obsessed by the Good Mother and the Terrible Mother, whom he came to call the Ecstatic Mother and the Teeth Mother, and by the Jungian idea that the interior of the soul is the feminine. "All of my poems come from the Ecstatic Mother; everyone's poems do," he wrote in a 1973 essay. "Men in patriarchies try to deny the truth that all creativity lies in feminine consciousness; it is part of the fight with the Mother." In the same year, however, Bly published the strongest of his many poems against the Vietnam war; the strongest was "The Teeth Mother Naked at Last," in which he saw man's inhumanity rooted in his allegiance to the Teeth Mother and her command to "dismember" the psyche.[24] This was a change from his earlier view that "Father consciousness" obstructed the painful but essential return to the Mother, and he seemed to be moving away from his pleasure in one Mother to voice his anger and fear connected with the other.

In recent years Bly has generated a number of encampments for men that have become a small but significant part of the men's movement. The camps try to help men return to some primal but nondestructive maleness, connected to nature, which the culture has buried in the psyche; it's not at all clear what has happened to the Ecstatic Mother in his mythology.

She is no more than an offstage presence in *Loving a Woman in Two Worlds,* Bly's latest book of poems. They differ from his earlier work in presenting real women, though they see them through the male poet's subjective eye more than they do as women with their own lives. Several poems show lovers as equals, several show the vulnerability of men, some show irony in relationships and some show the strength of women. I like these lines from "The Indigo Bunting":

> I love a firmness in you
> that disdains the trivial
> and regains the difficult.
> You become part then
> of the firmness of night,
> the granite holding up the walls.[25]

Two poets whose work first appeared in the seventies make the issues between men and women one of their themes, implicitly in their feelings or explicitly in their images. Robert Pinsky looks often at girls, women, most of all his daughter, seeing them as the independent beings they are by virtue of being human, which might even make it unnecessary to demand change in men or in society.[26] Michael Blumenthal is one of the best poets of the past twenty years—and probably the poet in whose work a line or metaphor shows him grappling, again and again, with the agonies that men and women go through as their traditional relations change. For example, from the poem "Kol Nidre":

> . . . I am eating cookies
> And reading the biography of Delmore Schwartz,
> another Jewish boy from Washington Heights whose father
> constantly threatened to die without dying, and whose
>   women
> drove him to cruelty with their relentless loving.

A second example, from the poem "Stones":

> We no longer build in stone—
> houses of rice paper, beds
> of feather. Manhood is the one stone we
>   still
> insist on, lifting it
>
> From abandoned quarries,
> carrying it on our backs
> even when we make love,
> until the woman beneath us
> calls passion a kind of

Suffocation, surfaces for air
like a young child whose head
has been pushed beneath the water,
a way to learn swimming.

Those poems are from Blumenthal's first book, *Sympathetic Magic.* In his second, *Days We Would Rather Know*, he moves from conflict between men and women to identification and integration. In "Couvade," for instance, a man "looks into the faces of his own wife/and child and staggers to bed in the sheer/empathy and pain of wanting to become them," and is rewarded after the birth: "And his son/will call him Father, and his wife: a man." In "Weeding," the poet sees that the task of weeding, called woman's work, brings him to become a woman, and says,

> I bend my body, lovely in its ribs,
> toward the earth again, so that the man
> and the woman who live inside it may find
> peace together, so that all that is separate
> inside my life might finally sing: the one
> song
> I have been practicing all these years, . . .[27]

Blumenthal matches Lowell, Ransom, Williams, and Yeats in showing that good poetry can and does deal, through feeling and through image, with the issues between men and women.

THEATER

Poetry is still usually written without regard to what is "publishable" even when the author wants to be published. Noncommercial novels are still published on occasion. But in theater and film, the creator's ability to fulfill his intentions is limited by a peculiar economics, the backers' perceptions of what the market will bear. These are often unconscious, irrational, or unrelated to the reality that others see, but they are controlling. But dramatists still write plays without thought of backers, which sometimes find backers all the same and are produced in Off-Broadway, Off-Off-Broadway, and regional theaters if not on Broadway.

Tennessee Williams wrote before women started to reshape American culture, and he never set out to address the issues between men and women. But one reason his plays resonate today is that they do look at those issues. Amanda in *The Glass Menagerie* irritates us with her silliness in one moment and evokes our compassion in another, but she is also powerful, modeled on Williams's own mother, whom he called "a little Prussian officer in drag," and her son Tom does not know how to deal with her except by abandoning her, one more hero who escapes women. Blanche in *A Streetcar Named Desire* is a decayed aristocrat; she asserts a status and a purity she is no longer entitled to and is destroyed by a working-class male, a painfully clear example of a powerless man asserting power over a woman.

Edward Albee goes further into a world where women try to escape the rules of society and the power of men. Martha in *Who's Afraid of Virginia Woolf* is a woman who tries to assert herself against the conventional standards that she constantly fails, against the academic environment her marriage has dragged her into, against her overall sense of worthlessness. She cannot overcome the myth of the feminine mystique, as women were beginning to do when the play entered the public consciousness in the sixties, and depends on her husband to maintain her sterile fantasies along with his own. She's a victim, which makes her another dubious candidate for feminist heroine, but a man created her and she keeps battling.

Few male playwrights since the early Albee have given their audience that much of the struggle between men and women. In plays as in novels, however, there are examples of men whose writing reflects the presumably rising consciousness of the culture. Paul Shyre, for example, wrote *Ah, Men*, a collage of male experiences with a musical binding, produced Off-Broadway in 1982. It portrays man as son, lover, husband, and father through the lives of Sean O'Casey, Eugene O'Neill, Groucho Marx, Clifford Irving, and the Ayatollah Khomeini, among others. Only O'Casey and George Burns show much sympathy with women. David Wiltse's *Doubles*, a hit on Broadway in 1985, reveals the men in a tennis foursome, who like the members of *The Men's Club* talk mostly about the women in their lives, who remain offstage. The play is amiable if sophomoric comedy, but its characters speak a language and seek male friendship in a way that would have been impossible before 1970. David Rabe's *Hurlyburly*, first produced in 1984, also speaks a new language and even reenacts the struggle between men and women, but it hardly shows a rising consciousness. The men treat the women onstage entirely as sex objects, and the women are so willing to be treated that way that I can't even say the play shows male hostility to change, only to women.

William Mastrosimone takes an almost opposite approach. His *Extremities* offers a woman who fights off a would-be rapist, makes him her prisoner, and threatens to bury him alive. Her female housemates are less melodramatic, even sympathetic to the prisoner. It's a play in which a male writer creates characters who voice different women's views, but the psychopathic quality he gives the heroine and the way he keeps her in her underwear for most of the first act make me wonder what his sexual politics really are, while I have no doubt of the politics John Irving shows in *Garp*. Susan Sarandon made the heroine an overwhelming and valiant figure in the 1982 production, undercutting that doubt about Mastrosimone, but in retrospect it's still there.

Sam Shepard, unlike the last four playwrights, is a major dramatist who in some plays does explore the world in which women seek independence, though like Tennessee Williams he probably never intended to. *Curse of the Starving Class,* first produced in 1977, is about the breakdown of a family trying to escape the descent into poverty. Father and son are both weak, and the mother is strong enough only to dream of selling the family sheep ranch and escaping to Europe, but the daughter is sturdy, sassy, unafraid. *A Fool for Love,* which opened in 1983, shows two lovers, who may also be brother and sister, resuming their unending and violent conflict in a motel room. Two other men appear—the woman's new boyfriend, weak compared to the main man, and a mysterious father figure who may be strongest of all. The woman doesn't win, but she certainly fights for herself.

Mac Wellman is an avant-garde playwright who doesn't get as close to explicit sexual conflict as Shepard does. But in a series of five plays his male and female characters are often truly equal in strength and weakness and the exploration of fear as they pursue "the subtle dialectic of gesture and spirit, parable and pratfall, dialogue and disorder." *Energumen,* the first play in the series, was produced at Soho Rep in New York in 1985.

Two English writers have done plays that deal more deliberately with the issues between men and women. David Hare's *Plenty,* produced in London in 1978 and in New York in 1982, struck many critics as a play about the decline of the British Empire. It's really the story of an Englishwoman who never lives up to the experiences of her youth with the French resistance in World War II, partly because of her own character and craziness, but partly because society and men won't let her do what she most wants. Hare, even more than Updike, is one of the rare men able to create a female character who is full of life, convincing even when you (or he) dislike her. His Susan decides to have a child, enlists a young working-class man to impregnate her, and fails to get pregnant. She lends a seventeen-year-old girl money for an abortion at the request of her friend Alice; Alice and the girl are lovers, and later so are Alice and Susan. She also gives Alice her home in Knightsbridge as a home for unmarried mothers. That's after she marries Brock, a diplomat whose career dies in large measure because she tries to save it. He is a decent man; in her frustration she drives him to drink and helps destroy his life even though, or perhaps because, she loves him. It's hard to decide which is more important in the play, the strong woman's ability to damage others or society's ability to prevent her from using her strength constructively.

Howard Brenton's *Sore Throats* was produced in 1979 in London and in 1983 in St. Louis. Jack, a London police man, leaves his wife, Judy, to live with a younger woman. He comes to her new flat in his police uniform to ask her to sign an agreement giving him half the money from the sale of the house they had owned together. They slash at each other with words about love and sex and money, words reflecting the centuries of male dominance that no marriage can escape. Judy talks of using the money to have an operation that might give her adders' heads for breasts, a tiger's head for a womb, surprises that would enable her to take revenge on a man. They talk past each other about their memories of their marriage and their expectations of the future; when Jack talks about his new chance for tenderness, he hits Judy in the mouth. She signs the agreement, but later, when the battle renews, she tears the paper up. In the second act, Judy and her roommate Sally talk about a trip to America, where they have gone through a procession of boys and men in an effort to learn what freedom—for one, from marriage, for the other from work and dating—really means. Jack comes in, carrying what seems to be a baby, and tells the story of the child's birth after a car accident. It turns out that Jack is carrying not a baby but bricks in the carry-cot. His lover did not die in the accident but left him to go off with another man, taking the baby with her. He says that since he couldn't have his daughter, he "nicked a few of her things." He asks, "Why can't men have wombs, breasts, the works." Sally replies, "Want the whole world, do you, mister?" Brenton here neatly reverses men's fear of the combination of two primal powers that they think modern women are demanding. Jack shows Judy that he still desires her sexually, and pleads for some of the money she still has from the house. She has converted it into cash, and starts tearing up the bank notes in front of him. Sally asks her if she is going to go back to work, and she says no, "I am going to be fucked, happy and free." This play does more than any other I have read or seen to depict the struggle between men and women.[28]

FILMS

In films even more than in theater, as I've noted, the creator—usually the director, in film, rather than the writer—is limited by economics, by money men's ideas about what will make more money. In this field people with money are indeed almost always male. Some of them are beginning to respond positively to the demands of women in the industry: the number of women making films as directors and producers, long minuscule, has begun to grow in the eighties. The number of films making women the objects of sex and violence is still huge,[29] and the number dealing with the issues between men and women is tiny, but I'm surprised that it's as large as it is. The films I discuss were all directed by men.

In the late sixties and early seventies, most films ignored the demands that women had begun to make in real life. The producers presumably believed that neither men nor women wanted the fantasy to come too close to a reality that produced so much anger and anxiety. One predominant pattern was increasingly violent machismo, as in *The Godfather* (1972). Another was escape into one variety or another of a man's world—not merely a world in which men dominated, but one in which all the significant relationships were between men and men, who often freed themselves from the stereotyped sex role of unexpressive strength and discovered each other. Obvious examples are *The Odd Couple* (1968), *Easy Rider* (1969), *Midnight Cowboy* (1969), or *Butch Cassidy and the Sundance Kid* (1969).[30]

Things began to improve in the late 1970s, when the mostly male commercial moviemakers realized there might be a market created or influenced by the women's movement. Among the results were *Julia,* with Jane Fonda as a successful playwright and Vanessa Redgrave as the eponymous anti-Nazi activist; *An Unmarried Woman,* with Jill Clayburgh as a wife who learns to fend for herself after her husband leaves her; and *Looking for Mr. Goodbar,* in which Diane Keaton searches for love in singles bars and finds death. Significantly, in all three of these examples the heroine is a woman with a career. The first two also have strong male characters who are genuinely supportive of the women. Richard Brooks, director of *Looking for Mr. Goodbar,* said that some of his friends called him "a traitor to our cause," and only half facetiously. *Goodbar* had no man of any positive substance in it, the heroine is hardly an independent woman, and the equation of casual sex with death is a notion that neither appeals to all women nor betrays all men. But Brooks intended to make a film about a strong female character, and he said in 1978, "It was women's organizations and the general outcry for realistic women figures on the screen that resulted in these new films."[31]

More recent films suggest that film directors are making more of an effort to look at the changes in relations between men and women, though the results show a full share of ambivalence and confusion. This was certainly true of the work of one cinema genius, Federico Fellini's *City of Women* (1980). His main character, Snaporaz (Marcello Mastroianni), is the hero of many earlier Fellini films, grown older. Pursuing the ideal woman, Snaporaz meets a variety of females who are stronger and more aggressive than he is, including a multifarious gang of furious feminists, and shows his own weakness and loses his own dignity in many ways. He also meets a satyrical guru, Dr. Xavier Zueberkock ("magic cock"), who celebrates his ten thousand sexual conquests in a temple attacked by the local female police force, but then gives up in exhaustion and prays to a statue of his mother. The film ends with Snaporaz sliding down an amusement park chute through his adult life to his childhood. Fellini clearly adores women, whom he mocks much less than he mocks men, but he is certainly ambivalent about both sexes' attempts to claim independence and power.

The biggest single category of films dealing with changes in gender dynamics is about the basic relationships of love and marriage: *Ordinary People* (1980), *Four Seasons* (1981), and *Terms of Endearment* (1983), for example. I find these the least satisfying of films about such changes because they usually ignore economic and social questions as though equality and independence were not affected by them. Ingmar Bergman's *Scenes from a Marriage* (1974) is an exception because it does deal with the characters' working lives and even more because of the director's genius in portraying profound human relations.

The troubled marriage in *Ordinary People* is a caricature. The wife-and-mother (Mary Tyler Moore) is strong, but anything but liberated. The husband (Donald Sutherland) is a conventionally sensitive male, and the psychiatrist (Judd Hirsh) is unconventionally, almost unbelievably sensitive. Still, it's a change from machismo. *Four Seasons* shows three married couples who are all friends, far more ordinary people than those in *Ordinary People;* the husbands show a variety of weaknesses as well as strengths and the wives a variety of strengths as well as weaknesses. This is more equality than moviegoers ever saw before 1970, but it never rises above the pleasant. Alan Alda wrote, directed, and starred in it. It's interesting that Alda, the male celebrity who has spoken most clearly in support of women on feminist issues, has never made a film that looks more sharply at the question of power between the sexes. *Terms of Endearment* never moved me, but it does give some flavor of reality in the relationship between rich widow Aurora Greenway (Shirley MacLaine) and former astronaut Garrett Breedlove (Jack Nicholson), who transform themselves from uneasy neighbors into adult lovers.

Several of the movies that deal with change are about role reversal, like *Mr. Mom* (1983), a comedy in which Michael Keaton is professedly happy to be a househusband but can't entirely conceal his anger about his wife's career and what it does to him. I give it C— as a film, but B+ for emotional realism.

The triumph in this category is *Tootsie* (1982), in which Dustin Hoffman plays Michael Dorsey, an actor who's talented but who can't get work, mostly because he's so perfectionist that directors and producers regard him as a pain in the ass. He disguises himself as a woman named Dorothy Michaels who lands a role in a soap opera, playing Emily Kimberly, a hospital administrator. Dorothy Michaels is also a pain in the ass, not because she is Michael Dorsey but because in character as Dorothy he can't help but speak out for her rights and all women's rights. He and she are both angry at the way men treat Dorothy, sexually and professionally.

Professionally, Dorothy has to deal with a soap opera director who thinks he knows how women feel and act. She drives him crazy by doing what she thinks is right in the role of Emily, down to bopping the old goat who plays chief surgeon. The director has to submit because the audience loves it, both the audience in the movie and the audience at the movie. Dorothy also demands that the director call her by her name, and not by the endearments that enable him to forget each woman's identity—one of which, of course, is "Tootsie."

Sexually, most men ignore Dorothy because she is homely. In publicity interviews Hoffman suggested that this was a devastating experience for him, even though as a man he had often committed that very sin. At least two men come on to her. One is the vain (and pathetic) old goat on the soap. The other man desires Dorothy honestly but without ever asking what she wants. She doesn't want him and she doesn't want the conventional marriage that is his ideal. Her feelings are there, but they get lost in Michael's panic—panic at the thought of a man asking to marry him, and panic because the man is the father of Julie, the young actress whom Michael falls in love with even as Dorothy gives her sisterly support.

When I saw the film, I wondered if feminists would object to their principles' being enunciated by what is, after all, a man in drag. In the event, many did. But my daughter-in-law, Barbara Jones, then an unemployed actress herself, said they shouldn't because Michael suffers the kind of rejection as an unemployed actor that society constantly inflicts on women. He has paid his dues.

When the film opened, Hoffman gave many interviews about the changes *Tootsie* had made in his life as a man. They sounded like very thin pop-psychology, and Arthur Bell wrote an article showing clearly that Hoffman's consciousness had risen only a couple of inches.[32] What's important, however, was that he was able to bring to life a character who did learn from "being" a woman, and that other men—director Sydney Pollack and writers Murray Schisgal and Larry Gelbart (though the writers needed help from a woman, Elaine May)—were able to help that act of creation. This did not happen in, say, *Some Like It Hot* (1960).

Tightrope (1984) is neither as much fun nor as good a movie as *Tootsie*, but it looks more closely at power, sex, and the dark side of change. Clint Eastwood plays a man with the Freudian name of Wes Block. On one level he is a vulnerable, hunted man whose wife abandoned him, leaving him with the care of two daughters (one played by Eastwood's own daughter, Alison). He plays football with them, cares for them tenderly, and has incestuous desires for them. On another level, the traditional Eastwood dimension, Block is a New Orleans detective investigating a series of murders of prostitutes. The murderer is in a sense his doppelgänger, who kills some of the women after Block has sex with them and handcuffs them—as Block did in making love. The man is forced to look at the way he intertwines sex and power. The case brings him to collaborate with, and then to love, a strong, feminist woman (played by Geneviève Bujold) who runs a rape-counseling center and teaches women karate so they can defend themselves. Eastwood's quintessential macho character is transformed before our very eyes into a man who struggles with his own vulnerabilities, with his most basic emotions, and with a woman who demands equality. Yet Eastwood gives the murdered women no complexity, no personality, no place in an economic or political world, so that even before they are murdered they have no life except as creatures whose deaths will help raise Block's consciousness and perhaps redeem him. The movie is fascinating, but it doesn't resolve the problems that it raises. In other words, it's a good symbol of male struggle with this kind of change.

Women and critics often criticize Brian de Palma's films, charging that they make women the victims of terror and violence and justify male dominance. It's not a surprising judgment after *Body Double* (1984), in which one man gazes through a telescope at a woman masturbating and later sees another man murder her with an electric drill strapped to his genitals. But Kate Ellis, a feminist writer, finds that de Palma's violence has consequences for those who commit it and those who merely observe it as well as for those it damages or destroys. It is far from the fantasy violence without consequences that reinforces a pallid machismo in so many movies and television programs (I do not believe that violent films cause violent acts in real life). Ellis also argues persuasively that *Body Double, Blow Out* (1981) and *Dressed to Kill* (1980) all portray inadequate, voyeuristic, or psychotic males who are helpless in coping with life compared to some of the women, most notably the prostitute played by Nancy Allen in *Dressed to Kill*.[33] Another woman reported finding real pleasure in the revenge shown in de Palma's *The Fury* (1978), in which Amy Irving plays a woman with psychokinetic powers who vaporizes an exploitative terrorist villain (John Cassavetes) merely by staring at him.[34] I believe de Palma does make many of his female characters equal to or stronger than his males, but his films too have only the thinnest economic and political contexts, and the dismal view of humanity that they suggest makes the women's strength a dubious asset.

Norma Rae (1979) and *Silkwood* (1983), in contrast, both tell the stories of women with specific real-life models who do live in economic and political worlds. One is a textile worker who becomes a union organizer, the other a plutonium plant worker who tries to expose her employer's disregard of radiation dangers. Neither woman subordinates her work or her public concerns to her private life. *Norma Rae,* directed by Martin Ritt and written by Irving Ravetch and Harriet Frank, Jr., is the softer of the two films, whose heroine is mother as well as worker, warm to other people despite her big mouth, and the film stops with her union's victory in a representation election. (Her real-life model was unemployed in 1985 and looking for help from star Sally Fields.) *Silkwood,* directed by Mike Nichols but written by two women, Nora Ephron and Alice Arlen, is a tougher film with a tougher heroine (Meryl Streep). She not only battles her bosses but isn't embarrassed to have a lesbian as a housemate and enjoys shaming an unfriendly fellow worker by flashing a bare breast at him in an antierotic, abrasive manner. The film ends with her death, like the real Karen Silkwood's, in a car accident that might just be murder by the nuclear fuel company, but it fudges the issue. Both pictures show the intersection of the class war between men and women and the class war between employer and worker, a rare focus for Hollywood.

John Sayles's films also take place in a realistic social and political context, though it's middle-class. They give a happy but far from rose-colored view of ordinary humanity and consistently show women as peers of men. In *The Return of the Secaucus Seven* (1980), the women are sometimes stronger and sometimes weaker than the men—but more often stronger, I thought after seeing it a second time in 1985. In *Lianna* (1983), Sayles gives a sympathetic portrait of a New Jersey housewife who becomes a lesbian, showing both the humor and the courage required. Sayles is the only male director I can think of who shows real identification with women in his films. His male characters show some anger and fear and anxiety, but his own are at a minimum.

TELEVISION

It's easy to think that television dilutes the ideas of women's independence and equality and men's feelings about them even more than films do, since television usually seems to dilute every idea that comes its way. But television knows that women and men in new roles and new relationships are part of its audience, and television's experience in producing programs that reflected change helped persuade some film producers to try movies with strong female characters in the late 1970s. The independent or working women on series like *The Mary Tyler Moore Show* and *Maude* helped pave the way for films like *Julia* and *An Unmarried Woman*. Those television programs did more than the films, however, to show the fear, anxiety, and envy that many men feel when women manifest their strength—in the Ted Baxter character on *Mary Tyler Moore* and Walt on *Maude*, for example.

Some soap operas also introduced feminist themes. Traditionally the soaps stick to tried-and-true formulas that seldom reflect reality, and successful programs like *Another World*, a Procter & Gamble mainstay, still do not allow a woman to have both a career and a happy marriage, as I noted in Chapter 7. But when the women's movement was having its biggest impact on public opinion, in the mid-seventies, there were significant departures from classical norms. Cathy Phillips, the heroine of *Search for Tomorrow*, had a legal abortion because a child would have interfered with her career as a lawyer. Then she quit her job in a small law firm because she was getting only menial legal tasks while her husband, with no better qualifications, was given more important work. Her husband was shocked at first, but later came to approve her decisions in both cases. Husband and wife later split up for classical soap opera reasons, however, when he had an affair with a woman he then had to defend on a murder charge. *One Life to Live* and *All My Children*, both created by Agnes Nixon but paid for by corporate money men, also presented many episodes about abortion, venereal disease, and career women. Things have changed a bit in the 1980s, with more focus on characters in their teens and twenties who face a more limited range of problems. Abortion is seldom seen as a desirable option in soapland in the era of Reagan and the right-to-life movement. But *All My Children* is still on the air and still occasionally realistic about men and women. *The Young and the Restless* is full of career women who are peers of the male characters, and other soaps sometimes deal with gender issues.

So do a few, a very few, recent or current prime-time shows. Most make only gestures. The evening soaps frequently have strong female characters like the Joan Collins role on *Dynasty* and the Jane Wyman role on *Falcon Crest*, but they are often unsympathetic, the men are seldom supportive of women, and the programs are so much a fantasy of a world of the wealthy that they reflect even less of the psychology of real people than the soaps. The crime and violence programs often show women with a façade of career or independence, but few of them make their women characters the equals of the men. Both types of program often make women the sexual, physical, or economic victims of the male villains.

The shows that do deal with gender issues often center on women who work because they need to. *Alice* and *One Day at a Time* spun comedy and drama out of the problems of working women with children. *Cagney & Lacey*, one of the largest-audience programs of 1985, shows the lives of two women detectives and their problems with work, men, children, disease, and other realities. The men were particularly supportive when Lacey had breast cancer. Mace Neufeld, one of the producers of this show, has also supported women filmmakers who find it hard to get backing, like the three who produced *Tell Me a Riddle* (1980). Another high-rated program, *The Cosby Show*, presents an idealized family that recalls some 1950s favorites in contemporary costume. Bill Cosby plays a father who knows best, but unlike earlier TV fathers, he is not just a wise man or arbitrator who comes home from distant tasks in time to solve problems. He is a doctor who is married to a lawyer, who does a major part of the child raising and often cooks dinner, who personifies the new father.

None of the current television programs I have mentioned shows much male anger or fear. The evening soaps and the thrillers often have macho characters who make women victims along with weaker men, but they seldom are responding to women who assert true equality. The programs that treat women with sympathy or respect make most of the recurring male characters supportive. Harvey, Mary Beth Lacey's husband in *Cagney & Lacey*, had a hard time when the program started, because he was unemployed and being a househusband while she was pulling in her detective's salary. A few male cops in the early days showed some dislike of women invading their man's world. But after the first year, most of the negative male feelings sank from view. I find this departure from reality intriguing. The producers must think their shows will be more successful if they avoid anxieties apart from those needed to create suspense in an episode.

COMICS

Comic books and comic strips are an essential part of American culture, in some ways a better mirror of changing reality than novels, films, or television programs—though it may take them longer to reflect the world as it really is. Today a higher proportion of comics than of those other cultural artifacts deal with women's claim to independence and equality, and often more positively.

In 1982 seven of thirty-eight strips in the Washington *Post*, 18 percent, were running episodes displaying some consciousness of change. In 1985 it had gone up to twelve of thirty-nine, or 31 percent, though there were slightly fewer explicitly feminist jokes or statements. These "comics," some serious, some funny, show career women, two-earner marriages, and men departing from traditional sex roles—or people of both sexes being made the butt of humor for voicing ideas that are feminist in some cases (not all female), male chauvinist in others (almost all male). There was some anxiety and disapproval in what I call comic strip soap operas, like "Mary Worth," but most of the emotions on display were positive. A comic page, after all, must be upbeat in its net impact. Other papers run the same strips, though none runs as many overall as does the *Post*, so none is likely to run as many with a raised consciousness. Only one of the strips I've seen, "Cathy," by Cathy Guisewite, is written and drawn by a woman.

The syndicators and the newspaper editors who buy their strips say this is a recognition of market demand, like the wave of movies with positive female characters in the late seventies. Most of these strips are products of the eighties, however. It apparently took the marketers a long time to realize what the market wanted, perhaps because the traditional remains popular at the same time. "Blondie," with her prototypical traditional marriage, now more than fifty years old, is still the best-read strip in the New York *Daily News;* Winnie Winkle started being a breadwinner in 1920 and is still going strong, but she seldom uttered a word that could be called feminist in all those years. Editors also say they welcomed the new strips about working women because a majority of their readers are women, but the news and feature departments of their papers started reflecting changes in work and home life ten years earlier than the comic pages did. The Washington *Post*, for all the awareness of women it started showing in the news, Style, and editorial pages in the late seventies, still didn't know what its readers wanted in the eighties. The *Post* canceled Greg Howard's "Sally Forth," a funny strip about a two-earner marriage, in 1982 only to restore it six weeks later after readers protested in what a *Post* editor called "thoughtful and interesting letters."

Stan Lee, the publisher of Marvel Comics, said he had always wanted to do comic books about female characters, and indeed had published them from the 1940s on, but was never able to make them sell well. One reason was that most comic book buyers were boys until the seventies. But in 1980, "Savage She-Hulk," literally a cousin of the Incredible Hulk, became a bestseller. In her natural state, she was a feminist and a criminal lawyer who always wore pants. Lee said, "I'm a great believer in equality, and I thought, 'Why does the woman always have to be a nurse or a secretary or a frivolous dilettante?' It occurred to me, 'Why not make her a bright and intelligent practicing attorney?' " But when a reporter asked him why Jennifer Walters always wore pants, Lee said, "Because pants tear best into the kind of skimpy costume Jennifer wears when she turns into the She-Hulk."[35]

Some of the reason for the delay was the long time it took male artists to raise their consciousness or realize what the market wanted. Mort Walker gave Lois Flagston, of "Hi and Lois," a job selling real estate after thirty years of traditional marriage. He says he made the change because women told him Lois was a terrible role model, because his son and daughter-in-law were facing the problems of a two-career marriage, and because he finally realized that many of his female neighbors in Greenwich, Connecticut, have jobs.[36] Walker has now turned Hi and Lois over to Dik Browne, but he still does "Beetle Bailey," a saga of army life. His heightened consciousness made him respond to feminist objections to Miss Buxley, General Halftrack's sexy secretary, and she has acquired a brain and an occasional feminist attitude in the past few years.

"Mary Worth" and "Judge Parker" are two comic strip soap operas that have been published for decades but keep developing contemporary scenarios. Judge Parker had to deal with an aggressive woman lawyer in 1982. Mary Worth usually finds a way to make sure that a working wife doesn't abandon or surpass her husband, but she doesn't suggest that the woman give up her career.

Newer, younger artists feel it's natural to bring newer, younger ideas to the comics page. Berke Breathed's "Bloom County" has a feminist schoolteacher, a male chauvinist promoter, a liberated male in a wheelchair, and a variety of children and talking animals who raise doubts about the whole human race and gender relations in every species. Howard's "Sally Forth" makes equal fun of husband and wife. I loved one strip in which daughter Hilary discombobulates her father by asking him if he feels that working fathers weaken the family structure or adversely affect a child's development. Bill Holbrook's "On the Fastrack" is a series of one-liners about office life in a company headed by a woman, who is as autocratic as any male chief executive.

Garry Trudeau's "Doonesbury," always topical and frequently political, makes fun of men and women in turn. In one of my recent favorites, Joanie finds her husband Rick, a reporter, at his computer on a Sunday and asks why. Rick says their baby son Jeffrey "said something amazing last night. I want to work it into the diary."

Joanie: "What diary?"

Rick: "I'm doing a diary for the Sunday section. On the new fatherhood. My editor feels there's a lot of interest in the current, more involved genera- tion of fathers. He asked me to keep an account of my experiences."

Joanie: "Uh-huh." Then, in the next panel, she says, "Listen, could you watch Jeffrey today? I've got a meeting."

Rick: "Sorry, Babe. I'm on deadline here." And the pretensions of many of the involved generation of fathers are laid bare for Trudeau's millions of readers by an involved-father artist married to a television news personality (Jane Pauley).

ADVERTISING

Advertisements provide another medium through which the culture expresses approval or disapproval of change in sex roles and gender power. Involved fathers are images of acceptance here, too: ad agency people recall a man diapering a baby as one of the first reflections of change in television ads, along with a woman driving a car. That was in the early seventies. A 1984 campaign showed a man driving a Peugeot to bring his newborn baby home from the hospital, to take his son for his first haircut, to pick up his daughter when she came home from college. Jay Jaspers, head of the creative group at Ogilvy & Mather that did that campaign, told me, "We wanted to place a foreign car in an American milieu, a middle-class milieu, to make it part of the likeability of the people. We talked about that, chewed on it, until we saw this meant we had to recognize that the responsibility of living as two people, as husband and wife, is a shared responsibility." Another Jaspers ad used three fathers on a bench with their babies, who were crawling or hanging in Snugglis, to sell financial services. Jaspers believes that ads must recognize that men are "evolving, gaining a new freedom, exploring more of their strengths and emotions than ever in the past."

The purpose, of course, is to sell goods. In one sense that makes advertising a good test: if marketers decide that they can sell products with images of men and women that show new sex roles and a new distribution of power, then change is really here. (Marketers often talk about roles and buying functions and almost never about power, but that's still what underlies or is implicit in the change in sex roles.)

But advertising people, still predominantly male despite the increasing number of women at high levels of the trade, are also the victims of the same combinations of emotions and the same perceptions of society that plague the rest of us. Betty Friedan drew attention to sex-role stereotypes in advertising in the ground-breaking feminist classic, *The Feminine Mystique,* in 1963. Ten years later, when the women's movement had already begun reshaping the overall culture, Rena Bartos of J. Walter Thompson screened 125 television commercials and found "perhaps nine" that gave even remote recognition to the contemporary woman.[37]

Things had improved a bit by the end of the decade, more in print than in television. I suspect that the combination of greater production expense and the assumption of low intelligence in the viewer kept TV from switching sooner. The voice-over, the voice of authority, was still male in 90 percent of television commercials in 1980, for instance—an increase from 84 percent five years earlier.[38]

Some advertisers had realized, however, that working women constituted an important market. United Airlines spent a quarter of its $2 million 1978 print budget on ads targeted to women travelers in women's magazines, for instance. American Express started ads, later translated to television, in which women used their credit cards to take men out to dinner. Oil companies ran ads showing women in nontraditional jobs, and insurance companies and national stockbrokers aimed ads at career women.[39]

But even today few advertisers are making use of images of change as much as Jaspers does. Some think it's enough to show men being stupid about detergents instead of women being stupid about detergents. Many are unable to discard sexist or sexy images of women. Nina Easton, a Ralph Nader associate, found that ads still present men as authority figures, wage earners, and doers, and women mostly as passive homemakers fretting about ring around the collar and feminine odor.[40] Women Against Pornography awarded nine plastic pigs in 1984 for ad campaigns that it considered "demeaning to women and girls," compared to a mere four Ms. Liberty awards for "prowoman ads." One of the pigs went to a Hanes Hosiery ad that showed a woman member of a formerly all-male club being ogled for her "smooth and silky legs." One of the Ms. Liberty awards went to an ad for Molyneux's Quartz perfume that showed a female pilot who is "always in charge." In 1985 Joseph Famolare had to give up an ad that aroused sharp protest from women's groups. It showed a woman wearing his wavy-soled shoes—a female runner crouched in starting position next to a man's hand holding a starter's gun. An Ogilvy & Mather survey found that 75 percent of women think that most ads insult the intelligence of the average consumer, while 50 percent think most ads are in bad taste. The comparable figures for men were 68 and 35 percent.[41]

Ogilvy & Mather didn't say what either sex thought of a Jaspers group ad for Paco Rabanne fragrance that fascinates me. Far from looking at man as father, it shows a man in bed alone in what appears to be an artist's studio, waking up to a message from the woman he spent the night with. She has left for what is clearly a business trip, but she can't wait to get back and smell him. The ad, in other words, shows a male sex object who isn't afraid of an aggressive woman and who isn't a slave to a conventional job. He has discarded fear and anxiety for relief, identification, and pleasure, in my terms. For a minute I wonder if change may already have a larger bridgehead in

American society than I usually think. Then I remember the vast majority of sex-stereotyped ads, completely in accord with the predominance of negatives in my interviews, the denial, hostility, and anxiety that turn up so often in books and plays and films. The Peugeot and Paco Rabanne men, the Molyneux women are not proof that the revolution has won its major battle. They are grounds for hope, in the same sense that John Irving and Clint Eastwood offer grounds for hope where you least expect it.

Chapter 15
DIVIDING LINES

Books and movies and advertisements, cultural artifacts of society, are part of the context in which the revolution in gender power and sex roles takes place. So are the various dividing lines that people see, or build, in a society.

I relied as much as possible in this book on individuals whose talk and actions would illuminate what happens at work and at home. They were all members of different groups defined by social dividing lines—class, race, region, age, and stage of adult development, sexual preference. Here I want to add some observations on those groups, those categories. My sample was not large enough or random enough to offer an opportunity for statistical comparisons, but I did form impressions.

CLASS

The class of gender crosses the boundaries of class defined by income, education, and power. Where the political and psychological dimensions intersect, men and women are indeed class enemies at many moments in their lives. (The oppressed class always sees the struggle more clearly than the dominant; so far, women have seen this more clearly than men.) But the human condition is that these enemies must love each other and often do.

The ways they love each other, the ways through this contradiction, this paradox, vary according to the familiar categories of class. Income and education do affect men's feelings about women's demands for independence and equality. So does power. Men treat women as equals more easily when they are sure of themselves and their money and power, or when questions of power are diffuse.

Blue-collar men feel the contradiction between their physical power and their place at the bottom of the male hierarchy, and they are more obvious than men in other classes about their need to treat women as underlings to compensate. They are more honest, or quicker to voice their anger and their fear, about changes in the balance of power and in sex roles, at work and at home. They find it harder than men with higher incomes and more education to overcome the traditions of their culture that prohibit treating women as equals, but some do so; at least one market researcher finds that blue-collar men express fewer traditional and macho values than stereotypes suggest, that some express higher expectations of intimacy and emotional support in relationships with women than middle-class men do.[1] This sometimes translates from talk into action. Lower-income men in my small sample and in advertising surveys sometimes do more housework than middle-class men, I suspect for the simple reason that their wives work but they still can't afford maids.

Middle-class and upper-class men are more affected by the psychotherapy subculture and by commercial trends, both forces that make some try, and others pretend to try, to understand and accept what women are doing. A higher proportion of middle-class men than either blue-collar or upper-class men is genuinely supportive of women at work. A higher proportion is also more likely to take a real share in, or real responsibility for, child care and housework. In both cases it's still a small minority that reaches the stage of association. Many upper-class men talk about their devotion to equality, but few give it in business management and only slightly more in the professions. In both groups their economic, command, and prestige power is real and they don't want to lose it. They are probably sincere when they talk about equality in their personal lives, and the proportion who treat their wives as equals, while small, may be as great as in the middle-class. But with upper-class men, I can't escape the feeling that it's more a matter of principle than practice because they hire maids and nannies, almost always female.

Middle-class and upper-class men, I found in my interviews, are more likely than blue-collar men to sense that there is something wrong about our effort to monopolize power, to keep women powerless. (It's harder for blue-collar men because they are further from real power.) Part of it is cognitive dissonance between our preaching democracy, human rights, and social mobility, and our practicing a kind of power politics that transforms gender and race into class. But I think our sense of wrong goes deeper than that. We know that mastery produces satisfaction, that competence means power and self-esteem. Conversely, we know that failure in mastery produces dissatisfaction, which turns into rage. We know that powerlessness, which we have made congruent with incompetence, is synonymous with low self-respect. We restrict women's mastery and deny them power even as they force us to recognize their competence.

RACE

The black experience of the gender revolution is different from white and Hispanic for several reasons. Black women have been working outside the home for so many generations that the idea of women in the workplace was not as revolutionary for them or their men as it was for other groups. Black women in general are still at the bottom of the economic ladder, but the proportion with better education, higher-status jobs, and higher salaries than men have is higher than it is among whites. This means the balance of economic and work power between men and women did not shift as dramatically for blacks as for others in recent years. Black women have been heading families in larger proportions for at least sixty years, so the balance of power at home did not shift so dramatically there either. In addition, the women's movement originated in and focused on the white middle class; it was the creation of white women whom many blacks see as a threat to black progress. So it did not touch black women as deeply as white, did not stimulate them to offer as many challenges as quickly to black men as white women did to white men.

Despite this, the balance at work and home for blacks *has* been affected by the changes of the past fifteen years. Many black men identify with women's demands as an outgrowth of the civil rights movement. The proportion who strongly resist women's demands is probably greater than the proportion of whites, however, if only because they are more conscious of how little power they have and are therefore more sensitive to every erosion in it. Many middle-class black men think they see women with money and power all around them, and they are often more intensely hostile than their white counterparts. Many black women have come to recognize what they see as a double oppression, racial and sexual. So do many black men, like the Atlanta banking consultant who said, "Men have no control now, and they're looking for control. . . . You can't deal with your boss because he's white, and you can't control the home place because your wife is making as much as you do."[2]

Among poorer blacks, many men simply do not "feel like a man" because of their inability to find a good job, earn good money, and do even half the providing for a family. They may feel impotent (and sometimes turn sexually impotent), or they may abandon the families they start and then feel even less like a man. They may displace their anger and resentment from the economy and the white world onto women—and all the more so when they see black women who earn decent money and provide single-handedly for families. The men's economic disability has many causes. Thomas Sowell, an economist, and William Wilson, a sociologist, are black conservatives who argue that the psychological legacy of the past is more important than anything in the society as a whole in blacks' failure to advance economically. Most blacks who have looked at the problem disagree, blaming continuing racial discrimination, real if not always intentional, visible in an array of facts:[3] black men show greater increases in rates of chronic disease and mental illness than white men. Blacks are imprisoned at a rate four or five times higher than whites (and prison is not a place that trains men in sensitivity to women). The unemployment rate for black men officially is twice as high as the rate for white men and in fact may be much worse than that. (There is nearly a one-to-one correspondence in the increase in unemployment among black men and the increase in female-headed families over the years, according to Walter Allen, a sociologist at the University of Michigan.) Government welfare programs give no money to mothers and children if there is a man in the house. Yet many black men continue to maintain a connection with children even when they abandon the family in form or in reality—a sign that it may be possible to draw them into one of the main channels for men's participation in the gender revolution.

Hispanic attitudes resemble whites' more than blacks' because the place of *la mujer* was so unquestionably in the home that the movement of women into the workplace was a dramatic change for Latins as it was for Anglos, indeed even more revolutionary in most Hispanic communities than in the majority society. The myth that women are not in the labor force persisted far longer for Chicanas than for Anglos, though today the proportions for all women sixteen and over are similar. Hispanic men and women both insist that Latin machismo and the importance of the family are often misunderstood by Anglos, but their more accurate versions still emphasize the traditional importance of the father and the confinement of the mother to home, even if she demonstrates real strength there. A Hispanic woman who achieves an income or occupational level higher than her husband's arouses more agony in her spouse than occurs in any other ethnic group. Mexican-Americans often go on to say that the rebellion against the forces of machismo and family by Chicana women has created a change that may be greater in the long run than the changes among Anglos. But the forces of change are attenuated by the Hispanic birthrate, 75 percent higher than that of the rest of the population (25.5 births per thousand compared with 14.7 for non-Hispanics), with a higher percentage born to women under twenty, which keeps more women from finishing high school and from finding better jobs. The birthrate of course reflects Catholic doctrine, but it also reflects the belief of many, perhaps most Hispanic males that manhood is demonstrated by the number of children a man has. My impression is that while the dynamics of power change among Hispanics resemble the Anglos', the proportion and the intensity of male resistance approaches the blacks'.

REGION

I did the interviews for this book in cities and suburbs in four regions to make sure I did not fall into the trap of identifying any one place with the whole country. They were the East (New York and Washington), the Midwest (Chicago, Detroit, and two smaller cities), the South (Atlanta, Dallas, and two smaller cities), and California (Los Angeles and the San Francisco Bay area). My impressions reflect the conclusions of experts on the census data that the United States is becoming ever more homogeneous in many respects, though diversity is growing in others. I found the highest percentage of opponents of change in the South and a greater proportion in the Midwest than on the two coasts. There was a higher percentage of supporters in the East and West, but the Midwest came close to them in the proportion of pragmatics. I can't prove, but I imagine, that my impressions reflect such facts as the increasing similarity of all regions in education and per capita income, or the higher proportion of older people in the South. And the census data, of course, say nothing about differences in cultural values among the regions.

My overriding impression was that none of the differences was significant. Ambivalents were the biggest single group in every region. Anger, fear, and anxiety and relief, admiration, and identification can be found with equal ease or difficulty around the country.

AGE AND STAGES OF GROWTH

I did not find, as some of my friends expected, that older men uniformly tend to resist and younger men to support what women are doing, as though revolution depended primarily upon youth. It's true that men in their twenties today grew up with feminism in the air they breathed, and with an informality between the sexes that has many causes besides feminism. Many of them are freer of sex-role stereotypes than older men are. In surveys they profess more support for the equality of women than do older men or the male population as a whole, and a few studies say that (in much smaller proportions) they are more likely to live up to their professions. It's also true that men in their sixties are often more devoted to, or more the prisoner of, the habits that go with the old stereotypes. But in every season of a man's life from his twenties through his fifties, I found opponents, ambivalents, pragmatists, and supporters.

Looking at men under thirty, I found more who speak in terms of equality than those in any other age group, of equality within marriage and equality for women at work. But there are just as many in this group who assume power or privilege as there are true egalitarians. Many expect their wives to have careers, for instance, but also expect those careers to take second place to their own. Many become angry or fearful when they compete against women in the workplace. The under-thirties are traditional in tending to start relationships and initiate sex more often than the women they know, as the few women I interviewed confirm. They are often unsure how to treat single women and more cautious—from fear or anxiety—about marriage, so they postpone it. (The proportion of men between twenty-five and twenty-nine who are single grew from 23 to 38 percent between 1960 and 1984.[⁴]) But young men are better able to say no to a woman's initiative than are their elders, and better able to maintain nonsexual friendships with women.

There are also some who reject tradition without moving toward equality —young men who seem ready to let women assume the kind of dominance that used to be male. I met two who talked about being househusbands; half-consciously they expect their wives to support them in a mirror image of the old wage-earner ethic, and they have no idea how much labor is involved in child raising. Three had little idea of how they wanted to earn a living, little concept of a career—like women before the recent changes. They are no doubt responding to the changes women are making, but hardly in an egalitarian fashion.

The most traditional of the under-thirties are blue-collar men for whom the factory is the place where they pass from the worlds of home and school, which they see as being run by women, to a world run by men. A woman personnel manager in the heavy equipment plant mentioned in Chapter 5, who dealt every day with the workers, saw this, and I heard her thought echoed in many men's conversations. She said:

Women who come to work in the factory are violating not only the man's sense of family but his sense of order in the world. Look at the world the man-child grows up in: up to the eighth grade it's run almost entirely by women—his mother and his teachers. Even in high school, there are a lot of women teachers—and the girl students affect the boys, whether they behave themselves or go wild. Graduation from high school and coming to work in the plant is graduation from a woman's world and coming into a man's world. When they see a woman at work on the line, it looks like, "Oh, Lord, here comes Mother back again."

Many of these men, even though they grew up in a world much influenced by feminist ideas, still see women primarily as sex objects, not as fellow workers. Many are more self-centered and less helpful than their elders to any peer; they give less support to women on the job than some older men who are uncomfortable with the female presence but have been conditioned both to help their buddies and to help ladies. And, as the personnel manager saw, many younger men think of the shop as the first place they will be members of a male world. Not all blue-collar men under thirty are like this, but many are—enough to remind people not to jump to conclusions or ignore the intersection of age with class.

Many men in their thirties, men born between 1945 and 1955, were closer to what had been predicted: old enough to have acquired traditional attitudes but young enough to have felt the impact of feminist charges and changes. Some tried to respond positively. Others were too unsure of themselves to resolve questions in a way that satisfied them or the women in their lives. Women looking at young men and at the thirties group often complain that they are getting neither what they asked nor the positive supports that accompanied the denial of equality in the old system.

Men in their late thirties and men in their forties were often in the position of marrying a homemaker and celebrating their tenth anniversary with a career woman. Some of these marriages ended in divorce, and the men in those that lasted probably struggled even harder to master the changing rules of the game. A *Ms.* magazine collective described both: "Some men who ran this gauntlet did not feel thanked enough. Some men who resisted change felt punished, angry, and occasionally guilty." That jibes completely with my interviews. *Ms.* added a point I didn't hear often, but which I find easy to believe: "Those feelings, once hidden, now surface as pained concern for the failures of feminism."[5]

Men under forty provide the members of two groups who have achieved prominence in the media, yuppies and new men. Both occupy a bigger place in middle-class consciousness than they do in the population. Yuppies account for only 4 percent of the baby boom, the seventy-six million people between the ages of twenty-one and thirty-nine. This figure comes from an advertising agency measure of the consumer population; what could be more appropriate? J. Walter Thompson U.S.A. defines yuppies as people in this age group who combine higher education (five years, on the average) and high income (a median of $39,100).[6] Despite the *u* for "urban" in yuppie, the agency finds that 56 percent of them live in the suburbs and only one in six is female. This figure may say more about their employers than about the yuppies themselves, but it provides an important reason for my observation that yuppies are unlikely to treat women as equals: they don't meet them as peers in large numbers.

Yuppies, by definition, are devoted to acquisitive and career pursuits, and appear (to me, at least) to be more selfish and narcissistic than the population as a whole. This may give them additional reason to postpone marriage and treasure the freedom of the single state. No doubt it also affects their behavior in marriage; I suspect that much of what I read about remodeling houses and finding new recipes for wholesome dishes reflects a yuppie attempt to substitute material ventures for some of the psychological effort needed to build intimacy and make a marriage last. I wonder if this makes for a more egalitarian marriage—it might, if the spouse were of the same kind—or a less. The first yuppies are now turning forty, and their behavior may change as they enter middle age and become more capable of thinking about others and integrating the masculine and feminine in themselves.

Thompson defines another 16 percent of the baby boom age group as would-bes, people with the same education as yuppies and presumably with yuppie values, but a median income of only $15,000—teachers, clergy, social workers, paramedics, college instructors. There's obviously considerable overlap between Thompson's would-bes and my service occupations, and a much higher proportion of would-bes than yuppies are women. Those two facts should make more of the male would-bes treat women as equals.

When I'm asked about yuppies, however, I think not only about that low 4 percent proportion of the baby boomers, but also of the downward mobility of the whole generation, including elite workers, workers, and housewives. Real after-tax income for families headed by a person aged twenty-five to thirty-four declined 2.3 percent between 1961 and 1982. The combined take-home pay of a two-earner couple in this age group is probably less than what each of their respective fathers earned on his own at the same age.[7] Now, that's a good reason for having no, or fewer, children. But—thinking back to my expectations of a group with a high proportion of women and a lot of service jobs—a man may not treat his wife as an equal if he earns no more than she does; it may only fuel his anger and his anxiety.

The new man is someone whom feminists, social scientists, and advertisers all search for. Barbara Ehrenreich describes the prototype as twenty-five to forty years old, single, affluent, and living in a city, "for it is among such men that the most decisive break in the old masculine values is occurring."[8] (I disagree on the single and I have doubts about the affluent.) He is usually able to choose his clothes, decorate his apartment, and cook for himself—abilities that certainly distinguish him from traditional man, even if, as Ehrenreich says, he uses these skills to demonstrate his class status. They also enable him to stay independent of the women who used to take care of his domestic needs, and he does indeed tend to avoid commitment, in the current phrase. "Sensitivity" is a touchstone for the new man, who claims that he knows how to be "in touch with his feelings." Ehrenreich has her doubts. "Quite possibly," she says, "as sensitivity has spread, it has lost its moorings in the therapeutic experience and come to signify the heightened receptivity associated with consumerism: a vague appreciation that lends itself to aimless shopping."

That fits with marketing definitions of the new man. Playboy Marketing Services describes him as single, separated, divorced, widowed, living with someone who works or married with a working wife, and making purchasing decisions. It estimated in 1984 that 64.9 percent of all men meet this definition, rather different from my estimate of 5 to 10 percent who genuinely support women's demands for independence and equality.[9] (See Chapter 17.) Advertising agencies describe him similarly, in terms of his willingness to do household chores (described in Chapter 9) and his propensity to make brand choices of products used in those chores, but they put him at 13 to 22 percent of all men.

All the surveys agree that men under thirty-five were more likely to show new-man characteristics than those over thirty-five. As I've said, I'm not so sure.

Hyatt & Esserman Research Associates did a poll for *Good Morning America* in 1980 that put the proportion of new men at 19 percent. They asked forty questions and defined the new man in terms of responses to the three that created the greatest division of opinion among the 752 men interviewed. The new man disagreed with the statement, "If women have children at home under six years of age, they should not work." He agreed that "when women marry, it's fine for them to keep their maiden names." And he agreed that "if both parents work, the wife and husband should take turns to stay home when the kids are sick."[10]

But two thirds of *all* men in the Hyatt & Esserman survey disagreed with the statement, "A man should never cry in public," and six out of seven agreed that men can be just as good at changing diapers as women. Those figures show how men in general have been affected by change. They are evidence for my feeling that it will be hard to reverse the revolution. But neither they nor the 19 percent of Hyatt & Esserman's definition of new men are going to make the revolution succeed. That will take another kind of man, or this kind of new man after he has gone through or been put through profound struggle with himself and society.

Some new men are certainly over thirty-five, even over forty. Older men do seem to find it harder than younger men to accept women on the job, but there are so many exceptions to this that I mention it only with reluctance. I found several older men who were genuinely supportive of women's demands for equality and choice. It takes a man who is relatively sure of his own competence, his own achievement, and his own masculinity to feel and behave positively about the changes women are making. Not every successful man is positive about these changes; many hate them as denials of their own lives and values, their own manhood. But a large proportion of those men who do like what women are doing are successful in their own terms. That means many of them are middle-aged.

Older men who are egalitarian and younger men who aren't don't constitute a historical anomaly as much as they illustrate the process of adult development that Daniel Levinson outlined.[11] A young man in his twenties, in early adulthood, is striving to take his place in the world as an adult male. He is apt to try to control or repress the feminine in himself. That often makes it harder for him to respond to women making changes, whom he sees as competing for places as adult "males." A man in his late thirties usually makes an intense effort to achieve a more senior, "manly" position in the world. That often makes him neglect or repress the feminine in himself and also makes him more hostile to women engaged in the same effort. In the forties, the period of the mid-life transition and the famous mid-life crisis, a man becomes more able to integrate the masculine and feminine in himself—and, if he is not too much the victim of tradition, more able to accept and support women's efforts to achieve independence and choice.

HOMOSEXUAL MEN

Many homosexuals, particularly gay activists, talk in convincing and fascinating detail about the ways that the women's movement gave them the courage to do two things: come out of the closet, and free themselves from the sexist culture in which they grew up. The two are intimately connected, but not identical; most gay men learn to accept and enjoy their sexual preferences before they discover the emptiness of conventional ideas of masculinity. Individual women inspired individual men to raise their consciousness (as happened to many straight men). Women's openness about sex encouraged gay men to be open about their sex lives. The collective militancy of the women's movement provided a model for the gay rights movement. The increasing numbers of gay men who have experienced these things identify strongly with women's demands for equality and independence. Steve Borst, an actor, spoke to me about both the personal and political aspects:

> There was one woman, there was an enormous amount of love between me and her. It was through her consciousness, her struggle to perceive herself as a valid human being who didn't have to put up with heckling in the street and the vagaries of relationships with men and things like that, that I began to understand my situation and apply those principles to my gayness as something that was part of my self, that could make me stronger as a person and in society. And there's a political level on which something like this happened to numbers of gay men. The development of the civil rights movements in this country started with blacks, went to women, then to gays, it was a progression from visibility to invisibility. The blacks were the most visible to straight white males, the women were harder for men to see, and before Stonewall in 1969 [the riot over police harassment that is usually considered the start of the gay liberation movement], the gays were invisible. Now we're visible, to ourselves and to everybody else.

Friendships like Borst's with straight women are very important to gay men. They seldom have deep friendships with straight men. Friendships with other gay men face problems and tensions similar to those of nonsexual friendships between heterosexual men and women: they might become sexual, which changes the nature of love and trust. Seymour Kleinberg believes from his own and others' experience that "the richest, least infantile, and most moral relationships gay men form are with women."[12] Both are struggling to realize their refusal to conform to the demands of traditional society. "Abandoning arbitrarily assigned, restrictive, sexual role-playing . . . she frees the male from an equally restrictive, equally arbitrary opposite role," John Rechy says, elaborating on the idea.[13] Women who have such friendships testify that the gay men neither patronize them nor treat them as objects as most straight men do.

Other gays say that it was their discovery, or rather their realization and fulfillment, of their homosexuality that enabled them to transcend traditional sex roles, to give up the efforts they had made since childhood to be "masculine" in the sense of repressing emotion or believing in "the system of leaders and followers," to "free the sister in ourselves" (an old slogan of the Gay Liberation Front).[14] They don't attribute this to friendship with a woman or the example of the women's movement. But a consciousness they think has been raised only through gayness still makes them identify with the changes of the gender revolution.

Gays learn early that they constitute an oppressed class, as women do. A few connect their oppression directly to their sexuality, which gives them something in common with a radical feminist like Ellen Willis. Kleinberg quotes a man who considered "the prodigality of gay promiscuity" as "a compensation for the injustices society has wished on us." Kleinberg says this struck him as more than mere defiance because it "implies that sexual obsession is not devoted exclusively to sensual pleasure but is much involved with an individual's sense of powerlessness."[15] Few straight men have reached an equivalent insight, which I think deserves to be included in revolutionary philosophy.

Homosexuals who give the women's movement credit for the start of their own liberation say that gays with other views probably make up a majority. Some compensate for their oppression by trying to dominate lesbians in gay activist groups, or women in their workplaces, acting very much like blue-collar workers or neurotically insecure men of any class in searching for people they can define as inferior—and finding women. An advertising man told me, "We want to be the equals of straight men, and if that means screwing women—figuratively—we'll do it."

Some gays would not care if they ever saw another woman. Some are clones who have adopted one variety or another of macho look, whether rigid Wall Street or heavy leather, and oppressive images of physical strength, sexual violence, and dominance. These two groups overlap; "the macho gesture is prominent in those gay bars and resorts where women are entirely absent," Kleinberg notes. He offers another important insight:

> The homosexuals who adopt images of masculinity, conveying their desire for power and their belief in its beauty, are in fact eroticizing the very values of straight society that have tyrannized their own lives. . . . The perversity of imitating their oppressors guarantees that such blindness will work itself out as self-contempt. . . .

While straight men define their ideas from a variety of sources (strength, achievement, success, money), two of those sources are always their attitudes toward women and toward paternity. It is no coincidence that the

same decade that popularized liberation for women and announced that
the nuclear family was a failure also saw men return to a long-haired,
androgynous style. If straight men are confused about their maleness, what
is the dilemma for gay men, who rarely did more than imitate these ideas?[16]

Kleinberg sees gays as tending toward one or another of two alternatives:
the macho life, or a species of feminism that derives from recognition of "the
common oppression" of homosexuals and women. Both tendencies show that
sexual preference does not insulate a man from the forces of change or the
question of gender power. Gay men are participants in the revolution and the
fight against it, and they, like straight men, must pay the costs even or especially when they struggle to make it work.

Chapter 16
THE TIMES WE LIVE IN

For every class and race and age group, women's demands for equality and men's feelings about change are forces that affect and are affected by the times we live in. Some people look at the past twenty years as a time of progress, some as a time of peril. Some look at the 1980s as years of regression and backlash, some as years redolent of the good old ways. There are men and women on both sides.

My own belief is that the backlash is real but that the underlying revolution is irreversible. It may reach fruition if believers keep fighting for it. If they don't, it may remain forever half-finished. But it will not vanish as though it had never been.

One reason the revolution is irreversible is that the number of men who welcome at least some of the changes in gender relations is increasing. The number is small, it's true, and ambivalents and opponents of change still combine to make a large majority (see Chapters 15 and 17). I believe it will require immense work by men and women to develop feelings in men of relief and identification and pleasure in the changes, to enable them to move from ambivalence to pragmatism or from pragmatism to support and association. A stampede toward dramatic change is highly unlikely. But I think the numbers of men who have already done some of these things have grown despite the backlash, and will keep growing.

The second reason that the revolution is irreversible is economic. The American economy has evolved to a point where few families can exist comfortably on one income, and few companies can function efficiently without their female employees. The number of women who work for pay has increased steadily since 1950, and 53.5 percent of all women aged twenty and more are now in the labor force. The proportion of men who hold any kind of job has been declining for more than twenty years, from 86 percent in 1960 to 78 percent in 1980 and slightly less today. The white male worker fell to a minority of the labor force for the first time in 1983. The U.S. Labor Department predicts that two thirds of the growth in the labor force between now and 1995 will be female.[1] These facts reflect employers' ability to pay women less than men as much as they do a change in sex roles. The balance may change if the ideas of equal pay and comparable worth win further victories and women's pay rises enough to reduce the benefit employers get from the female part of the labor force. But I don't think it will be reversed.

The more relevant question is whether corporations will change their ways to make it easier for both women and men to take care of their children, themselves or through others. Women will do better at every job, traditionally masculine or not, if their employers, usually male, reduce rather than exaggerate the conflict between work and parenthood. And the revolution (to repeat) will reach fruition only when men do half the child care. They never will unless their employers provide some combination of money, care facilities, and time off—and don't penalize them for using these new resources.

The historical trend may be moving in this direction; as I've noted, the number of employers providing child care assistance has tripled in three years. It's important that the number is increasing, but it's even more important that it's still only 0.03 percent of all employers. Resistance to this kind of change is a matter of corporate bookkeeping, visionary or myopic, that may be reinforced by the Reagan backlash but is not determined by it. Some companies are finding that assistance for child care and for other activities like education and recreation pays off in higher productivity. If more do, the trend will become less fragile, and the changes embodied in women's reach for masculine jobs and men's desire to share in child care will broaden and deepen.

A POWERFUL DIALECTIC

The third reason I think the revolution is irreversible is historical. The changes that women are making are part of a process of change that is centuries old. One part of the process can only be called negative and is often antifemale—the increasing weight of institutions, the weakening of individuals, the degradation of work and pleasure, and the decline of the family. It's the thesis in a dialectic of powerful momentum. The antithesis is a renewed development of the individual, the self, in which the women's movement plays a significant role but is often ignored. One possible synthesis, a happy alternative, is a world of newly strengthened individuals and newly reshaped institutions, in which men and women share power much more equally and equably than they do today.

Christopher Lasch draws an exaggerated but still essentially correct picture of the negative thesis in this dialectic.[2] Institutions like the state, the corporations, and other bureaucracies have grown stronger even as the values that once gave them legitimacy have eroded, disappeared, or changed shape. Individuals have grown weaker and more dependent on those arid forces. Their everyday competence has dwindled, the complementary traditions of self-help and self-denial have atrophied.

The degradation of work is part of this long change. It happened first through the development of factories two hundred years ago and then of assembly lines eighty years ago, and more recently through the growth of bureaucratic "service industries" whose tasks are often as meaningless and repetitive as those on assembly lines. The degradation of work, in other words, began long before the current women's movement—even when one recognizes that the movement of women into the workplace began about 1900, not in 1968. But men often displace anger at that degradation from its economic causes to other targets, like the presence of women in the workplace, and particularly in traditionally masculine occupations, in large numbers. The displacement is the easier because the arrival of women in an occupation often lowers its wage range, a mark of true degeneration, and because women provide so much of the work force for the developing service industries whose tasks men see as another kind of degraded and degrading work. The negative emotions mobilized in our unconscious by one profound force, the degradation of labor, intensify the emotions mobilized by another, women's challenge to millennia of male domination, and intensify them.

The degradation of work is accompanied by the degradation of pleasure, which takes on many qualities of work. Games used to embody important rituals and offer dramatic commentary on reality. Now they embody habits and offer banal escape from reality. The degradation of play thus becomes one more way of dissolving the boundary between work and play, a dissolution that men also see and fear in women's "invasion" of male occupations. Most of us tried and failed to bar that invasion, and we try, just as ineffectually, to bar their invasion of male sports. We don't look sharply enough at the real degradation of pleasure, which also affects our relations with women. We measure play by standards of achievement that we once used only for work—including standards of sexual "performance." Other forms of pleasure, like parties, acquire from work an aspect of social combat that often becomes war between men and women.

The degradation of work and of pleasure goes hand in hand with the decline of the family in which the individual once found meaning. The family has lost its productive function to the factories and much of its reproductive function to three different changes. Economic development made many children a burden rather than a necessity for survival. Scientific discoveries made birth control easy. Cultural change legitimized sex for pleasure rather than reproduction and undermined the traditional sex roles on which the traditional family depended. Women are often blamed for this decline because fewer of them are content to play only the family roles of wife and mother and nothing more. But the weakening of the family started well before large numbers of women went out to work for pay, and indeed was one of the causes of their doing so. The decline of the family is as much cause as effect of women's liberation.

Eighteenth- and nineteenth-century efforts to liberate women were in many senses responses to this process of degradation and decline. Abigail Adams's plea to her husband, John, to "consider the ladies," the feminization of culture in the Victorian era, and the seventy-two-year battle for women's suffrage were all attempts to change the pattern by which political and other institutions were developing. The successive ideals of "virtuous womanhood" in the closing decades of the nineteenth century, "educated motherhood" in the first decades of the twentieth, and "wife-companion" between the two world wars were attempts to cope with the decline of the family.[3]

So was the steady movement of women into the workplace from 1900 on, first a trickle and mostly single, later a flood and increasingly married. These women were trying to support themselves when their families could no longer do so adequately, long before psychological liberation became a factor. (The famous "Rosie the Riveter" jump in female employment during World War II was an exception to meet a temporary, nonfamily need of the state.) In every period a few sympathetic men joined in these efforts; some realized and some did not that this would mean changes in the distribution of power.

Singly and collectively these changes were the precursors of an antithesis to the process of degradation and decline, but neither they nor broader movements reshaped culture and economy enough to bring an antithesis to life. That has begun to happen in the past twenty or thirty years, even though the epoch of degradation still hasn't ended: the individual has responded to centuries of weakening with a new concern for the self, a new effort to develop the person.

Some of this concern is literally selfish, and more than selfish, narcissistic. But in some people it's a struggle to increase the sacred and expressive elements in an individual's life, to develop the self that cares for others and reaches beyond its own boundaries, as Daniel Yankelovich puts it.[4] Women who demand independence and equality at home and in the workplace often express the quest for both kinds of self-fulfillment. They want to develop the selves that the traditional culture limited, and they try to put into practice ideas, new and old, about commitment to others and to the community. So do the men who support change, whether it be commitment to a partner to do half the child care, or to a colleague to recognize her competence, or to a community to work for the prevention of rape and violence against women. (Yankelovich unfortunately ignores both these women and these men.)

The concern for the self that contradicts the earlier growth of institutions and decline of the individual is a major cultural change because it means abandoning the ethic of self-denial by which America grew. It is often visible in forms that verge on the banal, however. Joseph Veroff, Elizabeth Douvan, and Richard A. Kulka, the authors of the broadest look at the changes of recent decades, found that in 1976 people were measuring their well-being less in social terms than they had in 1957 and more in individual terms.[5] People speak less positively of marriage and parenthood, for instance, seeing those institutions as less critical for personal adjustment. Americans no longer depend on their spouses as exclusively as they did a generation ago. I'm sure that this particular freeing of the self reflects one effect of feminism on ordinary women and men, but the authors don't look very deeply at the connection between the attitudes they measure and changes in relations between the sexes.

They do say the movement of women into the workforce is the most profound change of the period they're studying. But they don't test for a link with the increase they find in the number of men who say that finding something wrong in social relationships at work is an important source of dissatisfaction on the job—from 10 to 19 percent over twenty years. I'm sure that this has a lot to do with men's unhappiness over the arrival of women in traditionally masculine jobs. Nor do they see a connection with the greater concern that people show about personal involvement in their jobs, the effort they make to use work for self-development despite the barren soil it seems to offer for that purpose—an effort that I think is also intensified by the presence of women in the workplace.

These different kinds of concern for the person not only constitute an antithesis in an ancient dialectic but suggest a range of syntheses that might truly reshape society, from a growth of narcissistic gratification to the development of a healthier self that reaches out to the community.

Lasch sees the age as one in which a narcissistic culture encourages the individual not truly to examine his life but to use the world as a mirror, not at all the same thing. It seems sad or even tragic to one who remembers when the world was an empty wilderness that the individual could shape to his own design.[6]

Lasch's vision is based on a confusion of a part of the population, a small part, with the whole. Yankelovich cites market surveys that show that 17 percent of working Americans, seventeen million people, place personal fulfillment above everything else—above money, security, performing well, or working at a satisfying job. He wrote before the media discovered yuppies, who insist that personal fulfillment must include money and career; some of his 17 percent no doubt became yuppies, who account for only 4 percent of the baby boom generation by one sophisticated reckoning.[7] Both Yankelovich's me-firsters and the yuppies are suffused with at least the potential for narcissism, but it's not so strong that it makes the establishment of a culture of narcissism inevitable. I'm happy it doesn't; I doubt that narcissistic women make good feminists, and I suspect that narcissistic men are strong opponents of women's demands for independence and equality. A narcissist culture would warp institutions and block both the women's and men's revolutions.

One alternative synthesis would elaborate Yankelovich's ethic of self-fulfillment, which develops the self so it cares for others. His market surveys suggest that 47 percent of the population is searching for community. Sometimes he sounds as though he's predicting that it will come to pass. Sometimes he says explicitly that he can't yet conclude that it is taking shape. He clearly hopes it will, however, as I hope that the revolution that women have started will come to fruition. My own vision of a positive synthesis involves less of a shift to vague ideals of altruistic fulfillment and more of a rebirth of competence, career, family, and community, all redefined to make men and women more nearly equal participants.

It won't be easy—in Yankelovich's version or mine. The old ways are still immensely strong at this moment in history, as every chapter in this book shows. Even where those ways are changing, neither care for the other nor equality of power among men and women are by any means assured. They are threatened by the potential for narcissism and by the tendency to escalate sexual antagonism to sexual combat. It happens faster than it did a generation ago—a negative consequence of the women's revolution and of men's response to it, and of the degradation of pleasure.

There's also another reason it won't be easy to reach a happy synthesis of equality between men and women: a few people are trying very hard to stop the revolution and move some steps back toward the old ways. They often seem to shape the policy of the United States government in the 1980s, and they often seem to have corporate profit considerations on their side. In their campaigns they evoke the powerful residues of emotion this book describes. I believe they won't succeed, but they increase the costs of change even more than the hostility and denial of men in general do.

WEIGHING THE FORCES

Any attempt to assess the forces of change and the forces of resistance in these times involves striking a succession of balances. At best, only 35 percent of men are supporters of women's claims to overall equality, or pragmatic about it—but the proportion who approve of their wives (or daughters or sisters or mothers) working for pay has been growing steadily for twenty years and reached an overwhelming 88 percent in a 1980 survey.[8] The number of men who support the presence of women in "a man's job" is undoubtedly smaller than those who welcome careers for women in their families. It varies with economic and educational class and type of work, but in corporations and law firms and hospitals it has been increasing for at least ten years. The number of men who support the promotion of women to high-level executive or professional jobs is even smaller, but it too is increasing steadily if slowly.

The proportion of men who really do an equal share of housework and child care is small, as I noted in Chapters 9 and 10, and only 14 percent said in one survey that they would choose homemaking if they had to choose between that and a paying job. (I'm surprised that it's as high as 14 percent.) But men have increased the amount of time they devote to housework by 20 percent over twenty years, four out of five fathers are present in the delivery room when their children are born compared to 27 percent a decade earlier, and the majority of fathers today change diapers.[9]

The balance is clearly that while the backlash is real and while we have a long way to go, more men accept change and more men support change than ten years ago, and significantly more than twenty years ago. Even the conservative newsmagazine *U.S. News,* surveying the American male in 1985, quoted experts as agreeing "that macho's rise is really only a blip in a long-term trend toward change."[10]

SOCIAL RESISTANCE

Despite these steady increases in the number of men who accept or support change, the resistance of the majority, the resistance charted in this book, is still strong in the 1980s. It is particularly powerful in social institutions. Two examples are worth a glance apart from the corporate and political worlds: organized religion and men's clubs.

There have been a number of gains for the concept of gender equality in religion in the past twenty years, like the ordination of increasing numbers of women as Episcopal priests, ministers in other Protestant denominations, and Reform and now Conservative Jewish rabbis. The United Methodists elected their first woman bishop in 1980, and the Episcopal House of Bishops voted in 1985 to support any diocese that chooses a woman bishop. A new translation of Bible readings to eliminate descriptions of God as only male was published in 1983 by the National Council of Churches.

But women still do not play major roles in the hierarchies of the religions that ordain women, or in shaping theology. The Lutheran Church in America refused to recommend the new Bible readings for use in its six thousand congregations because the translations were "inaccurate and sometimes written in a poor and inadequate linguistic style." Lutheran Bishop James R. Crumley, Jr., of New York was particularly troubled by the phrase "God the Father and Mother"—or "Mother and Father"—because it might make God appear "bisexual rather than asexual." I doubt he would have preferred "God the Parent," but I was struck by the fear of mother making yet another non-farewell appearance. Orthodox Jewry and the Vatican remain resolutely opposed to greater roles for women, the Church of Jesus Christ of Latter-day Saints (the Mormons) expelled Sonia Johnson for her criticism of the church's tactics against the Equal Rights Amendment, and Episcopal dissidents, mostly high church, formed their own group of churches that refused to accept women priests.

I interviewed the rector of one of those parishes, who described himself as a member of the Catholic element in the Episcopal church. He sounded sincere in his belief that Jesus used only men in the priesthood (though both the U.S. Catholic Biblical Association and the Pontifical Biblical Commission found nothing in the New Testament against the ordination of women). He also sounded sincere when he said, "I feel that the Lord made men and women different, that man generally has within his personality a sort of leadership factor, a dominant factor, and women have a submissiveness or adaptability about them which men find difficult." He mentioned several times that pagan priestesses served as sacred prostitutes, quoted some of his female parishioners as sensing that women priests were lesbians, and cited the example of a woman from his parish who had joined the Air Force—"she's sort of taken a masculine role"—but had written him that "she just couldn't receive communion from the hands of a woman." I thought this man of the Church sounded just like the men of the Army I had interviewed—and realized that he too feared the combination of female sexuality and power, not the power to kill in his case, but the power to save, which he believed in devoutly.

Catholic women are leaving the church in increasing numbers because they find it irrelevant to their lives, but Pope John Paul II has responded only by increasing the emphasis with which he urges women to stay within traditional church roles. American Catholic bishops held a conference in Washington in 1983 in which more than one hundred prelates met with fifty women to talk about the place of women in the modern church. It was plain there that many American bishops favor women's ordination for the priesthood but won't say so in public, and Auxiliary Bishop Austin B. Vaughan of New York, a conservative, complained that it "was stacked" in favor of feminists. But twelve hundred Catholic women, meeting in Chicago at the same time, demanded that the bishops go further and called for a church "with a vision of equal opportunity and a willingness not to oppose change."[11]

The bishops took a step in that direction in 1985 in a report written at the request of the Pope in preparation for a special synod called to examine the results of the Second Vatican Council of 1962–1965 "in light of new needs." The report said, "Particular attention must now be given to women, both lay and religious. Their role in the church and society must be clarified, their rights and dignity must be affirmed, and their advancement to positions of leadership and decision-making must continue. The church needs also to define the appropriate Christian stance toward the secular feminist movement."[12]

The report did not suggest the ordination of women, something which few Catholic male leaders have called for. An organization called Priests for Equality is said to have nearly two thousand members, and one of its advisers, the Reverend William J. Callahan, a former physicist, advocated the ordination of women and criticized the Pope's pronouncements on the subject. That impelled the Jesuits to "reassign" him away from his post with the group.[13]

The bishops' report seemed to me, however, to reflect in small but significant measure the thinking of Hans Küng, a theologian whom the Vatican regards as close to a heretic and who is director of the research project on "Women and Christianity" at Tuebinger University in West Germany. Küng notes that the church in this country would have to stop much of its work if women left it in greater numbers. They outnumber men in Catholic seminaries, where they serve as teachers and spiritual directors, and they do the work of parishes, hospitals, schools, and with the poor. Küng predicts that the Pope will lose his war against women and hopes "that a Pope who has so much devotion to Mary would comprehend the radical feminism of the Magnificat—Mary's prayer in Luke's Gospel. She prays that God 'will put down the mighty from their thrones and exalt the lowly.' This is probably wishful thinking, for the church has a long way to go to make this prayer a reality in its midst."[14]

Moving from the church to men's clubs feels a bit like moving from the sublime to the ridiculous, but the clubs are another place where the mighty don't want to leave their thrones. Here, too, at this moment in contemporary history, resistance to change is strong enough to remind the pilgrim that progress is difficult—even among men whose income and education (and sometimes their behavior in other places) suggest that they are likelier than others to welcome, or at least accept, many forms of equality for women.

Club members who oppose the admission of women claim they are only looking for a place to enjoy the camaraderie of their own sex. The Century Association is a New York club founded in 1847 to provide a place where "authors, artists and amateurs of letters and the fine arts" could receive both pleasure and enlightenment from one another's company. Some three hundred of its nineteen hundred members started a campaign in 1982 to admit women as members, on the assumption that it would increase the pleasure and enlightenment. A large number of members objected, charging that the admission of women "would drastically change the nature of the club and break down the effortless, unconstrained companionship among men and the casual freedom of association which over all the years has characterized The Century."[15]

Lewis Lapham, a Century member, suggested in a New York Times Op-Ed piece that men's clubs were part of the way that

> nature divides the whole of its creation into opposing forces (proton and electron, positive and negative, matter and antimatter, masculine and feminine) in order that their dynamic symmetries might decode and organize the unlicked chaos. The clarity of gender makes possible the human dialectic. Let the lines of balanced tension go slack and the structure dissolves into the ooze of androgyny and narcissism.[16]

I have had my own problems with people who want to dive into the ooze of androgyny (see Chapter 12), but it had never occurred to me that the admission of women to elite clubs would dissolve the boundaries between the opposing forces of nature. Lapham, however, was certainly demonstrating my contention that the threat to dissolve traditional boundaries between the genders engenders fear.

The *Times* ran an editorial by a writer who called herself "A Cultivated Woman," who articulated the fundamental problem that neither side of the Centurions had mentioned in their letters: men use their clubs as places where they tend to business, commercial or professional or political—to exercise power. Members, or their employers, regard club dues and expenses for food, drink, and use of the facilities as tax deductible—for more than 50 percent of revenues of many clubs in large cities. Society thus validates, and the taxpayer finances, institutions that discriminate against women and deprive them of power. Women therefore see the clubs, she wrote:

> as places in which deals are made, contacts established and friends and relatives given a boost. We see them, in brief, as part of an establishment from which we, and a lot of other people, have been excluded for a very long time. . . .
> Do we pose that much of a threat to male bonding? Or are we really a threat to—please be honest, gentlemen—a status quo that has served you very well?[17]

George Ball, former under secretary of state, still a distinguished investment banker, and long a Centurion, wrote a letter to the editor protesting that he had never made, or heard of anyone else's making, a single deal on the club premises. He also wondered if the editorial's "cultivated woman" might not be fictitious.[18] This turned out to be a male fantasy of denial that illustrates another of this book's basic points. Her second editorial was published the same day as his letter. She signed herself "A Non-Fictitious Woman" and suggested that if nobody ever made a deal at the Century, the members should be willing to forbid themselves, as a condition of membership, to deduct dues and the cost of meals at the club from their or their employers' federal income taxes.[19] The editorial writer was Mary Cantwell.

The role of men's clubs in the exercise of power is particularly obvious in Washington, D.C., where the Cosmos (which is not tax-exempt) and the Metropolitan clubs still refuse to have women members. (Senator Paul Simon, an Illinois Democrat, forced Laurence H. Silberman to resign from the Metropolitan in 1985 if he wanted to be confirmed for the position on the U.S. Court of Appeals to which President Reagan had nominated him.) Power is also part of the appeal of The Bohemians, in California, to which Ronald Reagan, George Bush, and many movers and shakers in the worlds of business and finance belong. The Bohemians were the object of considerable humor when members revealed that one reason they exclude women is that they pee against trees, and don women's costumes for the shows they stage, at the outdoor gatherings that they hold once a year.

There has been considerable progress, of course. The Duquesne Club in Pittsburgh, the University Club in Albany, the Players in New York have all admitted women in the past ten years. So have most of the athletic clubs that cater to business people; if they hadn't, they wouldn't have enough members to stay in business. New York City prohibits officials from conducting municipal business or spending city money at clubs with restrictive membership policies. A Maryland court ruled in 1984 that the Burning Tree Club, known as "the golf club of presidents" (of the United States), must admit women or lose its $180,000-a-year exemption from real estate taxes under a state law passed a year earlier. The Jaycees voted to admit women after the U.S. Supreme Court ruled that local chapters could not bar women in states that have antidiscrimination laws. But some Jaycee chapters disbanded or reconstituted themselves as independent, all-male clubs, or gave women applicants what one described as a "cold shoulder."[20] Resistance to the admission of women remains strong and sharp among many members of men's clubs.

BUSINESS RESISTANCE: COMPARABLE WORTH

In the world of clubs, resistance is usually expressed in terms that conceal the question of money, which proponents of change insist on revealing when they talk about tax deductibility. In the corporate and political worlds, questions of money usually conceal the dynamics of tradition and resistance to change, which are just as powerful as they are in the clubs. The psychological opposition to comparable worth is large, for example, but the billion-dollar costs are an even more immense obstacle. This isn't true of everyday resistance, like the feeling of men in middle management that they can once more make sexist jokes, repressed for a few years as unfashionable, in the presence of women, or return to biased hiring policies, ignoring laws still on the books against discrimination.

"Comparable worth" and "pay equity" are labels for the idea that a woman should get the same pay as a man not only for the same work, but also for different work that requires comparable knowledge and skills, mental ability and effort, responsibility, and perhaps working conditions. The idea became a cause for the American Federation of State, County and Municipal Employees (AFSCME), one of the few unions with a deep commitment to equality for women. It persuaded the state of Washington to do the first important study of comparable worth in 1974 for state jobs, but when Dixie Lee Ray—a woman and a Democrat—replaced Dan Evans as governor in 1976, she threw it out.

The Supreme Court opened the door to suits demanding comparable pay in a 1981 decision—a narrow ruling involving a woman guard in an Oregon prison, which merely said she was entitled to file suit. Pay equity soon became "the civil rights issue of the 1980s" in the eyes of both its supporters and its opponents, and a number of battles were fought. So far the idea has won more often than it has lost, but the decisive battle, in the Supreme Court, has not yet taken place.

San Jose, California, ended a nine-day strike by municipal workers in 1981 by agreeing to provide $1.5 million in pay adjustments to reduce discrimination against women. Colorado Springs, Colorado, and Pismo Beach, California, were the first American cities to adopt the idea, in 1982 and 1983 respectively, without facing either a union demand or a court case. Minnesota did a study in 1982 and agreed to spend $22 million to raise women's pay. Idaho, Iowa, New Mexico, and South Dakota have adjusted pay scales as a result of legislation or labor negotiations. AFSCME affiliates have filed suit in other states, counties, and cities, and at least twenty-five states and dozens of cities have voluntarily ordered studies of discrimination against women in the public sector. The city of Los Angeles adopted comparable pay in May 1985, and the state of New York agreed to pay more than fifty thousand women employees about $34 million in raises over two years to bring them into line with men in comparable jobs.[21]

AFSCME's first suit for comparable pay was filed against the state of Washington. In November 1983, U.S. District Judge Jack E. Tanner ordered that fifteen thousand women working for the state receive pay increases worth an estimated $642 million in back pay and $195 million in raises. The state, supported by the U.S. Department of Justice, appealed the decision, and in September 1985 the U.S. Court of Appeals for the Ninth Circuit overturned Tanner's ruling. A three-judge panel said the Washington legislature could enact a comparable worth plan if it chose to do so, but that Title VII of the 1964 Civil Rights Act "does not obligate it to eliminate an economic inequality which it did not create." Judge Anthony Kennedy used language that could devastate the theory of comparable worth when he said, "The state did not create the market disparity [in the pay of men and women] and has not been shown to have been motivated by impermissible sex-based considerations in setting salaries. . . . A study which indicates a particular wage structure might be more equitable should not categorically bind the employer who commissioned it. The employer should also be able to take into account market conditions, bargaining demands, and the possibility that another study will yield different results." Although the state sought the reversal, the Washington legislature indeed chose after the Tanner ruling to adopt a system of pay equity by 1993 and the state will continue the work of setting it up. AFSCME will appeal the Circuit Court ruling.[22]

Despite its victories, comparable worth has plenty of opponents. So far no private employer has agreed to pay on the basis of comparable worth, though it was a major element in the strike of clerical and technical workers against

Yale University in 1984. Industry groups like the National Association of Manufacturers, the U.S. Chamber of Commerce, and the delightfully named Equal Employment Advisory Council have spent millions to organize lobbying efforts against legislation that might give the idea broader scope and to study the problem of costs and of avoiding comparable-worth lawsuits. They are sure that comparable worth will raise labor costs and therefore prices, that firms will weed out low-skilled workers who can't justify the higher costs, and that this will ultimately harm the economy.[23]

Men in the public sector are sometimes dismayed, like police and fire fighters in Minnesota, whose unions broke with other state employee unions and lobbied against inclusion in the state's comparable-worth plan. Francis Fitzgerald of the Minnesota Association of Commerce and Industry reported, "The firemen went crazy because the point system classifies a librarian's job the same level as a fireman's job. One fireman testified that he knows a librarian's job is very dangerous—'a book could fall on her head.' " On the individual level too, however, feelings about change may be as much economic as psychological. Many men fear that the raises that go to women under comparable worth will come out of their future increases, or their very earnings. But William Callahan, leader of a public employees' union in San Jose, argued that "Contrary to popular belief, a lot of men support this, too. We see more and more two-paycheck families. Only they're really one-and-a-half paycheck families."

On the political front, President Reagan called the idea "nebulous and cockamamie." James L. Byrnes, a deputy associate director of the federal Office of Personnel Management, laid out a strategy in May 1984 for "pitting union against union on the issue and both against radical feminist groups." He was concerned particularly with a bill sponsored by Representative Mary Rose Oakar, an Ohio Democrat, that would require the federal government to identify and correct any discrepancies in pay between female-dominated and male-dominated government jobs. The bill showed no signs of passing, but the Reagan administration continued to worry, especially when Walter Mondale endorsed pay equity during the 1984 presidential election. William Niskanen, then the ranking member of the Council of Economic Advisers, called comparable pay "a medieval concept" whose "time has passed," speaking in a campaign debate. Clarence Pendleton, the chairman of Reagan's revamped Civil Rights Commission, called it "the looniest idea since Looney Tunes" in launching what was meant to be an objective study—which predictably rejected the idea by a five-to-two vote as an "unsound and misplaced concept" in April 1985.

The commission vote will have no effect on either the courts or the marketplace. But the Justice Department moved to transform the administration's attitudes into policy in August 1985. It filed a friend-of-the-court brief with the Seventh U.S. Circuit Court of Appeals in Chicago, siding with the state of Illinois in a suit filed by the American Nurses Association. The nurses were appealing a district court ruling that there was no basis in law for their claim of wage discrimination. The administration brief argued that comparable worth "would necessarily lead to a massive restructuring of our nation's economy and install the federal judiciary as a 'central planning commission' that establishes 'proper' wages for male and female employees."[24]

Despite the setbacks as I write, pay equity remains an issue on which change has overcome resistance more often than the reverse. Its ultimate fate is still to be determined.

THE POLITICAL BALANCE

I don't believe Ronald Reagan was elected *because* he opposes changes in the sexual balance of power like pay equity, but I suspect his huge majority drew many votes from men who wanted at least subconsciously to slow or stop change. In any case, he clearly opposes most of the specific changes that people are trying to make, and his election and reelection gave increased strength to those who want to mobilize government and society against the redistribution of power between the sexes. But once again, backlash is not the same thing as effective counterrevolution.

Particulars of politics, government, and judicial decisions in the eighties show both progress and setbacks on the path toward change. The death of the Equal Rights Amendment was pure setback. The Republicans ended their four decades' endorsement of ERA in the 1980 election campaign, and the Reagan administration welcomed its failure to pass state legislatures before the extended 1982 deadline, but neither party nor government brought that failure about. ERA died because its opponents used questions of sex (unisex bathrooms and homosexual marriages) and money (it would cost billions to enforce) to disguise what they saw very clearly was a matter of power, and to mobilize unsophisticated voters against it. They lobbied state legislators, mostly male, who saw a threat of retaliation at the polls that resonated with their own sexist resistance to change. Men played a very small role in the battle *for* the ERA. Few even tried, and the women's organizations generally made it their issue and rejected male help, as Barry Shapiro found when he organized MAN for ERA (see Chapter 13). NOW appointed a man to lead a 1981 campaign to organize male support for the ERA, but by then it was too late. Shapiro was right when he foresaw disaster unless men and women work together on issues of power. The defeat of ERA was an unqualified setback for the forces of change.

Many women and men saw the 1984 elections as a different test of progress. I would say the result was one step forward, one step back. In the presidential ballot the gender gap did not swing decisively against Ronald Reagan as the media had predicted. Women actually gave him a majority, though it was 2 to 9 percent smaller than the men's vote for him; the figure varies with the exit poll. The Democrats' nomination of Geraldine Ferraro for Vice President and their endorsement of the Equal Rights Amendment and free choice on abortion did not give them the advantage they hoped for. But Ferraro's candidacy did give women a new credibility in national politics. The Republicans exploited this more effectively than the Democrats. They commissioned television advertisements that appealed to women's concerns—inflation for older women, the pursuit of careers that profited from the Reagan economic recovery for younger women. They showcased women candidates. Representative Jan Meyers, a Kansas Republican, said Ferraro's nomination had "a very positive impact" on her campaign. On the other side, the women's vote was crucial to the election of two Democrats to the Senate, Paul Simon in Illinois and Tom Harkin in Iowa.[25]

Reagan was concerned before the election that he was perceived as antiwoman. This was undoubtedly one of the reasons that he appointed three women to high positions—Sandra Day O'Connor as the first woman on the U.S. Supreme Court, Elizabeth Dole as Secretary of Transportation, and Margaret Heckler as Secretary of Health and Human Services. They have followed conservative policies and voiced few if any feminist ideas, as was to be expected from Reagan nominees. But they still demonstrate female competence in government in a way that can only help achieve a more equable sharing of power in the long run.

That shows how people who oppose change often (if inadvertently) do things to encourage it. On the level of appointments as on the level of policy, however, backlash is stronger than progress. Reagan's choice of O'Connor, Dole, and Heckler is less important than the overall tally: he has named fewer women to the federal courts or meaningful positions in the federal government than Jimmy Carter did, making him the first president in more than a decade not to appoint more women to positions requiring Senate confirmation than his predecessor did. Indeed, in his second term Reagan has so far placed fewer women in high positions than he did in the comparable period of his first. Conservative Republican stars like former Jeane Kirkpatrick, former ambassador to the United Nations, and Faith Ryan Whittlesey, former head of the White House Office of Public Liaison, have borne witness to the administration's sexism.[26]

Reagan's appointments postpone the day when power is truly shared. He has also named many men who hope that day never comes. One case in which he failed to appoint a woman is a good example of resistance in another male. Helen Delich Bentley, who headed the Federal Maritime Commission under Richard Nixon and Gerald Ford, was considered for the position of Under Secretary of the Navy in 1981. She claimed the backing of Caspar Weinberger, Navy Secretary John Lehman, and several admirals. She was not appointed, however, because Senator John Warner, Republican of Virginia and a former Secretary of the Navy, put a hold on her nomination. He questioned her ability to climb on and off a ship and told her he didn't think the Navy was ready for a woman.[27] Bentley was elected to Congress from Maryland as a Republican on her third try, in 1984; obviously, some male voters, many of them Republicans, saw her qualifications. But some men in California are still resisting a woman in power. Reagan's Republican supporters there regard Rose Bird, the Chief Justice of the state, as too liberal, and have mounted a campaign to recall her in 1986. Nobody has ever challenged her competence, but she dislikes the death penalty and the campaign clearly exploits sexist emotions about a judge who can be portrayed as "soft"—on crime—because she is a woman.

More important than this *ad feminem* attitude are the policies of the Reagan administration, the laws of the U.S. Congress, and the decisions of the courts, particularly the Supreme Court, which play important roles in the shaping of society and of the thoughts and feelings of the people who make up the society.

The administration, in its eagerness to cut spending and reduce welfare, has cut social programs in ways that hurt poor women and families headed by women. I'm sure the policymakers would deny that they intended to oppress women, but the result is oppressive all the same, and I believe they would not have made the cuts so severely or so unhesitatingly if men had been the chief victims.

I have no doubt of conscious intent when I look at 1985 proposals to rescind rules that require government contractors to set numerical goals for hiring minorities and women. They would prohibit the use of statistics to detect discrimination. The proposals came from the Attorney General, Edwin Meese III, and his assistant attorney general for civil rights, William Bradford Reynolds, and were opposed by the Labor Secretary, William E. Brock. The AFL-CIO called them "a giant step backward in the fight against employment discrimination." They also turned out to be opposed by the National Association of Manufacturers and other business groups, and by corporations comfortable with the existing 1965 rules and with statistics that show progress. A compromise—unlikely to satisfy believers in affirmative action, but less obnoxious than the original proposal—was in the works as I finished this book.

Nor can there be any doubt of conscious opposition to change in Reagan's 1985 tax-reform proposals. The men in the Treasury Department would have given the largest benefits to high-income families with many children in which the mother does not work for pay. They also would have given significant benefits to middle-class families with two children and only one wage earner. But the proposals would have eliminated the existing two-earner tax deduction and converted the tax credit for child care expenses to a less valuable deduction. Either the proposals constituted a massive denial of everyday reality and the government's own figures—which show that only 10.7 percent of all households consist of an earning father, a stay-at-home mother, and children—or they were, as critics charged, a Reagan attempt to legislate a return to the traditional family structure, an act of hostility to women's economic independence. Conservative groups lent weight to the accusation by claiming that high taxation of families had forced women into the work force and that the Reagan proposals, which they welcomed, would give some mothers the option of staying home to care for their children. Members of House and Senate made plain that they would change this part of the tax reform to suit their middle-class constituents, who live in predominantly two-earner families.[28] The proposal thus became another case where a serious threat to change ran head-on into economic reality—an example of what I mean when I say the revolution is irreversible for economic reasons.

Congress in that case favored the status quo on taxes, but the two-earner deduction was a status quo that was itself an example of change. Congress has also moved directly for greater equality. It passed one economic equity act that many women saw as a "retail" substitute for the "wholesale" Equal Rights Amendment and will probably have passed another by the time this book appears. It has strengthened the enforcement of child support decisions in divorce cases, protected divorced military and civil service spouses on pension rights, and reformed private and public pensions to reflect the presence of women in today's workplace. Congress failed in one of its most important attempts at change, however—five bills were introduced in 1983 to end insurance rates that discriminate between the sexes, but none passed, largely because the insurance industry mobilized huge lobbying forces against them. States sometimes act for change where Congress does not, however. Hawaii, Massachusetts, Michigan, North Carolina, and Pennsylvania require "unisex" rates for auto insurance, and in 1985 Montana became the first state to bar discrimination on the basis of sex or marital status in any type of insurance.

Most legislative attempts to counter change have failed, like the Family Protection Act of 1981. Among other things, that would have amended federal law on child abuse to allow corporal punishment. It would have changed the tax laws to discourage women from working. It would have ended federal funding for educational materials that "tend to denigrate, diminish or deny the role differences between the sexes as they have been historically understood in the United States." It would also have denied federal funds to any person or organization that "presents homosexuality, male or female, as an acceptable alternative life style." It would be hard to imagine a clearer statement of opposition to change; it was almost too easy a target for people familiar with the changes that have already occurred, and it died in committee. An act to deal with teenage sex did pass, but not in its original form emphasizing chastity, that vanished icon. The most negative legislation that has passed Congress restricts federal funding for abortions.

ABORTION

Hostility to legal abortion is a major threat to the women's revolution—
Congressional hostility, the administration's hostility, and the hostility of the
many groups of the right-to-life movement. The administration's attitude is
its own ideology, of course, but it's also an attempt to satisfy the "pro-life"
forces that campaigned for Reagan and for many legislative candidates. These
forces oppose changes in the division of power as much as anybody in the
government does, but the need to satisfy constituents can and should be
distinguished from ideology. The desire to please supporters who are usually
labeled conservative led an unquestionably conservative government to take
an unusual step in July 1985: it appealed to the Supreme Court to reverse a
precedent for the first time since 1954, when the Court asked the Justice
Department for an *amicus curiae* brief in the famous school desegregation
case, *Brown v. Board of Education.* The Eisenhower administration favored
reversal of the old separate-but-equal precedent, which means it favored
change in a different field of power. The Reagan administration's unsolicited
brief sought the reversal of the 1973 *Roe v. Wade* decision that legalized
abortion, although the Court had affirmed *Roe* in a 1983 decision which
emphasized that adherence to precedent "is a doctrine that demands respect
in a society governed by the rule of law."

The administration brief seems to me to be a significant example of the
power of resistance, of hostility to women's freedom of choice. The public
sometimes sees the government's attitude that way because the organized
women's movement labels it clearly. Judy Goldsmith, the president of the
National Organization of Women when the government filed its friend of the
court brief, called it "a continuation of the Reagan administration's war on
women."

But the real army in this battle of the war is not government officials; it's
the antiabortionist movement, which has increasingly set the terms of public
debate on the issue as a matter of life and of fetal rights. Women's rights are
ignored more and more often, even by their supporters. Few pro-choice people articulate the idea that abortion is not only a matter for women with
unwanted pregnancies, but a matter of every woman's right to control her
fertility and for that matter to express her lust, a matter of sexual as well as
reproductive freedom. Without the right to choose abortion, a woman may
not be able to control her own life. And the fetus can enjoy none of its
putative rights unless it is inside the womb of a woman who might insist on
being consulted. It is also significant that while many prominent right-to-
lifers are women, the idea that fetal life entitles society to control women was
formulated by men. The people who have been convicted as the principal
bombers of abortion clinics are men. Barbara Ehrenreich and Ellen Willis

make these essential points with considerable force.[29] It seems very significant to me that almost no men make them (though Alan Otten summed the problem up concisely in a recent issue of the male-edited *Wall Street Journal*[30]). Abortion is or should be something that is almost as important to us as it is to the women we make pregnant. The right-to-lifers know it and studies of men whose partners have abortions show it. Men who support or are pragmatic about women's independence should favor free choice and speak our minds, or our independence will be curtailed, too.

Members of Congress have never come remotely close to reasoning like Ehrenreich's and Willis's, but so far enough of them know their constituencies to prevent a constitutional amendment that bans abortion from passing. (The pro-choice forces have seldom mobilized their strength as effectively as the antiabortion movement to elect or defeat candidates who agree with them, but public opinion polls still show a majority of Americans favoring legal abortion.) The right-to-lifers indeed have never been able to agree on the wording of an amendment that would gather maximum support. This particular path of the trend to change has therefore not been blocked, even though legislation like the Hyde Amendment bars the use of federal funds for abortions and thereby makes it harder for poor women to get them. The Supreme Court is unlikelier than Congress to think in terms of women's most basic freedoms; *Roe v. Wade* was decided on narrower and muddier grounds. But if the Court maintains the *Roe* precedent, it too will again be demonstrating that the revolution is irreversible.

THE JUDICIARY

Abortion cases are particularly important because the Supreme Court has a mixed record in the eighties on women's rights, which are really issues of equal opportunity and equal power. On the negative side, it has upheld statutory rape laws that punish only men for having sex with a minor of the opposite sex; upheld a state law requiring doctors to notify the parents of a minor in some cases before performing an abortion on her; ruled that a military pension (usually held by a man) may not become part of the property settlement in a divorce; upheld the constitutionality of an all-male military draft; made it harder for minorities and women to challenge discriminatory job programs and seniority systems; and narrowed the application of the 1972 education law, which prohibits sex discrimination by schools and colleges that receive federal financial assistance.

This last decision, the 1984 Grove City case, was important because it may make it harder to combat discrimination in many larger cases in other fields. The Court interpreted the intent of Congress one way despite a brief filed by fifty members saying that when it passed the law, it intended just the opposite. A bill to make that interpretation explicit and overturn the Court decision has been working toward passage ever since.

On the positive side, in addition to reaffirming that it is unconstitutional for states to ban abortion, the Court has ruled that in future, retirement plans may not give women and men unequal benefits. It has held that a nursing school cannot exclude men, in a decision written by Sandra Day O'Connor that emphasized "firmly established" principles requiring "exceedingly persuasive" justification for any gender distinction in a law. It has decided that law firms must comply with federal laws against discrimination in employment. It has held that employers cannot pay men and women unequal wages for jobs that are very much alike but not "identical in every respect," and that market forces alone do not justify lower pay for women doing substantially the same work as men. And the Court has ruled that employer health plans cannot exclude pregnancy coverage for a spouse whose other illnesses are covered. The practice, which many employers adopted to save money, discriminates against male employees by giving them less comprehensive coverage than their female colleagues, the Court said. It had ruled in 1976 that federal law did not require companies to insure female workers for pregnancy expenses; Congress, in one of its pro-equality moments, passed the Pregnancy Discrimination Act in 1978 to overturn that decision, and the Court had to follow suit.

On balance, I would say that the Burger Court has been a bit more negative than positive for changes in the distribution of power. But it has neither tried consciously to turn the whole tide back, nor done so unintentionally.

Lower federal courts and state courts have sometimes been more positive than the Supreme Court. The Third Circuit Court of Appeals decided against Grove City College and the government, and was reversed by the Supreme Court. U.S. District Court judge Henry F. Werker stopped the government from putting into effect the "squeal rule," which would have required family planning clinics to notify parents when their children received contraceptives. This seemed to run against the Supreme Court's reasoning on abortion notification. Lower courts have issued many rulings favoring class action suits by women against discrimination in employment; the administration is trying to confine such suits to the injured individuals, by federal regulation of contractors and by supporting suits by white males who claim they have been injured by quotas designed to increase the hiring and promotion of women and blacks.

The courts sometimes take two steps forward and a step back in the same case. Christine Craft, a television anchorwoman, sued her former employer, station KMBC in Kansas City, for sex discrimination. She claimed that her news director had told her that she was "too old, too unattractive, did not defer to men and did not hide her intelligence to make men look smarter." A U.S. District Court jury found that she had indeed been the victim of sex discrimination and awarded her five hundred thousand dollars. Judge Joseph

E. Stevens threw out that verdict, charging that the jury was affected by "pervasive publicity" about the case and that the verdict "is excessive and is the result of passion, prejudice, confusion or mistake on the part of the jury." He ordered a second trial and Craft won in that one too. Metromedia, the owner of KMBC, has appealed. The case seems to me to be a case history of male emotions about change, with pragmatic support in the jury victorious over hostility and denial of the men at the station—so far.

This chapter's summary of the times we live in supports my hypothesis that there's plenty of backlash against the idea of equality for women, but not enough to stop the world. The backlash makes itself felt in the minds and hearts of men, in important institutions like church and club and corporation, and in the overt and covert agendas of the Reagan administration. It provides many new examples of anger, fear, anxiety, envy, shame, and guilt; emotions are at work even or especially where people would deny it, as in the Supreme Court decisions on not drafting women and on notifying parents of a minor's abortion. The backlash threatens to block the movement toward the redistribution of power that has flowed from the manifold revolution of women and the (so far) miniature revolution of men.

But the backlash has not reversed those revolutions and appears unlikely to. Ambivalence and pragmatism are much bigger in the 1980s than either outright opposition (despite Ronald Reagan and John Paul II) or heartfelt support. Ambivalence may uncoil into backlash, but it's not the stuff of counterrevolution. Pragmatism, however, is enough to keep change rolling on its own momentum, if not to bring it to fruition.

Chapter 17
CONCLUSIONS

This book explores both the political and psychological dimensions of the changes in relations between men and women in America over the past twenty years. I call the sum of these changes a revolution, and I think they fit Hannah Arendt's definition of revolution: a new story, "a story never known or told before," whose aim is freedom.[1] She distinguishes between liberation, concerned with restoring rights that have been lost or abused, and freedom; liberation is a precondition of freedom, but freedom involves positive action in the larger community. The true American revolution, by her definition, was the elimination of mass poverty in colonial times. I would add two more: first, the cumulative effects of the century from the abolition of slavery to the civil rights movement of the sixties, a revolution in race relations; second, the events of the past twenty years that are still in the course of moving from women's liberation to a revolution in gender relations. None of the three, including the one that Arendt saw starting three hundred years ago, is yet complete. To reach fruition, the gender revolution must involve men more widely and reshape culture and society in some way comparable to those suggested in Chapter 16.

Women began this new story by claiming a bigger share in power than they have ever had—an equal share with men in political, economic, social, family, and sexual power, and the intellectual power to name and define. They not only demand this equal share, but in the process they also expose men's true powerlessness, the weakness that the majority of us disguise by identifying with the few, mostly male, who hold power.

In every chapter I've looked at a specific context in which men respond to these claims and revelations, at the ways men feel and behave in confronting these women. In some, I've looked at the ways we feel and the things we do on our own that affect the distribution of power. They all show that our "negative" feelings—our anger, fear, anxiety, envy, shame, and guilt—consistently (but happily not always) outweigh our "positives"—relief, pride, admiration, identification, and pleasure. Our hostility, our denial, and our transformation of women into beings that in our fantasies we can relate to in old, pre-challenge ways collectively outweigh our acceptance, our support, and our association with the women who challenge us.

These negatives sound like an old story, but they are part of the new one. I've looked closely at them because I think we need a better measure of them, a better map of the terrain inside our heads, our culture, our economy, and our society, because that terrain is one of the places where the new story will be played out. A better measure will help us transcend the enmity between men and women and the enmity between male supporters and opponents. And not only transcend the enmity, but alter it. Knowing the problems and the costs will make it easier to change not only our feelings and our actions but also the structures and the processes of society. It will help us join in the effort to complete the revolution.

"Measure" and "map" are inadequate metaphors. I've tried to put into scholarly journalism a mixture of systems and disorders that might be better seen in a novel or a hologram or a perpetually moving computer graphic. Whatever the form of art, it will show that the real issue is a question of power. We feel the emotions and act out the behaviors on the list I've just repeated because we don't want to share power with women. The most important reason that we don't is the fear of mother that is part of every child's psychological development and every culture's mythology.

This fear is reinforced by other emotions shaped by real and imagined differences between men and women and by millennia of male bonding, which combined to produce the ancient division of labor, the polarization of work and love, and the Chinese puzzle of traditional sex roles. All these forces lead us to dislike women in "a man's job"—a particular occupation or a particular place in the hierarchy. Acts and feelings vary with occupation, class, race, age, and sexual orientation; blue-collar men and professionals share key attitudes, for instance, and older men show more support for change and younger men less than many people expect. Men's struggle to support the revolution, unlike women's, relies on emotions that are thin and weak compared to the feelings that militate against change.

We usually support change at home more than at work if only because we love the women who are close to us and want to see them enriched in many senses, but the problem here is even more profound than at work, since it involves the combination of power and sex explicitly as well as covertly. The road to change we seem to take most often and like best is active fathering. We're still a long way, however, from the change that will mark the real victory of the revolution: the day when men do half the work of child raising from the moment of birth, freeing women from half that burden and changing the pattern of mothering that reproduces the fear of women in every generation.

The details of these conclusions are laid out in every chapter. I've saved two things for last, however. One is a figure, my guess at the answer to the question I'm often asked: How many men really support the changes women are making? How many men really fight for the revolution, for the redistribution of power?

My answer has to be that the proportion of all men who genuinely support women's demands for independence and equality is very small. I would guess from my interviews and from others' research that it's between 5 and 10 percent. Add in all the men who have found pragmatic reasons for accepting the changes that women are making and the level is probably still no more than 35 percent. Chapter 15 cites other estimates, from surveys by marketing firms, that range from 13 to 64.9 percent; the latter figure is based on a definition too superficial to be useful here. The order of magnitude in my impressions was confirmed by a poll of greater statistical respectability than mine: A New York *Times* national survey in 1983 found that 28 percent of American men felt that the women's movement had improved their lives, while 63 percent said it had not.[2] At the moment, ambivalents and opponents of a new distribution of power are still in the majority.

That often depresses feminists, women in general, and men who want to make change. It's an important fact. But it's even more important that the numbers of pragmatists and supporters are increasing, that more men accept and support change than ten or twenty years ago. (See Chapters 15 and 16.) The *Times* poll contained another confirmation of this: sixty-one percent of men and 51 percent of women said men's attitudes toward women had changed for the better over the previous ten years.

That's the first step toward the other definition I've been saving for the end: the answer to the question, is there a new man? If there is, what's he like?

There is, even if there aren't very many of him. Chapter 15 gave several answers derived from market research. Barbara Ehrenreich wouldn't let herself be imprisoned in those concepts and offered a better final description: a new man is one capable of appreciation, sensitivity, intimacy, plus commitment to a mate, to friends, to family, to a community and a vision of equality between men and women and of equality among men.[3]

I like that definition, with its echo of Yankelovich, but I think it needs to be given flesh and blood, heart and mind. In my definition, the new man is one who has abandoned or transcended most traditional male sex roles and the male attempt to monopolize power. He doesn't insist on being the sole or dominant earner of family income and he resists being a slave to his job even though he prizes competence and achievement. He believes that men are just as emotional as women and should learn to express their feelings, and he can talk about his own problems and weaknesses.

The new man supports women's quests for independence and equality with more than lip service. He works in his own workplace for equal pay for equal or comparable work and equal chances for promotion for his female col-leagues. He doesn't place his job ahead of his family *all* the time.

At home, if he's married, he recognizes his wife's career as equal in impor-tance to his own, and he trades off on transfers that mean promotion or on staying home from work with a sick child. Most important of all, he takes half the responsibility for house work and child care, in addition to doing half the work.

If he's single, he accepts a lover's business travel and late nights at the office with the same understanding he gives his own overtime. He takes care of himself physically, not just in trendy fitness, but in cooking and in cleaning as much as he relies on restaurant or maid. He takes care of himself emotion-ally, or at least doesn't rely exclusively on wife or lover or some other woman for emotional nurture.

Those qualities combine with Ehrenreich's vision to make up an extreme or ideal definition. The men in my 5 or 10 percent come close to it, or at least are moving toward it. It's hard work and struggle, but in the end, the result is worth it.

The struggle is visible in the negatives I've emphasized in every chapter. The individual angers and anxieties, the collective power plays, the deploy-ment of economic forces all show that change will be immensely difficult, toweringly high in social and emotional cost. But every chapter also gives detailed examples of new men, men moving toward acceptance and support, men finding pleasure and reward in the changes that women began. It is these men whose numbers are increasing, who are making it both a men's and women's revolution, the only thing that can give us an equal share in its fruits. Victory is not yet guaranteed, but the revolution continues.

NOTES

CHAPTER 1: WHY THIS BOOK

1. Ingrid Bengis, *Combat in the Erogenous Zone: Writings on Love, Hate & Sex* (New York: Alfred A. Knopf, 1972).

2. Daniel Levinson, *The Seasons of a Man's Life* (New York: Alfred A. Knopf, 1978).

CHAPTER 2: A FRAMEWORK OF IDEAS

1. In Western society, women frequently exercised a portion of real economic power, though they had almost no political power—in early medieval Europe, for example, and in colonial America. Other cultures in which women exercise some authority—non-Western and less developed—prove that male dominance is not quite so universal as many contemporary anthropologists think. But even in those societies, men occupy the main positions of leadership, just as they do in our own. Exceptions in the West are isolated and few in number, and like such historical examples as Elizabeth I and Catherine the Great or such modern ones as Golda Meir and Indira Gandhi, they rule through men. See Peggy Reeves Sanday, *Female Power and Male Dominance: On the origins of sexual inequality* (Cambridge: Cambridge University Press, 1981). See also Karen Sacks, *Sisters and Wives: The Past and Future of Sexual Equality*. Contributions in Women's Studies, no. 10 (Westport, Conn: Greenwood Press, 1979).

2. Elizabeth Janeway, *Between Myth and Morning: Women Awakening* (New York: William Morrow, 1975). See also her *Powers of the Weak* (New York: Alfred A. Knopf, 1980).

3. Janeway, *Powers.*

4. Dorothy Dinnerstein, *The Mermaid and the Minotaur: Sexual Arrangements and Human Malaise* (New York: Harper & Row/Colophon, 1977); and Nancy Chodorow, *The Reproduction of Mothering: Psychoanalysis and the Sociology of Gender* (Berkeley: University of California Press, 1978).

5. Janeway, *Powers.*

6. Wolfgang Lederer, *The Fear of Women* (New York: Harcourt Brace Jovanovich/Harvest, 1967).

7. Ibid.; and William Irwin Thompson, *The Time Falling Bodies Take to Light: Mythology, Sexuality and the Origins of Culture* (New York: St. Martin's Press, 1981).

8. The phrase is Dinnerstein's, *Mermaid.* See also Chodorow, *Mothering,* and Lillian B. Rubin, *Intimate Strangers: Men and Women Together* (New York: Harper & Row, 1983).

9. Rubin, *Intimate Strangers,* and Chodorow, *Mothering.*

10. Jay Rohrlich, *Work and Love: The Crucial Balance* (New York: Summit Books, 1980).

11. Dinnerstein, *Mermaid.*

12. Even Freud, whose ideas about aggression grew out of his theory of a death instinct, recognized that there was a positive side: "The instinct of destruction, moderated and tamed, and, as it were, inhibited in its aim, must, when it is directed towards objects, provide the ego with the satisfaction of its vital needs and with control over nature," in *Civilization and Its Discontents* (1930; reprint, New York: W. W. Norton, 1961). Erich Fromm, distinguishing destructive from "self-assertive" aggression, defined both as "moving forward toward a goal without undue hesitation, doubt, or fear." *The Anatomy of Human Destructiveness* (New York: Fawcett Crest, 1973). Satisfaction, control over nature, and goals are all aspects of work, but neither Freud nor Fromm made the explicit connection.

13. Eleanor Emmons Maccoby and Carol Nagy Jacklin, *The Psychology of Sex Differences* (Stanford: Stanford University Press, 1974). The endocrine association was confirmed by later tests of children whose mothers were treated during pregnancy with synthetic progestins to prevent miscarriage. The progestins tend to act like natural male sex hormones. Both boy and girl children of such pregnancies behaved more aggressively in standard tests than did siblings who had not been exposed to progestins. Jane Brody, "Male Hormones Tied to Aggressive Acts," New York *Times,* 7 March 1981.

Fromm, *Anatomy,* suggested that testosterone and aggression are linked because the anatomy of sex requires the male to be capable of penetrating the female even if she shows fear or resists; he then added that the male necessity to perform in the sexual act gives him more need than the female to demonstrate, to produce—in my terms, to work—and to have power.

14. Naomi Weisstein disputes the idea that males are more aggressive because of their higher testosterone levels. She points out that the studies of human societies were done mostly by men who were probably influenced by unconscious male biases, and that the linkage between testosterone levels and aggression has not been defined well enough to be of scientific value. Weisstein adds that if men are more aggressive than women, which she doubts, it may not be biological, but the result of the division of labor in human society before the technological age. (Personal communication with author.) The proof may not be as firm as Maccoby and Jacklin suggest, but their hypothesis is consistent with common experience and with my own perceptions.

15. See Dinnerstein, *Mermaid.*

16. Hannah Arendt, *The Human Condition* (Chicago: University of Chicago Press, 1958).

17. George Steiner, lecture at New York University, October 8, 1980. See also his *After Babel* (New York: Oxford University Press, 1975).

18. Arendt, *Human Condition.* The internal quotes are from Aristotle's *Politics.*

19. The boundary between what was private and female and what was public and male was not always easy to draw. David Herlihy says that in early feudalism, women's "extraordinary role in the management of family property" brought them into the public world. He describes them as administering an "inner" economy of the manor and managing social relations connected to it, while men ruled an "outer" economy of war and the acquisition of estates. Herlihy insists that "inner" and "outer" are not the

same as "private" and "public," that the "inner" economy was public as well as private because the private fief was a center of public life. David Herlihy, "Land, Family and Women in Continental Europe, 701–1200," in *Women in Medieval Society,* ed. Susan Mosher Stuart (Philadelphia: University of Pennsylvania Press, 1976).

I think this blurs a useful distinction. Men who intended to keep rule to themselves had no problem leaving to women an inner economy that was smaller and more concerned with labor than the outer economy.

But women do function in the public world of work in some premodern or pre-capitalist societies, where they are often equal members and decision makers in a community of owners of the means of production. Karen Sacks in *Sisters and Wives* calls them *sisters* and distinguishes them from *wives,* whose economic functions are determined by their relationships to their spouses.

20. Ruth Moulton, "The Fear of Female Power—A Cause of Sexual Dysfunction," *Journal of the American Academy of Psychoanalysis* 5, no. 4 (October 1977): 499–517.

21. 1 Cor. 14:34–35.

22. Sandra M. Gilbert and Susan Gubar, *The Madwoman in the Attic: The Woman Writer and the Nineteenth-Century Literary Imagination* (New Haven: Yale University Press, 1979).

23. Poem 613, Emily Dickinson, *The Complete Poems of Emily Dickinson,* ed. Thomas H. Johnson (Boston: Little, Brown, 1960). The poem was written about 1862 and first published in 1935.

24. See Cheris Kramarae, *Women and Men Speaking: Frameworks for Analysis* (Rowley, Mass.: Newbury House, 1981); and Robin Lakoff, *Language and Woman's Place* (New York: Harper & Row/Colophon, 1975).

25. Lederer, *Fear.*

26. Joseph H. Pleck, *The Myth of Masculinity* (Cambridge, Mass.: MIT Press, 1981).

27. Robert Brannon, "The male sex role: Our culture's blueprint for manhood and what it's done for us lately," in *The Forty-Nine Percent Majority: The Male Sex Role,* ed. Deborah David and Robert Brannon (Reading, Mass: Addison-Wesley, 1976). See also Robert Brannon, Samuel Juni, and K. Grady, "A Scale for Measuring Attitudes About Masculinity," unpublished paper.

28. Joseph H. Pleck, "Men's Power with Women, Other Men, and Society," in Elizabeth H. Pleck and Joseph H. Pleck, *The American Man* (Englewood Cliffs, N.J.: Prentice-Hall, 1980).

29. Male college students, for instance, confide in women friends more than in men friends. Mirra Komarovsky, *Dilemmas of Masculinity: A Study of College Youth* (New York: W. W. Norton, 1976).

30. Willard Gaylin, *Feelings: Our Vital Signs* (New York: Harper & Row, 1979).

31. Freud makes the point about the struggle against identification in "Analysis Terminable and Interminable," written in 1937. Jean Baker Miller notes that this implies the desire for identification in *Toward a New Psychology of Women* (Boston: Beacon Press, 1976).

32. Gaylin, *Feelings.*

33. Janeway, *Powers.*

34. This section is based on Gaylin's seven categories of pleasure. Gaylin, *Feelings.*

CHAPTER 3: A MAN GOES CRAZY

1. The A. K. Rice Institute is the American offshoot of the Tavistock Institute in England; its postulates are based on the work of Melanie Klein, Wilfred Bion, Margaret Rioch, A. Kenneth Rice, and others.

2. F. C. Redlich and Boris M. Astrachan, "Group Dynamics Training," in *Group Relations Reader*, ed. Arthur D. Colman and W. Harold Bexton (Washington, D.C.: A. K. Rice Institute, 1975).

3. Men and women behave differently in single-sex and mixed groups and respond in different ways to leaders of different sexes and styles. A woman leader who adopts a "blank screen" style, for instance, revealing little of her own feelings and not reciprocating the emotional behavior of the members, draws negative responses from both men and women. The reason may be that she disappoints their expectations that a woman will take an interested, nurturing approach even when she is in authority. But women displace their feelings of hostility to such a leader onto other group members more than men do. This reflects both the cultural inhibitions against attacking leaders that men share and the cultural discouragement of direct expression of aggression by women, to which men are not subject. Fred Wright and Laurence J. Gould, "Recent Research on Sex-Linked Aspects of Group Behavior," in *Group Therapy 1977: An Overview* (New York: Stratton Intercontinental Medical Book Corp., 1978).

4. Elizabeth Janeway, *Between Myth and Morning: Women Awakening* (New York: William Morrow, 1975).

5. Rosabeth Moss Kanter, *Men and Women of the Corporation* (New York: Basic Books, 1977).

CHAPTER 4: THE ARMY

1. Simone de Beauvoir, *The Second Sex* (New York: Alfred A. Knopf, 1957).

2. I am indebted to Helen Rogan, *Mixed Company: Women in the Modern Army* (New York: G. P. Putnam's Sons, 1981), for the idea of distinguishing between women's challenge to men's power in society and women's challenge to men's power in the Army.

3. Peggy Reeves Sanday, *Female Power and Male Dominance: On the origins of sexual inequality* (New York: Cambridge University Press, 1981).

4. Philip Caputo, *A Rumor of War* (New York: Holt, Rinehart and Winston, 1977).

5. Lesley Hazleton, personal communication to the author.

6. The Army estimated in 1980 that it had eighteen thousand single parents, more men than women; in 1985 it claimed it didn't know the precise figure and spoke only of thirty thousand "single-member sponsors," unmarried soldiers with people physically or financially dependent on them. Half of these were men with "only" financial responsibility for dependents, presumably children.

CHAPTER 5: BLUE-COLLAR WORKERS

1. *Detroit News,* 12 February 1981. Eyewitness report from the observer I am calling Kenneth McCann in my interview with him.

2. A government survey of utility companies, for instance, found that a higher proportion of blue-collar than white-collar workers failed to make women welcome in

their fields but said that white-collar resentment was higher in some cases. U.S. Department of Labor, Employment and Training Administration, R&D Monograph 65, *Women in Traditionally Male Jobs: The Experiences of Ten Public Utility Companies* (Washington, D.C.: Government Printing Office, 1978).

The Inner American, probably the broadest study of Americans' feelings about their lives, compared responses of representative populations in 1957 and 1976. All occupations reported more perceptions of problems at work in the latter year, but the rise was most dramatic among blue-collar workers of both sexes. There were also marked increases in seeing something wrong with social relationships at work in both high- and low-level jobs, but the most dramatic increase was among male laborers. The survey did not try to determine specific causes for these replies to broad questions, but I believe the women's invasion of male job fields must be one of the most significant. (Other important causes might be the increase in minority and immigrant jobholders with poor English, in some areas, and the changing culture of the "Me Decade.") The authors certainly consider the increase in the proportion of women who work one of the most important changes in American society over the two decades. Joseph Veroff, Elizabeth Douvan, and Richard A. Kulka, *The Inner American: A Self-Portrait from 1957 to 1976* (New York: Basic Books, 1981).

3. From tables for 1972–82 annual averages, and 1983 and 1984 annual averages, Bureau of Labor Statistics, *Employment and Earnings* (Washington, D.C.: Government Printing Office, 1984 and 1985).

4. Mary Lindenstein Walshok, *Blue-Collar Women* (Garden City, N.Y.: Doubleday/Anchor Books, 1981).

5. For testimony on workers' feelings about their assembly-line jobs and their employers, see Studs Terkel, *Working* (New York: Avon Books, 1975); Martin Douglas, "GM vs. Its Workers," New York *Times,* 15 February 1982, Op-Ed page; and Rick King, "In the Sanding Booth at Ford," *The Washington Monthly,* January 1976.

6. Blue-collar men have usually known their own importance to America, but they are emblematic because they are also important to people of other classes. Max Perkins, the scion of upper-class New England who edited not only F. Scott Fitzgerald and Thomas Wolfe but such masculine writers as Ernest Hemingway and Will James, wrote his friend Elizabeth Lemmon that his daughters had returned from a trip to Wyoming vowing that they would never marry "because cowboys couldn't support them and all Eastern men are as nothing beside them." Perkins added, "It's one reason we have wars: a man who wends his life with his knees crooked under a desk is only half a man, and we all know it. And Dr. Johnson said, when they were running down the military, 'If a general walked into this room now we'd all be ashamed.' And if a good workman, a mechanic, walked into a boardroom at a directors meeting, the directors would all feel ashamed. And if old Zimmerman, foreman at our press, a man like Adam Bede, in a striped apron, walked into our directors meeting we'd all feel ashamed. And that is true and must mean something, but what, I don't know." Letter quoted in A. Scott Berg, *Max Perkins: Editor of Genius* (New York: E.P. Dutton, 1978).

7. Lionel Tiger, *Men in Groups* (New York: Random House, 1969).

8. Ibid.

9. George P. Murdock and Caterina Provost, "Factors in the division of labor by sex: a cross-cultural analysis," *Ethnology* 12 (1973): 203–25, quoted in Peggy Reeves

Sanday, *Female Power and Male Dominance: On the Origins of Sexual Inequality* (Cambridge: Cambridge University Press, 1981).

10. Tiger, *Men in Groups.*

11. Ibid. William Irwin Thompson, *The Time Falling Bodies Take to Light: Mythology, Sexuality and the Origins of Culture* (New York: St. Martin's Press, 1981), offers a delightful gloss on Tiger in which the male bond is modified by the hominid shift from forest trees to the savanna and from the estrus to the menstrual cycle. In his scenario, females pull males away from the bond by "the remorseless power of pheromones" to fulfill their need for protective association with males. The females pull the males into new forms of social cohesion and restraint rather than acquiescing in forms that grow out of the male bond.

12. Lucy Gwin, *Going Overboard* (New York: Viking Press, 1982).

13. Lillian Breslow Rubin, *Worlds of Pain* (New York: Basic Books, 1976).

14. Georgina Smith, "Help Wanted-Female: A Study of Demand and Supply in a Local Job Market," quoted in Catherine Mackinnon, *Sexual Harassment of Working Women* (New Haven: Yale University Press, 1979). See also Henry Braverman, *Labor and Monopoly Capital: The Degradation of Work in the Twentieth Century* (New York: Monthly Review Press, 1974); C. Wright Mills, *White Collar* (New York: Oxford University Press, 1956); and Andrea Dworkin, "Phallic Imperialism: Why Economic Recovery Will Not Work for Us," *Ms.*, December 1976.

15. Brigid O'Farrell, "Affirmative Action for Women in Craft Jobs: Change in the small industrial workgroup" (Paper presented at the joint session of the Society for the Study of Social Problems and the American Sociological Association, New York, 25 August 1975).

16. Raymond M. Lane, "A Man's World: An Update on Sexual Harassment," *The Village Voice*, 16–22 December 1981; and "Female Miners Fight for Acceptance," *New York Times*, 11 October 1982. See also Merit Systems Protection Board, *Sexual Harassment in the Federal Workplace: Is It a Problem?* (Washington, D.C.: Government Printing Office, report no. 06200000058, 1981).

17. Lane, "Man's World."

18. Ibid.

19. Joseph Veroff, Elizabeth Douvan, and Richard A. Kulka, *The Inner American: A Self-Portrait from 1957 to 1976* (New York: Basic Books, 1981). The surveys also show that less educated people are likelier to say that divorce is never the best solution to marital problems and that parenthood "never" interferes with their lives.

20. "A.F.L.-C.I.O. Names a Woman as Member of Its Executive Board," *New York Times*, 22 August 1980; "Women Are Turning to Collective Action as a Key to Power and Protection," *New York Times*, 31 January 1985; and Peter Perl, "AFL-CIO Elects 4 Men to Executive Council," *Washington Post*, 31 October 1985.

21. "West Virginia Woman Accepted as the First to Head Mine Local," *New York Times*, 9 October 1978.

22. Judy Mann, "Parental Leave Needed," *Washington Post*, 25 October 1985.

CHAPTER 6: SERVICE OCCUPATIONS

1. Louise Kapp Howe, *Pink Collar Workers* (New York: G. P. Putnam's Sons, 1977).

2. Marvin Harris, *America Now: The anthropology of a changing culture* (New York: Simon and Schuster, 1981).

3. U.S. Department of Labor, Employment and Training Administration, R&D Monograph 65, *Women in Traditionally Male Jobs: The Experiences of Ten Public Utility Companies* (Washington, D.C.: Government Printing Office, 1978).

4. Tables for 1983 and 1984 annual averages, Bureau of Labor Statistics, *Employment and Earnings* (Washington, D.C.: Government Printing Office, 1985). Patrol figures from Police Foundation, quoted in New York *Times,* 11 January 1982.

5. Susan Ehrlich Martin, *Breaking and Entering: Policewomen on Patrol* (Berkeley: University of California Press, 1980).

6. Ibid. I have adopted many of Martin's ideas for this passage on the general nature of police work.

7. Tables for 1972–82 annual averages, and 1983 and 1984 annual averages, Bureau of Labor Statistics, *Employment and Earnings* (Washington, D.C.: Government Printing Office, 1984 and 1985). Carol Hymowitz, "More Men Infiltrating Professions Historically Dominated by Women," *The Wall Street Journal,* 25 February 1981.

8. R.G.S. Brown and R.W.H. Stones, *The Male Nurse.* Occasional Papers on Social Administration, no. 52. London, 1973. See also Bernard E. Segal, "Male Nurses: A Study in Status Contradiction and Prestige Loss," *Social Forces* 41 (1962).

9. American Nursing Association figures; Hymowitz, "More Men."

10. Bureau of Labor Statistics, *Employment,* table for 1984.

11. Paul Strassman, executive vice president of Xerox Corporation, quoted in Nancy Rubin, "Women Thrive on Technology," New York *Times,* 28 March 1982.

12. Robert Reinhold, "Women in Electronics Find Silicon Valley Best and Worst," New York *Times,* 1 March 1984.

13. Philip Kraft, State University of New York at Binghamton, quoted in Lillian B. Rubin, *Intimate Strangers: Men and Women Together* (New York: Harper & Row, 1983).

14. The Bureau of Labor Statistics classifies health, education, advertising, repair shops, and a host of other businesses as "other services." About 41 percent of the employees in this category earned less than thirteen thousand dollars in 1983, the latest figures available. Richard I. Kirkland, Jr., "Are Service Jobs Good Jobs," *Fortune,* 10 June 1985.

CHAPTER 7: BUSINESS MANAGEMENT

1. Anne Harlan and Carol Weiss, "Moving Up: Women in Managerial Careers" (Unpublished paper reproduced by Wellesley College Center for Research on Women, Wellesley, Mass., 1981). On the equal distribution of fear of success, see Marion M. Wood and Susan T. Greenfeld, "Women Managers and Fear of Success: A Study in the Field," in *Sex Roles* 2, no. 4 (1976).

2. Allan Sloan, *Three Plus One Equals Billions: The Bendix-Martin Marietta War* (New York: Arbor House, 1983).

3. Gail Sheehy in *Interview,* February 1983.

4. See Mary Cunningham with Fran Schumer, *Powerplay: What Really Happened at Bendix* (New York: Simon & Schuster/Linden, 1984); and Gail Sheehy, *Pathfinders* (New York: William Morrow, 1981).

5. Allan Sloan, *Three Plus One*.

6. Lisa Bernbach, "I'm Not Going to Let Them Change Me," *Parade*, 25 April 1982.

7. Robert Sam Anson, "Unlimited Partnership," *Savvy*, November 1982.

8. Ibid.

9. *Wall Street Journal* article quoted in Anson, "Unlimited Partnership."

10. Tom Morganthau with Hope Lampert, "Did Bill and Mary Blunder?" *Newsweek*, 11 October 1982.

11. Text of letter from Anson, "Unlimited Partnership."

12. Sandra Salmans, "Admired and Derided, Agee Surged to the Top," New York *Times*, 9 February 1983; Tim Metz, "Bendix-Marietta: Each One Eat One," *Wall Street Journal*, 8 August 1985.

13. Kirk O. Hanson, "Social Performance at ARCO," in *Participation III: Atlantic Richfield and Society* (Los Angeles: Atlantic Richfield Company, 1980).

14. For the best statement of token status as a force in its own right, and the estimate putting the barrier between 15 and 35 percent, see Rosabeth Moss Kanter, *Men and Women of the Corporation* (New York: Basic Books, 1977). For the first analysis of sexism past the token barrier, see Harlan and Weiss, "Moving Up."

15. Bureau of Labor Statistics figures show that in 1983 women under twenty-five earned 90 percent as much as men. Single women of all ages earned 87 percent as much as single men. Female lawyers earned 88 percent as much as male lawyers and female computer programmers 81 percent as much as male programmers. But in sales, where women are the larger group, they earned less than 50 percent as much as male sales clerks. The Rand Corporation predicted that women's wages would be no more than 74 percent of men's by the year 2000. William Serrin, "Experts Say Job Bias Against Women Persists," New York *Times*, 25 November 1984.

16. Harlan and Weiss, "Moving Up."

17. Ibid.

18. All the material in this paragraph comes from Beth McGoldrick and Gregory Miller, "Wall Street women: You've come a short way, baby," *Institutional Investor*, June 1985.

19. Ibid.

20. Harlan and Weiss, "Moving Up."

21. Ibid.

22. Alma S. Baron and Ken Abrahamsen, "Will he—or won't he—work with a female manager?" *Management Review* (published by the American Management Association), November 1981.

23. *Women in Management* (Washington, D.C.: U.S. Department of Labor, Women's Bureau, 1980).

24. Kanter, *Men and Women*.

25. Many of the ideas in this paragraph are derived from Janet M. Hively and William S. Howell, "The male-female management team: A dance of death?" *Management Review* (published by the American Management Association), June 1980.

26. Margaret Hennig and Anne Jardim, *The Managerial Woman* (Garden City, N.Y.: Doubleday, 1976).

27. Report by Madeline E. Heilman and Melanie H. Stopeck, describing New York University study, *Journal of Applied Psychology*, June 1985. "Sex Repel," describing test by Heilman and Lois Saruwatari at Yale, *Psychology Today*, December 1979.

28. A 1984 *Penthouse* survey showed that 96 percent of the respondents, men and women, said they had had sex with a co-worker. The sample is hardly representative and the statistics are questionable, but the survey can be taken as a sign of increasing acceptance. Brigitte Nioche, "What Men Want," *Penthouse,* May 1985. More serious evidence is provided by Srully Blotnick, whose survey found that 55 percent of female executives said they had had sex with a co-worker. Blotnick, "Sex and Success," *Savvy,* October 1985.

29. Robert Quinn, State University of New York at Albany, quoted in Georgia Dullea, "The Issue of Office Romances," New York *Times,* 17 May 1982.

30. Eliza G.C. Collins, "Managers and Lovers," *Harvard Business Review* 61, no. 5 (September–October 1983).

31. Srully Blotnick, "Sex and Success," *Savvy,* October 1985.

32. Merit Systems Protection Board, *Sexual Harassment in the Federal Workplace: Is It a Problem?* (Washington, D.C.: Government Printing Office, 1981). Of all victims who identified the level of the persons who bothered them, 65 percent of women said the harasser was a co-worker or other employee, while 37 percent said it was an immediate or other supervisor.

33. Bob Greene, "Sexual harassment: Both sexes can play," *Chicago Tribune,* 14 September 1981.

34. Christine Doudna, "Women at the Top," New York *Times Magazine,* 30 November 1980; and Marylin Bender, "When the Boss Is a Woman," *Esquire,* 28 March 1978.

35. Robert Schrank, "Two women, three men on a raft," *Harvard Business Review* 55, no. 3 (May–June 1977).

36. For further examples of men treating boss as mother, see Bender, "When the Boss Is a Woman," and Natalie Gittelson, *Dominus* (New York: Farrar, Straus & Giroux, 1978).

37. U.S. Department of Labor, Bureau of Labor Statistics, *Employment and Earnings* (Washington, D.C.: Government Printing Office, 1984 and 1985).

38. Figures from Catalyst, a non-profit organization that works to prevent gender from being a factor in careers, quoted by William Serrin, "Experts."

39. Jaye Scholl, "Corporations of the Year," *Savvy,* June 1983.

40. Muriel Fox, "Accelerating Women into the Corporate Power Structure" (Speech delivered at American Jewish Committee conference on Who Gets to the Top: Executive Suite Discrimination in the Eighties, New York City, 10 February 1984).

CHAPTER 8: PROFESSIONS

1. Figures for law and medicine in 1970 from Cynthia Fuchs Epstein, *Women in Law* (New York: Basic Books, 1981). Figures for all professions for 1984 and architecture in 1972 from the Bureau of Labor Statistics, *Employment and Earnings: 1984 Annual Averages* (Washington, D.C.: Government Printing Office, 1985). Figures for law schools, James P. White, memorandum to American Bar Association, 7 September 1984. Figures for medical schools, American Medical Women's Association. Figures for architecture schools, American Institute of Architects.

2. Lawrence Feinburg, "Women Being 'Drained' From Teaching," Washington *Post,* 17 March 1983, cites several studies. College Board test scores of education

majors have dropped more than those of other students, and the number of women earning education degrees dropped by more than a third during the 1970s. Women still hold 70 percent of teaching jobs.

3. Bradley Soule and Kay Standley, "Perceptions of Sex Discrimination in Law," *American Bar Association Journal* 59 (October 1973).

4. Gena Corea, *The Hidden Malpractice: How American Medicine Treats Women as Patients and Professionals* (New York: William Morrow, 1977).

5. Epstein, *Women in Law.*

6. Ibid. A nationwide survey of ninety-two of the country's hundred largest law firms showed that 5 percent of the partners were women in 1984. Kathleen Sylvester, "Women gaining, blacks fall back," *National Law Journal,* 21 May 1984.

7. Jill Abramson and Barbara Franklin, "Harvard Law '74: Are Women Catching Up?" *American Lawyer,* May 1983.

8. Dean Pohlenz in a telephone interview with the author; and Lindsey Miller-Lerman in Epstein, *Women in Law.*

9. Epstein, *Women in Law.*

10. Bruce Abel, "The Firms—What Do They Want?" *Harvard Law Record,* 12 December 1963, quoted in Epstein, *Women in Law.*

11. Corea, *Hidden Malpractice.*

12. Epstein, *Women in Law.*

13. Elizabeth Morgan, *The Making of a Woman Surgeon* (New York: G. P. Putnam's Sons, 1980).

14. Lisa Belkin, "A Group for Dual-Doctor Families," New York *Times,* 16 June 1985.

15. Louis Auchincloss, "Foster Evans on Lewis Boves," in his *Tales of Manhattan,* (Boston: Houghton Mifflin, 1967). Quoted in Epstein, *Women in Law.*

CHAPTER 9: MARRIAGE AND FAMILY

1. Figure on traditional families is for 1983; from Department of Labor, Bureau of Labor Statistics. Other figures from U.S. Bureau of the Census, Current Population Reports, ser. P-20, no. 398, *Household and Family Characteristics,* March 1984.

2. Daphne Spain and Suzanne M. Bianchi, "How Women Have Changed," *American Demographics,* May 1983. Data from Census Bureau reports.

3. Figures from National Center for Health Statistics. One cause of the decline was the tendency of young people to delay marriage for education and career. The average duration of marriages was 9.4 years in 1982, the same as in 1972. Associated Press, "Decline in Divorce is First in 20 Years," New York *Times,* 6 March 1985. The 1982 decline also reflected a tendency for the divorce rate to drop when the economy goes into recession, because more partners can't afford the expense of divorce. United Press International, "Divorce Appears to Dip With Economy," New York *Times,* 29 September 1982.

4. One study of thirty Boston-area divorces, for instance, found that the wives had wanted the marriages to end in eighteen of the cases, or 60 percent. Study by Janet A. Kohen, Carol A. Brown, and Roslyn Feldberg in George Levinger and Oliver C. Moles, eds., *Divorce and Separation* (New York: Basic Books, 1979). The proportion of women formally suing for divorce has gone up—from 65 percent in 1870, when the

divorce rate was only 0.3 per thousand people, to 73 percent in 1965. This suggests that the old double standard still determines much modern legality—that even when the husbands want to end the marriage, they still let the wives file for divorce for reasons of economics and reputation.

5. U.S. Bureau of the Census, Current Population Reports, ser. P-20, no. 382, *Households, Families, Marital Status and Living Arrangements: March 1983 (Advance Report)*. Issued July 1983. Unpublished Bureau of the Census reports say it was the same for 1984.

6. U.S. Bureau of the Census, 1984 update of Current Population Reports, ser. P-20, no. 382, *Households*.

7. U.S. Bureau of the Census, unpublished current population survey data, 1985.

8. Provisional data from National Center for Health Statistics.

9. U.S. Department of Labor, Bureau of Labor Statistics, *Employment and Earnings*, vol. 31, no. 12, December 1984; and Spain and Bianchi, *Demographics*.

10. Maureen Dowd, "Many Women in Poll Equate Values of Job and Family Life," New York *Times*, 4 December 1983.

11. Barbara Ehrenreich, *The Hearts of Men* (Garden City, N.Y.: Doubleday/Anchor Press, 1983).

12. See these surveys: Gallup Survey on the Emerging Male, *Redbook*, October 1976; Batten, Barton, Durstine & Osborne, Inc., "What Today's Man Wants From Today's Woman," *BBDO Research Report*, November 1979; Doyle Dane Bernbach Inc., "Husbands Say 'Don't Rock My Boat'," *Soundings from DDB*, 1980; Benton & Bowles, Inc., "Men's Changing Role in the Family of the '80s," *American Consensus Report*, 1980; Hyatt & Esserman Research Associates, *Good Morning America National Poll on Issues Concerning Men Today*, April 1980; Louis Harris and Associates, *The General Mills American Family Report 1980–1981;* Research & Forecasts, Inc., *United Media Enterprises Report on Leisure in America*, December 1982; and Beverly Stephen, "What Men Have to Say About Women," New York *Daily News*, 19 June 1983.

13. William J. Goode, "Why Men Resist," *Dissent*, Spring 1980. Goode also says that men do not, in general, feel threatened by competition from women in the workplace if we feel the competition is "fair," that is, open to the male superiority that we assume. He bases this on analysis of facts, of men's continuing dominance of the workplace and rising superiority in income compared to women. Those are unquestionably the facts. But Goode does not examine the fears men feel or express, which are hardly defined by the facts and which indeed impel us to struggle to maintain the reality of our dominance, as described in Chapters 5–9.

14. Philip Blumstein and Pepper Schwartz, *American Couples* (New York: William Morrow, 1983).

15. Peter Stein, ed., *Single Life: Unmarried Adults in Social Context* (New York: St. Martin's, 1981).

16. Ann Corbett, "Singles: The Great American Gender Gap . . . ," *Washington Post*, 14 July 1983. William Novak, *The Great American Man Shortage and Other Roadblocks to Romance* (New York: Rawson Associates, 1983).

17. Vivian Gornick, "Against Marriage," *The Village Voice*, 15 November 1983.

18. Eric Skjei and Richard Rabkin, *The Male Ordeal: Role Crisis in a Changing World* (New York: G. P. Putnam's Sons, 1981).

19. Blumstein and Schwartz, *American Couples*. See also N. T. Garland, "The

better half? The male in the dual profession family," in *Toward a Sociology of Women*, ed. Constantina Safilios-Rothschild (Lexington, Mass.: Xerox, 1972). Cited in Rhona and Robert Rapoport, *Dual-Career Families Re-examined: New Integrations of Work and Family* (New York: Harper & Row/Colophon, 1976). Garland studied fifty-three dual-career couples with both partners working in professions and found that in twenty, or 38 percent, the husbands were traditional and considered themselves the undisputed heads of family; twenty-seven, or 51 percent, were "neo-traditional," considered their careers more important than their wives', but still recognized their wives' right to fulfillment; five were "matriarchal," with the wife dominant; and only one was truly egalitarian. I suspect that a comparable study today would find fewer traditional, as many neotraditional, and more egalitarian.

20. See Lillian B. Rubin, *Intimate Strangers: Men and Women Together* (New York: Harper & Row, 1983).

21. Carin Rubenstein, "Real Men Don't Earn Less Than Their Wives," *Psychology Today*, November 1982, citing research by William Philliber of the State University of New York, New Paltz, and Dana Hiller of the University of Cincinnati, which was not published until 1983. The chance of divorce where both partners held high-level traditionally male jobs was 33 percent; where the woman held a traditionally female job, it was 15 percent.

22. Rubin comment quoted in Mary Bralove, "For Middle-Aged Man, A Wife's New Career Upsets Old Balances," *The Wall Street Journal*, 9 November 1981.

23. This paragraph builds on ideas from Willard Gaylin, *Feelings* (New York: Harper & Row, 1979); Andrew Tolson, *The Limits of Masculinity: Male identity and women's liberation* (New York: Harper & Row/Colophon, 1977); and Nancy Chodorow, *The Reproduction of Mothering: Psychoanalysis and the Sociology of Gender* (Berkeley: University of California Press, 1978).

24. Gaylin, *Feelings*.

25. Linda Lytle Holmstrom, *The Two-Career Family* (Cambridge, Mass.: Schenkman Publishing, 1973), was among the sociologists who disproved Talcott Parsons's theory that competition was inevitable in two-career marriages. Holmstrom found competitiveness in only seven of her thirteen two-career couples. I found it in twenty-six of thirty-eight two-career couples. Other researchers like Blumstein and Schwartz affirm its prevalence.

26. Blumstein and Schwartz, *American Couples*.

27. Caroline Bird, *The Two-Paycheck Marriage: How Women at Work Are Changing Life in America* (New York: Rawson, Wade, 1979).

28. Rosanna Hertz of Northwestern University, study of twenty-one couples in the Chicago area cited in "Money, Power and the Family Budget," New York *Times*, 6 March 1983.

29. Harry Maurer, *Not Working: An Oral History of the Unemployed* (New York: Holt, Rinehart and Winston, 1979).

30. Blumstein and Schwartz, *American Couples*.

31. U.S. Bureau of the Census, Current Population Reports, ser. P-60, no. 145, *Money, Income and Poverty: Status of Families and Persons in the U.S.* 1983. In 2.3 million of these couples the wife was the sole wage earner. Families in which the wife earned more had a lower median income than did families in which the husband earned more.

32. Rubenstein, "Real Men." Zimmerman quoted in Doris Deakin, "Couples: Two-Career Marriage Woes," Washington *Post,* 24 May 1984.

33. Rubenstein, "Real Men."

34. Joan Frazier, "Banking on Women," *New Times,* 18 April 1975.

35. Research by Thomas Stanley of Georgia State University, Atlanta, described in Ed Bean, "Riddle: Why Won't a Typical Millionaire Take You for a Ride in His Fancy Car?" *The Wall Street Journal,* 10 May 1985.

36. Sheila Weller, "Women Who Support Men," *Ms.,* July 1979.

37. For further examples of conflict and further insights into all the subjects in this chapter, see Rubin, *Intimate Strangers.*

38. See, for example, the study by Wenda Brewster-O'Reilly, Stanford University School of Education, cited in "A Woman's Work Is Never Done," New York *Times,* 6 March 1983.

39. Naomi Gerstel and Harriet Gross, *Commuter Marriage* (New York: Guilford Press, 1984). Studies by Barbara Bunker and Virginia Vanderslice of the State University of New York at Buffalo, Elaine A. Anderson and Jane Spruill of the University of Maryland, and Fairlee Winfield of Northern Arizona University cited in Jewell Parker Rhodes and Edwardo Lao Rhodes, "Commuter Marriage: The Toughest Alternative," *Ms.,* June 1984; and Jonathan Dahl, "As Long Distance Marriages Rise, Some Couples Actually Prefer It," *The Wall Street Journal,* 24 June 1985.

40. Conference Board report quoted in Glenn Collins, "More Corporations Are Offering Child Care," New York *Times,* 21 June 1985.

41. Catalyst, "Preliminary Report on a Nationwide Survey of Maternity/Parental Leaves," 1984. While Catalyst had a very high response rate, 28.7 percent, I suspect that the companies that did not respond were much less likely to offer paternity leave, so the true national percentage is probably much lower than 36 percent. Estimate on placement help by Alissa Hicks of Catalyst, extrapolating from "Human Factors in Relocation," 1983.

42. See Joseph H. Pleck, Michael E. Lamb, and James A. Levine, "Facilitating Future Change in Men's Family Roles," in *Men's Changing Roles in the Family,* ed. R.A. Lewis and M. Sussman (Binghamton, N.Y.: Haworth, in press). And Joseph H. Pleck, *Working Wives, Working Husbands* (Beverly Hills: Sage, 1985).

43. Gayle Kimball, *The 50-50 Marriage* (Boston: Beacon Press, 1983).

44. Doyle Dane Bernbach Inc., "Husbands." Blumstein and Schwartz, *American Couples,* found that even among couples who say housework should be shared equally, 44 percent of wives and only 28 percent of husbands spent eleven hours a week or more on housework. Among the cohabitors, who resemble my two-career married couples, 78 percent of the women and 67 percent of the men endorse equal sharing of housework. But 42 percent of the women and only 21 percent of the men do more than ten hours of housework a week.

Blumstein and Schwartz's research on gay male couples gives further insights into the strength of traditional sex roles in men. Many of these couples have problems allocating household tasks because both men feel too busy with their jobs and are disinclined to do "women's work." Both heterosexual and homosexual men feel that a partner who is successful in a paid career should not be burdened with housework. Sometimes that takes the form of understanding for an achieving wife or gay lover who does few home tasks, sometimes the form of an achiever's unwillingness to do the chores himself.

45. Brewster-O'Reilly, "Woman's Work"; and Hertz, "Money."

46. Pleck, *Working Wives.*

47. Blumstein and Schwartz, *American Couples.*

48. Pleck, *Working Wives.*

49. Author conversation, September 1981, with Sue Goff-Timmer, Institute for Social Research, University of Michigan, quoting from her dissertation then in progress.

50. Mike McGrady, *The Kitchen Sink Papers: My Life as a Househusband* (Garden City, N.Y.: Doubleday, 1975).

51. Blumstein and Schwartz, *American Couples,* found that in the majority of married couples, the man was work-centered and the woman relationship-centered. But in 25 percent of the couples in the study both partners were relationship-centered; in 13 percent the husband was but the wife was work-centered; and in 6 percent both were work-centered. Among cohabitors, a greater percentage of men were relationship-centered than among married couples.

52. Ibid.

53. Rapoport and Rapoport, *Dual-Career Families.*

CHAPTER 10: THE NEW FATHERING

1. The first two studies are the same reviewed by Joseph H. Pleck, *Working Wives, Working Husbands* (Beverly Hills: Sage, 1985). The estimate of more involved fathering is that of Michael Yogman, director of the Infant Health and Development Program at the Children's Hospital Medical Center in Boston, and James Levine, director of the Fatherhood Project at the Bank Street College in New York. Michael D'Antonio, "The Pressure to Be Super Dad," *Newsday Magazine,* 6 January 1985.

2. Joseph H. Pleck, "Husbands' Paid Work and Family Roles: Current Research Issues," prepared for *Families and Jobs,* ed. Helena Z. Lopata and Joseph H. Pleck, vol. 3 of *Research on the Interweave of Social Roles* (Greenwich, Conn.: JAI Press, 1983).

3. Research by Thomas W. Draper and Tom Gordon described in "Real Men Don't Rub Backs," *Psychology Today,* September 1983.

4. Daniel Yankelovich, *New Rules: Searching for Self-Fulfillment in a World Turned Upside Down* (New York: Random House, 1981).

5. Andrew Cherlin and Frank Furstenberg, Jr., "Fathers Who Don't Pay," *Washington Post,* 23 March 1984. That article cites a survey of children of divorce mentioned in next sentence: Frank Furstenberg, Jr., of the University of Pennsylvania, James L. Peterson, and Nicholas Zill. The study cited in this paragraph on men whose relations with children improve after divorce: E. Mavis Hetherington, Martha Cox, and Roger Cox, "Divorced Fathers," *Family Coordinator* 25, no. 4 (October 1976), special issue on fatherhood.

6. James A. Levine, now head of the Fatherhood Project at the Bank Street College of Education, quoted in Glenn Collins, "A New Look at Life with Father " New York *Times Magazine,* 17 June 1979.

7. Ruth Moulton, "The Fear of Female Power—A Cause of Sexual Dysfunction," *Journal of the American Academy of Psychoanalysis* 5, no. 4 (October 1977): 499–517. For the earlier theory of the "good and bad breast," see Melanie Klein, "Envy and

Gratitude," (1957), in *Envy and Gratitude and other works 1946–1963*, (New York: Delacorte, 1975).

8. Dorothy Dinnerstein, *The Mermaid and the Minotaur: Sexual Arrangements and Human Malaise* (New York: Harper & Row/Colophon, 1977).

9. Lillian B. Rubin, *Intimate Strangers: Men and Women Together* (New York: Harper & Row, 1983).

10. Dinnerstein, *Mermaid*.

11. See Jessica Benjamin, "Master and Slave: The Fantasy of Erotic Domination," in *Powers of Desire: The Politics of Sexuality*, ed. Ann Snitow, Christine Stansell, and Sharon Thompson (New York: Monthly Review Press, 1983).

12. Rubin, *Intimate Strangers*.

13. Karen Horney, "The Dread of Woman," in *Feminine Psychology*, (New York: W. W. Norton, 1967).

14. Ross D. Parke, *Fathers* (Cambridge, Mass.: Harvard University Press, 1981).

15. Frank A. Pedersen et al., "Variation in Infant Experience Associated with Alternative Family Roles," in *Families as Learning Environment for Children*, ed. L. Laosa and I. Sigel (New York: Plenum, 1982).

16. John Munder Ross, "In Search of Fathering: A Review," and Stanley I. Greenspan, "The Second Other," in *Father and Child: Developmental and Clinical Perspectives*, ed. Stanley H. Cath, Alan R. Gurwitt, and John Munder Ross (Boston: Little, Brown, 1982).

17. Parke, *Fathers*.

18. David B. Lynn, "Fathers and Sex-Role Development," *Family Coordinator* 25, no. 4 (October 1976), special issue on fatherhood.

19. James M. Herzog, "On Father Hunger: The Father's Role in the Modulation of Aggressive Drive and Fantasy," in Cath, Gurwitt, and Ross, *Father and Child*.

20. Ross, "In Search."

21. Letty Cottin Pogrebin, New York *Times*, 8 September 1983, "Hers" col.

22. Jane Lazarre, "Fathers as Mothers: On Being a Father in the Year of the Woman," *The Village Voice*, 22 September 1975.

23. Martin Greenberg and Norman Morris, "Engrossment: The Newborn's Impact upon the Father," in Cath, Gurwitt, and Ross, *Father and Child*.

24. Calvin A. Colarusso and Robert A. Nemiroff, "The Father in Midlife: Crisis and the Growth of Paternal Identity," in Cath, Gurwitt, and Ross, *Father and Child*.

25. Ibid.

26. Stanley H. Cath and James M. Herzog, "The Dying and Death of a Father," in Cath, Gurwitt, and Ross, *Father and Child*.

27. Robert Meister, *Fathers: Daughters, sons, fathers reveal their deepest feelings* (New York: Richard Marek, 1981).

28. Lee Salk found similar feelings in his collection of twenty-eight interviews, *My Father My Son: Intimate Relationships* (New York: G. P. Putnam's Sons, 1982).

29. Mike Clary, *Daddy's Home: The personal story of a modern father who opted to raise the baby and master the craft of motherhood* (New York: Seaview Books, 1982).

30. Joseph F. Riener, "Those Mixed-Up, Painful Feelings of Being a Parent," Washington *Post*, 10 January 1982.

31. Kenneth Pitchford, "The Manly Art of Child Care," *Ms.*, October 1978.

32. The Fatherhood Project, *Fatherhood U.S.A.* (New York: Garland Press, 1983).

33. Conference Board survey described in Glenn Collins, "More Corporations Are Offering Child Care," New York *Times*, 21 June 1985.

34. Judy Mann, "Who Cares?" Washington *Post*, 12 March 1982.

35. Gail Scott, "Issues: 'Crayons in the Boardroom'," Washington *Post*, 8 June 1983; and Glenn Collins, "Employers Offering Seminars to Help the Working Parent," New York *Times*, 23 June 1983.

36. Dean Rotbart, "Doctor's Husband," *The Wall Street Journal*, 13 April 1981.

37. Edward Tivnan, "About Men: End of a Line," New York *Times Magazine*, 11 March 1984.

38. Zick Rubin, professor of social psychology at Brandeis University, quoted in Margot Slade, "A Father's Warmth for a Son," New York *Times*, 11 February 1985.

39. Study of time by Michael Lamb of the University of Utah Medical Center and study of appropriate toys by Judith Langlois of the University of Texas at Austin, cited by Glenn Collins, "Parley Explores the Father's Role," New York *Times*, 9 December 1984.

40. Nancy Chodorow, *The Reproduction of Mothering: Psychoanalysis and the Sociology of Gender* (Berkeley: University of California Press, 1978).

41. The phrase "desexualized affection" comes from Marjorie Leonard, "Fathers and Daughters," *International Journal of Psycho-Analysis* 47 (1966): See also Signe Hammer, *Passionate Attachments: Fathers and Daughters in America Today* (New York: Rawson Associates, 1982).

42. Associated Press, "Father's Roles and Incest," New York *Times*, 13 December 1984.

43. William S. Appleton, *Fathers and Daughters* (Garden City, N.Y.: Doubleday, 1981). See also Hammer, *Passionate Attachments*.

44. See Judy Klemesrud, "Older Fathers: Becoming a Parent After 50," New York *Times*, 7 January 1985.

45. Daniel Levinson, *The Seasons of a Man's Life* (New York: Alfred A. Knopf, 1978).

CHAPTER 11: SEXUALITY

1. Michael Castleman, *Sexual Solutions* (New York: Simon and Schuster, 1980). Augmented by my conversations with Michael Castleman.

2. Jack Litewka, "The Socialized Penis," *Liberation*, March/April 1974, reprinted in Jon Snodgrass, ed., *For Men Against Sexism* (Albion, Calif.: Times Change Press, 1977).

3. Ibid.

4. Ibid.

5. See Ellen Morgan, "The Erotization of Male Dominance/Female Submission," *The University of Michigan Papers in Women's Studies* (Ann Arbor, Mich.: University of Michigan, 1975). Kissinger remark quoted in Du Pre Jones, "The Sayings of Secretary Henry," New York *Times Magazine*, 28 October 1973.

6. See Constantina Safilios-Rothschild, *Love, Sex, and Sex Roles* (Englewood Cliffs, N.J.: Prentice-Hall, 1977).

7. See Alan McEvoy and Jeff Brookings, *If She Is Raped: A Book for Husbands, Fathers and Male Friends* (Kalamazoo, Mich.: Learning Publications, 1984).

8. Jessica Benjamin, "Master and Slave: The Fantasy of Erotic Domination," in *Powers of Desire: The Politics of Sexuality,* ed. Ann Snitow, Christine Stansell, and Sharon Thompson (New York: Monthly Review Press, 1983).

9. Ibid.

10. Ibid.

11. See Deirdre English, "The Fear that Feminism Will Set Men Free," in Snitow, Stansell, and Thompson, *Powers of Desire.*

12. See Jane E. Brody, "Why a Lag in Male-Oriented Birth Control?" New York *Times,* 16 October 1983.

13. Kinsey and Hunt tabulated in Anthony Pietropinto and Jacqueline Simenauer, *Beyond the Male Myth* (New York: New York Times Books, 1977). Philip Blumstein and Pepper Schwartz, *American Couples* (New York: William Morrow, 1983). Third survey cited is part of Research & Forecasts, Inc., *Where Does the Time Go? The United Media Enterprises Report on Leisure in America* (New York: United Media Enterprises, 1982).

14. On the psychological side, see Avodah K. Offitt, *The Sexual Self,* rev. ed. (New York: Congdon & Weed, 1983).

15. Ellen Willis, "Women Are Denied the Right to Express Lust," *Ms.,* March 1982. This article was transcribed from Willis's responses to an interviewer's questions.

16. Pietropinto and Simenauer, *Male Myth.*

17. Ibid.

18. Lonnie Barbach and Linda Levine, *Shared Intimacies* (Garden City, N.Y.: Doubleday, 1980).

19. Pietropinto and Simenauer, *Male Myth.*

20. Blumstein and Schwartz, *American Couples.*

21. Survey of 65,396 men and 14,928 women, *Playboy,* January 1982.

22. Linda Wolfe, *Women and Sex in the 80s: The Cosmo Report* (New York: Arbor House, 1981).

23. Lynn Atwater, *The Extramarital Connection: Sex, Intimacy and Identity* (Irvington, N.J.: Irvington Publishing, 1981).

24. Ibid.

25. Morton Hunt, *Sexual Behavior in the 1970s* (Chicago: Playboy Press, 1974), quoted in Jonathan Gathorne-Hardy, *Marriage, Love, Sex & Divorce: What Brings Us Together, What Drives Us Apart* (New York: Summit Books, 1981).

26. Blumstein and Schwartz, *American Couples.*

27. Ibid.

28. Offitt, *Sexual Self.*

29. Castleman, *Sexual Solutions.*

30. William H. Masters and Virginia E. Johnson, *Human Sexual Inadequacy* (Boston: Little, Brown, 1970). See also Gail Sheehy, *Passages: Predictable Crises of Adult Life* (New York. E.P. Dutton & Co., 1976).

31. James T. Yenckel, "Private Lives: Confronting Impotence," Washington *Post,* 16 August 1983.

32. Offitt, *Sexual Self.*

CHAPTER 12: THE MOVEMENT

1. Robert Brannon, "Changing Men, Changing Women," in *Beyond Sex Roles*, ed. Alice Sargent, 2d ed. (St. Paul, Minn.: West, 1985), estimates that fifty thousand men have taken part in men's consciousness-raising groups. It would be stretching a point to say that all fifty thousand have been touched by the men's movement, but it's also true that some men who have been affected have never been in C-R groups. Maximum attendance at any national men's meeting was about seven hundred at the Fifth Men and Masculinity Conference in Los Angeles in December 1978. Perhaps two thousand different people attended the first ten M&M Conferences. The National Congress for Men had local component organizations whose total membership I would guess was somewhere between two and five thousand, and Free Men claims as many as three thousand members, but the two groups overlap. The books mentioned in this chapter have sold, collectively, several hundred thousand copies, but few readers' lives are changed by most books.

2. Ibid.

3. Scholars define movements in terms like these: "a group of people who are organized for, ideologically motivated by, and committed to a purpose which implements some form of personal or social change; who are actively engaged in the recruitment of others; and whose influence is spreading in opposition to the established order. . . ." (L. P. Gerlach and V. H. Hines, *People, Power, Change: Movements of Social Transformation* (Indianapolis: Bobbs-Merrill, 1970.) This certainly describes the women's movement and excludes the men's, which has neither implemented much social change nor spread significantly. But I think such a definition needs the idea of passion to distinguish between forces like the women's movement and the civil rights movement in the United States, on the one hand, and less driven groups that lobby, oppose, or express alienation on the other.

4. See Alan E. Gross, Ronald Smith, and Barbara Strudler Wallston, "The Men's Movement: Personal vs. Political," in *Social Movements of the Sixties and Seventies*, ed. Jo Freeman (New York: Longman, 1983).

5. Jack Sawyer, "On Male Liberation," *Liberation* magazine, Aug.–Oct. 1970, reprinted in *Men and Masculinity*, ed. Joseph H. Pleck and Jack Sawyer (Englewood Cliffs, N.J.: Prentice-Hall, 1974).

6. Gene Marine is a professional writer whose interest in the women's movement evaporated as he went on to other subjects—and perhaps as his marriage broke up, he told me in 1977.

7. The phrase about contradiction and class enemies is from Ellen Willis, "Nature's Revenge," New York *Times Book Review*, 12 July 1981.

8. Marc Feigen Fasteau goes about the furthest when he says, "Innovations like sensitivity training will only become effective when competitive, hierarchical, and authoritarian attitudes toward work are tempered by the kinds of changes instituted in the General Foods experiment [which gave teams of workers increased responsibility for segments of the production process in a plant that workers also helped design] and by analogous shifts in individual values in both the executive and the blue-collar ranks." Marc Feigen Fasteau, *The Male Machine* (New York: McGraw-Hill, 1974).

9. Jon Snodgrass, ed., *For Men Against Sexism* (Albion, Calif.: Times Change Press, 1977). That reprinted John Stoltenberg, "Toward Gender Justice," which charged that patriarchy made "power, prestige, privilege and prerogative" over women the

cultural norm of male identity; and Steven Dansky, John Knoebel, and Kenneth Pitchford, "The Effeminist Manifesto," in which gay men called for "gynarchism"— women seizing power—and offered to take upon themselves a share of "the day-to-day life-sustaining drudgery that is usually consigned to women alone," particularly the work of raising children.

Glen Bucher, *Straight/White/Male* (Philadelphia: Fortress Press, 1976), called on men to accept their guilt as oppressors of women and to bear witness to straight, white, male privilege, both in a Christian manner. Another anthology, *The Women Say/The Men Say*, edited by Evelyn Shapiro and Barry M. Shapiro (New York: Dell/ Delta, 1979), looked harder at politics and work than had any men's movement book and collected some ideas for changing the system. But its subtitle was "Women's Liberation and Men's Consciousness," and only a third of its authors were men.

Among the social psychologists whose works are important to the men's movement are Joseph Pleck, Robert Brannon, and Robert Lewis. See Brannon, "Changing Men"; Pleck and Sawyer, *Men and Masculinity;* Joseph H. Pleck, "Men's Power with Women, Other Men, and Society: A Men's Movement Analysis," in *The American Man,* ed. Elizabeth H. Pleck and Joseph H. Pleck (Englewood Cliffs, N.J.: Prentice-Hall, 1980); Joseph H. Pleck, *The Myth of Masculinity* (Cambridge, Mass.: MIT Press, 1981); Deborah S. David and Robert Brannon, eds., *The Forty-Nine Percent Majority: The Male Sex Role* (Reading, Mass.: Addison-Wesley, 1976); and Robert A. Lewis, ed., *Men in Difficult Times: Masculinity Today and Tomorrow* (Englewood Cliffs, N.J.: Prentice-Hall, 1981).

10. I attended two regional pro-feminist conferences (one of them not a men's meeting, strictly speaking, but a conference called "Men and Women in Struggle for Community" in Oakland in 1977, which included people from the men's, women's, and new left movements) and the second, third, sixth, eighth, and tenth national Men and Masculinity Conferences. I also attended the first and third national meetings of the National Congress for Men, described later in this chapter.

11. Alan E. Gross, Ronald Smith, and Barbara Strudler Wallston, "The Men's Movement: Personal or Political?" (Unpublished 1980 version of the paper in Freeman, *Social Movements),* found that at Knoxville in 1975 every session focused on personal experience even though some had political implications. At the second conference, at State College, Pennsylvania, in 1976, 69 percent of the sessions were in the personal growth category and 31 percent oriented to political, social, or instrumental activity. At Des Moines in April 1977, 64 percent of the eleven major workshops and 26 percent of the sixty-nine minor sessions were political. At Los Angeles in December 1978, 55 percent of the major sessions and 46 percent of the minor were political. At Milwaukee in October 1979, only 32 percent of the workshops were political—but there were other channels for political concern. I calculated on the same basis that 34 percent of the workshops at the seventh M&M conference and 37 percent at the eighth were political—but only 22 percent at the tenth, which taken as a whole was the most political M&M conference yet.

12. Jane Lazarre, *The Mother Knot* (New York: McGraw-Hill, 1976).

13. Gross drew part of his evidence from the reaction of his own C-R group when he came back from the Knoxville M&M conference and told members about it. They showed "a frankly stated disinterest in becoming actively involved" in national conferences or a national movement. He reported a similar lack of interest in a regional

center to serve as a clearinghouse for men who might ask to be referred to C-R groups and for guest speakers or films. See Gross, Smith, and Wallston, "Men's Movement."

14. Ibid. The authors estimate that at the St. Louis and Los Angeles meetings the proportion of homosexuals rose to 45 percent, perhaps because those conferences were scheduled over Thanksgiving and Christmas holiday periods when married men would stay at home with their families. Others who attended those meetings dispute the estimate.

15. Ibid.

16. Emma Goldman never used these words, so far as is known. In her autobiography she says, "I was one of the most untiring and gayest" at dances intended to persuade girls to join a cloak-makers' strike in 1889. A comrade told her it did not behoove an agitator to dance with such reckless abandon. "I insisted that our Cause could not expect me to become a nun and that the movement should not be turned into a cloister. If it meant that, I did not want it. 'I want freedom, the right to self-expression, everybody's right to beautiful, radiant things.'" (Emma Goldman, *Living My Life* [New York: Alfred A. Knopf, 1931], vol. 1.) I am indebted to Alix Kates Shulman for helping me find this passage.

17. Pleck, *Myth.*

18. Fasteau, *Male Machine.*

19. Brannon and other critics of traditional sex roles speak of an androgynous society that offers a fascinating challenge to traditional assumptions about male and female and the social order—in a science-fiction novel by Ursula K. LeGuin, *The Left Hand of Darkness* (New York: Ace Books, 1969/76). It is a delightful novel that does indeed show the foolishness of unquestioned sex roles. But the mutant humans on the planet Winter that LeGuin calls androgynes are not merely psychologically capable of being both masculine and feminine. They are biologically capable of being both—as much hermaphrodite as androgyne. They are sexually neutral for twenty-one or twenty-two days of their month. Then they enter estrus, and if they find a partner, they become either male or female, hormonally and by extruding or enveloping the necessary sex organs. They have no control over which sex they become and it may vary from month to month. If one is female in a given month and is impregnated, he/she can bear a child. The earthly explorer who is narrator of one chapter warns that if an earthly ambassador is sent, he "must be warned that unless he is very self-assured, or senile, his pride will suffer. A man wants his virility regarded, a woman wants her femininity appreciated, however indirect and subtle the indications of regard and appreciation. On Winter they will not exist. One is respected and judged only as a human being. It is an appalling experience." Q.E.D.

20. Daniel Levinson, *The Seasons of a Man's Life* (New York: Alfred A. Knopf, 1978).

21. The idea that competition and achievement are oppressive was reflected at several conferences. The ideology was expressed by Jack Sawyer: "The male sex role oppresses by leading men, simply in order to achieve their own personal ('masculine') identity, to accept a competitive system where they learn to value themselves by their achievement compared with others, and at the same time to deny their own emotional life." (Jack Sawyer, *On the Politics of Male Liberation.* [Broadside distributed at Third National Men and Masculinity Conference, Des Moines, 1977.])

22. At the banquet of the first meeting of the National Congress for Men, Thom Thompson, a Baltimore marriage counselor and member of Free Men, the largest and

best-known cluster in the no-guilt wing, explained its workings to a woman who didn't know the organization. One of his points was, "We don't talk about women much." A few minutes later he objected when I said, "Free Men usually ignore women."

23. Herb Goldberg, *The Hazards of Being Male* (Plainview, N.Y.: Nash Pub., 1976).

24. Herb Goldberg, *The New Male* (New York: William Morrow, 1979).

25. Herb Goldberg, *The New Male-Female Relationship* (New York: William Morrow, 1983).

26. Goldberg, *New Male.*

27. Richard Haddad, "Concepts and Overview of the Men's Liberation Movement" (Address delivered at the University of Wisconsin-Extension on October 9, 1979), published in *American Man* 1, no. 2 (Spring 1980).

28. See Sheila M. Rothman, *Woman's Proper Place: A History of Changing Ideals and Practices, 1870 to the Present* (New York: Basic Books, 1978).

29. National Commission on the Observance of International Women's Year, *"To Form a More Perfect Union . . .": Justice for American Women* (Washington, D.C.: Government Printing Office, 1976).

30. The divorce reformers are just becoming aware of books like Mel Roman and Patricia E. Raley, *The Indelible Family* (New York: Rawson Wade, 1980), and Mel Roman, *The Disposable Parent: A Case for Joint Custody* (New York: Holt, Rinehart & Winston, 1978), which provide some context for their movement. Few of these men have read Ross Parke's *Fathers* (Cambridge, Mass.: Harvard University Press, 1981), James A. Levine's *Who Will Raise the Children?* (Philadelphia: J. B. Lippincott, 1976), or any of the other books that show fathers can be just as nurturing to their children (apart from breast-feeding) as can their mothers.

31. Address delivered to National Congress for Men, June 13, 1981, copyright 1981 by Fredric Hayward.

CHAPTER 13: THE MEN OF THE MOVEMENT

1. I interviewed sixteen men who were or had been active in the movement. Ten were in the pro-feminist wing and six on the no-guilt divorce-reform side. Nine of the sixteen came into the movement because of their wives, eight of them pro-feminist and one no-guilt. Sometimes the women demanded that the men make specific changes in their behavior. Sometimes the men responded to changes that the women's movement had made in their wives' consciousnesses. Two of the nine were motivated by problems their wives encountered at work and in graduate school. Three were motivated not only by their wives, but also by experiences in their own work—one by editing a book with feminist essays that inspired him, one by becoming first excited and then disillusioned by affirmative action programs, and one by making sex roles his academic specialty. Five of the nine were still married to the same women when they talked to me. Two of the four divorced men in this group thought their wives had treated them badly, but all nine still wanted to change either male roles or the whole system. Of the other seven, three came to the movement as a result of their experiences in the divorce process, making the proportion twelve out of sixteen motivated by events in their marriages. The wives whose behavior made these three angry with the divorce system were hardly feminists, but two of the three had developed sympathies

for independent women that would have seemed unlikely when they first went into divorce court. Three men became active in the movement as a result of experiences at work. One of these responded positively to women who became supervisors in the "people's health clinic" where he worked (though he had earlier been sensitized by living with women in a 1960s commune and lobbying for the admission of women to an Ivy League men's college). One was stimulated by the demands made by women in community- and union-organizing. One responded negatively to women bosses who he felt discriminated against him because he was male. The last of my sixteen joined the movement because he had decided he would never fit masculine stereotypes and desperately needed permission and approval not to—and to feel that he was nonetheless a worthwhile human being.

2. I asked Ellie for an interview to get her perspective on what had happened between her and Phil. She refused to talk to me.

CHAPTER 14: THE CULTURE GAP

1. George Stade, *Confessions of a Lady-Killer* (New York: W. W. Norton, 1979).

2. George Stade, "Men, Boys and Wimps," New York *Times Book Review,* 12 August 1984.

3. American women, male clergy, and popular writers took over a good part of the public mind in the nineteenth century by a process that Ann Douglas calls "the feminization of American culture." It enabled both lady and clergyman "to cross the cruel lines laid down by sexual stereotyping. . . . She could become aggressive, even angry, in the name of various holy causes; he could become gentle, even nurturing, for the sake of moral overseeing." These changes were sentimental rather than real. Women gained no power outside the realm of popular culture; the process provided no serious obstacles to the evils it ostensibly opposed, from slavery to industrialization, and it produced no serious art (though some artifacts, like *Uncle Tom's Cabin,* had serious political consequences). This was the beginning of the split between mass and high culture. The great male writers of the Victorian era in America were part of the high culture. Their art did not appear to deal with the same subjects as that of the "female scribblers" (Nathaniel Hawthorne's phrase), and they had few readers. (Ann Douglas, *The Feminization of American Culture* [New York: Alfred A. Knopf, 1978]).

4. Stade, "Men." It seems remarkable that in this essay, Stade makes no mention of Douglas, his colleague at Columbia, a woman who preceded him in this exploration.

5. Philip Roth's, *Portnoy's Complaint* (New York: Random House, 1969); *My Life as a Man* (New York: Holt, Rinehart and Winston, 1974); and *The Anatomy Lesson* (New York: Farrar, Straus & Giroux, 1983).

6. C. D. B. Bryan, *Beautiful Women; Ugly Scenes* (Garden City, N.Y.: Doubleday, 1983).

7. Leonard Michaels, *The Men's Club* (New York: Farrar, Straus & Giroux, 1981).

8. John Updike, *The Witches of Eastwick* (New York: Alfred A. Knopf, 1984).

9. Andrea Stevens, "A Triple Spell," New York *Times Book Review,* 13 May 1984.

10. Alan Saperstein, *Mom Kills Kids and Self* (New York: Macmillan, 1979).

11. Avery Corman, *Kramer versus Kramer* (New York: Random House, 1977); and Robert Miner, *Mother's Day* (New York: Richard Marek, 1978).

NOTES 427

. John Irving, *The World According to Garp* (New York: E.P. Dutton, 1978); and *The Cider House Rules* (New York: William Morrow, 1984).

13. Thomas Berger, *Regiment of Women.* (©1973; New York: Dell, 1982). Lawrence Sanders, *The Passion of Molly T.* (New York: G.P. Putnam's Sons, 1984).

14. See Robert Dunn, "Fiction that Shrinks from Life," New York *Times Book Review,* 30 June 1985.

15. "No Second Troy," from W. B. Yeats, *Collected Poems,* definitive edition (New York: Macmillan, 1956).

16. "Chanson" and "The Monstrous Marriage" are in William Carlos Williams, *The Collected Later Poems* (New York: New Directions, 1963). "The Ivy Crown" is in William Carlos Williams, *Pictures from Brueghel: Collected Poems 1950–1962* (New York: New Directions, 1962 and 1967).

17. The poems mentioned are in John Crowe Ransom, *Selected Poems: Third edition, revised and enlarged* (New York: The Ecco Press, 1978).

18. "Mermaid" is in Robert Lowell, *The Dolphin* (New York: Farrar, Straus & Giroux/Noonday, 1973); "Jean Stafford, a Letter," is in Robert Lowell, *Day by Day* (New York, Farrar, Straus & Giroux, 1977).

19. See Allen Ginsberg, *Collected Poems 1947–1980* (New York: Harper & Row, 1984).

20. Charles Bukowski, *War All the Time* (Santa Barbara: Black Sparrow Press, 1984).

21. Hugo, Koertge, Stafford, and Beecher are among the poets in Edward Field, ed., *A Geography of Poets* (New York: Bantam Books, 1979).

22. These poems are all in Mark Strand, *Selected Poems* (New York: Atheneum, 1981).

23. "The Bath" is in Gary Snyder, *Turtle Island* (New York: New Directions, 1974). "To Hell With Your Fertility Cult" is in Snyder, *The Back Country* (New York: New Directions, 1968).

24. The essay and "Teeth Mother Naked at Last" are in Robert Bly, *Sleepers Joining Hands* (New York, Harper & Row, 1973). I am indebted to the insights into Bly contained in Richard Jones and Kate Daniels, eds., *Of Solitude and Silence: Writings on Robert Bly* (Boston: Beacon Press, 1981).

25. Robert Bly, *Loving a Woman in Two Worlds* (Garden City, N.Y.: Doubleday/Dial, 1985).

26. Robert Pinsky, *Sadness and Happiness* (Princeton: Princeton University Press, 1975); Pinsky, *An Explanation of America* (Princeton: Princeton University Press, 1979).

27. "Kol Nidre" and "Stones" are from Michael Blumenthal, *Sympathetic Magic* (Huntington, N.Y.: Water Mark Press, 1980). "Couvade" and "Weeding" are from Michael Blumenthal, *Days We Would Rather Know* (New York: Viking-Penguin, 1984).

28. Stanley Kauffmann led me to this play in his review from *Saturday Review* (July–August 1983), reprinted in his *Theater Criticisms* (New York: Performing Arts Journal Publications, 1983).

29. The National Coalition on Television Violence estimates that horror, slasher, and violent science fiction films rose from 6 percent of box office receipts in 1970 to 30 percent in 1985. This does not distinguish the sex of the victims of violence, but I feel certain the proportion of women has not diminished.

30. See Molly Haskell, *From Reverence to Rape: The Treatment of Women in the Movies* (New York: Holt, Rinehart and Winston, 1974). She also notes some partial exceptions in this period: Paul Newman's *Rachel, Rachel,* John Cassavetes's *Faces,* and Ronald Neame's *The Prime of Miss Jean Brodie* dealt sympathetically with women, but they were repressed and unglamorous women. In *My Night at Maud's* (1969), Eric Rohmer created a female character of intellect, energy, and generosity— and then had the hero reject her for an unknown blond, seen from a distance, whose purity turns on acquaintance into suspicion and prudishness.

31. Joan Mellen, "Hollywood Rediscovers the American Woman," New York *Times,* 23 April 1978.

32. Arthur Bell, "Toot, Toot, 'Tootsie' Hello," *The Village Voice,* 28 December 1982.

33. Kate Ellis in a talk to Philadelphia Women's Studies Conference, Philadelphia, Pa., 16 March 1985.

34. Ari Korpivaara, "Grossed Out on the Summer's Top-Grossing Film," *Ms.,* August 1985.

35. Judy Klemesrud, "Female Superheroes Get Star Roles in the Comics," New York *Times,* 4 January 1980.

36. Jonathan Friendly, "Women's New Roles in Comics," New York *Times,* 28 February 1983.

37. Anna Quindlen, "Women in TV Ads: The Old Image Lingers," New York *Times,* 16 May 1978.

38. Judy Klemesrud, "Voice of Authority Still Male," New York *Times,* 2 February 1981.

39. Barbara Lovenheim, "Admen Woo the Working Woman," New York *Times,* 18 June 1978.

40. Nina Easton, *Women Take Charge* (Washington, D.C.: Center for Study of Responsive Law, 1983).

41. Ronald Alsop, "Despite Less Blatant Sexism, Ads Still Insult Most Women," *The Wall Street Journal,* 1 August 1985.

CHAPTER 15: DIVIDING LINES

1. Barbara Ehrenreich, "A Feminist's View of the New Man," New York *Times Magazine,* 20 May 1984, and "Blue-Collar Lovers and Allies," *Ms.,* September 1985.

2. Diane Weathers, "A New Black Struggle," *Newsweek,* 27 August 1979.

3. See Ronald Smothers, "Concern for the Black Family: Attention Now Turns to Men," New York *Times,* 31 December 1983.

4. Census Bureau figures quoted in Alvin P. Sanoff et al., "The American Male," *U.S. News & World Report,* 3 June 1985.

5. Nancy Chodorow et al., "Feminism 1984: Taking Stock on the Brink of an Uncertain Future," *Ms.,* January 1984.

6. The study also lists elite workers, 3 percent of the total, with a median income of $34,852 but no higher education, and workers, 55 percent of the total, with no higher education and a median income of $10,036. Housewives and students account for the remaining 22 percent. Bert Metter and Peter Kim, "The New American Consumer" (Unpublished study by J. Walter Thompson U.S.A., New York, 1985).

7. Bureau of Labor Statistics and Census Bureau data quoted in Phillip Longman, "The Downwardly Mobile Baby Boomers," *The Wall Street Journal*, 12 April 1985.

8. Ehrenreich, "New Man."

9. Anthony Astrachan, "Overview: Marketing to Men," *Advertising Age*, 4 October 1984.

10. Ibid.

11. Daniel Levinson, *The Seasons of a Man's Life* (New York: Alfred A. Knopf, 1978).

12. Seymour Kleinberg, *Alienated Affections: Being Gay in America* (New York: St. Martin's Press, 1980).

13. John Rechy, *The Sexual Outlaw* (New York: Dell, 1977). Two books describe friendship between women and gay men: Rebecca Nahas and Myra Turley, *The New Couple: Women and Gay Men* (New York: Seaview, 1979); and John Malone, *Straight Women/Gay Men: A Special Relationship* (New York: Dial, 1981).

14. Jeff Keith, "My Own Men's Liberation" (Article distributed at a Men and Masculinity Conference).

15. Kleinberg, *Alienated Affections*.

16. Ibid.

CHAPTER 16: THE TIMES WE LIVE IN

1. Andrew Hacker, "Women vs. Men in the Work Force," New York *Times Magazine*, 9 November 1984.

2. Christopher Lasch, *The Culture of Narcissism: American Life in an Age of Diminishing Expectations* (New York: W. W. Norton, 1979).

3. See Sheila M. Rothman, *Woman's Proper Place: A History of Changing Ideals and Practices, 1870 to the Present* (New York: Basic Books, 1978).

4. Daniel Yankelovich, *New Rules: Searching for Self-Fulfillment in a World Turned Upside Down* (New York: Random House, 1981).

5. Joseph Veroff, Elizabeth Douvan, and Richard A. Kulka, *The Inner American: A Self-Portrait from 1957 to 1976* (New York: Basic Books, 1981). The authors, present or former associates of the Institute for Social Research at the University of Michigan, questioned 2,267 adults, a huge representative sample, in 1976, and compared their findings with a similar sample studied in 1957.

6. Lasch, *Culture of Narcissism*.

7. Bert Metter and Peter Kim, "The New American Consumer" (Unpublished study by J. Walter Thompson U.S.A., New York, 1985). It defines yuppies as people with five years of higher education and a $39,100 median income. There are 3.1 million in a baby boom generation of 76 million.

8. Virginia Slims poll, prepared for the President's Advisory Committee for Women by the Public Agenda Foundation, a subsidiary of Yankelovich, Skelly and White, Inc., New York, December 1980, cited in Deborah Durfee Baron and Daniel Yankelovich, *Today's American Woman: How the Public Sees Her*.

9. From a survey by the Los Angeles *Times*, 1 November 1984, and various surveys quoted in Alvin P. Sanoff et al., "The American Male," *U.S. News & World Report*, 3 June 1985.

10. Ibid.

11. Kevin Klose, "U.S. Catholic Feminists Gather to Counter Papal Conservatism," Washington Post, 13 November 1983; and Kenneth A. Briggs, "Catholic Bishops Meet to Discuss Role of Women," New York Times, 14 November 1983.

12. William R. Greer, "Catholic Bishops Say Women's Role Should Be Larger," New York Times, 16 September 1985.

13. George Vecsey, "Jesuit Official Disciplines a Priest for Outspoken Views on Women," New York Times, 26 November 1979.

14. Hans Küng, "Will the Pope Win Over Women?" New York Times, 11 November 1983.

15. "Century Club: Male Bastion Is Challenged," New York Times, 12 January 1983.

16. Lewis H. Lapham, "La Différence," New York Times, 4 March 1983.

17. Editorial, New York Times, 13 January 1983.

18. Letter from George Ball, New York Times, 24 January 1983.

19. Editorial, New York Times, 24 January 1983. This account is indebted to Nat Hentoff, "A Non-Fictitious Woman vs. the Good Old Boys," The Village Voice, 22 February 1983.

20. James Barron, "Some Units of Jaycees Rebel Against Admitting Women," New York Times, 10 September 1984.

21. There are useful journalistic summaries of the issue in Kathy Sawyer, "Court Faces Issue of Equal Pay for Comparable Work," Washington Post, 4 June 1981; Walter Goodman, "Equal Pay for 'Comparable Worth' Growing as Job-Discrimination Issue," New York Times, 4 September 1984; Cathy Trost, "Comparable Pay Still Faces Test, but Foes See Trouble Ahead," The Wall Street Journal, 10 May 1985; and Carol Lawson, "Women in State Jobs Gain in Pay Equity," New York Times, 20 May 1985.

22. Associated Press, "U.S. Court Upsets Pay Equity Ruling for Women," New York Times, 5 September 1985.

23. See Robert J. Samuelson, "The Fiction of 'Fairness'," Washington Post, 17 April 1985.

24. Howard Kurtz, "Justice Dept. Opposes Nurses 'Comparable Worth' Lawsuit," Washington Post, 17 August 1985.

25. Bill Peterson, "Reagan Did Understand Women," Washington Post, 3 March 1985; and Ellen Hume, "Some Women Politicians Are Backing Away from Feminist Label to Expand Base of Support," The Wall Street Journal, 3 April 1985.

26. Jane Mayer, "Women Charge They Don't Get Their Share of White House Jobs," The Wall Street Journal, 10 September 1985.

27. Judy Mann, "Naming Woman to Court May Be More Bilge," Washington Post, 24 June 1981.

28. Dale Russakoff and Keith B. Richburg, "Reallotting Families' Tax Loads," Washington Post, 2 June 1985; and David E. Rosenbaum, "Doubts About 'Neutrality' Threaten the Tax Plan," New York Times, 30 June 1985.

29. Barbara Ehrenreich, "Is Abortion Really a Moral Dilemma?" New York Times, 7 February 1985; and Ellen Willis, "Putting Women Back into the Abortion Debate," The Village Voice, 16 July 1985.

30. Alan L. Otten, "Women's Rights vs. Fetal Rights Looms as Thorny and Divisive Issue," The Wall Street Journal, 12 April 1985.

CHAPTER 17: CONCLUSIONS

1. Hannah Arendt, *On Revolution* (New York: Viking, 1963). The analysis is indebted to Daniel Yankelovich, *New Rules: Searching for Self-Fulfillment in a World Turned Upside Down* (New York: Random House, 1981).

2. Judy Klemesrud, "Americans Assess 15 Years of Feminism," New York *Times,* 19 December 1983.

3. Barbara Ehrenreich, "A Feminist's View of the New Man," New York *Times Magazine,* 20 May 1984.

INDEX